Being Hindu, Being Indian

ADVANCE PRAISE FOR THE BOOK

'*Being Hindu, Being Indian* may well be the definitive biography of Lala Lajpat Rai. Not only is it very comprehensive, each phase of his life being fully contextualized, but it is also remarkably nuanced, defying simplistic interpretations. Vanya Vaidehi Bhargav, indeed, shows that Rai was as complex as his epoch, when various nationalistic forms of identity politics crystallized in India'—Christophe Jaffrelot, professor of political science, Sciences Po, and author of *The Hindu Nationalist Movement in India*

'Lala Lajpat Rai is one of the most fascinating figures of modern India. To enter into Lajpat Rai's complex and nuanced thinking is to enter into some of the deepest questions that defined modern India. This book is a wonderful starting point to understand why Rai ended up with the positions he espoused. It brilliantly rescues him from both the condescension of the Left and the misappropriation of the Right'—Pratap Bhanu Mehta, author of *The Burden of Democracy*

'Vanya Bhargav's expansive study of one of India's most important political and intellectual figures of the twentieth century directs us away from easy conclusions about his connections to longer-term trajectories of Hindu and Indian nationalism. Instead, Bhargav presents a comprehensive study of Lala Lajpat Rai's nationalist thought over different phases of his life, bringing into relief its fluidity, complexities and nuances, as well as significant differences with Hindutva or forms of secular Indian nationalism. This will be essential reading for anyone wishing to explore the complicated transitions in early-twentieth-century Indian political thought, especially in the crucial later decades of Lajpat Rai's career, as he transitioned between support for the Khilafat movement to support for the Hindu Mahasabha in the 1920s. One of the book's greatest contributions lies in its suggestion that scholars need to differentiate between different "secularisms", some of them emanating from within Hindu ideas of the nation'—William Gould, professor of Indian history, University of Leeds, and author of *Hindu Nationalism and the Language of Politics in Late Colonial India*

'This meticulous reconstruction of older debates on India's nationhood is also a product of toil and solid reasoning. Vanya Bhargav argues persuasively that while Lala Lajpat Rai, this stalwart figure from undivided Punjab with its Muslim majority, was a firm defender of Hindu rights, he never held that India or its territory belonged exclusively or specially to Hindus'—Rajmohan Gandhi, professor, University of Illinois Urbana-Champaign, and author of *Patel: A Life* and *Punjab: A History from Aurangzeb to Mountbatten*

'A compelling and fine retelling of Lajpat Rai's life of politics and ideas. Bhargav asks the difficult questions of religious identity and political power as navigated by Lajpat Rai that left a rich but complex legacy. With deftness and delicacy, the book retraces fundamental debates on nationalism and communalism in a bygone turbulent era as it shows their lasting significance. The book repositions the long-forgotten Lajpat Rai as embodying a unique politics with sharp and even urgent lessons for politics today'—Shruti Kapila, professor of history and politics, University of Cambridge, and author of *Violent Fraternity*

'This excellent book reshapes our understanding of Lajpat Rai's intellectual and political life as a complex thinker who carried multiple flags of nationalism in India. Bhargav offers innovative and compelling interpretations of what being Hindu and being Indian meant for Rai as he navigated a world for and against Hindutva. This is a well-researched work of intellectual history that will be essential reading for anyone interested in the ideas that shaped Hindu nationalism'— Vinayak Chaturvedi, professor of history, University of California, Irvine, and author of *Hindutva and Violence: V.D. Savarkar and the Politics of History*

Being Hindu, Being Indian

LALA LAJPAT RAI'S
IDEAS *of* NATIONHOOD

Vanya Vaidehi Bhargav

PENGUIN
VIKING
An imprint of Penguin Random House

VIKING

USA | Canada | UK | Ireland | Australia
New Zealand | India | South Africa | China | Singapore

Viking is part of the Penguin Random House group of companies
whose addresses can be found at global.penguinrandomhouse.com

Published by Penguin Random House India Pvt. Ltd
4th Floor, Capital Tower 1, MG Road,
Gurugram 122 002, Haryana, India

First published in Viking by Penguin Random House India 2024

ISBN 9780670094073

Typeset in Minion Pro by MAP Systems, Bengaluru, India
Printed at Thomson Press India Ltd, New Delhi

www.penguin.co.in

Contents

Part 3: War Years in Exile and the Khilafat Movement

Part 4: The Turbulent Twenties

Author's Note

I have long harboured the passion to write history that is accessible to the public. As a student, I was frequently frustrated, discouraged and alienated by jargon-filled, abstract and, frankly, dull academic writing. It is a skill to convey complexity while writing clearly. Equally, I have experienced the thrill when scholars communicate a complex history or concept in an accessible manner and change the way I see the world.

Yet, to write for the public is not an easy choice for a historian. It means publishing with a non-academic press. Publishing with academic publishers, like Oxford or Harvard University Press (and peer-reviewed journals like the *Journal of Asian Studies*, to give only one example), is considered by many universities and research institutes as an infinitely more reliable path to an academic job and a regular income. Academic publishers are often seen as providing more credibility. To write for the public is, therefore, often risky for a scholar, especially a young one. Writing for the public is a skill and art distinct from contributing original research to a specialized body of knowledge (and a debate) on a specific topic that several historians have contributed to over the years. It requires you to simplify and explain to those who may not know as much about a particular topic. To endeavour to contribute originally to a very specialized body of historical knowledge (in my case, a vast body of scholarship on Hindu nationalism) and also convey this knowledge to a non-specialist public is extremely hard. So, partly, the answer to the frequently asked question 'Why don't more historians write for the public?' is that doing so involves doing two jobs at once and, often, for the salary of one!

Despite the risks and challenges of this endeavour, I am grateful for the opportunity to share with the public whatever I have learnt and understood through my scholarly research. Too often have I been alarmed by the astoundingly simplistic manner in which so many non-specialists understand history, and simultaneously amazed by how many intelligent scholars, having become so siloed in academia alongside their peers, are surprised when the realization dawns upon them that what they treat as historical 'common sense' is, quite understandably, not obvious for the much larger numbers among us who are not exposed to academic research (and not only by choice but due to societal and policy-related structural reasons).

Anti-intellectualism and the denigration of expertise represent a severe threat to the discipline, and to historical knowledge and understanding. Those who do not care to train themselves in the methods and approaches of history believe they are equal to experts who spend decades reading, corroborating and interpreting primary sources and secondary historical scholarship. Ignorant pseudohistory is successfully masquerading as 'history' on countless blogs, websites, YouTube channels, podcasts, WhatsApp forwards, 'news' channels, and even some newspapers and books. Partisan propagandists are being accepted as historians, and historians are being touted as propagandists. Myth often passes as objective historical fact and history dismissed as mere subjective opinion. Those lacking knowledge of the historical discipline, training and method are confusing pseudohistory with history. At such a time, it is vital to try and bridge the glaring gap between expert historians and the public. This book is one such attempt.

I hope to not only tell the story of the ideas of Lajpat Rai but also convey some sense of how complex history can be. It is certainly not as simple as the narratives we find in WhatsApp forwards, what our politicians and relatives tell us, or even what we read in many of our school textbooks. It is not about determining who the hero was and who the villain. Events have not only one person or community to blame; they do not have one cause but many. As a working rule, the more complex the explanation or story, the more you may trust it. History teaches that we may need to acknowledge that those we admire can be deeply flawed, and that even those we thoroughly dislike may have once done some good. Individuals, religion, society, and politics, ideas and concepts are not timeless. They keep changing. We need to muster a lot more imagination than we think we do to grasp the ways in which our past societies, polities and norms differed from our present realities. To assume timelessness is to be what historians call 'ahistorical' and to lack a historical sensibility. To straightforwardly read back contemporary reality into the past of any country (e.g., the modern democratic political form) is to be what historians call 'anachronistic'. And change is often not linear but can be zigzag, messy and chaotic.

I also hope to advance public understanding about the complexity of the discipline and profession of history. The degree of specialization in history is stunning and massively underestimated by non-specialists. In my experience, those who stopped studying or seriously reading history after class ten often assume that all of history can fit into a single textbook. This is like mistaking a world map for the world itself. History is staggeringly larger than that textbook we left behind all those years ago. It is specialized according to geographical regions. These may be broader than the nation state: there are historians of South Asia, Central Asia, Southeast Asia, Europe, the Americas, Africa and Oceania. History is specialized according to nation-state frames: there exist historians of India, Britain, China, Afghanistan and Monaco, ad infinitum. According to subnational regions: historians of Bengal, Orissa, Madras, Kerala, the North-east, etc. There are historians of London, Baltimore, Delhi, Bombay, Calcutta, Lahore, ad infinitum. History is specialized according to time periods: different historians specialize in prehistoric India, ancient India, medieval India, early modern India, modern India and post-Independence India. Historians specialize in political, military, intellectual, social, religious, cultural, economic, environmental, gender, imperial and global history, ad infinitum. Within the (still very broad) subfield of the political history of modern India from the 1880s to 1947, some specialize in the early 'national' politics of the 1880s, some in religious reform in the 1880s, the British Empire's foreign policy in the 1880s, in white racism or de-industrialization or land relations in the same decade, revolutionaries in the early 1900s, the foundation and composition of the early Muslim League, caste movements in the early 1900s, tribal movements in the 1910s, peasant politics in the 1910s, the impact of the First World War on Indian society, constitutional reforms in 1919, the 1919 Jallianwala Bagh massacre, Gandhi's Kheda Satyagraha, the Khilafat/non-cooperation movement, communal riots in the 1920s, Congress politics in the 1920s, Muslim politics in the 1920s, the revival of the Hindu Mahasabha in the 1920s, the Rashtriya Swayamsevak Sangh's politics, the Nehru Report, the rise of communism in the 1920s, tribal, peasant and caste movements in the 1920s, revolutionary politics in the 1920s, the two civil disobedience movements, labour and peasant movements in the 1930s, the communal tangle in the 1930s, the Congress ministries in 1937–39, the relations between the Congress and capitalists, Congress–labour relations, India during the Second World War, the Quit India movement, Azad Hind, the INA trials, peasant rebellion in the 1940s, the Cabinet Mission Plan, communal tangle and negotiations in the 1940s, Partition, and so on, and so on and so on. Historians are researching the lives and politics of Tilak, Savarkar, Tagore, Bose, Nehru, Azad, Gandhi, Ambedkar, Periyar, Jinnah, Bhagat Singh and countless other lesser-known figures. This is still leaving many, many, many research areas out (that full list will make up innumerable books).

No historian is a master of all. Yet good historians know quite a lot about their specialist sub-subfield. And to acquire this specialist understanding, they inevitably have to rely on the knowledge produced by historians outside their sub-subfield and subfield. History is an interconnected, collective enterprise. Good historians not only build upon the knowledge they receive but develop a more expansive understanding of the broader field of history—a historical sensibility better than that of a non-historian.

True, historians can get some details wrong, miss nuances and even be mistaken in their interpretations. This is why historians often contest one another. While their mutual criticisms may sometimes be prompted by non-academic considerations, these are more often a vital means to produce better historical understanding. Good history is about getting closer to the complex truth. That often involves debate. Anyone can choose to enter the debate. But to be taken seriously as a credible 'peer' (a fellow historian)—or even a credible reader of history—one has to first put in a lot more effort and read a lot more to understand history as a discipline, method and sensibility. For example, to understand the complex phenomena of the partition of the subcontinent, one needs to come to grips with the vast body of scholarly debates about it. To read one book on Partition is merely to skim its surface.

This book's purpose will be well served if others use it as a stepping stone to reach greater depth on the issues it raises and examines. I look forward to more nuanced understandings of Lajpat Rai's thought and of nationalism in general. Equally, I hope future scholarship is undertaken in a spirit of graceful and constructive revisionism rather than petty demolition. And that whatever knowledge my research has produced is not discarded but is built upon even as it is scrutinized and challenged. I will be mighty pleased if historians and the wider public engage with this book in the same scholarly spirit in which it was written.

Introduction

In popular imagination, Lajpat Rai, one of the giants of the anti-colonial struggle, is always linked to Bhagat Singh. It was to avenge his death that Bhagat Singh assassinated Saunders, an act for which he was hanged. Lajpat Rai, in the mind of the public, is almost always remembered as a great leader who sacrificed his life for the nation, falling victim as he did to a brutal assault by lathi-wielding agents of the British colonial state. Indeed, Hindi films such as the many Bhagat Singh movies and that contemporary classic of youth disaffection, *Rang De Basanti*, all correctly portray Lajpat Rai as a stalwart against British imperialism.[1] Many Indians will also recall that Lajpat Rai, along with Bal Gangadhar Tilak and Bipin Chandra Pal, was part of the 'Lal–Bal–Pal' triumvirate of 'extremist' leaders who, as opposed to 'moderates' like Gopal Krishna Gokhale, advocated more radical methods to achieve India's freedom. Lajpat Rai's standing as a fervent freedom fighter is attested to by the tributes paid to him annually on 28 January, his birth anniversary, by politicians across the spectrum.[2]

But Lajpat Rai is also known in another avatar: as an ideological ancestor of Hindutva, the Hindu nationalist ideology first elaborated properly by Vinayak Damodar Savarkar in his 1923 tract *Hindutva: Who is a Hindu?* Proponents of Hindutva today make a clear and assertive claim on Lajpat Rai as one of their own. Through its tenures since its thumping electoral victory in 2014, members of the Bharatiya Janata Party (BJP), including Prime Minister Narendra Modi, pay tribute to Lajpat Rai on his birth anniversary every year. In 2015, during her election campaign, Kiran Bedi, the BJP's chief ministerial candidate for Delhi, tied her party's scarf around his statue in New Delhi.[3] In 2016, the minister of state for culture and tourism inaugurated an exhibition on Lajpat Rai to commemorate his 150th birth anniversary.[4] The same year, the weekly organ of the Rashtriya Swayamsevak Sangh (RSS), *Organiser*, paying homage to Lala Lajpat Rai, described him as championing a politics more akin to its own rather than the 'anti-Hindu', 'pro-Muslim' nationalism of the Indian National Congress under Gandhi and Nehru.[5] Alongside Savarkar, the prophet of Hindutva, Keshav Baliram Hedgewar, the founder of the RSS, and the likes of Subhas Chandra Bose and Bhagat Singh, Lajpat Rai is named by the Hindu Right as one of the Hindu 'heroes' neglected by the Congress party and secular historians.[6] This ideological family also remembers him as a Hindu leader who contested Gandhian ahimsa (non-violence) as a dangerous means of protesting against tyranny.[7]

Interestingly, this Hindu nationalist claim on Lajpat Rai as their icon is confirmed by dominant interpretations of the man in historical scholarship. The ideas of V.D. Savarkar and M.S. Golwalkar, viewed as the founding fathers of this ideology, dominate scholarship on Hindu nationalism.[8] But Lajpat Rai too appears briefly in such studies. For instance, in Christophe Jaffrelot's seminal history of the Hindu nationalist movement from 1925 to the 1990s, he is viewed as a 'proto-Hindu nationalist' who, in 1909, articulated an earlier, nascent form of the ideology which Savarkar then developed fully in his 1923 *Hindutva* tract.[9] In his more recent work, Jaffrelot devotes more attention to Lajpat Rai, viewing him more boldly as playing a pivotal role in the birth of Hindu nationalism, an ideology later fine-tuned by Savarkar.[10] This broadly aligns with the view of Chetan Bhatt, another scholar of Hindu nationalism, who views Lajpat Rai as an exponent of a Hindu nationalism with strong ideological continuity with the Hindutva nationalism of Savarkar and the RSS.[11]

The same impression of Lajpat Rai is found in scholarship that views him as an important figure but is less focused on him.[12]

This interpretation of Lajpat Rai ends up leaving out much nuance and complexity. I first began suspecting something was amiss when, wanting to gain a deeper understanding of politically ascendant Hindu nationalism, I started reading *The Collected Works of Lala Lajpat Rai*.[13] In one of its fifteen volumes, I chanced upon documents which revealed that contrary to what I had assumed about the proponents of Hindu nationalism, Lajpat Rai had supported the Khilafat movement led by Gandhi and a section of Indian Muslim leaders. I was intrigued. How was a purported forefather of Hindutva supporting a Pan-Islamic movement in defence of an Islamic Caliphate? I found writings in which Lajpat Rai wholeheartedly approved of Congress–Muslim League cooperation, attempted to endow Hindus and Muslims with bonds of common belonging, and revised his understanding of India's medieval history to emphasize peaceable coexistence rather than conflict between Hindus and Muslims. Despite our strides in our attempts to understand Hindu nationalism, were we historians missing out on some nuance and complexity? This must, at least in some way, be inevitably limiting our understanding of an ideological and political constellation which remains deeply relevant to the history and politics of India today. Would not a better understanding of the nationalist thought of Lajpat Rai yield something of significance intellectually and politically? And so began my research into Lajpat Rai's narratives of nationalism developed over forty years from the 1880s up to 1928, the year he passed away.

In his pioneering book on Hindu nationalism, Jaffrelot's view of Lajpat Rai as a forerunner of Savarkar is based on Rai's speech at the first conference of the Punjab Hindu Sabha in 1909. Here, Lajpat Rai articulated the notion of a 'Hindu nation'. The use of this concept is assumed to reveal Rai's espousal of an earlier ('proto') form of the Hindutva nationalist ideology that Savarkar elaborated in 1923. But was Rai's 'Hindu nationalism' in these years really equal to a nascent form of Savarkarite Hindutva? And did Rai completely reject 'Indian nationalism' during this period? Jaffrelot's study made valuable contributions to our understanding of several aspects of Hindu nationalism. But all products of research have some limitations. Many of Jaffrelot's readers may come away with the impression that this single speech by Lajpat Rai, where he articulates the notion of a 'Hindu nation', represents his entire nationalist thought. Given his elaboration of an 'Indian nationalism' and his support for the Khilafat movement, things were evidently more complicated. Did Lajpat Rai shift his views on nationhood and, if so, why? What was the content and nature of his new nationalism? Additionally, one obvious problem with treating Lajpat Rai as an ideological precursor to Savarkar is that many of the ideas he articulated in the last decade of his life, the 1920s, coincided with and even succeeded the writing and publication of Savarkar's *Hindutva*. How can the nationalist thought Rai articulated after *Hindutva*'s publication be its antecedent?

Still, the Hindu Mahasabha is noted to have 'acquired a clearly Hindu nationalist orientation in the 1920s'[14] when it adopted Hindutva as its creed.[15] Given that Lajpat Rai emerged as a prominent Hindu Mahasabha leader from 1924 until his death in 1928, it may be reasonable to assume that he must also have championed Hindutva during his Mahasabha years. But did he? Why did Rai join the Hindu Mahasabha after elaborating an 'Indian nationalism' and supporting the Khilafat movement? Did this mean he ultimately retracted the accommodative Indian nationalism he had articulated just a few years ago? Or did it continue to affect Lajpat Rai even as a Hindu Mahasabha leader in the mid-1920s? I began to realize that the absence of a contextualized study of Lajpat Rai's 1909 speech and, more importantly, the lack of a comprehensive study of his nationalist thought over different *phases* of his life, had facilitated the assumption that Lajpat Rai's nationalist thought embodied Hindutva in its nascent form. My research brought into relief its fluidity, complexities and nuances, as well as significant differences with Hindutva.

To be sure, in his more recent work, Jaffrelot's reading of Lajpat Rai as a pioneer of Hindu nationalist ideology, later elaborated more fully by Savarkar, is backed by evidence that goes beyond his 1909 speech. It includes his association with the Punjab Hindu Sabha, whose ideological charter was marked by anxieties about Hindu numerical decline, Christian conversions and the introduction of separate electorates for Muslims.[16] Jaffrelot goes further back to Lajpat Rai's close association, from the 1880s to the 1900s, with the Arya Samaj which, he argues, 'was a vehicle for what was virtually Hindu nationalism',[17] and to Rai's elaboration of a history marked by an 'ideological anti-Islamism' central to Hindu nationalism.[18] Lajpat Rai's nationalist thought certainly displayed many of these features at particular historical junctures. But once again, to read these selected expressions as supporting evidence for the argument that Lajpat Rai was a founder of 'Hindu nationalism', a monolithic ideology which attained full fruition in Hindutva, leaves out significant complexity and fluidity that marked Lajpat Rai's ideas on nationhood through his life. A systematic study of Rai's thought through different phases of his political life reveals nationalist narratives with differences with Hindutva. These differences carry significant intellectual and political implications.

Similarly, although Chetan Bhatt claims to reject a teleological[19] narrative tracing the historical development of Hindu nationalism, he succumbs to precisely such an account when he refers to Lajpat Rai's thought as a 'phase' in the development of Hindu nationalist ideology.[20] For Bhatt, Lajpat Rai expresses a series of 'gestatory' (or embryonic) ideas of the Hindu nation that found their way 'virtually unchanged' into Savarkar's Hindutva and the RSS's nationalism and is therefore seen to elaborate virtually the same variety of Hindu nationalism.[21] That certain ideas articulated by Lajpat Rai may have been borrowed or built upon by Savarkar need not make him a proponent of Hindutva. This is possible for two reasons. First, Rai may have articulated other important ideas alongside his articulation of a 'Hindu nation' which make his 'Hindu nationalism' distinct from Hindutva. While elaborating his Hindutva ideology, Savarkar may have left these particular ideas out or indeed added some new ones of his own that made Hindutva distinct from Lajpat Rai's Hindu nationalism. Second, after articulating ideas about a Hindu nation, Lajpat Rai may have himself proceeded to later express substantially different ideas about nationhood, even as Savarkar and others drew upon his earlier ideas of Hindu nationalism.

To be sure, Bhatt's argument about Lajpat Rai's nationalist thought is not just based on his articulating embryonic ideas that find their way into Hindutva. Examining these ideas, he makes an independent, bolder case for a strong 'convergence' in their 'substantive ideological content'.[22] But this argument makes sense only because several ideas of Lajpat Rai that complicate this narrative have been overlooked. Strangely, Bhatt mentions the existence of 'epistemological discontinuities' between Lajpat Rai and the Savarkarite/RSS variety of Hindu nationalism, but ultimately inexplicably dismisses them to argue in favour of strong ideological continuity.[23] For example, even while noting that after 1924 Lajpat Rai formulated the idea that Hindus and Muslims shared a 'composite nationality', this is brushed aside without explanation with a statement that he had, in previous years, already declared that he was a 'Hindu nationalist'.[24] Rai's articulation of the notion that Muslims constituted an integral part of the 'Indian nation' and his dismissal of the idea of Hindu Raj ultimately get trivialized as they are surrounded with quotations showing his support for Hindu *sangathan* (consolidation) and his participation in the Hindu Mahasabha. His 'Hindu communalism' is thus seen to nullify the intellectual significance of his belief that Hindus and Muslims constituted an 'Indian' nation, and to automatically prove his Hindu nationalism, one that is virtually indistinguishable from Hindutva. Of course, the very lack of analysis of such discontinuities is what causes Lajpat Rai's thought to be subsumed into the Savarkarite/RSS school of Hindutva nationalism, and into 'Hindu nationalism' more generally.

Resisting the Pigeonhole

The absence of a comprehensive study of Lajpat Rai's nationalist thought has facilitated his evaluation as a predecessor of Savarkar, which has in turn inhibited the study of his thought in its own right. This book undertakes the first comprehensive and systematic examination of the nationalist thought of Lajpat Rai. Unlike previous scholarship whose assumptions or interpretations are based only on selective portions of Lajpat Rai's nationalist thought, this work is based on a sustained analysis of his entire oeuvre on nationhood. In doing so, it strongly contests dominant interpretations that iron out the intellectual shifts, fluidity and complexity in Lajpat Rai's thought to evaluate him as Savarkar's precursor, either sharing deep ideological affinities with Hindutva or even representing some nascent, softer variety of it. This book further challenges even the assumption that Lajpat Rai's nationalist thought can be satisfactorily described as representing a non-'exclusivist' (or non-exclusionary) variety of Hindu nationalism.[25] Although this allusion to internal differentiation within 'Hindu nationalism' is a welcome step in the right direction, such an evaluation of Lajpat Rai's thought continues to obscure the myriad, distinctive ways in which he conceptualized nationhood throughout his life.

But just as my study refuses to flatten out the complexities of his thought and place it in the 'Hindutva' or even the broader 'Hindu nationalism' camp, it also resists an earlier scholarly tendency to ignore his ideas about Hindu nationhood to argue that his body of thought represents a form of 'Indian nationalism', although admittedly with a conceptually puzzling 'communal' twist.[26] This scholarly stance is best represented by Gyanendra Pandey, a historian who, in the early 1990s, pioneered the analysis of the discourses of Indian 'nationalism' and 'communalism' as they emerged in colonial India. Pandey viewed Lajpat Rai as being among those (Indian) 'nationalists' who saw service to religious 'communities' as compatible with and even necessary for service to the Indian nation.[27] His championing of a politics of a Hindu 'community' in the 1920s, through the Hindu Mahasabha, is also perfunctorily interpreted in light of this framework. While correctly recognizing that Lajpat Rai expressed a politics of the Hindu community alongside the idea of an 'Indian nation' that included Muslims, this scholarship fails to illuminate the much more complicated relationship between

Lajpat Rai's simultaneously expressed notions of an 'Indian nation' and a 'Hindu community'. Moreover, in contrast to scholarship which ignores his articulations of the 'Indian nation' and evaluates him simply as a Hindu nationalist, these scholars erred in the opposite direction; they failed to explore Lajpat Rai's ideas about Hindus constituting a nation and pigeonholed all his diverse ideas into a single 'Indian nationalism'.

I am not the first to notice the more complicated nature of Lajpat Rai's thought. John Zavos, another scholar of Hindu nationalism, admits this complexity when he states that Lajpat Rai was both a 'Hindu nationalist' and a 'genuine Indian nationalist'.[28] Cursorily adducing Rai as an example, Zavos argues that the 'competing ideologies' of Hindu and Indian nationalism could simultaneously be expressed by the same person, blending and clashing in cultural and political contexts. But beyond rightly noting that figures like Lajpat Rai expressed both a 'Hindu' and an 'Indian nationalism', Zavos's study is unconcerned with exploring the texture of such complex thought. Then, we have Neeti Nair, a historian who has researched Hindu politics in colonial Punjab, who goes further than most in recognizing that Lajpat Rai shifted positions, and held complicated and even inconsistent stances.[29] But Nair's work is primarily concerned with uncovering the complexities of Punjabi Hindu politics in colonial India. It is not conceived as an intellectual history whose primary focus is to explore and understand the nature and meaning of ideas. While noting several of Lajpat Rai's shifting positions, Nair's work does not undertake a deeper, sustained examination to tease out their texture, meaning and intellectual implications. Previous scholars such as Jaffrelot, Bhatt and others who initiated research on Lajpat Rai's nationalist thought laid the basic ground for future researchers like me to deepen their understanding of it. This is true even though, due to their focus on unearthing a larger story, these scholars arrived at what was ultimately an incomplete, much-reduced picture of Rai's thought. This book builds on such research. It also recognizes the contribution of scholars like Zavos and Nair towards opening up space to acknowledge the complexity and nuances in Lajpat Rai's nationalist thought. While doing so, it goes further to offer a comprehensive and textured study of Lajpat Rai's oeuvre on nationhood.

My study shows that for a large part of his life, from the 1880s to 1915, Lajpat Rai was caught in a dilemma about how to define nationhood in India. At different historical junctures, he expressed different nationalist narratives, some grounded in the notion that 'Hindus' along with 'Muslims'[30] and other communities formed a single Indian nation, and others in the idea of Hindus constituting a separate nation. During this period, despite intermittent challenges, the existence of the Empire was largely taken for granted. The concept of the 'nation' in its nationalist political–statist sense—which holds that all communities deemed 'nations' must possess a self-governing state of their own—was gaining ground, but had not yet become dominant. Reflecting this hybrid reality, Lajpat Rai shifted between using the term 'nation' in its nationalist sense and its pre-nationalist sense to signify a cultural community without connotations of statehood. Shifting between these two senses of the 'nation', Lajpat Rai was conflicted about whether India was inhabited by one 'nation' or more. He moved between articulating an 'Indian' and a 'Hindu' nation, sometimes even expressing both concepts together, although in two different (nationalist and pre-nationalist) senses. He, however, clearly prioritized strengthening his imagined 'Hindu nation'.

By 1915, changes in personal, domestic and global contexts fundamentally and irreversibly changed Lajpat Rai's concept of nationhood. As the imperial world order appeared to weaken after the First World War, he could more vividly and realistically imagine 'nations' as self-governing political formations, in fully political and statist terms. The logic of superior nations having any moral right to rule over other inferior nations gave way to an imagination where all nations had an equal and inalienable right to self-government. Lajpat Rai now began to use the term 'nation' consistently in only its full-fledged nationalist political–statist sense. He also ceased to equate 'nations' with religio-cultural communities. He decided firmly that there existed in India only one nation and not more, and that this was the 'Indian nation' encompassing India's various religious communities. Lajpat Rai elaborated a full-bodied idea of an Indian nation, attempting to bind together India's Hindus and Muslims through common culture, ancestry and history. Moreover, contrary to the assumptions of current scholarship, even in the 1920s, when Lajpat Rai emerged as a prominent Mahasabha leader and is believed to have espoused a 'Hindu nationalism', he fervently championed an 'Indian nationalism'. Rather than ironing out these complexities and changes in Lajpat Rai's nationalist thought, my research has taken them seriously.

One of this book's central aims is to show that even when Lajpat Rai articulated his most robust 'Hindu nationalism' in the first decade of the twentieth century, it diverged from Savarkar's Hindutva in important ways. Lajpat Rai viewed Hindus and Muslims as separate 'nationalities' and converged with Savarkarite Hindutva when he took 'Hindu culture' to constitute the core of the Hindu nation.[31] Lajpat Rai's 'Hindu nationalism' also shared Hindutva's view that the Hindu nation was crystallized in Hindu historical resistance against the foreign Muslim enemy. Yet, even then, Lajpat Rai stood at quite a distance from Hindutva. He envisioned a friction-ridden yet cooperative relationship between the Hindu and Muslim 'nationalities' within a common state. His ability to see the Muslim nation existing robustly alongside the Hindu nation was vastly different from Savarkar's demand that to become part of the Hindu nation, Indian Muslims and Christians must abandon all marks of their religion and culture and assimilate into 'Hindu culture'.[32] Lajpat Rai's Hindu nationalism lacked Savarkarite Hindutva's desire for Hindu cultural supremacy and its aversion to religio-cultural diversity.

Unlike Hindutva, Lajpat Rai's Hindu nationalism ultimately envisioned the eventual unification of Hindu and Muslim 'nationalities' into a broader 'Indian' nation. Even when Rai espoused his semi-political Hindu nationalism, when he used the concept of the nation in its political–statist sense, he articulated an 'Indian nation' including Hindus and Muslims (and other religious communities).

Savarkar's Hindutva treated Muslims and Christians as second-class citizens of an India that belonged to Hindus, belying his ostensible concession of citizenship rights and reservations to Muslims. Lajpat Rai contemplated Muslim reservations without harbouring dreams of Hindu supremacy and domination. Rai's nationalism, of course, also diverged from Golwalkar's Hindu nationalism, which refused to concede to minorities even citizenship rights, envisioning them as living under complete Hindu domination. Lajpat Rai's early-twentieth-century 'Hindu nationalism' may have contributed to the more extreme Hindu nationalisms of the 1920s and 1930s. But his own Hindu nationalism needs to be understood independently of teleological ties to them.

By 1915, when Lajpat Rai committed himself to using the term 'nation' to signify only one large cultural community which needed to express itself in an independent state, he elaborated a richly textured nationalist narrative firmly grounded in the notion that Hindus and Muslims constituted a single 'Indian nation'. He went to great lengths to prove their common Indian nationhood by constructing for them a shared hybrid ancestry and a pluralist culture, and by rewriting India's 'Muslim' history. By unearthing this narrative, my research shows that whether or not Hindutva further developed the 'Hindu national' ideas articulated earlier by Lajpat Rai, his own 'Hindu nationalism' gave way to a rich, distinctive Indian nationalist narrative. Indeed, his new conceptualization of nationhood led him to support the Pan-Islamic Khilafat movement led by Gandhi and a section of the Indian Muslim leadership from 1919 to 1921. Contrary to what may be assumed about a supposed forefather of Hindutva, during the Khilafat movement, rather than expressing a Hindu nationalism fearful of Muslim religiosity and suspicious about their 'extraterritorial loyalties', Lajpat Rai's Indian nationalism urged Hindus to respect Muslim religious sentiments and sympathies towards the Ottoman caliphate and the Muslim world. It also strove to promote trust between India's Hindus and Muslims. In proffering reasons for why Hindus must support this 'Muslim' cause, Lajpat Rai, much like Gandhi, stressed that 'Hindu–Muslim unity' was crucial for

both Indian national identity and Indian self-government. As we can
see, pigeonholing Lajpat Rai's entire thought as 'Hindu nationalism'
obscured a historical–intellectual juncture when a Hindu political
figure like him enthusiastically supported Pan-Islamism as necessary
for Indian nationalism.

This book further seeks to challenge historical scholarship
which assumes that when, in the chaotic and violent aftermath of the
Khilafat movement, Lajpat Rai joined and led the Hindu Mahasabha,
he elaborated a Hindu 'communalism' that was equivalent to 'Hindu
nationalism'. It will show that in the mid-1920s, in response to
changed political contexts, Lajpat Rai elaborated yet another new and
distinct 'Indian' nationalist narrative. The militant Hindu politics he
sought to engineer through the Mahasabha aimed at establishing a
radically 'secular' state and politics—free of all markers of religion—
which he now considered a crucial precondition for the foundation
of a united Indian nation. From the more trust-based and other-
embracing secular Indian nationalism he articulated during the
Khilafat movement, Lajpat Rai moved to a more distrustful and
hard-line secular Indian nationalism that was explicitly hostile to
community-based politics. His vehement opposition to the politics of
the Muslim community meant that a move from 'Hindu nationalism'
to a 'secular' Indian nationalist conception does not always involve
a move towards a politics more accommodative towards Muslim
demands. Even so, like his militant Hindu politics, his secular Indian
nationalism had integrity and meaning. Grounded in moral and
political values, it was not just a ploy to institute Hindu majority
domination. As a Mahasabha leader, he also remained willing to
relinquish his radically 'secular' vision of state and politics to concede
reservations to the Muslim 'minority' if this was required for Indian
national unity.[33]

Lajpat Rai's ability to shift between 'Indian' and 'Hindu'
nationalism in the earlier part of his life, and his change to consistently
articulating Indian nationalist conceptions later, shows that he
was not hemmed in by a single ideology of nationalism. This book
takes Rai for what he was: a source of multiple ideas of nationhood.

Lajpat Rai remained intellectually flexible and kept the debate about nationhood open for a long time before firmly settling into the conception of a single Indian nation. The greater degree of oscillation in the earlier part of Lajpat Rai's life was made possible by the fact that during these years the concept of the 'nation' itself was in flux and 'in the making' in broader public discourse. The political–statist notion of nationhood was undoubtedly around and even strongly held by some political actors. But it was less widespread and had not begun to resolutely challenge the idea of Empire. The pre-nationalist sense of nation still circulated. This allowed Lajpat Rai's shift between nationalist and pre-nationalist meanings of 'nation', and between articulating an Indian and Hindu nation. Towards the latter part of his career, as the concept of the 'nation' in its political–statist sense became more stable and predominant in public discourse, Lajpat Rai grew less experimental about whether India was one nation or two. This book offers insight into a critical juncture when fluidity regarding conceptions of nationhood became increasingly scarce. People settled into believing unwaveringly either that the territory of India was inhabited by one diverse Indian nation, or only one Hindu nation, or two nations, one Hindu and one Muslim.

The 'Hindu' and 'Indian' nationalist narratives that Lajpat Rai expressed at different times were made available to others in the public domain and went in many directions. If the 'Hindu nationalist' ideas he articulated in the early part of his life can be seen as the nascent stage of an ideology that eventually crystallized into full-blown Hindutva, many of his 'Indian nationalist' ideas bore sufficient resemblance to the 'Indian nationalism' articulated by Nehru and other 'Indian nationalists' in the Congress to suggest that they might have also been built upon by the latter. Consequently, if his 'Hindu nationalist' thought is included in the pre-history of Hindutva, his 'Indian nationalism' can similarly be included in the pre-history of the official Indian nationalism of the Congress.[34]

Yet, my aim is not to free Lajpat Rai from the clutches of those interested in drawing up a lineage of Hindutva so he can be appropriated for a history of the Congress or secular Indian nationalism more broadly. Instead, my research seeks to break free of such teleological interpretations, which only obscure the nuances, complexity and distinctiveness of Rai's thought. Considering the different narratives of nationhood he articulated in different phases of his life as equally integral to his 'nationalist thought', it analyses each in its own right, independent of the body of ideas it possibly ultimately contributed to in later decades. Rather than seeking to dislodge Lajpat Rai from the category of 'Hindu nationalism' to re-lodge him under a self-explanatory 'Indian nationalist' umbrella, I wish to highlight that catch-all categorizations of the entirety of a political actor's thought—without a granular examination of its nuances and subtle textures at particular historical junctures, and without proper consideration of the shifts and changes in it across time—can obscure the complexity, fluidity and distinctiveness of their thought.

To be sure, the fluidity in Lajpat Rai's thought still occurred within broad intellectual parameters. His different Hindu and Indian nationalist narratives converged in being attached to the notion of 'Hindus' as an important grouping, respecting India's diversity, lacking an expectation of cultural assimilation or homogeneity, desiring cooperation with Indian Muslims within a common Indian polity, assuming a 'Hindu majority', and being open to conceding reservations for Muslims in acknowledgement of their fears of Hindu domination. By recognizing the commonality between Lajpat Rai's 'Hindu' and 'Indian' nationalist narratives, my research supports the work of scholars like William Gould and John Zavos which challenges assumptions about a hard boundary between 'Indian nationalism' and 'Hindu nationalism'.[35] In showing that Rai's articulation of a secular Indian nation could coexist with his Hindu 'communal' politics, it also partly agrees with scholarship—best represented by Ayesha Jalal—which contests assumptions about mutual exclusivity between secular Indian nationalism and such politics.[36] Rai's thought shows that 'Hindu nationalism' and 'Indian nationalism' can be expressed by the same person, and share intellectual ground. And that the same holds for 'Indian nationalism' and 'Hindu communalism'.

Yet, while welcoming the contribution of recent scholarship that highlights overlaps between 'Indian nationalism' and 'Hindu nationalism/communalism', my study of Lajpat Rai's thought seeks to push back against any impression that these ultimately constitute more or less the same position. I wish to deliberately resist predominant tendencies to read Gould's argument, that certain forms of self-avowed Indian nationalism were in the last instance nothing but a particular (non-Hindutva) variety of Hindu nationalism, as revealing that secular Indian nationalism was nothing but a thinly veiled form of Hindu nationalism.[37] I also wish to challenge the misconception promoted by the otherwise important research of Jalal and others that secular Indian nationalism can be easily championed alongside Hindu majoritarian communalism and, due to its foundation upon an engineered Hindu majority, is compromised by Hindu communalism—once again ultimately amounting only to a thinly disguised form of it.[38] Lajpat Rai's thought in the mid-1920s shows that his strategy to organize a 'communal' politics to achieve his ideal of a 'secular' Indian nation threatened to undermine the latter. Equally, despite his Hindu politics, his secular Indian nationalism continued to possess integrity and positive significance for minorities. My analysis of Lajpat Rai's simultaneous articulation of Hindu politics and a secular Indian nationalism recognizes the internal tension that marked this complex stance, and therefore the tension that continues to exist between the categories of 'secular Indian nationalism' and 'Hindu communalism'. Taking Lajpat Rai's 'Hindu communalism' seriously need not nullify the significance of his secular 'Indian nationalist' narratives. Such reductionism, following from a rightful attempt to dismantle hard binaries, can be as problematic and misleading as the drawing of strict binaries.

This book argues against such intellectual reductionism and the pigeonholing of all of Lajpat Rai's ideas into either Hindutva or a moderate variety of Hindu nationalism, or indeed secular Indian nationalism. Doing this has prevented us from noticing the subtleties, nuances and distinctiveness of Rai's thought at particular junctures. For example, they have prevented us from recognizing the

distinctive texture and nature of the 'Hindu nationalism' he regularly
articulated before 1915, and its difference from Hindutva. They have
prevented us from noticing shifts and changes in his thought across
time. For instance, we failed to heed Lajpat Rai's distinct 'Indian
nationalist' narratives during the Khilafat movement and even his
Hindu Mahasabha phase. The internal complexity, fluidity and
dynamism of Lajpat Rai's nationalist thought make it resistant to
easy overall categorization. If one has to make such an evaluation,
one can only say—rather vaguely—that *taken collectively*, the distinct
and internally complex narratives that Lajpat Rai articulated in his
political life remain an intellectual position distinct from Hindutva,
the moderate varieties of 'Hindu nationalism' and the Congress's
official ideology of 'Indian nationalism'. The important takeaway really
is that blanket, catch-all categorizations of Lajpat Rai's nationalist
thought have prevented us from properly understanding it, and from
forensically examining its contours and textures as articulated in
different phases of his life. Each of his nationalist narratives requires
granular scrutiny before being evaluated in light of the categories of
'Hindu nationalism' and 'Indian nationalism' (categories which are
internally differentiated, lie on a continuum, and may, but also may
not, overlap significantly). This book constitutes the first attempt
to arrive at a fuller, richer understanding of a distinctive body of
nationalist thought that, given Lajpat Rai's stature and influence,
doubtlessly shaped the intellectual milieu of India both during his
lifetime and beyond it. More broadly, it seeks to bring attention to
the diverse, internally complex ways in which nationalist narratives
can be articulated; although they might have several concepts in
common, the different meanings attributed to these concepts and the
various ways in which these are structured in relation to each other is
what makes each nationalist narrative distinctive.

Some Subplots

As sorts of subplots, this book also sheds light on the changes
that certain key elements of Lajpat Rai's nationalist narratives
underwent over time, opening up space for readers and researchers

to contemplate the broader implications of these intellectual paths. These trajectories will be visible across the chapters of this book. For instance, Lajpat Rai began by attempting to forge Hindu unity by de-emphasizing theological details and emphasizing only the broadest and simplest theological tenet of the Arya Samaj: Vedic monotheism.[39] Over time, as he felt it would be unable to perform this task (given the tremendous plurality of Hindu religiosity), he dropped references to Arya Samajist theology to arrive at an internally diverse, catholic conception of Hinduism.[40] The Arya Samaj was now conceived as one of Hinduism's many sects. The persistent imperative to include progressively larger numbers of people within his definition of the 'Hindu nation' eventually compelled Lajpat Rai to subordinate even his newly conceived, internally differentiated Hinduism to the secular categories of Hindu 'history' and 'Hindu culture'.[41] His move from theology to secular 'Hindu culture' made possible both a 'Hindu nation' and a Hindu majority.[42] After 1915, when Lajpat Rai elaborated a full-bodied Indian nationalist narrative, secular Hindu culture was conceived in a more capacious manner, in terms of a timeless entity that defined even Muslims and Christians as members of the Indian nation.[43]

At the same time, he advocated an Indian nationalist culture composed of elements of both Hinduism and Islam, and Hindu and Muslim culture. In the end, Lajpat Rai required that all religions, including this catholic Hinduism, be subordinated to the Indian nation, and that all marks of religion—even its secularized forms[44]—be divorced from the political domain as the means to build a peaceful, cooperative and stable Indian nation.[45] This vision of a 'secular' Indian nation–state[46] now rested on the assumption of a Hindu majority 'community', itself conceived in secular rather than theological terms. Across Lajpat Rai's Hindu and Indian nationalist narratives, then, a gradual movement occurred towards a progressive de-emphasis on religious theology in favour of the progressive culturalization and secularization of Hindu religion. This process first facilitated a Hindu majority and then simply assumed it. Here, Lajpat Rai participated in a broader phenomenon to which both Indian nationalists in the Congress and Hindutva nationalists contributed.

Even those Hindutva nationalists who desired a theocratic state gave up the idea due to the theological diversity of Hinduism. To facilitate a Hindu majority, theology must be sacrificed for a secular culturalist vision. Interestingly, contrary to the argument that Indian nationalism was contaminated by Hinduism, my study of Lajpat Rai reveals that it was often Hindu religion that was either instrumentalized or abandoned for the sake of secularized Hindu and Indian nationalist narratives. Importantly, it also illustrates that Hindu or Indian nationalisms predicated on such a creation of a Hindu majority, while open to critique, do not always end in a Hindutva-like desire for Hindu majoritarian domination or aversion to diversity.

Another subplot discernible in the background is Lajpat Rai's early attachment to ascendant modern ideas of democratic political representation and self-rule. He quickly grew attached to its anti-aristocratic numerical logic, whereby numbers ('one person, one vote') determined political influence for the first time in history. With his belonging to an all-India Hindu majority making this easier for him, Lajpat Rai adhered to the logic and language of democracy both as a 'Hindu nationalist' and as an 'Indian nationalist'.[47] In showing that it is possible to be a democrat both as an Indian and Hindu nationalist, this book hopes to help us analytically differentiate between different types of Hindu nationalists: those committed to the core democratic principles of equality, freedom and inclusion, and those using the rhetoric of democracy instrumentally while in reality being guided by the anti-democratic impulse to institute majority domination and treat some groups as if they are less free and equal, and do not belong.[48]

A third subplot relates to caste. Like the many political actors who conceived Indian politics in Hindu–Muslim terms, Lajpat Rai's invocation of the Hindu nationality/community and the Muslim nationality/community as the natural and primary building blocks of India often entailed the omission of not just theological, regional, linguistic and class differences but also caste cleavages. His 'Hindu nationalist' narratives at times presumed the inclusion of low castes and even rationalized the caste hierarchy.[49]

But at other junctures, caste cleavages, the invisibilization of which sometimes helped animate the notion of a Hindu majority, would be exposed and would cause anxiety about the fragility of this notion. Lajpat Rai's Arya Samajist background then allowed caste hierarchy to be explicitly acknowledged as a problem, leading him to espouse radical caste reform to produce a majority Hindu 'nationality' on a stronger footing.[50] Yet, in his final 'Indian nationalist' narrative, the felt urgency of defending this Hindu majority from the perceived threat of the Muslim community could make him abandon caste radicalism and adopt a more conciliatory attitude towards 'orthodox' Sanatanist Hindus (i.e., Hindus claiming to defend *sanatan dharm* or the eternal, timeless Hindu religion).[51] Lajpat Rai's intellectual trajectory on caste reveals that 'Hindu nationalism' can variously involve conservative or radical attitudes to caste, and that 'secular Indian nationalism' can entail a more conservative stance towards caste as compared with 'Hindu nationalist' positions.

Finally, we come to the subplot of Punjab. This book examines Lajpat Rai's nationalist thought primarily from the point of view of his attempt to forge a unified Hindu community and negotiate a political relationship with Muslims at an all-India level. His provincial Punjabi background is not its central focus. But, of course, it informed many of the positions he assumed. Lajpat Rai's association with Punjab's Arya Samaj was clearly reflected in his initial formulation of Hinduism.[52] It also influenced his initial construction of Hindu history.[53] At the same time, as his dilution of Arya Samaj tenets in favour of Hindu culture shows, from the very beginning, Lajpat Rai displayed a strong tendency to transcend the regional to forge an all-India Hindu 'community' or 'nationality' in the all-India political context. His Arya Samajist background, with its radical approach to caste reform, once again revealed itself as he strove to engineer a strong all-India Hindu majority 'nationality'. The influence of Punjab disappeared altogether when he re-imagined the relationship of Hindus and Muslims in India in the light of his newly acquired internationalist perspective during the war years and the Khilafat movement. And it would reappear to forcefully shape his nationalist thought in the post-Khilafat turmoil in the mid-1920s. Now, his belonging to a Hindu minority in Muslim-majority Punjab played a vital role both in his fearful turn to a vigorous Hindu politics (which he spearheaded through the Mahasabha) and his ability to consider Muslim demands for safeguards arising out of fears of Hindu majority domination. Lajpat Rai's ability to identify with both a Hindu-minority status in the Punjab, and a Hindu-majority status at the all-India level made it possible for him to hold both these intellectual positions.

This book's primary aim, however, remains unchanged: to follow Lajpat Rai through different junctures in his life as he struggled to define broader 'Hindu' and 'national' identities, and consistently attempted to answer questions such as: 'What does it mean to be Hindu?', 'What does it mean to be a nation?', 'Is being national the same as being Hindu?' and 'What is the best way to relate Hindu identity to Indian national identity in a manner that is fair to both Hindus and others?' As mentioned, in doing so, Lajpat Rai offers us a body of nationalist thought distinct from the Indian nationalism of Gandhi and Nehru, and the Hindutva of Savarkar and the RSS. Understanding Lajpat Rai's thought can yield intellectual–political insights relevant for India today. It can help secular Indian nationalists grasp the nuances of the positions perceived to be on the Right and help Hindutva sympathizers better comprehend their opponents, and assume alternative positions previously invisible to them. This book aspires to promote understanding and dialogue between divided and estranged Indians, and thus contribute to de-polarization and consensus building. It does so in the hope that, despite disagreements, members of 'the world's largest democracy' will not treat each other as irreconcilable enemies, but be committed to understanding each other with as much empathy and good faith as they can muster. It is based on the premise that people committed to democracy manage intellectual–political conflicts without treating their adversaries as fundamentally less worthy, as permanent enemies. And that they believe in conversation and persuasion rather than force and violence.

Approach and Sources

Quentin Skinner, the renowned intellectual historian,[54] has warned fellow intellectual historians that ideas must not be treated as if they are launched in a vacuum, detached from their political and intellectual contexts.[55] The proper way of doing intellectual history, he argues, is to not just analyse an individual's ideas but to place them in their political and intellectual context, and to grasp what they are doing in those contexts.[56] This is how the intended meaning of an individual's thought is recovered. Against current scholarly trends, I take special care to take Skinner's approach seriously and give a fuller picture of the political and intellectual contexts in which Lajpat Rai's thought actively emerged. I hope to shine light on how different types of contexts—political and intellectual, broader (long-term, macro) and narrower (immediate, micro)—inform the ideas of a politician–thinker like Lajpat Rai.

However, the book primarily aims to highlight the distinctive texture, analytical nuances, ideological fluidity and even internal tension that can inform the thought of a politician–thinker. Lajpat Rai's nationalist thought was marked by a significant degree of fluidity, a result of the particular type of political thinker he was, one who articulated a specific kind of thought. This point needs elaboration. Of course, even the seemingly abstract thought of political thinkers, who can be called theorists or philosophers, is also an intervention in a political and intellectual debate, can change over time and be internally contradictory.[57] But such thought—or rather, such theory or philosophy—is often produced in relative independence from everyday practical politics, aspires to a high level of generality and abstraction, and is obsessively, self-consciously concerned with clarifying the meaning of words and concepts, and their relationships to other concepts. This results in a relatively high degree of coherence and consistency. This is the kind of scholarly political theory or philosophy produced by political thinkers like Thomas Hobbes who wrote a systematic treatise like *The Leviathan*. Lajpat Rai did not produce this kind of systematic political theory or philosophy.

A second type of political thought is produced by political thinkers who are not scholars but fully active political actors. Their political thought is articulated in the thick of practical politics, with the desire to actively influence and change it. As an inevitable outcome of its direct, active engagement with politics, a relatively higher degree of fluidity and internal tension is present in this type of thought as compared to the thought of political philosophers. Nevertheless, it still remains relatively stable and independent in the face of changing political contexts. A product of relatively deep, self-conscious reflection on the world, it generates or elaborates a broader political and ethical vision. Though not the more scholarly political theory of Hobbes, its reflective vision gives such political thought a relatively high level of coherence and consistency. This is the kind of political thought produced by thinkers like Gandhi.

Lajpat Rai represents a different, third type of political thought. Unlike Hobbes and like Gandhi, he is immersed wholly in practical politics. His political thought is expressed in the thick of practical politics, with the desire to actively influence and direct it. But he allows his political thought to be shaped by changing political contexts to a higher degree than thinkers like Gandhi. For instance, Lajpat Rai's nationalist thought was reshaped to a significant extent in response to a major global event (e.g., the First World War), political–intellectual realignments of other political actors (e.g., the Muslim League's political reorientation and desire, by 1915, to cooperate with the Congress), changed personal context (e.g., his stay abroad, away from India) and domestic political events (e.g., the disintegration of the Khilafat movement and the riots that followed). Like Gandhi, Lajpat Rai was also guided by ethical concerns. He remained firmly rooted within a loose moral compass which sought to ensure that Hindus and Muslims could live together with dignity and justice within a larger Indian nation and/or polity. However, unlike Gandhi, he did not self-consciously and consistently weave these into a systematic political and ethical vision. Instead, he saw himself as straightforwardly driven by political goals: anti-colonialism, defining a 'Hindu' and 'national' identity, and forging a 'Hindu' and 'national' unity. He did not have a broader, comprehensive, explicitly articulated ethical vision which he felt must consistently guide his ideas and positions as a political actor. In other words, he was not always compelled to judge whether his ideas and positions as a political actor were consistent with this vision. Due to this, there exists a higher degree of fluidity to the point of even expressing and vacillating between mutually conflicting ideas at a given historical juncture.

Despite its claims of universal application, Skinner's method for intellectual history presupposes that our object of study would be the *relatively* more systematic, high-theoretical political thought of political thinkers like Hobbes and Niccolo Machiavelli, or even Rabindranath Tagore and Gandhi. Beyond a point, it appears not to be particularly helpful in studying political actor–thinkers like Lajpat Rai whose struggle and experimentation with different political ideas make their thought relatively less systematic, less canonical, more organic, radically contextual (informed by frequent references to multiple, often fast-changing political–intellectual contexts) and more malleable. This greater changeability is what makes the political thought of figures like Lajpat Rai both extraordinarily fascinating and difficult as objects of study. To understand Rai's thought, I had to shift to an approach more sensitive to political embeddedness, radical contextuality,[58] intellectual flexibility and even inconsistency.[59] This book hopes to offer some guidelines on how to study and understand such ideologically flexible, pragmatic, organic, contextual and quotidian political actor–thinkers.

Without denying the differences between thinkers like Lajpat Rai and Gandhi, I do not wish to overstate them either. One reason why Gandhi's thought—or even Nehru's or Savarkar's—appears relatively more systematic is because these figures have been primarily understood through their isolated texts rather than the totality of their texts and quotidian utterances expressed in different contexts over time—i.e., through the kind of approach I have chosen to study Lajpat Rai. Despite its more systematic nature, because they too—like Rai—were political actors responding to different political events, and the ideas and actions of other political figures, their political thought also inescapably acquired some degree of instability and dynamism. In all humility, I hope my more contextual, fluidity-sensitive approach serves as an exemplar to better understand the political thought of other politically embedded actor–thinkers too.

My archive consists chiefly of the largely untapped writings and speeches of Lajpat Rai over a roughly four-decade long period that spanned his active political life. This includes a wide range of textual material, including books, tracts and pamphlets authored by Lajpat Rai; his articles, 'letters to the editor', interviews to the press, 'open letters' to certain prominent political personalities and public speeches published in newspapers such as the *Tribune*, the *Panjabee* and the *People*, among others, and occasionally his private correspondence. I have relied on these sources as compiled in the fifteen volumes of *The Collected Works of Lala Lajpat Rai*, which has collated, along with Lajpat Rai's published books and pamphlets, primary material held by multiple archives, including the Nehru Memorial Museum and Library and the National Archives of India in New Delhi, the Dwarka Das Library in Chandigarh, the Punjab Municipal Library in Lahore, the British Museum and Library in London and a number of libraries in the United States of America. The books, tracts and pamphlets authored by Lajpat Rai were not canonical works of a high-theoretical nature but are useful for gleaning his relatively more deliberate reflections on the main questions and problems that moved him. This was sometimes also true for lengthier articles that he published in newspapers as part of a 'series'. But much of the primary material for Lajpat Rai consists of shorter articles and public speeches, mostly (although not always) containing political thought that was much more embedded in and informed by the minutiae of everyday politics, and therefore much more quotidian in nature. As suggested above, the nature of such primary textual material posed unique challenges in terms of demanding the reconstruction of multiple, fast-changing contexts to which Lajpat Rai often only cursorily referred, assuming the familiarity of his audience or readership, a familiarity which the present reader of his speeches of course often no longer possesses. It also often required me to piece together snippets of his thoughts on a particular theme expressed disjointedly, unsystematically across multiple speeches or sometimes found in speeches on different, seemingly unrelated themes. The overwhelming majority of Lajpat Rai's writings and speeches are in English. For the few writings originally in Urdu, I have relied on translations by Jai Ratan of the Sahitya Akademi as produced in *The Collected Works*. To provide intellectual context for Lajpat Rai's political ideas, I have gone beyond primary sources directly related to him to utilize the speeches and writings of his interlocutors in explicit or implicit political–intellectual debates.

Outline of the Book

Because the broad nationalist narratives that Lajpat Rai articulated unfolded chronologically, in engagement with evolving political contexts, they are best understood as an unfolding story running through real historical time. And so, against the current trends in the discipline of history, this book follows a chronological rather than a purely thematic approach.[60] Each of the book's four parts cover the nationalist narratives that Lajpat Rai articulated in four distinguishable phases of his intellectual life.

Part 1 highlights the nationalist narratives articulated by Lajpat Rai in the first two decades of his political life, the 1880s through the 1890s. Starting with his coming of age in colonial Punjab, Chapter 1 sheds light on his turn to the Arya Samaj in the early 1880s, and what this meant for his views on religion. Chapter 2 explores Lajpat Rai's reaction, in the late 1880s, to Sir Syed Ahmad Khan's rejection of the Congress and its demand for elective representation. A Muslim aristocrat from an older generation, Khan held that Indians on legislative councils must be nominated on the basis of ancestry and historically proven political abilities. Arguing against Khan, Lajpat Rai insisted that representatives for Indians must be elected from a wider pool of the Indian people. He articulated an incipient concept of the 'Indian nation' in its modern nationalist–statist sense, and his imagined 'Indian nation' included different religious communities.

Chapters 3 and 4 follow Lajpat Rai as he articulates a different conception of nationhood in the 1890s. Chapter 3 highlights how Rai's desire to lay claim to a broader 'Hindu' identity led him to define Hinduism in terms of simple Vedic monotheism, and also to turn to secular categories like 'Hindu culture' and 'history'. Showing that by the 1890s Lajpat Rai had begun to explore the idea of a 'Hindu nation', Chapter 4 examines the contours of Rai's Hindu nation. It does so also by analysing Rai's construction of India's history, the aim of which was not to demonize Muslims, but to impart a sense of pride to the 'Hindu nation'.

Part 2 unveils the nationalist narratives elaborated by Lajpat Rai between 1900 and 1915. Chapter 5 shows that for various reasons, he began this intellectual phase by explicitly rejecting the Congress's notion of a common 'Indian' nation to elaborate a robust notion of 'Hindu nationality'. Nevertheless, his Hindu nationality existed alongside India's other 'religious nationalities' and could even potentially unite with them in a future Indian nation. To prove the existence of the Hindu nationality, he advanced a historical narrative of Hindu resistance to 'foreign' Muslim rule. As shown in Chapter 6, Rai also claimed that rather than rely on Western concepts, Hindus should draw upon the resources already available within Hinduism to build a social and national spirit among themselves. Further, he argued that just as the internal diversity within Islam or Christianity did not thwart Muslim or Christian nationality, likewise Hinduism's immense diversity was no impediment to the existence of a Hindu nation.

Chapter 7 examines Lajpat Rai's conception of Hinduism and nationhood as articulated after the Swadeshi movement (1906–08) had opened up possibilities for more agitational and militant modes of politics. Recognizing that an essential feature of the nation was that it possessed collective political agency, Lajpat Rai turned to the Bhagavad Gita to show that Hinduism contained resources for confrontational, even violent, political action to reclaim a measure of power for the nation.

Chapter 8 explores Lajpat Rai's ideas of nationhood in the context of the 1908–09 Muslim League demand for separate electorates and 'weightage' (i.e., 'weighted' representation of a community in excess of its numerical proportion in British India's population). It shows that Lajpat Rai's opposition to separate electorates was driven by his belief that by assuming the permanently separate political interests of Hindus and Muslims, they foreclosed the possibility of a single Indian political nation in the future. He returned to the conception of the 'Indian nation' he had articulated in 1888. By rejecting 'weightage' and asserting the legitimacy of the numerical criterion, Lajpat Rai also revealed his inclination to believe that this Indian nation would function best within a broadly liberal–democratic framework.

Chapter 9 reveals that in 1909, in attempting to realize his most robust Hindu nation, Lajpat Rai abandoned his attempt to find Hindu nationality in Hindu religion and made secular 'Hindu culture' the centrepiece of his Hindu nation. It will be shown that despite appearances of strong similarity, Lajpat Rai's Hindu nationalism remained distinct from the Hindutva nationalism that Savarkar conceptualized roughly a decade later. The larger part of this chapter also highlights that between 1909 and 1914, Lajpat Rai considered a radically egalitarian attitude to caste as crucial for building a strong Hindu nation, which in turn he considered essential for building the future Indian nation.

Part 3 follows Lajpat Rai's discourse on the nation between 1915 and 1922. Chapter 10 argues that during Lajpat Rai's exile between 1915 and 1919, he rejected the idea that India was inhabited by separate 'religious nationalities'. He now separated 'religion' from the idea of nationhood and used the term 'nation' to signify only one larger 'Indian' community encompassing both Hindus and Muslims. In other words, he abandoned the idea that there were two separate cultural nations, one Hindu and the other Muslim, which could then unite in a larger political entity called the 'Indian nation'. Instead, he articulated a full conception of Indian nationhood in which one Indian nation in the cultural sense dreams of full self-government for itself. Lajpat Rai sometimes proved the existence of this Indian nation by insisting that Hindus and Muslims shared Aryan ancestry and a secular 'Hindu culture', defined as the essence of the Indian nation. Despite being sometimes grounded in Hindu assumptions, Lajpat Rai's new Indian nationalism did not aim to stamp out India's religio-cultural diversity to realize Hindu cultural homogeneity. Significantly, at other times, Lajpat Rai attempted to endow Hindus and Muslims with a common nationality by asserting their common racially mixed Aryan–Mongolian ancestry. He also wished India's public culture to be a pluralist mix of both 'Hindu' and 'Muslim' cultures. Chapter 11 shows that Lajpat Rai's new 'Indian' nationalism was also evident in his rewriting of India's history, through which he sought to emphasize the indigenous nature of 'Muslim' rule.

Chapters 12 and 13 unveil Lajpat Rai's ideas on nationhood as articulated in 1920–21 in the midst of the Khilafat agitation. Far from what might be expected of a man regarded as the intellectual precursor of Savarkar, Lajpat Rai was more Gandhian in his wholehearted embrace of the Khilafat slogan of Hindu–Muslim unity. He exhorted Hindus to support the Khilafat cause of Indian Muslims, emphasizing that this would strengthen Hindu–Muslim unity, crucial for the identity and autonomy of the Indian nation. Hindus were also enjoined to unite with Muslims to save the Ottoman Caliphate because it was the guardian of the Indian nation. This section argues that Lajpat Rai saw Pan-Islamism as necessary for the Indian nation.

Part 4 focuses on the post-Khilafat period that saw galloping mistrust between Hindu and Muslim leaders and the eruption of violent riots at the popular level. Chapter 14 elucidates this new context, and Chapter 15 shows how Lajpat Rai first responded to it by demanding the reform of religions for the sake of securing a united Indian nation. However, Chapters 16 and 17 reveal that after the 1924 Kohat riot, Lajpat Rai joined the Hindu Mahasabha to articulate a Hindu politics geared towards opposing Muslim demands of communal representation and separate electorates, and inaugurating a radically 'secular' state and politics. This, he now believed, was essential to realize a united, firmly grounded Indian nation. At the same time, Rai could shift away from this hard-line 'secular' Indian nationalism to concede limited communal representation to Muslims. Much of his Mahasabhaite politics aimed at opposing perceived Muslim attempts to extend communal representation beyond what he believed were reasonable limits, which he feared would bring Muslim domination, wreck the Indian nation and encroach upon the rights of the Hindu community.

Chapter 18 explores Lajpat Rai's ideas on Hindu sangathan, arguing that for him, it entailed on the one hand, resistance to Gandhian ahimsa and the inculcation of physical culture and, on the other, a symbolic organization of the Hindu community that sacrificed caste reform. It emphasizes that although Lajpat Rai often spoke of sangathan as if it was taking place in a non-'political' realm, it was driven by the political aims of maintaining a Hindu majority and establishing a secular Indian nation–state. Chapters 19 and 20 show that Lajpat Rai often underlined the non-political nature of sangathan and the limited nature of the Mahasabha's politics because he saw himself as spearheading a temporary 'communal' politics, which had to remain subordinated to Congress's Indian nationalism. They illustrate that in the 1920s, Lajpat Rai, as an influential leader of the Mahasabha, did not turn to Savarkar's ascendant Hindutva nationalism, but aimed to realize a vision of secularism. This secularism was attached to the notion of a Hindu majority and attempted to limit separate Muslim representation, but also respected India's diversity and remained willing to accommodate checks against Hindu domination.

Part 1: The Late Nineteenth Century

1

Towards the Arya Samaj

By 1820, the English East India Company had conquered most of the Indian subcontinent. Having conquered Bengal and Mysore in the previous century, the Company steadily extended the frontiers of its empire, absorbing the Marathas, Delhi and Awadh. But it was only with the death of Ranjit Singh in 1839 that the British turned their attention to the north-west. First conquering Sindh in 1843, the Company dealt a crushing blow to the Sikh Empire in the Anglo–Sikh War of 1849.[1] With the conquest of Punjab, the entire Indian subcontinent came under the control of the British. As a strategic region which mustered the least resistance during the 1857 revolt, Punjab enjoyed certain advantages. But these were outweighed by the much harsher system of governance that the British adopted in Punjab. Impatient with constitutional procedures, the British administration in Punjab relied on direct, personal and paternalistic rule by officials, and often fell back on military force. It was in this sternly ruled British Punjab that Lajpat Rai was born on 28 January 1865.

Born in the small village of Dudhike in Ferozepur district in central Punjab, Lajpat Rai received his early schooling in Rupar (Ambala district), where his father served as a Persian instructor.[2]

His itinerant father then moved the family to Shimla, Ambala city and finally to Jagraon. Apart from this familial wandering, little Lajpat also found himself caught in a religious conflict playing out within his family. Born into the Agarwal Baniya caste, Lajpat Rai had a paternal grandfather who was a Swetambara Jain, a mother who was a follower of Sikhism and a father who was nearly a Muslim. Having undergone a Persian schooling, and inspired by the 'lofty character' of his teacher, a *maulvi*, Lajpat Rai's father Radha Krishan had become 'a believer in Islam, according to the Sunni school'.[3] He took a keen interest in the teachings of different religions, but recited the namaz, observed Ramzan fasts and cultivated acquaintances among the *ulema* and maulvis.[4] After the influential Muslim aristocrat–official and thinker Syed Ahmed Khan began propounding his reformist, rationalist interpretations of Islam in the 1860s–70s, Radha Krishan became a 'Muslim of the Syed Ahmad School'.[5] His allegiance to a reformed Islam made him averse to certain rituals and customs of Hinduism, particularly idol worship, which he denounced in the published organ of the Brahmo Samaj of Lahore.[6] Radha Krishan's beliefs frequently caused conflict with his wife, Gulab Devi, who was repulsed and upset by her husband's Islamic ways.[7] The fear of Radha Krishan taking the final step of a formal conversion and the consequent disintegration of the home loomed over the family.[8]

During Lajpat Rai's childhood, his father got him interested in studying religion, particularly the Quran. Young Lajpat also observed the namaz and sometimes kept Ramzan fasts. Radha Krishan and Lajpat's participation in Islam partly reflected the persistence in British Punjab of an older Persianate world[9] which had infused all of Punjab from the eleventh to the late eighteenth century, manifested in Punjab's Muslim-majority population.[10] Over the centuries, Hindus had adjusted to this Persianate world, learning Persian and partaking in many aspects of this Persianate culture. In fact, like Lajpat Rai, other future leaders of the Arya Samaj such as Guru Dutt Vidyarthi and Lala Hans Raj also had fathers who were immersed in this Persianate world, possessing knowledge of Persian and an interest in Islam.[11] But now, this world was fading. For a section of the Muslim intelligentsia, British conquest once again reminded them of their weakness, something keenly felt since the collapse of the Mughal Empire and the rise of the Sikhs under Ranjit Singh. A new threat was felt from the unprecedented flow of Christian missionaries into Punjab following the British conquest, as well as from socio-economically upwardly mobile Hindu intelligentsia. Although Hindus had not politically ruled over the Punjab since the thirteenth century, and were, like Sikhs, a minority in the province, they were a fairly large minority and were adjusting successfully to the new world of the British Raj.[12] Through the 1850s, the Government of Punjab initially relied on an imported Bengali middle-class elite to fill subordinate posts in administration. Bengal, the first region to be conquered, had been the first to acquire a Western-educated Indian intelligentsia, which was required to fill the lower rungs of imperial administration. Following British power as it moved through the Gangetic plain, several Bengalis settled in Punjab throughout the 1850s. But soon the government established educational institutions to train young Punjabis to fill these subordinate posts. Taking advantage of the introduction of English education, upper-caste Punjabi Hindus rose to form a new class of anglicized Punjabis. In fact, due to the decline of the Brahman and Kshatriya castes in Punjab from the days of Mughal and Sikh rule, this Punjabi Hindu intelligentsia was dominated by merchant and trader castes like Khatris, Agarwals and Aroras.[13] As Jaffrelot argues, these already dominant Hindu trading castes now utilized English education to translate an economic dominance into a sociocultural one.[14]

Lajpat Rai, an Agarwal Baniya by caste, would have spent his childhood unaware of these larger currents in Punjab. But it was his socio-economic background that partly explains the arrival of the sixteen-year-old Lajpat in Lahore in 1881 to acquire a higher education at the Government College. Despite severe financial strain, his parents were determined to give him a college education, and Lajpat Rai enrolled for an Arts degree and simultaneously opted to study Law. In doing so, he joined the tiny minority of Indians who were able to take advantage of the new English-medium college education,[15] and the first generation of Punjabi Hindus who were surging ahead of the Punjabi Muslim majority.[16] To relieve financial pressure on his parents, Lajpat Rai decided to focus primarily on Law, in order to qualify as a *mukhtar* (junior pleader) and earn a living. In fact, when he acquired his licence for mukhtarship in 1883, he cut short his college education to begin his legal practice in Jagraon. These two years (1881–82) in college in Lahore, the cultural capital of Punjab, changed the course of his life. For it is in these years that Lajpat Rai joined the Arya Samaj, beginning his long association with this organization and movement that would shape his thought in fundamental ways.

In fact, after arriving in Lahore, Lajpat Rai had first joined the Brahmo Samaj at the behest of his father. Radha Krishan never converted to Islam and would, by the mid-1880s, turn to Vedantic philosophy in Hinduism about which he read copiously in Urdu.[17] But in the early 1880s, his strong criticism of certain aspects of contemporary Hinduism seemed to align with the Brahmo Samaj just enough to urge his son to join it. When the Bengali middle-class elite migrated to Punjab throughout the 1850s to fill the lower posts in the imperial bureaucracy, they brought new ideas into the province, and dominated its social and intellectual world. The Brahmo Samaj, founded in 1828 in Calcutta, travelled to Punjab, and established itself in Lahore in 1863. This was a socio-religious movement started by Rammohun Roy (1774–1833) to reform Hinduism in light of British imperial and Christian missionary criticism of it. As Lajpat Rai had been receiving his early education as a 'sickly schoolboy'[18] in the 1870s, the Brahmo Samaj was translating its literature into Punjabi, Hindi and Urdu to propagate its ideas in Punjab. Prominent Brahmo leaders like Debendranath Tagore (father of poet Rabindranath Tagore) had visited Punjab twice in the early 1870s to develop the movement, and a small socially significant number of educated Punjabis began to participate in the Brahmo Samaj. But by 1881–82, the brief two-year period which saw Lajpat Rai join and quickly leave it, the Brahmo Samaj had splintered and declined into an organization of Bengalis alone, with Punjabi Hindus leaving it in droves to join the new movement on the rise in Punjab: the Arya Samaj.

Interestingly for a movement that gained its widest success in Punjab, the Arya Samaj had in fact been founded in 1875 by a Gujarati, Swami Dayanand Saraswati (1824–83). Raised as a Shaivite Brahmin, Dayanand was unconvinced by the idolatrous Hinduism of his family and left in search of *mukti* (liberation). Although in search of individual liberation, he found a guru at Mathura whose teachings quickly convinced him of the need to reform Hinduism itself. The basic tenet of Dayanand's teachings was that the degeneracy of Hinduism was due to Hindus turning away from the Vedas, and that regeneration lay in a return to the Vedas.[19] While Lajpat Rai was attending school in East Punjab, Dayanand was travelling the north of India, meeting and learning from Brahmo reformers like Debendranath Tagore (1817–1905) and Keshub Chandra Sen (1838–84) and Muslim reformers like Syed Ahmad Khan (1817–98). After writing his reform programme in *Satyarth Prakash* (Light of Truth) in 1875, he proceeded to Bombay where he won some support and established the Bombay Arya Samaj. But it was only when he travelled back north in 1877, this time to Lahore, that Dayanand's Arya Samaj developed into a full-blown movement. Dayanand spent only a year in Punjab from April 1877 to July 1878, but this was enough to trigger a radical transformation among Punjabi Hindus. In 1877, when Lajpat Rai was a twelve-year-old in high school, the Lahore Arya Samaj was established, and Dayanand travelled throughout Punjab, setting up its branches. The Samaj attracted many local reformers, and weaned away Punjabi Hindu intellectuals from the Brahmo Samaj. By the time the seventeen-year-old Lajpat Rai officially joined the Arya Samaj in 1882,[20] seven years after its foundation, the Arya Samaj was a flourishing socio-religious movement in Punjab and North-Western Provinces (now Uttar Pradesh).

A week after joining the Samaj, Lajpat Rai was sent by Sain Das, president of its Lahore branch, to the North-Western Provinces as part of an Arya deputation. In 1883, his new guru, the founder of the Arya Samaj movement, Swami Dayanand, died suddenly.

A heartbroken Lajpat Rai delivered an impassioned speech at the local Arya Samaj, establishing his position as a 'front-rank speaker of the Samaj'.[21] When Lajpat Rai moved in 1884 from Jagraon to Rohtak as a mukhtar, he continued to divide his time between mukhtar work and the Rohtak Arya Samaj, of which he became secretary.[22] Here, he qualified as a *vakil* (lawyer), a higher status in the legal profession, but remained more interested in raising funds for a movement rapidly gaining ground among Arya Samajists who, encouraged by the success of Syed Ahmed Khan's Muhammadan Anglo-Oriental College (today's Aligarh Muslim University), wished to establish a Dayanand Anglo-Vedic (DAV) College to honour the memory of Swami Dayanand.[23] This is what Lajpat Rai was doing when the Indian National Congress was founded in 1885. Moving to Hissar in 1886 as a vakil, he spent his free time infusing life into the Hissar Arya Samaj, of which he soon became the secretary. Here, he helped a handful of local Arya Samajist leaders to popularize the Samaj among the wider populace, particularly Jat peasants.[24] While a DAV High School had been opened at Lahore that year, at Hissar Lajpat Rai raised funds for the establishment of a DAV College. Lajpat Rai was no ordinary member of the Arya Samaj, closely involved as he was in its organization and expansion in the 1880s. Intimately associated with the Samaj through the 1880s–90s, Lajpat Rai's thought was inevitably influenced by it.

* * *

Before attempting to understand what Rai's decision to join the Arya Samaj reveals about his religious views, we must understand the broader context of late-nineteenth-century British India in which this organization—or movement—was born. Although the term 'Hinduism' was first coined and used only in the early nineteenth century, Hindu beliefs and practices—relatively coherent and cohesive despite their startling diversity—had begun gradually acquiring a more self-conscious identity vis-à-vis Islam in the period between 1200 and 1500.[25] But by the time the Arya Samaj was established, these beliefs and practices had undergone a significant transformation. Hinduism turned into a considerably more unified system of 'religion', with much more well-defined boundaries than before.[26] The most decisive catalyst for this hardening of boundaries was Hinduism's encounter with British colonialism, which brought new ideas and forms of knowledge, novel state practices, a new culture and religion, and new means of communication.[27] When the English East India Company mutated from a trading company to a ruling power in the late eighteenth century, it decided to rule Indians according to Indian law. Unlike how the British understood their own society, they saw religion as the primary unit of Indian society, and—despite Indian self-perceptions to the contrary—classified the Indian population into two main religious groups.[28]

The company state therefore bifurcated personal or family law (relating to marriage, inheritance, caste and other religious customs) into new, scripture-based 'Hindu' and 'Muslim' law. As a result, a new homogenizing tendency within 'Hindu' and 'Muslim' law was inaugurated (where 'Hindu' and 'Muslim' law became increasingly internally homogenous or uniform). People were also now compelled to declare themselves as Hindu or Muslim in everyday disputes, producing a stricter demarcation between Hindus and Muslims than had hitherto existed.[29] These communally bifurcated personal laws ensured that indigenous socio-religious reformers limited their efforts exclusively towards members of their own community, giving rise to separate 'Hindu' and 'Muslim' public spheres.[30] The cohesiveness of modern Hinduism, and its sense of separation from others, was accentuated. The boundaries of modern Hinduism were further intensified by the novel colonial state practice of the decennial (ten-yearly) census, begun in the last quarter of the nineteenth century. In contrast to censuses in Britain, which took territorial location and occupation as their categories of analysis, the colonial census took religion as the primary category of classification for Indian society.[31] To count the numbers of 'Hindus' and 'Muslims', census officials defined Hinduism (and Islam) in a standardized, homogenous   manner,   which   also   hardened   its   boundaries vis-à-vis Islam (and vice versa). Members of India's religions were marshalled into 'communities'—mapped, counted and compared to one another.[32] These colonial–administrative ways of thinking and organizing information were increasingly imbibed by Hindus (and Muslims) in the nineteenth century.[33] New means of communication such as the railways and telegraph, as well as a booming print culture across India, encouraged Hindus in different parts of India to re-conceptualize Hinduism in all-India, 'national'—rather than local or regional—terms. The increased cohesiveness of Hinduism, as a single religion for all Hindus, was increasingly being imagined at a pan-Indian level.

Hinduism was radically transfigured in the nineteenth century in another important way. British scholar–officials and Christian missionaries, on the one hand, and Hindus, on the other, attempted to understand Hinduism in light of Christian or Western forms of thought.[34] Having never encountered a religion like Hinduism, British colonial officials and scholars attempted to understand it and sought out comparable features with Abrahamic faiths familiar to them, and sometimes ended up redefining and representing Hinduism in their light.[35] Ignoring the plethora of oral, local and vernacular Hindu beliefs and practices, they saw its true form as located in one or more of its ancient, classical texts or scriptures.[36] While in the decades following the conquest of Bengal in the mid-eighteenth century, British perceptions of Hinduism had comprised of wonder, appreciation and admiration,[37] by the mid-nineteenth century, corresponding with Britain's increased imperial domination over India (and the advent of race science), British official–scholars and Christian missionaries began to unleash vituperative criticism upon Hinduism for its lack of conformity to Abrahamic traditions. Contemporary Hinduism was portrayed as degenerate, disorganized and inferior, with idol worship, polytheism and the caste system picked out for special censure.[38] The minority of middle-class Hindu subjects with access to the colonial system of education were exposed to both reformulations of Hinduism in the light of Christian or Western ideas and concepts, and its scathing evaluations vis-à-vis the Christian West.[39] They were taught the merits of English culture and Christianity, a process which sometimes entailed a denigration of Hinduism.[40] This disparagement of Hinduism coincided with Hindus increasingly conceptualizing it in more cohesive terms, as having more fixed boundaries vis-à-vis other religions. Attacks on Hinduism were therefore felt more keenly and collectively now. Sections of the Hindu intelligentsia responded to such criticism and creatively re-thought Hindu beliefs and practices in their light.[41] They often defended Hinduism while simultaneously re-imagining and re-formulating aspects of it in engagement with Western categories and the Western conception of religion. For some reformist Hindus, this meant partially emulating some features of Abrahamic traditions, such as their emphasis on exclusive monotheism (the belief in one true God) and a single infallible revealed scripture or Book.[42] The colonial encounter sparked Hindu efforts to creatively redefine and reform Hinduism to make it correspond more closely with Christianity or Abrahamic traditions more generally. This process was not one of passive imitation of non-Hindu, Western forms of thought. Hindus possessed considerable agency, resisted many aspects of missionary polemic, and actively drew on and experimented with the pre-colonial Sanskrit textual canon. The creative reformulated and re-invented forms of pre-colonial Hindu religion in light of the Western, colonial, Christian encounter was a genuinely Hindu construction.[43] Criticisms about the chaotic, disorganized nature of Hinduism, as compared to Christianity, also resulted in many Hindus elaborating more forcefully and clearly the core beliefs and practices that bound Hindus together, and in attempts to unify and organize Hinduism.[44] This sometimes entailed attempts to iron out its internal diversity, and portray it in homogenous and undifferentiated terms, which also marked it off as sharply distinct from other religions. In some cases, there was also new emphasis on the exclusive truth of a single God or text while declaring those of other religions as false, or at least incompletely true.[45]

Yet, attempts to portray Hinduism as homogenous and the growing sense of pan-Indian Hindu unity hid underlying differences. In redefining Hinduism in engagement with Western/ Christian ideas, Hindus often disagreed over what in fact constituted its core features. Several Hinduisms were imagined. As we will see, some grounded Hinduism in the Upanishads,[46] while many others sought refuge in the Puranas.[47] Still others argued that Hinduism had nothing to do with scriptures at all. Some Hindus considered Krishna as the one true God, while others allowed polytheism. Some saw going to temples and praying before images and idols as modes of worship integral to Hindu tradition, while others decried these as a corruption of true Hinduism. In fact, the nineteenth century was marked by a vibrant culture of public debate or 'religious controversy' that raged in the Indian subcontinent from Bengal to Bombay.[48] Impassioned, heated debates over the nature of Hinduism occurred not just between Hindus and others, but among Hindus themselves.

The messy, lively dynamism of this debate among Hindus was manifested in the plethora of organizations that emerged during this century, beginning with the Brahmo Samaj and the Dharma Sabha, more active in its earlier and middle decades, and organizations like the Tadiya Samaj, Arya Samaj, the Sanatan Dharma Sabhas, the Dev Samaj and the Ramakrishna Mission, popular during the 1870s and beyond. And this was in North India alone. This internal debate and contestation reflected the diverse ways in which different groups of Hindus were negotiating being Hindu, as they struggled to meet the challenges thrown up by modern, colonial times.[49]

Both the Brahmo Samaj and the Arya Samaj had been founded in this context of increasing consolidation of pan-Indian Hinduism and internal debate and contestation within it, as Hinduism was creatively redefined in engagement with colonial modernity. The Brahmo Samaj, which Lajpat Rai had briefly joined in Lahore half a century after it was founded in Calcutta in 1828, represented one of the first attempts to radically reformulate Hinduism in light of Western/Christian ideas. Responding to British colonial and Christian missionary criticism of the polytheism, idol worship and ritualism of Hinduism,[50] Rammohun Roy, the architect of early Indian liberalism, had argued that 'Real Hindooism', which he anchored in Upanishadic Vedanta, consisted of monotheistic worship of a single formless God through reason, rather than the polytheistic idol worship of many gods and goddesses through devotion. Blaming Brahmins for misleading Hindus into these corrupt practices and excessive ritualism, this religious reformer sought to reform Hinduism by restoring Hindus to what he saw as the faith of their ancient ancestors.[51] Roy attacked certain social practices resulting from what he considered a corruption of true monotheistic Hinduism: caste discrimination, female infanticide and sati (the immolation of widowed women on their husband's funeral pyre).[52] Already by 1830, the Brahmo Samaj's position on sati was being opposed by the Dharma Sabha of Calcutta, which considered this practice of widow-burning as integral to Hinduism.[53] But such was the internal debate among Hindus that soon after the Brahmo Samaj established its first branch in Punjab in Lahore in 1863, differences within Brahmos themselves resulted in a split in the movement. In the 1850s, Debendranath Tagore, who led and popularized the Brahmo Samaj after Roy's death, had responded to Western critiques of Roy's interpretation of the Vedanta by abandoning textual authority altogether while defining Hinduism. Yet, he had still seen the Brahmo movement as rooted within Hinduism.[54] In the 1860s, the Samaj's leader, Keshub Chandra Sen, was urging Brahmos to abandon caste completely and draw explicit inspiration from Christian theology. In 1866, differences over this led the majority of Brahmos to follow Sen into a new organization called the Brahmo Samaj of India, with Tagore's Adi ('original') Brahmo Samaj, consisting of mainly his relatives and friends.[55] Despite this major schism, the Brahmo Samaj had expanded in Punjab in the early 1870s, with a small but significant number of reformist Punjabi Hindus participating in it, and drawing the fury of 'orthodox' Hindus by their insistence on widow remarriage, communal meals and opposition to the sacred thread and other established forms of Hindu worship.[56]

But, as already mentioned, and signified by Lajpat Rai's switch from one to the other, by the early 1880s, the Brahmo Samaj in Punjab was being strongly challenged by the Arya Samaj. Given Lajpat Rai's

close association with the Arya Samaj throughout the late nineteenth
century, one needs to understand the particular contours of Arya
Samaj's religious outlook to gain insight into Rai's view of religion.
This is particularly important since primary sources for Lajpat Rai's
views on religion in the 1880s are largely unavailable—lost due to
police searches during his lifetime, family disputes after his death and
the violent upheaval of Partition. His religious thought in the 1880s
must be reconstructed by understanding the distinctive religious
world view of the Arya Samaj, for which one must rely mainly on
historical research on the Arya Samaj. These are supplemented by
two books Lajpat Rai wrote on Swami Dayanand and the Samaj in
1898 and 1914 respectively.

    The Arya Samaj, and Lajpat Rai, insisted that the Vedas, India's
oldest religious texts,[57] contained the word of God, all divine
knowledge and perfect Truth.[58] The Samaj specifically insisted
that the Vedas—by which was meant the four *Samhitas* i.e., the
Rigveda, Yajurveda, Samaveda and Atharvaveda—alone contained
divine revelation.[59] While these were 'absolutely authoritative',
other historically more recent texts like the Puranas, Tantras,[60] and
even the wider Vedic corpus including the Upanishads—called the
Vedanta, or the 'end of the Vedas'—were not.[61] For Arya Samajists like
Lajpat Rai, the Tantras and Puranas were false, poisonous creations
of man.[62] The Upanishads, Brahmanas and Dharmashastras, also
human creations, were sacred 'only to the extent that they were
consistent with . . . the Vedas'.[63] Arya Samajists defined themselves
against and drew the ire of the self-proclaimed 'orthodox' Hindus
who claimed to defend *Sanatan Dharm* (the eternal, continuous
tradition of Hinduism) and considered the Puranas as divine
alongside the ancient Vedas.[64] In locating divinity solely in the
Vedas, Arya Samajists also differentiated themselves from Hindu
reformers like the late Rammohun Roy and Swami Vivekananda
(1863–1902) who grounded Hinduism in the Vedanta, and even
more definitively from those like Vivekananda's guru, the great
mystic Ramakrishna Paramhansa (1836–86) who drew inspiration
from the strikingly transgressive Tantras.[65]

Arya Samajists believed that it was because Hindus had begun to follow false texts that Hinduism had degenerated into its present corrupted form.[66] In its attempt to reform Hinduism to the version it believed was found in the ancient Vedas, it attacked various contemporary popular practices it considered indecent or immoral. For instance, the Arya Samaj condemned the singing of what they considered 'obscene' songs during ceremonies or festivals, excessive mourning, public bathing, pilgrimages, horoscopes, liquor drinking and meat eating.[67] They even shunned popular Holi celebrations as disgraceful, vulgar and obscene.[68] But, like the Brahmos, they singled out for special attack contemporary Hinduism's polytheism, its worship of many gods and goddesses. Insisting that the ancient 'Vedic Religion' was monotheistic, they affirmed belief in only one Supreme God.[69] In fact, the Vedas speak of many gods.[70] But for Arya Samajists, contemporary Hinduism's polytheism was a deviation from Vedic religion.[71] Lajpat Rai even quoted the German orientalist celebrity–scholar Max Müller (1823–1900) to argue that Vedic monotheism was comparable to that found in the Quran and that 'even the Bible does not contain such a clear enunciation of the concept'.[72]

The Arya Samajist attack on many popular Hindu practices was actually shared by Sanatanist Hindus,[73] with some agreeing with its insistence on monotheism.[74] But such Sanatanists did not accept the Arya Samajist assertion of the exclusive divinity of the Vedas or its belief that it was the turn to 'false' Puranas that had led to these practices and to polytheistic worship. Still, what really offended Sanatanists was the Arya Samaj's fierce assault on idol worship (*murtipuja*), something the Arya Samajists shared with Brahmos. Arya Samajists taught that Vedic religion entailed the belief that God was formless. This meant the rejection of incarnation—the notion that God could assume physical form in a human being,[75] of holy men and also worship through idols and temples.[76] In a few instances, new enthusiasts of the Arya Samaj had thrown their idols in the Ravi River or smashed them in local bazaars.[77] Instead of idol worship, the Samaj argued that the Vedas enjoined the performance of the five

Mahayajnas or 'principal religious practices', which included the Deva *yajna* or *homa* fire ceremony and the Brahma yajna which Lajpat Rai described as including 'the worship of God, morning and evening, by contemplation, communion and prayer' and 'the regular reading of some portion of the scriptures [Vedas] once a day'.[78] Thus, contrary to the elaborate ritualism actually found in the Vedas,[79] the Arya Samaj shunned elaborate, Brahmin-led ritualism as the fraudulent trickery of priests—what Dayanand had scornfully called 'pope-*lila*' (priestcraft).[80] Instead, they presented Vedic religion as consisting of simple rituals that did not require the services of Brahmin ritual specialists. In espousing a Vedic monotheism grounded in simple abstract worship, the Arya Samaj diverged from Sanatanist Hindus who justified existing ritual practice and, even when committed to monotheism, pressed that this one true God was a personal God who must be worshipped through *bhakti* (pure devotion) offered to His idols or images.[81] For Sanatanists, the Vedas, Puranas and Smritis prescribed idol worship as the sole path to God, and Arya-inspired iconoclasm was sacrilegious.[82]

The Arya Samaj shared with the Brahmo Samaj an insistence on monotheism and a rejection of idolatry, the latter leading them both to cause great offence to 'orthodox' Sanatanist Hindus. Why then were Punjabi Hindus like Lajpat Rai abandoning Brahmoism for the Arya Samaj by the early 1880s? Increasingly conscious of their position in Punjab as a minority community, the sense of insecurity felt by the Punjabi Hindu intelligentsia had been heightened after British annexation and the expansion of Christian missionary activity in Punjab post-1857. While relations between the colonial state and Christian missionaries in the rest of British India were complicated and often conflictual, Punjab's government was distinctive in its encouragement of missions promoting a uniquely aggressive brand of Christianity.[83] The anxieties felt by many Punjabi Hindus were aggravated by their colonial education. Contrary to what one may expect, the new class of anglicized Punjabi Hindus opposed British attempts to restrict English education in Government College (Lahore) in favour of

vernacular and classical education. They instead demanded an
expansion of English education from which they were benefiting
as a new elite.[84] At the same time, however, they harboured fears
of becoming culturally deracinated through this education. In light
of these cultural anxieties elicited by British conquest, missionary
expansion and English education, the Brahmo Samaj's syncretic
teachings emphasizing the universal truth of all religions and its
open appreciation of Christianity under Keshub Chandra Sen
was seen to be an inadequate defence of Hinduism.[85] The answer
to these anxieties of Punjabi Hindus was finally provided by the
wandering *sanyasi* from Gujarat: Dayanand Saraswati. His Arya
Samaj pushed an image of the Brahmos as being too Europeanized,
too close to Christianity and as having shunned their ancestral
faith, while presenting itself as rooted in indigenous religion.[86]

This self-presentation of Arya Samajists as more authentically
Hindu than the Brahmos, however, needs to be qualified. Rammohun
Roy had certainly accepted colonial–official and Christian missionary
denigration of contemporary Hinduism for its polytheistic excess
and idolatry, and their representation of abstract monotheism
as the superior and 'natural' form of belief. Internalizing the
supposed superiority of idol-free monotheism, he had appropriated
it for the true Hinduism he saw as embodied in the philosophical
Upanishads.[87] This had partly been his way of asserting the standing
of Hinduism vis-à-vis Christianity, often presented as the superior
faith in the colonial context.[88] Under its new leaders, Brahmos
continued to construe Brahmoism as a bulwark against Christianity
but had no qualms in advocating reform by entirely eschewing textual
authority and even openly drawing from religions like Christianity.[89]
They denied the presence of God's wisdom in the texts of any one
religion, and insisted that it could be found in all religions through
the capacity of intuition present in all humans equally.[90] While this
resulted in Arya Samajist criticism of Brahmos as less authentically
Hindu than themselves, Arya Samajists had themselves internalized
official–missionary criticism of contemporary Hinduism for its
idolatrous polytheism, and moved closer to Christian, Western forms

of religion as they redefined Hinduism in terms of a supposedly superior abstract monotheism.[91]

Both Brahmoism and the Arya Samaj drew on pre-colonial Hindu traditions and reinterpreted and reinvented them in light of their engagement with Protestant Christianity. Both were products of the Hindu–Christian/European encounter, neither more authentically indigenous or more foreign than the other. The crucial difference was that while Brahmos always saw their redefined monotheistic Hinduism as compatible with the belief that the divine truth of the single Supreme God was found in all religions, Arya Samajists presented the reformulated monotheistic Hinduism as located in the ancient Vedas, in turn portrayed as the exclusive source of God's wisdom. If Brahmo assertions about divine truth in all religions, and its appreciation of Christianity, made Punjabi Hindus nervous about the possibility of cultural abandonment, they could now embrace even more radical reformulations of Hinduism—made to correspond more closely with the Christian tradition—all the while still claiming to follow the original Hinduism embodied by the Vedas. The Brahmo assertion that abstract monotheism was preached by original Hinduism challenged the view that monotheism was a monopoly of Christianity. But the Arya Samajist claim that Vedic monotheism was the exclusive location of all divine truth proclaimed Hinduism's superiority vis-à-vis Christianity, considered a particularly threatening force in Punjab. The religious ideas of young Lajpat Rai were greatly influenced by the Arya Samaj, which sought to define itself against the Brahmos—as more grounded in India's indigenous religion, and as a better defence against Christianity—even as it was itself a product of the nineteenth-century encounter between pre-colonial traditions and Christian, Western notions of religion.

2

Defending the Congress against Sir Syed

When the Indian National Congress was founded in 1885, as recounted in the previous chapter, the twenty-year-old Lajpat Rai had been engrossed in Arya Samajist activities. But that did not necessarily mean that he remained oblivious to political developments. Here, we look at his brief intervention in political affairs in 1888 and 1889. While some fellow Arya Samajists declared the new Congress movement suspect, Lajpat Rai was curious. When one Ali Mohammad Bhimji was touring Punjab in 1888 on behalf of the Congress, Lajpat Rai invited him to Hissar and arranged a public meeting. But it was the opposition to the Congress from the eminent Syed Ahmad Khan, that drove Lajpat Rai's first intervention in overtly political all-India affairs.[1]

Even in the late eighteenth century, strong regional patriotisms had already emerged, as had a broad sense that the people inhabiting Hindustan constituted a loose 'community' who shared bonds of emotion and sentiment.[2] This notion of Indians as a broad community, gradually sharpened under Company Raj throughout the early nineteenth century, had manifested itself in the 1857 Revolt in which numerous princes and commoners came together in acts of resistance against the British. But it was only in the latter third of the nineteenth century, with the expansion of Western education, print culture and new communication systems (like the telegraph and railways),[3] that members of the newly emergent Western-educated, upper-caste middle class from different presidencies of British India began to clearly and forcefully articulate the idea that the people of India constituted a 'nation' bound by a distinctive culture defined against the West.[4]

By the late 1860s and certainly by the 1870s, such individuals also began to organize politically to speak on behalf of the Indian nation, crystallizing their growing belief that the people of India constituted a modern political community possessing common political concerns.[5] This was evident in the language of new organizations like the Poona Sarvajanik Sabha (founded in 1870 and led by Mahadev Govind Ranade), the Indian Association (founded in 1876 by Surendranath Banerjea), the Bombay Association (which got a new lease of life in 1876 when Dadabhai Naoroji took charge of it) as well as several newspapers in circulation in the 1870s.[6] They organized themselves around all-India 'national' issues, and attempted to break regional barriers. But as the political demands of these associations were ignored, and particularly after witnessing how naked racial hysteria by Englishmen resident in India led to the withdrawal, in 1884, of a proposed bill allowing Indian judges to try Europeans in small towns, an intensified clamour emerged for an all-India 'national' organization.[7] The result was the formation of the Indian National Congress (INC) in 1885, in which politically conscious people from different parts of India could unite for collective action.

The sense expressed by Dadabhai Naoroji (1825–1917) in 1867 that 'the nation is now becoming gradually assimilated for political purposes'[8] increased dramatically with the foundation of the INC. While it eventually became the longest-lived national movement in the modern colonial world, at the time of its foundation the INC was one among a few attempts to rise above provincial politics to organize an 'Indian national' politics. In its early years, it remained a ramshackle experiment by a small number of urban middle-class professionals. Its most prominent leaders included Naoroji,

W.C. Bonnerji, Surendranath Banerjea, M.G. Ranade, D.E. Wacha, P.S. Mehta, Madan Mohan Malaviya and Baddrudin Tyabji, all of whom belonged to this class of middle-class professionals. Beginning as a meeting of seventy-two delegates, by its third session in 1887 its delegates numbered about 600. But great hope, enthusiasm and even euphoria had accompanied the foundation of the INC. The Bombay Presidency Association hailed its birth as 'an epoch in the political history of our countrymen'.[9] Various organs of the Indian press viewed the foundation of the Congress as 'an event of the highest significance' (*Indu Prakash*), marking 'the birth of national unity' (*The Hindu*) and a new 'era in the history of Indian political unity' (*Indian Nation*).[10] There was a sense that 'what in 1885 was little more than an experiment, in 1887 bore every appearance of a permanent National Institution'.[11] Clearly, the consecutive, annual political meeting of delegates from different parts of India seemed to symbolize something unprecedented and momentous.[12] It certainly signified the concrete materialization of the idea which had been floating around, at least since the middle of the nineteenth century: that the people of India, despite all differences, constituted a 'nation' in the *political* sense, that they were united by common political concerns and must act as a single self-organizing political agent.

When this new, potentially permanent 'Indian National' political organization consistently demanded the introduction of elective representation in the imperial and provincial legislative councils—a demand for limited self-government for the Indian nation—it made a mark. Of course, limited self-government was 'requested' very much within the British Empire to which Congressmen remained loyal. The political culture of questioning the very legitimacy of the British Empire had not yet taken shape.[13] The Congress asked not for independence but for the amelioration of certain undesirable aspects of British rule in India, and for the British to fulfil their own oft-stated objective of regenerating India. Still, in a context where British imperialists insisted that Indians did not constitute a nation and that Indian society was unsuited for elections, the Congress's demand for elective representation signified a more assertive stance that the

'Indian nation' constituted a discrete political unit that ought to be self-governing to some extent.

The British Indian government tried to deny its import, with Viceroy Dufferin publicly dismissing Congressmen as a 'microscopic minority'.[14] Some scorned the idea that the people of India with all their divisions constituted a nation.[15] Other Englishmen were more alarmist, arguing that the Congress would inevitably develop into 'a deadly engine of sedition', lead to a mutiny like in 1857 and to 'the massacre of Englishmen, their wives and children'.[16]

Quite apart from British officials, stern opposition to the Congress also came from another quarter—from Sir Syed Ahmed Khan. Hailing from the North-Western Provinces (now Uttar Pradesh), Sir Syed was an influential aristocrat–official who had led the movement for Muslim modernism and, towards this end, had founded the now decade-old Muhammadan Anglo-Oriental College at Aligarh in 1875.[17] This had been his response to the British treatment of Muslims following the 1857 revolt. Despite Hindus (including the princely elite like the Rani of Jhansi) playing as much of a role, the British had suspected Muslims, particularly Muslim aristocrats, of being moved by a nostalgia for 'their empire', and being the prime culprits, turning it from a sepoy mutiny into a political conspiracy to destroy the Raj.[18] The British response had been brutal: the last Mughal, unwillingly used by the mutineers as a symbol of their resistance, was tried and exiled to Rangoon, his sons and grandsons summarily executed. There were several such executions of the Muslim aristocratic elite in Delhi which, as the centre of Mughal culture, was destroyed. Such repression impelled introspection among the elite Muslim leadership and forced them to stomach the fact that the British were here to stay on their own terms.

Having earlier dismissed English/Western culture as barbaric and uncultured, the Muslim intelligentsia was now compelled to take it seriously. Some had reacted by turning to fundamentals of the traditions of the Prophet (seen in the Deobandi movement started in the 1860s). Others like Sir Syed responded by leading a reform movement aimed at demonstrating, to the horror of *sharia*-minded Muslims,[19] that Islamic theology was compatible with Western modernity, knowledge and science.[20] The Aligarh college symbolized his philosophy of Muslim reformism, and aimed to make English education and Victorian morals attractive to the Muslim aristocracy so they could overcome, what he believed, was their backwardness and take up positions in the colonial bureaucracy.[21] Already a well-known public figure by the late 1860s, Sir Syed's fame rose with the establishment and success of his Aligarh college, an example of an educational institution set up by an Indian that provided an education that was neither like government-run institutions, largely British and threatening cultural alienation, nor like *madrasas*, completely cut off from modern, English education and the opportunities they brought within the Empire; instead, the Aligarh college provided an English education with room for Islam.[22] It was this great Indian Muslim reformer, who had inspired both Lajpat Rai's father as well as his guru Dayanand Saraswati, who now in 1887 roundly denounced the Congress.

Sir Syed remained conspicuously aloof for the first two years of the existence of the Congress. But in December 1887, as seventy-nine other Muslim delegates attended the Congress at Madras, presided over by Badruddin Tyabji, the prominent Bohra Muslim Congressman from Bombay, Sir Syed publicly denounced it at Lucknow and urged Muslims to oppose both this 'Indian national' organization as well as its demand for elective representation. In Sir Syed's own province, his public opposition was followed by a vigorous attack on the Congress by the United Indian Patriotic Association, which included prominent North Indian Hindu *taluqdars* (landed aristocrats) and the Raja of Benaras.[23] Interestingly, the head of the 'orthodox' Deobandis issued a fatwa cautioning Muslims not to associate themselves with the activities of Sir Syed, and stating that cooperation with Hindus was permissible in worldly affairs provided it did not violate the basic principles of Islam. Individual Muslims would indeed participate off and on in Congress sessions.[24] Even so, meetings were held in several parts of India in 1888 to voice Muslim support for Sir Syed's stand.[25]

Such opposition to the Congress prompted a flurry of activity among its supporters. In the North-Western Provinces, the twenty-seven-year-old Madan Mohan Malaviya increased efforts to popularize it.[26] Tyabji wrote to Sir Syed, stressing that Muslims must join the Congress and support its programme.[27] In Punjab, Sir Syed's anti-Congressism had drawn even those individuals who had so far remained indifferent to the Congress.[28] Among those infuriated by Sir Syed's opposition was a twenty-three-year-old vakil in Hissar who had so far held Sir Syed in great esteem: Lajpat Rai. So shocked and disappointed was young Lajpat that, in late 1888, shortly before attending the fourth Congress session at Allahabad, he shot off a series of public 'Open Letters' to the septuagenarian Sir Syed.

Signing them off as 'Son of an old follower of yours', according to Lajpat Rai's own account, these letters, the first time he had written on affairs which were not merely local or provincial, were discussed throughout the country, and made his name more known in Indian political circles.[29] As Lajpat Rai arrived in Allahabad in December 1888 to attend his first Congress session, an event he would later remember as the beginning of his political life,[30] he was enthusiastically received at the railway station by A.O. Hume (1829–1912), the Englishman who had helped found the Congress, the young but already distinguished Malaviya and several Congress volunteers. Written between October–December 1888, the contents of Lajpat Rai's letters to Sir Syed reveal how Rai imagined *nationhood* in relation to his nascent ideas regarding *political self-government* and *representation*.

To fully understand Lajpat Rai's stance, we must first properly grasp the position he was refuting. Lajpat Rai attacked Sir Syed for what he considered a volte-face: How could this great man, who had himself earlier spoken of Hindus and Muslims as one 'nation' and demanded political representation for it on councils, now suddenly deny they constituted a nation and oppose the Congress for demanding political representation for it? During his public career, Sir Syed had often harshly criticized government policies and seemed to have supported causes like those championed now by the Congress.

These had included the right of Indian judges to try Europeans, greater Indianization of the civil services and the introduction of local self-government.[31] Lajpat Rai pointed out in one of his letters, that in his 1858 essay *The Causes of the Indian Revolt*, published a year after the Mutiny, Sir Syed had argued for the admission of 'natives' or 'Hindustanees' into the Legislative Council of India.[32] So, in opposing the Congress's demand for elective representation had Sir Syed really undertaken a complete reversal?

Contrary to Lajpat Rai's retrospective reading, Sir Syed's call for the inclusion of Indians had never been a plea for some limited form of democratic political representation or self-rule by an 'Indian nation'. 'Natives' on councils were not envisaged as being *elected* by 'the people' to represent them and take decisions on their behalf. Instead, they would be *nominated* by the government to advise it, with the aim of strengthening and preserving British rule in India.[33] Of course, at the time, Sir Syed had been unique in his audacity in asking for even such a form of 'native' representation from the British Government in India which ruled India as a highly centralized autocracy of hierarchically organized officials headed by the viceroy and secretary of state.[34] Nevertheless, these representatives were envisaged as acting not for the Indian people but merely as sources of information about them in order to render British rule more effective.[35] Moreover, as he envisioned Indian political representation, not any and every 'native' was eligible for this role; only those belonging to socially eminent groups would be granted representation on imperial councils. Born into a noble family which had served the Mughals,[36] Sir Syed was influenced by a particular strand in the Mughal view of governance which held that the basis of strong, secure government was the ruler's ability to establish ties of loyalty with significant lineage groups.[37] Granting socially eminent 'natives' representation on councils was about giving them some share in political power rather than representing 'the people' in the sense of acting for them or articulating their opinions or interests.

Sir Syed's opposition to the Congress and its demand for the elective principle—the principle of choosing one's political representatives through voting—was impelled by his aristocratic belief that Indian representatives in legislatures be nominated by the ruling British government according to their 'high social position' as determined by ancestry; they had to be 'great *Raises*'[38] ('respectable' noblemen) of 'good breeding'.[39] The elective principle would put Indians on councils according to their 'ability', thus propelling men of 'low caste or insignificant origin' into positions affecting the lives of the aristocratic Indians with ruling lineages:

> Would our aristocracy like a man of low caste or insignificant origin, though he be B.A. or M.A., and have the requisite ability, should be in a position of authority and have the power in making the laws that affect their lives and property? Never! Nobody would like it (Cheers) . . . Think for a moment what would be the result if all appointments were given by competitive examinations. Over all races, not only over Mohamedans but over Rajas of high position and the brave Rajputs who have not forgotten the swords of their ancestors, would be placed as a ruler a Bengali who at sight of a table knife would crawl under his chair . . .[40]

Far from demanding democratic–political self-rule for the 'Indian nation', Sir Syed desired that Muslim notables along with Hindu Rajas and Rajputs represent the 'natives' and be consulted by the British as they ruled over the peoples of India. He found unacceptable and scoffed at the elective principle that would put Bengalis of 'insignificant origin' in positions of authority over Muslim and Hindu aristocrats of ruling heritage. Here, Khan was not unlike Hindu notables like the Raja of Benaras who, supporting Sir Syed's opposition to the Congress, dismissed democracy as an 'occidental idea' unsuited to India and against the religious beliefs of Hindus and, in a similar vein to Khan, asked: 'How would you care to have Kalvars and Mochis [lower castes of liquor distillers and cobblers] as our legislators?'[41] For him, the current defect in British government was precisely that it was too 'democratical [*sic*]', appointing individuals regardless of social position. These men together were similar to aristocrats in Britain, France or America who, in the previous century, and even in this one, had resisted moves towards greater democratization by claiming hereditary social distinction.[42] Shunned as the rule of the poor or the mob which was untrustworthy and lacking moral knowledge, the concept of democracy had been thoroughly discredited for two millennia after a limited form of it was first practised in Athens in the sixth century BCE.

Rule by monarchies in conjunction with aristocrats, considered a natural elite with innate superiority by virtue of their military prowess and hereditary social status, had been the norm for most of human history. The notion of rule by the people had once again begun acquiring a small measure of respectability only after the American and French revolutions in the late eighteenth century.[43] Even then, aristocracies in America and Britain had remained powerful, declining in America only from the 1830s onwards with Jacksonian democracy and in Britain, even more recently, when the Reform Acts in the 1860s and 1880s progressively diminished their political power and enfranchised larger numbers of ordinary working-class people. Much as aristocrats in the West were discomfited by this momentous historical shift, Syed Ahmed Khan resisted the Congress demand for the introduction of elective representation by asserting the high social status, military and governing expertise, and hereditary right of rule of the Hindu and Muslim aristocracy.

Interestingly, Sir Syed had seen his claims about the foreign, conquering lineage of Muslims as parallel to similar claims about the foreign, conquering Aryan ancestry of high-status Hindus.[44] But he seemed to suggest that Muslims were particularly suited for representation on councils by virtue of their descent from a ruling race.[45] He emphasized that Muslims, who had conquered and ruled over India and other countries, knew the art of political rule.[46] In a letter to his friend, the poet Altaf Husain Hali, he had explained his opposition to the extension of elective representation to India: 'I am a Muslim, an inhabitant of India and descended from Arabs . . . the Arab people neither seek nor do they desire that instead of ruling themselves, someone else should rule them.'[47] Sir Syed's discomfort with elective representation, then, was driven by an unwillingness to accept that under such a system the Muslim 'ruling race', instead of having a special relationship with the political order, would be subject to the rule of others. Yet, while Sir Syed appeared to speak of political rule by 'Muslims' in general, he meant to refer only to the Muslim aristocracy; as his disdain for 'men of low-caste origin' shows, the majority of *low-caste* Muslim farmers, artisans and labourers were far from his mind when he lamented the prospect of the ruling race of 'Muslims' being subjected to others. In fact, his opposition was also fuelled by an anxiety about an older aristocratic elite, to which he belonged, losing ground to a new elite—the rising middle class, whom the Bengali Hindus, despite their so-called 'insignificant' origin, epitomized.[48] His aversion to elective representation stemmed from his fear that the modern system of education had produced a new Bengali Hindu elite which was rising in the rungs of administration and was already felt to be too close to the British rulers.[49] The new system, based on meritocracy and elected political representation that the presently Bengali-dominated Congress demanded, would further encourage the British to rely on this new elite rather than the older aristocratic elite to which he belonged. A history of military expertise and experience in governance by the Muslim aristocracy was adduced to assert its superiority over the new Bengali middle-class elite, and deny the latter's recent claims to political power via meritocracy.

But another reason behind Sir Syed's opposition to elective representation was his fear that it would produce unjust political outcomes in a country with innumerable social cleavages and inequalities:

> The system of representation by election means the representation of the views and interests of the majority of the population . . . in a country like India, where caste distinctions flourish, where there is no fusion of the various races, where religious distinctions are still violent, where education in its modern sense has not made an equal or proportionate progress among the population . . . the larger community would totally override the interests of the smaller community.[50]

Interestingly, despite conceiving of them as a ruling race, Sir Syed also held, in line with British officials like W.W. Hunter who popularized this idea in the 1870s,[51] that Muslims were in decline, had fallen behind Hindus in wealth, English education and government employment[52] and were 'plunging into an abyss of wretchedness'.[53] Indeed, at least in Sir Syed's own North-Western Province, urban growth due to industry and commerce had mainly benefited Hindu traders and moneylenders.[54] Educational statistics at the time also revealed that for various reasons 'Muslims', taken as an aggregate, were lagging behind 'Hindus' in government-sponsored English education.[55] This in turn meant losing posts in the colonial administration, which now required some knowledge of English.[56] This sense of decline was further exacerbated by a new assertive Hindi-speaking Hindu middle class challenging the status of Urdu, the language of the Hindu and Muslim aristocratic elite, as the language of the colonial courts and administration.[57] Sir Syed's Aligarh college had been conceived as an effort to arrest this very decline of Muslims. And so, his logic went, until Muslims had recovered, in any new system of political representation in which representatives were elected from a wider pool of 'natives', eligible on the basis of education and property ownership (the criteria affirmed by the Congress), Indian Muslims were bound to lose out.

And then, Sir Syed's anxiety about Muslims being marginalized in political representation was further aggravated by another belief:

> Let us suppose first of all that we all have universal suffrage as in America and that everybody, *chamars* [a Dalit caste] and all, have votes. And first suppose that all the Mahomedan electors vote for a Mahomedan member and all Hindu electors vote for a Hindu member . . . it is certain that the Hindu member will have four times as many because their population will have four times as many . . . and now how can the Mahomedan guard his interests? It would be like a game of dice in which one man had four dice and the other one only one.[58]

Thus, his opposition to the Congress demand for elective representation was also grounded in the fear that if the pool of natives from which political representatives were drawn was expanded beyond aristocrats to include anyone who was educated and owned property, and potentially later to every man in India, numbers would begin to matter. In such a system, Hindus, with their numerical majority, would dominate political representation on councils. Although, as we saw above, Sir Syed could conceive aristocratic elites as sharing similar political interests, he could also at other times assume that Hindus and Muslims would always see themselves as sharing political interests with their respective co-religionists rather than with each other. Sir Syed feared that the numerical preponderance of Hindu voters in a system of elective, democratic representation would result in Hindus ruling over Muslims. A modernist in his educational outlook, he drew upon a pre-modern, aristocratic notion of representation to resist the modern, elective form of representation. This was partly his way of refusing the reduction of India's Muslims—counted as one-fifth of British India's population at the time—to a permanently beleaguered minority in a democratic polity.

Prior to the formation of the Congress, Sir Syed had spoken of an Indian *qaum*, a word he himself translated as 'nation'. In a speech he delivered in 1884 at Gurdaspur, quoted by Lajpat Rai in one of his letters, Sir Syed exclaimed:

> Oh Hindus and Mussulmans, do you inhabit any other country than India? Do you both not live here on the same land and are you not buried in this land or cremated on the *ghats* of this land? You live and die here. Therefore remember that Hindu and Mussulman are words of religious significance, otherwise Hindus or Mussulmans, and Christians who live in this country constitute one nation. When all these groups are called one nation, then they should be one in the service of the country, which is the country of all.[59]

That Hindus and Muslims constituted one Indian nation had been clearly expressed by Sir Syed. Yet, the same speech starts with a reference to the presence in India of the Hindu and Muslim 'nations': 'By the grace of God, two nations [Hindus and Mussulmans] live in India at the moment and they are so placed that the house of one adjoins that of the other . . .'[60] In several of his speeches prior to the foundation of the Congress, his imagined Indian qaum had been conceptualized as constituted by two smaller Hindu and Muslim 'nations', with the word 'nation' being used in two senses.[61] The Indian 'nation' was conceived as a territorially bounded community, composed of the Hindu and Muslim 'nations', with the term used in the sense of cultural communities or stock (communities of common descent or ancestry).[62] In neither case was the term 'nation' used in its modern national*ist* sense, with connotations of popular self-government and statehood. The Indian nation was not conceived as a sovereign people who must eventually find political expression in a self-governing nation–state. And while his conception of the Muslim 'nation' (as stock) doubtlessly had a political dimension too, since he saw its members as having broadly common political concerns and possessing a special relationship to the political order, this was not a conception of Muslim nationhood in a nationalist sense. 'Muslims', even if distinguished from 'Hindus' as a politically distinct descent group, were, as we saw, still conceived as a people who would themselves be ruled over (along with the majority of other Indians, Hindu or otherwise) by Muslim and Hindu aristocrats of high birth. The Muslim nation was not conceived as a sovereign people deserving self-government.

In his anti-Congress speeches of 1887–88, Sir Syed resisted the idea, expressed forcefully by the Congress, that the people of India only formed one single Indian nation, and that this was the only nation in the subcontinent. He insisted that the people of India were not so united as to form one nation the way the people of England or Scotland did, and continued to assert that India was inhabited by 'two different nations'—the Hindus and Muslims,[63] if not more.[64] At times, he held on to the concept of a Muslim 'nation' but asserted that Hindus were not one: 'The Hindus of our Province [the United Provinces], the Bengalis of the East, and the Mahrattas of the Deccan

do not form one nation.'[65] This belief is also evident in his use of
the term 'nation' for 'Bengalis'.[66] If Sir Syed still held that India was
a qaum, he clearly still conceived it as a territorial community itself
composed of at least two, if not more, smaller nations/stocks.[67] And
still, in neither case, did he use the term in the modern, nationalist
political–statist sense: neither the Indian qaum nor the Hindu,
Bengali or Muslim 'nations' were ever conceived as politically self-
ruling in even any limited form; they were to be ruled over by great
raises knowledgeable in the art of political rule. Uncomfortable
with the Congress's suggestion that India was inhabited by a single
Indian nation alone, Sir Syed resisted the use of this term in its new
nationalist–political sense, which implied that the members of this
Indian nation were equal and united by common political concerns.
India was, at best, a (territorial) 'nation' of different 'nations' (stocks)
with significant cleavages and deep inequalities between them, which
needed to be addressed. The elective system was not imagined by him
as a step towards political self-rule by 'Indian nation'; it would always
result in the 'Hindu' or 'Bengali' nation (by which he often meant
the new Hindu or Bengali Hindu elite) ruling over what, in such a
system, would be the disadvantageously placed Muslim nation/stock
and, worse, its Muslim aristocracy with its apparently natural gift for
political rule.

Syed Ahmed Khan's rejection of the Congress's nationalist
conception of the Indian nation was an extension of his resistance
to the transition—which he could anticipate—to a form of political
thought and action in which power was derived from and legitimized
by 'the people' and, therefore, a Hindu majority. His repudiation of
this Indian nationalist frame, and assertion of the right of high-born
Muslims to assist British rule (along with well-born Hindu Rajas and
Rajputs) over the Indian populace, therefore entailed a refusal of a
new form of Muslim minorityhood. That is, it resisted the eclipse of
a form of politics which had existed for centuries both in India and
beyond, which relied on a minority of privileged hereditary elites,
and according to which 'Muslims' could exist as a privileged minority
or at least demand parity with Hindus. And it refused the transition

to a new, modern form of politics predicated on notions of formal equality, merit and on numbers and ideas of popular–democratic and national sovereignty, in which 'Muslims' would be reduced to a new kind of politically marginalized minority.

In the four open letters Lajpat Rai wrote to Sir Syed, he accused him of rescinding his principles; a man who had demanded representation on councils for the Indian nation was now opposing the Congress for doing the same. But Sir Syed and the Congress worked with two different notions of representation. In his first letter, Lajpat Rai attributed Sir Syed's opposition to 'imbecility due to old age' or to 'tomfoolery' guided by his 'selfish greed'.[68] This illustrates his initial inability to fully comprehend Sir Syed's aristocratic conceptualization of political representation, with *'raises'* of the Hindu and Muslim 'nations' being nominated by the British government to share in its rule over the rest of the Indian 'nation'. Yet, as his second letter shows, Lajpat Rai not only quickly understood Sir Syed's preference for the method of nominated representation but also rejected it unequivocally:

> Can men like Raja Shiva Prasad and yourself be properly considered as representatives of the people, and can the method of selection, by which you were sent to the Council Chamber, be accepted as of any value? Could Raja Peary Mohan Mukherjee and other native members have consented to the raising of the Salt tax if their fate was dependent on the voices of the people, whose throats were to be cut by that obnoxious measure etc. etc.? Then the correct solution is this and no other, that the people must be represented by their own elected delegates . . . totally independent of government approval or disapproval.[69]

Lajpat Rai objected to Indian representation on councils via official nomination as a 'downright farce'; since these Indians were not chosen by 'the voices of the people', they did not act for them, and sometimes even engaged in political behaviour that harmed them. The high social position of such men, which for Sir Syed qualified them for legislative council positions, was regarded by Lajpat Rai as a drawback, preventing them from empathizing with the miserable conditions of other 'natives'.[70] Election, the act of choosing representatives by vote, was considered essential for any genuine political representation of 'the people' in councils. Lajpat Rai was clearly driven by the idea that 'the people' must have a say, via representatives elected by them, in government and in political decisions that affected them.

However, at this historical juncture, Lajpat Rai did not demand a fully democratic form of political self-government. Indeed, in the 1880s, Congressmen accepted the British imperial argument that India needed to be prepared for self-government, which would be granted sometime in the future when India was deemed ready for it by the British.[71] Lajpat Rai supported a Congress whose leaders and delegates—whether Banerjea, Ranade, Malaviya, Gopal Krishna Gokhale or Bal Gangadhar Tilak—presently demanded only that half the members of legislative councils be elected representatives of the people.[72] And although Lajpat Rai stressed the need for elected representatives chosen by 'the people', he seemed presently satisfied, as were other Congressmen, with a franchise greatly limited by education and property qualification.[73]

Property ownership as a qualification for enfranchisement had been part of the history of the rise of democracy in the West. It had been legally abolished in the US only in the 1830s. In Britain, the 1867 Reforms had enfranchised large sections of the British working class, but some form of property ownership continued to limit male franchise (and would do so till 1918). In 1888, 40 per cent of British adult males were qualified to vote.[74] The franchise that the Congress demanded for colonized India was nowhere close to this mark, likely adding up to less than 1 per cent of the population. A minuscule number of educated, propertied Indians were conceived as automatically representing the votes—or the political opinions and interests—of uneducated, poor Indians imagined as incapable of representing themselves. In other words, in this political vision, only men with education and property would have the vote and be elected as Indian political representatives. In 1888, much like the main Congress stalwarts, Lajpat Rai articulated a

severely restricted conception of democratic–political self-government
(at least for now).

Nevertheless, his position still constituted a departure not only
from Sir Syed but also, as is clear from the names he mentions in
the above quote, from Hindu *zamindars* (landowners) who, having
led and dominated older political associations like the British
Indian Association (BIA), had worked with notions of nominated
representation similar to Khan; they believed that the landed
aristocracy, as 'natural leaders' of the Indian people, was fit to
represent them.[75] Holding on to pre-modern conceptions of political
representation, these men did not believe that India's 'people' needed
to have any voice whatsoever in who governed them and how;
they never envisaged even a very restricted notion of popular self-
government by 'the people' of India. In contrast, Lajpat Rai, like
the men who currently dominated the Congress, rejected this older
notion of representation devoid of the notion of popular self-rule,
to espouse the modern principle of elected representation. The
expansion of political representation beyond the 'high-born' still
entailed representation by only a slightly enlarged (and still extremely
small) group of individuals, now composed of educated middle-class
property-owners. But what was new was the felt need to justify this
group's claim to political representation through its apparent closer
proximity to 'the people'. This was in turn seen as making them more
authentically of the people. Unlike Khan, Rai's modern conception
of representation entailed the belief that the political opinions and
interests of 'the people' had to necessarily be represented, in however
indirect or mediated a manner, in their government. Of course,
just as Khan's social position had played into his opposition of the
notion of democratic representation, Lajpat Rai's membership of
the aspirational, educated upper-caste middle class played into his
opposition to the older system of nominated political representation
that had excluded this class from political rule. And into his belief in
the notion—once again becoming acceptable after having fallen into
disrepute for centuries—that the power of rulers comes from the 'the
people', who must have a voice in their government, if only through

a severely limited, doubly indirect form of popular, democratic self-government.

While criticizing Sir Syed's opposition to the Congress's demand for elective representation, Lajpat Rai also addressed the occasionally aggressive pride with which he had recently spoken of Muslims as a conquering race:

> Sir Syed Ahmed feels extremely proud of his ancestors, not because they were men who contributed to the well-being of humanity, not because they taught the lesson of equality to the world, not because they were followers of a book, said to teach the oneness of mankind, the equality of mankind, but because they were conquerors, which in the strict sense of the word, means dacoits. What were men like Timur and Nadir Shah if not the heads of looting...[76]

He chided Sir Syed for pouring scorn on Bengalis:

> The Syed inveighs at Bengalees because their forefathers never injured any section of the human race by their sword, because they never turned out to be aggressors! ... It is the standing glory of the ancient Indians that no foreign nation ever had an occasion of being deprived of their liberties by them. Nobody in the world can deny the undaunted courage and the war-like spirit of the ancient Rajputs, who, notwithstanding this, never thought it proper to disturb the peace of a neighbouring people. No race ever complained of its having been ruined by a Rajput invasion.[77]

Lajpat Rai inverted the image of Muslims as a proud, conquering race by painting Timur and Nadir Shah as nothing but 'dacoits'. This attempt to puncture the pride that might accrue from the notion of the historical role of Muslims as conquerors, along with his defence of 'Bengalis', implicitly refuted Sir Syed's assertion that the ruling lineage of Muslims qualified them for political rule more than others of so-called 'insignificant origin'. For Lajpat Rai, the ruling lineage of Muslims did not naturally grant them voice in the political order. Instead, precisely because of their 'insignificant' origin, 'Bengalis'—by which Lajpat Rai, much like Sir Syed, meant the new Bengali Hindu elite to the exclusion of the low-caste Bengali Muslim peasant majority—were more in touch with the needs of 'the people'. And so, their association with the government, through their election, was more in line with Lajpat Rai's desired objective of self-rule by 'the people'.

At certain junctures, Lajpat Rai rightly noted that what troubled Sir Syed most was the progress of 'Bengalis': 'He does not seem to oppose the National Congress in fact, but the Bengali element predominating in it. The progress of the Bengali, the superiority of his abilities, and his taking a lead in every national movement pains the poor Syed to the core of his heart.'[78] At the same time, as we can see from Lajpat Rai's attempt to defend Bengalis by defending the peaceful rule of 'ancient Indians'/'ancient Rajputs', he evidently read Sir Syed's contempt for Bengalis as an attack on Hindus collectively, and saw himself as offering a defence of not just Bengalis but Hindus at large. Sir Syed was indeed troubled by the rise of not only the Bengalis but a wider Hindu middle class. While at times he emphasized that both the Muslims and the Hindus of his province would not be able to compete with Bengalis, at others he urged Muslims to guard against the actions of both 'Bengalis' and 'Hindus'.[79] He pointed out that Congress schemes would only benefit 'Bengalis, Mahrattas and Brahmins'—the caste elite that for him often defined 'Hindus'—while injuring the Muslim 'nation'.[80] As noted before, Sir Syed's opposition to elective representation was driven by the anxiety that in a system in which representatives were elected from a wider pool of natives, and in which education, wealth and numbers would matter, the Hindu majority would have overwhelming political advantage. His response was to question whether Hindus constituted a nation and imply that unlike Muslims they were inexperienced in the art of political rule.[81] This subtle denigration of Hindus did not go unnoticed by Lajpat Rai, who concurrently defended other Hindus along with 'Bengalis'. His support for the principle of elective representation was likely also an implicit refutation of the view that 'Muslims'—whether only its aristocracy or also other classes—alone were entitled to share in the government by the British. Despite their lack of history of conquering other 'nations', Hindus too possessed the capacity for political rule, a fact particularly manifest in Rajput history. Yet, despite this history, it was the felt inability of Hindus to make as strong a claim as Muslims of a robust, continuous history of political rule that likely also attracted Lajpat Rai to elective, democratic representation as a means by which Hindus might once again have access to the political order.

In instances when he read Sir Syed's opposition to the elective principle as an assault on 'Hindus', and defended the latter by adducing Rajput history, Lajpat Rai of course forgot that Sir Syed had evaluated Hindu Rajas and Rajputs as worthy of ruling over the people of India alongside Muslim '*raises*'. He had himself rhetorically asked Rajputs whether they could live under the rule of 'Bengalis'. Thus, while Sir Syed pushed for a cross-community alliance of aristocrats, Lajpat Rai, in highlighting a Rajput history to defend 'Bengalis', made an implicit plea for the Hindu capacity for political rule. Importantly, though he utilized Rajput history, his dismissal of even Hindu aristocrats, noted above, as unrepresentative of 'the people', shows that his support for elective political representation was impelled by the desire that not just Hindu Rajputs but the wider Hindu 'people' have a voice in political rule, albeit of course through their more enlightened middle-class representatives. His support for the elective principle contained within it the tacit hope of bringing a small measure of popular self-rule by Hindus.

Nevertheless, Lajpat Rai did not demand this limited self-rule for a *Hindu* nation. In his fourth 'open letter' to Sir Syed, he extensively quoted from the latter's speeches from 1884 to remind him of the meaning he had once attached to the word 'nation'.[82] Lajpat Rai produced Sir Syed's words, quoted earlier, from his Gurdaspur speech.[83] He then reproduced another speech the Syed had delivered at Lahore in 1884 in which he had remarked:

In the word NATION I include both Hindus and Mahomedans, because that is the only meaning which I can attach to it (i.e. NATION or *qaum*)... With me it is not so much worth considering what is their religious faith, because we do not see anything of it. What we do see is that we inhabit the same land, are subject to the rule of the same Governors; the fountains of benefits for all are the same, and the pangs of famine also we suffer equally. These are the different grounds upon which I call both those races which inhabit India by one word, i.e. Hindu, meaning to say that they are the inhabitants of Hindustan. While in the Legislative Council, I was always anxious for the prosperity of this nation.[84]

Lajpat Rai presents Sir Syed as having reneged on his earlier conception of Hindus and Muslims forming one Indian nation, to talk of separate Hindu and Muslim 'nations'. This either deliberately misrepresented Sir Syed's use of the word 'nation', or—more likely—simply misunderstood it. As noted, Sir Syed had always imagined India as a 'nation' of different 'nations'. His imagination of the continuance of the British Empire meant he had no conception of national self-rule or a nation–state.[85] His lack of a modern, nationalist–statist conception of the 'nation' (wherein every nation–people had to ultimately find political expression in a state of its own) allowed him to imagine India as a country of multiple 'nations'. Nevertheless, Lajpat Rai's extensive quotations of Sir Syed's words regarding the existence of an Indian qaum and his assessment of it as a sign of his 'former greatness' confirm Rai's own belief that India contained not different nations but a single Indian nation whose members included both Hindus and Muslims. Unlike Sir Syed, Lajpat Rai had begun to imagine, if only in the very distant future, the end of Empire and progress towards some form of self-government. Beginning to conceive of nations in a nationalist/ statist sense, i.e., believing that every nation–people must one day be self-ruling and have its own government, he held that in India this self-rule would be by the *Indian* nation. To him, the introduction of the elective principle was an essential step towards some measure of self-rule by this Indian nation.

At the same time, just as Sir Syed had imagined his (pre-nationalist) Indian 'nation' as composed of different 'nations', Lajpat Rai imagined his (nationalist) Indian 'nation' as consisting of different 'communities'. One of the reasons why Sir Syed resisted any sort of self-rule for the Indian nation as a whole was that he believed this would result in an unequal distribution of political power between what he thought was the larger, stronger Hindu community/nation and the smaller, weaker Muslim community/nation. Lajpat Rai, cognizant of Sir Syed's worry, responded in the following manner:

> The nation consisting of Hindus, Mahomedans, Christians and others cannot be said to be progressing unless all the component parts of it contribute towards the progress of the whole; thus the progress of the Mahomedans, being an integral part of the 'whole', must necessarily form an important part of the progress of the nation. But one cannot mean to stop the progress of the whole because that part has not kept pace with the others. The desire of Sir Syed Ahmed to arrest the progress of the whole Indian nation unless the Mahomedans become capable of equally competing with other communities is simply absurd and expresses his utter ignorance as to how a nation politically advances . . . the Syed has in his reply shown himself to be completely ignorant of the meaning of nationality. The Syed represents the nation to be a bride, having two eyes, Hindus and Muslims, thus dexterously excluding Christians, Parsis and others. Just suppose for a moment that both the eyes of a person are defective, the one to a lesser degree and the other a greater one. No reasonable man in the world will allow his better eye of the two not to recover its normal strength unless the other also recovers fully.[86]

Lajpat Rai clearly recognized that Syed Ahmed Khan's opposition to the elective principle stemmed from his anxiety that the Muslim 'community' lagged behind Hindus—it had not 'kept pace' in terms of education and wealth and was thus presently incapable of 'equally competing with other communities'. Yet, he did not allay Sir Syed's fears that the introduction of the elective principle in legislative councils, as a step towards Indian national self-rule, would produce unjust political outcomes for Muslims as opposed to Hindus. He simply rejected the suggestion that the elective principle be halted till the Muslim community had caught up or because it would benefit it less than others.[87] Accepting Sir Syed's premise that Hindus were ahead of Muslims, he argued that this 'better eye' too had to recover its 'normal strength', and presented progress towards Indian national self-rule (via the elective principle) as an indispensable first step towards the political recuperation of the Hindu community. These statements implicitly admitted that Indian national self-rule might indeed come at the cost of the Muslim community and to the benefit of the Hindu community. Lajpat Rai was offended by Sir Syed's suggestion that Hindus and Muslim constituted not only one Indian 'nation' but, first, two different 'nations'. But nowhere did he attempt to show how self-rule by the 'Indian nation' would bring the political advancement of *both* the Hindu and Muslim 'communities' that he insisted constituted it.

This was unlike the senior Congressman Surendranath Banerjea who, in a speech in October 1888, went to relatively greater lengths to 'appeal' to the 'Mohammedan community and Sir Syed himself, arguing that Congress demands would benefit 'Hindus and Mohammedans alike', even contending that 'they will benefit the Mohammedan a great deal more than the Hindu'. Banerjea noted individual instances of Muslims having done well in university and civil services examinations to demonstrate the advances the community had made in 'English culture and English education', as a way of emphasizing its potential for succeeding in systems based on meritocracy and election. He additionally also pointed out that the Congress had introduced a rule whereby if Muslim delegates objected to a question nearly unanimously, it would not be discussed. Banerjea ended his speech by reminding his audience of the history of 800 years of amity and goodwill between Hindus and Muslims, relations which had survived even the end of the Mughal Empire, by insisting that the Congress was open to all, and once again appealing to Hindus and Muslims as brothers who should set aside their differences for the sake of the larger national family.[88]

Lajpat Rai's nonchalance towards Sir Syed's anxieties about the adverse consequences of elective representation for the Muslim community resulted from his holding a democratic/elective conception of political representation, different from Sir Syed's aristocratic/nominated conception. But it was equally an outcome of Lajpat Rai conceiving political representation differently from Sir Syed in a further, second sense. Sir Syed visualized political representation as a descriptive mirror of various communities in Indian society, and saw political interests as a feature of religious communities. He subscribed to what may be called a descriptive, community-based notion of representation.[89] In contrast, Rai revealed his conception of political representation at the fifth Congress session in 1889: 'I am Hindu; in the Punjab, the Hindus are in a minority, and so far as I am concerned, I should be quite content to be represented by any good Mahomedan or Sikh member.'[90] This was what may be called a non-descriptive, territorial conception of political representation, which assumed that political interests were not just features of religious communities, and that political representatives could act for the interests of any individual or group within a territory, even other than of their religious community. Holding that Hindus, Muslims and Parsis were 'one people and one nation', guided by a 'feeling of Indian brotherhood', he believed that as members of one Indian nation, they should conceive themselves as sharing substantial political interests and acting for each other. Departing from Sir Syed's premise that Hindus would always conceive themselves as sharing more political interests with other Hindus than with Muslims, Lajpat Rai did not take seriously his very real apprehension that numerical preponderance of Hindu voters in a system of elective representation would result in Hindus ruling over Muslims. If animated by the feeling that all Indians constituted one nation, the elective principle would only result in a form of Indian national self-rule, with members of the Indian nation representing in councils and thus acting for other members of the Indian nation.

As he saw it, even if the elective principle brought to power mostly Hindu members of the Indian nation, they would act for its Muslim members. This was interesting for someone who himself imagined the Indian nation as a political community composed not of individuals but distinct religious 'communities'. While members of these 'communities' were seen as quite distinct and autonomous in the *non-political* social or cultural domain, Lajpat Rai asked them to act as Indians politically, with no explanation as to why or how they should cease to function as members of their respective 'communities' once they entered the political domain. It was their different—descriptive/community-based vs non-descriptive/territorial—conceptions of political representation that also led one man to refuse elective representation as a pre-determination of Muslim minoritization at the all-India level, and the other's insouciance about such apprehensions to eagerly embrace both elective representation and the idea of future self-government by an Indian nation.

Of course, Lajpat Rai's belonging to the numerically stronger Hindu community allowed him to assume this benign view of non-descriptive/territorial representation and Indian national self-rule. In what was to become a standard Indian nationalist argument by the mid-twentieth century, Lajpat Rai saw Sir Syed's apprehension about whether non-Muslims could represent them as signifying only 'prejudice' and an as yet insufficiently developed feeling of 'Indian brotherhood'.[91] He did not theoretically acknowledge that at least sometimes members of a 'community' might legitimately share some political interests only with each other, such that only a member of that community could represent it. He also did not acknowledge that the interests of the Indian nation may indeed sometimes end up being defined by elected Hindus in terms of the interests of their majority community in ways that could politically marginalize minority communities. Nevertheless, that Lajpat Rai did not fear the political consequences of the elective principle for the Punjabi Hindu minority, to which he also belonged, reveals his general commitment to the principle that as Indians, Hindus and Muslims could and should represent each other when they embodied Indian national self-rule in councils.

Interestingly, despite his belief that descriptive, community-based notions of political representation reflected an inadequately developed larger Indian national consciousness, at the 1889 Congress session Lajpat Rai ultimately supported a resolution that affirmed that 'minorities shall be represented by men of their own particular sections' in proportion to their population.[92] Rai was unwilling to halt the rolling out of the elective principle or progress towards Indian national self-rule to protect any perceived interests of the Muslim community. But he was open to an election-based arrangement that safeguarded them even if he disagreed with such a community-based conception of political interests and representation. The concession of community-based representation according to numerical proportion (in other words, reservations) was an attempt to mitigate fears that the elective principle would result in Hindu majority rule under the guise of Indian national self-rule. Some Hindu participants in the Congress, like Malaviya, chose to remain silent on the issue of communal representation for minorities.[93] Lajpat Rai, cognizant of his own minority status as a Punjabi Hindu, was more sympathetic to Muslim fears of being minoritized under Indian national self-rule. He allowed himself to depart from a purist Indian nationalism (one that wished to remain unblemished by community-based politics) which stoked fears of Hindu majority rule. Instead, he articulated an Indian nationalism which sought limited self-rule for the Indian nation in a form that ensured that this would be the rule of Hindus along with Muslims and other smaller minorities. Just like Syed Ahmed Khan, the young Lajpat Rai's intellectual positions—his nationalist conception of the Indian nation, and commitment to democratic and non-descriptive/territorial forms of representation—also embodied a refusal. Together, they rebuffed Khan's stance against the transformation of Muslims from a privileged aristocratic minority to a 'minority' in the modern sense of the word, which signified disadvantage and vulnerability. Rai embraced the historical shift to a modern form of politics in which the power and legitimacy of rulers was derived from the people. His dismissal of claims to political representation based on social superiority, ruling lineages, military valour and statecraft was a logical outcome of this position. He welcomed and affirmed the new democratic notion of representation and the modern, nationalist conception of the Indian nation and the transition to a mode of politics which would reduce 'Muslims' to a new kind of vulnerable 'minority'. Within this new democratic, nationalist framework, with its logic of majorities and minorities, he was willing to countenance, very early on in the late nineteenth century, a limited form of descriptive, community-based representation for minorities to safeguard their political interests from Hindu majority domination.

3

Holding on to Hindu-ness

After his first intervention in all-India politics in 1888–89, Lajpat Rai remained relatively quiet on the all-India political front, attending only two of the next ten annual sessions of the Congress, which many Punjabi Hindus saw more as an organization of Bengali and Bombay politicians. The 1890s, a decade during which Lajpat Rai transformed from a twenty-five-year-old young adult to a more mature thirty-five-year-old, were spent immersed in the activities of the Arya Samaj. Returning from Hissar to Lahore in 1892, he was particularly involved in the educational activities of the new DAV college which he helped found in 1888. As we saw in the first chapter, as an Arya Samajist, Lajpat Rai equated religion with one text, the Vedas (the four Samhitas), which he believed preached abstract monotheistic worship of a single attribute-less God. In response to the challenge posed by the European Christian encounter, he responded by articulating a Vedic monotheism. The 1890s saw him de-emphasize theological detail even as he spoke of Hinduism and the Hindu community.

Like all other Arya Samajists, Lajpat Rai was scathing in his criticism of several aspects of contemporary Hinduism, most notably its textual plurality, polytheism and idol worship. But he refused to eschew 'Hinduism' in favour of a separate 'Vedic religion'. Here, he differed from other Arya Samajists. This became clear when bitter disagreements among them, in the late 1880s, resulted in an acrimonious split in the Samaj in 1893.[1] One faction, soon to be known as the 'Gurukul Party', insisted that all fifty-one doctrines (*siddhant*) outlined by Swami Dayanand, including and especially his opposition to meat eating, be binding on Arya Samajists.[2] For them, vegetarianism was the mark of a moral man, and they insisted that no 'flesh-eater' be admitted as a member of the Samaj.[3] To create a moral community of Aryas strictly committed to the Swami's fifty-one doctrines, the Gurukul Party was willing to sacrifice the integrity or 'wholeness' of Hinduism. The other faction, later known as the 'College Party', passionately argued that since Dayanand was merely a great man and not infallible, neither his teachings nor his interpretation of the Vedas was binding on Arya Samajists. Although Dayanand had espoused vegetarianism, it was not a key tenet of the Vedic religion and was not binding. This faction openly rejected vegetarianism as a condition of Arya Samaj membership; an Arya Samajist only needed to subscribe to the ten principles (*niyam*), the general manifesto of the organization.[4] A struggle broke out within Arya Samaj organizations such as the Lahore Arya Samaj and the Arya Pratinidhi Sabha (Arya Representative Assembly).

Thrown into the midst of this controversy upon his return to Lahore, Lajpat Rai sided with the College Party. In fact, after the struggle over the Lahore Samaj ended in the defeat and ousting of the 'non-vegetarian' College Party and the latter founded an alternative Samaj at Anarkali (a suburb of Lahore), he served as its president. The split resulted in the Gurukul Party dominating the original Lahore Samaj and the Arya Pratinidhi Sabha, and the College Party retaining control of the recently established DAV college. The two factions of the Samaj continued to denounce each other through the 1890s.

While sources for Lajpat Rai's own views at the time of the split are unavailable, a speech in 1893 by Lala Mulraj, a prominent leader of the College Party, indicates the general stance of the faction to which he belonged. Mulraj wished to place the Arya Samaj on 'a broad and catholic basis'—requiring its members to only express belief in one God and the Vedas. Divisive doctrinal requirements were to be avoided to ensure that that diverse religious groupings of Hindus could see themselves as belonging to one common religion.[5] In his own 1914 book on the Samaj, Lajpat Rai wrote that only three of the ten niyams contained any doctrinal teaching. These were: a belief (1) that God was the source of all true knowledge, (2) in the worship of this single omniscient, formless God alone, and (3) that the Vedas were the Books that contained this true knowledge. He wrote:

> This, surely was the simplest of creeds, to which no Hindu, at any rate, should have any difficulty in subscribing . . . [it was] intended to keep all dogma in the background and to free the Principles from any controversial matter. It is said, in fact, that the object was to make the Arya Samaj as Catholic as it possibly could be without sacrificing its Hindu character.[6]

Although a strict vegetarian himself[7], Lajpat Rai had supported 'the individual's right of private judgement' in this regard.[8] Unlike the Gurukul Party, he did not stress the particularities of Arya Samajist doctrine and practice, at the cost of the Samaj's separation from the larger entity known as 'Hinduism'.[9] Rai was among those Arya Samajists who de-emphasized Arya Samajist theology precisely so they could continue to lay claim to the larger category of 'Hinduism' and the entity it represented.

In his 1898 biography of Swami Dayanand, Rai insisted that the Samaj's founder had intended to institute neither a new religion separate from Hinduism nor a new sect within it.[10] He merely wished to 'purge Hinduism of all the evils that had found admittance into it'.[11] In short, he had merely wished to reform Hinduism. Several Hindu reformers, like the Brahmo Samajist Keshub Chandra Sen and Prarthna Samajist Mahadev Govind Ranade (1842–1901), often explicitly conceived Hinduism's 'reform' as requiring the deliberate, self-conscious adoption of external (European liberal or even

Christian) elements.[12] But Dayanand and his followers like Lajpat Rai conceived the 'reform of Hinduism' as a 'return' to the ancient 'Vedic religion'. The latter—reformulated as abstract monotheistic worship—was imagined as nothing but the uncorrupted, pure, original and true form of Hinduism.[13] As an Arya Samajist wishing to hold on to a 'Hindu' identity, Lajpat Rai's definition of 'Hinduism' was influenced by the Arya Samajist religious outlook. But he concluded that the only way he could successfully balance both identities, without sacrificing one for the other, was to substantially dilute much of the prickly, intricate Arya Samajist tenets of 'Vedic' theology and define Hinduism in terms of the Samaj's broadest, most basic tenet: abstract Vedic monotheism. Minimizing the Arya Samaj's Vedic theology was essential to make room for the largest possible number of Hindus to identify—despite the stunning diversity in their beliefs and practices—with Rai's Arya Samaj-inflected definition of Hinduism.

. Imbibing British criticism, Lajpat Rai saw contemporary Hinduism's ritualistic and idolatrous polytheism as a source of disarray, and abstract monotheism as a source of unity, zeal and strength.[14] For him, 'returning' to abstract Vedic monotheism, to Hinduism's supposedly original form, was the best means of transcending Hinduism's complicated religio–theological diversity, and achieve Hindu unity. Therefore, while some elementary theology appeared in Lajpat Rai's thought, the imperative of engineering a Hindu unity fuelled its dilution and attenuation. Religious theology—in the form of belief in one God and the Vedas as the sole source of His wisdom—became a means to bolster Hinduism's worth vis-a-vis Christianity (and, as evident from his comparison of Vedic monotheism with the Quran, Islam),[15] and to strengthen the integrity and unity of the single entity called Hinduism. Beyond emphasizing abstract Vedic monotheism towards this purpose, Lajpat Rai remained largely uninterested in the intricacies of Arya Samajist articulations of Vedic theology.

Arya Samajists like Lajpat Rai were not the only Hindus to respond to assumptions about the superiority of Christian and

Islamic monotheism by appropriating monotheism for Hinduism.[16] Brahmo Samajists like Rammohun Roy had already done so at the dawn of the nineteenth century. The difference, apart from Roy basing his monotheistic Hinduism in the Vedanta, was that, for Roy, this monotheism was meant to foster unity not of Hindus alone but of all religions. By Lajpat Rai's time, it had become common to foster collective unity among Hindus by refashioning Hinduism as a monotheistic faith. Even some Sanatanist Hindus were doing so. The father of modern Hindi, Bharatendu Harishchandra of Benaras, who claimed to represent sanatan dharm, the unbroken Hindu tradition, redefined Hinduism as a monotheistic faith, although one centred on bhakti and image-worship to a personal God. Despite Harishchandra's emphasis on Vaishnava bhakti and image worship, he shared with Lajpat Rai the aim of formulating a monotheistic Hinduism to foster Hindu unity.[17] Similarly, Bal Gangadhar Tilak (1856–1920), emerging as a Hindu leader from Maharashtra, was attempting, through his Ganapati festival, to redefine Hinduism as a congregational religion, seeking to achieve through the refashioning of practice (rather than theology) the same end—Hindu unity.[18] Lajpat Rai participated in a larger phenomenon, occurring in different parts of India in the late nineteenth century, in which Hinduism was being creatively re-imagined to foster Hindu unity and pride. As a Punjabi Arya Samajist, his own distinctive attempt to achieve this end involved de-emphasizing elaborate doctrinal points of Arya Samajist theology, and reformulating Hinduism in terms of the Arya Samaj's broadest tenet of abstract Vedic monotheism.

A Secular Education for Hindus: Language, Culture and History

Lajpat Rai's inclination to de-emphasize Arya Samaj theology to engineer a Hindu unity was visible in the educational curriculum he envisioned in the 1890s for DAV College, established in 1888 to honour the Samaj's founder. He advocated a 'Vedic' education geared less towards theology than secular instruction in what he considered the language, culture and history of Hindus. But before elaborating on the content of the education Lajpat Rai sought to promote, we need to understand the context in which it was being proposed.

Colonial education at the school level was carried out in the vernacular medium till high school (in Punjab, young Lajpat had received Urdu-medium instruction in school).[19] However, textbooks, supervised by the colonial state, incorporated European subjects drawn from European educational curriculum, and sought to impart 'European' knowledge and British Victorian moral values.[20] History textbooks, even when in the vernacular medium, followed European models of historiography (history writing). They invariably drew upon English histories of India and were positively biased towards the 'British period'.[21]

If the number of Indian subjects receiving this new colonial education at the school level was small, those with access to English education at the college level was minuscule. Despite opposition from British orientalist official–scholars who wished Western knowledge to be grafted onto Orientalist learning and taught in the vernacular,[22] Macaulay's famous 1835 Minute on Education decided that colonial higher education would only teach Western texts. These texts imparted a liberal, literary (as opposed to scientific) education in the English medium, and were considered a repository of the best of European thought.[23] While this English education reached only a microscopic minority, it was guided by the stated objective of producing a loyal class of Indian intelligentsia which was, in Macaulay's words, 'Indian in colour and blood but English in taste, in opinions, in morals and in intellect'.[24] The system of modern, Western education in the English medium, then, asserted the superiority of liberal cultural values, even if only to a tiny minority of Indians.[25] University syllabi included subjects such as English literature, European history, moral philosophy, logic and political economy (both of which had John Stuart Mill as required reading). These introduced Indians to new modes of Western thought.[26] Histories of India were taught but were written by European writers, based on European conceptions of history, and presented the colonial interpretation of Indian history.[27]

Universities offered Persian, Arabic and Urdu, as well as Sanskrit as
an option for Hindus, whose study, contrary to what is sometimes
assumed, continued during the colonial period.[28] Lajpat Rai had
himself assumed the study of Arabic and Persian before giving it up in
favour of Sanskrit at the insistence of his Arya Samajist friends.[29] Yet,
despite the continued study of Sanskrit, the victory of the 'Anglicists'
in 1835 had been accompanied by an insistence on the superiority of
English, Western knowledge, liberal cultural values and institutions,
and the neglect of indigenous knowledges (medicine, astronomy,
history, geography and so on), which were variously condemned as
'superstitious', 'primitive', 'mythic' and untrue.[30]

Many members of the Indian intelligentsia—within or outside
the Congress, Hindu or Muslim—considered this new liberal, literary
English education as the greatest blessing of British rule. It gave them
access to modern European knowledge, and enabled the moral,
social and political regeneration of Indians.[31] Yet, some members of
the same class—Muslims in the North-Western Provinces or Hindus
in Punjab—also felt its culturally alienating effects.[32] In 1893, Lajpat
Rai would allude to this in a tract titled *A Historical Glance at
Sanskrit Education in the Dayanand Anglo-Vedic College.* For him,
colonial education, largely lifted from British curricula, ignored 'our'
achievements in knowledge and culture, and fully suited neither the
'temperament, outlook and spirit of our people' nor the 'political,
social and cultural needs of our country'.[33] Just as Sir Syed had done
with his Aligarh College, Lajpat Rai (along with other Punjabi Hindu
Arya Samajists) wished to rectify what he called the 'defective', 'highly
lopsided' Western education provided by the government.

Vedic education was the answer to this perceived problem. But
unlike the Gurukul Party (named after the Gurukul this faction
established at Kangri, UP), Lajpat Rai and his College Party did
not emphasize a rigorous religious education for Hindus.[34] Rai's
relative disinterest in what he called 'Vedic theology' is evident
in his *Historical Glance* tract where he states his wish to 'avoid' its
systematic teaching as a separate subject at the DAV College.[35]
Satisfied with the teaching of Vedic theology in Arya Samaj's weekly

sermons, he opposed its introduction as a subject at the College. The same relative indifference towards theology is evident in his wish that *Sandhya*, prayers involving the recitation of Vedic mantras at particular junctures of the day, not be performed during college hours as this forced even students averse to prayers to pretend to pray merely to retain their place in the college, thereby encouraging the habit of hypocrisy.[36]

But if not Vedic theology, what was the content of the 'Vedic' education that Lajpat Rai wished to impart? For him, Vedic education entailed 'the promotion of our own language and culture on a national scale'.[37] This meant the teaching of the Vedas, something ignored in government-run education, a greater emphasis on ancient Sanskrit than in government universities, and the propagation of 'our national language' through 'the study of Hindi literature and the [*sic*] allied culture'.[38] Lajpat Rai's view of Hindi as the language of Hindus was the result of a broader process, first initiated by British officials and missionaries, and subsequently encouraged by the Hindi movement begun in the North-Western Provinces (UP) in the 1860s.[39] This movement, spearheaded by Bharatendu Harishchandra,[40] was now being led by the young UP Congressman Malaviya.[41] This involved the splitting of the Hindustani language, with a roughly equal number of Sanskrit and Persian–Arabic words, to create a modern (more Sanskritized) Hindi and (more Persianized) Urdu as the national languages of Hindus and Muslims respectively.[42] By the 1880s, this process was complete. Despite his own ignorance of it, Lajpat Rai (along with the rest of the Punjab Arya Samaj) came to unquestioningly view and promote Hindi in the Devanagari script as the language of Hindus.[43] The 'Vedic' education Lajpat Rai envisioned for Hindus clearly entailed the teaching of Sanskrit and Hindi languages and literature, which he in turn equated with the promotion of Hindu 'culture'.

Lajpat Rai had harboured anxieties about the eagerness of Indians to imbibe English culture.[44] Still, opposing the Gurukul Party that strongly prioritized an elaborate curriculum of Sanskrit and Vedic studies,[45] Lajpat Rai resolutely insisted on an English education

alongside Vedic education—the indispensable importance of the
'Anglo' in Anglo–Vedic.[46] Despite his criticism, and much like the
'moderates' who currently led the Congress, Rai considered English
education as the greatest blessing of British rule.[47] Addressing the
Gurukul Party, Rai emphasized that even Swami Dayanand was 'not
quite happy with institutions . . . which taught only Sanskrit' and had
believed that 'the recent enlightenment and so-called renaissance
had come from the West, mainly through the English language'.[48]
The Swami had appreciated the importance of English education
for the 'rejuvenation of the nation'. For Lajpat Rai, then, English
education was critical for collective enlightenment, renaissance and
rejuvenation. His appreciation of 'liberal education'[49] suggests that he
partly attributed this collective 'rejuvenation' to Western liberal values
that English education imparted. Therefore, contrary to whatever
hopes the British may have harboured while introducing it[50], Lajpat
Rai was among those Indians who saw English liberal education as
crucial for encouraging a collective reawakening among Hindus.[51]

Rai stressed that 'it is English education which had enabled
us to realize our position, and impress on us the fact that unless
we progress with the times, we will be left behind in the march of
nations'.[52] Having read numerous histories of India and Europe
written by European writers,[53] Lajpat Rai saw English education as
vital for imparting a historical consciousness. History as a subject,
conceived in European terms and deploying European methods—i.e.,
articulating a strictly linear, 'factual' account rather than a cyclical one
expressing a general historical memory—had indeed been central to
the new system of education.[54] While intended to justify British rule,
colonial histories had also imparted a consciousness of historical
depths and trajectories, frequently associated with the development
of nation–states.[55] The tripartite chronological division of Indian
history into Hindu, Muslim and British periods further accentuated
community consciousness.[56] Histories written in the vernacular
evidently produced a similar effect. Lajpat Rai would later recall
that it was from *Qasis-i-Hind* (Judges of India), a book written by
his Arabic teacher, the renowned Urdu writer and poet Mohammad

Hussain Azad, that he learnt to appreciate India's pre-Islamic past, admire 'Hindu valour' and 'be proud of Hindus'.[57] Nevertheless, it was with English education that he associated this new historical consciousness. And so, for him, along with a Vedic education in their language and culture, Hindus needed an English liberal education which, through its teaching of 'history', could revitalize them.

In fact, Lajpat Rai believed that imparting a knowledge of history, particularly of one's 'community and country', should be the main purpose of education. In a book he wrote for school students in 1898, entitled *A History of India*, he stated:

> A man having no knowledge of the history of his country and society has got no right to be called educated. It is desirable for every man to be familiar with the history of the religion and customs and moral, social and political development of his community . . . Only by knowing the history of his country and community can he know about attributes which distinguish his society from the people of other societies.[58]

In the preface to the same book, he outlined why an education in this particular 'history' was important. First, it promoted understanding of the distinctiveness of Hindu identity. Second, it induced attachment and pride in one's religion and community.[59] And finally, it provided knowledge of the path laid down by their 'ancestors' which must be emulated to overcome the present Hindu decline.[60] Such 'history' showed a path towards the collective regeneration of Hindus. Therefore, for Lajpat Rai, apart from instruction in their language, an education for Hindus had to include knowledge of their 'history', viewed as a crucial vehicle to endow them with a collective identity of which they could be proud.

To foster Hindu unity, Lajpat Rai de-emphasized elaborate Arya Samajist Vedic theology and utilized its attenuated tenets to arrive at a broadened definition of Hinduism. Towards the same end, he also advocated an education for Hindus geared less towards theology than secular instruction (secular in the sense of not being strictly related to the divine or sacred) in what he considered the language and history of Hindus, both considered central aspects of the unspecified Hindu 'culture' he sought to promote. 'Religion' itself was largely detached from its associations with divinity, faith, worship, doctrine and practice, and reduced to the language and history of Hindus as a key aspect of their culture. Although he did not use the concept of culture frequently at this historical juncture, Rai's use of it indicates his incipient participation in a new, modern discourse of 'culture' steadily rising to prominence globally since the mid-nineteenth century. In the eighteenth century, the term 'culture' had been used almost synonymously with 'cultivation'. It had been used by Enlightenment thinkers to connote a general process of intellectual, spiritual and material progress and self-development of all of humanity towards a 'civilized' or 'cultivated' state (where often this 'culture'—as universal civilization—of course referred only to the particular culture of Europe).[61] From the late-eighteenth century, the term had undergone a semantic shift, such that by the mid-nineteenth century it no longer signified only the collective self-cultivation of humanity (culminating in the high point of European culture).

Now, the term was increasingly used in the plural, and to signify the diversity of life-forms—'ways of life'—of different peoples.[62] This modern meaning of 'culture', signifying a distinctive way of life, began to take root from the mid-nineteenth century. It was in this pluralized sense that Lajpat Rai fleetingly used the term culture in the 1890s, largely in the anthropological, more descriptive sense (which allowed even 'savages' to have their own culture—or 'way of life')[63] but possibly with some residues of the other, value-laden sense of the term, signifying the objectified results of cultivation like (Hindu) philosophy, history, literature and so on. The concept of culture had first been used in India by the Bengali social critic (and author of the Bengali poem we know as 'Vande Mataram') Bankimchandra Chatterji in the 1880s. Seizing this global concept, Chatterji had redefined Hinduism in terms of 'culture', with the Bhagavad Gita's advocacy of desireless action (nishkama karma) as the path to the cultivation of innate capacities.[64] Now, a decade later, Lajpat Rai of

Punjab similarly participated in a discourse of 'culture', although only transiently and inchoately. But while Chatterji had emphasized Krishna of the Gita as the model of culture as self-cultivation for the whole of humanity, Lajpat Rai addressed Hindus and gestured more vaguely to their (objectified) culture as supposedly embodied in Hindi/Sanskrit and the history of their 'ancestors'.

By the late nineteenth century, the imperatives of fostering a unified, regenerated Hindu community were causing religious theology to lose ground to broadly secular categories like 'history' and 'culture' in Lajpat Rai's Hindu thought. The Gurukul Party would also attempt to fortify a united Hindu community by emphasizing a shared language, history and culture of Hindus.[65] But its insistence on an elaborate list of Arya tenets ran counter to this project. By leaving theology largely to the Gurukul Party Arya Samajists, Lajpat Rai and his College Party more assertively resisted the shift of the Arya Samaj out of the Hindu fold. They simultaneously attempted to lay claim to the latter by going down what may be called a secular, culturalist path. In this manner, they participated in, and even spearheaded, a phenomenon in the late nineteenth century by which Hinduism was, to some extent, being desacralized, decoupled from religious faith and ritual practice, and reconfigured in terms of a broadly non-religious, secularized 'culture'. This culturalization—and indeed, secularization—of Hinduism meant that in some instances it was no longer strongly tied to religious faith, practice and dogma, but still functioned to provide a sense of collective belonging.[66] Indeed, its internal religious diversity was one reason why some actor–thinkers like Lajpat Rai downplayed its religious elements and were beginning to look towards secular history and culture as a means of providing this sense of belonging.[67]

4

History, Community and Nation

In the preface to his 1898 book *A History of India*, Lajpat Rai stated that 'it is desirable for every man to be familiar with the history of the religion and customs and moral, social and political development of his community'. He often referred to Hindus as a 'community'. This was also evident in his campaign for the Hindu Orphan Relief movement in 1897–99, where he appealed to the 'Hindu community' to help provide relief to famine-stricken Hindu orphans, and prevent them from 'falling into the hands of missionaries'.[1] In *A Historical Glance* he promoted Hindi as part of DAV education by referring to it as 'our national language';[2] he had also argued that Swami Dayanand realized the value of English education for rejuvenating 'the nation';[3] then, in 1899 he praised English education for making 'us' realize that 'we' were falling behind in the 'march of nations'.[4] So, Lajpat Rai clearly also referred to a 'nation'. But he was ambiguous about what this term referred to. For instance, in a work published in the mid-1890s, he wrote about the nation thus:

> My countrymen . . . have no idea about those noble thoughts and qualities which have sustained our nation . . . There is no better subject for a people than the history of their past. This is quite

true for a nation that has marched downward from its zenith . . .
which declined after reaching the zenith of its glory and which in
its heyday was at the top of the world . . . that nation's knowledge
was the highest . . . so far as the testimony of history goes, this
nation is the most ancient of all . . .[5]

Was this now a reference to an exclusively Hindu nation or the same
Indian nation he had written about in his letters to Sir Syed? The
question is important since the latter means that he was defining
the objective characteristics—its language, culture and history—of
this 'Indian' nation in mainly Hindu terms, in a manner implicitly
exclusionary towards India's Muslims. On the other hand, in case
the reference is to a Hindu nation, this should lead us to ask: What
about Indian Muslims? Are they included or excluded from the
Hindu nation? The exclusive focus on Hindus and Muslims in these
questions is unavoidable. Rai's mind worked primarily through
a Hindu–Muslim lens, and often ignored India's Christians in its
political imaginations. As we shall see later in this chapter, Lajpat
Rai's conceptualization of India's history reveals that he often saw
Sikhs, the other important minority in his province of Punjab, as
simply Hindu, disregarding tendencies among many Sikhs of this
period to assert their separate identity from Hindus.

In his 1896 biography of Giuseppe Mazzini, the propagandist
and champion of Italian nationalism, Rai painstaking detailed the
political life of Mazzini, 'one of the most outstanding men of the
nineteenth century'.[6] He did so in the hope of inspiring his own
countrymen to make sacrifices for the nation. Interestingly, in doing
so, he forwarded Sir Syed as an exemplar:

One should give money generously for the welfare of the country
and bear the consequent hardships, if any, with a smile. Even if
a handful of such well-meaning persons come forward it augurs
well for the future of the country. Even today our country is
not lacking in such exemplary people, Sir Syed Khan being one
of them among Muslims. In Hindus also there are several such

people. My object in writing these pages is to present before you such examples for your edification, and if by my writing I can induce you to emulate them I will consider that my effort has been well rewarded. You may also tread the thorny path of sacrifice in the cause of the country and put on a pedestal those who have already trodden this path.[7]

Elsewhere, Rai wrote of the 'Hindus and Mohammedans of India'.[8] Rai clearly still saw India's Muslims as firmly holding their place within India. For him, they could contribute and were contributing to the welfare and progress of India, and could also be commended as exemplary models for emulation to the unnamed 'nation' he addressed. So, did Lajpat Rai speak of an Indian nation which included Muslims? Or a Hindu nation which could learn from Muslims who were excluded from this nation, even as they lived in India? An examination of Lajpat Rai's discourse on the nation during this decade does not answer this question definitively. One possibility is that Rai meant an Indian nation defined in largely Hindu terms, but which included Muslims and conceded their contributions to India. The other is that he now used the term nation to refer to an exclusively Hindu nation, while still seeing Muslims as belonging equally to India, possibly beginning to view them subconsciously as a separate nation. While Lajpat Rai himself does not clarify this, given his writings in the coming decade, it is possible that he was beginning to move towards believing the latter. Perhaps Sir Syed's resistance to the idea that Hindus and Muslims constituted a single Indian nation (rather than, first, distinct nations themselves) had made Rai unsure of the very idea of nationhood he had defended so strongly in 1888–89. At the same time, he had, on occasion, explicitly referred to a 'Hindu nation' in the mid-1880s too, before writing his open letters to Sir Syed where he had strongly defended the idea of an Indian nation.[9] After his brief political intervention through his open letters, he seemed to once again pick up that idea, wanting to take it further and give it more flesh. At a time when Rai was still in the process of developing his ideas of nationhood, he may have

even simultaneously expressed two shifting ideas of nationhood—
one expressed in the overtly political domain in the late 1880s (the
Indian nation), and the other in another sociocultural domain in the
1890s (the Hindu nation). Sir Syed's resistance to the notion of an
Indian nation and Rai's distance from the Congress or other overtly
political affairs in the 1890s may have only nudged him further to
concentrate on building a robust Hindu community or 'nation' in
the less-overtly-political sociocultural domain.

Lajpat Rai still continued to use the word 'community' for
Hindus (and Muslims), and presumably often imagined these
as existing in an Indian nation, just as he had in his letters to Sir
Syed. But it was possible that he now began to play with the notion,
closer to the one Sir Syed had espoused, that India was inhabited
by separate 'nations'. Largely aloof from overt political affairs during
the 1890s, and correctly perceiving the political supremacy of the
British Empire as being at its apex, when Rai articulated the idea of
nationhood in the sociocultural domain, he used the term as it most
often had been in the nineteenth century: in the non-statist sense of a
cultural community.

To be sure, this definition of the 'nation' as a cultural community
could also have latent political dimensions, but it was non-statist
in that the Hindu nation was not imagined as needing political
expression in a state of its own. Muslims could be excluded from
his definition of the 'Hindu nation'. But in the context of British
imperial supremacy, and precisely because the word nation was
not used in its nationalist–statist sense, such exclusion had few
negative consequences. Within the British imperial state, India
could be imagined as a country wherein both Hindus and Muslims
constituted self-contained and exclusive (cultural) 'nations' which
could exist independently, and perhaps also cooperate, if required,
politically. Lajpat Rai's fuller elaboration of a Hindu (cultural) 'nation'
in the 1890s likely subconsciously assumed the existence of another
Muslim (cultural) 'nation', even if he did not state this explicitly at
this juncture. As stated before, during the 1890s, he did not name
the nation he spoke about, signalling a state in which ideas were in

the process of being formed, were in flux and in a state of being only half-articulated.

In imagining India as consisting of more than one nation, Rai represented a broader intellectual tendency in the nineteenth century where efforts to unify the Hindu 'nation' coexisted with it being imagined alongside a Muslim 'nation'. This was true for Tilak as he organized his Ganapati and Shivaji festivals in Maharashtra,[10] Malaviya as he aimed at Hindu unity through the Madhya Hindu Samaj in the United Provinces[11] and for Bharatendu Harishchandra as he endeavoured to forge a united Hindu religious front through his Tadiya Samaj.[12]

If we agree with scholars who view the simple assertion of the cultural distinctiveness and unity of one's imagined nation as a form of 'nationalism',[13] Lajpat Rai was articulating a non-statist Hindu cultural nationalism. Yet, this Hindu nationalism assumed the full-bodied existence of Muslims in India, possibly viewed them as another 'nation', and—as Rai's welcome acceptance of Sir Syed's contributions to India reveals—certainly saw them as possessing the same right to cultural self-assertion as Hindus. Indian Muslims were accepted as a given in the Indian polity; their cultural self-assertion welcomed as contributing to 'India'. The primary aim of Lajpat Rai's Hindu nationalism was to inspire the Hindu nation to realize its true inner worth and potential and feel a sense of pride in its distinctive identity, rather than to demonize Muslims.

This is clear in his construction of India's history, which he considered essential for his project of fostering a collective Hindu identity and pride. Lajpat Rai's historical narrative in fact seems more a response to British discourses that denigrated Hinduism and Hindus. Even sympathetic Orientalist scholars like William Jones (1746–94), H.T. Colebrooke (1765–1837) and Max Muller,[14] who painted a romantic, glorious picture of India's ancient past, had portrayed contemporary Hinduism as debased and marked by absurdities—such as polytheism, idolatry, belief in the transmigration of the soul, decadent ceremonies, blood sacrifices, the caste system and social practices like sati and child-marriage.[15] While in very ancient times, the ancestors of Hindus may have been the embodiments of morality, knowledge, wisdom and pure religion, Hinduism and Hindus had subsequently degenerated terribly. James Mill's *A History of India* (1818), the hegemonic textbook of Indian history throughout the nineteenth century,[16] went further to deny Hindu greatness even in ancient times. Contesting scholars like Jones who emphasized a high state of civilization at least in ancient India, Mill rubbished the idea of India's ancient past as a golden age, stating that its achievements were driven by irrational pursuits (such as astrology) and configured by a primitive priestly despotism antithetical to progress.[17] Believing that humanity could only progress from primitive barbarism to a higher state of knowledge and civilization, Mill dismissed the idea that any valuable wisdom could be learned from India's ancient past. For him, Indians needed to be liberated from their own barbarous past through the civilizing, modernizing mission of the British Empire.[18] Modern Hindus were often decried in British imperial discourses as effeminate, passive, lazy and deceitful.[19] Some, such as the British historian John Robert Seeley, with whose writings Lajpat Rai was acquainted, argued that Hinduism was hopeless as a uniting principle that could produce a potentially self-ruling nation.[20] Sometimes, Hindus were also portrayed as having possessed no agency historically, and no politics, such that in their history, kingship and the state had been unimportant.[21] Instead, caste and religion had swallowed up the political, leaving behind a society, a Brahmin-led theocracy, that was changeless and also eternally conquerable.[22] Such portrayals of Hindus and Hinduism contrasted with depictions of Muslims and Islam. To be sure, European writers remained deeply distrustful of Muslims, and frequently drew on their now prejudiced views about Islam in the 'Near East', and particularly about the Ottoman Empire, to portray Muslims as despotic, fanatical and violent.[23] And at least initially, European writers had often projected onto the Ottomans what they had feared and despised in their own absolutist states.[24] Yet, Muslims were sometimes still considered as worthy opponents, whose religion was free of the absurdities that marked Hinduism, and whose history deserved respect.[25]

Deliberately and inadvertently, persistent negative portrayals of contemporary Hindus and Hinduism in British imperial discourse served to legitimize British rule.[26] While sympathetic Orientalist scholars saw the British Empire as helping Indians (Hindus) rediscover their own ancient past, others like Mill saw the British imperial mission to modernize and morally uplift them.[27] At times, the British imperial state was even portrayed as the 'manly' protector of Hindu women from effeminate Hindu men, with effeminacy itself represented as the cause of the subordination of Hindu women.[28] Such criticism was partly imbibed by many middle-class Hindu subjects of the British Empire, including Lajpat Rai, injuring their self-esteem and pride. It is possible that some also implicitly responded to ideas espoused by Muslim aristocrats like Sir Syed who, with their own fears of minoritization in mind, sometimes proclaimed Muslims to be a 'nation' familiar with political rule, while stating that Hindus were neither a nation nor—although here he had excluded Hindu aristocrats—knew the art of rule.

Lajpat Rai's narrative of 'history' implicitly challenged such discourses, and sought to dispel the worthlessness, inferiority and humiliation felt by Hindus. But to do so, Lajpat Rai did not draw on the 'degenerate' Hindu present whose reality he largely accepted uncritically. With the colonial experience having robbed him of the ability to evaluate Hindus largely on his own terms, or in terms of indigenous epistemic (knowledge-related) frameworks, Lajpat Rai remained under the spell of British discourses about Hindu degeneracy.[29] At the same time, like several Arya Samajists, he drew on Orientalist narratives to contrast a glorious ancient Vedic past against the picture of contemporary degeneracy.[30] As evident from his biography of Swami Dayanand, Lajpat Rai constructed the ancient Vedic past as an age when Indian society and polity were infused with the 'Vedic religion'.[31] In his view, during the Vedic age, the ancient ancestors of Hindus, the 'Aryans', followed Vedic monotheism. Reflecting the influence on him of another crucial element of the Arya Samajist religious outlook—anticlericalism— Lajpat Rai saw the Aryans as rejecting mediators between themselves and God. This made them intolerant of human claims of infallibility and therefore of attempts to dominate them:

> A man who firmly believes that he can find God through his own knowledge and devotion and without the help of any intermediary can never accept any extraordinary rights of any king, nor can he accept the theory that people should be divided in two classes, one class having the right to rule over the other and the other being obliged to be ruled.[32]

Despite the vital role accorded to priesthood in ancient Vedic rituals,[33] the Arya Samaj in the nineteenth century held that the 'Aryans' of the Vedic age had rejected Brahmins as intermediaries between God and themselves. Lajpat Rai utilized this Arya Samajist view to argue that the Aryans' rejection of Brahmin priesthood had made them intolerant of political domination and fostered their fierce political self-reliance.[34] Even after the Vedic age, 'the period of the compilation of the Brahmanas' still retained some essence of the Vedic religion, and Aryans continued to vanquish enemy kingdoms and rule over India.[35] Even 'much of the north-west, including Afghanistan and a part of Turkistan' was under Aryan rule, which was marked by neither fears of foreign invasion nor of internal revolt. Contrary to the theme of war that appears in one and dominates the other, for Lajpat Rai, during the 'age of the Brahmanas depicted in the Ramayana and Mahabharata', India was paradise—a land of righteous action, prosperity and happiness.[36] It was also a period of great learning, with several achievements in grammar, astronomy, mathematics, music and metaphysics, with 'Vedic knowledge' serving as the source.

From Enlightenment thinkers like Voltaire to the German Romantic thinker Herder in the eighteenth century, to the Orientalist scholars beginning with William Jones to those belonging to later generations like H.T. Colebrooke and Max Muller, these thinkers were part of a tradition of European Orientalist scholarship that conjured up a picture of India's Vedic past as a utopian paradise when ancient Aryans epitomized the purest religion and the highest moral wisdom; their society was endowed with all the wealth, power and beauty that nature could bestow.[37] In constructing a glorious, ancient Aryan past in which Hinduism and Hindus were completely unlike their supposed contemporary forms, Lajpat Rai echoed Orientalist narratives.[38]

Lajpat Rai was still unable to break free of colonial epistemic frameworks. Yet, rather than being uncomplicatedly derivative of Orientalist narratives, he utilized them for his own purpose. The idealization of India's Aryan past by European thinkers and scholars had served their own aims: to launch attacks on their church and the Catholic clergy, refute Jewish claims to authority as the founders of original true religion and precursors of Christianity or offer a corrective to the inner life of Europe.[39] And also, of course, to justify empire. Rai utilized the Orientalist trope of India's ideal Aryan past to instil pride and self-confidence in his imagined Hindu 'nation' in the context of colonial humiliation. By positing that Hinduism and Hindus had achieved self-rule and greatness in the ancient Aryan past, Lajpat Rai challenged views, current among British imperial (and possibly, to a lesser degree, some Muslim aristocratic) circles, that Hindus had not known self-government.

In turning to an idyllic Aryan past to bolster Hindu self-esteem, Lajpat Rai contributed to broader discourses articulated by several prominent Hindus both before and during his time. Among others, Rammohun Roy, Swami Dayanand, Ranade, Surendranath Banerjea and Tilak had all turned to the Orientalist trope of the Aryan golden age as a response to colonial domination and inferiorization.[40] For instance, for Roy, the Aryan past was marked by the prevalence of pure monotheism and the absence of ritualism and practices like sati and idolatry.[41] For the Maharashtrian social reformer Ranade, it conjured up a time when women enjoyed freedom, and polygamy, infant marriage, and incestuous marriage were not practised. To Banerjea, the Aryan forefathers (which included Valmiki, Vyas, Panini, Gautam Buddha, Shankaracharya) were great at literature, science and war, and in bravery and morality outstripped all other

Asiatic races.[42] Roy and Ranade also attempted to boost Hindu self-respect by expressing the notion (first popularised by European orientalists like Max Muller) that Hindus belonged to the same 'Aryan' family as the British.[43] These were attempts to establish the parity of Hindus vis-à-vis their British conquerors, in a context where 'race science' frequently emphasized differences and innate British and European superiority. Dayanand had taken forward the trope of the golden Aryan Vedic age by asserting that it was marked not only by idol-free monotheism but also the Aryans' commitment to scientific and social progress. It further constituted the centre of all knowledge and righteousness and was the fountainhead of all religions.[44] Others like Tilak aimed to achieve the same end by retaining the notion of a common Aryan family but ultimately praising the Indian/Hindu 'section' of Aryans for having both preserved the original Aryan civilization and ruled over the non-Aryan 'savages' they encountered in India upon their migration.[45] Here, Tilak, like Dayanand, attempted to assert the superiority of Vedic India vis-à-vis Europe.[46] Lajpat Rai's view of the Aryan past as a time when Hindus were guided by pristine monotheism, ruled over India and beyond, and led a life of peace, prosperity, righteousness and high learning was intended to bolster Hindu self-confidence in the face of colonial humiliation.[47] The same function was served by his portrayal of Hindus and Europeans as descendants of common 'Aryan' stock.[48] Rai's insistence that the Vedic monotheism of the ancient Hindus was the original source of other religions of the world was perhaps also intended to declare Vedic Hindu superiority vis-à-vis Europe.[49]

Lajpat Rai's attempt to restore dignity and instil pride in Hindus continued in his historical construction of India's medieval and early modern period. In the nineteenth century, nationalist histories naturalized the thesis that Hindus had suffered a political defeat at the hands of Muslims. Yet, this narrative of defeat was often ambiguous. For instance, Lajpat Rai rejected the narrative that Hindus had ever suffered total political defeat. In his book *Shivaji* (1896), he highlighted that while no independent Christian kingdom had existed in the medieval Turkish empire in Europe, in India 'when Muslim rule was at the zenith of its glory, independent Hindu states existed both in northern and southern India, maintaining their independence in the face of the Muslim sword'.[50] These continued to exist till the British arrived in India.[51] To substantiate his claim, he pointed to Rajputana, which had 'remained independent for nearly three hundred and fifty years after the founding of Muslim rule'.[52] Shivaji, the late-seventeenth-century Maratha warrior–hero, was similarly hailed as having resisted Muslim rule to lay the foundation of a major Hindu kingdom.[53] Here, Lajpat Rai, a Punjabi, drew on a symbol of Maratha self-rule which, having first been popularized by Maharashtrian leaders like Ranade, was being reinvented by the mid-1890s as a symbol of Hindu self-rule by others like Tilak.[54] Apart from the Maratha Empire, the Sikh kingdom was also appropriated for this narrative of historical Hindu rule.[55] This was in defiance of those Arya Samajists as well as Sikhs who wished to keep the Sikh and Arya/Hindu identities separate.[56] Lajpat Rai also drew attention to the complete independence of 'a large part of the Deccan' till the fourteenth century, reminding his readers that its southern part remained under Hindu rule till the sixteenth century.[57] Thus, by pointing to several separate, smaller kingdoms in various regions of India—the Marathas in Maharashtra, Sikhs in the North-west, and others in the Deccan—Lajpat Rai attempted to construct a narrative of Hindu rule to challenge the thesis of Hindu defeat. An assertion that even the apex which Muslim rule had attained under Akbar was impossible without the 'goodwill and sword of Hindus' sometimes supplemented this history of Hindu kingdoms.[58] This narrative of cooperation further attempted to mitigate the force of the defeat thesis by pointing to Hindu assistance in the success of Muslim rule.[59]

But Lajpat Rai ultimately did not deploy these themes further to build a narrative that radically rejected the narrative of Hindu defeat. The refusal to do so resembled much of the nationalist history written in the nineteenth century. As the scholar Partha Chatterjee has pointed out, despite the presence of several kingdoms, this national history held that, in truth, there was always one realm that extended over the same area as the country and was symbolized by the capital or throne.[60] The realm constituted the generic sovereignty of the country, and the capital or throne represented the centre of sovereign statehood. Since the country was India, there could only be one true sovereignty that extended over its territory, represented by a single capital or throne at its centre. Therefore, the defeat in 1192 of Prithviraj, the king of the Rajput Chauhans, and the capture of Delhi was interpreted as the end of a whole period of history, and the battle of Plassey signified the end of Muslim rule and the beginning of British rule. This trivialized the continued existence of various, relatively autonomous Rajput realms in the North[61] and other southern kingdoms throughout the long, medieval 'Muslim' period.[62] Following this logic, despite proudly noting the presence of several medieval and early modern 'Hindu' kingdoms, Lajpat Rai still held that the true realm, which coincided with India's limits, and constituted the generic sovereignty of the country, was 'Muslim', symbolized by the 'Muslim' capital or throne. He seemed to consider the Rajput, Sikh, Maratha and Deccan kingdoms as ultimately subsidiary to the true realm that remained in the hands of Muslims. In the end, for him, the inability of Hindu kingdoms to overthrow Muslim rule and capture this realm constituted a definitive form of defeat.

Lajpat Rai therefore ultimately found himself unable to deny that Hindus had suffered defeat. As Chatterjee argues, in contrast to the pre-modern Puranic historiography which had explained the rise and fall of kingdoms in terms of divine will, those schooled in colonial education were introduced to a new European historiography which explained the fate of kingdoms in terms of human struggles for power.[63] This conceptual shift had made it possible to speculate about the political conditions that led to victories and defeats. Conjecture about the reasons behind the political defeat of Hindus now became possible and was common in this period. Lajpat Rai fully participated in this conceptual shift and sought to understand the reasons for Hindu defeat. It is this part of his historical narrative that shows that its primary purpose was to instil pride and self-confidence in the Hindu 'nation', rather than to foster antagonism towards Muslims. Rather than naming 'Muslim rule' as the chief cause of 'Hindu decline', he settled on explanations that went far beyond Muslim oppression and conquest.

Muslim conquest was explained by the former's superiority in education, military skill and religious zeal. But these were only the immediate reasons. The deeper cause behind Hindu defeat was their own 'religious degeneration' which had made them 'unfit to face harsh realities',[64] and had begun long *before* the arrival of the Muslims. From his Dayanand biography, it is clear that Lajpat Rai held that the decline had already begun in the 'age of the Brahmanas' whose authors had 'forgotten the real meaning of the Vedic mantras', which was suffocated under the 'chains' of elaborate rituals.[65] The Vedas were further ignored by scholars of subsequent schools of philosophy who even questioned the existence of God.[66] This was followed by 'Aryavarta' or India coming under the sway of Buddhism, which Lajpat Rai held responsible for initiating the worst kind of idol worship.[67] Despite Buddhism being a 'godless creed', Buddha's followers raised him to the status of God, giving rise to the practice of worshipping statues of great men after their death. To meet this challenge, the votaries of the Vedic religion started depicting Rama and Krishna as *avatars* or incarnations of God[68] and advocating the worship of their images, resulting in the creation of the Puranas.[69] Although Buddhism was eventually defeated by the monk–philosopher Sankaracharya, he mistakenly treated the Upanishads on par with the Vedas to expound monism—the oneness of Brahma (the formless 'creator') and *jiva*— that was nowhere mentioned in the Vedas.[70] The defeat of Buddhism did not lead to the reinstatement of the true Vedic religion found in the Samhitas. Moreover, despite himself believing in monism and one formless Brahma, Sankara allowed those who were unable to comprehend Him in this form to worship different gods, thereby encouraging false polytheism.[71] By not insisting on monotheism, he was complicit in the continued 'Aryan' ignorance of the 'real' Vedic religion, the root cause of their decline.[72]

Lajpat Rai held that while the persistence of some form of theism, after the defeat of atheistic Buddhism, did result in Hindu achievements in literature, scholarship and fine arts, a 'fresh process of decline' was inevitable due to the acceptance of false Puranic beliefs as truth. The result of the nation 'turning away from its real God' was that the Puranic period was marked by sectarianism, caste distinctions and Brahmins using rituals and ceremonies to tighten their grip on Hindus to the extent that they repeatedly 'became a prey to foreign invasions [sic]'.[73] The 'Puranic' period saw the abandonment of scholarly pursuits and the adoption of all sorts of evil acts of 'debauchery and promiscuity', for which Tantric literature was created as justification.[74] With Puranic thought degenerating into such 'disgusting' practices, the 'Aryans' fell further 'into a pit of ignorance and became a prey to false and debilitating religious beliefs' far removed from the true Vedic religion.[75]

It was at this time that the 'Puranic' Hindus encountered Islam and Muslims. To be sure, Lajpat Rai portrayed the spread of Islam before it reached India in a manner borrowed from Orientalist discourse. As we have seen, steeped in prejudices and stereotypes that now marked many European assessments of the Ottomans, this discourse portrayed Muslims as despotic, fanatical and violent.[76] Rai's narrative abounds with violent images of swords, fire, trampling and pillaging as he wrote of the intolerant, bloodthirsty, cruel and marauding 'soldiers of Islam' setting out on 'campaigns of conquest'.[77] But instead of labouring on violent atrocities against and oppression of Hindus by Muslims, Lajpat Rai's narrative argued that the chief cause of the defeat of Hindus by Muslims was the superior monotheism-inspired zeal of the latter, which the idolatrous polytheistic 'Puranic Hindus' could not withstand.[78] In other words, the chief cause of the defeat of 'Hindus' by 'Muslims' was their allowing the degeneration of their true Vedic religion into polytheistic worship of idols, avatars and great men, excessive ritualism, a reliance on false texts and philosophical nitpicking. In particular, he singled out Brahmins as responsible for this decline: their attempt to control other Hindu castes through elaborate rituals and ceremonies and a monopoly of Vedic knowledge contributed to the eventual degeneration of the Vedic religion and to wider Hindu amnesia regarding their true religion.[79]

Interestingly, in holding Brahmins responsible for Hindu amnesia about Vedic religion, Lajpat Rai differed quite significantly from Tilak who praised Brahmins for their 'super-religious fidelity' in preserving Vedic traditions through their 'specially cultivated memory'.[80] Or Ranade who refrained from blaming Brahmins.[81] The broad anti-Brahminical thrust of Lajpat Rai's mytho-historical account of 'Hindu decline' drew on Dayanand Saraswati,[82] with the exception that for Dayanand the Brahmin-led decline began with the Mahabharata war.[83] Scholars have read Arya Samajist historical narratives, including Lajpat Rai's, as constructed against the Muslim other, reflecting an 'ideological anti-Islamism'.[84] But in Rai's case, his Arya Samajist background prompted him to assign responsibility for Hindu 'decline' ultimately to Hindus (particularly, Brahmins) themselves. Contrary to constituting the *consequence* of Muslim rule, Hindu decline—the degeneration of their religion—long preceded it and in fact had even made it possible.

In not making Muslim rule central to his explanation of Hindu decline, Lajpat Rai differed from Arya Samajists like Gurukul Party leader Lala Munshi Ram (later known as Swami Shraddhanand) who squarely blamed Hindu decline on Muslim invasions.[85] He was also unlike several Hindus beyond the Samaj ranging from Bankimchandra Chatterji[86] and other Bengali writers to authors of nationalist history textbooks for Bengali schools who similarly blamed Muslim rule for Hindu decline and emasculation.[87] Yet, Lajpat Rai was not alone in attributing Hindu decline to causes other than Muslim rule. For Bharatendu Harishchandra, Hindu decline was caused by their move away from the true religion of their Aryan ancestors, which for him was monotheistic worship based in Vaishnava bhakti.[88] Ranade pegged it on the collective corrupting influence of barbarian 'non-Aryan races' like the Scythians and Mongolians who had conquered North India, the aboriginal Dravidians in the South, and Jainism and Buddhism *along* with Islam.[89] Like Lajpat Rai, these men blamed Hindu decline on either Hindus themselves or on several factors preceding and additional to Muslim rule, rather than solely on Muslim conquest and oppression. In taking the 'Muslim' period as merely one, almost incidental element in a larger story about Hindu decline, these historical narratives avoided making the demonization of Muslims their primary objective. Lajpat Rai's historical narrative, along with that of these men, reveals that, contrary to the assumptions of some scholars,[90] a strand of Hindu discourse in the nineteenth century, despite dwelling on Hindu decline, was not guided by antagonism to Muslims.[91]

Lajpat Rai's construction of a glorious Aryan past was meant to restore Hindu national pride in the context of primarily British imperial discourses regarding the degeneration of Hindu religion as well as the political incapacity of Hindus. In his attempt to bolster Hindu self-confidence, he strove to challenge the conventional thesis of Hindu defeat by Muslims. As we saw, Lajpat Rai was not averse to describing Islam in negative terms. His tract on Shivaji chronicled Aurangzeb as a treacherous enemy of Hindus and lauded Shivaji for challenging Muslim rule and standing up for his 'Hindu *jati*'.[92] Yet, Rai's endeavour to contest the defeat thesis highlighted instances of Hindu rule in the past, rather than fantasies about collective Hindu resistance to the Muslim other. Ultimately relenting to the notion of Hindu defeat, he attributed this to a protracted process of decline that began prior to Muslim rule and for which he blamed Hindus (or, more accurately, Brahmins) themselves. Lajpat Rai's historical narrative shows that in the nineteenth century, not all 'nationalist' histories grounded in a glorious Aryan past, challenging the thesis of Hindu defeat or dwelling on Hindu decline, were constructed in active opposition or hostility to Muslims. Some simply aimed at arousing a sense of collective self-reflection and agency among the Hindu 'nation'. Lajpat Rai's refusal to articulate his 'Hindu nationalist' historical narrative in terms primarily antagonistic to Muslims fits well with his view of them as a group with whom Hindus could coexist and cooperate in a common polity.

Part 2: The New Century

5

Rejecting the Congress's Indian Nationalism

After returning to Lahore in 1892, Lajpat Rai had remained immersed in the affairs of DAV college as a member of the 'College Party' of the now deeply split Arya Samaj. As evident in his writings, his thought in the 1890s was still marked by a pan-Indian, 'national' imagination. Yet, after surging in 1888–89, Lajpat Rai's interest in the INC appears to have ebbed during the 1890s. Out of the eleven annual Congress sessions held between 1890 and 1900, he attended only two—in 1893 and 1900, both in Lahore. In his autobiography written in 1914, Lajpat Rai attributed his indifference towards the Congress during the 1890s to the influence of his friends in the Arya Samaj. They believed that while the Congress was busy 'speechifying', India would become stronger only through self-help and education. Some held that the Congress was chasing unity with Muslims at the expense of Hindu solidarity.[1] At the 1893 session in Lahore, he spoke mainly on the importance of technical education, and developed contacts with two delegates from Poona: Gokhale and Tilak.[2] At the 1900 session, he moved a resolution demanding that the Congress dedicate half a day of its three-day annual meeting to discussing industrial and educational problems.[3] The Congress, barely active in Punjab, was losing its initial vitality and beginning to stagnate.[4]

Like Tilak, the increasingly popular star of Maharashtra with whom Lajpat Rai was now developing closer relations,[5] and Aurobindo Ghose—a Bengali in the employ of the Maharaja of Baroda who was himself influenced by Maharashtrian radicalism—Lajpat Rai too had grown impatient with the current mode of Congress politics.[6] From their specific provincial platforms, these men were starting to voice the opinion that more action was needed beyond annual meetings where delegates passed resolutions and were content with patient petitioning and constitutional agitation—the chosen methods of Congress veterans like Dadabhai Naoroji, Surendranath Banerjea, Pherozeshah Mehta, Ranade, as well as younger Congressmen like Malaviya and Gokhale who were close to this oligarchy which controlled the Congress during this period. What was required was selfless, 'active' political work which would draw in 'the masses'.[7]

Before attending the Congress session in Calcutta in December 1901, thirty-six-year-old Lajpat Rai wrote a newspaper article titled 'The Defects of the Congress and Remedies'. He intended it as a constructive critique of an organization to which he himself belonged, and whose existence he still considered valuable. Rai pointed out its organizational defects and suggested solutions. But the article also elaborated upon what Rai considered another principal defect of the Congress—its conception of nationhood. In doing so, he revealed how far he had travelled since he first forcefully articulated his conception of nationhood thirteen years ago, at the callow age of twenty-three, in his letters to Sir Syed.

In this 1901 article, for the first time, Lajpat Rai explicitly and publicly rejected the notion of Indian nationality. Calling it a 'false idea',[8] he described the Congress's attempt to unite Hindus and Muslims as 'forced', 'premature', 'chimerical' and 'futile'.[9] Muslims, he argued, believed that Hindus could never be their equal in the 'scale of nations', and considered themselves superior both physically and, by virtue of belonging to a race of rulers, in administrative capability.[10] Even the humble *julaha* (a particularly low-ranking low-caste Muslim weaver) claimed superiority in the art of governance and dreamt of dominating Hindus. With the exception of 'a good many far-seeing men', Lajpat Rai argued, a large class of educated Muslims remained aloof from Hindus, believing that their political prospects improved if they existed as a separate 'nationality'.[11]

Sir Syed's remarks regarding the existence of separate Hindu and Muslim 'nations' and the ruling ancestry of 'Muslims' had clearly stayed in his mind (even though Syed's view of political rule had ignored low-caste Muslims and potentially included Hindu aristocrats). Rai was probably aware of similar views expressed by several prominent members of upper-caste Muslim organizations which existed before the Muslim League was founded in 1906. Through the 1890s, they expressed the view—in opposition to Muslims affiliated with the Congress—that Indian society was divided along racial, caste and religious lines, and that the politics of Hindus and Muslims would always be determined by their religious values and affiliations.[12] Discourse regarding the descent of Muslims from historically and socially pre-eminent groups and a ruling race also continued in upper-caste, *sharif* ('respectable', 'high-born') Muslim circles.[13] Such views at least partly reflected their fears of Hindu majoritarian domination as a consequence of elective representation, introduced in a very limited form at local and provincial levels. This new form of political representation had resulted in a progressive and sharp decline in Muslim representation vis-à-vis Hindus throughout the decade.[14] And so, rather than constituting an argument to seek domination over Hindus, assertions about the ruling lineage of Muslims were often (even if not always) an intellectual manoeuvre to stall the rapid political marginalization of Muslims under the system of elections. The history of Muslim rule was used to circumvent a system that assigned political importance by numerical weight, and to demand political parity with Hindus.[15]

Nevertheless, such discourse was plainly read by Lajpat Rai as evidence of the disdain most Muslims felt towards Hindus, with the stereotype of the fanatical Muslim julaha, birthed by colonial officers in the nineteenth century, being drawn on by Rai in support of his claim.[16] Caste-based social and political divisions among Muslims were overlooked. Upper-caste Muslim political discourse converged with a negative stereotype about the low caste julaha's fanaticism to produce in Rai's mind a generalized image of the 'Muslim' attitude towards Hindus. Given what he saw as the contemptuous distance kept by Muslims from Hindus, he believed it 'suicidal' for Hindus to force a union with them.[17]

In fact, the thought of actively attracting Muslims to their organization had receded from the minds of most Congressmen by the 1890s, only to be rekindled after the formation of the Muslim League in 1906.[18] But despite the Congress being a predominantly Hindu organization—'already accused of being a Hindu Congress', according to Surendranath Banerjea[19]—what bothered Lajpat Rai was the Congress's anxiety to speak for all Indians. He felt it was sacrificing 'Hindu interests' for its 'false idea of nationality'.[20] Interestingly, Rai shared this unease with many prominent Muslims who feared that distinct Muslim interests would be submerged in a general 'Indian' nationalism. Of course, the difference was that Muslim distrust of Indian nationalism stemmed from their minority status and from the predominance of Hindus both within the Congress and in India. The Congress was suspected of claiming to represent the 'Indian nation' even as it really spoke only for the Hindu majority. Lajpat Rai, on the other hand, harboured anxiety about the loss of Hindu particularity to a transcendental 'Indian' nationalism despite the preponderance of Hindus both within the Congress as well as the general populace:

> . . . let not this general assembly stand in the way of Hindu progress and . . . lull them to sleep over their interests as such, make them forgo the opportunities of furthering their unity, inter se, and neglect the placing of it on a firm, sound and unassailable basis.[21]

Rai suggested the formation of an all-India 'Hindu political or semi-political congress or conference'.[22] Like the Congress, this Hindu organization would meet annually to exclusively serve 'Hindu nationality' and its specific interests.[23] These included the propagation of Sanskrit, Hindi and the Devanagari script, 'common text-books', protecting Hindu orphans from 'proselytising agencies of other denominations' and, if necessary, recording protest against confidential government circulars which aimed at favouring other communities at the expense of Hindus.[24] The reference to confidential circulars alluded to the Punjab government's policy to give priority to Muslims in subordinate administrative posts to reverse the trend of Hindu officials appointing them all too rarely. This effectively translated into efforts to covertly ensure that these posts were filled by an equal number of Hindus and Muslims.[25] Apart from the position of upper-caste Muslim organizations, it was also clearly the perceived threat that Lajpat Rai sensed as a Hindu from the British policy in Punjab of deliberately favouring Muslims that had convinced him of the need to articulate and strengthen a separate 'Hindu nationality'.

In advocating the idea of a separate 'Hindu nationality', Lajpat Rai differed from the main leaders who then headed the Congress. Gokhale, now rising within the Congress hierarchy, continued to speak of 'the mass of the people of India' as one single nation,[26] holding that the Congress had helped 'weld together' a scattered people 'to create, throughout India, a sense of nationality' and had enabled 'India, for the first time in her history, to breathe and feel like one nation'.[27] His statement in 1905 gives a further glimpse into how he envisioned nationhood:

> The growth during the last fifty years of a feeling of common nationality, based upon a common tradition, common disabilities and common hopes and aspirations, has been most striking. The fact that we are Indians first and Hindoos, Mahommedans, Parsees or Christians afterwards, is being realised in a steadily increasing measure, and the idea of a united and renovated India, marching onwards to a place among the nations of the world, worthy of her great past, is no longer the idle dream of a few imaginative minds, but it is the definitely accepted creed of those who form the brain of the community—the educated classes of the country.[28]

This echoed the language of earlier veterans like Dadabhai Naoroji who spoke of 'a national life beyond a sectarian life',[29] and Surendranath Banerjea who proclaimed: 'Who constitutes the nation? Not surely the Hindus and Mohamedans alone, but Hindus, Mohamedans, Parsis, Christians, Sikhs . . . I claim for the Congress that its programme is the most catholic, the most comprehensive, the most admirably suited to the varied requirements of the different sections of the great Indian community.'[30] Gokhale's mentor, Justice M.G. Ranade, who had died earlier that year, had always spoken of Hindus and Muslims as 'communities' belonging to one Indian nation.[31] Malaviya similarly continued to refer to the nation in terms of an 'Indian voice'.[32] Though Tilak too would soon give a public call to unite Hindus into a 'mighty nation',[33] Lajpat Rai was the first to call for the formation of a pan-Indian, explicitly political (or, as he said, 'semi-political') Hindu congress to promote the interests of 'Hindu nationality'. His call occurred several years before the creation of Punjab's Hindu Sabhas in 1907–09, and a full fourteen years before the foundation of the Hindu Mahasabha in 1915.[34]

Yet, Lajpat Rai saw Hindu nationality as existing alongside what he considered India's two other main 'religious nationalities': the Muslims and Christians. And although he felt that an 'immediate' and 'complete' union of these 'nationalities' was fanciful and futile in the present circumstances, he kept open the possibility of their 'union' in the future. He saw himself as aiming at a less superficial union than the one apparently attempted by the Congress. A 'concrete' union was possible only if there existed a 'common danger and the conviction that they cannot overcome it . . . but by uniting . . . against a common foe'.[35] Although it was presently lacking in India's religious nationalities, the realization that they needed to unite against an external enemy common to India's 'religious nationalities'—the British—could render possible the Indian nation. A second prerequisite for Indian unity was that the Congress leave deliberation, on subjects that caused 'reasonable friction' between different religious nationalities, with their respective organizations, which would themselves be strong and united.[36] India's nationalities needed complete freedom to 'strengthen' themselves without harming others,[37] their equal strength constituting a necessary condition for their future union into an Indian nation.

This was precisely why a Hindu political organization exclusively in service of the Hindu nationality was vital. Without it, the position of the Hindu nationality would remain weak, and an enfeebled Hindu nationality would only diminish prospects of union with the Muslim nationality. Writing five years before the Muslim League's foundation, he found the Islamic *anjumans* (associations) which promoted Muslim 'national' interests as a welcome step towards this future Indian union.[38] For the same reason, Lajpat Rai could admire the Muhammadan Anglo-Oriental College as a sign of Muslim 'national zeal' and the Central Hindu College of Benaras as a 'tangible sign of a growing sense of religious nationality' among Hindus.[39] Here, Lajpat Rai echoed Tilak who held that the strengthening of the Hindu nation through his Shivaji festival was entirely compatible with the Muslim nation launching an Akbar festival with the same aim. Akbar was imagined not as a symbol of Hindu–Muslim unity, but as a 'Muslim' hero. Yet, this utilization of Hindu and Muslim symbols to strengthen separate nations, Tilak held, would not 'make the existence of amicable relations between the two nations an impossibility in the future'.[40] Lajpat Rai's own continued hope for a future Indian union is evident in the fact that during Rai's visit to the United States in 1905, he spoke admiringly of 'the spirit of unity and nationality that obtains here amongst a mixed population composed of all nations of the earth' and urged India to learn this lesson from America.[41]

In positing a vision in which political interests were extensions of religious affiliations, it was Lajpat Rai who ultimately undertook a volte-face from his position in 1888, something he had ironically accused Sir Syed of. Having vehemently disparaged such reasoning, the young Lajpat had advanced a vision of India's religious communities as possessing substantially common political interests by virtue of being members of a single Indian nation. This no longer seemed to hold true for him. Instead, the idea of a common Indian nationality sounded like a farce to him. Hindus, Muslims and Christians shared more in common with their co-religionists than with each other. In suggesting that Hindus and Muslims deal with their political issues internally or in a federal way, Lajpat Rai prefigured the logic of the Muslim League, which would later argue that Muslims, as a 'community' or 'nation', had distinct political interests that needed articulation and fostering by its own separate political organization. This organization would then negotiate with the Hindus for the sake of Indian unity. When in the 1930s the League would insist that Muslims were a separate nation (still, in a non-statist sense), it broadly built upon the same federal logic which Lajpat Rai too had articulated at the turn of the century.

Historian Gyanendra Pandey pioneered the analysis of the discourse of Indian nationalism in late-nineteenth and early twentieth-century colonial India. He argued that during these years many nationalists, including Lajpat Rai, imagined the Indian nation as consisting of different 'religious communities', and saw service to the community as compatible with or even implying service to the Indian nation.[42] In fact, Lajpat Rai—and evidently others like Tilak—imagined India as inhabited not by one Indian nation (composed of different communities) but by different 'religious nationalities'. Nevertheless, Pandey's argument holds true for these two men in that both saw the 'strengthening' of these 'nationalities' not as undermining prospects of a future Indian unity but as its essential prerequisite. At the same time, a difference persisted between these men and other Congressmen who were deeply anxious that separateness beyond a point, and particularly its politicization, would hinder India's progress. For instance, Ranade had discouraged attempts by Hindus and Muslims to treat their interests as separate, and believed that India's progress was impossible unless they were impelled by a common desire for a 'fusion of thought and feeling'.[43] In contrast to Rai (and Tilak), men like Ranade saw separateness beyond a point as hindering rather than strengthening Indian nationhood. Still, despite Lajpat Rai's willingness to countenance separate 'semi-political' nationalities, it is noteworthy that he accepted the Congress's existence to express the 'joint aspirations' of Hindu, Muslim and Christian religious nationalities who were seen to share some common interests over and above their substantially separate 'national' interests.[44]

Affirming Hindu Nationality: History and the Embrace of Internal Diversity

The 'proof' that Lajpat Rai adduced for the existence of Hindu nationality came from history. This was revealed in his response in 1902 to a newspaper article written by an anonymous 'Hindu nationalist' who claimed that nationalism was a modern, European concept which Hindus needed to appropriate.[45] Lajpat Rai disagreed, claiming that Hindus had historically possessed a sense of nationality. As proof, he alluded, as he previously had, to Hindu nationality as embodied in ancient 'Aryan' rule. But now his repertoire of ancient 'Hindu' kingdoms expanded more assertively to include the mythological Pandavas of the Mahabharata,[46] as well as the empires of Ashoka and 'Vikram'. The latter may have referred to Chandragupta II, the Gupta king who ruled over the Gangetic plains between 375 and 415 CE and had assumed the title of Vikramaditya.[47] On the other hand, the Puranas, as *itihas*, are seen by many upper-caste Hindus as the annals of tradition, and are chronicles of gods and kings, and semi-mythological accounts of dynasties. They contain stories about the mythological king, Vikramaditya.[48] It is quite possible that Rai drew on Puranic mythology when he referred to king Vikram.

Interestingly, the Mauryan emperor Ashoka (268–232 BCE), whose empire had virtually covered the entire subcontinent, was included by Lajpat Rai in his narrative of Hindu nationality. This was despite Ashoka's embrace and propagation of Buddhism, a faith which, in the previous century, Rai had viewed as contributing to Hindu decline.[49] Early medieval kings such as Siladitya (a possible reference to Harshavardhana, the seventh-century ruler of north India) and Bhoja (the ninth-century Gurjara–Pratihara ruler of western India)[50] were also included. Falling silent on Hindu decline, Rai's historical narrative was now less apologetic; it more confidently invoked a more full-bodied image of past Hindu rule. The idea of Hindu national existence, however, was not only buttressed by illuminating a 'history' of past Hindu rule but also by highlighting Hindu resistance to 'foreign' Muslim rule. Rajput and Maratha kingdoms were now not just brought forth as examples of Hindu rule but framed as resistance to 'foreign yoke'.[51] Lajpat Rai also explicitly dwelt on the 'Hindu emperor', Prithvi Raj (Prithiviraj Chauhan), who had 'twice command[ed] the united services of almost the whole nation in his noble and valiant defence of the empire and motherland', embodying the 'heroic stand which the nation made against the foreigner'.[52] He further highlighted that 'Hindus of all classes' had united to repel one of the invasions by the Ghaznavid Turks. Lajpat Rai's portrayal of a Hindu nation uniting in resistance to a Muslim conqueror glossed over the conflicts between the Chauhans, the Paramaras and Chaulukyas; the refusal of the ruler of Kanauj to come to the aid of Prithvi Raj in his battle against the Ghaznavids, and the presence of Hindu generals and Jat soldiers in Ghaznavid armies.[53] Nevertheless, for Lajpat Rai, his communally framed history of Hindu empires and Hindu resistance to 'foreign' Muslim rule demonstrated that Hindus constituted a nation.[54]

Interestingly, for Rai, contemporary foreign British rule remained insufficient to advance an argument for why Hindus and Muslims in the present must unite as members of a common Indian nationality. But the trope of 'foreign' Muslim rule in medieval times was enough for him to gloss over historical differences among Hindus to argue for the existence of their common Hindu nationality. In conceiving Muslim rule as a foreign other against which the 'Hindu nation' united, Rai diverged from several Congress veterans. As we saw in Chapter 2, Surendranath Banerjea painted a history of 800 years of amity and goodwill between Hindus and Muslims. Similarly, Ranade had considered Muslim rule in India as the common past of Muslims and Hindus. For him, Mughal rule had 'refined the tastes and manners' of Hindus, and improved their art of war and government. Historical contact between Hindus and Muslims spawned a fusion of thoughts that benefited both and created a united India.[55] Gokhale depicted Muslim rulers as making India their home and contributing to its wealth.[56] In arguing that Hindu nationality was crystallized in Hindu resistance to 'foreign' Muslim rule, Lajpat Rai prefigured the history that would be expounded two decades later by V.D. Savarkar in his 1923 tract *Hindutva*.[57]

Further along in the 1902 newspaper article, Rai flatly asserted that 'disputes' or even 'strife' among Hindus did not disprove the existence of Hindu nationality:[58]

> ... the idea of nationality does not necessarily imply a complete union amongst all its members on all matters, social, religious or political; nor does it suggest the existence of a state of perfect concord and harmony among its members or leaders, or the freedom of the latter from all human weaknesses such as lead personalities to indulge in strong or even abusive language amongst, and towards, each other.[59]

He argued that to expect complete unity was to expect the impossible and ignore human nature.[60] Randomly lumping together what he considered older and newer nations, and a religion-centric conception of nationhood with ethno-linguistic and territorial ones, he stated that, despite internal differences, the Romans, Greeks, Muslims, English, Germans, Americans, French, Swiss, Italians and Dutch were all 'splendid and noble types of nationality'.[61] As long as they did not exceed their limits, differences, controversy and mutual criticism were necessary for the healthy growth of nationality.[62] Hindus could bitterly conflict and yet constitute a nationality. Instead of something to be overcome or erased, deep difference and even disunity among members of the Hindu nationality was not just acceptable but also desirable. Internal diversity among Hindus, often a thorny problem for those asserting that Hindus constituted a nation, was turned by Lajpat Rai into a virtue. Once again, just as in his conceptualization of history, present difference between Hindus and others precluded the existence of an 'Indian nationality', but difference and even conflict among Hindus was easily accommodated to arrive at a 'Hindu nationality'. This was because contemporary Hindus, despite their internal acrimony, supposedly still possessed a sufficient sense of unity to combine against a common enemy:

> ... it is sufficient for the growth of nationality, if the different parts that claim shelter of its ways have a sense of unity, which is

sufficient to make them combine against a common enemy and a common danger . . . Let us keep one ideal before us. Let our ideal be sufficiently high to cover all, sufficiently broad and extensive to include all, who take pride in one common name, a common ancestry, a common history, a common religion, a common language and a common future.[63]

So, just as in his narrative of history where the Muslim enemy had crystallized Hindu nationality, a nameless common enemy in contemporary times—standing for the British or India's Muslims—was sufficient to generate a Hindu nationality. In his instrumental use of an 'enemy' to play down internal diversity among Hindus and furnish their common nationality, Lajpat Rai once again prefigured Savarkar's *Hindutva*.[64] He also did so when, to define Hindu nationality, he emphasized ethno-linguistic and religious singularity, notions borrowed from European conceptions of nationhood.

Interestingly, at this juncture, nineteen-year-old Savarkar's own ideas on nationhood were quite far from *Hindutva*. Five years from now, he would finish writing his analysis of the 1857 revolt in his *Indian War of Independence*.[65] While Rai in 1902 was clearly writing the history of a Hindu nation, a history he saw as partly crystallized in resistance to the historical Muslim enemy, Savarkar would soon write a history of the Indian nation, romantically conceiving the 1857 revolt as ushering in a new era where Hindus and Muslims would end previous historical enmity in favour of 'mutual friendship', and unite into a common Indian national brotherhood.[66] Rather than viewing them as a 'foreign' historical enemy, in his account of the revolt, Savarkar would conceive Muslims as patriotic, 'national' heroes, whose deep faith in Islam coexisted alongside powerful love for the Indian soil and feverish commitment to securing India's freedom from the British.[67] While Rai's history of the Hindu nation was aligned in opposition to the historical Muslim enemy, Savarkar conjured a history of the Indian nation, where Hindus and Muslims became natural 'national' allies in their fight against the common British enemy, who conspired to 'trample the Hindu religion and the Muslim faith'.[68] With hindsight one can say that in 1902 the thirty-seven-year-old Rai was out-Savarkar-ing Savarkar, articulating a Hindu nationalism that came much closer to 1920s Hindutva than the young Savarkar's own then-current Indian nationalism. While Savarkar furnished a history that enabled Hindus and Muslims to imagine themselves as commonly belonging to an Indian nation, Rai rejected the idea of a common Indian nation, and produced a history that made feelings of common belonging more difficult.

Yet, despite convergences, Lajpat Rai's Hindu nationalism in 1902 differed from the Hindutva nationalism Savarkar would articulate in the 1920s. Savarkar would blame Ashokan non-violence and humanity, and Buddhist conceptions of universal brotherhood, for emasculating Hindus and making them susceptible to foreign invasions.[69] Rai incorporated the Buddhist Ashoka in his history of Hindu rule and, unlike Savarkar in his later Hindutva avatar, did not lament historical non-violence with the aim of producing violent Hindu militancy in the present. Unlike the future Hindutva-championing Savarkar, Rai also did not portray Muslim rulers as motivated by a desire for religious and political domination, the eradication of Hindu religion or the oppression of Hindus.[70] Rai's Hindu nationalism converged with Savarkar's Hindutva nationalism in imagining the crystallization of Hindu nationality in resistance to the historical 'foreign' Muslim enemy. But it did not—as Savarkarite Hindutva would—ceaselessly labour to present the entire Indo-Muslim millennium as a long period of incessant 'indigenous' Hindu resistance and warfare against the 'foreign' Muslim invaders.[71] Rai's portrayal of Muslim rulers as 'foreign' may have discomfited some Muslim leaders, but it also aligned with the claims of many high-status, high-caste *ashraf* Muslims.[72] Moreover, its intention was not to provoke antagonism or animosity towards them. Rather, past Muslim rulers were useful to prove the historical existence of a distinct Hindu nationality. Nor did Rai's turn-of-the-century Hindu nationalism foreclose the future possibility of Hindus uniting with Muslims in an Indian national unity if and when realization dawned on both communities that the British were their common, external enemy.

In *Hindutva*, Savarkar would ultimately foreclose the possibility of Hindus and Muslims constituting a common nation. India's

Muslims and Christians were excluded by him in his definition of Hindutva or 'Hindu-ness' despite his own admission that they partly met the 'essentials' of Hindutva he had outlined. He granted that they met the *first* criteria of Hindutva of living in the territory of India because they themselves or their forefathers had been born in India.[73] Another important part of this 'first' essential of Hindutva, which related to territory and geography, was love for and attachment to the Indian/Hindu homeland and fatherland.[74] Savarkar allowed that the majority of Muslims and Christians may love India as so.[75] Interestingly, according to Savarkar, the majority of Muslims and Christians also met the *second* criteria of Hindutva— of possessing what Savarkar considered 'Hindu blood'.[76] This was by virtue of them being descendants of Hindu converts.[77] Hindus, Muslims and Christians shared a common bloodline and belonged to the Hindu race. Some like the Khoja and Bohra Muslims even met his *third* criteria of being attached to what Savarkar considered 'Hindu culture' or Hindu 'civilization' (what he would translate as 'Hindu Sanskriti').[78] This included the literature, art, history, heroes, cuisines, laws, rites, rituals, customs, festivals, ceremonies and sacraments of Hindus.[79]

But Savarkar would write that, having 'adopted a new cult', most Muslims and Christians had disowned, and ceased to be attached to, their erstwhile Hindu sanskriti.[80] They now saw themselves as 'belonging to a cultural unit altogether different from the Hindu one'.[81] Their new culture, and the new 'outlook' it endowed them with, had little in common with that of Hindus.[82] This was the major reason why Muslims and Christians, despite their consideration of India as their fatherland and their possession of virtually 'pure Hindu blood', could not be included in the fold of Hindutva, Hindu-ness or Hindu nationhood.[83] Savarkar admitted that Bohras and Khojas, and some Christian communities, basically met the three essentials of Hindutva—love for fatherland, Hindu blood and love for Hindu Sanskriti.[84] But they could not be included in his definition of the Hindu nation. To exclude them, Savarkar would turn to what he considered an extremely important 'religious aspect' of the third essential of Hindutva, which was Hindu Sanskriti.[85] This was the consideration of India as not just a fatherland but also a holy land.[86] Savarkar would link the territory of India exclusively to Hindus (within whom he included Sikhs, Buddhist and Jains), linking the land not just to the founders, seers, godmen, gurus and prophets of the religions of these 'Hindus' but to the historical sacrifices that Hindus had allegedly made for it.[87] For Hindus, India was not just their fatherland but also their holy land.[88] On the other hand, even those Muslims and Christians, who considered India their fatherland, possessed Hindu blood and were shaped by and attached to Hindu culture, could ultimately not be considered part of the Hindutva nation, because they did not consider India their holy land.[89]

Overlooking the numerous sacred sites of Muslims and Christians within India, Savarkar would argue that since their holy lands (such as Mecca, Medina, Jerusalem or the Vatican) lay outside India, their 'mythology and Godmen, ideas and heroes' were not 'children of the soil'.[90] This is why the outlook of India's Muslims and Christians smacked of 'foreign origin'. Additionally, according to Savarkar, 'naturally' they gave more love and loyalty to their holy land than their fatherland. And so, 'their love [towards India] was divided'.[91] Thus, Savarkar laboured to decisively exclude all Muslims and Christians from his definition of the Hindutva nation, by arguing that most of them had disinherited the 'Hindu culture' indigenous to India, and all of them had holy lands outside India, which made their religion and culture 'foreign' to India and divided their love and loyalty to it. For the later Savarkar who expounded Hindutva, Muslims and Christians could not be part of the Hindutva nation unless they proved their undivided love and loyalty to India by recognizing only India as their holy land, and abandoning their devotion to holy lands outside it.[92] That their main sacred sites lay outside India, and that many of their holy figures or myths were linked to such 'extra-territorial' places, was beyond the control of most Indian Muslims and Christians, who were (and are) born into and inherited these religious traditions. Yet, this accidental fact inevitably meant that to prove their undivided love and loyalty to India, Muslims and Christians were required to abandon their religions, which had supposedly made them disown the Hindu cultural heritage of India, a key essential of Hindutva nationhood, and adopt cultures 'foreign' to India. Abandoning their holy lands and their religions, and adopting 'Hindu culture and history' were both essential requirements for them to be included in the Hindutva nation, which had a supreme claim upon India.[93]

In 1902, Lajpat Rai's Hindu nationalism certainly excluded Muslims and Christians from its definition of the Hindu nation. Yet, it did not require them to renounce their religions to unite with Hindus in a common 'Indian' or 'Hindu' nation. Instead, the Muslim and Christian nationalities were free to express their religiosity and strengthen themselves, which was considered an essential prerequisite for forging any common Indian nationality in the future. In its clear attempt to articulate and consolidate a Hindu nation, Rai's nationalism in 1902 was certainly closer than even young Savarkar's nationalism to the latter's post-First-World-War Hindutva nationalism. Yet, it still retained significant differences with Hindutva, most notably in its comfortable and full acceptance of India's religio-cultural diversity and attachments to holy sites outside India.[94] Interestingly, this challenges the view of the scholar Chetan Bhatt who interprets Rai's turn-of-the-century nationalism as eliding the distinction between a 'Hindu' and an 'Indian' nationalism, and as therefore 'virtually equivalent to that of Savarkar'.[95]

Here, it might be productive to compare Rai's nationalism to the nationalisms that would be elaborated by Aurobindo Ghose and Bipin Chandra Pal (B.C. Pal) during and after the Swadeshi movement (1905–08). Both deeply religious and spiritual men, they believed in the religious basis of Indian life. Deploying Hindu religious imagery, symbols and idioms to articulate and revitalize an 'Indian' nation, they defined its core in terms of a Hindu spiritual essence. Ghose's Hindu-tinged 'Indian' nationalism undoubtedly privileged Hinduism, regarding it as ultimately superior to other faiths by virtue of its spirituality and universalism.[96] But, as pointed out by historian Peter Heehs, the Hindu universalism at the centre of Ghose's Indian nationalism was imagined as a seed for a new faith that included the best aspects of Islam and Christianity, and his deeply religious nationalism never sought to actively stigmatize or exclude India's non-Hindus.[97] Similarly, Pal's Hindu-leaning 'Indian' nationalism invoked the cult of Kali and Krishna, and also privileged Hinduism.[98] Yet, he spoke of a federated Indian nationality and invited every community to address the problem of composite nationality from the viewpoint of their own community.[99]

Unlike Ghose and Pal who would work with notions of an 'Indian' nation, Lajpat Rai explicitly rejected the idea of an Indian nation in 1902 and did not articulate a Hinduized Indian nationalism, grounded in a superior Hindu essence or defined through Hindu religious imagery or symbols, which could potentially alienate India's Muslims and Christians. In fact, unlike Ghose or Pal, he made no attempt at all to endow India's religious communities with any sense of a common nationality, whether through Hinduism or any other means. Instead, he saw India's Hindus, Muslims and Christians as separate religious nationalities, completely excluding each from the other's nation. So, the question of foisting a Hindu essence on others, or Hindu supremacism while defining Indian nationhood, did not arise. And just as Pal's Hindu-tinged 'Indian' nationalism would comfortably invite India's non-Hindus to develop a composite Indian nationality from their own point of view, Rai's 'Hindu nationalism' allowed Muslim and Christian nationalities to strengthen themselves just as he was attempting to do for the Hindu nationality. Here, Rai presaged Pal's federal logic, with the difference that while Pal imagined a federated Indian nationality (with Hinduism as its bedrock), for Rai it manifested in a multinational Indian polity (without any common national essence at all). A significant difference between the nationalist imaginations of these men was that while Ghose and Pal required Indian nationalism to be grounded in a deep spiritual religiosity, this was wholly unnecessary for Rai's Hindu nationalism. Making no appeal to Hindu spirituality, the latter instead looked back to a history of Hindu rule and resistance against a foreign enemy and to a common will in the present to unite against a common enemy, a theme incidentally absent from the nationalisms elaborated by Ghose and Pal.[100]

6

Defending Hinduism from Other Hindus

By 1904, it appears that thirty-nine-year-old Lajpat Rai found the spirit of Hindu nationality in Hinduism itself. He laboured to define Hinduism as a 'social faith',[1] containing ideas of 'social unity' and 'social responsibilities and obligations',[2] which he in turn saw as evidence of Hinduism's possession of the notion of 'national responsibilities' and 'a spirit of nationality'.[3] In an article he wrote for the *Hindustan Review and Kayastha Samachar* in April 1904 titled 'The Social Genius of Hinduism', Lajpat Rai argued that Hinduism contained the 'social ideals' set forth by two British public intellectuals, Herbert Spencer and Benjamin Kidd, both exponents of Social Darwinist thought. This reflects Rai's acquaintance and engagement with this body of thought which, scientifically discredited since the mid-twentieth century, had originated in Britain and rapidly gained popularity throughout the late nineteenth and early twentieth century across the globe from Europe to the United States as well as the colonized world. Social Darwinism had arisen in response to Charles Darwin's (1809–1882) groundbreaking ideas about the evolution of species through natural selection, as expressed in his *Origin of Species* (1859) and *The Descent of Man* (1871). His idea—that organisms changed and thrived through the natural selection of favourable characteristics—challenged Christian Biblical ideas about the fixity of species and the divine organization of the world. The assumption that humans had evolved from apes ran counter to the belief that the earliest humans were given civilization by God. These earth-shattering ideas divided the scientific community but were also picked up by several non-scientist intellectuals who used Darwinian ideas about the natural world to explain everything from society to culture, to politics, business and ethics.[4] This was Social Darwinism. The term itself reflects how thoroughly porous the boundary between evolutionary biology and sociology (the study of society) was at the time.

The key to Social Darwinism was the belief that Darwin's ideas about natural evolution could be used to explain human society: that the process of natural selection, including competition and the struggle for existence, ultimately weeded out degenerate failures and promoted those with superior traits—be they individuals, classes, nations, races or species, and that evolution meant constant progress and improvement, which in turn was an inevitable law of nature.[5] Herbert Spencer (1820–1903) was the great popularizer of Darwin's ideas, and the foremost exponent of Social Darwinism. In fact, it was he who coined the term 'survival of the fittest'. Spencer believed that social and political progress was a 'natural law'. For him, humans were inevitably evolving from a barbaric, militaristic society to a civilized, industrial society. This change was spurred by individuals and social institutions. For this reason, he attacked any interventionist policies by the state (such as those designed to help the poor) as hindering the natural progress of humans towards a better future.[6] In Europe and America, Spencer's belief in radical individualism and laissez-faire liberalism attracted the most attention. The latter philosophy was enthusiastically drawn on by rich industrial magnates on both sides of the Atlantic. In America, John Rockefeller and Andrew Carnegie used Spencerian language to justify the growth of (what was actually monopolistic) big business in terms of the natural law of 'the survival of the fittest'.[7] But as historian Christopher Bayly has argued, beyond the West, most notably in China and India, it was often Spencer's understanding of polity and society as organically evolving beings that resonated the most.

Historians of India have largely focused on the influence of Spencerian thought on radical anti-colonial Indian nationalists, who were attracted to extremism or revolutionary violence. One such man was Shyamji Krishnavarma (1857–1930), who had settled in London with the explicit purpose of countering British imperialism through relentless propaganda, and would very soon become a patron of revolutionary activities in London, Europe and India.[8] Following Spencer's death, Krishnavarma instituted the first Herbert Spencer Lectureship at the University of Oxford in 1904.[9] He also founded the the Indian Sociologist journal, which is judged by some scholars as having played a critical role in popularizing Spencer's ideas among Indians.[10] Lajpat Rai would meet Krishnavarma in 1905 during a trip to England, even staying at his newly inaugurated India House, a hostel which by the end of the decade came to be identified as a hotbed of radical revolutionaries (including V.D. Savarkar). While the two men would agree on the cause of Indian self-government, Rai later recalled their relations as being marked by friction, and referred to Krishnavarma as a miserly, conceited autocrat intolerant of any dissent.[11] He would also recall disliking the acerbic manner in which the latter decried Congressmen like Gokhale. More relevant here is that the thirty-nine-year-old Lajpat Rai expounded his social Darwinist interpretation of Hinduism before he met Krishnavarma. He seems to be among a diverse range of Indians (including Congress moderates such as K.T. Telang and M.G. Ranade) whose political thought drew on Spencer's ideas before the foundation of The Indian Sociologist and by the time Krishnavarma set up his Lectureship in 1904. At the same time, it is possible that Rai's invocation of Spencer in April 1904 was prompted by Krishnavarma's announcement of his Spencer Lectureship in 1903, which had been widely reported in the press, and may have sparked curiosity in Spencerian ideas.[12]

But more interesting than determining what prompted Rai to invoke Spencer is examining why he was deployed, how and for what purpose. Intellectual historian Shruti Kapila dwells on the curiosity of why radical revolutionaries committed to the politics of violent change were attracted to Spencer, a liberal associated with social evolution (rather than revolution). She concludes that it was Spencer's antipathy towards the state and his belief in the powers of the social order that appealed to individuals like Krishnavarma. This was due to the belief that the state was associated with British colonialism and had led to cultural loss, and that Indian efforts to enact political change through the state could only produce political and cultural servitude. Such radical nationalists were attracted to the Spencerian idea that the real agents of change were the individual and society, and that meaningful change did not require dependence on the state.[13] Although Rai came to admire revolutionaries, he would never be one himself, and would never completely renounce faith in effecting change through constitutionalism. Yet, it was perhaps because he shared their belief in the limited Indian capacity to effect meaningful change through the colonial state that he was similarly attracted to the Social Darwinist notion of individual-driven and society-driven change. Non-state social institutions could be forces of change. In his April 1904 article, Lajpat Rai set out to prove that Hinduism was that institution. It met the evolutionary 'social ideals' advanced by highly esteemed Social Darwinists, and possessed resources for individual, social and national regeneration.[14]

Along with ideas about competition, struggle and survival, what Lajpat Rai gleaned from Social Darwinism was the notion of 'altruism'. He read the evolutionary social ideal set forth by Spencer as one in which the individual develops an 'altruistic instinct' whereby he attains the highest pleasure in 'voluntarily sacrificing himself in the interests of the social organism'.[15] Here, the interests of each 'citizen' merged with those of the 'citizens at large', making the social organism 'socially efficient'. Lajpat Rai quoted Spencer's *Data of Ethics* (1879), which contained the most sustained and influential theoretical discussion of 'altruism' yet published, and had become the definitive statement of the evolutionary approach to ethics.[16] It was once again Spencer's writings which had popularized the concept and language of altruism first in Britain and then elsewhere in the 1870s.[17] While other words like 'benevolence' had been used in earlier debates about acting for the good of others versus one's own self-interest, these words and these debates focused on individual behaviour; the new language of altruism provided the latest scientific and philosophical terminology to address such questions, and marked a shift in emphasis from discussions of the morality of individuals to the morality of classes and nations.[18] In Britain, the language of altruism helped people position themselves in debates regarding the two most pressing issues of the time: empire abroad and poverty at home.

But what were Spencer's own ideas about altruism? In his view, both egotism and altruism were natural to humans since the dawn of time, but human society would naturally evolve and progress from a predatory, uncivilized and egotistic society to an industrial, civilized and altruistic one.[19] While he sometimes opposed aggressive British imperialism using the language of altruism, Spencer was not in fact an enthusiast of altruism as a social ideal. As mentioned above, he viewed the new Liberal interventionist state policies of poverty relief as a kind of socialist interference in individual freedom and as stymieing natural social evolution towards a better, more properly altruistic future.[20] Spencer criticized Christianity for promoting a forced, extreme altruism (where one must love one's enemy as oneself) as an ethical ideal in the present. This would promote inferior, degenerate classes. The correct ideal was a continuous compromise between egotism and altruism.[21] His *Data of Ethics,* which Lajpat Rai mentioned, rejected both extreme egotism and extreme altruism and argued for a compromise as the only possibility. Still, what Lajpat Rai held onto in Spencer's ideas, and construed as his 'social ideal', was the higher level of altruism Spencer assumed would be naturally biologically attained by humans in the future, in which the individual sacrificed his or her interests for the social organism.

Rai also referenced Benjamin Kidd's (1858–1916) global bestseller *Social Evolution* (1894) to argue that his social ideal required members of the social organism to sacrifice their individual good not just for the good of the whole but also in 'the interests of the generations yet unborn'.[22] Kidd's theory of how societies evolved was inspired by the famous scientific experiments of German naturalist August Weismann (1834–1914).[23] The central plank of evolutionary moralism, till the 1880s–90s, was the belief that acquired characteristics were heritable (passed down from one generation to the next). This belief assumed that mental traits acquired through education and other agents of moral improvement were passed from parent to offspring, such that there was a biological reason to believe that each new generation would be more morally elevated than the next. Weismann's experiments included mice with their tails cut off repeatedly producing offspring with full-length tails. This was taken to prove that only the immortal 'germ plasm' passed unchanged from organisms to their offspring. Acquired characteristics were not heritable, and so there was no biological reason to believe that human society would inevitably progress to higher and higher levels of morality.

Inspired by Weismann, Kidd derided Spencer's dream of a biologically determined altruistic society in the future. For him, progressive altruism was not promised by biological evolution but could only be fostered by cultural means. In fact, for him, altruistic feelings were not produced by biological evolution at all; they were produced by social evolution. Altruism had to be cultivated by religion, and more specifically by Protestant Christianity. Kidd believed that Darwin and Weismann had shown that competition was what guaranteed the progress of a race. But there was no good reason for individuals to submit themselves to a harsh, competitive social environment and sacrifice themselves for the progress of the race; following the dictates of reason, humans tended to act in their self-interest. However, since science required individuals to sacrifice their interests for the progress of the human race, individuals needed to be persuaded to become less rational. Equating religion with irrationality, Kidd argued that irrational religion was necessary for individuals to become less selfish and more altruistic, which would in turn foster fairer competition, the condition necessary for the progress of human societies. So, Spencer believed in the biological nature of altruism and the natural progress of humans towards higher levels of morality. He did not believe it had to be fostered externally, and criticized extreme altruism whether through state policy or as represented in Christianity as harmful for human progress. On the other hand, contesting Spencer, Kidd rejected any biological basis for altruism and moral evolution, and held that it had to be and should be fostered through Christianity for the sake of human progress. It was in this context that Kidd had advocated an extreme altruism in which individuals were to sacrifice their interests even for the sake of the as-yet-unborn, the idea upon which Lajpat Rai drew in 1904.[24]

To show that Hinduism met the evolutionary 'social ideals' advanced by Spencer and Kidd, Rai quoted selected translations of numerous Hindu texts—the Rigveda, Atharvaveda, the Manusmriti, the Ramayana, Mahabharata and 'Chanakya's *Niti-shastra*' (the *Arthashastra*). The Rigveda, which contains the world's oldest poetry, mostly comprises praises to Vedic gods and early contemporary local chieftains, as well as some speculative hymns. It is also pervaded by the theme of warring tribes, with conflicts occurring between both Aryas (an ethnic or cultural term for the speakers of Indo-Aryan languages) and Dasas/Dasyus (which may either represent the aboriginal people or earlier pre-Vedic Indo-Aryan immigrants), as well as among Arya tribes themselves.[25] Overlooking these aspects, Rai pointed to a hymn in the later Book 10 of the Rigveda Samhita, which divided society into four varnas—what he himself translated as 'castes'—and saw this as evidence of the 'unity of the social organism'.[26] For him, the four castes, 'as individual units of one organism', performed separate functions, and expressed 'the mutual interdependence of all parts of society', 'a complete system of social duties', and the 'essential oneness of the whole'.[27]

The Manusmriti, the ancient Brahminical dharmic legal text written between 200 BCE and 200 CE, which Lajpat Rai associated with 'orthodox Hindus', was utilized by him to substantiate his reading of the caste system as reflecting Hinduism's 'original social conception'.[28] Rai noted its advocacy of 'vast and rather astounding inequalities of treatment between Brahmins and shudras, verging in places almost on inhumanity and cruelty'.[29] Even so, what was more important for him at present was to emphasize what he considered its emphasis on the 'service of others' and the 'social good of the whole community'. For Rai, this was evident in the Manusmriti enjoining members of each caste to do their duty not only for themselves but for other castes: 'The Brahmin is enjoined to study not for the benefit of his soul only, but to teach others as a purely social duty. In the same way, it was the duty of Kshatriyas to protect all . . . the duty of the Vaishya was to produce and trade for all and that of the Shudra to labour for all [sic]'.[30] The caste hierarchy advocated in the Manusmriti, which Rai fleetingly did note with some alarm, was thus ultimately ignored in favour of an interpretation which emphasized social harmony. For Lajpat Rai, the shlokas in the Manusmriti embodied an 'altruistic morality' underlining that the 'welfare of all' was dependent on individuals performing their social duties conscientiously.[31] Sidestepping their Brahmin-centricism,[32] Rai pointed to shlokas emphasizing the duties of hospitality and charity as evidence of the Manusmriti's altruistic morality.[33] In Rai's interpretation, the legendary Manu's laws on marriage even reflected an anxiety for 'the welfare of unborn generations',[34] meeting Benjamin Kidd's altruistic ideal.

Lajpat Rai carefully cited selected hymns of the Rigveda and Atharvaveda (the fourth Veda) to remind Hindus of their exhortations to 'assemble, speak together', have a 'common mind' and 'common purpose', to 'agree and be united', and 'love one another'.[35] Some of these hymns addressed Vedic gods, and others were part of charms to promote unanimity in the assembly and concord in the family. In Rai's interpretation, they aimed to inculcate 'effective social organisation' and a 'common national purpose'.[36] Lajpat Rai held that the 'actual working' of this 'spirit of unity' could also be found in the Hindu epics, the Ramayana and Mahabharata. He finally ended his citations of Hindu scriptures with a verse from Chanakya's *Arthashastra* (350 BCE–250 CE) which urged one to 'sacrifice a member for the sake of the family, a family for the sake of a village, a village for the sake of a district'.[37] The ancient text was intended as an elaborate treatise on statecraft designed for use by kings. Lajpat Rai employed it to support his argument that different sacred texts of Hinduism contained the 'germs and foundations' of the highest Social Darwinist ideals.[38] This, for him, was evidence of their possession of the notion of 'social or national responsibilities', and proof of the existence of a 'spirit of nationality' among ancient Hindus.[39] The sociality or strong social orientation of the ancient Hindu faith, which had once constituted ancient Hindus into a nation, had the potential to once again make a nation out of present-day Hindus.[40]

In emphasizing Hinduism's social and national nature in his 'Social Genius' article, Lajpat Rai explicitly aimed to refute those 'Hindus educated on western lines' who, urged by 'some eminent Hindus of the western Presidency', believed that 'the genius of Hinduism is essentially individualistic and antisocial' and that Hinduism could offer no resources for 'reforming' the social.[41] It is not immediately clear which Hindu reformers from the Bombay Presidency this specifically referred to. Those like K.T. Telang and Ranade, fierce critics of certain aspects of Hindu society, had urged followers to desist from viewing it as a 'festering mass of decay and corruption' from which they must separate.[42] Ranade, now deceased, had interpreted Hinduism's evolution and growth as a process whereby it had continuously adopted new ideas from outside and from other faiths, and urged that the absorption of Western ideas and rationalism was in line with this historic spirit.[43] Yet, he also maintained faith in several Hindu institutions. This desire to strike a balance between criticism-driven change and preservation, and the unwillingness to break from the Hindu community, was similar to Lajpat Rai's approach.

Rai's allusion may then have been to the increasingly vocal line taken by reformers like Narayan Chandavarkar (1855–1923), who strongly criticized Ranade for his cautious approach when he was alive and had assumed leadership of the Indian National Social Conference after his death in 1901. This group abandoned the *shastric* (Hindu text-based) approach to reform to declare their faith in 'reason', and urged more rationally motivated and more radical breaks with Hindu 'traditions'.[44] Lajpat Rai saw himself as countering the alleged belief of such Hindus that social orientation, absent in Hinduism, must be borrowed from the West, particularly via what Rai saw as the Western concept of 'reason'.[45] He rejected reason as the sole source for building or reforming the social, and to prove his point adduced Benjamin Kidd's argument that 'uncontrolled reason' resulted in excessive individualism and antisocial tendencies.[46] As we saw, Kidd had argued that human progress required society to be persuaded to become less rational and more religious and altruistic. The equation that Kidd drew between religion and irrationality, altruism and irrationality, and selfish individualism and rationality had been criticized by several commentators.[47] Such criticism notwithstanding, Lajpat Rai seized on Kidd to argue that reason promoted excessive individualism and to reject it as a sole source for rejuvenating Hindu society. Ignoring Kidd's particular emphasis on Christianity, Rai grasped his broader stress on religion to assert that ancient Hinduism already possessed resources to rebuild a new social or national orientation.

An excessive reliance on 'reason' was problematic in Lajpat Rai's eyes also because it was viewed as Western. In a 1904 article titled 'Reform or Revival?' Lajpat Rai made a bid to promote a measure of conciliation between Hindu 'reformers' and Hindu 'revivalists' who attacked each other publicly with great acrimony. He tried to shine light on the substantial common ground between the rational approach to reform often adopted by 'reformers' and the *shastric* approach of the 'revivalists'. But Rai argued that the reformer's appeals for reform on grounds of 'utility' were less popular with Hindu society than the revivalist's appeals for the same reforms via references to the Hindu shastras and the Hindu past. The term 'utility' was a reference to Utilitarianism, a nineteenth-century British moral philosophy which held that what mattered morally was utility or happiness, and the right action in any situation was that which maximized the total amount of utility and happiness [which is why the English utilitarian Jeremy Bentham (1748–1832) had talked about the 'the greatest happiness of the greatest number'].[48]

Central to utilitarianism was the rigorous use of reason to determine morality and maximize utility or happiness. Rai held that while both were worthy of respect, the appeal of the reformer to the 'rational' was less popular than the revivalist's appeal to the 'national'.[49] In fact, 'reformers' like Ranade had in previous years disparaged the notion that national regeneration was possible only through 'cold calculations of utility' and without drawing on religion.[50] The opposition Lajpat Rai drew between reformer–utility–rational versus revivalist–religion–national was therefore reductive to begin with. But what is more interesting is that in Rai's formulation, Hindu scriptures were temporarily equated with the national and indigenous, and reason with non-native, European foreignness. While Rai welcomed both approaches to the reform of Hindu society, his rebuttal defended the revivalist, shastric approach against 'reformer' criticism, and clearly rejected utilitarianism and reason as an exclusive basis for social reform. Interestingly, this was despite the Utilitarian implication that the individual good would have to be sacrificed if this maximized overall happiness, a principle that came close to Rai's own portrayal of the social ideals of Hinduism. Ironically, Spencer, whom Rai had interpreted as upholding the ideal of selfless sacrifice for the other, had accused Utilitarians of promoting an extreme ideology of 'pure altruism'.[51] Lajpat Rai did not reject rationality completely, and pointed out that the Punjabi Arya Samajist efforts at reform were both 'national' and 'rational', dependent on scripture and reason.[52] Still, what is noteworthy is Rai's disinclination to admit reason as the sole basis for reform due to its apparent associations with Europe, and its allegedly non-national and foreign nature.

As we saw, the equally Western concept of altruism was appropriated without difficulty from British evolutionary sociology and presented as the defining feature of ancient Hindu texts. Lajpat Rai's own criticism of 'reason' and argument for finding 'social' and 'national' ideals in the religion of Hinduism drew on the arguments of British public intellectuals like Kidd. And Lajpat Rai found within ancient Hindu texts a faith corresponding with Social Darwinism and nationalism, both modern ideologies originating in the West.

Still, in continuing to reference ancient Hindu texts, even as he found modern Social Darwinist and nationalist ideals within them, Lajpat Rai saw himself as asserting the 'national' over the 'Western'. Because these ideals were imagined as integral to ancient Hinduism, the desirable change towards greater social and national cohesiveness could be seen as consistent with original, true Hinduism and not a departure from it towards the 'West'.

In arguing for Hinduism's social and national spirit, Lajpat Rai abandoned his earlier Arya Samaj-inflected definition of Hinduism as Vedic monotheism. Reflecting his acceptance of the Arya Samaj as merely one of Hinduism's many sects, he now moved beyond the Vedas to openly embrace Hinduism's multiple, non-Vedic texts. He thus moved further away from, and even drew sharp criticism from, the Gurukul Party that continued to reject 'Hinduism' in favour of ancient 'Vedic religion' and the term 'Hindu' in favour of 'Arya'.[53] Lajpat Rai's public embrace of various Hindu texts reflected his move towards a more catholic, broad-based conception of Hinduism. Collapsing the religious into the social, which in turn was identified with the national, he now elided theology to define Hinduism as a 'nationality' or as a 'national' spirit. Hinduism—de-linked from notions of divinity and sacredness—was therefore further secularized as nationalism. This helped sidestep Hindu theological diversity and encompass an even greater number of individuals than earlier within his definition of Hinduism. As we saw, in labouring to prove that Hindu shastras already contained the national spirit, Lajpat Rai also adduced the caste order as evidence of Hinduism's 'social' (and 'national') unity. Since 1900, many Arya Samajists, including the Gurukul Party leader Lala Munshi Ram (later known as Swami Shraddhanand), were opening up Vedic practice to the so-called low castes and Untouchables.[54] Lajpat Rai's Arya Samajist background too made him note the 'cruel and inhumane' injunctions against lower castes in the Manusmriti. Yet, his 'Social Genius' article demonstrates his ability to gloss over the hierarchy, inequality and exploitation entailed in the caste system, to arrive at a symbolic Hindu unity.

In defining Hinduism as quintessentially social and national, Lajpat Rai again sidestepped religious–theological differences among Hindus. But his subsequent writings reveal that religious diversity among Hindus remained a persistent thorn in his project of forging a 'Hindu nation'. In an article titled 'Hinduism and Common Nationality', he wrote:

> It is often said that Hinduism is not the name of a particular religion, nor that of a religious nationality, and that it does not represent one set of beliefs, common to all who call themselves Hindu, and that therefore it is perfectly idle to appeal to Hindus in the name of a common nationality. It has become almost fashion to insist that the term Hinduism is too vague to be properly defined, and that there is hardly anything substantially common which binds one Hindu to another in the ties of national brotherhood. Hinduism, in short, is said to be more often a congeries of different religions and sects holding diverse and not unoften [sic] diametrically opposite views on matters of faith and doctrine. Hinduism is said to include and cover almost every form of religious faith known to or practiced by mankind from the purest monotheism to the lowest form of animism, polytheism, hedonism, pantheism, in fact all sorts of isms. There is a fairly large class of Hindus who suffer from want of faith in the potentialities of their religion to unite them or inspire them to the lofty ideals of a great religious platform whereupon to bring together a Hindu union.[55]

Lajpat Rai expressed disagreement with these unnamed individuals who, he argued, were so despondent about the prospects of Hindu unity in the face of Hinduism's confounding theological diversity that they recommended the conversion of Hindus to Christianity. Refuting such doubts, he pointed to the differences within its 'sister faiths', Christianity and Islam:

> These two latter contain as many varieties and shades of religious beliefs and doctrines in themselves, if not more, as Hinduism

does, of course, giving due consideration to the ages of these three religions. If the Hindus have got their *Vedantists*, the Muhammadans have their *Sufis* and the Christians have those who have raised the banner of higher Christianity. If Hindus have their Trinity in Brahma, Vishnu and Shiva, the Christians have theirs in Father, Son and Holy Ghost. If the Hindus have got their Avatars, the Christians have (besides the great incarnation of God in the body of Christ) their Popes and Saints. If the Hindus believe in different deities, there are Muhammadans and Christians who believe in Saints, *Walis*, *Mahdis*, &c., &c . . . If there are Hindus who are steeped in superstitious beliefs and observe many gross forms of worship, there are millions and millions of Muhammadans and Christians also, particularly the latter, whose religious practices are as gross as those of the multitudes of Hindus. If there are fables in the Puranas, there are equally ridiculous stories in the Quran and the Bible.[56]

Lajpat Rai quoted German Sanskritist Theodor Goldstücker (1821–72) to highlight the 'hundreds of creeds' within Christianity, each of which 'claims to be in exclusive possession of Christianity', and whose 'difference was so essential that it was strong enough to perpetuate the most inveterate animosities and to result in wars the like of which cannot be traced in the history of any other creed'.[57] Islam too contained 'as many varieties and shades of religious beliefs and doctrines . . . if not more, than Hinduism does'.[58] Interestingly, though scholars have noted the tendency of Hindu nationalists to attribute an exaggerated cohesion and unity at least to Islam if not Christianity,[59] Lajpat Rai emphasized internal differences and discord within them in order to avow the existence of a Hindu nation despite internal discord. He hoped to show that Hinduism was not unique in possessing a perplexingly 'endless variety of religious beliefs' within it.[60] If internal diversity and even discord within Islam and Christianity did not disqualify them as 'religious nationalities', why should it do so for Hinduism? Hinduism was as much a religious nationality as Christianity and Islam.[61]

Lajpat Rai argued that Islam and Christianity accommodated even 'scoffers, agnostics and sceptics' who questioned the divinity of the Quran and the Bible but still clung to 'the outer form of religion, the very essence of which they take pleasure in decrying'.[62] Countless individuals who did not consider the Bible as divine revelation stayed within 'the pale of outward Christianity' and remained as Christian for 'purposes of religious rites and ceremonies, baptism, marriage etc.' as those who believed that 'every letter of the Bible was spoken by God Himself'.[63] Lajpat Rai appeared to suggest that atheists should not be barred from membership to the 'Hindu nationality' as long as they clung to Hinduism's 'outer form'. Belief, worship and ritual or practice were now de-emphasized ever more strongly as Lajpat Rai defined Hinduism. It was instead defined in broadly non-religious, cultural terms to facilitate belonging even without believing.[64] More than a decade later, Savarkar would privilege 'Hindutva' as a category over 'Hinduism' because while Hinduism signified 'religious dogma', Hindutva was broad enough to include even non-believing Hindus.[65] Lajpat Rai did not transcend Hinduism through a secular category like Hindutva; he simply attempted to redefine 'Hinduism' itself in secularized terms. Nevertheless, crucial differences still remaining,[66] Rai foreshadowed Hindutva in this one significant respect of de-emphasizing religiosity while defining Hindu-ness.

To be sure, even now Rai insisted, once again citing Goldstucker, that the great bulk of Hindus did in fact consider the Vedas as the 'pivot on which all religious questions of Hindu India rest'.[67] Lajpat Rai's Arya Samajist background prompted him to keep the Vedas as the central external marker of an internally differentiated Hinduism. But no mention was made of the theological or ritual content of the Vedas; they simply served as a skin-deep identity marker around which Hindus, despite their deep diversity, could rally as a national community. Tilak similarly argued that Vedantists, Shaivas, Vedics and Vaishnavas should see themselves as Hindus just as Catholics, Protestants, Puritans and such other 'cults' regarded themselves as Christians.[68] He struggled to consolidate Hinduism's 'different sects' into a 'Hindu nation' by suggesting that they were united by common

allegiance to the Vedas, the Gita and the Ramayana.[69] Lajpat Rai, the
Punjabi Arya Samajist Hindu, did the same by zeroing in on the Vedas.
Having de-emphasized active faith and observance to facilitate a
collective Hindu identity that encompassed Hinduism's tremendous
internal diversity, Vedic religious texts were still anxiously invoked
in an effort to strengthen this Hindu identity. Yet, the Vedas were
invoked in a desacralized form, without emphasizing their sacred
or religious content. The ostensibly 'religious' Hindu identity still
had little to do with religiosity, and was ultimately still conceived in
largely secularized terms; it functioned as an indispensable marker
of communal and national belonging rather than an expression of
religious faith.

7

'Extremist' Politics: The Gita and the Possibility of Violence

As we saw in Chapter 5, by the turn of the century, Lajpat Rai—along with Tilak, Aurobindo Ghose and B.C. Pal—had begun to demand that the Congress move beyond gradualist, petition-based politics. Rai had also publicly criticized the Congress in 1901. But within three years, he once again resumed contact with the organization. He was among the group of politically minded Punjabis who sought to persuade the Congress to establish both an internal constitution and a political machinery, so it could conduct coherent and sustained political work throughout the year.[1] The thirty-nine-year-old Lajpat Rai was a prominent leader of the Punjabi delegates who attended the Congress's annual session in Bombay in 1904. Here, Lajpat Rai was selected along with Gokhale, with whom he was developing a close equation, to go to England as part of a Congress deputation in view of the impending general elections there.[2] The Congress's old guard had concluded that given the intransigence of the British government in India, their efforts should be directed at the English parliament and British public. It was particularly hopeful about the anticipated victory of the Liberal Party, the first since the formation of the Congress, which they believed would improve chances of constitutional reforms for India.

The hope that Congressmen had from Britain's Liberal Party was based on their divergent perceptions of Conservative and Liberal viceroys in India. For instance, the Conservative Lord Lytton (who served between 1876 and 1880) had dismissed English-educated Indians as 'Babus, whom we have educated to write semi-seditious articles'.[3] On the other hand, the Liberal Lord Ripon (who served from 1880 to 1884) spoke of the 'increasing . . . necessity of making the educated natives friends instead of enemies of our rule', and had introduced local self-government.[4] By 1885, many politically conscious Indians had become alert to differences between the Conservative and Liberal Parties in British politics, and distinguished between the authoritarianism of the Conservatives (also called the Tories) and the relative responsiveness of the Liberals.[5] But in fact, over the course of the 1890s, differences between Tory and Liberal attitudes to India had become less clear. The period saw a Tory viceroy agree with his Liberal predecessor that introducing an elective element in the provincial councils would deflate the Congress, and a Liberal viceroy appease the Lancashire cotton lobby and refuse to introduce elections in Indian legislatures.[6]

Lajpat Rai seemed to have grasped this by 1904, believing that a victorious Liberal Party would be no different from the Conservatives when it came to British imperialism in India. Nevertheless, he agreed to be part of the Congress deputation and, between May and October of 1905, visited several counties in England and Scotland explaining Indian grievances and claims to the British public. During his six-month-long trip Lajpat Rai established contacts with members of Britain's Labour Party, founded a decade before in 1893. Presumably because many of its socialist members expressed internationalist and anti-imperial sentiments,[7] Rai viewed it as the only political formation from whom Indians could expect sympathy for their cause. But the Labour Party was powerless. And so, Lajpat Rai continued to strongly believe that Indians primarily needed to organize political action in India itself.[8]

The opportunity for this arrived in 1905 itself, while Rai was still in England, when Lord Curzon, the conservative viceroy of India, announced the decision to partition Bengal. The partition of Bengal into eastern and western sections was intended to undermine the power of the well-educated, high-caste Bengalis of Calcutta who had been at the forefront of Congress politics. This was done by cutting them off from the estates they owned in the Muslim-majority eastern part, lumping East Bengal with Assam, and overwhelming the population of West Bengal with people from Orissa and Bihar.[9]

The partition provoked the first major nationalist movement of mass protest in India: the Swadeshi movement of Bengal.[10] And it quickly opened up possibilities for the more agitational and confrontational modes of politics advocated by 'Lal–Bal–Pal' and Aurobindo Ghose. In defiance of the Bengal government's ban on public assemblies, mass meetings and protests were held in halls, theatres, temples, community grounds and private residences, soon spilling onto the streets of Calcutta. Calls emerged for a boycott of British goods and their replacement by swadeshi or Indian-made ones, resulting in the picketing of shops selling foreign goods. There was also a clamour to establish a system of national education rooted in Bengali. The Swadeshi movement continued into 1906, led by Congress veterans like Surendranath Banerjea and younger upcoming radical leaders like Pal and Ghose. In April 1906, a Congress-led procession with cries of 'Bande Mataram!' (a slogan banned by the British government in the wake of recent protests) was lathi-charged at Barisal in East Bengal, and Banerjea was arrested. Following this, radicals like Pal and Ghose took charge, touring the area and delivering fiery speeches. Protest meetings were held all over Bengal and began spreading to other Indian provinces as well. In May 1906, the Maharashtrian radical leader Tilak arrived in Calcutta, with thousands gathering to hear him speak.

The Bengal radicals now suggested Tilak's name as president of the Congress session due to be held in Calcutta in December 1906. But by now, a clear division had emerged between 'moderate' Congress veterans (like Surendranath Banerjea, Dadabhai Naoroji,

Pherozeshah Mehta, Gokhale and Malaviya) and the radicals (like Pal, Ghose, Tilak and Lajpat Rai) who soon became known as the 'extremists'.[11] Following his return to India in November 1905, Lajpat Rai had tried unsuccessfully to urge the Congress to initiate a popular demonstration coinciding with its imminent December session in Benaras.[12] Gokhale's presidential speech at the session had supported swadeshi and boycott.[13] But he persuaded his friend Lajpat Rai to withdraw his opposition to a resolution welcoming the Prince of Wales to India.[14] Rai's more assertive stance was defeated but an informal alliance had been formed between the radicals from Punjab, Maharashtra and Bengal against the Congress's old guard.[15] When Tilak's name was advanced by the Bengal extremists in 1906 as President for the 1906 Calcutta session, this was opposed by the moderates.[16] They ultimately successfully pushed for Naoroji, the author of the 'drain of wealth' theory, and widely respected Grand Old Man of Indian Politics that no one wanted to oppose.[17]

But rather than personal rivalries, real differences divided the moderates and extremists. Despite their critiques of British colonialism, which linked India's poverty to British rule, the moderates collectively still reposed faith in the British claim that its imperialist aim was to gradually devolve power to Indians and help India become a self-governing state within the empire, along the lines of white colonies like Australia and Canada.[18] To achieve this, they believed they had to appeal to liberal political opinion in Britain through petitions and resolutions,[19] and pressurize the British government in India through criticism within legislative councils. Ultimately, the 'moderates' believed it was crucial to keep a dialogue open with the British. While they agreed to swadeshi, they remained wary of boycott, considering it too belligerent towards the British. Some 'moderates' were also concerned that a boycott forced the poor to buy low-quality and more expensive swadeshi goods, and that the boycott of government-funded educational institutions would deprive young Indians of the qualifications they needed.[20] The 'moderates' were criticized by the 'extremists' as being too timid and ineffective. The extremists may have differed on their ultimate goal—Rai and Tilak found self-government with the empire acceptable, while Pal and Ghose called for absolute independence.[21] But they agreed on the urgent need for a sustained agitational campaign against the British through a boycott of British goods and institutions, their replacement with swadeshi alternatives, and through confrontational meetings and processions—a programme called 'passive resistance'.[22]

The moderates succeeded in having Naoroji as president for the Congress's December 1906 session. But the Partition of Bengal had strengthened the hands of radicals within and outside the Congress. In December 1906, Lajpat Rai and Tilak addressed a mammoth public meeting in Calcutta, advancing the 'extremist' programme.[23] At the 1906 Congress, as the moderates attempted to limit protests to Bengal and the Partition issue, extremists like Pal called for an all-India campaign of boycott and swadeshi.[24] Meanwhile, the campaign of passive resistance continued into 1907 in Bengal, remaining strongest in Calcutta and the eastern part of the province.[25] The authorities attempted to curb these novel protest meetings with repressive ordinances, dispersed peaceful meetings with brutal lathi charges and charged leaders and journalists with sedition. In Maharashtra, 'extremist' fervour in 1907 was witnessed in the rising popularity of Tilak's radical journalism, bonfires of foreign cloth and the picketing of liquor shops.[26]

In Punjab, the early months of 1907 saw protests against new regulations which took away some of the existing rights of peasants, and steeply raised the tax on water.[27] Peasants suspected that corrupt officials would use the new rules to demand higher bribes despite the recent plague outbreak and crop failure. Unlike in Bengal and Maharashtra, where the Swadeshi movement remained largely confined to the middle and upper classes, in Punjab, leaders from these backgrounds were able to successfully connect their cause with that of the peasantry.[28]

Lajpat Rai participated in the peasant protests, linking them to the wider assertive agenda of the Swadeshi movement.[29] As it turned sporadically unruly, the governor of Punjab, Denzil

Ibbetson, concluded that the agrarian agitation was part of a secret plot to violently overthrow the British government. He asked the Government of India for jurisdiction to ban public meetings, close hostile newspapers and arrest anyone inciting peasants not to pay taxes.[30] In May 1907, convinced that he had masterminded the agrarian agitation, the British government deported the forty-two-year-old Lajpat Rai, without trial, to Burma's Mandalay Fort Prison.[31] The central government would find no evidence for charges that Rai had made seditious speeches, advocated illegal or violent methods, or tampered with the loyalty of native troops.[32] But till his release in November 1907, Rai would spend the next six months in the Burmese prison. It was from here that he wrote a lengthy article titled 'The Message of the Bhagwad Gita'.[33]

In 1904, Lajpat Rai had already established that Hinduism possessed 'social' or 'national' content. Now, following the Swadeshi agitation, he more keenly realized that an essential feature of a national community, as distinct from other communities, was that it possessed collective agency, the capacity to collectively *act* in order to achieve a measure of self-government. He now sought to show that Hinduism sanctioned collective political action, and possessed resources to support this 'active' conception of nationality. He had not found this notion of political action in the Vedas, Brahmanas, Upanishads or the Manusmriti. But he found them in a segment of the ancient Mahabharata epic—the Bhagavad Gita.

Instead of portraying the Vedas as the central pivot of the Hindu 'nationality', as he usually did, in this essay, Lajpat Rai portrayed the Gita virtually as its nucleus.[34] This, interestingly, corresponded with Rai's embeddedness within a particular historical juncture between 1880 and 1910 when the Gita saw a steep rise in circulation and influence both in India and the West, and in its perceived importance within modern Hinduism.[35] Rai explained that while the Vedas remained a sealed book for the majority, the Gita was more 'open and intelligible'. It was the most popular sacred book of Hindus, read by all *sampradays*,[36] whether orthodox or heterodox, 'reformed or unreformed'.[37] Even bitterly conflicting Hindus accepted it as their 'common object of veneration'. Though all Hindus did not find it infallible like the Vedas, it was revered as a gospel of 'very high' authority. It was with this justification that Lajpat Rai squared his Arya Samajist background with his utilization of this non-Vedic, Vaishnava text.[38] In assertively drawing on the Gita, he diverged from the Arya Samaj's founder Swami Dayanand who had expressed ambivalence towards it.[39]

Before showing that the Gita contained resources for collective political action, Lajpat Rai had to deal with alternative schools of interpretation over the Gita's essential teaching. The Gita, composed between 200 BCE and 200 CE, was a response to prevalent theories of action in ancient India.[40] These stressed that since desire-based action leads to bondage to the cycle of rebirths in this world, the best path was to leave desire-based action and all attachments, and thus renounce the world. With this position represented by Arjuna's indecision about entering into war and his throwing down of his weapons, Krishna proposes a new theory of action in the Gita while persuading Arjuna to fight: one should not renounce action but should act without attachment to the results of the action. Arjuna should fight the war but without concern for victory or anxiety about defeat. For action with control over one's mind leaves open the path to liberation. Krishna then discusses the different paths to spiritual realization—including the discipline of action (*karma yoga*), the discipline of knowledge (*jnana yoga*) and the discipline of devotion (*bhakti yoga*), praising all as worthy. Through medieval times, different commentators disagreed over the true message of the Gita. Some Vedantic philosophers like Ramanuja stressed that it privileged the discipline of devotion as the path to individual salvation. Others like Sankara believed that knowledge was superior to action and required renunciation of the world.[41]

Acknowledging these different schools of interpretation, Lajpat Rai summarily disregarded broad philosophical disputes regarding the Gita as hair-splitting.[42] However, he pronounced the probable correctness of those whom he called the Yogis—who held that the Gita gave 'foremost place to yoga and action'—over the Sankhyas—who believed it established 'the superiority of jnana [knowledge] over all other ways of knowing and realizing the supreme soul'.[43] The Lord, he says, gives 'a decisive opinion in favour of 'Yoga by action' (karma yoga) in preference to 'renunciation of activities'.[44] For Rai, most of the chapters of the Gita were 'only an amplification of Karma yoga'—the performance of karma or action 'without attachment to its fruits'.[45] Quoting British theosophist Annie Besant's recent and widely influential translation, Lajpat Rai noted Arjuna's confusion as to why Krishna had enjoined him to perform 'this terrible action (i.e., war)'.[46] He then reproduced Krishna's reply that man never rose to perfection through renunciation, and that he who sat 'controlling the organs of action but dwelling in his mind on the objects of senses' was less worthy than he who, controlling the senses, 'with the organs of action without attachment, performed yoga by action (karma yoga)'.[47] Krishna had therefore exhorted Arjuna to 'perform thou right action, for action is superior to inaction'.[48]

In advocating this 'activist' interpretation of the Gita as against medieval Vedantic interpretations that emphasized the renunciation of worldly action, Lajpat Rai echoed previous Indian commentators like Bankimchandra Chatterji[49] and Vivekananda as well as British theosophists like Annie Besant.[50] In doing so, he also anticipated later prominent commentators such as Tilak,[51] Aurobindo Ghose[52] and Gandhi.[53] Indeed, Lajpat Rai's elision from historiography on the modern commentaries on the Gita is surprising, given that he seems to be the first among the 'extremist' political leaders to publish a somewhat systematic exegesis on the Gita, and to assert that it taught detached action, not renunciation. Following Rai's political trajectory, Tilak would pen his own widely influential *Gita-Rahasya* from Mandalay prison in 1910–11 after his arrest in 1908 in the aftermath of the Swadeshi agitation.[54] Ghose had made a similar activist interpretation of the Gita in remarks scattered across a few articles around the same time as Rai, but these had not amounted to a systematic account. Like Rai and Tilak, he would (re)turn to the

Gita more fully during his imprisonment in the Alipur bomb case in 1908–09. But his resulting more systematic commentary, written between 1916 and 1920, as he transformed from a revolutionary to the 'yogi of Pondicherry' and international spiritual guru, contained a radically revised interpretation of the Gita. Ghose now saw it as teaching not strident political action but a universal spiritual truth to be embraced by humanity as a whole.[55] Through his 1907 essay, Lajpat Rai fully participated in the intellectual move of responding to the new political possibilities opened up by the Swadeshi moment by attempting to find within the Gita, and thus within Hinduism, resources for more assertive, confrontational and 'masculine' political action.

Lajpat Rai also stressed that the chief purpose of the Gita was to 'persuade Arjuna to fight'.[56] Arjuna's moral dilemma about whether killing one's kin or elders whom one loved and respected was sinful, even when this was required by one's *dharma* or duty, was resolved by Krishna's reply that it was not.[57] Krishna declared:

. . . one's individual dharma is the supreme law of his life . . . Everything must be subordinated to it . . . The slaying of one's nearest and dearest relative, not to speak of any enemy, is not sinful if one cannot perform one's duty (Dharma) but by slaying him. One's dharma cannot be anything but righteous. Hence anything which is necessary to be done in the performance of Dharma cannot be sinful. [58]

In Rai's view, then, the Gita sanctioned violence and killing if one had exhausted all other means to perform one's dharma or if one's duty required killing.[59] If certain that one cannot perform one's duty 'without running the risk of doing what otherwise appears to you to be sinful', one must do so.[60] Indeed, the Gita deemed such violence 'righteous'. In fact, abjuring duty—out of considerations of love, mercy, or 'injury to self or other'—was sinful and unrighteous.[61] The performance of one's dharma, even if it entailed violence and killing, would lead to salvation—the realization of the Supreme Soul and complete freedom from births and deaths—and 'the state of supreme bliss (*paramananda*)' that accompanied it.[62] Conversely, betrayal of dharma ensured one's destruction.[63] This, for Lajpat Rai, was the essence of the message of the Gita.

That Lajpat Rai was adapting this message of the Gita to contemporary nationalist concerns is evident from his use of the following sentence: 'A patriot warrior commits no sin in killing the enemies of his country in fair fight.'[64] It was the dharma of the 'patriot warrior' to defend his country against its enemies, and if this dharma required killing, this was morally righteous, not sinful. Lajpat Rai interpreted the Gita, and thus Hinduism, as permitting violent political action to reclaim a measure of political power for the nation. Here, his commentary diverged from the 'activist' interpretations of earlier commentators which, despite their emphasis on political action, had not used the Gita to provide such a pointed and explicit moral justification for political violence. In this aspect, Rai of course differed significantly from Gandhi who would interpret the Mahabharata allegorically as the eternal inner spiritual battle between dharma and adharma within every individual's soul, and Krishna's call to Arjuna to fight as an injunction to individuals to overcome inner tendencies to act according to self-interested desires and instead ground their actions in disinterested duty. For Gandhi, the Gita taught detachment to the fruits of action, whereas violent action in service of the nation implied attachment and was therefore fundamentally opposed to Krishna's teachings regarding rightful action.[65]

It was of course Arjuna's particular position as an 'Arya–Kshatriya',[66] a member of the warrior caste, that made fighting a righteous war (*dharmayuddha*) his 'individual dharma'.[67] Fighting was not everyone's dharma but the particular, individual dharma of Kshatriya warriors, which they were obliged to perform despite recognition of the superiority of a Brahmin's dharma.[68] But Lajpat Rai saw in the warrior Arjuna an analogy for 'present-day Indians'. Like Arjuna, they were currently plagued by 'doubt' regarding their duty and were showing 'chicken-hearted scepticism' at the time of action,[69] when they should be more masculine and militant. As Krishna's message had dispelled the 'demon of doubt'[70] that had threatened to lead Arjuna astray, so too would it dispel the doubt and 'unmanliness' of modern Indians. That Lajpat Rai was drawing this equation is evident in the concluding paragraph of his commentary where he addressed 'present-day Indians':

> . . . disinterested performance of one's duty, without attachment to its fruit, at any cost and any risk . . . this is the message for the descendants, successors and countrymen of Krishna and Arjuna, swayed as they are, at present, by the forces of ignorance, superstition, chicken-heartedness and false ideas of Dharma and Karma. In unswerving loyalty to this truth - at any cost and under any circumstances - lies the salvation of the present-day Indians. If ever any nation stood in need of a message like that of Krishna, it is the Indians of to-day. If ever the inheritors of Krishna's name and glory stood in need of a sound doctrine to lead them to success and prosperity amidst adverse circumstances of the greatest awe-inspiring and fear-generating magnitude, it is now. Let them invoke his aid by acting up to his message and we are sure all their doubts will be dispelled, their unmanliness gone and the road to success and glory gained but surely. It will a shame if the countrymen of Krishna let any false ideas of *Yoga* prevail amongst them or let any false doctrines of renunciation (*sanyaas*) and relinquishment (*tyaag*) enfeeble their arms. If no false notions of *Dharma* are allowed to paralyse their minds and their hands, we are confident their future is as assured as was the victory of Arjuna over the mighty forces of Duryodhana, even though the latter had the bodily support of a Bhishma and a Drona.[71]

Lajpat Rai's assertion that the Gita and, by implication Hinduism, permitted conditional violence (violence under certain conditions) was similarly linked to the new post-Swadeshi context, which saw anti-colonial politics beginning to sporadically assume the form of individual acts of violence against the British. Although such anti-British violence began making an impact only from 1908 onwards, a little after his commentary was written, Lajpat Rai seemed to sense the emergent trend to view violence as a possible mode of anti-colonial politics. His interpretation of the Gita, as sanctioning righteous violence, justified it. Since 1905, Lajpat Rai had frequently referred to both the partition of Bengal and the government's repressive response to the Swadeshi agitation as a form of Russian-style 'despotism', 'autocracy' and 'military terrorism' that functioned in blatant disregard of 'the strongly-expressed opinion of the whole nation'.[72] This more 'despotic' character of the British government may well have provoked Rai and his 'extremist' colleagues' turn to the Gita as a means of legitimizing violent political action. Indeed, as intellectual historian Robert Upton has demonstrated, in the spring of 1908, following an anti-colonial assassination attempt by the revolutionary Khudiram Bose, and in remarks that would lead to his own arrest and imprisonment for sedition, Tilak would explicitly argue that the British colonial state's 'autocratic' and 'despotic' foisting of the Partition of Bengal on the people in complete disregard of their sentiments had driven Bengali youth to lean on violence as a means to reform colonial government.[73] Like Rai, Tilak wrote of the government's use of 'Russian methods', to which, he argued, a reciprocal response in the style of Russian subjects (i.e., anarchic revolutionary violence) must be expected.[74]

Shruti Kapila has interpreted the Gita's theme of killing of kin in Tilak's 1908 commentary as evidence of his exhortation to Hindus to direct political violence against their brothers, Indian Muslims, as a means to restore moral and political order.[75] This reading is disputed by Upton who argues that Tilak's sanction of violence in his *Gita-Rahasya* was intended to legitimize violence against the colonial state, a fact noted by colonial officials.[76] While a reading of Hinduism as sanctioning conditional fraternal violence created the future possibility of it being marshalled against India's Muslims, this was clearly not the intent behind Lajpat Rai's use of the Gita in 1907. He had participated in the agrarian protests in Punjab alongside Muslim (and Sikh) zamindars, collaborating with leaders such as Mian Sirajuddin, Chaudhuri Shahabuddhin and Mohammad Shafi.[77] In his 'Story of My Deportation', published in 1908, he appreciated the Muslim merchants of Ahmedabad and Surat who had objected to the lie of the Anglo–Indian press that Muslims were happy with his deportation and had no sympathies with him.[78] Rai also recalled that:

> The journey [from Lahore to Mandalay] was uneventful except for touching marks of respect and regret shown by Mohammedan constables forming part of my escort . . . on board the streamer, they talked with me freely and I can never forget the depth of feeling displayed by a young Mohammedan constable having a most handsome and prepossessing appearance. While deeply regretting my misfortune and almost weeping over it, he gave expression to his own and to his country's feeling of helplessness in words of deep and sincere pathos . . . for the first time in my life, perhaps, did the noble purity of the Indian mind, uninitiated in the hypocritical gloss of Western civilization, burst upon my soul in its full and original grandeur.[79]

Rai was hardly about to follow up on these thoughts and experiences with a justification of fraternal violence against Muslims. His imagined target in his essay on the Gita was clearly the British symbolized by the 'mighty forces of Duryodhana'. For him, the Gita's sanction of conditional righteous violence against one's dearest kin meant an even bigger sanction to a patriot–warrior's violence against an enemy like the despotic British government. Lajpat Rai's anti-colonial attitude was recognized by the British when they deported him. A telegraph Viceroy Minto wrote to Secretary of State Lord Morley a day before Lajpat Rai's deportation referred to him as 'a revolutionary and political enthusiast inspired by the most intense hatred of the British government'.[80] The centrality of the Gita in Lajpat Rai's new politics represented an intensification of Lajpat Rai's developing anti-colonial position.

Yet, to read Rai's concluding entreaty to Indians to heed Krishna's message as a nationalist call to arms would be simplistic. In the introduction to 'Story of My Deportation', he addressed his countrymen, warning that nations were 'not made or saved by dare-devil methods', that 'unnecessary sacrifice of life and energy' was a 'great and heinous crime', and that 'Indians . . . had no right to throw away their lives like mad men'. 'An honourable life,' he continued, 'was infinitely superior to a death under a short-bred impulse', and it was a 'pure waste . . . to allow their ranks to be thinned by recklessness'. What was required was a clear, bold vision, but this prospect was hindered by 'irresponsible talk of undisciplined enthusiasm, much less by violent methods'.[81] He went on: '. . . the British laws are so far sufficiently wide and liberal to leave a good margin for steady and zealous work along constitutional lines. Let us therefore studiously keep ourselves within the law.'[82]

These warnings against violence were based more on considerations of strategy than morality. His essay on the Gita clearly shows that Rai held no *principled* opposition to political violence, considering it morally legitimate and even necessary under certain conditions.[83] Yet, even in this essay, his justification of violence was conditional—violence was to be resorted to only after all other means to pursue one's righteous duty had been exhausted. Violence was not Rai's preferred mode of politics; he still argued for the primacy of non-violent, legal and constitutional politics, but that which was much more assertive, energetic and popular–agitational than the cautious, gradualist legislative politics of the main 'moderate' leaders of the Congress. In the Bhagavad Gita, Lajpat Rai had found the justification for the most extreme form of political action, namely political violence and war. As he saw it, if this was so, less extreme forms of assertive non-violent political action by Indians to reclaim political power that legitimately belonged to the nation had even greater justification. Here, Lajpat Rai differed from the revolutionaries of the Anushilan Samiti and Yugantar, as well as India House in London—including Krishnavarma and Savarkar— who read the Gita to justify their belief that insurrectionary political violence was the best, most natural mode of anti-colonial politics.[84] They used Krishna's urging of Arjuna to fight in a righteous battle to justify their belief that independence was to be gained *only* by anti-colonial revolutionary violence, and by training themselves in the use of lathis, swords, guns and bombs. Contrary to the members of such clandestine groups, Lajpat Rai's insistence that the resources of political violence were contained in the Gita was less a direct or immediate call to violence than an indication of his belief that the resource for this political possibility existed in Hinduism. The emphasis on the existence of the possibility of political violence was intended to serve as an inspiration for a more assertive, confrontational but largely non-violent, collective political action.

8

Opposing the Muslim League

The 1906 victory of the Liberal Party in Britain, combined with the unease of the British government of India over the Swadeshi unrest, created conditions that led the British to contemplate further constitutional reforms for India. The government had increased the number of nominated Indian representation in councils in 1892, and since 1904 the Congress had again begun pushing for greater elected Indian representation. Urgently feeling the need to rally the more moderate and loyal sections of Indian opinion in the face of Swadeshi ferment, by mid-1906, the new Liberal Secretary of State for India, Lord Morley, announced his intention to consider the Congress demand. By 1906, the moderates and extremists were squabbling over whether greater confrontation with the British would help or hinder reforms, and over whether Indian nationalism should confine itself to the demand of gradual constitutional reforms or go beyond it. Meanwhile, the prospect of further reforms was creating deep unease among prominent spokespersons from the Muslim community. In October 1906, they anxiously organized a deputation to meet the Viceroy, Lord Minto, in Simla to advance some demands of their own.[1]

The 'high-born', high-caste members of the deputation, who would organize themselves into the All-India Muslim League by December, no longer insisted, as Syed Ahmed Khan had, that the natural right of '*raises*' [noblemen] to political rule nullified the need for elective political representation. They now accepted the principle of elective representation, but wanted to reconfigure the elective system to ensure particular outcomes for Muslims through two electoral devices, which they now demanded: *separate electorates* and *weightages*. Contrary to the wishes of many other 'traditional' and 'modern' Muslims, who did not support separate Muslim electorates,[2] the years between 1907 and 1909 witnessed growing public clamour by these spokespersons for the Muslim community, mainly through the Muslim League, for these demands. Eager to cultivate indigenous support wherever possible in the aftermath of the Swadeshi agitation, the British colonial government grew increasingly inclined to concede some of these demands to gain the support of these prominent Muslims.[3]

At first, neither Lajpat Rai nor any of the main Congress leaders seem to have paid much attention to the new contours of Muslim politics. Immediately following Lajpat Rai's release from the Burmese prison in November 1907, the INC split at its Surat session in December, a result of disagreements between the 'moderates' and 'extremists' over the extent and form of confrontation with the British government. The moderates, preferring a more cautious approach, had been concerned that 'extremist' belligerence was stiffening British attitude, delaying constitutional reforms, and dividing the Congress when it needed to put up a unified front. The extremists had denounced the gradualism of moderate leadership, accusing it of betraying the nationalist cause.[4] The split in the Congress ultimately resulted in the virtual ousting of the radical 'extremists' such as Tilak, Pal and Ghose from the Congress, and its retention in the hands of 'moderates' like Mehta, Banerjea, Gokhale and Malaviya (with the latter announcing his desire not to be seen with Tilak on any platform ever again!).[5] Lajpat Rai had sympathized with extremist criticism of moderate politics, but was on good terms with moderates like

Gokhale and respectful of Mehta, Banerjea and Malaviya. Considering himself part of neither camp, he had attempted to play peacemaker.[6] Interestingly, the extremists led by Tilak had suggested Lajpat Rai's name as president for the 1907 session, but since this was opposed by the moderates, he had declined to stand if it meant becoming party to a factional politics which could fracture the Congress.

Following the split, the Congress sent Gokhale to England in 1908, where he spent the year directing its efforts towards influencing Lord Morley and his Liberal Party regarding the timing and shape of the constitutional reforms. Meanwhile, the anti-colonial assassination attempt by the revolutionary, Khudiram Bose, in the spring of 1908[7] provided the government with the pretext to crack down on extremists.[8] The year saw the arrests of Tilak and Ghose for sedition and subversion of British rule, respectively, as well as the prohibition of public meetings and free assembly, curbs on 'seditious' writings and the censorship of the press, and deportations without trial.[9]

B.C. Pal was imprisoned and subsequently forced into self-imposed exile in England in the same year.[10] Demoralized by political inactivity resulting from the Congress split and government repression,[11] Lajpat Rai left in August 1908 for England, where he spent the next several months explaining to the British press and public the injustices of British rule and the Indian demand for a greater measure of self-government. Here, he also observed the suffragettes who campaigned for voting rights for women, and met Gokhale, the exiled B.C. Pal, Shyamji Krishnavarma, and even the Russian anarchist–communist prince Pyotr Kropotkin.[12] It was only in early 1909, as it became clear that the British were acceding to the Muslim League's demands for separate electorates and 'weightages', that Lajpat Rai felt compelled to intervene in the debate on Muslim political representation.

Twenty years earlier, in his one-sided engagement with Sir Syed, Rai had defended the Congress's demand for limited political self-rule and articulated the concept of a *single* 'Indian' nation. In Chapter 5, we saw that, by the turn of the century, he had spurned the notion of Hindus and Muslims constituting a common Indian nation, and instead defended the concept of a Hindu nation. His 'Hindu nation', while certainly political, had been articulated in detachment from political thinking regarding questions of (limited) self-government and political representation. Now, eight years later, the prospect of further constitutional reforms combined with new Muslim demands compelled him, once again, to return to questions of self-government and political representation. He was also driven to rethink the relationship between Hindus and Muslims and his conception of nationhood in light of these questions. Rai's intervention in politics to oppose both demands of the Muslim League saw him shift back to the conception of Indian nationhood he had publicly rejected in 1901.

Prominent Muslim notables who led the 1906 Simla Deputation to Viceroy Minto and then formed the nucleus of the newly founded Muslim League, echoing the logic of the colonial state,[13] insisted that, unlike the nations of Europe, India was composed not of a homogenous people but a diversity of religious communities, and that in Indian politics individuals primarily acted as members of distinct communities rather than as autonomous individuals. To substantiate their argument, they pointed to the existing system of (limited) elective representation in India which saw Hindu voters returning Hindu candidates, and the Hindu majority securing the greatest political representation.

These upper-caste spokespersons for the Muslim community therefore demanded the upfront political recognition of communities as the main units of representation. In their view, communal representation not only respected political reality but was also desirable in its nurturing of communities from which individuals drew nourishment. These men argued that truly fair representation required that electorates be organized along religious or communal lines (rather than territorially i.e., having a variety of individual and group interests within a territorially organized constituency—the system we have in place today).[14] To be sure, they admitted that Hindu and Muslim 'communities' or 'nationalities' had *many* common and even identical interests as fellow countrymen, which needed to be safeguarded by representatives of these interests. But these men pressed that Muslims were a 'distinct community' or 'nationality' with *additional, special* interests that were not shared by other communities.[15] These special interests, they argued, were neglected under the system of elective representation via communally mixed electorates, as the latter was dominated by the Hindu majority and allowed the emergence of only those Muslims who were willing to sacrifice 'their right of private judgement' and vote with the majority.[16] As historian Farzana Shaikh has argued, for these men, mere elected status did not signify true representation of Muslims because a Muslim elected from a mixed electorate was 'a mere mandatory of the Hindu majority'.[17] The election of 'really representative men', who could legitimately represent the special interests of Muslims, required that eligible Muslims be organized into exclusive electoral colleges (or electorates).[18] Separate electorates embodied the idea that a true Muslim representative was one who was elected only by the community of Muslims (and not by others), and was accountable exclusively to the Muslim community (and not to others).[19] In this political schema, Hindus were perfectly entitled to similarly elect their own representatives. The demand for separate electorates ultimately revealed the belief that notwithstanding any overarching political interests that Hindus and Muslims might have in common, and which they could represent for each other, Muslims had a significantly *larger* number of political interests exclusively in common with members of their own 'community'/'nationality'. Only a Muslim elected exclusively by Muslims could represent these more substantial political interests they shared as one 'community'/'nationality'.[20]

When in November 1908 Secretary of State Lord Morley suggested a scheme based on mixed electoral colleges,[21] the language of the Muslim League grew bolder. At the League's 1908 session, Maulana Mohamed Ali, the Aligarh graduate who was rising to political prominence and would lead the Khilafat movement a decade later, reiterated that in India the lines of cleavage between various political interests were 'denominational' rather than 'territorial'; Hindus and Muslims stood for 'a different outlook on life, different mode of living, different temperament and necessarily different politics'.[22] Whatever Muslims may share with their Hindu countrymen, they shared significantly more with other Muslims, a fact that any system of elective representation needed to respect. The Aga Khan, the influential leader of India's Shia Ismailis, also argued that differences between Hindus and Muslims were not just religious but also 'historical and social, racial and physical', and that the 'political order' needed to reflect 'the wide differences which separate Hindus and Mussulmans at the present time'.[23] In making his case for separate electorates, Sayyid Ali Imam, the eminent Bihari barrister leading the League's negotiations with the Government of India, and the League's president in 1908, went as far as to declare that Hindu and Muslim 'communities' had 'nothing in common in their traditional, religious, social and political conceptions'.[24] The history of India, he argued, including Akbar's experiment in 'unification', had shown that differences in religious and political beliefs of both communities were too strong to be reconciled.[25] The Muslim League objected vehemently to the 'promiscuous system' of mixed electoral colleges and insisted on a 'purely denominational system of representation' (separate electorates) 'from the lowest rung . . . to the top' to guarantee the 'true representation' of Muslims.[26]

As Farzana Shaikh argues, this insistence on separate electorates affirmed that the political interests of Muslims could only be determined through a consensus arrived at exclusively by Muslims.[27] This assertion, that the true political interests of Muslims could not meaningfully be determined by a political consensus arrived at by Hindus and Muslims together, negated (not completely but) to a substantial extent the notion of their constituting a common political society.[28] In demanding separate electorates, the Muslim League leadership echoed the late Sir Syed in rejecting the idea epitomized by the Congress that India was a country inhabited by *only* a single, supreme Indian nation whose members had common political interests *overriding* those they shared with their co-religionists. Instead, it asserted the presence, and primary importance, of distinct Hindu and Muslim political 'communities' or 'nationalities'—which could nevertheless cooperate politically in the legislative councils of the British Empire on the commonalities they did share. Interestingly, in doing so, the League, to some extent, both mirrored Lajpat Rai's intellectual position of 1901 and confirmed the very reason he had given for assuming it. Rai had then publicly rejected the Congress's idea of an Indian nation as a false, futile, even fantastical idea, refusing to even attempt to realize such a reality as long as 'Muslims' remained aloof from 'Hindus'. He had instead urged that the separate Hindu and Muslim (and Christian) religious nationalities strengthen themselves as a necessary precondition for them to unite in the future into a common Indian nation. Now, eight years later in 1909, the Muslim League demanded that the electoral system institutionalize this very political vision through separate electorates. Lajpat Rai, on the other hand, not only virulently opposed this idea but, in doing so, returned to the idea of nationhood he started out with in 1888.

In February 1909, Lord Morley accepted separate electorates by drawing a parallel with Catholics and Protestants in Britain and Ireland:

The Mohammedans protested that Hindus would elect a pro-Hindu [Muslim] . . . just as I suppose in a mixed college of 75 Catholics and 25 Protestants voting together, the Protestants might suspect that the Catholics voting for the Protestant would choose what is called a Romanticising Protestant, and as little of a Protestant, as they could find. Suppose the other way, in [Catholic-majority] Ireland there is an expression, a 'shoneen' [a pejorative term connoting an Irish person prone to Anglophile snobbery]– that is to say a Catholic who, though a Catholic, is too friendly with English Conservatism and other influences which the [Irish] Nationalists dislike. And it might be said, if there were 75 Protestants against 25 Catholics, that the Protestants when giving a vote in the way of Catholic representation, would return 'shoneens'.[29]

Morley emphasized that the world was not without a precedent for the idea of a 'separate register'. In Cyprus, the British had established a Legislative Council in 1882 to which Greek/Christian and Turkish/Muslim members were elected on the basis of separate electoral lists. In 1905, in Bohemia in the Habsburg Empire, Germans and Czechs were granted separate voting rolls such that they voted separately for their own candidates even while living in the same political districts.[30] Lord Morley embraced the League's demand that the same mechanism be applied to India.

Importantly, Morley also accepted the second demand of the Muslim League: 'weightage' (i.e., 'weighted' representation of a community in excess of its numerical proportion in British India's population).[31] The Muslim leadership had noted rightly that Indian Muslims were 'a minority . . . in itself more numerous than the entire population of any first-class European power, except Russia'. British India was indeed home to the world's largest Muslim population, totalling sixty-two million, more than the populations of Great Britain, France or Germany. It was argued that the present system of elective representation was unjust as it did not capture and reflect this numerical strength. Muslim Leaguers asserted that the present shares of political representation were based on unfairly inflated Hindu population figures, arrived at through the inclusion of the population of parts of Burma and of 'uncivilised portions . . . [including] Animists and other minor religions'.[32] Yet, the League leadership further protested that if the people of India were being granted their representatives 'in the State', the Muslim numbers in proportion to the total population of India were, in any case, an inadequate basis for determining Muslim share in political representation.[33] Muslim political representation must also be 'commensurate . . . with their political importance'.[34] In estimating the latter, due weight had to be given to 'the position they had occupied in India a little more than a hundred years ago, of which the traditions have naturally not faded from their minds'. Additionally, the Muslim community's contribution to 'the defence of the Empire' also had to be taken into account.[35] Interestingly, this was not unlike the arguments about the history of

Sikh political rule and services to the empire which would be advanced by Sikh leaders a decade later as they demanded separate and weighted representation.[36] Some Muslim Leaguers reminded the government of the vital importance of the loyalty of the Muslim community to the 'prestige and stability' of British rule.[37] Others defined the Indian Muslim community's unique political importance in terms of its link to the history of the wider Pan-Islamic world stretching from Southeast Asia to the Middle East.[38] These arguments were put forward strongly against Morley's 1908 scheme which had proposed, along with mixed electoral colleges, reserved seats for Muslims according to their numerical proportion in the population.

The Muslim League saw itself as reluctantly adjusting to an already unfolding political reality and advised that 'representative institutions of the European type' be adopted in India with caution.[39] While Sir Syed had used the historical rule of Muslims to completely reject the elective system where an arbitrary numerical criterion would determine access to political representation, the Muslim League advanced the same argument to insist that numbers *alone* should not determine political representation. Like Sir Syed, the 'high-born' leaders of the League were unmoved by even the very restricted notion of *popular, democratic self-government* expressed by the middle-class Congress elite in the imperial context. Though the League rejected the notion of a single Indian nation in the modern nationalist–political sense (i.e., a political community aspiring to common statehood), it did not fully conceive of Muslims as a 'nation' in a modern nationalist–political sense either. Instead of holding that the Muslim 'nation' must have some limited voice in their government (limited Muslim national self-government), the League's 'high-born' leadership wanted assured access to the extremely limited political opportunities opened up in the Empire through the new elective system.

Much like Sir Syed, the League's position partly also resulted from fear of the consequences, for Muslims, of adopting the numerical criteria which underlay elective representation. The demand for weightage, which resisted a democratic–political system based on numbers alone, was its innovative way of offsetting

the minority status that would accrue to Muslims in a system of
limited self-government within the Empire and then with the
unfolding of popular or democratic self-government. While
the political realities of colonial India were nowhere close to
complete democratic self-government, the Muslim League, even
under the still massively restricted property-based franchise, could
anticipate its consequences for Muslims, believed to be lagging
behind Hindus in economic and educational terms.[40] Arising
out of similar apprehensions about prospective marginalization,
demands for weightage would become more common in colonial-
era Indian politics over time. As noted, it was demanded by
Sikh leaders a decade later.[41] Two decades later, B.R. Ambedkar
(1891–1956) would demand weightage for 'Depressed Classes',
dismissing the notion of minority representation according to
population as merely something 'intended to provide political fun'
since it was ineffective in actually preventing the majority from
blocking the minority's efforts to safeguard or improve its position.[42]
Weightage would also be demanded by Anglo–Indians.

It was partly the same fear of minoritization that prompted the
League to resist the notion that only a single Indian nation existed in
India. The single-nation logic would bring Hindus and Muslims into
the majority–minority framework, the very outcome that the League
wished to offset. It therefore insisted that Hindus and Muslims
constituted two (sometimes overlapping but generally) radically
distinct political 'communities'/'nations', an idea embodied in the
demand for separate electorates. To reiterate, this early version of the
two-nation theory was completely detached from any conception
of separate statehood (the Muslim 'nationality' was not imagined as
finding true political expression in a state of its own). Indeed, the
Muslim League's leaders—not unlike many Hindu political figures
of the time—still took for granted the Empire's existence. But clearly,
this desire to halt the minoritization and marginalization of Muslims
effectively explains not only the League's resistance to the demand
for self-government for an 'Indian nation' but also its declaration of
loyalty to the Empire.

The demand for separate electorates embodied the repudiation of the political supremacy of an 'Indian nation' and the contrary insistence on Hindus and Muslims primarily constituting separate political 'nationalities'. The demand for weightage was accompanied by supremacist arguments about the historical and political importance of Muslims, being deployed to reject the numerical criteria of Western liberal democracies, and resist the status of a political minority. These positions did not reflect an intrinsic incompatibility between India's Muslims, on the one hand, and Indian nationalism and liberal democracy, on the other. Several Muslims, including Abul Kalam Azad, Dr Sayyid Mahmud and Mohammad Ali Jinnah,[43] opposed these demands and many of the arguments that underpinned them.[44] For some of the prominent Muslims who did articulate the aforementioned arguments, these were at least partly also attempts to circumvent a system of representation which, given their scattered population distribution, often resulted in Muslim representation far below their numerical strength.[45] For many, these may have also constituted part of an early, novel attempt to craft for India the beginnings of what would today be called a *consociational* democracy.

Such a system rejects dominant liberal assumptions of non-descriptive political representation (i.e., that political representatives can and should act for different individual or group interests) and instead affirms descriptive representation (i.e., that political representatives can and should act only for their own respective identity-based groups). It also refuses to leave the fate of political representation of various identity-based groups up to the quantitative aggregation of individual political preferences or votes (as in the case of dominant conceptions of liberal democracy). Instead, consociational democracies seek to guarantee adequate political representation to significant identity-based groups, often in disregard of strict considerations of their numerical strength. Here, a kind of power-sharing agreement is imagined between autonomous groups ('communities' or 'nationalities') as a necessary path towards political coexistence and cooperation.[46] This sort of political arrangement had been attempted in Canada in the nineteenth century, and would be adopted in the Netherlands from the next decade.[47] Several decades after Muslim Leaguers first began toying with the idea of a similar political system for India, in the second half of the twentieth century, consociational democracies would be established in Switzerland, Austria, Belgium, Lebanon, Cyprus, South Africa, Malaysia, Bosnia and Herzegovina, and Northern Ireland.[48] While in particular forms and in particular countries, such political arrangements would be tremendously successful in promoting inclusion, equality, justice and peaceful cooperation between diverse groups, in other forms and contexts they would be less successful. Here, they would come to reify and sharpen identity-based cleavages instead of softening[49] them, reduce incentives for cross-communal cooperation, freeze and institutionalize polarization, and lock individuals into particular identity-groups while constraining their political choices.[50] Way back in 1909, some mainstream Hindu politicians were inadequately sensitive to the fears that drove the Muslim League's demands. But the wariness of a number of them towards these demands was guided by similar concerns about the sharpening and solidification of cleavages.

On 21 February 1909, a month after the London branch of the Muslim League led a deputation to Morley to protest against his November 1908 scheme of mixed colleges,[51] Lajpat Rai first intervened in the controversy over the League's demands. He did so by writing, from England itself, an article for *The Mahratta*, a weekly once edited by Tilak who, now languishing in prison, could not participate in these debates.[52] Rai began his attack on separate electorates in the following manner:

> It is relevant to inquire on how many occasions within the last 47 years or so, ever since the Indian Councils Act of 1861 came into force, the Legislative Councils of India had to deal with questions exclusively or specially affecting the Muslims of India as distinguished from their non-Muslim countrymen. It might also be important to know how many times, if at all, there was a

conflict of opinion between Hindu and Mahomedan members of these Councils. It is not perhaps so well known, as it ought to be in this country, that in all matters of inheritance, marriage, divorce etc. Hindus are governed by the Hindu law and Mahomedans by the Mahomedan law. The Legislative Councils are not supposed to meddle with or modify the provisions of any of these laws. Besides, even independently of this, there is little or no chance of any measure coming before the councils by which the interests of one religious community may be more injuriously affected than those of the other.[53]

Interestingly, like the Muslim League, Lajpat Rai continued to affirm a substantial degree of separateness between Hindu and Muslim 'communities': Hindus and Muslims had exclusive or special interests as members of their respective 'communities', which they shared only with their co-religionists and not with each other. But, for him, these additional interests were already safeguarded through separate personal laws. Apart from these special community-based interests protected by law, the political interests of Hindus and Muslims were not necessarily opposed to or distinct from each other. He denied the existence of a large and significant number of political questions 'exclusively or specially affecting the Muslims'. So, unlike the League, he believed that Hindus and Muslims could share many, substantially overlapping political interests, and that, given that separate personal laws already protected the exclusive interests of Hindus and Muslims, separate electorates were not required for this purpose.

Elsewhere, Lajpat Rai explicitly repudiated the Aga Khan, who led the League's campaign for separate electorates, arguing that a 'denominational electorate' and the extension of 'denominational representation' to the lowest levels would scatter 'seeds of discord and disunion' far and wide.[54] He remarked that given the Aga Khan's own cherished ideal of uniting Hindus and Muslims into one nationality, the modus operandi he had chosen to realize this union was counterproductive. In an interview to *The Times* in February, the

Aga Khan had indeed stated that he looked forward to the ideal of 'an eventually united people of one nationality, among whom religious differences, now so acute, will have minor significance in social and political life, as they have, for instance, in the United States, between Christians and Jews'.[55] But as Lajpat Rai pointed out, he also demanded separate electorates. This was not a contradiction for the Aga. While cherishing 'the ideal of a united people in India', he maintained that the new political order must reflect the wide differences between Hindus and Muslims. For him, British rule had organically brought about a measure of 'unifying change'; this process, a 'work of time', was not to be forced by the 'artificial stimulus' of political arrangements which would only exacerbate divisions. 'An Act of Parliament', he had stated, 'cannot weld into one, by electoral machinery, two nationalities so distinct as the Hindus and Mohammedans'. For Lajpat Rai, it was the very community-based political arrangement of separate electorates that politically divided Muslims from Hindus, and made disunity a foregone conclusion. To realize 'national political purposes', the 'Hindu politician' had to 'obliterate all religious distinctions' and therefore oppose separate electorates.[56]

For Lajpat Rai, territorially based mixed electorates allowed Hindus and Muslims to see themselves as members of not permanently distinct political communities but a single common political community. Separate electorates presupposed that individual political actors were perpetually and exclusively members of their respective 'communities'. Mixed electorates, on the other hand, allowed Hindu and Muslim political representatives, chosen together by both Hindus and Muslims, to be responsible to a variety of individual or group interests, including the interests of both 'communities'. Mixed electorates were a crucial vehicle for Hindus and Muslims to act as members of a higher common Indian political nation. This was certainly an interesting position assumed by a man who, in 1901, had rejected the idea of Indian nationality in the immediate term, arguing that Hindus and Muslims were different 'religious nationalities'. His call then for an all-India Hindu 'semi-political' congress to serve the Hindu nationality seemed to have conceded that these nationalities possessed at least *some* distinct political interests. In a context where the Empire had begun to be challenged by the incipient idea of the 'nation' in its nationalist–political sense but was also still very much a political reality, Lajpat Rai used the term 'Hindu nationality' variously, sometimes to connote simply a cultural community, but sometimes also to signify a 'semi-political' community. Yet, this 'Hindu nation', even when imagined in a political sense, was never conceived of in the full nationalist–political sense. And interestingly, when, in 1909, he was again compelled to seriously conceptualize nationhood in the unambiguously statist context of political representation and self-government, he returned to his original 1888 conception: that for political purposes Hindus and Muslims constituted one single Indian nation.

In implicitly disregarding the Muslim League's insistence on the existence of separate political communities/nationalities, he somewhat concurred with Hindu Congressmen like Madan Mohan Malaviya, president of the 1909 session at Lahore, who espoused a purist vision of a single Indian national political community.[57] Malaviya stressed that the Congress's aim was to 'eradicate' all possible race-related, creed-related and provincial 'prejudice' to consolidate a sentiment of nationality among all Indian people.[58] He insinuated that Muslims were putting their 'community' over the 'nation', and wholeheartedly urged them to realize that since the lot of Hindus and Muslims had been 'cast together in this country', they could not build a common (Indian) national life separately.[59] Yet, perhaps because of his own previous scepticism about it, Lajpat Rai adhered to a less purist conception of the Indian nation. While his expressed desire to 'obliterate religious distinctions for national political purposes' seems to indicate a relatively less diversity-sensitive, homogenizing Indian nationalism, his explicit affirmation of separate, communally bifurcated personal laws suggests a more nuanced Indian nationalism which respected a significant degree of religio-cultural difference and autonomy, and comfortably accepted its legal institutionalization.

At the same time, Rai differed from other Congressmen like Gokhale, to whom he had grown close. Gokhale publicly expressed his discomfort with what he thought was the League's treatment of Hindus and Muslims as two 'watertight' compartments. He proposed that even if separate electorates were accepted, elections through mixed electorates must be part of the political system at some level to provide an opportunity for 'composite action by all communities' as members of one political nation. Yet, in conceding separate electorates Gokhale was quickly willing to also consider the League's logic that respecting a large measure of political distinctness between Hindus and Muslims could—by promoting greater representation, equality and inclusion—itself be a step towards the eventual creation of a united Indian nation.[60]

Lajpat Rai stated that the goal of the Hindu politician was 'an actual democratic form of government, with no distinction of Hindu, Mahomedan, Parsi, and the rest', and added that 'nothing can be more disastrous to the success of representative institutions than their constitution on a denominational basis'.[61] Separate electorates then were, to him, disastrous for the incipient democratic political institutions being introduced in India. Conversely, for him, the absence of religious distinctions in politics was absolutely necessary for democratic self-government. Although he did not elaborate, he may have been animated by the belief that democratic government— rule by 'the people' through election—must ensure that the political interests of the 'people' were not permanently bifurcated on community lines, such that they lacked the freedom to choose who among 'the people' represented them on a particular issue. To him, democratic rule by 'the people' would necessarily allow Hindu and Muslim members of 'the people' to unhinge their political interests from their 'communities', shift and share them, and choose their representatives freely. This freedom to choose representatives from across communities would represent real electoral choice and therefore actual democratic self-rule.

Rai's invocation of 'actual democracy', as a form of government devoid of any religious community-based political distinctions, drew on the dominant conception of liberal democracy, one that formally took individuals, rather than groups, as its basic political unit, and conceived of political equality as the determination of political representation through an aggregation of equally weighted votes (one-man–one-vote) cast in territorial (rather than communal) electorates.[62] While particular forms of community-based representation can clash with democracy, as we saw, democratic principles can be compatible with particular political arrangements that guarantee group- or community-based forms of representation. Nevertheless, the particular liberal–individualist conception of democracy that Lajpat Rai espoused construed the institutionalization of community-based political representation, particularly through separate electorates, as detracting from democratic principles.[63] As in his engagement with Sir Syed, Rai's membership of the emergent Hindu middle class, and a 'community' which could function as a numerical majority, played an important part in his articulation of the concept of one 'Indian nation' and a liberal–individualist (as opposed to community-based) conception of democratic representation.

Lajpat Rai also responded to the Muslim demand for weightage. The upper-caste Muslim League had backed this demand by glossing over caste among Muslims and portraying them as a monolithic 'community' descended from a ruling race. Lajpat Rai punctured the weightage claim by exposing caste distinctions among Muslims:

> Hindu converts to Islam generally kept their caste intact, and are to this day bound by their caste rules, somewhat modified by the change of their religion; and even the foreign Muslims, who came from Arabia, Persia, or Afghanistan, are still tenacious of their caste distinctions . . . Arguments cannot convince me, in the face of facts to the contrary, that a high-caste Mahomedan will sit on the same *dastarkhan* [tablecloth], eat from the same plate, or smoke the same *huqqa* with a Mahomedan *Chura* or *Mossalli* [low caste Muslims] . . . there are many Mahomedan castes of which the members do not generally marry out of the

caste . . . The fact remains that the high-caste Mohamedans who
are advancing an extraordinary claim for larger representation
in the Legislative Councils are few in comparison to the bulk of
the Mahomedan community in whose name they speak. However
the argument drawn from the political and historical importance
of the Mahomedans in Indian history may apply to the Syeds,
Moguls, Pathans, Lodhis, Tuglaks, and Gauris, it cannot apply
to those castes which have never had political power in India,
or elsewhere.[64]

Indeed, as medieval historian Raziuddin Aquil points out, the vast
majority of Muslims in medieval India were indigenous converts
from lower caste and tribal groups, without access to political power.
The medieval period had therefore been a glorious golden age for
a minority of Muslim immigrants and their Hindu collaborators,
not for the majority of Indian Muslims—a fact which incidentally
challenges the clear-cut and misleading Muslim domination vs
Hindu subjugation binary through which India's medieval history is
often misunderstood.[65]

By highlighting the low-caste majority among India's Muslims,
with its supposed lack of ruling lineage, Lajpat Rai rebutted a central
premise of the League's demand for weightage. Interestingly, rather
than making a democratic argument about equality, Rai refuted the
claim for Muslim weightage by deploying and affirming the League's
hierarchical caste logic. He further opposed the notion that Muslims
be granted weightage on grounds of their loyalty and military
service.[66] He found it incredulous that 'special representation' could
be granted as a 'reward' for this, and asked why weightage should not
then be extended to the Sikhs, Gurkhas, Rajputs and Jats, who had
also served in 'military expeditions on the North-West Frontier, in
Egypt, China and Abyssinia'. Lajpat Rai also attempted to highlight
what he thought was the arbitrariness of this criteria demanded by
the League:

    . . . it has been admitted that even in the Punjab the Sikhs and
    Hindus are better educated and more enterprising, and that they

are 'more affluent' than their Mahomedan countrymen. They are better agriculturalists, and as good, if not better, soldiers. But under Lord Morley's scheme the Mahomedans of Punjab will have a larger number of seats on the Legislative Council of that Province than their Hindu and Sikh countrymen, because they are numerically in a majority.[67]

Stressing that the *numerical* criterion was the only legitimate criterion for determining the extent of political representation, he posed the following question: 'Does the All India Muslim League seriously think that backwardness in education, want of organization and want of enterprise are substantial grounds for claiming a larger representation than their *numbers* entitle them to?'[68] Lajpat Rai refused to concede arguments for 'weighted' Muslim representation based on what he considered were arbitrary criteria—their alleged historical and political importance, loyalty to the Empire or contemporary educational 'backwardness'. Such criticism of the concept of Muslim weightage on the assumption that the numerical criterion was the legitimate basis for political representation was also evident in the language of Gokhale[69] and Malaviya,[70] and reflected the general stance of many Hindu Congressmen. Malaviya was unable to comprehend why Muslims were politically more important than other 'communities' in India, and why they must be granted representation on this basis.[71] Gokhale admitted that Hindus were at an advantage vis-à-vis Muslims in numbers, education and wealth but, much like Lajpat Rai, refused to see these as sufficient grounds for Muslim weightage. He focused on refuting the League's reasoning based on Muslim historical rule, loyalty and the Indian Muslim link to a global community. He refuted the first reason by emphasizing Hindu rule in India for centuries before Muslims, and the second by pointing to the emergence of Muslim critics of the British government (revealing his awareness of the younger generation of Muslim leaders who would soon move closer to the Congress).[72] He dismissed the third reason adduced by the League by arguing that Indian Christians and Buddhists too possessed links with global communities. Even Congressmen like Gokhale, who were sympathetic to the League's position, aligned with Lajpat Rai in dismissing these criteria as irrelevant to the question of political representation. By tying political representation to numbers, these Hindus, along with Lajpat Rai, were affirming the liberal–individualist democratic logic emerging within the Empire.

Yet, Lajpat Rai insisted that the Hindu politician 'does not seek a Hindu majority crushing Mahomedan or other minorities'.[73] In a testimony to his sincere commitment to the numerical criterion, he counted Muslims as one-fourth of the population and was willing to countenance, just as in 1889, a representative system in which this 'minority' obtained 'proportionate representation'.[74] His support for Morley's 1908 scheme that guaranteed this showed his willingness to grant reservations for the Muslim 'minority' according to their demographic strength.[75] Contrary to his own expressed desire to 'obliterate' all religious distinctions in politics, Rai was willing to countenance the institutionalization of religious differences not only through separate laws, but also through guaranteed community-based political representation via the mechanism of reservations. Clearly, even as Rai opposed the League's demands for separate electorates and weightage, his opposition did not amount to an integrationist, diversity-insensitive Indian nationalism. Instead, it was one that still entailed a significant measure of respect for the notion of Muslims as a distinct political community, as long as it functioned within a framework of mixed (or joint) electorates and, by implication, took Indian nationhood to be the primary and overriding political identity. Despite his insistence that true democracy must be devoid of all religious-based political distinctions, he was ultimately willing to depart from a strictly liberal–individualist conception of democracy towards one that accommodated community-based political representation, so long as the latter did not take the form of separate electorates and, by implication, negate what he and many others globally considered the foundations of liberal democracy.

9

Hindu Nationalism and Caste Radicalism

After his return from England in the spring of 1909, Lajpat Rai once again felt alienated from the moderates-dominated Congress. The grant of separate electorates and weightage to Muslims had caused significant resentment among the Hindus of Punjab, Lajpat Rai's province. Hindus were calculated as a minority of roughly 40 per cent in Punjab, and urban, educated Hindus felt particularly resentful as these new political devices challenged their political preponderance in urban areas.[1] At its December session, the Congress would express disapproval of religion-based electorates and what it believed was the grant of excessive representation to Muslims, and also specifically of their adverse impact on Hindu minority representation in Punjab.[2] Still, a feeling was emerging among many Punjabi Hindus that the Congress was failing to speak for their interests, and that they needed to organize themselves separately.[3] This is possibly because of Gokhale's increasing willingness to accept separate electorates as a means to allay the Muslim League's fears and create what he thought were conditions for stronger Indian national unity.[4] In line with the prejudicial colonial view of Indian society, the 1909 'Morley–Minto reforms' emphasized religion as the primary political identity in defiance of suggestions by a variety of Punjabis of all religions in

favour of class and occupational identities. As historian Neeti Nair
has shown, they had the effect of deflecting political energies from
the anti-colonial politics seen in the 1907 rural movement in Punjab
towards community-based politics.[5] Lajpat Rai's changing political
thought reflected this shift.

In July 1909, Lajpat Rai urged the Congress not to hold its
forthcoming session in Lahore as planned, to give Punjabi Hindus
time to come to terms with their 'defeat'. Despite having himself
spoken of an Indian nation earlier that year, when he argued against
separate electorates, he now warned that, at this juncture, the
Congress's claim to speak for both Hindus and Muslims as constituents
of one Indian nation would aggravate Hindu–Muslim tension in
Punjab; it was repudiated by Punjabi Hindus and questioned by the
bulk of Muslims.[6] As Madan Mohan Malaviya presided over the
1909 Lahore Congress, Lajpat Rai stayed away, choosing instead to
participate in the first Hindu Conference of the Punjab Hindu Sabha,
an organization floated by Lala Lal Chand, a College Party Arya
Samajist, in the wake of the Reforms to specifically safeguard Hindu
interests. In his speech at the conference, Lajpat Rai once again
returned to the idea of a 'Hindu nation', arguing that the sense in
which the Congress used the term 'nation' was not its only meaning:

> It may be that the Hindus, by themselves, cannot form themselves
> into a nation in the modern sense of the term, but that is only a
> play on words. Modern nations are political units. A political unit
> ordinarily includes all the peoples who live under one common
> system and form a state. The word nation and state when thus
> considered are practically interchangeable phrases. That is the
> sense in which the expression is used in connection with the
> proceedings of the 'Indian National Congress'. That is, no doubt,
> one use of the word and the one which is commonly adopted
> in modern political literature. But that is not the only sense
> in which it is or can be used. In fact the German word 'Nation'
> did not necessarily signify a political nation or a state. In that
> language it connoted what is generally conveyed by the English

expression 'people', implying a community possessing a certain type of civilisation and culture. Using it in that sense there can be no doubt that Hindus are a nation in themselves because they represent a type of civilisation all their own.[7]

Like Savarkar in the 1920s and RSS chief M.S. Golwalkar in the 1930s, Lajpat Rai in 1909 was influenced by Swiss jurist Johann Kaspar Bluntschli, an exponent of German ethnic nationalism.[8] Lajpat Rai quoted Bluntschli's *The Theory of the State* (1875–76) to argue that a 'people'/nation came into being not through voluntary agreement or social contract but through a 'slow psychological process' in which 'a mass of men' developed 'a type of life and society which differentiated them from others and became the fixed inheritance of their race'.[9] Nations formed over time as their distinctive 'accumulated culture' was passed down from one generation to another and became 'hereditary'. Lajpat Rai wished to show that neither community of religion nor language were necessary features of nations, but that 'the essence of a people lies in its culture'.[10] The Hindu people constituted a nation because they shared a common 'Hindu culture', which he left largely undefined except stating that it was easily distinguishable from 'Semitic and other non-Aryan cultures' and European culture (although he did identify similarities between Aryan Hindu culture and European culture, which was held in high esteem in the colonial context).[11] In distinguishing 'Aryan' from 'Semitic' cultures, Lajpat Rai drew on European thinkers. But while Max Muller and the German philosopher Friedrich Nietzsche (1844–1900) conceived this distinction in linguistic or racial terms[12]—i.e., in terms of Aryan vs Semitic linguistic families or Aryan vs Semitic races—Lajpat Rai made 'culture' the basis of classification.

Like many North Indian upper-caste Hindus, Lajpat Rai seemed unaware that his trope of Aryan Hindu culture may alienate south Indians and lower-caste Hindus who saw themselves as descendants of non-Aryan Dravidians. Nevertheless, he clutched onto non-European Aryanism alongside non-Semitism as he attempted to define 'Hindu culture'. Rai dismissed notions of 'racial superiority' and 'racial purity'[13] while simultaneously stressing the common racial origin of Hindus.[14] To bolster his claim about the existence of a Hindu nation, he marshalled the supposedly common Aryan racial origin of Hindus. But, for him, it was still 'culture' rather than racial origin that constituted a nation's essence. Racial terms—Semitic, non-Aryan—surfaced as Lajpat Rai attempted to distinguish Hindu 'religion' from Hindu 'culture', and groped for something against which to define this nebulous 'Hindu culture' he sought to make the defining essence of the Hindu nation. But for him, ultimately, the 'spirit of Hindu culture which gives us the right to call ourselves a people' was 'reflected in our literature, especially in our epic poetry' and 'our festivals and social practices'.[15] Rather than race, a culturalized Hinduism, recast as 'Hindu culture', and de-linked from its religious significance, emerged as the core of the Hindu nation.

Having fleetingly used the category of 'culture' in the 1890s in its newly modern and anthropological sense (signifying a 'way of life' rather than collective cultivation), Rai now explicitly and firmly made it the centrepiece of his definition of the Hindu nation. As we saw in previous chapters, Lajpat Rai had already moved quite far from his initial Arya Samaj-inflected formulation of Hinduism to increasingly capacious definitions which accepted internal diversity and included larger numbers. Now, in the wake of the British concession of separate electorates and Muslim weightage, Lajpat Rai realized that grounding Hindu nationhood in a common religious basis rooted in the Vedas would:

> . . . necessarily exclude those who do not subscribe to the scriptural authority of the Vedas, such as our friends of the Brahmo Samaj, the Jains and some Sikhs. But so far as I understand the aim of the leaders of the present Hindu movement, such exclusion is far from their desire. I presume that they wish to include everyone who calls himself a Hindu within the folds of their movement . . . the Hindu movement inaugurated by the organisers of this Conference does not contemplate the exclusion of anyone who is prepared to sail under the Hindu flag . . .[16]

It was to provide his hitherto most catholic definition of the Hindu nation that Lajpat Rai based it in 'Hindu culture':

> For the bulk of our people the problem is easily solved by their taking their stand on the Vedas and making them the rallying point of all their efforts after unity and reform. For others who cannot accept the authority of the Vedas as scriptures binding on them, it is quite sufficient if they were to studiously retain, and laboriously maintain, the distinguishing features of Hindu culture in their thought and life.[17]

By making Hindu culture its centrepiece, Lajpat Rai's 'Hindu nation' now actively included religious groups like the Sikhs, Jains and Buddhists. This was unlike Tilak whose definition of the Hindu nation excluded them.[18] A secularized notion of 'Hindu culture' now assertively superseded even that surface-level marker of Hindu religion that had till now remained in his definition of the Hindu nation: the Vedas. The resolute substitution of Hindu 'religion' with secular 'Hindu culture' as the core of his definition of the Hindu nation constituted Lajpat Rai's hitherto most strident claim on the notion of a Hindu majority. As mentioned, it facilitated the inclusion of Sikhs, Jains and Buddhists into this catholic 'Hindu nation' but kept out India's Muslims and Christians, who were assumed to partake not in Hindu culture but Muslim and Christian cultures. Here, Rai's Hindu nationalism converged with the Hindu nationalism Savarkar would elaborate roughly fifteen years later in his 1923 *Hindutva* tract. In 1909, Savarkar was in fact smuggling guns and bomb manuals to India, apparently even manufacturing bombs himself to realize his goal of anti-colonial insurrectionary violence.[19] That year also saw the publication of his *Indian War of Independence* which articulated the idea of an 'Indian nation' based on a natural Hindu–Muslim alliance.[20] But in *Hindutva*, he would de-emphasize religious belief and make 'Hindu culture' an indispensable 'essential' of his Hindutva nation to circumvent the problem of internal religious diversity among Hindus and produce a broad, catholic definition of Hindu nation which excluded Muslims and Christians.[21]

Prominent scholars of Hindu nationalism have read Rai's 1909 speech at the Provincial Hindu Conference as an expression of 'Hindu nationalism'.[22] Importantly, they have interpreted it as marking the 'birth' of Hindu nationalist ideology, holding that Rai's Hindu nationalism was the seed of Hindutva, representing only an early embryonic form of the latter, and bound to grow into it over time.[23] The straightforward labelling of Rai's nationalist thought in 1909 as 'Hindu nationalism' and its assessment as the early, nascent form of Hindutva presumes that Rai's nationalism is not significantly different from later Hindutva. 'Hindu nationalism' was indeed the title of Lajpat Rai's speech as it was published in the *Punjabee*. The above-mentioned convergence of Lajpat Rai's Hindu nationalism with Savarkarite Hindutva also seems to prove correct the interpretation of these scholars. Yet, despite its seeming affinity with the Hindutva ideology of later years, the Hindu cultural nationalism espoused by Lajpat Rai in 1909 remained distinct in significant ways.

As we have seen, Savarkar's Hindutva would demand that Indian Muslims abandon their religion and sympathy for any holy places outside Indian territory to assimilate into the Hindu cultural nation. Rai's self-proclaimed 'Hindu nationalism' in 1909 did not demand that Muslims abandon their religion and cultures and assimilate into Hindu culture. Just as in 1902, it imagined a Muslim 'religious nationality' as robustly existing alongside the Hindu nation. Lajpat Rai believed this Muslim nation was justified in expressing its religiosity (presumably including its reverence for extraterritorial holy places), and wished to grant it a 'free hand to strengthen' itself.[24] Rather than demanding religious abandonment and cultural assimilation, Lajpat Rai's Hindu nationalism accepted India's religio–cultural diversity. Unlike Savarkar's future Hindutva nationalism, Rai also did not labour to portray Hinduism and Hindu culture as native to India, and Islam/Muslim culture and Christianity/Christian culture as foreign to it. Unlike it, he did not attempt to establish the supreme claim of Hindus, and their religion and culture, over the land of India. [25] This involved a fuller acceptance of India's religio–cultural diversity.

As Savarkarite Hindutva would, Rai's Hindu nationalism saw Hindus and Muslims as separated by radical religious and cultural differences such that, for him, they even formed different 'nationalities'. The Hindu–Muslim political relationship was also still imagined as being marked by competition, rivalry, friction and probably even acrimony. Rai seemed to believe that recent developments had proved right the view he had articulated in 1901–02.[26] The upper-caste spokespersons of the Muslim community repudiated a union with Hindus, closed their ranks in the Muslim League and thereby gained politically. Hindus, guided by the false idea that Hindus and Muslims already constituted a united Indian nation, had lost ground. Instead of repeating the 'parrot-cry' of Indian national unity, they needed to realize that the best way to realize a united Indian nation in the future was to first strengthen the Hindu nation:

> I am firmly convinced that it is impossible to build an Indian nation from above. The structure must be built from below. It is rather putting the cart before the horse in expecting Hindus and Mahomedans to unite and make a common cause, before bringing about a sense of unity and solidarity amongst the different sections of the Hindu community itself.[27]

But he took care to clarify that 'by aiming at unity and solidarity amongst the Hindus, we do not contemplate a blow at Indian unity.'[28] In 1901–02, Lajpat Rai had rejected the present existence of an Indian nation, and had seen the unity of the Hindu 'nation' or 'community' as a necessary step towards realizing any future possibility of the formation of a united Indian nation with the Muslim and Christian 'religious nationality'. Now, in 1909, he explicitly and more positively declared: 'the political salvation of India must come out of a combination and union of all the communities into one national whole. The goal may be a distant one, but that decidedly is the goal.'[29] As compared to 1901–02, when he had even dismissed

the notion of an 'Indian nation' as fantastical, by 1909, Lajpat Rai
had clearly become more certain that the ultimate political end
'decidedly' was and 'must' be to forge an overarching *Indian* nation.
While he still prioritized the unity of the Hindu nation, he stressed
its compatibility with the notion of a broader 'Indian nation'. The
strengthening of the 'Hindu nation' was imagined as occurring
alongside efforts to similarly strengthen the Muslim nation, with both
seen as essential prerequisites for forging a future 'Indian nation'.[30]
Rai's imagination of the strengthening of the 'Hindu nation' as a
route towards the larger project of forging the 'Indian nation' was
unlike the Savarkarite vision in *Hindutva,* which would reject the
possibility of Hindus and Muslims coexisting in a common 'Indian
nation' with whatever religious and cultural differences existed
between them. The only possibility was for Muslims to adopt Hindu
culture and assimilate into India's only, or at least most supreme,
Hindutva nation.

In 1909, the forty-four-year-old Lajpat Rai articulated his most
robust cultural conception of the Hindu nation. Hindus were imagined
as 'nation' in what he considered the German sense of the term,
constituting a distinct 'people' with a distinct culture. The Hindus
were a distinct 'nation' and 'people', with these concepts signifying a
cultural community. This German-influenced cultural conception of
the 'Hindu nation' was certainly not apolitical. But even now, it was
not imagined in its full-fledged, modern nationalist–statist political
sense, embodying the belief that every 'nation' must politically express
itself in a self-governing state over a particular territory. Rai's 'Hindu
nation' was neither imagined as having superior claims over India's
territory, nor as deserving a self-governing state of its own over this
land. Lajpat Rai's politically charged cultural 'Hindu nation' existed
alongside a similarly conceived Muslim nation, and imagined their
future political union in a larger 'Indian nation'. It was this Indian
nation which was imagined in the modern nationalist–statist sense,
as possessing connotations of statehood (self-government). Thus,
whenever Rai used the term 'nation' in this modern, fully nationalist
sense, in relation to statehood—which he himself considered its

'modern', commonly accepted political sense—he continued to adhere to the ideal of an 'Indian' nation, including Hindus and non-Hindus.

The cultural commonalities that bound the 'Indian nation' together were not yet conceivable to Lajpat Rai, and were therefore left un-articulated. He thus did not express a cultural identity for his weakly imagined 'Indian nation'. Still, Rai's lack of demand for cultural assimilation and lack of assertion of superior claims for Hindu culture over India had meaning. Such a demand and assertion would have made hierarchy, supremacy and domination central to his nationalism. Their lack implied they were not. As Lajpat Rai had clarified in his intervention in the separate electorates controversy only months ago, he did 'not seek a Hindu majority crushing a Mahomedan or other minorities'.[31] His imagined 'Indian nation', which needed to be forged and was seen as deserving political expression in a future self-governing state, was predicated on a basic respect for India's pluralism.

In retaining the goal of forging a larger Indian nation, Lajpat Rai differed not just from the future Savarkar but from the Punjab Hindu Sabha leader, Lala Lal Chand, who rejected what he called the Congress's 'self-effacing' concept of a common 'Indian' nation, calling it an 'impossible ideal'.[32] He exhorted Hindus to form a separate nation, even urging the substitution of Congress committees by Hindu Sabhas, goading the Hindu nation to meet Muslims with an 'aggressive attitude'. This Hindu nationalism sought to *displace*, rather than serve, Indian nationalism.

Lajpat Rai's idea that Hindus and Muslims formed two separate 'nations' also diverged from that of some Hindu Congressmen like its current president, Malaviya. To be sure, albeit doing so from within the Congress, Malaviya articulated ideas very much like Lajpat Rai's. This can be seen, in Malaviya's justification, during his presidential address, of Punjab's Hindu Sabha movement in its protest against what he called the 'unjust preferential treatment' shown to Muslims, and his desire that it work according to the Congress's ideals of Indian nationalism. Yet, at this juncture,

Malaviya expressed consternation that the Hindu Sabha was urging Hindus to 'abandon the hope of building a common national life, and devote themselves to promote the interest of their own community as Mahomedans have tried to promote those of theirs'.[33] He implored the Hindu Sabha to safeguard Hindu interests without feelings of 'narrow sectarian jealousy', with the desire to win over their Muslim brothers, and without departing from the noble ideals and principles of the Congress. Malaviya, unlike Rai, continued to adhere to the Congress's view that Hindus and Muslims presently constituted one single Indian nation.

Gokhale, as its most prominent representative in India and Britain, continued to forcefully articulate the Congress's position on nationhood, firmly conceptualizing the diverse peoples living within British Indian territory, regardless of religious differences, as constituting a common Indian nation. Rather than defining this nation in terms of an ancient Hindu culture, Gokhale saw it as being forged from and enriched by diverse cultures.[34] Still, for him, belonging to this common overarching Indian culture was insufficient to create the Indian nation; what was required was individual political consciousness of belonging to and wanting to belong to an Indian nation, and a will to contribute to its present and future progress.[35] At the close of the first decade of the twentieth century, Gokhale carried out his politics—demanding an enquiry into excessive public expenditure by the British government, higher employment of Indians in the civil services, the introduction of universal, free and compulsory education, and self-government within the Empire— with the aim of realizing and strengthening this Indian nation.[36] As is clear, this notion of an Indian nation was articulated by the Congress in defiance of ideas about nationhood expressed by members of both the Muslim League and the Hindu Sabha, including Lajpat Rai. In fact, by 1909, Gokhale had pronounced the 'Hindu League' and Muslim League as anti-Muslim and anti-Hindu, respectively, apparently declaring both as anti-national.[37]

* * *

The 1909 reforms clearly added an urgency to Lajpat Rai's efforts to achieve Hindu national unity, evident in his insistence on a Hindu culture that transcended differences of religion and language. But now he also strove to achieve Hindu unity via the route of caste.[38] He noticed that the Muslim League's argument for weightage had been accompanied by references to the Hindu caste system; Muslim weightage was presented as a necessary corrective to the unjust inclusion of low castes in the category of 'Hindus' for purposes of representation, which greatly inflated Hindu numbers in comparison to Muslims. The weightage demand was made alongside suggestions that these 'uncivilized' classes be detached as a bloc from the category of Hindus.[39] Responding to the League's political language, Lajpat Rai wrote his first article on 'Depressed Classes' in mid-1909, and argued that neglecting these classes was 'politically unsound' as it had enabled Muslims to push for the exclusion of 'Untouchables'[40] from the category of 'Hindus' while counting the latter for purposes of representation, and facilitated the League's demand for weightage.[41] Henceforth till he left India in 1914 for what would turn out to be a five-year period, Lajpat Rai, under heavy surveillance by the British for suspected links to 'revolutionary' activity,[42] and disillusioned by the 'moderate' Congress, remained aloof from overt politics. He concentrated instead on strengthening the Hindu nation/community by tackling the problem of caste divisions within.

To be sure, even in the previous century, Lajpat Rai had approved of granting low castes the right to recite Vedic mantras and held that 'everyone had the right to seek guidance and gain knowledge from them'.[43] This denied Brahmins' privileged access to the Vedas, their role as intermediaries between the individual and God, and in turn the assumption upon which their role rested: their superiority by birth.[44] Although this disregard for the idea of differential access to the Vedas had reflected his openness towards the possibility of a more egalitarian[45] Hindu nation/community, Lajpat Rai had not dealt with the caste system within Hinduism in a serious, sustained manner. As we saw, in 1904, he even rationalized caste hierarchy in an attempt to prove that the Hindu shastras contained a national faith. His return to the issue of caste in 1909 was a departure in that it was the first time he seriously contemplated the issue in its own right and shifted towards a radically egalitarian notion of the Hindu nation/community.[46]

Lajpat Rai now more explicitly attacked 'the unquestioned authority of the mere Brahmin by birth'.[47] He argued that a child born to Brahmin parents had no inherent social superiority nor the right to preach religion.[48] A man's position as Brahmin was determined not by birth but by his knowledge of the Vedas. And since everyone had the right to read and interpret the Vedas directly for themselves,[49] everyone had an 'equal right to become Brahmins'. He further argued that the Vedas—'the original source of Hindu religion'—revealed that the ancient social organization of Hindus embodied an open, flexible caste system wherein individuals could rise according to 'merit' to the highest religious and social positions.[50] Non-Vedic textual traditions of Hinduism such as the Itihasas and the Puranas showed that the merits of an individual's action did not pass on to his descendants.[51] At times Lajpat Rai even asserted that any individual, irrespective of caste, could become a Brahmin by the force of his 'personal character', 'conduct and achievements'.[52] With moral conduct being a measure of merit, the latter was sometimes defined in religious terms. But Lajpat Rai often also defined 'merit' independently of any emphasis on the acquisition of divine Vedic knowledge or moral conduct, suggesting its conceptualization in largely secular terms. This allowed for greater caste mobility. By retaining the category of the Brahmin as well as the notion of becoming one by 'merit'—defined in religious or secular terms— Lajpat Rai appeared to legitimize some form of social hierarchy. But the principle of equal opportunity it entailed provided for greater mobility that undercut the notion of a rigid, hereditary hierarchy.

Lajpat Rai emphasized that the Laws of Manu defined Vratyas as Hindus who had lost their status by failing to perform certain religious rites.[53] The 'Depressed Classes' were vratyas whose ancestors had lost their original caste status precisely through such 'non-observance'. Rather than considering them inherently impure by birth or permanently outcaste due to the commission of a sin, such classes could be 'readmitted' simply by performing certain religious rites.[54] Lajpat Rai was soon asserting that apart from permitting upward mobility by 'merit', Hindu shastras also sanctioned the shuddhi[55] of the so-called untouchables by reinvesting them with the sacred thread, and that the shastras contained 'concrete evidence' of ancient Brahmins 'assimilating' non-Brahmins in this manner.[56] For him, because the sacred thread was an 'unmistakable symbol of purification', and the only visible marker that differentiated upper and lower caste Hindus, it was extremely effective in raising the latter's social status.[57] Indeed, as religious studies scholar C.S. Adcock argues, although the shuddhi of low castes has been viewed by scholars as constituting merely a nominal change in their status,[58] it could also entail a dissolution of low-caste status, bestowing them their rightful place in Hindu society.[59] In 1912, while in the United Provinces, 'the home of Hindu orthodoxy', Lajpat Rai challenged 'the pundits' to excommunicate him for his personal reclamation of 'a number of Doms, one of the lowest untouchable castes in the UP'.[60]

Lajpat Rai further argued that in ancient times, contemporary caste taboos did not exist: 'The Hindu Shastras are replete with such examples. It appears that in ancient times . . . whatever their vocation, it did not matter where they [the people] lived and what they ate, where they married and with whom they established relations. Nothing was done under compulsion. But now it is not so.'[61] He urged that these 'shackles' needed to be 'broken in theory and in practice'. Along with other high-caste Arya Samajists, he himself ate food cooked by Doms and drank water brought by them.[62] Even from the Manusmriti, which would be publicly burnt in 1927 by Ambedkar for its sanction of caste hierarchy and violence towards lower castes, Lajpat Rai gleaned evidence of the prevalence of inter-caste marriages: 'Manu takes special pains to fix the caste status of the offspring of mixed marriages . . . which conclusively establishes the prevalence of these marriages at the time of the compilation of the present Manu-Samhita.'[63] This disregard for the taboo on inter-caste marriage was significant considering the view of many

'Dalit' intellectuals (including Ambedkar) that the sexual regulation entailed in endogamy was the very essence of caste hierarchy.[64]

Finally, Lajpat Rai argued that it was because the ancestors of Hindus had maltreated Depressed Classes that they had been reduced to the subordinate position they occupied for centuries. The implication was clear: caste inequalities were a socially constructed problem, not given by birth. If so, no amount of shuddhi would bring about the 'real uplift' of the Depressed Classes; this was merely one of the many superficial remedies pursued by leaders of the 'Hindu community'.[65] What was 'urgently needed' was their education. This would 'produce leaders and reformers' among them and ameliorate their social status.[66] Considering it shameful that Hindus considered the so-called 'Untouchables' polluting and denied them opportunities to improve their position, Rai asserted the 'right' of every human to be judged by merit and not birth, and appealed to caste Hindus to establish schools for 'Untouchables'.[67] Lajpat Rai was clearly willing to countenance the possibility of lower caste education resulting in a more egalitarian socio-economic structure. Referring to the Ludhiana Municipal Committee's refusal to let Ramdasis use the municipal water tap as an illustration of the 'fatal egotism and brutal callousness' of caste Hindus, he asserted the need to educate Depressed Classes to arouse awareness of the wrong done to them by 'arrogant Hindus'.[68] Ignorance hindered their social uplift as it permitted the perpetuation of caste Hindu prejudice against 'social intercourse' with them; the removal of this ignorance through education would make upper-caste prejudice disappear.[69] Lajpat Rai's focus on education as a means of dismantling caste hierarchy bore some resemblance to the late-nineteenth-century non-Brahmin leaders of Jotirao Phule's Satyashodhak Samaj (Truth-Seeking Society). They too had pushed for education among low castes to intellectually emancipate them from the doctrines of Brahminical Hinduism.[70] Lajpat Rai's stance was also significant given the long-standing demand of 'Dalit' publicists for equal access to education that they believed would help demystify Brahmin trickery at the heart of their continued dehumanization.[71]

Lajpat Rai also appealed to caste Hindus on the basis of secular moral principles, urging, out of a sense of 'humanity' and consideration for 'human rights', the relaxation of the 'cruel' and 'shockingly unjust' hereditary caste hierarchy.[72] In challenging caste hierarchy on grounds of humanity and human rights, Lajpat Rai overlapped with early low-caste intellectuals such as Gopal Baba Walangkar (1840–1900) and Phule (1827–90), the latter being influenced by the works of European religious radicals like Thomas Paine.[73] Lajpat Rai may have drawn on ideas of humanity that appeared in the political thought of the ascendant 'Labour and Socialist circles'[74] he encountered on his 1905 visit to England, and with whom he interacted closely during the early 1910s.[75]

Lajpat Rai declared, 'We are living in a democratic age. The tendencies of democracy are towards the levelling down of all inequalities.'[76] His enthusiasm for the political mobilization of 'the masses' during the Swadeshi agitation had reflected his keenness to include the subaltern in an expanded definition of 'the people'. Conceiving of democracy in terms of greater collective agency of 'the people' in this expanded sense, he used its egalitarian pull to argue for greater equality between castes. Likening upper castes to 'slave-owners' in a way reminiscent of Phule's 1873 work *Gulamgiri* (Slavery),[77] Lajpat Rai implored them to end the oppression of Depressed Classes and 'treat all equally'.[78] For him, this move towards greater caste equality was demanded by the principle of 'social justice',[79] the link between justice and equality once again likely reflecting the influence upon him of British socialist thought.[80] Finally, Lajpat Rai sometimes also argued for civic equality for low castes based on an implicit notion of liberal–democratic citizenship. For instance, the Ludhiana Municipal Committee's refusal to allow Ramdasis the use of a municipal water tap was, for Lajpat Rai, particularly unjust since this denied a 'public' facility to 'tax-payers': 'Just think of the arrogance and inhumanity of a decision refusing a tax-payer the use of a municipal water tap . . . Hindus refusing the use of a public water-stand to a brother Hindu . . . is a sight to make the gods weep.'[81] These principled arguments were bolstered by highlighting the practical futility of attempts to maintain caste taboos in the face of upper-caste use of modern technologies and innovations like the railways, modern medicine, aerated water and public taps which rendered touch anonymous[82]—an argument also made by early lower-caste intellectuals like Walangkar.[83]

Lajpat Rai further strengthened his moral appeal by arguing that one needed to heed the plight of Depressed Classes on grounds of 'expediency'; neglect was causing them to convert out of Hinduism to Islam and Christianity. He quoted the 1901 and 1911 census to support his claim that Hindus were in numerical decline as compared to Muslims and Christians whose numbers were rising.[84] Rai was participating in the discourse centred on Hindu demographic decline that was becoming dominant among many prominent caste Hindus. In fact, his public interest in this theme coincided with the publication, in the Punjabi press,[85] of a series of articles on the same topic by a Bengali Hindu, Lieutenant–Colonel U.N. Mukherjee, who predicted that the slower growth rates of Hindus will eventually lead to their disappearance.[86] Hindus were portrayed as a 'dying race . . . surrounded by an already overwhelming and progressively expanding numbers of Muslims, who, in their self-engineered growth, suck out the life-blood of their rivals'.[87] Lajpat Rai did not explicitly mention Mukherjee but was probably aware of the debate. In any case, unlike Mukherjee who pointed to a catastrophic picture of steady decline and doom, Lajpat Rai dismissed the idea that an Islamic or Christian revival by mass conversions threatened Hinduism.[88] Even so, individual conversions resulting in Hindu numerical decline made him anxious.[89] Lajpat Rai noted that the majority of individual converts belonged to the Depressed Classes.[90] While he did see Islam and Christianity as some sort of threat, he insisted that the fault was not that of 'Islamic and Christian preachers' whose attempts to convert these 'outcastes' were entirely legitimate.[91] To his mind, the absence within Islam of taboos on commensality (the practice of eating together) made it appear to low castes a more merciful faith.[92] Similarly, Christianity offered them independence, self-respect, education and equality in church services.[93] Lajpat Rai's discourse is remarkable for its virtual absence of stigmatization of Muslims and Christians; instead he praised Islam and Christianity for their admirable egalitarian ethic. Nor could the Depressed Classes be blamed for leaving the Hindu fold:

> The community was the mother, its members her children. That mother could not be unjust to any class . . . if that mother did not treat the depressed classes with an impartial eye, she had no claim upon them and they had a right to leave her and cut off connection with her.[94]

After conversion, these Classes received food, a higher status and 'left a society that hated them'.[95] Given this, they could not be blamed if they separated from Hindus and converted to other religions.[96] Lajpat Rai declared that the fault was 'entirely that of the Hindus', who were callous, cruel, intolerant and inhuman in their attitude towards these classes. By attributing Hindu numerical decline to upper-caste discrimination, Lajpat Rai differed from U.N. Mukherjee,[97] who blamed low-caste Hindus for their laziness and incapacity to unite, and attributed Muslim proliferation to the Muslim male desire for Hindu widows.[98] For Lajpat Rai, the process of Hindu numerical decline could be reversed only when upper-caste Hindus stopped mistreating the 'Depressed Classes'.

Of course, it is true that 'expediency' of maintaining Hindu numbers was an explicit aim behind Lajpat Rai's efforts to dismantle the caste hierarchy. He openly stated that numbers were the greatest strength of Hindus—the source of their power and influence—which was not shared by any other community.[99] The attempt to transform the relationship between castes coexisted with his desire to maintain a 'majority community', on the basis of which Hindus demanded political rights.[100] Despite sharing affinity with 'low caste' intellectuals, Lajpat Rai differed from them in one significant respect: for him, the welfare of lower castes was always subsidiary to the primary aim of maintaining the integrity and majority of the Hindu nation/community. Still, his appeals for caste reform on grounds of political expediency do not negate the significance of his principled appeals. As he clarified:

> Morality requires that we should take to the work of elevating the depressed classes out of a sheer sense of justice and humanity regardless of outside considerations. But to appeal in the name of expediency, when the latter strengthens the demands of morality and humanity, involves no breach of principle.[101]

Moreover, notwithstanding his intention to maintain a Hindu majority, Lajpat Rai's attitude to caste hierarchy is significant in light of historian John Zavos's claim that, by the 1910s, the dominant position in the ideology of Hindu politics emphasized the 'horizontal' approach to Hindu unity. This entailed sidestepping the thorny issues of caste division, hierarchy and oppression by simply binding together different castes in the name of being all-embracing and tolerant.[102] Lal Chand, the Hindu Sabha's main leader, clearly embodied this intellectual position:

> It is not stressed that the feet be given the status of the head, but it is certainly enjoined that their position as essential parts of the 'sacred' living body be duly recognised, that they be not neglected and do receive their proper share of nourishment, education and enlightenment, to enable them to perform their own function to the best advantage of the community and the body politic.[103]

Projecting the Hindu community as a living body, Lal Chand rationalized it as an organic whole in which each of its constituent, hierarchically arranged castes had a function.[104] In sharp contrast to this blatant advocacy of caste hierarchy, Lajpat Rai, having grown distant from the Hindu Sabha movement by 1910, complained sarcastically of its superficial attitude towards caste:

> People look forward to the newly started Hindu Sabha to take up the matter in right earnest, but it appears that the august body

is engaged in more important work than the uplifting and the elevation of Depressed Classes is supposed to be. They seem to care more for Legislative Councils and things of that nature than for the danger which the Hindu community runs by neglecting the backward classes.[105]

By 1911, U.N. Mukherjee had also eschewed caste reform to recast Hinduism as embodying an idealized pluralism, justifying caste hierarchies and even untouchability as a part of an organic 'Hindu' whole.[106] As historian P.K. Datta shows, this was Mukherjee's response to the challenge posed by the Gait Circular, a note released by the government in 1910 which threatened to exclude low-caste groups from the category of 'Hindus' for census enumeration. Lajpat Rai, on the other hand, was grateful that the Circular had galvanized 'orthodox' Hindus into sympathy with the 'Depressed Classes' and warned against the danger of apathy setting in again.[107] Instead of eschewing caste reform, he accelerated his efforts to transform caste hierarchical relations in the years following the Gait Circular, articulating his most radical ideas about caste equality in 1913–14. And so, despite his association with both the Hindu Sabha movement and the College Party of the Arya Samaj, viewed by scholars as proponents of a politics of horizontal unity which papered over hierarchical caste divisions among Hindus,[108] Lajpat Rai propagated what Zavos has called the 'vertical' approach to Hindu unity. This sought to bring about Hindu unity by actively transforming lived relations between caste Hindus and the Depressed Classes.[109] He was one of the first well-known caste Hindu political leaders of his time who sought to achieve the unity (and majority) of the Hindu nation/community by transforming the lived relations between high and low castes, and thereby move assertively towards an *egalitarian* notion of this Hindu nation/community.[110]

Part 3: War Years in Exile and the Khilafat Movement

10

A New 'Indian' Nationalism in Exile

From 1909 to 1913, Lajpat Rai had remained largely aloof from the Congress controlled by the moderates. After his initial participation, his interest also waned in the Punjab Hindu Sabha, which he claimed was overly concerned with winning legislative seats than strengthening a Hindu community or nation by dismantling caste hierarchies. Apart from focusing on the latter, Lajpat Rai made a trip to England in 1910, contributed to the development of the Ayurvedic and Technical departments at DAV College, and was elected to the Municipal Council of Lahore in 1913. According to his biographer, his work with the colonial regime (in which he focused on free primary education in Hindi and electric street lights, among other things) led British officials to soften their image of Lajpat Rai as a political conspirator or revolutionary, and they now began to view him as a reasonable man.[1] On his own admission, and not unrelated to the surveillance he had been under, during these years Rai, for the most part, avoided saying anything 'unpleasant on political subjects'.[2] This changed with his election (alongside, among others, M.A. Jinnah)[3] to a Congress deputation to England following its 1913 Karachi session.

Arriving in England in May 1914 for what he thought was a six-month trip, Lajpat Rai spent time mingling with leading socialist politicians and intellectuals including Keir Hardie, Sydney and Beatrice Webb, and George Bernard Shaw, and got interested in the British labour and trade union movement.[4] He had plans to proceed to Europe, but these were thwarted when the First World War broke out in July. So, Lajpat Rai remained in England, writing a book on the history of the Arya Samaj and his autobiography *The Story of My Life* (both of which have been important sources for this book).[5] Unable to return to India even after six months, Lajpat Rai decided to cross the Atlantic, and landed in the United States of America in late November. Apart from six months in Japan in the latter half of 1915, Lajpat Rai spent the next five years, till December 1919, in the United States.

Living in New York City for the most part, he came in contact with several progressive circles. Armed with a letter of introduction from Sidney Webb, Lajpat Rai met the renowned Columbia University economist Edwin R. A. Seligman, who introduced him to other members of the University and other personalities in New York.[6] Seligman invited him to attend the annual meetings of the American Economic, Sociological and Statistical Association in Princeton. In New York, Lajpat Rai met the journalist and editor of the progressive liberal magazine *New Republic*, Walter Lippmann.[7] He acquainted himself with progressive intellectuals from Harvard, Stanford and the University of California, Berkeley.[8] Eager to grasp the workings of American society and politics, Lajpat Rai travelled across the States, visiting various cities including Boston, Washington, Chicago, Atlanta, New Orleans, San Francisco, Los Angeles and Berkeley.[9] Keen to understand the 'Negro problem', Lajpat Rai came in contact with NAACP (the National Association for the Advancement of Colored Peoples) founders W.E.B. Du Bois and Oswald Villard, the African–American educator Booker T. Washington of the Tuskegee Institute, and the first African–American president of Morehouse College, John Hope.[10] During his travels to the South, Lajpat Rai was shocked to witness the unabashed racism of Jim Crow America. Attending a screening of D.W. Griffith's *Birth of a Nation* (which he wrote of as a 'play of the Ku Klux Clansmen' [*sic*]), he noted the frenzied passion this film aroused in the audience, which 'reached the highest pitch of race hatred'.[11] Lajpat Rai recorded his impressions about America in a book written in 1915 titled *The United States of America: A Hindu's Impressions and a Study.*[12]

Both during his travels and his stay in New York City, Lajpat Rai came in touch with Indian diasporic circles, meeting young Indian students and many Ghadar revolutionaries (of whom he remained critical).[13] He met the young M.N. Roy, one of the central figures of early Indian communism,[14] twenty-five-year-old B.R. Ambedkar (a PhD student of Seligman's at Columbia University),[15] and Rabindranath Tagore on his brief visit to the States.[16] During his long stay in New York, Lajpat Rai cultivated and maintained friendships with Irish–American anti-imperialists, several liberal and socialist intellectuals, and feminist activists like Agnes Smedley and Henrietta Rodman.[17] Many of these individuals would associate themselves with the India Home Rule League of America that Lajpat Rai founded in October 1917 to 'spread correct knowledge of Indian affairs in America' and win the sympathy of Americans for the Indian cause.[18] In 1918, Rai also established *Young India*, a monthly publication he wrote for and edited from New York till he left America in late 1919.

As interesting as Lajpat Rai's activities, experiences, interactions and reflections about America was the significant shift in Lajpat Rai's *conception of nationhood* that is noticeable from early 1915. In the past, he had occasionally—as in 1901—dismissed the notion of Indian nationality as a false idea.[19] At other times, as in 1909, he affirmed his belief in an overarching Indian nation that accommodated Hindus and Muslims.[20] Either way, he remained strongly tied to the notion that Hindus and Muslims constituted separate cultural nations. Even as he ultimately envisioned them as constituting a common, overarching 'Indian' political community or nation (in its modern nationalist sense, with connotations of self-government and statehood), Lajpat Rai struggled to articulate and imagine what, if anything, Hindus and Muslims shared in common culturally and historically as 'Indians'. Indeed, despite affirming the idea of a common Indian nation, and in turn implicitly conceding the notion of Hindus and Muslims being bound by common political interests, he often saw the discrete Hindus and Muslim cultural nations as mostly having distinct (and often competitive) political interests. Rather than elaborating a thickly textured, common Indian national cultural identity for Hindus and Muslims over and above their particular religious or cultural identities, or attempting to unite them, he argued that the separate cultural and even political strengthening of India's Hindu and Muslim nations was the best means to strengthen the Indian nation; Lajpat Rai's first and overwhelming priority, then, remained to articulate a common national identity for Hindus, and to strengthen and unite this 'Hindu nation'. Broadly, then, till now, Lajpat Rai had remained much more a 'Hindu nationalist' than an 'Indian nationalist' (even though, as we have seen, his Hindu nationalism remained distinct from the Hindutva nationalist ideology Savarkar was about to elaborate).

This is what changed in early 1915, from when Lajpat Rai's vision of nationhood underwent what seems like a perfect inversion. The fifty-year-old Rai now explicitly criticized 'religious nationalism' and 'communal patriotism' as 'false ideas', and consistently insisted that India's Hindus and Muslims belonged to a single 'Indian' nation.[21] While we examine the intricate texture of Rai's new 'Indian nationalism' in more detail below, we must first ask what precisely triggered this change. One answer to this question is that Rai's changed geographical location and new remoteness from India provided him with a new global sense through which differences between Hindus and Muslims began to look less significant, inducing him to shift to a different conception of nationhood. Indeed, a slight shift began to occur whilst he was in England itself. In his book on the Arya Samaj, written in England in late 1914, he had already felt it necessary to conclude it with a warning to the Samaj:

> The Arya Samaj has to remember that the India of today is not
> exclusively Hindu. Its prosperity and future depends upon
> the reconciliation of Hinduism with the greater *ism* – Indian
> nationalism – which alone can secure for India its rightful place in
> the comity of nations. Anything that may prevent, or even hinder,
> that consummation is a sin for which there can be no expiation.[22]

Even in previous years, Rai had occasionally stressed that attempts
to strengthen the 'Hindu nation' were and would be compatible
with a larger Indian national unity. What changed now was a lack
of insistence that this Indian nation would be built by strengthening
a Hindu nation, and the greater urgency Rai felt to warn *Hindus* of
the need to realize that Hinduism must be reconciled with a 'greater'
Indian nationalism. The superordinate importance and priority
given to the Indian nation was new. From 1915 onwards, Lajpat Rai
would imagine the Indian nation more vividly, and conceptualize its
members as possessing many more, thicker bonds of cultural and
political unity than he had been able to imagine before.

If geographical remoteness had triggered this intellectual shift,
what pushed it much further was the new political context emerging
in India: the reorientation of the Muslim leadership. As we saw in
Chapter 8, since its foundation in 1906, the League had continued the
policy of early Muslim leaders like Syed Ahmad Khan—of rejecting
the claim of the Congress to represent the common political interests
of an 'Indian nation'. Even as it frequently admitted that Hindus and
Muslims shared several common interests, the League's leaders had
emphasized that Hindus and Muslims possessed their own special
political interests and were therefore distinct 'communities' or
'nationalities'.[23] This political imagination had driven the League's
rejection of mixed electorates with its assumptions of a common
political society, and its belief that separate electorates, in which
only Muslims voted for Muslims, were crucial to ensure 'true'
representation of Muslim political interests (with Hindus also
electing their own representatives exclusively). Broadly like the
Congress 'moderates' (and indeed several Arya Samajists and Punjab

172 Being Hindu, Being Indian

Hindu Sabha members) in their declaration of loyalty to the British Empire, the Muslim League had differed from the Congress in its lack of any leaders resisting the Empire using a modern conception of a nation—whether Indian or Muslim—imagined as self-governing in the future.

This had changed by the end of the first decade of the twentieth century, when a younger generation of Muslims—represented by the brothers Mohamed (1878–1931) and Shaukat Ali (1873–1939),[24] and the young Abul Kalam Azad[25] (1888–1958), among others— began to feel alienated by British policies inside and outside India, leading them to question the political stance of the League's old guard. In India, the British government's 1911 annulment of the partition of Bengal had caused resentment among prominent Bengali Muslims who had benefited from the creation of a separate province in 1905.[26] The government's refusal in 1912 to accept a Muslim university at Aligarh without effective government control had angered several Western-educated Muslims in the United Provinces.[27] In 1913, the government's demolition of the *wuzu khana* (washing place) of a mosque in Kanpur and its indiscriminate firing on protestors further embittered the new Muslim leadership.[28] On the international front, this newly prominent 'Pan-Islamic' section of Indian Muslim leadership was upset with Britain's tacit approval of attacks on the Ottoman Empire by Italy and the Balkan countries in 1911–12 and with British ministers making speeches approving the idea of Christian powers partitioning the Ottoman Empire.[29] Since the 1880s, several prominent Indian Muslims had begun to espouse Pan-Islamic ideas, viewing themselves as part of a global Muslim community sharing a common Islamic civilization, with the Ottoman caliph as its spiritual head and the Ottoman Empire as its temporal or material embodiment. At least partly, Pan-Islamism was their means of elevating the esteem of Indian Muslims in the context of British imperialist ideas persistently asserting the superiority of Western civilization while emphasizing the inferiority of Muslims.[30] The Ottoman caliphate–empire, the last remaining independent Muslim power in a world dominated by Europe, was a symbol of the glorious Islamic civilization, from which they could draw pride and confidence. Pan-Islamism is also what they found comfort in as they grappled with the formal end of Mughal rule in India and faced the prospect of their increased marginalization in politics.[31] For some, paying allegiance to the caliph, a symbol of Islam, was simply a manifestation of their religious faith. Unsurprisingly, Britain's outright declaration of war against the Ottomans in 1914 deeply disturbed this section of Indian Muslims. Britain's policies in India and abroad led a new generation of Indian Muslims to repudiate the old guard's policies of loyalism towards the British and aloofness from the Congress. The British government's harassment of the Pan-Islamic 'Muslim' press, and its internment of the Ali brothers and other Pan-Islamists in 1914–15 further intensified this trend towards rapprochement with the Congress.[32] Now, these Pan-Islamic sections of Indian Muslim leadership aligned with men like Mohammad Ali Jinnah (1876–1948), Wazir Hasan (1874–1947) and Mazharul Haq (1866–1930), who already desired greater collaboration between the League and the Congress, and between Hindus and Muslims.[33] The movement for reconciliation accelerated in 1915 partly due to the determined efforts of men like Jinnah and Haq who outmanoeuvred the League's deeply resistant loyalist old guard to create a committee to jointly draft a reforms scheme with the Congress.[34]

The Congress itself had aided this process by a series of overtures to the League since 1910. Gokhale had already expressed his willingness to accept separate electorates to 'remove the feeling of soreness in the minds of minorities.'[35] In 1912, the Congress president publicly recognized the expediency of granting 'communal representation'. In 1913, the Congress was headed by a Muslim president, and held its session in the 'conspicuously Muslim city' of Karachi.[36] By 1915, the politically ascendant Anglo–Irish Theosophist leader Annie Besant (1847–1933) was emphasizing the need for the Congress and the League to produce a joint reforms scheme.[37] Before his death in 1915, Gokhale drafted a scheme with the Aga Khan, who had also begun to think that after 1909 Muslims had a satisfactory basis from which to negotiate with the Congress.[38] Recently released from jail, B.G. Tilak indicated his acceptance of separate electorates in 1914,[39] and declared that 'a considerable section of the educated Mahomedans have begun to perceive . . . the necessity of political agitation along Congress lines and it would be a fault of the Congress if it does not meet them halfway'.[40] The new spirit of Hindu–Muslim cooperation was evident in the support sought and received from both Hindus and Muslims for Tilak's and Annie Besant's new 'Home Rule' agitations (demanding Home Rule within the empire).[41]

The cumulative significance of these developments impacted Lajpat Rai early on in his years of wartime exile spent in America. Writing his book, lengthily titled *Young India: An Interpretation and a History of the Nationalist Movement from Within* (1916), in 1915, he noted with great satisfaction that 'the younger generation of Mohammedans, so thoroughly filled with the idea of nationalism', had defied staunch opposition from the 'ultra-loyalist' old guard to unite with the Congress over the demand for Home Rule and to jointly draft a scheme satisfying 'both the great religious communities inhabiting that great country'.[42] The united support received by Besant's Home Rule League from Hindus and Muslims represented for him a great advancement in 'Indian nationalism'. A consistent critic of the old Aligarh policy of aloofness from the Congress, Lajpat Rai was delighted at what he saw as the 'entirely changed attitude of the Mohammedan community'. He remarked that now even 'educated Muslim separatists' saw the 'policy of separation from the Hindus' as harming their community, realizing that it was possible for them to be 'Mohammedans in religion and Indians in politics'. In Rai's interpretation, it was British aggression towards the Ottomans which had deeply offended Indian Muslims, and 'done wonders in nationalising' them. This trivialized the several other 'domestic' reasons (mentioned above) for why Indian Muslim increasingly felt disaffected with British rule in favour of one reason—their Pan-Islamic sympathies. Still, what is interesting is Lajpat Rai's view of Pan-Islamism as having 'nationalized' Indian Muslims and as being beneficial for Indian nationalism.[43] Clearly, for him, Muslim willingness to unite with Hindus as members of one nation was crucial for the success of Indian nationalism. Probably alluding to himself, Lajpat Rai argued that the abandonment of Muslim 'separatism', which he reductively saw as the only cause of anti-Muslim sentiment among Hindus, had softened the stance of Hindus towards them too.

Apart from ignoring other reasons for anti-Muslim prejudice among Hindus,[44] Lajpat Rai also exaggerated the extent of change in Indian Muslims. Like Rai, the newly dominant Muslim leadership also read Congress–League cooperation and their agreement over self-government as signalling the dawn of a new Indian nationalism. Azad and Jinnah saw these events as heralding a 'new spirit', a 'new-born movement' towards 'national unity', and the evolution of a 'common Indian nationality'.[45] The Muslim League's new constitution now referred to the unity of Hindu and Muslim 'communities' as 'national' unity, assuming the oneness of nationhood in India. Mohamed Ali, the increasingly popular ex-Aligarhite champion of Pan-Islamism, echoed this language, speaking of an 'Indian nation' and referring to Muslims firmly as a 'community'.[46] For some Muslim figures like Azad, this shift in larger political discourse merely aligned with their pre-existing political imagination and already-held views that the League's policy of separation and loyalism was mistaken.[47] But several members of the Muslim League still evaluated the earlier policy of political isolationism as having been beneficial in protecting Muslims, a foundational precondition for the evolution of Indian nationalism, deeming harmful only its persistence or excess.[48] By uniting with Hindus over the demand for self-government, these Muslim personalities were certainly at the forefront of encouraging this new nationalism, but they continued to see Hindus and Muslims as distinct political communities within the larger 'Indian' political community or 'nation'.

Lajpat Rai seems not to have noticed this continuity amidst change. Nevertheless, the shift in Muslim political discourse towards speaking resolutely of one 'Indian nation',[49] whose unity and autonomy were to be sought jointly with Hindus, which Rai had noted, was real. And it propelled him to reconfigure his own nationalist thought, to firmly and more confidently re-imagine Hindus and Muslims as members of a common 'Indian nation'. Having once spurned the notion of an 'Indian' nation as futile as long as the Muslims rejected it and conducted their politics separately,[50] he saw the new Muslim willingness to conduct their politics in tandem with Hindus as meeting the crucial precondition for the birth of an authentic 'Indian' nationalism, which he could now also champion.

The rapprochement between the Congress and the League culminated in the 'Lucknow Pact' of December 1916. Apart from a joint declaration of complete self-government as the eventual goal of both bodies,[51] this 'Pact', achieved mainly through the efforts of Jinnah and Tilak,[52] saw the League compromise by accepting Muslim political representation below their numerical proportion in the Muslim majority provinces of Punjab and Bengal, and the Congress by accepting separate electorates and weightages for Muslims in minority provinces.[53] As Hugh Owen, the historian who has most closely analysed the Lucknow Pact, has argued, the Lucknow Pact would help create an atmosphere of mutual trust between Hindus and Muslims, laying the ground for their future cooperation in the Rowlatt and Khilafat campaigns of 1919–22.[54] While Owen interprets Lajpat Rai's absence at Lucknow as a factor facilitating the Pact, in fact, watching from afar, he celebrated it as proof of the common Indian national spirit that moved both Hindus and Muslims.[55] In cursorily endorsing the Pact, Rai consented to this very political imagination that underlay it: a conception of the Indian nation as comprising distinct Hindu and Muslim political communities. In doing so, he disregarded his own disparagement in 1909 of separate electorates as harmful for Indian nationhood.[56] As you may notice in the course of this chapter, Rai's sanction of the Pact was also in tension with the religion-transcending Indian nationalist vision he would articulate in another book in the same year. The euphoric sense of being present in a wholly novel political moment, pregnant with the possibility of consolidating the Indian nation, led Lajpat Rai to not only overestimate the extent of change in Muslim political discourse, but occasionally also articulate conflicting positions on whether or not religion should be mixed with politics. This internal tension would remain in Lajpat Rai's new Indian nationalist thought until the mid-1920s, when he would attempt to resolve it. But, for now, it lay dormant, its existence entirely compatible with his eagerness to unite Hindus and Muslims into a single 'Indian nation'.

Quite apart from the changed political context in India, Lajpat Rai's altered nationalist stance was also rendered possible by an event originating far away from India: The First World War. As we saw above, Lajpat Rai reductively saw the offence caused to Indian Muslims by British aggression towards the Ottomans as the key reason for the new 'national' attitude,[57] and viewed his own changed stance as a response to this. But the war did not reshape his nationalist imagination only through this circuitous route; it also did so by endowing him with a new international perspective. The brutal recklessness with which European powers sought to self-aggrandize and destroy each other in an all-out war made Lajpat Rai, like many anti-colonial thinkers of his time, question much more assertively the assumption of the moral and cultural superiority of Western civilization.[58] From late 1914, he began to deny with more confidence than before that only Europe and the 'modern West' had things to teach the 'East' or 'Asia'; the latter was not just as worthy as the West but in certain crucial matters worthier because it had more to teach Europe—for example, how to use power ethically to serve rather than exploit humanity.[59] Even in the 1890s, Lajpat Rai, as an Arya Samajist, had occasionally asserted Vedic Hinduism's superiority vis-à-vis Europe in the religious domain (by stressing the superiority of Vedic monotheism). But as the First World War radically shook Europe's claims to moral superiority, he more forcefully proclaimed the superiority of the East/Asia over the West. Rather than possessing a more superior form of something Europe had (monotheism), the East/Asia was projected as possessing something that Europe lacked (i.e., an ethical mode of conducting politics). And rather than claiming that India was superior in a spiritual domain isolated from the political domain, India and Asia were now projected as possessing superiority in the political domain itself. India was also not just superior in the past; in certain crucial matters, Asia, inclusive of India, was superior now.

By dramatically denaturalizing ideas of European/Western superiority, the war enabled Lajpat Rai to strike at the intellectual foundation of the Eurocentric imperial world order: the assumption that the culturally and morally superior European nations were ruling over the rest of the world to civilize its peoples.[60] He now more forcefully criticized European imperialism for its 'tyrannical', 'brutally exploitative' and even 'criminal' treatment of Asia and Africa.[61] While Lajpat Rai had been a virulent critic of British rule in India even in the past, often condemning it as an 'autocracy' or as Russian-style 'despotism',[62] what was new was his understanding of imperialism as a contingent, distorted and illegitimate organization of the global order. The global event of the war allowed Lajpat Rai to move from focusing on Britain's oppression of India towards recognizing imperialism more clearly as a larger European problem, one which afflicted the entire Eurocentric international order as presently configured. Indians were not unique victims of despotic rule; other Asian and African countries similarly suffered under the unjust, unequal imperial world order. This new understanding of India's shared experience of colonial subjugation with others was signalled by the increased prominence in Lajpat Rai's political vocabulary of the categories of 'the East' and 'Asia', which first clubbed India alongside Japan and China, but soon also Burma, Indo-China (Vietnam), Ceylon (Sri Lanka), Persia (Iran) and Turkey.[63]

This radical moral delegitimization of the existing world order was accompanied by the new-found realization, in the wake of the war, that it was perhaps not as strong and stable as had been widely believed. By 1915, Lajpat Rai was noting that the Germans had shattered the myth of British invincibility[64] and indeed in the early war years it often seemed like Britain was losing the war.[65] Yet, even with the possibility of an Allied victory, the war raised expectations that its end would bring substantial changes in the maps of Europe, Asia and Africa,[66] and that the world was on the eve of a great reconstruction.[67] Lajpat Rai remarked that Indians had now fought valiantly alongside and against whites, which had given them confidence in their fighting prowess, and destroyed the myth of white superiority.[68] This would lead Indians to demand a radical change in their political status. So would the growing belief that their hardships and sacrifices during the war, both at the front and at home, would reap rewards.[69] The expectation of a changed post-war world was heightened by Lajpat Rai's wartime residence far from India, in the United States and Japan, which forced him to pay greater attention to the rising ferment against European imperial encroachment in countries outside India, an education probably reinforced by his meetings with nationalists from other countries like China.[70] Rai's five-month stay in Japan between July and December 1915, where he came in contact with prominent Pan-Asianists like Okawa Shumei,[71] particularly convinced him that the war was a harbinger of a new Asian awakening against European imperial domination.[72] Anticipating a new post-war world order, Lajpat Rai himself began to articulate a Pan-Asian vision, calling on Japan to lead Asia and work for its liberation.[73] In any case, he predicted a transnational movement towards Asian unity, and a protracted struggle for freedom in Asia,[74] which would produce a worldwide revolution against the imperial world order.[75]

The new world order inaugurated by this Pan-Asian struggle would consist of 'free states' based on the principles of humanity and universal brotherhood.[76] In short, the war enabled Lajpat Rai to vividly imagine an alternative, egalitarian world order in which despotic imperial rule was unacceptable and 'home rule' in India and other Asian nations was mandatory.[77] Towards this end of realizing the new world order, Lajpat Rai latched onto not just Pan-Asianism but also subsequent developments in world politics and global discourse. As the United States entered the war in April 1917, and began to appear as a potentially major player at the peace table, Rai implored it to strive for 'such international re-arrangement of the world as would take the power of exploitation from all powerful and imperialistic nations and which would confer equal opportunities of development and progress on all the peoples of the earth for themselves and for common humanity.'[78] A few months after the Bolshevik Revolution later that year, Lajpat Rai attended a Conference of Radical Socialist and Labour Organizations in New York. In his speech, he drew on Bolshevik rhetoric, particularly the words of Leon Trotsky, to argue for an international order grounded in the equality and brotherhood of nations.[79] Throughout 1918, despite knowing that US President Woodrow Wilson had not intended it for colonized nations, Lajpat Rai seized his rhetoric of 'self-determination' to argue for a new international order organized on this principle.[80] When the war ended in November, he hoped that the new League of Nations which Wilson planned to establish, would wash away the *ancien régime* of empires, and their tradition of treating colonial conquests as legitimate spoils of war, to create precisely such a world of equal, self-determining nations.[81]

With the existing world order itself in need of a complete overhaul, Lajpat Rai came to believe that India had hitherto been too insular in its attempts to fight the British within India, failing to understand the importance of 'world forces'.[82] Indians needed to 'think and act internationally',[83] make India's battle against Britain's imperialism part of a Pan-Asian struggle against European imperialism, where it would join other colonized nations to engender a change in the international system. It was towards the same end that Indians needed to enlist the sympathy of the newly emergent and apparently more progressive world power, America. This is what Lajpat Rai doggedly attempted after he returned to America from Japan in late 1915, first through articles in the *New York Times* and progressive publications like the *Evening Post*, the *Nation*, the *New Republic* and the *Masses* throughout 1916, and later through the India Home Rule League of America which he founded in October 1917.[84]

This new broadened internationalist perspective led Lajpat Rai to now view the religious differences between India's Hindus and Muslims as trivial. Rather than frittering away their energies in petty mutual quarrels, these fellow victims of British imperialism had to sink their differences, unite and join other world forces to smash the entire global imperial order. This realization, which struck him in early 1915, kick-started his re-imagination of nationhood in India. This process was encouraged by the increasingly urgent imperative to prove that Indians, despite their diversity, did constitute a nation and did meet the newly emergent international standard of national 'self-determination'.[85] It was further reinforced by his prolonged stay in the United States, during which he studied it closely, taking particular interest in 'the process which had led to the fusion of different races from which the population had originally sprung into one nation'.[86] The picture of America as a country with a 'great free mixture of nationalities',[87] a diverse society constituting itself into a single political community ('one nation') was likely on his mind when he wished that India 'assimilate' some of America's 'ideas and ideals'.[88]

It is unclear what role Rai's social milieu in America played in his new imagination of India's Hindus and Muslims as members of one nation. As noted, whilst in America, Lajpat Rai interacted with several progressive liberal, socialist, radical, pacifist, anti-imperialist and even feminist intellectuals.[89] But his affiliation with them seems to mostly be an outcome of their support for Indian self-government, often an extension of their broader anti-imperialism. Moreover, American progressives were a diverse lot; some whom he met—like the sociologist Edward A. Ross—held racist beliefs and held exclusionary views about immigration, while others—like the NAACP co-founders Oswald Villard and W.E.B. Du Bois, and Booker T. Washington—combated racism and held more egalitarian views. At least explicitly, his closer interactions with such egalitarian progressives led Lajpat Rai to reflect more deeply on racial discrimination in America and make parallels with British–Indian and inter-caste relations, rather than Hindu–Muslim relations.[90] Nevertheless, it is possible that contact with the more egalitarian, inclusive strand of American progressive thought, particularly that which had begun to conceive of human nature as a product of environment and culture (rather than race) may have further encouraged the new nationalism he began articulating in light of changed Indian and global contexts.[91]

A New Indian Nationalism in Exile

What then was the substance of Lajpat Rai's new nationalism? As he moved towards imagining India as part of a new world order of equal, self-governing nation–states, his use of the term 'nation' decisively shifted to now consistently refer only to the modern, fully nationalist sense of this term. In other words, henceforth Lajpat Rai's use of the term 'nation' referred *exclusively* to a self-governing political community, rather than *also* to a politico–cultural community without connotations of self-government. As he made this decisive intellectual shift, Rai refused to continue to see Hindus and Muslims as separate 'religious nationalities'. In his book *The Problem of National Education* (1918), he now judged the nationalism promoted by the Arya Samaj and Sir Syed's Aligarh College as 'narrow', 'openly sectarian' and not 'truly national'.[92] Lajpat Rai reneged on his earlier equation of the 'nation' with religious communities. His assertive move towards conceiving the nation exclusively in its fully nationalist, statist sense, with connotations of self-government, was accompanied by a shift towards firmly and consistently conceiving it in more expansive terms—for him, 'the nation' now signified *only* one supreme political community of 'Indians', encompassing all of India's inhabitants, irrespective of religious (and other) differences.

As Lajpat Rai declared elsewhere: 'I do not admit that India is not a nation or that sameness of language, religion or race is necessary for a political national existence [*sic*].'[93] He clearly refused to equate the statist concept of the nation with the Hindu community. Holding that 'religion is a matter of individual faith and taste; and with the common civil life of the country, religion does not and should not interfere',[94] he wished 'religion' to be expelled from this idea of the 'nation'. Having once argued that the Indian nation could only be built 'from below' by *strengthening* religious 'nationalities', Rai now argued that it needed to be built by individuals completely *transcending* religion at the political level so as to recognize their political (and economic) commonalities as 'Indians':

It must form an important part of the active teaching of patriotism
in India to impress on the mind of young children the fact of
their common country, of their common political and economic
interests, of their common history and of their common destiny ...
To be Indians, first, last, and all the time, in all political and
economic matters and in our relations with non-Indians . . .[95]

When addressing Indians in his *Problem of National Education* book,
Lajpat Rai advocated that they needed to proactively fortify the Indian
nation. But when countering British imperial discourse proclaiming
India's ineligibility for self-government (because it was not one
but many nations),[96] Rai abandoned suggestions to strengthen the
Indian nation through a religion-transcending politics and simply
pointed to proofs of the Indian nation's self-evident existence. This
was manifest in a pamphlet titled *Self-Determination for India*,
published in 1918 by Rai's India Home Rule League of America.[97]
The pamphlet backed its assertion that 'the whole of India is one
nation' through an early use of a phrase which would become a
cliché in official Indian nationalist discourse in later decades: 'unity
in diversity'. The first proof of Indian nationhood was provided by
India's natural geography that apparently marked it off from the rest
of the world. This claim was substantiated by adducing the following
statement from Vincent Smith's *Early History of India* (1904)
which had overtaken James Mill as the new hegemonic history of
India:[98] 'India, encircled by seas and mountains, is indisputably a
geographical unit.' This was followed by British geographer George
Chisholm's assertion that 'there is no part of the world better marked
out by nature as a region by itself than India exclusive of Burmah'.[99]
British colonialist scholars often asserted that nationhood was a
Western attribute unlikely to be found or replicated in the East.[100] In
defiance, the pamphlet deployed their writings to claim that India's
nationhood was defined by nature itself. By making unchanging
geographical unity a defining feature, this Indian nationhood
included within it all individuals touched by India's geography,
irrespective of religious and cultural differences.

But the next proof adduced by the pamphlet appears to take Rai's 'Indian' nationalism very much in the direction of Hindu nationalism: 'ethnologically they [the people of India] belong to the same Aryan race.' The pamphlet argued that long before Alexander's invasion in the fourth century BCE, 'the Hindu religion [had] absorbed into its fold all the non-Aryan races, with the result that Hindu culture became the predominant culture of India'.[101] Thus, prior to Muslim rule, Hinduism had 'assimilated' the non-Aryan races and their culture resulting in India being inhabited by an Aryan race and infused by its 'Hindu culture'. The advent of Islam in India, following the Muslim 'invasion' and Mughal rule, did not change the fact that the majority of Indian Muslims were descendants of Aryan Hindus who, although they had embraced a different faith, continued to remain influenced in non-religious matters by the 'immemorial Hindu culture' of their ancestors (and also their regional cultures).[102] The pamphlet quoted British anthropologist and colonial–official Herbert Risley's *People of India* (1908) to posit that 'beneath the manifold diversities of physical and social type, language, and customs and religions, which strike the observer in India, there can still be discerned a certain underlying uniformity of life from the Himalayas to Cape Comorin'.[103] Lajpat Rai was happy to believe that this uniformity was provided by India's timeless Hindu culture.

He refused to equate his now-firmly-held statist conception of the 'nation' with a particular religious community. In *The Problem of National Education*, Lajpat Rai even articulated a religion-transcending, individualistically grounded Indian nationalism (i.e., an 'Indian nationalism' that required individuals to completely transcend their particular religious identity at the political level to recognize their commonalities as members of the Indian nation). But in elaborating the distinctive identity of this Indian nation in *Self-Determination for India*, Lajpat Rai seemed to do so in terms of a race and culture defined as Hindu. The pre-Muslim 'non-Aryan' races and their cultures had been 'absorbed' by the Aryan race and its 'Hindu' religion, making a homogenous 'Hindu' culture the predominant culture of India. A timelessness was attributed to this culture, which was seen as binding the nation even after the advent of Islam in India.[104] This implicitly denied that the culture of the imagined Indian nation was shaped, even in part, by Muslims (or indeed any non-Hindus). Islam appears as having minimal influence on the secular or profane culture of Muslims. The latter was seen as the creation of neither Muslims, nor Hindus and Muslims together, but mainly of India's ancient, unchanging Hindu culture.

In earlier years, Lajpat Rai had strived to arrive at a 'Hindu nationality' either by strongly de-emphasizing theology as he defined Hinduism or by transcending Hinduism itself in favour of a more encompassing secular 'Hindu culture'. Now, he spoke interchangeably of 'Hinduism' and 'Hindu culture' (imagined in broad homogenous rather than internally plural terms), and imagined this secularized Hindu culture as forming the core of his newly imagined 'Indian nation'. While Rai identified Hinduism with Hindu culture, a sharp cleavage was drawn between the religion and culture of Indian Muslims; they followed Islam in religious matters but were defined more by the secular Hindu culture that defined the Indian nation. In earlier years, the culturalization and secularization of Hinduism, its reconfiguration as 'Hindu culture', had served to include within his 'Hindu nation' various religious groups like the Sikhs, Jains, Buddhists and Brahmos, despite their religious differences, with followers of Hinduism. But it had simultaneously served to exclude Muslims and Christians from this broadly defined 'Hindu nation'. Now, this 'Hindu culture' appeared as the essence of the 'Indian nation'. But it was imagined more capaciously, as something with which even Muslims and Christians could identify, even as they continued to follow a different religion. Put differently, earlier, 'Hindu culture' had served to transcend religious diversity among followers of Hinduism and between them and Sikhs, Jains and Buddhists to forge a 'Hindu nation'. Now, it served to transcend religious diversity between Hindus, Muslims and Christians to render an 'Indian nation' possible.

At first glance, the pamphlet's claim that most Indian Muslims descended from Aryan ancestors appears similar to the claim made by the newly prominent Bihari Muslim barrister and Congressman,

Mazharul Haq, in his presidential speech to the Muslim League in 1915, which Lajpat Rai reproduced enthusiastically in *Young India*. Referring to Muslim 'invaders' who had made India their home, Haq argued:

> From time to time their number was strengthened by fresh blood from Arabia, Persia and other Muslim lands, but their ranks were swollen mainly by additions from the people of the country themselves. It is most interesting to know that out of the present seventy millions [*sic*] of the Muslim population, those who have claimed descent from remote non-Indian ancestors amount only to eight million. Whence have the remaining millions come, if not from Indian ranks?[105]

The notion that some Indians were of 'non-Indian' descent, possessing blood from 'Muslim lands', but that most were descendants of 'people of the country', of 'Indian' ancestors, appears strikingly similar to the narrative in the *Self-Determination for India* pamphlet. But while both viewed the majority of Indian Muslims as descendants of an indigenous, non-Muslim race, Haq designated this race as 'Indian', not 'Aryan'. While Haq underplayed religious differences between Muslims and Hindus by pointing to their common 'Indian' race, Rai's pamphlet did so by pointing to their common 'Aryan' race and Hindu culture. Haq's imagination lacked the Hindu assumptions that tinted the latter. By endowing Indian Muslims with an 'indigenous' Aryan lineage, Lajpat Rai's nationalism also ignored the claims of some high-status *ashraf* Muslims about the foreign descent of Indian Muslims. Such claims were determined by the origin of Islam in Arabia and the will to assert genealogical links with the Prophet and the early Islamic community. Indian Muslims, with their originally foreign lineage, had settled in India and shaped its culture alongside Hindus. To be sure, in departing from his earlier conception of Muslims as possessing foreign origins and including them in his notion of the Aryan race, Lajpat Rai aligned with the genealogies constructed by colonial scholars and also many *ashraf* Muslims who distinguished between their own high-born, foreign origins and the indigenous, even Hindu, origins of the majority of low-caste Muslims.[106] Though nowhere identical to it, Rai's narrative also shared interesting affinities with ideas later articulated by Abdul Ghaffar Khan (1890–1988), popularly known across India as 'Frontier Gandhi'. Though referring to Pashtun Muslims alone, Khan would argue that while they had embraced Islam, Pashtuns had descended from Aryans and possessed a Hindu–Buddhist lineage and heritage. He would even boldly claim that the Pashtuns were the original Aryan progenitors of India's pre-Islamic civilization.[107] Of course, Rai was not making a claim about any present-day Muslim group being the founders of Hinduism. But he somewhere converged with Khan in providing Muslims with an Aryan Hindu lineage. Rai's bequeathing of Aryan origins to India's Muslims, while problematic, was intended to assert the indigeneity or indigenous nature of Muslims, and bestow Hindus and Muslims with a sense of belonging to a common ancestral community.[108] In doing so, Lajpat Rai also refused the very myth that would be used by certain Hindus to proclaim that the foreignness of Muslims excluded them from Hindu or Indian nationhood.

But considering Rai's membership to the Hindu majority, this kind of Indian nationalism, steeped in notions of Aryan race, and particularly in locating the essence of nationhood in Hindu culture, appeared to gloss over diversity, and remained potentially alienating for several Muslims. It also appears to share some ground with Savarkar's Hindutva ideology, written in *Hindutva: Who is a Hindu?* in 1921 but conceptualized during these very wartime years.[109] Despite naming their nations differently—'Indian' and 'Hindu'—both Rai's wartime nationalism and Savarkarite Hindutva made Hindu culture their defining core, and seemed to include Muslims in the nation only when they were seen to identify with its Hindu essence.

Yet, crucial differences remained. Involved in manufacturing bombs and smuggling pistols and bomb manuals to India, Savarkar's eagerness for anti-colonial violence had led to his arrest in 1910 for, among other charges, 'procuring and distributing arms' and 'waging war against the King in India'.[110] He was sentenced to two life terms in 1911 and sent to Cellular Jail in the Andamans. Whilst in the prison, Savarkar renounced the Indian nationalism he had articulated in *Indian War of Independence* and moved towards Hindutva, the Hindu nationalist ideology that has inspired several generations of Hindu nationalists right until today. Some attribute Savarkar's intellectual shift to his experience of discrimination at the hands of certain Muslim warders at the jail.[111] Others view it as a response to rising Pan-Islamic fervour among prisoners.[112] According to his most recent biographer, Savarkar had begun expressing fears regarding Pan-Islamism ever since the Ottomans entered the war in 1914.[113] Now, in his mind, 'the Muslims in India might find their devil's opportunity to invite the Muslim hordes from the North to ravage India and to conquer it'.[114] In the Hindutva ideology he was now conceptualizing, Savarkar's definition of Hindu nationhood required India's Muslims to renounce attachments to their holy lands outside India, and give up all marks of their religious and cultural identity to assimilate completely into Hindu culture.[115] On the other hand, Lajpat Rai welcomed the heightened Pan-Islamic fervour of the younger generation of Indian Muslims as beneficial for Indian nationhood. His Indian nationalism, despite its Hindu assumptions, demanded neither the abandonment of extraterritorial holy lands nor assimilation into Hindu culture, constituting a significant analytical difference with Hindutva not to be trivialized. Rai easily included Indian Muslims in the Indian nation along with their extraterritorial attachments.[116] And while he may have clutched at the tropes of Aryan race and Hindu culture to justify his new-found conviction that Hindus and Muslims constituted one nation, his lack of demand of assimilation from Muslims meant a practical acceptance of religio-cultural diversity. If the Hindu assumptions of Rai's Indian nationalism ultimately make it a 'Hindu nationalism', it still remained distinct from Savarkarite Hindutva. Rai's nationalism was not a soft version of Hindutva, which implies a toned-down version of essentially the same content. It constituted a distinctively different position—a non-assimilationist,[117] diversity-accepting Hindu nationalism.

Moreover, in his other writings, Lajpat Rai was humming a rather different tune. For instance, in *The Problem of National Education*, he insisted that:

> No Indian, Hindu or Mohammedan, ever attaches any importance to his racial origin or to the racial origins of the rest of his countrymen. *There is no country on the face of the globe which has a pure race.* The sons of man have so freely mixed and mingled in the past, that racial distinctions are only a matter of imagination and conjecture. More often than not they are a cloak for political dominance and economic exploitation . . . In India there is no race conflict. Hindu and Mussulman and Christian are all a racial 'mix up' [*sic*]. The Mussulman descendants of Persia, Afghan, Turkaman [*sic*], Mogul and Arab invaders have a great deal of Aryan blood in their veins and the Hindu descendants of the Aryans have a great deal of Mongolian blood. The Anglo-Indians, too, have all these veins. It is stupid and mischievous to talk of race conflict in India. Mother India knows and recognises no race distinctions.[118]

Here, Lajpat Rai dismissed as fiction the idea of a world of nations comprising single, pure races. Disclaiming the view that Indian followers of different faiths descended from common Aryan ancestors and belonged to a single Aryan race, he instead pronounced that they possessed both Aryan and Mongolian blood. India was not a land of different, conflicting Hindu and Muslim races; it was inhabited by a racially mixed population marked by the absence of racial conflict. By emphasizing the common, jumbled racial origins of Hindus and Muslims, Lajpat Rai implicitly refuted claims that stressed the foreign origins of present-day Muslims as against the indigenous Aryan origins of Hindus. He further produced the following quotation from an essay titled *Patriotism, National and International* (1917) by the America-born Jewish scholar Charles Waldstein:

All these ethnological pretensions and passions—and this is one of
the distinctive features of the modern conflict of 'races'—are based
upon the achievements of and results of modern ethnological
study, the youngest and least accurate of the modern sciences. In
federation with the revised study of philology, comparative religion
and anthropology, the *ethnological politician and agitator* found
fertile field, especially for internal disintegration and antagonism,
in the inner life of modern states (*in most cases neither consciously
nor unconsciously quite free from considerations of material
interest and greeds* [*sic*]) in the antagonism between Aryanism
and Semitism.[119]

Waldstein, the classical archaeologist, erstwhile professor of Art
at the University of Cambridge, and believer in international
cooperation, had, in his previous works, expressed misgivings
about the prevalence of 'ethnological chauvinism' in European
nations which impeded humanitarian brotherhood and destroyed
goodwill within nations.[120] His latest book on patriotism continued
these themes in the context of the war,[121] arguing that politicians
were manipulating the inexact, unreliable discipline of ethnology
to arouse conflict within modern states. Lajpat Rai clarified that
although Waldstein's remarks referred to the role of race theories
in provoking anti-Semitism and internal conflict within states,[122]
such theories were also used by imperialist nations to politically
dominate and economically exploit other nations, a point ignored
by Waldstein. Race theories indeed had an intimate relationship
with imperialism in Asia and Africa from the mid-nineteenth
century onwards.[123] Lajpat Rai's realization that imperialists
exploited categories like race to dominate India compelled him to
dismiss notions of racial purity and celebrate Indians as a 'racial
mix-up' [*sic!*].

Interestingly, Lajpat Rai matched his ability to jettison the idea
of racial purity with his willingness to drop the idea of cultural
homogeneity, thereby completely eschewing European romantic
models of nationality. In his 1915 review of Sister Nivedita's book

Footfalls of Indian History (1915), Rai lauded her argument that India was an 'organic synthesis', a seamless 'whole' which transcended the diverse 'fragments' that composed it and 'moulded' their identity with its national character.[124] He also appreciated the following words on India by this Irish-born disciple of Swami Vivekananda:

> Has she or has she not her own touch that is unmistakable? . . . Even in decorative matters the thing is that Indian [*sic*] cannot be mistaken for a product of any other nationality . . . In form, in costume, in character and, above all, in thought, the thing that is Indian is unlike any un-Indian thing in the whole world.'[125]

Lajpat Rai approved Sister Nivedita's thesis that India 'lives' as an 'individual unit' which, despite borrowing elements from 'world-culture', was determined to 'assimilate and nationalise' these.[126] Instead of insisting on Hindu culture as a unifying force, Lajpat Rai sometimes chose to affirm India's national cultural unity in abstract, indeterminate and even mystical terms. The unnamed indeterminacy of the overarching distinctiveness of Indian culture that 'moulded' and 'assimilated' its diverse components into a nationality likely served to encompass India's diversity rather than tacitly refer to Hinduism. This is suggested by Lajpat Rai in the same review:

> The present writer [Lajpat Rai] has expressed several times that these national festivals are the milestones on the road to national life, landmarks in the history of the nation, and he is glad to notice there is a conscious awakening to their value and significance in the life of the nation. The Hindus and Muslims would do well to take part in each other's festivals instead of making them the occasion of breaking each other's heads. With the exception of a very few festivals, most of the Hindu and Mohammedan festivals can be given an all-India character. One cannot understand why Mohammedans cannot take part in celebration of *Basant Panchami, Bisakhi, Dussehra* and *Diwali*; nor why Hindus cannot join in the celebration of *Muharram* and the *Shab-i-Barat*.[127]

In recommending that Muslim festivals be celebrated as 'national' festivals, Lajpat Rai clearly expressed his desire that aspects of Muslim culture be celebrated as constitutive of India's publicly expressed 'national' culture. In *The Problem of National Education*, he included Muslim personalities in his pantheon of national icons, insisting that 'we modern Indians can be as well proud of a Hali,[128] an Iqbal, a Mohani[129] as of Tagore, Roy[130] and Harish Chandra.[131] We are proud of Syed Ahmed Khan as of Rammohun Roy and Dayanand'.[132] Similarly, he approvingly quoted the following words from the book *India and the Future* written by British journalist William Archer after his recent visit to India:

> The educated Mussulman does not withhold his admiration from the religious, philosophic, and epic literature of the Hindus. He takes pride in it as the literature of India; just as the educated Hindu reckons the Taj and Fatehpur Sikri among the glories, not of Muslim, but of Indian architecture.[133]

Here, Muslim architecture was acknowledged as Indian culture. Unlike the *Self-Determination* pamphlet which appeared to deny space to Muslim culture, Rai's other writings acknowledged and promoted what he considered Muslim culture as Indian national culture. In *Young India,* in his approving quotation of Haq's 1915 speech, he was able to acknowledge that Indian civilization and even Hindus had been enriched and reshaped anew through contact with the splendour of Muslim culture:

> The Muslims enriched the hoary civilisation of India with their own literature and art, evolved and developed by their own creative and versatile genius. From the Himalayas to Cape Comorin the entire country is studded with those gems of art which remind us of the glorious period of Muslim rule. The result was a new civilisation which was the outcome of the combined efforts of all the peoples of India and the product of the two great civilisations in the history of the world . . . Ethnology and folklore of India

eloquently speak of manners and customs showing influence of one people upon the other.[134]

The words with which Lajpat Rai ended his review of Vincent Smith's latest book, this time on the Mughal emperor Akbar, clearly revealed his desire that Islam and Islamic culture be constitutive of Indian national culture:

> In his person, Akbar *combined the best elements of real Islam and real Hinduism.* That in itself is an evidence [sic] of Akbar's greatness of soul. May his memory inspire his countrymen, Hindu and Mohammedan, in building the future national edifice in such a way as to combine not just *the best of the two old cultures*, but also the best of the new one, that has since been born in the West, from which India is drawing copiously.[135]

Lajpat Rai's desire to deliberately fashion a pluralist Indian national culture is also apparent in his treatment of the question of national language. In previous years, he had promoted Hindi as the national language of Hindus. Even now, when desperate to prove Indian nationhood in the face of imperialist denial, as in *Self-Determination for India*, he could affirm that India's only sacred language, Sanskrit, provided unity to linguistically diverse Indians.[136] But in his more reflective book addressed to Indians, *The Problem of National Education*, he clearly wrote:

> I may assume that the country will readily adopt Hindustani as the future national language of India, if the Hindus and Mussulmans could come to an agreement on the question of script. The adoption of Hindustani as a national language does not in any way affect the provincial vernaculars. The provincial vernaculars must be the medium of instruction in primary schools of each province, with the addition of Hindustani as an All-India language, the Hindus learning it in Deva Nagri and the Mussulmans in Urdu characters.[137]

Though at least Tamil would have found place among provincial vernaculars, like most North Indian politician–thinkers, Lajpat Rai sidestepped the issue of Dravidian languages when it came to the question of national language. But within this North Indian-centric vision, his promotion of Hindustani in both scripts as the national language shows that when it came to practically crafting national culture in the present, Lajpat Rai did not aim to pass off some homogenized Hindu culture as Indian national culture.[138] Theorists and scholars of nationalism today argue that conceptions of the nation, which sincerely celebrate diversity in public culture, alone allow for a genuine multiculturalism.[139] In desiring both a syncretic Indian national culture and Hindustani as India's national language, Lajpat Rai advocated what we today might call a multicultural national identity. In fact, even *Self-Determination for India*—which built a case for Indian nationhood by stressing India's geographical unity and its linguistic, racial and cultural homogeneity—ended with the assertion that what made a people a nation were not such *objective* criteria but the 'desire' to be one, a *subjective* criterion. It quoted an essay titled *Nationality* written in 1862 by Lord Acton, the nineteenth-century politician and professor of Modern History at Cambridge, to state that:

> A nation is no longer what it had been in the ancient world, a progeny of common ancestors, or the aboriginal product of a particular religion, a result of merely physical and material causes, but a moral and political being; not the creation of a geographical or physiological unity, but developed in the course of history by the action of the state . . . it is derived from the state and is not supreme over it.[140]

In contrast to its own earlier argument of the Indian nation as naturally and ethnically given, the pamphlet now asserted that all modern nations, rather than constituting given entities that preceded the state, were in fact its products. Under a state, people gradually 'became animated with sympathies which make them cooperate with one another more willingly than with other people and desire to be under the same government.'[141] Such a 'desire for cooperation exists throughout India' and had been 'accelerated and accentuated by British domination.'[142] Thus, Indian national consciousness, likely still assumed to have been set in motion by successive states earlier, had been hastened by British colonialism. The Lucknow Pact between the Congress and the League was adduced as an example of this accelerated desire among Hindus and Muslims to settle differences and cooperate politically as Indians. The text went on, 'so intense was the feeling of unity throughout India that any attempt to divide the country into independent states would provoke indignant responses'.[143] This intense *desire* to be a united Indian nation made the Indian people a nation. Thus, to make his case that the people of India constituted a single Indian nation, Lajpat Rai could use narrower, objective ethno-linguistic criteria in the style of German Romantics, with some problematic implications for India's Muslims, but also equally underplay these and give weight to a subjective criterion of the kind stressed by the famous nineteenth-century French philosopher, Ernst Renan. One of the earliest thinkers of nations and nationalism, Renan emphasized that what made nations were not any objective criterion like race, language, religion or geography, but the subjective feeling and desire of wanting to be a nation. Though ignoring the fact that some might not consent to the notion of one Indian nation[144]— relying on the subjective criterion allowed Lajpat Rai to more easily posit a united Indian nation which accommodated India's startling religious, linguistic and cultural diversity.

Addressing an Indian audience in *The Problem of National Education*, Lajpat Rai conceded that this subjective criterion was not already met and that Indian national consciousness had to be actively inculcated. Yet, he revealed the same contented embrace of India's deep diversity: 'every child should be taught in so many words that every human being born in India, or of Indian parents, or who has made India his or her home, is a compatriot, a brother or a sister, regardless of colour, creed, caste or vocation.'[145] In attempting to forge the Indian nation, Lajpat Rai allowed the inclusion of every individual born in India, and choosing to reside in and love it as their home. Lajpat Rai's definition was commodious enough to accommodate the Anglo–Indian community and even those without 'Indian' lineage such as Annie Besant and Sister Nivedita, whom he referred to as India's 'adopted children'.[146] This broad and accommodative conception of Indian nationhood readily included India's Muslims and Christians, with all their religio-cultural differences, a vision quite distant from a definition of Indian nationhood that demanded that non-Hindus first declare their love for Hindu culture or acknowledge their essential Hindu-ness. Similarly, Lajpat Rai's assertion that the 'essential' unity of the Hindus, Muslims, Christians, Buddhists, Parsis, Sikhs and Jains of India[147] affirmed the unity of the Indian people as an axiom, requiring no demonstration.[148] He recommended Radhakumud Mukherjea's *Fundamental Unity of India* (1914) which, as its title suggests, made similar assertions, as a textbook for all national schools and to be read by every patriotic Indian.[149] This manoeuvre—of simply asserting the self-evident, fundamental unity of Indians—circumvented the prickly problem of explaining how the Indian nation could exist amidst staggering diversity even as the latter was seamlessly accommodated into the definition of the Indian nation.

Indeed, Lajpat Rai's aversion to homogeneity was evident in his authorization of the following statement in *Self-Determination for India*:

> . . . to require races of India to coalesce into a nation with one religion and one tongue, is midsummer madness. It would revive the medieval idea of one empire, one people, one church. The world is now happily rid of such tyranny. America presented to the world the principle of federalism, the last of the political principle, but the richest in promise of peace and freedom.[150]

Inspired by the administrative federalism of the United States, the pamphlet welcomed federalism as a solution to the conundrum of

India's famed religio-cultural diversity.[151] A future autonomous federal government for the Indian nation would grant autonomy to the culturally diverse regions that composed it. Dedicated to self-government for the Indian nation, Lajpat Rai also committed himself to granting partial self-rule to its constituent cultural units. Federalism would realize a culturally plural Indian nation that embraced diversity, protecting the smaller cultural units from being overridden and threatened. Importantly, since a federal plan would grant more autonomy to provinces, and since Bengal and Punjab, the North-West Frontier Province and Baluchistan were Muslim-majority provinces,[152] championing federalism inevitably meant supporting a notion of Indian nationhood that accommodated significant Muslim cultural autonomy. Clearly, despite his desire that religion be transcended at all political levels, Lajpat Rai could afford religio-cultural diversity considerable space for political expression at the provincial level. It was perhaps precisely because he was willing to provide religion such political expression that he desired its transcendence at all other political levels, particularly what he considered the supreme level of political identity: Indian national identity.

So, whilst in America, Lajpat Rai firmly and explicitly rejected the isolationist religion/religious community-based definitions of nationhood he had so frequently articulated in the decades before. Instead, he articulated ideas around what may broadly be called a secular 'Indian' national identity. As alluded to at the start of this chapter, Lajpat Rai's new ideas harboured an internal tension that he would seriously attempt to resolve only in the mid-1920s. In *Self-Determination for India*, his acceptance of the Lucknow Pact sanctioned a conception of a secular Indian nation in which Hindus and Muslims could function as distinct religio-political communities. The supreme secular Indian national identity was seen as legitimately existing alongside narrower, sub-national[153] religion-based political identities. His preference for a federal India similarly permitted the expression of sub-national, religion-based provincial or regional identities alongside the overarching secular

Indian national identity. But in *The Problem of National Education* he articulated the hope that overriding secular Indian national identity would be grounded in a complete rejection of all religion-based political identities. Even so, this internal tension within Rai's new nationalist thought—about the extent to which the secular Indian national identity could permit narrower religion-based political identities—was compatible with, and coexisted with, his sincere desire to see Hindus and Muslims united under the supreme secular Indian national identity.

But things were still a little more complicated. Lajpat Rai renounced his erstwhile isolationist 'Hindu nationalism', and rejected religion-based definitions of nationhood. But his now firmly adopted religion-transcending and secularized 'Indian' national identity could sometimes take his new, ostensibly secular Indian nationalism in the direction of what can actually legitimately be called Hindu nationalism. As we saw in the *Self-Determination for India* pamphlet published by his Home Rule League, Lajpat Rai could endorse attempts to unite Hindus and Muslims into a single Indian nation by invoking Hindu tropes of an Aryan race and Hindu culture. So, while he seemed to keep religion separated from the 'Indian' national identity, Lajpat Rai could sometimes still affirm definitions of Indian nationhood that took 'Hindu culture' to be India's essence. In its privileging of a timeless Aryan Hindu culture as India's national essence, and implicitly denying that India's Muslims (and several other religious and non-religious communities) had similarly shaped Indian national culture, Lajpat Rai's new ostensibly secular Indian nationalism could occasionally swing towards becoming a kind of Hindu nationalism. As we saw, however, this Hindu nationalism remained distinct from Savarkar's newly articulated Hindutva nationalism. The latter sought a culturally homogenized Hindu nation which included Muslims and Christians only on the condition of complete assimilation into 'Hindu culture'. On the contrary, in the *Self-Determination* pamphlet, these Hindu tropes were used to urgently convince a foreign readership that Hindus and Muslims shared, despite their religious differences, an overarching sense of belonging to a common national community. Potentially alienating, and stopping short of articulating India's national identity in more fully inclusive terms, Rai's reliance on Hindu tropes did not reflect a desire to supress diversity and impose a Hindu racial lineage or culture on India's non-Hindus. This is further confirmed by the fact that these tropes were readily dropped in the *Self-Determination* pamphlet in favour of a subjective criterion for nationhood, federalism and a dismissal of homogeneity as 'madness'. The different intent behind the Hindu assumptions of Rai's 'Indian' nationhood—to provide an overarching unity to Hindus and Muslims while practically accepting a large degree of diversity—clearly differentiated Lajpat Rai's new Hindu-leaning 'Indian' nationalism from Savarkar's Hindutva nationalism.

The story of Lajpat Rai's new 'Indian' nationalism did not end here. In *The Problem of National Education* and his book reviews, Lajpat Rai dismissed the idea of an Aryan race to speak of Hindu and Muslim Indians as an Aryan–Mongolian racial admixture. He jettisoned the assumption that Indian Muslims were merely shaped by India's essentially Hindu culture, making little contribution to this national culture. Instead, he conceived Indian national culture in broader, more fully inclusive terms, acknowledging Muslim contributions to it, and envisioning a genuinely pluralistic public culture for his Indian nation, that was more concretely respectful of Muslim cultural differences and deep diversity at large. As we saw, in *The Problem of National Education,* Lajpat Rai once briefly also declared that 'religion is a matter of individual faith and taste; and with the common civil life of the country, religion does not and should not interfere'.[154] Desiring that 'religion' be expelled from the idea of the 'nation', Lajpat Rai here seemed to advocate that religious communities be transcended altogether to make a common civic–political culture (rather than multi-religious culture) the basis of Indian nationhood. On several occasions during the war years, Lajpat Rai entirely abandoned his Hindu assumptions in an endeavour to elaborate an even more fully accommodative, inclusive and pluralist conception of Indian nationhood. These aspects of his new nationalist thought cannot be categorized as a 'Hindu nationalism' of even the above-mentioned non-Hindutva, diversity-accepting variety. It was instead a properly secular and pluralist Indian nationalism, which attempted to unite India's Hindus and Muslims under a secular Indian national identity, by unearthing and crafting for them a common secular pluralist national culture which they could share. Rai's turn towards this genuinely secular, pluralist Indian nationalism was reflected in his reinterpretation of Indian history, particularly India's 'Muslim' history, to which we shall now turn.

11

Revisiting India's History: Indigenizing 'Muslim Rule'

As we saw in Chapter 5, in a 1902 newspaper article titled 'Hindu nationalism', Lajpat Rai had claimed that Hindus had historically possessed a sense of nationality, and advanced as proof a historical narrative of ancient and early medieval Hindu empires as well as Hindu resistance to 'foreign' Muslim rule.[1] Even then Lajpat Rai's history had lacked the Savarkarite Hindutva emphasis on ceaseless, inevitable conflict and warfare between Hindus and Muslims, nor had it viewed Muslim rule as marked by the intention to defile and eradicate Hinduism, or dominate and humiliate Hindus.[2] Still, his argument had broadly presaged, by two decades, the narrative of Indian history constructed by Savarkar from the war years—in its assumptions that Hindu nationality crystallized during resistance to Muslim rule, of the indigenous nature of the Hindu nation against the foreignness of Muslims, and its presentation of the historical relationship of Hindus and Muslims as consisting merely of opposition. This historical narrative had matched Lajpat Rai's conceptualization of Hindus and Muslims as separate, competitive 'nationalities', and his indifference towards providing them with a common identity or unity.

201

After 1915, Lajpat Rai moved in a different direction. In light of his new 'Indian' nationalist imagination, he felt the need to revisit and reinterpret the medieval Persianate period[3] of India's history. Rather than underscoring how the Hindu nation was actualized while resisting Muslim rule, this new historical narrative attempted to counter portrayals of Muslim rule as foreign and as a period marked by domination, oppression and antagonism. The period of 'Muslim rule' was re-imagined as one involving socio-cultural interaction, political equality, religious tolerance and concord, and even exemplifying virtuous Indian self-governance.

To be sure, in his account of India's past in *Young India*, Lajpat Rai retained his earlier narrative of pre-Muslim 'native' Hindu rule.[4] He insisted that 'the idea of universal sovereignty over the whole of India under one paramount power' was known to Hindus; 'Chandragupta, the Hindu' had established a complex, modern administration in North India from Assam to Afghanistan, and under Ashoka 'the whole country was consolidated under one imperial sway'.[5] The two most famous Maurya kings—one likely Jain, and the other Buddhist—were incorporated into Rai's narrative of Hindu rule. It was asserted that before the thirteenth century 'no foreign rule had been imposed upon it from without', such that the mainland remained under 'native rulers and native laws', and it took 'the Muslims' four hundred years to establish their first kingdom in India. This retained the nativity of Hindus and continued Lajpat Rai's earlier attempts to contest discourses that denied Hindu experience in political rule.

Lajpat Rai also continued to deny narratives that interpreted 'Muslim rule' as implying the complete political defeat of Hindus, underscoring that the first three of six centuries of 'Muslim rule' remained confined to the North. Even when Akbar consolidated the whole country, fierce resistance was offered by the valiant Rana Pratap of Udaipur, who gained the sympathy of the 'patriotic Hindus' in Akbar's court. Writing of the Sikhs, Rajputs and Marathas in the eighteenth century, Lajpat Rai maintained that 'Muslim supremacy was destroyed by the Hindus and not the British'.[6] The insistence on 'independent' Hindu political rule in the South, 'Hindu' compassion for Rana Pratap's resistance to Akbar, and the final Hindu challenge to Muslim authority continued his earlier attempts to bolster Hindu self-esteem, and maintained a distinction between Hindus and Muslims problematic for any attempt to construct for them a common ancestry or history as Indians.[7]

However, Lajpat Rai qualified this discussion with elaborate intellectual manoeuvres aimed at indigenizing 'Muslim' rule (i.e., emphasizing its indigenous, non-foreign nature):

> Yet it is not right to say that the Muslim rule in India was a 'foreign rule'. The Muslim invaders were no doubt foreign in their origin, (just as the Normans and Danes were when they came to England), but as soon as they had settled in India, they adopted the country, made it their home, married and raised their children there, and *became sons of the soil*. Akbar and Aurangzeb were as much Indians as are today the Moguls and Pathans in Delhi or elsewhere. Sher Shah and Ibrahim Lodi were not more foreigners in India than were the descendants of William the Conqueror or successors of William of Orange in Great Britain. When Timur and Nadir Shah and Ahmad Shah Abdali attacked India, they attacked a kingdom which was ruled by *Indian* Muslims. They were as much the enemies of the Mohammedan rulers of India as of the Hindus. The Muslims, who exercised political sovereignty in India from the thirteenth up to the middle of the nineteenth century A.D., were Indians by birth, Indians by marriage and Indians by death. They were born in India, they married there, there they died, and there they were buried.[8]

After annexing or subjugating significant parts of present-day Tajikistan, Iran and Iraq, Russia, Syria, Turkey and Egypt, the Central Asian conqueror Timur had invaded India and sacked Delhi in 1398–99, clashing with the Tughluqs of the Delhi sultanate, and destroying their power and prestige. A little more than three centuries later, in 1739, the Persian warlord Nadir Shah would similarly sack Delhi, after defeating a Mughal army under Mohammad Shah, a post-Aurangzeb-era Mughal emperor. Then, in 1748, Ahmad Shah Abdali, the powerful Afghan warlord, raided North India, attacking Mughal governors as much as the Marathas.[9] Lajpat Rai was broadly correct when he clarified that these had been instances of non-Hindustani 'Muslims' attacking Hindustani 'Muslim' sultans. He was also largely correct in viewing the Mughals as Indian. Having appropriated much of India's pre-Persianate culture, the Mughals had seen themselves as Hindustani kings and wished to be seen by others as such.[10] And a similar desire to stress their nativity to their Hindustani homeland was also witnessed during the pre-Mughal Delhi Sultanate era.[11]

Lajpat Rai drew on British history, specifically themes of the gradual amalgamation of the foreign Norman conquerors into Britain, to emphasize the eventual Indianization of the once-foreign Muslim invaders. Although propagated in a different century in a different context and for entirely different purposes, Lajpat Rai's intellectual manoeuvres to underplay the conventional trope of 'the Muslim conquest'[12] resembled attempts by English parliamentarians in the seventeenth century to downplay and legitimize the Norman conquest in 1066, and refute claims that the Normans had a relationship of pure domination over the Saxons.[13] The Stuart king, James I, and his supporters had asserted his absolute right to rule over England by insisting that, as the leader of the Normans, he possessed this right by the Norman conquest of England. The parliamentarians, wishing to limit the power of the monarchy, refuted this discourse by 'dressing' the conquest in legitimacy, arguing that the first Norman King, William 'the Conqueror', had not conquered England but in fact had inherited the right to rule it from previous Anglo–Saxon kings by making himself part of their system of monarchy and its own unique laws. This is virtually how Lajpat Rai now saw India's Sultanate and Mughal emperors. Without suggesting direct influence, it is interesting to note the striking affinity between Lajpat Rai's words and those of a seventeenth-century English politician–historian who asserted that 'William did not conquer England: it was the English that had conquered William'.[14] In his 1918 review of Vincent Smith's

Akbar, Lajpat Rai endorsed Smith's statement that while Akbar conquered India, 'it cannot be denied that Akbar was also conquered by India'.[15] Whether or not Smith was influenced by earlier British discourses, he used a remarkably similar language whilst writing about Akbar. Affirming Smith, Lajpat Rai was possibly indirectly influenced by diffused British discourses legitimizing the Norman conquest as he reinterpreted 'Muslim' rule in India. Just as English parliamentarians had once underplayed the Norman conquest to limit the power of the monarch, just so Lajpat Rai now reinterpreted and minimized the significance of the 'Muslim' conquest by asserting the acquired indigeneity of Indian Muslims.

In Lajpat Rai's new understanding of Indian history, the story of 'Muslim' rule was not one of conquest and domination but of racial and cultural intermingling whereby Muslim rulers lost their alien foreignness. He substantiated this by contrasting the indigenous nature of 'Muslim' rule with the foreign, colonial nature of British rule. India's Muslim rulers rarely ruled it as a foreign country using 'servants from Arabia, Persia or Afghanistan' (as the British did by recruiting officials from Britain), and did not discriminate socially or politically against their Hindu subjects:

> Their bias, if any, against the Hindus was religious, not political. The converts to Islam were sometimes treated with greater consideration than even the original Muslims – Akbar, of course, did away with that distinction – but even the most bigoted and the most orthodox Mohammedan ruler of India was not possessed of that kind of social pride and social exclusiveness which distinguishes the British ruler of India today. If the racial question ever came to prominence during Mohammedan supremacy in India, it was not between Hindus and Mohammedans, but between Mohammedans and Mohammedans, as for instance between *Tuglaks* and *Pathans*, or between *Moguls* and *Lodis* . . . In the reign of rulers like Sher Shah, Akbar, Jahangir, and Shah Jehan, the Hindus were eligible for highest offices under the crown next after the princes of the royal blood. They were governors of

provinces, generals of armies, and rulers of districts and divisions. In short, the distinctions between Hindus and Muslims were neither political nor social.[16]

In Lajpat Rai's view, in contrast to the racial arrogance and exclusivity of the British who treated Hindus as social inferiors and debarred them from most political positions, India's Muslim rulers displayed no such prejudice or hubris and recruited Hindus to high political posts; unlike the British even their army had been 'wholly Indian'. Meritocratic openness under 'Muslim' rule—having produced a 'Hindu' prime minister, commander-in-chief, finance minister and governor of Kabul[17]—had reached its peak under Akbar who made Hindus see him as 'their own', and who even had intimate friendships and marital relationships with Hindus.[18] Indeed, even the early Ghaznavid armies had Hindu generals and Jat soldiers. Under the Mughals, Rajputs were a vital component of the administrative nobility and military elite.[19] And as Lajpat Rai rightly acknowledged, Akbar had married the daughters of Rajput chiefs and placed them socially on a par with other women of the court, which in turn had led to the diffusion of Rajput values in Mughal culture.[20] The indigeneity of Muslim rulers was further proved by Rai who argued that, rather than exhibiting conceit, they contributed to the evolution of Indian culture:

> They brought their own language and literature with them. For a time, perhaps, they transacted all government business through that language, but eventually they evolved a language which is as much Indian as any other vernacular spoken in India today. The groundwork of this language, which is now called Urdu or Hindustani, is purely Indian.[21]

This difference was also reflected in the policies of Muslim rulers which aimed not at exploiting India in the interests of a foreign country but at benefiting India:

Every penny of the revenues they raised in India was spent in India . . . Looked at from the economic point of view, the government was as much indigenous as under Hindu rule . . . They had no Lancashire industries to protect, and were under no necessity of imposing excise duties on Indian-made goods . . . The Muslim rulers of India had no anxiety for, and were in no way concerned with, the prosperity of the labouring classes of Persia or Afghanistan. If anyone sought their patronage, he had to come and settle in India. So their government was an Indian government and not a foreign government . . . Her revenues were spent for her own benefit. She had her industries and manufactured the goods she consumed. Anyone wanting the privilege of trading with India under special terms had to obtain sanction with her government, as the East India Company did.[22]

Lajpat Rai concluded that prior to British rule India had never been a 'dependency' controlled by a far-off, alien, 'non-Indian' nation:

History does not record a single instance of India being ruled from without, by a people of purely non-Indian blood and in the interests of another country and another people, before the British. India was always an empire by herself. She was never part of another empire, much less a dependency. She had her own army, her own navy, her own flag . . . There was no India Office in Arabia or in Persia or in Kabul, to which the people of India looked for initiative in the affairs of their native land . . . India, under the British is, however, entirely different.[23]

Muslim rule was contrasted with British rule in India to highlight that just as assertions of racial and social exclusiveness by the British made them foreign, their absence made Muslim rule indigenous. Unlike India's British rulers, its Muslim rulers led governments by and for Indians, which were therefore Indian governments. Thus, Britain served two crucial functions for Lajpat Rai's historical narrative.

England's historical assimilation of the initially 'foreign' conquering Norman race helped him reinterpret the 'Muslim' conquest of India and refute the foreignness of Muslim rule. Additionally, the British conquest of India, with its assertions of racial and social exclusivity, served to highlight its foreign nature against which was contrasted the indigenous nature of Muslim rule in India, symbolized by its openness to racial and sociocultural intermingling. Muslim rule was re-imagined as a sort of self-governing Indian empire–nation, with its distinct institutions and emblems—'her own army, her own navy, her own flag'.[24] Instead of standing alongside British rule as an example of foreign rule, Muslim rule now became a continuation of the indigenous rule of India's Hindu rulers. The 'Muslim' period of India's history travelled away from its British period and towards its 'Hindu' period.

Successive British colonial historians of India stressed the theme of 'Muslim' tyranny and violence as a means of rationalizing the British occupation of India. The British were portrayed as having liberated India from eight centuries of terrible Muslim rule.[25] In presenting Muslim rule as Indian self-rule, Lajpat Rai de-emphasized the violence associated with Muslim rule in these British colonial histories, as well as the Hindu/Indian nationalist discourses that drew on them.[26] In *The Problem of National Education,* he clarified that earlier 'Muslim' raids and invasions into 'India', when 'long trains of slaves taken by Mahmud and others', occurred when Muslims had no presence in India, and that 'general massacres ordered by Tamerlane [Timur] and Nadir Shah' spared neither Hindus nor Muslims.[27] He contested Vincent Smith's accounts of the assassinations allegedly ordered by Akbar, arguing that they were based on 'the flimsiest possible evidence',[28] and criticized Smith's 'undue' censure of Akbar for inflicting barbarous punishments on his enemies.[29] Lajpat Rai even protested that there was 'no authentic record of Aurangzeb having ordered any general massacre of the Hindus in any part of the country'.[30] His reconstructed history of 'Muslim' rule was shorn of images of violence and barbarity. It simultaneously downscaled narratives of Hindu–Muslim conflict by placing it in the comparative context of Christian sectarian conflict in Europe:

A careful scanning of the history of India for the last thousand years, from the invasion of Abdul Qasim[31] [*sic*] to the disappearance of the last vestige of Mogul sovereignty shows nothing which by any stretch of imagination may be compared with the conflict between Roman Catholicism and Protestantism which raged in Europe for over four centuries. Is there anything in Indian history which can be cited as parallel to the massacre of St. Bartholomew's Day in France, or to the orgies committed by rival sects in Holland, Spain, Italy, Germany, and even Great Britain and Ireland, in their frenzied attempts to extirpate one another?[32]

His comparison of Hindu–Muslim relations to Christian sectarian conflict already imputing an in-built intimacy, Lajpat Rai underlined their relative peaceful coexistence under Muslim rule. He not only lauded Akbar for his interest in and patronage of all faiths,[33] but questioned whether 'even Aurangzeb' had ever seriously tried to 'overpower and outcast' Hinduism.[34] Vincent Smith was criticized for claiming that under the Delhi sultans, the 'public exercise of Hindu religion was illegal', 'frequently treated as capital offence'.[35] Quoting William Archer, he argued that Muslim princes had ruled over Hindu subjects as Hindu princes had ruled over Muslims—with a 'very tolerable impartiality of rule or misrule'.[36] Rai concluded that 'Hindus had come to realise that, after all, the Mohammedan rule in India was not so bad or tyrannical and oppressive as they were told by interested historians' and that 'even Aurangzeb was not, after all, as bad as they had supposed him to be'.[37]

Lajpat Rai challenged British imperialist discourses, which contrasted an India in which Hindus and Muslims were historically locked in religious bigotry and conflict,[38] with Europe as the locus of enlightenment and civilization.[39] He instead conjured late medieval/early modern Europe as a site of religious conflict and dogmatism, against which the 'Muslim' period of Indian history was contrasted as a site of peaceful pluralism. While Europe had ruthlessly stamped out religious diversity, India's Muslim rulers had not. Thus, just as Lajpat Rai affirmed America's federalism as a model for realizing a culturally plural polity, and Britain's history to tackle the Muslim conquest of India, he pointed to Europe's wars of religion to highlight the relative peace and tolerance under India's 'Muslim' period.

Instead of massacres, conflict and oppression, Lajpat Rai's history of the 'Muslim' period evoked images of peace, fairness and even benevolence. Refuting Vincent Smith's evaluation of Akbar's rule as representing a 'vast multitude of petty local despotisms' kept in order by 'an overpowering autocracy', Lajpat Rai proclaimed that this was a better description of British rule in India.[40] He constructed Akbar's reign as a period of good statesmanship, brilliant and efficient administration, and economic abundance—conveying images of order and prosperity.[41] In doing so, he again diverged from British as well as Indian/Hindu nationalist discourses which presented Muslim rule in India as a period of despotism, misrule and anarchy.[42]

Motifs of historical Muslim violence and oppression against Hindus had the potential to arouse resentment and animosity at worst and otherness and estrangement at best. By positing an alternative history of 'Muslim' rule marked by fairness towards Hindus, Lajpat Rai implicitly nudged Hindus to view Muslims as a community whom they could trust, live with peacefully and unite with for common action.[43] This reconfiguration of India's history encouraged present-day Hindus and Muslims to recognize each other's worth, 'take pride' in each other's history and culture[44] and see themselves as sharing a common Indian identity. While his newly imagined Indian nation led him to readjust his historical narrative, revising the latter in turn enabled him to rationalize, legitimize and fortify his reinvented Indian nation. As these words from *The Problem of National Education* show, Lajpat Rai was conscious of the role rewriting history could play in fostering present Indian national unity:

> The teaching of Hindu-Mohammedan unity can be greatly facilitated by the writing of special and carefully worded theses on the lives of our national heroes. Lives of Shivaji, Pratap, and Govind Singh, as well as those of Akbar, Sher Shah and Shah Jahan, must be carefully written . . . they should be scrupulously

true, but written from a broad, patriotic and national point of view. They should be a composite production of patriotic and scientific history. Hindus should learn to take pride in the achievements of Mohammedan heroes, saints, and writers, and the Mohammedans in those of the Hindus.[45]

Rewriting history to foster a national identity and unity was of course not unique to India. In the nineteenth century, Britain had seen similar attempts to revise history to forge a British national identity that included the Scots, the Welsh and the Irish alongside the English.[46] Even real historical conflicts between the Scots and the English were deliberately ignored to create a British national identity and unity in the face of constant wars with France. A reconfigured history—of the Normans and Saxons (from whom the English claimed ancestry) eventually setting aside their enmity in the interest of national unity—was advanced to foster British national unity in the present.[47] Lajpat Rai's reinterpreted history of Hindu–Muslim relations intended much the same for his newly elaborated Indian nation in the early twentieth century, although he in fact moved closer to, rather than further away from, how professional historians today understand India's medieval history.[48]

To be sure, residues of an earlier historical imagination remained. Apart from the motif of Hindu resistance to Muslim rule, Rai's narrative still sporadically associated the 'Muslim' period with medieval decline and stagnation. In one newspaper article, he claimed that the position of Indian women had declined since Vedic times, 'the worst changes having occurred under the influence of Moslem dominance'.[49] In his review of Smith's *Akbar* he pronounced that there was 'great truth' in Smith's remark that the 'Mohammedan period' was 'necessarily a chronicle of kings, courts, and conquests, rather than one of national and social evolution'.[50] Here, despite his elaborate indigenization of India's 'Muslim' rulers in *Young India*, he also referred to Akbar as 'a foreigner, in whose veins there was not a drop of Indian blood'.[51] But rather than belying his endeavour, these remarks highlight both the fragility of Lajpat Rai's new vision, and the genuine and enormous effort he had mustered elsewhere to break out of his older mode of thought to forge a new, shared Indian national identity for India's Hindus and Muslims.

In the previous chapter, we saw that during his self-imposed exile in America, Lajpat Rai attempted to bolster a common secular Indian national identity for India's Hindus and Muslims by fashioning for them a common pluralist national culture. He clearly also strove to do so through a reinterpretation of India's history. Manan Ahmed Asif, an intellectual historian of medieval Hindustan, has argued that the partition of the Indian subcontinent in 1947 was ultimately the outcome of anti-colonial actors, both Hindu and Muslim, progressively internalizing British colonial discourse about the foreignness of Muslims to India, and considering the medieval period of Indian history as one of despotism and decay.[52] Yet, during the war years, Lajpat Rai strove to challenge this narrative of the history of India. Evidently aware that it was India's medieval period that generated acrimony, estrangement and bitterness, he turned to it and launched a reinterpretation of it, puncturing the idea of an oppressive and violent Muslim colonialism over India and its Hindu inhabitants, and emphasizing the nativity of Indian Muslims.[53] If historical narratives of separation—or, histories of 'perverted sectionalism', as one concerned historian in the 1930s would put it[54]—produced real-life separation between India's Hindus and Muslims, Lajpat Rai arduously attempted to prevent this outcome. He did so by arguing that both Hindus and Muslims belonged to India, and seeking a way of thinking about India's history that could thwart separatism,[55] and realize unity instead of division.[56] In doing so, Lajpat Rai, the man so often considered a forefather of Hindutva, in fact stepped into the prehistory of another body of ideas—that of secular nationalist history-writing, of which Jawaharlal Nehru's *Discovery of India* (1946) is conventionally considered a foundational text, and which would come to underpin the official ideology of the post-independent Indian nation–state.[57] In his critical analysis of what he calls 'communal' and 'secular' history-writing, historian Neeladri Bhattacharya has noted, in a descriptive vein, that communal histories view Hindus and Muslims as irreconcilably opposed to each other and as sharing little in common, and emphasize a history of discord and antagonism. On the other hand, secular histories have attempted to highlight the porosity of boundaries between Hindus and Muslims, and have attempted to highlight a history of concord, harmony and togetherness. While communal histories have heard only voices of sectarianism, secular histories have searched for histories of tolerance.[58] A full three decades before the-much-younger Nehru would embark on a similar project, Lajpat Rai attempted to craft a historical narrative which aimed, as Bhattacharya puts it, 'to constitute memories that would make intercommunity dialogues and understanding possible'.[59] His reinterpretation of India's medieval history aimed to strengthen the common, overarching secular Indian national identity which he now believed united—and must unite—India's Hindus and Muslims.

12

Supporting the Caliphate

When in 1919, in collaboration with Mohandas Karamchand Gandhi (1869–1948), a section of the Indian Muslim leadership launched the Khilafat movement, Lajpat Rai was still in the United States. The movement aimed to defend the Ottoman caliphate and empire. As briefly mentioned in Chapter 10, since the late nineteenth century, a section of prominent Indian Muslims had begun to espouse Pan-Islamic ideas, viewing themselves as part of a global Muslim community that shared a common Islamic civilization, with the Ottoman caliph as its spiritual head and the Ottoman Empire its temporal embodiment.

Throughout history, the idea of the caliphate has been the subject of divergent interpretations and has been put into practice in vastly different ways. The original caliphate (632–661 CE) was founded after the death of Prophet Mohammad in 632 CE when his close companions assumed leadership of the relatively small early Muslim community in Medina.[1] This early caliphate was grounded in the belief that caliphs represented the deceased prophet and, as his temporal successors, must lead the Muslim community.[2] The early caliphate was marked by the reigns of four successive loosely elected caliphs, by Arab expansion, intra-Muslim violence and even violent mutinies against and assassinations of some caliphs.[3] The subsequent Syria-based Ummayid caliphate (661–750 CE) itself emerged out of a caliph's assassination.[4]

The Ummayid caliphate was grounded in the belief that caliphs represented not the prophet but God.[5] This new interpretation indicates that the caliphate was already being transformed by the end of the seventh century. The Ummayid dynasty's adoption of Persian and Byzantine imperial practices, and its opulence too, revealed the Ummayid caliphate's divergence from the early caliphate.[6] The Ummayid caliphate converged with the early caliphate, however, in witnessing expansion (now into North Africa, the Andalusia, and parts of Asia) but also intra-Muslim conflict and internal rebellion. The Abbasid dynasty (750–1258 CE) emerged out of rebellion against the Ummayids, and also claimed to represent the ideal of an Islamic caliphate.[7] But the Iraq-based Abbasid caliphate represented a distinct polity, famous for its patronage of arts, sciences, learning and culture, and its cultural diversity and inclusivity.[8] During this period, an independent Ummayid emirate was also established in Andalusia and another in Morocco.

After the Abbasids lost political authority in the tenth century, the next three centuries saw Muslim sultanates and dynasties—like the Buyids, Samanids, Ghaznavids and Seljuks—pay homage to a greatly diminished caliphate in Baghdad in return for his recognition of the legitimacy of their independent kingdoms.[9] Rival caliphates emerged in North Africa and Spain. The political and legal theory of the caliphate evolved in this period, but was incongruent with the political reality of different power centres across Muslim societies.[10] In 1258 CE, the Mongols defeated the powerless Abbasids, assassinated the caliph and ended their caliphate in Baghdad.[11] Some descendants of the Abbasids continued to claim the title of caliph but without holding power.[12] A synthesis of Mongol and Muslim traditions again altered the meaning of the caliphate, and Mongol governance respected religious differences.[13] Major Muslim-ruled empires across Eurasia henceforth followed this legacy of syncretism.[14]

Muslim rulers after the fifteenth century—whether the Safavids in Persia, the Ottomans in Anatolia or Mughals in India—built significantly different empires, but all ruled on the basis of this syncretic vision.[15] They also ruled according to inherited kingship practices and their own innovations, with their polities diverging from the early caliphate, and the Ummayid and Abbasid caliphates.[16] The Egypt-based Mamluk Empire hosted the symbolic Abbasid caliph in Cairo. Protecting the holy cities of Mecca, Medina and Jerusalem, he claimed religious but not political authority, and did not claim to create a united Muslim community under one caliph. The Mamluks' provision of refuge to a powerless, symbolic caliph ran contrary to all earlier theories of the caliphate.[17]

When the Ottoman Empire toppled the Mamluks in Egypt in 1517, the Ottoman sultan did not initially claim the title of caliph for himself. He hosted the last Abbasid caliph in Istanbul for a decade.[18] But as the Abbasid caliphate disappeared once and for all, the powerful Ottoman sultans, who now ruled over Islam's holy cities, came to be seen as the most legitimate heirs to the caliphate.[19] Yet, till the nineteenth century, caliph was only one of the titles used by the sultans, who primarily called themselves khans and shahs. Drawing on Mongol legacy, they even used the title Caesar and portrayed themselves as inheritors of the Roman Empire to bolster their legitimacy.[20] Importantly, Muslims outside Ottoman lands did not see the Ottomans as exclusive caliphs of the world's Muslims.[21] Instead, different sultanates often tried to claim the title of caliphate for their own political purposes. For instance, in the sixteenth century, the Moroccan monarch declared himself caliph.[22] Before the nineteenth century, there was also no conception of the Muslims of the world comprising a global community united by a common religion and civilization.[23] Instead, there was awareness of the religious, cultural and political–governmental diversity that marked different Muslim-ruled empires.

In India, some sultans of Delhi had offered symbolic allegiance to the Abbasid caliphs, both before and after Abbasid power crumbled in 1258, but ruled their polities independently.[24] The Mughals disregarded Ottoman claims to the caliphate, and assumed the title of caliph to establish their legitimacy and enhance their reputation as just rulers.[25] The belief among several upper-caste, upper- and middle-class Indian Muslims in the late nineteenth century that the Ottoman sultan was the spiritual head of Islam was then indeed a novel idea, arising only after the British abolished symbolic Mughal authority in 1857.

This acknowledgement of the Ottoman sultan as the caliph was also a consequence of changes in the imperial world order. Till the late nineteenth century, the Ottoman Empire was still a member of the European club of empires, competing or allying on equal terms with the Habsburgs, the French, the British and the Russians.[26] The imperial balance was upset when European powers started shifting from an older imperial logic to a new one based on Christian and Muslim identities.[27] The British had allied with the Ottomans against the Russians in the Crimean War of 1854, and the Ottomans had backed the British during the 1857 revolt in India, in which many Indian Muslims had participated.[28] But by the late 1870s, Britain began speaking of saving Christian populations from Muslim tyranny under the Ottomans.[29] Its withdrawal of support to its former ally in its war against Russia in 1878–88 enabled the defeat and substantial weakening of the Ottoman Empire. European powers also began to support Christian nationalist revolts against Ottoman 'Muslim' rule, spoke of dismantling the Ottoman Empire, while themselves encroaching upon Ottoman territories such as Algeria, Tunisia and Egypt.[30] The Ottoman sultan now began advancing his claim as the caliph of Islam as he attempted to bolster his position as his empire declined vis-à-vis expansionist European powers.[31]

This development interacted with the dramatic expansion of European rule over Muslim societies in Africa and Asia in the late nineteenth century.[32] Muslim intellectuals across these societies now encountered discourses about the inferiority of Muslims, Islam and the Islamic civilization.[33] It was while countering such discourses that Pan-Islamic ideas of a 'Muslim world', united by a common religion and civilization, were born. These were reinforced by shared experiences of European racism, and unprecedented levels of inter-connectivity enabled by the new communication and transportation technologies of the nineteenth century.[34] Several Muslim intellectuals across Eurasia and Africa looked to the Ottoman sultan as the spiritual leader of this newly imagined Muslim world, while mostly still seeing themselves as subjects of European empires.[35] European treatment of the Ottoman Empire symbolized the humiliation of Muslims under European empires, and the Ottoman caliph reminded them that Muslims deserved to be treated with dignity.[36]

Even in the early twentieth century, while attempting to recover their position in the imperial system, the Ottomans used the idea of the Muslim world to argue that the British Empire's vast Muslim population made Britain a natural friend of the caliphate.[37] Even after the Young Turks took power in 1908, they initially used the office of the caliphate to pursue Ottoman–British rapprochement and maintain the imperial world order.[38] Some British officers similarly continued to hope that friendship with the Ottomans would keep Muslim subjects loyal.[39] And many Muslims across the British Empire hoped that better relations with the Ottomans would lead to better treatment of them as imperial subjects.[40] In India, sympathies with the Ottoman caliph (as protector of the holy cities) coexisted with continued loyalty to the British Empire.[41]

By the close of the first decade of the twentieth century, however, this position had become increasingly difficult to maintain. The loyalty of a younger generation of Indian Muslims was increasingly strained by British policies in India. The British government's annulment of the partition of Bengal in 1911 caused resentment, as did its refusal in 1912 to accept a Muslim university at Aligarh without government control. Its demolition of the wuzu khana of the Kanpur Mosque and indiscriminate firing on protestors in 1913 further embittered the new leaders of Muslim opinion. The loyalty of these Indian Muslims was further strained by British policies towards the Ottomans. In 1911, Italy invaded the Muslim-dominated Ottoman province of Libya, and the British refused to support the Ottomans in the face of this Italian aggression.[42] By 1912–13, such tacit approval of big imperial powers of further European colonization of Muslim lands encouraged the small Balkan states to ally against Ottoman rule and Muslim presence in Europe more generally.[43] This resulted in the massacres and expulsions of Balkan Muslims. As the Balkan coalition emerged victorious, the Ottomans were forced to cede almost all the European territories they had controlled for 500 years. The inability of European states to prevent the massacres and their acceptance of them encouraged the perception among Ottomans that a new crusade was underway.[44] The pro-British policy of new Young Turk rulers of the Ottoman Empire was now even more strained.[45] And as a result of these events, Pan-Islamic sentiments intensified globally,[46] also animating a section of Indian Muslim leaders more than they had ever before.[47] The cumulative force of British policies in India and abroad had begun to push these leaders towards greater cooperation with the Congress and Hindus.

When the First World War broke out in 1914, the Ottomans and the British faced each other as enemies. As part of their war propaganda, the Ottomans drew upon the nineteenth-century notion of a 'Muslim world', calling upon it to revolt against European colonial rule. The British government countered Ottoman propaganda by promising that, given the political and non-religious nature of the war, Britain would leave the institution of the caliphate and Muslim holy cities untouched, and thereby refrain from interfering with the religious duties of its Indian Muslim subjects. Rather than following Ottoman propaganda, prominent Indian Muslims warned the British government that their loyalty was conditional upon Britain's assurances regarding the caliphate and holy cities.[48] Still, the British felt threatened enough to intern Pan-Islamic leaders like the Ali brothers in 1915.[49]

Whatever moderation remained rapidly eroded when, as the war progressed and Britain marched towards victory, it disregarded its promise, supporting an Arab revolt against the Ottomans in 1916 and cutting off the Ottomans' physical links with the holy cities of Mecca and Medina. This undermined a key pillar of the Ottoman claim to the caliphate—the sultan's sovereign rule over these holy cities.[50] By 1917, the British had wrested not just Mecca and Medina from Ottoman control but also Jerusalem.[51] Fears heightened that the European powers sought to displace the Ottomans from West Asia and dominate it themselves.[52] When the war ended in 1918 with Turkey's defeat, and peace terms were negotiated in early 1919, it became increasingly clear that Indian Muslim fears about the dismemberment of the Ottoman Empire and the dismantling of the caliphate by the victorious European powers were coming true. At this juncture, the Pan-Islamic Indian Muslim leadership—including the Ali brothers, Azad, M.A. Ansari[53] and Hakim Ajmal Khan,[54] among others—sidelined the Muslim League and pure constitutionalists[55] like M.A. Jinnah to launch the mass-based Khilafat movement.[56] The movement aimed primarily to pressure the British to preserve the boundaries of the Ottoman caliphate–empire, and keep *Jazirat ul-Arab* (the Arabian Peninsula), containing Muslim holy cities, under the Ottoman caliph's control.[57]

The Indian Muslims who held that the Ottoman sultan was the caliph of Islam did not wish to become political subjects of the Ottoman Empire.[58] For some, paying allegiance to the caliph, the spiritual head of Islam and also the custodian of Islam's holy sites, was part of their religious obligation as Muslims.[59] To defend the caliphate was therefore to defend Islam. For many, including Azad and the Ali brothers, defending the caliphate was a way of compelling the British to respect the principles of religious freedom and religious toleration guaranteed by secular British constitutionalism.[60] For Azad, the young journalist–writer, erudite scholar of Islamic law and ethics, and 'chief theoretician' of the movement,[61] the caliphate was also required to implement a grander project of Islam-derived humanitarianism.[62] But as alluded to already, apart from religion-related reasons, the Pan-Islamic sympathies of many Muslim intellectuals inside and outside India were a response to colonial humiliation, a means to elevate the self-esteem of Muslims in the face of British imperial ideas that emphasized the superiority of Western civilization and the racial–civilizational inferiority of Muslims.[63] The Ottoman caliphate–empire was the last remaining independent Muslim power in a world dominated by Europe, the symbol of the past glory of the Islamic civilization, a source of Muslim self-confidence. It was also what gave some Indian Muslims comfort as they grappled with the formal end of Mughal rule and the prospect of their marginalization in Indian politics.[64] An important symbol and source of Muslim self-confidence was threatened, and the Khilafat movement sought to thwart this danger.

The Pan-Islamism of some Khilafat leaders aimed at simply giving India a role in shaping the British Empire's foreign policy. Yet, that of many others turned increasingly anti-imperial or—as in the case of individuals like Azad—fused with their already existing anti-imperial sentiments. This Pan-Islamism/anti-imperialism sought to challenge the Eurocentric imperial world order, and generate a new post-war world that accorded India and the Muslim countries dignity and equal status vis-à-vis European nations.[65] Pan-Islamic concerns blended with attempts to unite Indian Muslims to facilitate their participation in the 'Indian national' resistance against British imperialism on an equal footing with Hindus.[66] For some Muslims like Azad, their concern about the threat to the caliphate and to Islam's potential for universal humanism coexisted with their use of Quranic arguments to encourage Muslims to unite with Hindus as equal members of a plural Indian nation, and to protest against British colonial injustices and for India's freedom.[67] Pan-Islamic concerns and the desire to strengthen 'Hindu–Muslim unity' for a collective anti-imperial Indian struggle for swaraj (self-rule) similarly coexisted in the thinking of the Ali brothers, M.A. Ansari and Ajmal Khan.[68] Guided by a combination of religious–theological, symbolic, anti-imperial and nationalist reasons, a section of Western-educated Indian Muslims joined hands, in early 1919, with traditionally educated but eclectically minded men like Azad to mobilize the Khilafat movement. The movement also saw such leaders temporarily ally with a section of the ulema and Sufi pirs concerned about the fate of Islam's holy places.[69]

Muslim leaders of the Khilafat movement were supported by Gandhi, who expressed sympathy with the 'Khilafat wrong'. Returning home in 1915, after living in South Africa for twenty years, Gandhi had entered Indian politics as a leader already well-known and respected in political circles for his non-violent resistance against British racist discrimination in that part of the empire. Believing that the Indian nationalist movement must be rooted in the rural countryside amongst the toiling masses, Gandhi spent the next three years assisting—quite successfully too—peasant struggles in Champaran (Bihar) and Kheda (Gujarat).[70] After being invited in April 1919 by some young radical nationalists to assume leadership in all-India politics, the fifty-year-old launched the Rowlatt Satyagraha to protest against and civilly disobey legislation aiming to extend the extraordinary emergency powers the British government had temporarily assumed during the war.[71]

Named after Sydney Rowlatt, the head of a government-appointed 'sedition committee' established to investigate 'criminal conspiracies', and which then recommended these measures, the 'Rowlatt Acts' aimed to counter radical anti-colonial nationalists through detention for up to two years without trial.[72] Gandhi's Rowlatt Satyagraha involved fasting, hartals, public mass meetings, rallies and marches, and intended to also non-violently break specific laws (concerning liquor, salt and the publication of banned literature). Agitations took place in Amritsar, Lahore, Delhi, Bombay city, Ahmedabad, Madras city, Calcutta, and parts of Bihar and the United Provinces, and a remarkable degree of Hindu, Muslim and Sikh cooperation was witnessed.[73] Hindu–Muslim fraternization was symbolized starkly by Muslim dignitaries urging an Arya Samajist sanyasi, Swami Shraddhanand, to deliver a speech from Delhi's Jama Masjid.[74] The Satyagraha was met with repression by the British colonial state, which censored the press, shot protestors in Delhi, arrested Gandhi and the Punjabi leaders Saifuddin Kitchlew and Satyapal, and banned public meetings. In April 1919, Amritsar saw the infamous Jallianwala Bagh massacre of a crowd of peasants peacefully calling for the repeal of the Rowlatt laws and protesting against the brutalities of the previous days. This was followed by a rule of extreme repression and terror in Punjab, which included arbitrary arrests, torture, forced crawling, whipping, public flogging, incarceration in cages, confiscation of property, curfews, a news blackout, and even the bombing of Gujranwala city by the Royal Air Force. There were also police firing against sympathetic demonstrators in Calcutta.[75]

But before all this occurred in early 1919, Gandhi had already made contact with the Ali brothers (whilst they were in jail) and M.A. Ansari, and been quickly convinced that the Khilafat issue was a genuine grievance.[76] Gandhi extended support to the Khilafat cause because he sincerely believed it was a legitimate issue concerning the religious faith of India's Muslims.[77] His support resulted equally from his conception of the Indian nation and how it needed to be strengthened.[78] Long before Lajpat Rai's stay in America provoked his decisive shift toward it, Gandhi's experience of living abroad and leading the Indian community there had shaped his conception of the 'Indian nation'.[79] Hindu and Muslim members of the Indian minority in South Africa were less politically divided by religion than they were in their own country, and collectively struggled to demand citizenship rights from the British Empire as Indians rather than asking for religion-based safeguards as they did in India.[80] For Gandhi, these diverse communities with radical religious differences could, and did, constitute a single Indian nation.[81] For him, the maintenance and strengthening of this Indian nation required, not dwelling on a common culture or history, but rather participation in a common struggle for truth, and an everyday moral politics of neighbourliness and friendship (*mitrata*) between Hindus and Muslims.[82] The latter entailed deliberate sharing in each other's suffering, which would in turn produce a collective sensibility among them. It was also for this reason that he was determined to work with Indian Muslims just as he had in South Africa,[83] and why he declared support for the Khilafat grievance, with which he deeply sympathized.

Many Indian Muslims had been aghast at the draconian Rowlatt Acts and Punjab atrocities. While the Ali brothers and Azad were under arrest in 1919, Ansari and Hakim Ajmal Khan were among the many Khilafat agitators who plunged into public, non-violent mass protests against these British colonial injustices—its '*Nadirshahi* rule' as Khan called it.[84] As the following statement by Khan shows, the sudden surge in Pan-Islamic sentiments among several Indian Muslims, in the face of threats to the Ottoman caliphate, had coexisted with commitment to their Indian 'motherland':

> I am aware that the exceptional nature of events now happening in the Muslim world has led me to dwell at length on topics of exclusively Muslim interest, but I have done so advisedly and in the confident hope that it cannot, at this time of day, lead any one to doubt the Musalmans' vivid consciousness of the solemn duty they owe to their motherland. As children of the soil, they know and fervently desire to fulfil their duty to the country of which they, in common with Hindus, Christians, Parsis and other communities are the proud inheritors . . . For India the unseen future holds a magnificence and splendour compared with which the most glorious grandeur of her past will be but small. Let all hands of men as well as of women join to unveil that vision.[85]

Ansari similarly declared, in the midst of the Khilafat campaign, that 'a true Mussulman is always a good Nationalist', and made a strong plea for India's 'self-determination'.[86] The widespread Hindu–Muslim cooperation during the 1919 demonstrations against the Rowlatt Acts and Punjab atrocities was reflected in slogans of 'Hindu–Mussulman ki jai!'.[87] Gandhi's support to the Khilafat cause further cemented the already developing Muslim cooperation with Hindus, the combined outcome of Pan-Islamic concerns and anger at British injustices in India.

As the Khilafat movement was intensified in late 1919, the hartals and mass meetings across India were addressed by Hindu and Muslim leaders like Ansari and Shraddhanand, and attended by members of both communities.[88] With Gandhi, Shraddhanand, Jawaharlal Nehru and Malaviya present, an all-India Khilafat conference held in

November decided that Muslims would boycott events to celebrate peace and the war's end, and withdraw cooperation from the British government if the caliphate was jeopardized in the peace settlement. By the end of the year, Gandhi had announced that Hindus would support Muslims in the just cause of the Khilafat.

On his return from his five-year exile in the United States in February 1920, Lajpat Rai found an India marked by a new mass assertiveness. Most of 1920 saw Gandhi negotiate with Muslim leaders over the precise programme of the 'non-cooperation' movement planned against the British government. A 'Khilafat day' was organized in late March, and several Khilafat conferences ultimately decided on a four-point programme for non-cooperation. This included the renunciation of imperial titles, resignations from government service, resignations from the police and military, and the non-payment of taxes.[89] Then, in May, the Hunter Commission Report on the Punjab disturbances was published. It did not go far enough in acknowledging British atrocities in Punjab.

The same month also saw the publication of the Treaty of Sevres, which dictated the terms of peace to defeated Turkey. The treaty rolled back the frontiers of the once-great Ottoman Empire, leaving the Turks in control of a small territory. Erstwhile Ottoman lands, removed from Turkish control, were divided into British, French, Greek and Italian zones. The holy places of Islam were removed from the caliph's custody.[90] The treaty stunned Khilafat leaders, and drew the sympathy of more Hindu leaders for the Khilafat cause.[91]

Adding the promotion of swadeshi goods, and the boycott of government schools and colleges, law courts and legislative council elections to their programme,[92] Gandhi and the Khilafat leaders launched the Non-cooperation Movement on 1 August 1920 (a day which also saw the passing of B.G. Tilak). The non-cooperation programme was officially adopted by the now-Gandhi-influenced Congress at the end of the year.[93] The intertwined all-India Khilafat and non-cooperation mass movements continued for fourteen months, throughout 1921 and into early 1922, when the Chauri

Chaura incident impelled Gandhi to call it off. The mass upsurge saw the participation of a variety of now-well-known political personalities—Motilal Nehru (1861–1931) and his thirty-year-old son Jawaharlal[94] (1889–1964) in the United Provinces; 'Deshbandhu' C.R. Das[95] (1870–1925), B.C. Pal (1858–1932) and the twenty-year-old Subhas Chandra Bose (1897–1945) in Bengal; thirty-five-year-old Rajendra Prasad (1884–1963) in Bihar; C. Rajagopalachari (1878–1972) and forty-year-old 'Periyar' E.V.R. Naicker (1879–1973) in Madras;[96] and the forty-four-year-old Vallabhbhai Patel (1875–1950), by now Gandhi's trusted lieutenant in Gujarat.[97]

Way back in 1915, the same year that Gandhi returned to India but had as yet turned neither to all-India politics or the Khilafat issue, Lajpat Rai had noted from America the rising Pan-Islamic fervour among the younger generation of Indian Muslims, and welcomed it as beneficial for his newly imagined 'Indian' nationalism.[98] When he returned to India in February 1920, his optimism about Pan-Islamism and his new Indian nationalism made him receptive to the Khilafat movement. Much like Das, Pal and Motilal Nehru, Lajpat Rai had expressed initial doubts about some points in Gandhi's proposed non-cooperation programme.[99] However, having always agreed with non-cooperation in principle, Lajpat Rai threw himself behind the Gandhi-led movement with full fervour when it was launched in late 1920.[100] His doubts regarding the precise means of non-cooperation had in any case remained independent of his stance on the Khilafat, for which he had expressed sympathy at several points in the year. As president of the Congress's special session at Calcutta in September, the fifty-five-year-old Lajpat Rai—erstwhile 'Hindu nationalist'— was encouraging Hindus to support the Khilafat movement.[101]

Scholarship on Hindu nationalism has typically portrayed the standard Hindu response to the 'Muslim' cause of the Khilafat as primarily consisting of apprehension or opposition, sparking feelings of alienation, inferiority, vulnerability and resentment.[102] The Khilafat movement is viewed as the catalyst for the rise in popularity in the 1920s of the Hindutva nationalism of Savarkar and K.B. Hedgewar's RSS (National Volunteers Association) founded in 1925.[103] This straightforward leap from Khilafat to Hindutva has promoted the impression that the insecurity felt by many Hindu political actors after the movement was the sole Hindu response during it. Another body of scholarship researching the Khilafat movement has acknowledged the 'fairly widespread feeling of cooperation', 'remarkable Hindu–Muslim amity' and 'fraternisation' during the Khilafat/Non-cooperation movement.[104] It mentions prominent 'Hindu' political figures—such as Lajpat Rai, Swami Shraddhanand, Malaviya and the Nehrus—as participating in Khilafat-related protests, conferences and deputations.[105] Yet, these histories almost give the impression that these Hindus acted unthinkingly, without articulating any ideas in support of the Khilafat cause. Figures like Lajpat Rai still occasionally emerge as fearing Gandhi's efforts to forge a Hindu–Muslim front.[106] Gandhi therefore appears as an exception in urging Hindus to champion the Pan-Islamic cause of Muslims.[107] The textures of the intellectual positions of other Hindu political figures on the Khilafat cause have remained largely unexplored. The rest of this chapter and the next one take a step towards filling this gap by excavating Lajpat Rai's reasons for urging Hindus to unite with Muslims in their fight for the Khilafat.[108]

Hindu–Muslim Unity, Pan-Islamism and the Indian Nation

In the speeches he delivered in the weeks following his return to India, Lajpat Rai frequently emphasized the importance of 'Hindu–Muslim unity' as the 'foundation'—the premise or starting point—of India's 'swaraj'.[109] He argued that by separately hankering after 'crumbs' for their respective 'communities', Hindus and Muslims had facilitated their collective oppression by the British and prevented their attainment of nationhood. To end this subjugation, narrow, competitive religious community-based politics needed to be transcended. United political action was required to 'take the whole loaf together', a metaphor for collective struggle for self-government, the latter being beneficial for both Hindus and Muslims as constituents of the Indian nation.[110]

The Lucknow Pact, which had created conditions for Hindu–Muslim cooperation, and which Rai had welcomed, had been the outcome of a religious community-based politics. Rai had possibly overlooked this fact in the heat of a mass movement, with this representing a genuine inconsistency in his thought. On the other hand, he was possibly making a distinction between two kinds of religious community-based politics. One, an isolationist politics where Hindus and Muslims competed with each other and worked against the idea of an Indian nation—the type of politics he disapproved of. And two, the politics embodied by the Lucknow Pact which saw Hindu and Muslim politics attempt to compromise and find common ground, and strengthened the Indian nation—a politics he approved. It is possible that he still consciously approved of the Lucknow Pact's vision of an Indian nation consisting of distinct religio-political communities, and demanded a broader religion-transcending, common and overarching 'Indian national' politics. Perhaps he still approved of the Lucknow Pact precisely because he believed it had finally ended competitive religious community-based politics and created the space for a robust Indian national politics. Lajpat Rai's stance on the extent to which he wished religion to be separated from politics remained ambiguous. With this ambiguity marking his nationalist thought, he asked Hindus and Muslims to transcend isolationist or exclusivist religion-based politics and participate in a collective struggle for Indian self-government as members of the Indian nation.

Lajpat Rai urged Hindus and Muslims to unite by sacralizing two events of the previous year: Shraddhanand's speech at the Jama Masjid[111] and the heroic 'martyrdom' of Hindus and Muslims at Jallianwala Bagh.[112] He saw Hindu and Muslim victims of the massacre as having died together for the 'sacred' cause of India's liberty.[113] They were exhorted to turn Jallianwala Bagh into a permanent memorial to the 'martyrs' and a holy place of 'political pilgrimage', which would engender common contemplation and veneration of the Indian nation, and remind them to end their

Swami Dayanand Saraswati
(1824–83), founder of the
Arya Samaj, which Lajpat Rai
joined in 1882

Sir Syed Ahmed Khan (1817–98) (*centre*), to whom the twenty-
three-year-old Lajpat Rai wrote his four open letters in 1888

Lajpat Rai, as a young man

Lala Munshi Ram (later, Swami
Shraddhanand) (1856–1926),
who led the Gurukul Party of
the Arya Samaj after the Samaj's
split in 1893

INDIAN NATIONAL CONGRESS GROUP, BOMBAY, DECEMBER 1904.

Front Row.   From left to right.   Dinshaw Edulji Wacha (ex-President), Sir William Wedderburn, Bart. (ex-President), Sir Phirozeshah
        M. Mehta, K.C.I.E. (ex-President), Sir Henry Cotton, K.C.S.I. (President), Samuel Smith, M.P., Surendro Nath
                                Banerjea (ex-President), and J. N. Ghosal.
Second Row.   From left to right.   F. J. Lalji, H. A. Wadia, N. M. Saker, R. K. Cama, the Hon. G. K. Gokhale, M. Viraraghava Chariar,
        the Hon. G. K. Parekh, Shamrao Vithal, S. C. Sarbadhikari, and Hasan Budrudin Tyabji.

Top leaders of the Indian National Congress, 1904; the photo shows
Pherozeshah Mehta (1845–1915), Surendranath Banerjea (1848–1925) and
G.K. Gokhale (1866–1915), but other important leaders, like Dadabhai
Naoroji (1825–1917) and M.M. Malaviya (1861–1946) are absent

The Lal–Bal–Pal trio: Lala Lajpat Rai (1865–1928), B.G.
Tilak (1856–1920) and B.C. Pal (1858–1932)

Lajpat Rai

Lajpat Rai, undated photo

Lajpat Rai (*centre*) meets Indian students, including the twenty-year-old Jawaharlal Nehru (*first from the left*) (1889–1964) at the University of Cambridge, 1909

Lajpat Rai at a meeting of the Fabian Society, a British socialist organization committed to a gradualist and reformist approach towards establishing socialism

H.M. Hyndman, a Marx-inspired British socialist whom Lajpat Rai befriended on his 1905 visit to England

Ramsay MacDonald, a prominent Labour politician who would become Britain's first Labour prime minister in 1924; Lajpat Rai developed a friendship with him in 1909–11

Lajpat Rai (*right*) in 1918; the young man on the left is
N.S. Hardikar, his secretary in the US

Lajpat Rai in the United
States of America

Walter Lippmann, American journalist and editor of the progressive liberal magazine the *New Republic*; Lippmann hosted Lajpat Rai at important venues in New York, provided advice about how to publish articles in American magazines and helped Rai expand his network in the US

W.E.B. Du Bois, African–American activist and co-founder of the National Association for the Advancement of Colored Peoples (NAACP), whom Lajpat Rai befriended soon after arriving in the US in 1914

quarrels and unite in its service.[114] Jallianwala Bagh, where the 'mingled blood' of Hindus and Muslims had flowed, symbolized the common suffering and sacrifice of Hindus and Muslims under the British. Consciousness of shared experience of suffering under British colonialism would produce a common national sensibility in Hindus and Muslims.

Lajpat Rai's emphasis on Hindu–Muslim unity was not guided simply by an instrumentalist desire to win self-government. At the welcome meeting held in his honour when he landed in Bombay in February 1920, he had proclaimed:

> My friends, I must tell you that henceforth we should recognise it as a fundamental doctrine that the unity of Hindus and Mohammedans will be a great asset to our political future. In this unity we shall not be guided by temporary benefit of this community or that. We shall not adopt it as a measure of political expediency. But we shall adopt it as a fundamental doctrine of our faith to stick to it, to our deathbeds, until we win our freedom. Not till then only, but thereafter too, we shall live in this country as brothers determined to win. That is one of the fundamental doctrines that we must adopt as the first article of our political faith.[115]

Hindu–Muslim unity was a crucial normative end valued for its own sake, encouraged purely on moral grounds regardless of considerations of convenience, advantage, utility or profitability. Rather than a cold, contractual alliance between the two 'communities', it must be a felt unity infused with the consciousness of constituting a single nation. By underlining that Hindu–Muslim unity was not only essential for swaraj, but also a normative ideal in itself, Lajpat Rai's thought came remarkably close to Gandhi's.[116] Having in previous years frequently argued that the path to building the Indian nation lay through first strengthening the unity of Hindus and the separate unity of Muslims, Rai now for the first time firmly made Hindu–Muslim unity an essential prerequisite to forge the Indian nation.

Precisely because Hindu–Muslim unity was central to both
the autonomy and the identity of the Indian nation, Lajpat Rai
claimed Hindus must support their 'Mohammedan brethren' on the
'Khilafat question'.[117] Hindu support was crucial to convince their
Muslim brothers of their sincere desire for friendship, and to further
'cement the Hindu–Muslim entente'.[118] The term 'entente', seemingly
borrowed from the Triple Entente powers (Britain, France and Russia),
symbolized an agreement to end mutual conflict to fight a common
opponent. Although upon his arrival in India he had argued against
grounding politics in religion, Lajpat Rai unflinchingly accepted
the Khilafat cause as an entirely legitimate religious and political
issue for Muslims.[119] He himself nowhere clarified this ostensible
tension in his thought. But, as mentioned, Lajpat Rai clearly stood
most resolutely against a religious community-based politics which
he considered isolationist, one that stayed aloof from Hindus and
rejected the idea of a common Indian nation. A religious politics
around the cause of the Khilafat was not an isolationist religious
community-based politics that kept its distance from Hindus and
sought to secure Muslim political interests vis-à-vis Hindus. Instead,
it aimed to preserve the very foundation of a threatened Islam,
was bringing Muslims closer to Hindus and was strengthening the
Indian nation. Lajpat Rai comfortably assented to a religious politics
aiming to safeguard the Islamic faith as long it was conducted within
the framework of Indian nationalism. And so, as president of the
September 1920 Calcutta Congress, he proclaimed that 'the vast
majority of Sunni Muslims' took the Turkish sultan to be their caliph,
the successor of the prophet, and that Islam required him to be 'the
head of a large, powerful and independent state'.[120] He agreed with
the contention of those Pan-Islamic Indian Muslims who claimed
that the Treaty of Sevres, signed in August by a defeated Turkey,
palpably 'violated the fundamentals of Islam'.[121] As Lajpat Rai saw it,
by drastically reducing the territorial power of the caliph, the Treaty
prevented Muslims from fulfilling their religious obligations. In
other words, the practice of the Islamic faith required the Ottoman
caliph's rule over a large, powerful independent state.

In believing that the religious obligations of Muslims required the existence of the caliph and the caliphate, Lajpat Rai echoed Indian Muslim Khilafat leaders. For instance, Azad declared that the caliphate was instituted by God to secure obedience to Him, and that obedience to it was a religious obligation for all Muslims.[122] Mohamed Ali likewise announced that Islam demanded 'allegiance' to the caliph, the centre of the Islamic world.[123] Similarly, in holding that the religious obligations of Muslims required the caliph to exercise temporal power over a sovereign state, Lajpat Rai similarly echoed this Muslim leadership.[124] The Khilafat deputation to the Viceroy in January 1920 stated: 'temporal power is the very essence of the institution of the Khilafat, and the Mussulmans can never agree to any change in its character or to the dismemberment of its Empire.'[125] As stated earlier, apart from religious–theological reasons, Indian Muslim sympathies for the Ottoman caliphate–empire were also animated by its symbolic importance at a time when Islam's power had dramatically declined worldwide and in India.[126] They were also driven by anti-imperialist dreams for a post-war world order in which the Muslim world and India would have a status equal to the West, and were moved by the desire to agitate against the British colonial oppression and for Indian swaraj. Still, what is significant is Lajpat Rai's acceptance of Indian Muslim iterations that their Islamic obligations required the existence of the Ottoman caliphate–empire. Like Gandhi (and, it seems, quite a few other Hindu leaders),[127] he was at ease with such Muslim religious beliefs. The Treaty of Sevres had given an enormous fillip to the Khilafat movement, which now aimed to restore the much-reduced Ottoman caliphate–empire to its former status, and also insisted that this was possible only with Indian self-government.[128] Lajpat Rai, as Congress president, justified this re-energized, intensified Pan-Islamic, anti-imperial movement in support of a Muslim caliphate–empire.

He urged Hindus to support the Khilafat question as 'trustees of the honour of Islam'.[129] For him, Hindus had to support the Khilafat issue even if they saw it as a religious cause confined to Muslims. Hindu–Muslim unity was not just about acting unitedly for shared causes, but also mutually supporting each other's causes not immediately identified as one's own. Like Gandhi, then, Lajpat Rai conceived Hindu–Muslim unity as going beyond having a single, unified mind to entail mutual empathy, obligation and reciprocity.[130]

In articulating this idea of 'trusteeship', Lajpat Rai seemed to draw on imperial language recently institutionalized in international society by the newly founded League of Nations' system of mandates. Mandates were conceived as an alternative to empire, whereby conquered territories were not 'annexed' but divided between the Allied powers who would act as 'trustees' of the native population.[131] This imperial concept of trusteeship possessed connotations of superior peoples obligated to rule over backward peoples for their welfare.[132] Gandhi occasionally used the concept for the imperial relationship between Britain and India, and to highlight the unjust treatment of the British who were meant to be the 'trustees' of India/ Indians.[133] Lajpat Rai stripped this concept of its paternalistic, inegalitarian connotations, instead using it to encourage reciprocal obligation between Hindus and Muslims as equal members of the Indian nation. Hindus were trustees of Islam as Muslims were trustees of Hindu institutions. As its trustees, Hindus were obligated to assume responsibility for Islam, and support their Muslim fellow-nationals in their religious cause.

In his newly established Lahore-based newspaper *Bande Mataram*, Lajpat Rai argued against certain unnamed Hindus who questioned the need to partake in a religious question of Muslims. He wrote: 'The Khilafat with which the destiny of seven crore Muslims is linked becomes a national question for us. If we have to work side by side with them for the progress of our country and nation, it becomes our duty to respect their religious sentiments'.[134] This being the case, the 'unjust and immoral' attempt to encroach on the religion of 'our Muslim countrymen' was to 'trample upon *Indian* religious susceptibilities'.[135] Here, mutuality was translated as single-mindedness such that offence to Muslims could be immediately identified by Hindus as an offence to themselves. This argument again echoed Gandhi, who asked Hindus to support the Khilafat movement because any question affecting Indian Muslims affected the whole nation of which they were a part, and because as members of one Indian nation they had to share in the sufferings of their countrymen.[136]

Occasionally, Lajpat Rai asked Hindus to unite with Muslims in support of the Khilafat cause because, for him, it simply *was* an Indian cause. Before and during the war, the British had promised 'his Majesty's most loyal Moslem subjects' that the 'Holy Places will be immune from attack and molestation' and the institution of the caliphate honoured.[137] But on their path to victory, Britain broke its pledge. While Gandhi saw these as unchristian violations of promises to 'Moslem India' in blatant disregard of its religious sentiments,[138] Lajpat Rai, in his speech as Congress president, had interpreted them as the breaking of a promise made to India by which Britain had obtained Indian help in the war against Turkey.[139] Gandhi asked Hindus to support their Muslim fellow Indians on the religious question of the Khilafat, and even do so as part of their dharma (religion/moral duty).[140] For Lajpat Rai, the breaking of the Khilafat pledge represented a humiliating violation of a promise made to Hindu and Muslim members of the Indian nation. A collective protest by them demanding the fulfilment of the British promise regarding the caliphate and the Ottoman Empire represented a united assertion of the dignity of the Indian nation.

For Lajpat Rai, support for the Khilafat would aid the cause of the Indian nation from another direction. This is evident from his response in *Bande Mataram* to arguments advanced by some Hindus that they should keep away from the Khilafat cause as the Pan-Islamic sympathies of Indian Muslims made them conceited, inflated their sense of their 'political importance' in negotiations with the government, and made them aloof from India and hostile to Hindus.[141] Unlike Gandhi, who remained silent on these Hindu anxieties, Lajpat Rai addressed them, perhaps because he was himself previously offended by the distance the Muslim leadership had maintained from the Congress and Hindu leadership. He emphatically maintained that instead of rendering them aloof, the 'religious zeal'

Muslims felt towards the Khilafat caused them to renounce the policy of aloofness charted by Syed Ahmed Khan and his Aligarh College in the 1880s, and assume their 'rightful place' in Indian national politics. The realignment of Muslim politics resulted not solely from Pan-Islamic religious fervour, but a combination of factors: the rise of a new generation of Muslim leaders, some of whom already conceived nationhood in non-religious territorial terms; British policies in India, which caused resentment, and League–Congress compromise over political representation in the Lucknow Pact. Still, reductive explanations notwithstanding, what is noteworthy is Lajpat Rai's view of Muslim religious fervour—and for a 'Pan-Islamic' cause extending beyond the borders of British India—as contributing to, rather than detracting from, Indian nationalism. Considering this development as 'beneficial to the Hindus', he urged them to encourage the process by which India's Muslims increasingly saw themselves as constituting the Indian nation together with Hindus.[142]

In another interesting argument for why Pan-Islamism was beneficial to the Indian nation, Lajpat Rai seized on what he considered the irrational British fear of Pan-Islamism as a force that would drive Indian Muslims to conspire with Muslim powers abroad to facilitate India's invasion. Since the nineteenth century, as the Ottoman Empire weakened more than ever before in the new Europe-dominated imperial world order, and two-thirds of the world's Muslims came under European rule, Muslim intellectuals across the world countered European racist–imperialist discourses about Muslim and Islamic inferiority by articulating Pan-Islamic ideas.[143] These discourses expressed concern about the fate of the 'Muslim world'; articulated ideas about the history, civilization and achievements of the Muslim peoples; the essential civility, rationality and unity of Islam and Muslims; and the Ottoman sultan as caliph and spiritual leader of Muslims across the world. These ideas intended to assert the equality and dignity of Muslims as subjects or citizens of their empires. But Pan-Islamic (and also Christian evangelical) articulations of a continuous Muslim world spread between China and Europe—inhabited by a great mass of Muslim populations, and united by Islam and the Islamic civilization—increasingly made European colonial officers nervous, even paranoid, about Muslim revolts against Western hegemony.[144] British anxieties heightened as the content of some Pan-Islamists abroad (like the itinerant Persian propagandist–activist Jamal-ud-din al-Afghani) and now even in India, with the world's largest Muslim population, turned increasingly anti-British.[145]

As Lajpat Rai saw it, British fears regarding the Pan-Islamism of Indian Muslims checked the 'oppressive tendencies' of the British, compelling them to treat Indians justly.[146] The common benefits that Pan-Islamism delivered to Hindu and Muslim members of the Indian nation required Hindus to support it. Rather than stoking Hindu fears of Pan-Islamism, Lajpat Rai persuaded Hindus to unite with Muslims in wholeheartedly supporting it. Like Gandhi, he viewed Muslim countries abroad not as a threat to but rather as an advantage for the Indian nation.

13

Pan-Islamism, the World Order and India

In supporting a movement aimed at preserving the Ottoman Empire, Lajpat Rai seemed to compromise his position as an anti-imperialist. He attempted to wriggle out of this by arguing: 'I do desire the destruction of imperialism but I do not desire the destruction of some empires for the benefit of others.'[1] Speaking at the Calcutta Congress after the Treaty of Sevres was signed, he argued that the dissolution of the Turkish empire, now 'hardly in a better position than the Nizam of Hyderabad', had led not to the freedom of Syria, Palestine and Mesopotamia (Iraq) but their absorption into the French and British Empires. 'Arabia and Kurdistan and Armenia' were reduced to 'vassal states'.[2] 'Muslim independence' was 'entirely gone', swallowed up by European imperialism. It was hardly 'in the interest of humanity', he claimed, that some empires be dissolved for the 'enlargement and glorification of others'. Therefore, he supported the restoration of the dismembered Ottoman Empire as a counterweight to European imperialism.

A few months earlier, in *Bande Mataram*, Lajpat Rai had qualified his support for the Ottoman Empire with the following argument.[3] After urging Hindus not to uncritically accept what he considered the exaggerated, hypocritical anti-Turkish propaganda of European nations motivated by their own imperialist designs, Lajpat Rai reiterated his principled opposition to the rapacity of big states.[4] His support for the Ottoman Empire was tempered by its conceptualization as a sort of loosely decentralized, federal caliphate composed of self-governing countries. Expressing support for the self-government of 'Arabia, Iraq, Anatolia and such other countries', he argued that their independence could be safeguarded from 'enemy powers' only if they were under the paramount control of one caliph. The caliphate's overarching paramountcy was crucial to protect these countries from European imperial expansion. Underplaying the imperial logic of the Ottoman Empire itself, Lajpat Rai saw his own support for the Khilafat as animated by anti-imperial solidarity: 'Being slaves ourselves, is it not our duty to sympathise with those who are putting up a grim fight to see that their freedom does not slip out of their hands?'[5] Lajpat Rai proclaimed that 'any further extension of the British Empire in Asia is . . . fatal to the liberties of the human race'.[6] By maintaining a balance of power in the international order and protecting Muslim countries, the federal Ottoman caliphate would safeguard the rest of humanity from European imperialism.

We saw in Chapter 10 that, for Lajpat Rai, the war had radically unsettled ideas of a culturally and morally superior Europe possessing the right to rule over the rest of the world. This enabled him to more assertively attack the entire Eurocentric colonial world order as illegitimate and unjust.[7] A new consciousness of a shared suffering of colonial subjugation with other Asian (and African) countries, signalled by the increased prominence in his vocabulary of the category of 'the East' and 'Asia', had also led him to conceive the battle against British imperialism in new international terms. During the war, he had envisioned India joining a Japan-led Pan-Asian struggle against the Eurocentric imperial world order to inaugurate an egalitarian world order consisting of self-governing nations. But after the war, as it became clear that the victorious powers sought to maintain a world order grounded in imperial hierarchies, Lajpat Rai embraced the Pan-Islamism espoused by many Indian Muslims to continue his struggle for an egalitarian world order. As indicated by his increased use of phrases like 'the Muslim countries of Western Asia' and geographic terms like 'Muslim Asia' and 'Central Asia', he viewed these Muslim countries as sharing with India, China and Japan an 'Asian' identity defined against Christian Europe.[8] To preserve the Ottoman Empire (re-imagined as a federation of self-governing Muslim Asian countries) was to bolster a fortress protecting Asian independence from European imperialism. Hindu support for the caliphate was critical for India to play its role in this Asian anti-imperialist movement for a more egalitarian, just world order. Clearly, Lajpat Rai's reasons for why Hindus should support the Khilafat movement went beyond strengthening Indian national identity and unity to include a greater anti-imperialist internationalist agenda.

Of course, this internationalist argument for Pan-Islamism was also a nationalist argument for India's autonomy. The preservation of the Ottoman empire would check further British imperialist expansion in Asia, which Lajpat Rai believed was 'detrimental to the interests of India'.[9] In his Congress speech, he noted with foreboding what followed the dismantling of the Ottoman Empire: the establishment of 'British suzerainty in Arabia', the 'British occupation of Mesopotamia', involving the 'practical absorption of Persia (Iran) and Central Asia . . . into the British empire'. [10] He also feared the future annexation of Afghanistan. The destruction of the Ottoman Empire was facilitating British expansion into Muslim West Asia, not only harming the interests of the 'Muslim world',[11] but further facilitating India's subjugation:

If the British imperialist has no scruples using Indian troops in Egypt, Persia, Arabia, Mesopotamia, Syria and Central Asia, why will he have any in using troops he raises in these countries against us? . . . If the Muslim population in these countries continues to resist British attempts at occupation which they are likely to do for years, the Indian army will be in constant requisition to fight their battles in these regions, which means a constant and never-ending drain on our resources, both human and economic. The best interests of India therefore require that the Muslim countries of Western Asia should remain free and independent. Their amalgamation into the British Empire even under the pretence of mandatory jurisdiction is likely to be extremely harmful to us.[12]

In the loss of freedom of Muslim Asia, Lajpat Rai saw the loss of India's freedom.[13] A restored Ottoman Empire, protecting the freedom of Muslim Asia, would thus safeguard India from further imperialist oppression. With the Muslim world a citadel protecting it, Lajpat Rai saw Pan-Islamism as beneficial for the Indian nation. In conceiving Muslim countries as a defensive barrier for India, Lajpat Rai again shared ground with Gandhi, who argued:

> Not only has this great friendship between India and Mussulman states around it removed for all time the fear of Mussulman aggression from outside, but it has erected around India a solid wall of defense against all greed from Europe, Russia or elsewhere. No secret diplomacy could establish a better entente or a stronger federation than what this open and non-aggressive treaty between Islam and India has established. The Indian support for Khilafat, as if by a magic wand, converted what was once the Pan-Islamic terror for Europe into a solid wall of friendship and defense for India.[14]

Interestingly, Rai's erstwhile 'extremist' associate B.C. Pal, back in politics for one last time before withdrawing completely a year later,[15] and known for having previously linked Hinduism with nationalism,[16] also saw the Ottoman Empire as a check against European military and cultural imperialism which endangered India's national autonomy.[17] The support of these men for the Ottoman caliphate–empire was guided by the aim of protecting India. Like Lajpat Rai, Gandhi and Pal also saw the Khilafat issue in internationalist terms. Gandhi argued that Hindus must join the Khilafat struggle to produce a better world, and Pal considered it as benefiting humanity at large.[18] Yet, Gandhi conceived Hindu support for the caliphate in terms of Hinduism fighting to defend

Islam and 'emancipate Christianity' from its lust for power.[19] By saving both Islam and Christianity, Hindus would help establish the unity and truth of all religions, and thus help create a better world. Pal similarly supported the caliphate and held that 'the destruction of a single religious faith was a challenge to his own religious faith and humanity at large'.[20] Both conceived the international aims of the Khilafat struggle in religious terms. At least on one occasion, Lajpat Rai, too, portrayed this anti-colonial international struggle in religious terms:

> So long as Christianity in its crusading zeal keeps spreading its tentacles from one country to another, I do not believe that restraining other religions from doing so will do any good to the world. Christianity's present-day pursuits, methods and attitudes are against the teachings of Christ. If people religiously followed Christ's teachings, peace would be restored to the world. But today's Christianity is brimming with the idea of imperialism and world domination. Under these circumstances, it is wrong to think that Muslim religious frenzy is fraught with danger to the world.[21]

A world in which Islam, whose power was embodied in the Ottoman Empire, served as a counterweight to imperialist Christianity was better than one with unmitigated domination by Christianity. Yet, unlike Gandhi and Pal, Lajpat Rai only temporarily couched in religious terms his largely secular anti-imperial internationalist and nationalist agenda. His support for the Khilafat was never animated by the aim of rescuing or emancipating any religion or uniting the world's religions.

Indian Nationalism in Service of Islam and the Muslim World

While, to Hindus, Lajpat Rai emphasized the Pan-Islamic Khilafat cause as a means to serve the Indian nation, in addressing Muslims, he argued that serving the cause of Indian freedom was equal to serving Islam. Writing in the Lahore-based *Tribune* three months after the Treaty of Sevres was signed, he argued that the loyalism of some Muslims to the British government had 'dishonoured their spiritual head and desecrated their holy places'. This loyalist 'apostasy from Islam' was the key reason why their Khilafat demands had been ignored, and had caused 'the wreck of the Khilafat'.[22] In their loyalism, some Muslims had failed to realize that 'the political freedom and power of Islam outside India was in danger so long as India was unfree' under British rule.[23] The British used India to extend their Empire and deprive Muslim countries of political power. Six months later Rai reiterated in *Bande Mataram* that Muslim loyalism, by strengthening the British empire in India, had harmed the political power of Islam abroad.[24] He insisted that Indian Muslims would have rendered 'better service to Islam beyond India' had they joined the more assertive, anti-British Congress 'from the very beginning in full force and in greater numbers'. Indian nationalism was conceived as beneficial to Islam, by which Rai meant both the religion and an imagined geopolitical space comprising the world's Muslim countries—what he at least once, elsewhere, called the 'Muslim world'.[25] The anti-imperial Indian nationalism of the Congress was projected as beneficial to the Islamic faith and the imagined geopolitical unit of the Muslim world loosely united by it. Lajpat Rai therefore actively encouraged Indian Muslims to unite with Hindus over the cause of Indian freedom. *The Tribune* reported that in December 1920, he spoke to students of Delhi's Muslim National University, soon renamed Jamia Millia Islamia, an independent institution founded in October in the context of anti-imperial non-cooperation (and through the combined efforts of the Ali brothers, Azad, Ansari, Ajmal Khan, Gandhi and the young Zakir Hussain):[26]

Lajpat Rai . . . referred to the [loyalist] policy of old Aligarh and termed it the negation of the very basis of Indian freedom. He expressed his great joy and approval at the assault made by the students of the Muslim National University on the policy

of the old college, which he called the citadel of reaction and
fashionable superstition . . . He urged them to prepare themselves
for emancipating India. He emphasised the necessity of closer
Hindu-Muslim unity and said that the cause of Muslim Asia was
the cause of India as well, for the independence of Islam and India
are interdependent.[27]

Lajpat Rai's attribution of the European imperialist decision to
partition the Ottoman Empire was not factually grounded. He may
have disregarded that rather than propagating superstition, the
Aligarh college had in fact been guided by Muslim reformism based
on rationalist, modernist principles.[28] He may not have heeded that
Aligarh loyalism had partly reflected aristocratic disdain for the
conception of popular self-rule implicit in the modern concept of
the nation and partly fears of Muslim minoritization[29] that might
result from accepting 'Indian national self-government'. Rai also
overlooked the fact that 'loyalism' had not been unique to Aligarh
Muslims or the Muslim League. Several 'moderate' Congressmen
had believed that India still had much to gain from the British
connection. After the 1907 anti-colonial agitation in Punjab, several
Punjabi Hindus and a section of the Arya Samaj had distanced
themselves from Rai's own anti-colonial activism and declared
loyalty to the British.[30] The All-India Hindu Sabha, newly founded
in 1915, had declared its intention to 'loyally cooperate' with the
government and remain aloof from Congress non-cooperation.[31]
Fearing that self-government would result in Brahmin domination
over non-Brahmins, the newly founded Justice Party in Madras and
the Non-Brahmin Party in Maharashtra called for the extension of
British rule.[32] Lajpat Rai ignored these facts as he invoked Muslim
loyalism while addressing Indian Muslims. Even so, his repeated
portrayal of Indian nationalism being in the interest of Islam and
the Muslim world, and vice versa, is remarkable.

Lajpat Rai claimed that Britain had captured all routes to India
earlier under Muslim possession, and subjugated Islam precisely to
keep India in its clutches. Consequently, the freedom of the Islamic

world was seen as the means by which to end India's unfreedom. But conversely, ending India's subjugation was viewed as necessary to end Islam's suppression. India's freedom was required to realize Islam's freedom:

> The political freedom of Islamic countries like Afghanistan, Persia, Central Asia, Mesopotamia, Syria, Turkey, Egypt etc., depends on a joint democratic rule in India of the Hindu, Muhammadan and other communities, whether the rule be within the British empire or outside it. If India is not strong enough to maintain its freedom, foreign powers will continue to cast avaricious glances towards it. If India cannot maintain its freedom, the freedom of Central and Western Asia will also be in danger. The present condition of Asia is such that it is necessary for India to gain liberty for the sake of the freedom of Central and Western Asia.[33]

Arguing that Indian freedom and consequently the 'joint democratic rule' by Hindu and Muslim Indians would end British imperialist subjugation of 'Muslim' Asia, Lajpat Rai portrayed free India as its guardian. Not only was the Muslim world a defensive barrier for India but, conversely, in a post-Ottoman world only a self-governing Indian nation could protect the Muslim world. And so, Muslims were exhorted to unite with Hindus against British imperialism in the cause of 'national' self-government. Portraying Muslim–Hindu unity for Indian self-government as crucial for Islam and the Muslim world, Lajpat Rai portrayed Indian nationalism as serving both.

In addressing Indian Muslims during the Khilafat movement, Lajpat Rai's language was akin to that used by younger Muslim leaders like Mohamed Ali and Azad. For Mohamed Ali, the only way to 'save Islam from danger' was to 'side with Hindus and first secure the freedom of your own country'.[34] Similarly, Azad, more than two decades younger than Rai, viewed the British as part of a European Christendom which was waging a crusade against Islam in parts of Africa and Asia, and saw British injustices in India as violating the ethical principles of Islam. He exhorted Indian Muslims to unite with

Hindus in an anti-colonial struggle against unjust British rule and for Indian freedom, conceiving it as an ethically grounded *jihad* in defence of Islam.[35] Although the term jihad today is instantaneously equated with religious war, Azad had initially conceived it as an 'internal' struggle of his personality, and then as a struggle against the 'medievalism' of the ulema and their ideas of Islamic jurisprudence and customs. During the Khilafat movement, he used the term to mean not warfare but a collective struggle, largely through the written and spoken word, against the oppression and injustice of British imperialism, which was in turn seen as violating Islam's ethical principles.[36]

Discouraging the term jihad, Lajpat Rai's view of Indian nationalism as a service to Islam broadly aligned with that of prominent Khilafat leaders.[37] In occasionally using differentiated languages while addressing Muslims and Hindus, using a primary (though not exclusively) religious language for the former and a primary nationalist one for the latter, Lajpat Rai was broadly similar to Azad who once asked his Muslim readers to 'remember that the struggle for freedom is a patriotic duty for the Hindus. For us Muslims, it is a duty enjoined by our religion'.[38] Like Rai, Azad disapproved of his co-religionists expressing loyalty to the British, reprimanded them for their aloofness from the Congress, and asked them to perform their religious duty by uniting with Hindus in the national struggle for freedom and self-government.[39] The Khilafat movement therefore saw influential Hindu leaders like Lajpat Rai intellectually align with Muslim leaders in portraying Muslim unity with Hindus for the cause of Indian nationalism as a duty to Islam.

The Muslim World as Unthreatening

Intellectual historian Cemil Aydin has argued that the idea of a 'Muslim world'—that Muslims across the world are united by shared habits, concerns and politics differing from others—is a modern notion, born in the nineteenth century.[40] It was articulated as a response to European imperialist discourses which classified 'Muslim' subjects as different and inferior in racial and civilizational terms. Several Muslim intellectuals across European empires contested this inferiorizing discourse and, in doing so, often articulated the notion of a Muslim world as a geopolitical entity united by a common faith and a glorious Islamic civilization. While Aydin argues that this illusory idea of a Muslim world often cut off Muslims from non-Muslims in their own empires and countries, this had not been the case for many Khilafat leaders in India. They espoused the notion of a Muslim world while simultaneously pressing for the need for Muslims to unite with Hindus for the cause of India's swaraj. As for Lajpat Rai, he seems to have explicitly used the term 'Muslim world' only once during the Khilafat movement.[41] Still, he frequently enough referred to the conglomeration of Muslim countries in West Asia as a geopolitical space loosely united by Islam. At the same time, he recognized political divisions among Muslim countries and, interestingly, even lamented as 'unfortunate' the absence of a unified Muslim world.[42] He did not uncritically assume a false global Muslim geopolitical unity. So, Lajpat Rai participated in the modern discourse around a Muslim world but without expressing the notion in a very strong sense, wherein this world was imagined strongly united by Islam, possessing no divisions, and dividing Muslims from non-Muslims. Lajpat Rai saw Indian Muslims as identifying with the Ottoman caliphate–empire and the Muslim world outside India. However, during his years in the United States, he had fashioned a culturally pluralist and historically more inclusive 'Indian' national identity which Hindus and Muslims could share in common. Neither then nor during the post-war Khilafat movement did he view Indian Muslim affiliation to a wider Muslim world as precluding their belonging to the Indian nation.

Arguing that both India and the Muslim world were exploited by British imperialism to keep each other under subjection, and that their freedoms were mutually dependent, Lajpat Rai emphasized their shared experience of injustice and the necessity of a shared struggle by Hindus and Muslims for the freedom of India and the Muslim world. Instead of seeing India and the Muslim world in opposition to each other, he stressed their interdependence. So, Hindus and Muslims could serve the Indian nation by supporting Pan-Islamism and support Pan-Islamism by serving the Indian nation.

Lajpat Rai's vision of India and the Muslim world as each other's guardians endowed him with an equanimity about the existence of Islam beyond India, completely devoid of the suspicion and fear it was currently arousing in some Hindus. This is best exemplified by Savarkar's *Hindutva* which, by 1921, was fully conceptualized and written out as a tract.[43] A little more than a decade ago, Savarkar's *Indian War of Independence* had proclaimed that faith in the 'doctrines of Islam' was 'in no way inconsistent or antagonistic to, a deep and all-powerful love of the Indian soil'.[44] He wrote: 'That a Mahomedan dominated by an uncommonly spiritual impulse, can . . . by the very fact of his being so dominated, be also a patriot of the highest excellence, offering his very life-blood on the altar of Mother India, so that she might [lift] her head as an independent and free country; and that the true believer in Islam will feel it a pride to belong to, and a privilege to die for, his mother country!'[45] But as we saw in Chapter 10, by 1914, Savarkar had started expressing fears that Indian Muslims were trying to use their Pan-Islamic linkages to invite the establishment of Muslim rule in India.[46] In *Hindutva*, thirty-eight-year-old Savarkar clearly expressed his new belief that Indian Muslim devotion to Islam's holy sites outside India divided their love for their 'fatherland', overrode their loyalty towards India, and posed a threat to Hindus:

> . . . though Hindusthan to them [Indian Muslims and Christians] is Fatherland as to any other Hindu yet it is not to them a Holyland too. Their Holyland is far off in Arabia or Palestine. Their mythology, Godmen, ideas and heroes are not children of the soil. Consequently their names and their outlook smack of a foreign origin. Their love is divided.[47]
>
> Look at the Mohammedans. Mecca to them is a sterner reality than Delhi or Agra. Some of them do not make a secret of being bound to sacrifice all India if that be to the glory of Islam or could save the city of their prophet . . . O Hindus, consolidate

and strengthen Hindu nationality; not to give wanton offence to
any of our non-Hindu compatriots in fact to anyone in the world
but in just and urgent defence of our race and land; to render it
impossible for others to betray her or to subject her to unprovoked
attack by any of those 'Pan-isms' that are struggling forth from
continent to continent.[48]

Savarkar overlooked distinctive South Asian variants of Islam born
on 'Indian' soil and possessing a presence there for at least a thousand
years.[49] He ignored the several sites in South Asia that India's Muslims
considered sacred. Savarkar also conflated the religious devotion of
Indian Muslims to holy sites in 'foreign' Muslim lands as proof of
their political allegiance to them.[50] Their supposed political loyalty
to the Muslim world was seen as diminishing and superseding their
political loyalty to India, which was rendered vulnerable to their
Pan-Islamic complicity with the supposedly aggressive designs of
the Muslim world. As we have seen, Savarkar could accommodate
Indian Muslims (and Christians) in his definition of nationhood
only if they renounced their attachments to holy places outside India,
and treated only India as a holy land. On the other hand, Lajpat Rai
saw Muslim devotion to sacred sites abroad and even their concern
for the fate of the Ottoman caliphate–empire as separate from their
political allegiance. He accommodated India's Muslims in his idea
of the Indian nation without demanding that they renounce any
extraterritorial religious attachments. Any attachments Indian
Muslims had to the wider 'Muslim world', however thick or thin,
were seen not as a threat to India but as helping in propping up allies
against European imperial aggression.

Lajpat Rai's composure about Pan-Islamism was evident in his
response to the 'Afghan invasion' controversy. In April 1921, in a
speech delivered in Madras city, Mohamed Ali, eager to emphasize
Indian Muslim devotion to India's freedom, had announced that
if any power invaded India to subjugate it, Muslims had a duty to
lead the resistance. But, he said, if the same power—for instance,
Afghanistan—invaded India to help overthrow British rule, Muslims
must assist it.[51] Ali's statement provoked serious anxiety among some

Hindus about Indian Muslims aiding an Afghan invasion of India to impose 'Muslim rule' in India.

What was this talk of an Afghan invasion of India? To understand it, we need to briefly delve into British–Afghan–Indian relations. In the nineteenth century, it was in fact imperial Britain which had invaded Afghanistan twice and from 1878 maintained it as a semi-independent buffer state protecting India from the threat of Tsarist Russian expansionism.[52] The Amir of Afghanistan, himself fighting British imperial domination during the First World War, had temporarily allowed anti-British Indian revolutionaries on its soil. Some of them, including Raja Mahendra Pratap and the Ghadarite Mohammed Barakatullah, had travelled to Kabul to seek Afghan (alongside Turkish, German, Russian, Chinese and Japanese) help to overthrow British rule.[53] These anti-revolutionaries even established a self-proclaimed 'Provisional Government of India' in Kabul in early 1916.[54] But the Amir ultimately refused to ally with anti-British forces and the efforts of these revolutionaries to engineer a revolt against the British were soon crushed.[55] Three years later, following the crumbling of the Tsarist empire in Russia, Afghanistan's new Amir sought to wrest from the British its fully independent status and, in the spring of 1919, attacked British India. The much weaker Afghanistan was quickly defeated by the all-powerful British Empire in 1919, although it successfully wrested for itself complete independence. In the following years, the British occasionally viewed Afghanistan with suspicion for encouraging trouble on India's north-west border, raised the bogey of an Afghan invasion, but ultimately did not see Afghanistan as a real military threat to their occupation of India.[56] Afghanistan had itself been its semi-colony until recently and, particularly after its post-war annexation of erstwhile Ottoman territories, Britain possessed the world's largest empire and most powerful army and navy. The likelihood of Afghanistan invading and occupying British India was therefore slim.

Moreover, during the brief Anglo–Afghan war, most Indian Muslims had remained unconcerned. Some deemed the Amir's actions as egregious and irrelevant to their concerns for the Ottoman caliphate and Islam's holy places.[57] British intelligence reports stated that among Indian Muslims there was a 'shade of resentment at his [the Amir's] presumption in meddling in India's domestic affairs and imagining that Afghan rule would be acceptable to any class'.[58] Some educated Muslims stressed that while 'Pan-Islamism' was a 'distinct ideal', 'few wish to replace English rule with any other rule'. M.A. Ansari declared that it was the duty of 'all true and patriotic Indians, whether Hindu or Muslim,' to resist any 'foreign invasion on [sic] our motherland'.[59] In 1920, Central Khilafat Committee, the main Muslim political organization leading the Khilafat movement, attempted to alleviate potential Hindu concerns, reiterating that Muslims wished to serve their religion and country of birth at the same time, and that they did not 'desire to oust England and introduce a Mohammedan or any other power to rule over India'.[60]

Some did believe in the legitimacy of seeking Afghan assistance to liberate India. But as historian Maia Ramnath has demonstrated, even Hindu revolutionaries had previously sought the help of Muslim countries for the cause of Indian liberation.[61] In 1909–11, Bhagat Singh's uncle, Ajit Singh, who was deported to Burma with Lajpat Rai in 1907, and other Hindu and Muslim revolutionaries, had attempted to use Turkey, Egypt, Morocco and Iraq as bases for their activities, seeking the help of the authorities and the nationalists of these countries for their revolutionary efforts. During the First World War, the prominent Ghadarite Har Dayal travelled to Istanbul and sought Turkish (and German) help to spread Pan-Islamic propaganda among Indian soldiers in the region and encourage an invasion of India via Afghanistan.[62] Other Hindu revolutionaries had sought Turkish (and German) help to spread appeals of Pan-Islamic jihad and anti-British nationalism among Indian Muslim pilgrims in Mecca and soldiers in the Middle East. Some Ghadarites had been captured and executed in Iran for jointly fighting with Turks against the British. Other Hindus had sought foreign help from non-Muslim countries. Maharashtrian Hindu politicians, including Tilak, had previously sought help from the Hindu kingdom of Nepal to liberate India from colonial domination through an armed rebellion, and

Hindutva exponents would, within a few years, even be dreaming of a Hindu king from Nepal presiding over an independent India.[63] Two decades later, Subhas Chandra Bose would see it fit to encourage a German-, Italian- and Japanese-led invasion of India to liberate it.

In approving an Afghan invasion of India to overthrow British rule in 1921, Mohamed Ali differed from Ghadarite revolutionaries like Har Dayal mostly in that his statement remained fanciful rhetoric rather than being translated into action. The same fancifulness distinguished Ali from Bose's future efforts to actively encourage much more powerful, expansionist imperialist foreign states than Afghanistan to invade India and free it. Ali's statement had clarified that Muslims must resist any power invading India to subjugate it. His enjoining Muslims to assist Afghanistan if it invaded India to overthrow the British clearly attempted to prove his anti-colonial dedication to Indian freedom/self-government. Ali would reiterate that for him Muslim rule could never count as true swaraj:

> If the reign of the Sikhs is established in India it would not be called swaraj but it would be the rule of the Sikhs. If the Rajputs win, it would not be swaraj but the rule of the Rajputs. If the Mahomedans win it would be the rule of the Mahomedans, but it would not be called swaraj, and if the Hindus win, it would be called the rule of the Hindus, but it would not be called swaraj. Swaraj means the rule of all—the rule in which all are united, in which all are treated like brothers and equals. Such is the swaraj we now want to establish.[64]

But in light of the Muslim-ness of Mohamed Ali and Afghanistan, and the history of medieval Persianate rule in India, Ali's statement created a stir among a number of Hindus. One lead article in the Allahabad-based, English-language daily the *Leader* charged 'Muslim non-cooperators' with 'virtually soliciting' an Afghan invasion of India, warning of its consequences for India and its Hindu population.[65] Several articles censured the Ali brothers for their 'zealous' friendship with Afghanistan and dealing with 'foreign states' to redress grievances instead of confining themselves to India. They questioned the sincerity of their 'nationalism' and desire for swaraj.[66] One pronounced that Saifuddin Kitchlew, another Khilafat leader, could not give allegiance to any government in India which was not entirely Muslim and that to him, swaraj meant an India controlled by the caliph.[67] Mohamed Ali's statement also caused deep consternation among prominent Hindu leaders. Malaviya hurriedly clarified that he would oppose any such invasion by rendering help to the British government.[68] Swami Shraddhanand published a story about an alleged Afghan emissary meeting the Ali brothers and securing an assurance from them of Hindu and Muslim support in case of India's invasion, clarifying that he would oppose such a jihad.[69] Shraddhanand concluded that 'Muslims only want to make India and the Hindus a mere means of strengthening their own cause. For them Islam comes first and Mother India second.' He was now contemplating whether Hindus should not work for 'their own *sangathan* [consolidation]'.[70] B.S. Moonje, the Nagpur leader soon to emerge as a militant Hindu Mahasabha leader, expressed concerns about Islamic rule in India and the need for Hindus to 'raise their heads' to thwart such attempts.[71] B.C. Pal now feared that an Afghan invasion could incite 'our Muslim population' to revolt and cause the establishment of 'Moslem Raj at Delhi'. Indeed, the controversy changed B.C. Pal's stance towards Pan-Islamism, which he now saw as a 'great menace to Indian nationalism'.[72]

Intervening in this controversy in May 1921, Lajpat Rai first clarified that Hindus could not trust any foreign power 'whether Islamic or otherwise', nor wanted any foreign nation 'even if it be a Muslim one' to establish its rule over India.[73] Yet, he dismissed allegations that the Ali brothers had 'invited' the Amir of Afghanistan to invade India, insisting that Mohamed Ali had merely announced that 'if the Amir declared *jehad* [on British India] he will not help the Government of India', a position Lajpat Rai considered 'natural' for an emotional 'Muslim nationalist' committed to the non-cooperation programme. Interestingly, rather than suspecting them, Lajpat Rai expressed admiration for those 'Muslim nationalists' who allegedly declared it their duty to help 'the Muslim crusaders'. However, clearly attuned to the disproportionate power imbalance between a European imperial power like Britain and countries like Afghanistan, he considered this outside the scope of 'practical politics'.[74] As much as pragmatism, however, Lajpat Rai's nonchalance is explained by his statement that he 'did not in the least suspect Mohammadan nationalists who declare that they do not desire that the Amir of Kabul establish his rule in India'.[75] A year earlier, at the Calcutta Congress, Rai had dismissed similar fears expressed by Hindus regarding the alleged Muslim desire for 'Muslim sovereignty in India': 'How long are we going to be afraid of shadows and be deceived by imaginary fears set before us as a justification of despotic rule?'[76] Now, again in 1921, Lajpat Rai argued that the 'imaginary matter' of the Afghan invasion—'this ghost'—had been raised by the British to weaken the strong, growing unity between Hindus and Muslims and divert attention from non-cooperation.[77] He advised Hindus to establish 'complete friendship' with Indian Muslims, and repose in them 'complete confidence'; the removal of 'such doubts, misgivings and prejudice as had taken possession of their minds' was essential to overthrow British rule. Hindus were to declare that they were 'in every way and under all circumstances prepared to cooperate with the Muhammadans till the Muhammadans liberate the Caliphate from the control of non-Muhammadans'.[78] So, even as other prominent Hindu leaders began to feel threatened by Pan-Islamism, Lajpat Rai refused to see a fifth columnist conspiracy to establish Muslim domination in India, and urged Hindus to follow him in reposing their faith in the Pan-Islamism and nationalism of India's Muslims. For him, the freedom of India and the Muslim world required 'complete and permanent' trust between Hindus and Muslims, which:

> . . . cannot be complete and permanent so long as the Hindus do
> not assure the Muhammadans that the freedom of India is not
> synonymous with Hindu rule and so long as the Muhammadans
> do not assure the Hindus by their conduct that their attempt to

secure liberty for India does not mean that an Islamic power, external or internal, should establish its rule in India.[79]

Rather than exclusively focusing on Hindu fears, Lajpat Rai also attempted to allay Muslim fears regarding the possible equation of freedom with 'Hindu rule', a response perhaps to anxieties reignited among some Muslim leaders, whether or not illegitimately, by Gandhi's use, in a recent speech, of the word *dharmaraj* to denote self-government.[80] Instead of fearing Pan-Islamism, an Afghan invasion or the establishment of Muslim rule in India, Lajpat Rai seemed more afraid of fears of Muslim domination among Hindus, on the one hand, and Hindu domination among Muslims on the other. Both would erode the trust so crucial for Hindu–Muslim unity and consequently Indian freedom.

* * *

Lajpat Rai had already articulated broad ideas around a secular 'Indian nation' whilst in exile in the United States. His new secular Indian nationalism was ambiguous about the extent to which it permitted a religious community-based politics. Rai's embrace of the Lucknow Pact accepted a conception of a secular Indian nation in which Hindus and Muslims could function as distinct religio-political communities. The supreme secular Indian national identity was seen as legitimately existing alongside narrower, sub-national religion-based political identities. Elsewhere, he had articulated the hope that the overarching secular Indian national identity would be grounded in a complete rejection of all religion-based political identities. This unrecognized and unresolved internal tension in Lajpat Rai's secular nationalist thought had coexisted and was compatible with Rai's efforts to strengthen the secular Indian national identity, by highlighting for Hindus and Muslims a pluralist national culture and more harmonious history which they could share.

On his return to India, Lajpat Rai made a bid to actively strengthen the supreme secular Indian national identity during the

Khilafat/non-cooperation movement. He attempted to do so by discouraging isolationist or separatist religious community-based politics, and instead encouraging Hindus and Muslims to unite as members of the Indian nation. Much like Gandhi, he sought to make inter-religious/Hindu–Muslim unity essential to Indian national identity and for Indian swaraj. In the heat of a mass movement, the Indian nation was to be realized and materialized not by recalling a shared culture or history, but by Hindus and Muslims joining hands in a common struggle against British colonial injustices and repression. In fact, Rai's secular Indian nationalism emphasized a relationship of trust, mutuality and reciprocal obligations between Hindus and Muslims. As during the war years, this secular nationalism remained internally conflicted regarding the extent to which it permitted a religious community-based politics. It remained unclear whether Rai wanted Hindus and Muslims to completely transcend such a politics or still permitted religious community-based politics as long as it was not isolationist or competitive but worked in tandem both with each other and a broad Indian nationalist politics. This internal tension continued in Rai's nationalist thought during the Khilafat years as he attempted to consistently bolster an overarching secular Indian national identity.

Still, Rai's secular Indian nationalism clearly and consciously sanctioned a particular kind of religious politics. This was one oriented towards saving a religion perceived as under threat. In the contingent historical moment when, following the First World War, important Islamic institutions, symbols and sacred sites were perceived as threatened by European imperialist aggression, Rai's secular Indian nationalism permitted a religious politics geared towards protecting Islam, including an Islamic caliphate–empire and holy places outside India. Gandhi often appears in histories as the sole political actor articulating such a discourse during the Khilafat movement.[81] However, clearly Hindus like Lajpat Rai also explicitly enjoined a moral politics of Hindu–Muslim reciprocity, both as a moral end in itself and as crucial for buttressing the secular Indian nation.[82] Rai stressed that bolstering the identity and unity of the secular Indian nation required Hindus to respect Muslim religious sentiments, and support their troubled Muslim fellow-nationals in a politics oriented towards safeguarding Islam, including its extraterritorial embodiments. Rai's secular Indian nationalism defined the Indian national identity in secular–plural terms i.e., as delinked from any one religion. But it did not demand a complete, indiscriminate separation of religion from politics. Instead, it allowed religious politics as long as it did not undermine this overarching secular Indian national identity, united Indians across religions rather than divided them, and served swaraj rather than empire. Lajpat Rai's secular Indian nationalism was comfortable with Indian Muslim sympathies with extraterritorial Islamic symbols, institutions and holy places. It was also at ease with the existence of a 'Muslim world' outside India. The latter was conceptualized as an internally differentiated, even fragmented geopolitical conglomerate, loosely, rather than strongly, united by Islam.

In international terms, Lajpat Rai's secular Indian nationalism visualized the Muslim world not as a threat to India, but as its friend, with both locked in an alliance of mutual protection against global European domination. Whatever sympathies Indian Muslims expressed towards a broader Muslim world were not seen by Rai as cleaving them off from India or other Indians, but as coexisting with their commitment to Indian nationalism. Rai's secular Indian nationalism accepted Indian Muslim sympathies with the Muslim world, and held that supporting this world bolstered prospects for the success of a united, autonomous secular Indian nation. Hindus were consequently urged to realize the exaggerated, even false nature of their fears about the Muslim world, and view it as a partner in a common fight against the really more threatening Europe.

Part 4: The Turbulent Twenties

14

Violent Turmoil

The Khilafat/non-cooperation movement, spearheaded by the Gandhi-led Congress and the Central Khilafat Committee, lasted for more than a year, with the most success seen in the boycott of government schools and colleges, the setting up of national educational institutions, and the boycott of foreign cloth and liquor.[1] By the end of 1921, the government finally responded to this energetic, growing mass movement with a familiar response—repression. In September, it arrested the Ali brothers, Saifuddin Kitchlew and four others—including the Shankaracharya of Sharadapeeth—on charges of conspiracy to tamper with the loyalty of the troops. In July, during a Khilafat conference in Karachi, these men had supported a fatwa calling on Muslims to stop serving in the army and for the British to be driven out of India.[2] The 'Karachi Seven', as they were called, were sentenced to two years imprisonment in October.[3]

In November, political meetings and volunteer organizations were banned in various parts of India, and numerous arrests were made. In UP, Congress prepared lists of volunteers ready to go to jail, with Motilal Nehru heading the list. The arrests began in early December. In UP, Motilal and Jawaharlal Nehru were arrested along with fifty-five members of the UP Provincial Congress Committee.[4]

In Bengal, Congress volunteers and similar organizations were declared unlawful, prosecutions were initiated against leading politicians and newspapers, and public meetings banned for three months. On the orders of C.R. Das, many Congress activists in Bengal courted arrest, and soon Das, Azad, Subhas Chandra Bose and other top leaders were arrested. More than a thousand arrests were made subsequently.[5] During December and January, about 30,000 activists were imprisoned across India, with some arrested only for wearing the Gandhi cap, selling khadi or shouting 'Mahatma Gandhi ki jai!'[6] The crackdown indicated the government's sense of alarm about the movement's growing strength.[7] Fifty-six-year-old Lajpat Rai too had been arrested in early December for holding a Congress meeting in Punjab as part of the same clampdown.[8]

Even before this crackdown on the movement's leadership and volunteer cadre,[9] cracks had begun to appear in the fragile 'Hindu–Muslim entente', with trust gradually eroding on both sides.[10] As we saw in the previous chapter, Mohamed Ali's statement in April 1921 that he would assist an invading Afghan army aiming to overthrow British rule had caused consternation among some Hindu leaders, including Malaviya and Shraddhanand, and in some Hindu-owned newspapers.[11] In May, Gandhi had persuaded the Ali brothers to publicly apologize for any pronouncements which may have been construed as violent.[12] This was part of an understanding with Viceroy Reading, who agreed in return to drop proceedings against the brothers. Although the latter complied, they felt the apology made them appear weak before the government and their followers. They began to lose trust in Gandhi and his uncompromising insistence on non-violence. To recover lost ground, the brothers repeated their intention to non-violently subvert the army with or without the Congress's approval.[13] But by June, the Khilafat Committee, led by the Ali brothers, had begun to demonstrate an increasing impatience with Gandhi's cautious non-violent non-cooperation.[14] In a speech, Mohamed Ali emphasized the brothers' devotion to Gandhian non-violence, but clarified that Islam permitted violence in self-defence, and reserved the right to use violence against the British if non-cooperation failed.[15] This had been the context in which, during the Khilafat conference in Karachi in July, the Ali brothers had openly declared their intention to provoke disaffection among Muslims in the British Indian army.[16] The conference also stated that they would declare India's independence at the Congress's next session. These collective pronouncements—for which the Karachi Seven were arrested in September—had made Gandhi, fearful that an untrammelled mass movement might lead to violence and government repression, fairly uncomfortable.

Then, in August, the Mappila rebellion (in the Malabar region of what is now Kerala) had witnessed the predominantly Muslim Mappila peasants revolt against their mostly Hindu landlords. Although Lajpat Rai had remained calm in the face of this rebellion,[17] it eroded trust between certain sections of Hindu and Muslim leadership. The revolt resulted from a combination of complex factors: the Mappilas constituting an economically impoverished, marginalized peasant community with a long history of armed rebellion against authority; agrarian discontent and an incipient famine; the Mappilas now including a sizeable number of recently demobilized soldiers who fought in the First World War, and having been trained in the use of arms and concerted action; the Mappilas using the Khilafat/non-cooperation movement as a pretext to champion a form of non-cooperation that condoned violence as a means of demanding redressal from their Hindu landlords; the government's mishandling of agrarian discontent, its repression of political meetings by Congress and Khilafat non-cooperators, and its silencing of these moderating voices and, finally, an eventual trigger involving the alleged desecration of a mosque.

The government rightly reported that the revolt involved the destruction of Hindu temples along with estates, and included forcible conversions and the proclamation of 'Khilafat kingdoms'.[18] But it discounted economic motivations to lay blame solely on religious fanaticism, the political atmosphere created by the Khilafat/non-cooperation movement and more specifically on Mohamed Ali's speech referencing the Amir of Afghanistan in Madras in

April.[19] Congress and Khilafat leaders disowned the Mappila rebels and their violence, arguing that the revolt was rooted primarily in the economic grievances of the Mappila peasants rather than religion and the non-cooperation movement. They blamed the government for prohibiting their political meetings and preventing them from preaching non-violence.[20] Abul Kalam Azad and Abdul Bari proclaimed that forced conversions were against Islamic law.[21] On several occasions, Hakim Ajmal Khan similarly proclaimed forced conversions to be un-Islamic, and condemned and shamed those Mappilas who had engaged in forceful conversions.[22] Gandhi and the Ali brothers appealed to the Mappilas to renounce violence but, in a telling revelation of how difficult it is for leaders of mass movements to always control their 'followers', they were denounced as infidels by the Mappilas.[23] The Central Khilafat Committee urged Muslims to abstain from cow slaughter as a goodwill gesture towards Hindus. But much of the ulema leadership hardened its opinion, refusing to believe the accounts of forced conversions carried in the press and demanding a proper investigation.[24] In the end, a section of Hindu leadership and public opinion grew more sceptical of 'Muslim' intentions.[25] For them, the Mappila revolt raised the spectre of an organized Muslim community poised to wipe out Hindus.[26]

In fact, the Khilafat/non-cooperation movement continued with great enthusiasm even after the Mappila rebellion. Arrests of the Karachi Seven had been followed by Gandhi and other Congressmen offering themselves up for arrest and issuing statements against the government.[27] In September–October, in support of the Karachi Seven, the remaining Indian Muslim leadership organized a campaign which proclaimed from every soapbox the Karachi conference resolutions and fatwa calling on soldiers and the police to resign from service. This fatwa campaign generated great enthusiasm among Muslims, and resulted in a notable number of resignations of Muslim policemen.[28] Stalwarts of the movement dedicated their energies to try and save the broad Hindu–Muslim concord which had been threatened by the Mappila rebellion.[29] Azad continued to function as an effective leader of the Khilafat/non-cooperation movement in the

absence of the Ali brothers, urging Indian Muslims to work under
the direction of, and join, the Congress for communal harmony,
non-cooperation and swaraj.[30] In November, several hartals were
successfully organized by Congress and Khilafat volunteers across
India to protest against the visit of the Prince of Wales.[31] People
excitedly waited for Gandhi to launch his planned campaign of mass
civil disobedience, including non-payment of taxes, as the last stage
of non-cooperation.[32]

But matters deteriorated rapidly after the arrests of the
movement's top leadership, including Lajpat Rai, in November–
December 1921. Tensions heightened between the Gandhi-led
Congress and the more radical sections of Muslim Khilafat leaders
who remained outside jail. Hasrat Mohani, one of these leaders,
argued that non-violent non-cooperation should be scrapped in
favour of a declaration of 'complete freedom' from Britain, and the
use of violence, if necessary.[33] He and some ulema insisted that Islam
sanctioned violence under certain conditions. This was stridently
opposed by Khan and Ansari, and of course Gandhi, revealing the
tensions developing between the moderate and radical sections of
Indian Muslim leadership, and between the Congress and Muslim
hardliners. In a letter to Gandhi, Abdul Bari, another prominent
radical Khilafat leader, remarked that compete freedom for India
was impossible in the near future because Hindus were not interested
in a total break with the British.[34]

Then, as preparations for mass civil disobedience were reaching
their peak, in February 1922, some of Gandhi's followers burnt to
death twenty-two policemen at Chauri Chaura (in UP). Fearing that
the movement was veering towards uncontrollable violence, Gandhi
decided to call off the Khilafat/non-cooperation movement.[35] This
sudden decision was met with despair, disillusionment, anger and
resentment from many leaders of the movement, Hindu and Muslim.[36]
Gandhi was soon arrested and tried for exciting disaffection against
the government under Section 124A, and sentenced to six years in
prison.[37] With its main leaders in jail and the programme suspended,
the Khilafat/non-cooperation movement lost its momentum, and

the broader 'Hindu–Muslim entente' crumbled.[38] Enthusiasm and euphoria curdled into despondency, resentment and squabbling. Most of 1922 saw sections of Hindu and Muslim leaders blaming each other for lack of commitment to the cause of Indian freedom.[39] Although moderate Khilafat/Congress leaders like Ansari and Khan disagreed vehemently with this evaluation, others like Bari complained that Gandhian non-violence, which had effectively ended the non-cooperation movement, had failed Muslims.[40] Mohani declared that the burden of both non-cooperation and the arrests connected with it had been borne largely by Muslims, and that Hindus had let them down by calling off the movement. These radical Khilafatists, along with many ulema, soon deserted the Congress.[41]

As already hinted at, dissensions re-surfaced not only between sections of Hindu and Muslim leaders but also within what had always been various other precarious coalitions which had propelled the Khilafat/non-cooperation movement.[42] The tenuous alliance *among* Muslim Khilafat leaders was shattered. While the Khilafatists and ulema led by Bari and Mohani abandoned the Congress, several others, among them Ansari and Khan, stayed with it, trying to maintain the link between the Khilafat movement and the Gandhian programme of non-violent non-cooperation.[43] Factionalism soon split the Khilafat Committee.[44] By late 1922, fifteen years after it had first split in Surat in 1907, the Congress too splintered into ideological factions. The 'No-changers', including C. Raja, Sardar Patel and Rajendra Prasad, vociferously resisted any change from Gandhi's programme of non-cooperation (including council boycott) with the British. On the other hand, the 'Swarajists', led by C.R. Das and Motilal Nehru, and supported by Patel's elder brother Vithalbhai,[45] now wished to depart from Gandhian non-cooperation, fight elections, enter legislative councils and oppose the British from within.[46] The issue soon also divided the Pan-Islamic Muslim leadership. Some like Ansari and the Ali brothers (once they returned from jail) chose to follow Gandhian non-cooperation. Others like Hakim Ajmal Khan and several 'secondary leaders' of the Khilafat movement—mainly erstwhile followers of Mohamed Ali—began to disentangle themselves from Pan-Islamic affairs and soon joined the 'Congress-Khilafat-Swaraj Party', which was formed in December and favoured council entry.[47] Those Congress and Khilafat leaders who tried to maintain Hindu–Muslim unity were weakened by this internal fragmentation, and were now more strongly challenged by those uncompromising Hindus and Muslims who had always questioned or opposed such unity.[48]

Meanwhile, 1922 also saw a rise in Hindu–Muslim tension on another plane. The Mappila rebellion provided the Arya Samaj the opportunity to revive and popularize its shuddhi movement, which had been dormant for a decade.[49] With some press organs exaggerating and sensationalizing the number of forced conversions,[50] shuddhi activists were sent to Malabar to reclaim Hindus who had been forcibly converted.[51] Shuddhi also resolved more broadly to 'reclaim' Indian Muslims, who were touted the descendants of original Hindus who had converted out of Hinduism.[52] This alarmed many Muslims—including sections of the ulema—who became concerned about the fate of Muslims in India.[53]

The year's end then saw a Hindu–Muslim riot in Multan in southern Punjab.[54] According to one police report, following the riot, the Hindu Raksha Dal of Multan directed Hindus to boycott Muslim labourers and shopkeepers, and some Muslims responded by refusing to eat anything touched by Hindus.[55] The Multan riot was partly what led Malaviya—the 'moderate' constitutionalist working closely with Jinnah until just a year ago—to revitalize the All-India Hindu Mahasabha.[56] Founded in Hardwar in 1915, the Mahasabha had not been an all-India organization but a body of urban-based, upper-caste educated middle class (and predominantly Sanatanist) Hindus from UP and Punjab.[57] It had also been quickly marginalized by developments at the all-India level. The Tilak- and Jinnah-engineered Lucknow Pact between the Congress and the League had ignored the Mahasabha and its opposition to the Pact.[58] It was further politically sidelined, just as the League was, by Tilak's Home Rule agitation in 1918 and Gandhi's mass agitations of 1919–22.[59] Many Punjabi Hindus and especially Arya Samajists like Shraddhanand had turned away from it and towards Congress-led agitation.[60] Several Mahasabha leaders had wished to work the Montagu–Chelmsford Reforms, and disagreed with Gandhian non-cooperation, and with Congress's composite nationalism and desire for unity with Muslims. The Hindu Mahasabha had therefore held aloof from Gandhi's anti-colonial Khilafat/non-cooperation movement.[61] In fact, it politically collapsed between 1917–20 and ceased to function normally till 1922.[62]

Now, in December 1922, the Mahasabha drew up plans to strengthen its organization and extend it across India.[63] It was attracting prominent Arya Samajist Hindus, including those who had taken little interest in it before.[64] The Mahasabha now launched the sangathan movement, calling on Hindus to organize in 'self-defence', in direct response to the Mappila revolt and the Multan riot.[65] After the Multan riot, some organs of the north Indian Hindi press were also declaring that Hindu unity was much more important than Hindu–Muslim unity.[66]

In December 1922, a few months after the riots in Multan, fifty-seven-year-old Lajpat Rai wrote a private letter from Lahore Central Jail to C.R. Das, whose stance on council entry he was now beginning to agree with.[67] In it, he expressed serious doubts regarding the possibility of Hindu–Muslim unity:

> I have devoted most of my time during the last six months to the study of Muslim history and Muslim law and I am inclined to think that it [Hindu-Muslim unity] may be neither possible nor practicable. Assuming and admitting the sincerity of the Mohammedan leaders in the non-cooperation movement, I think their religion provides an effective bar to anything of the kind. You remember the conversation (I reported to you at Calcutta) which I had with Hakim Ajmal Khan and Dr. Kitchlew. There is no finer Mussalman in India than Hakim Sahib, but can he or any other Muslim leader override the Quran? . . . I can only hope that my reading of Islamic law is incorrect and nothing will relieve me more than to be convinced that it is so. But if it is right, then it

comes to this, that although we can unite against the British, we cannot do so to rule India on democratic lines. What then is the remedy? I am not afraid of seven crores of the Indian Mussalmans, but seven crores plus the armed hosts of Afghanistan and Central Asia, Arabia, Mesopotamia and Turkey will be irresistible. I do honestly and sincerely believe in the necessity and desirability of Hindu-Muslim unity; I am also fully prepared to trust the Muslim leaders, but what about the injunctions of the Quran and Hadis? The leaders cannot override them. Are we then doomed? I hope not. I hope your learned minds and wise heads will find some way out of this difficulty. If so, do kindly communicate your views to me.[68]

In believing that the Quran forbade Muslims from uniting with Hindus or ruling alongside them in a democracy, Lajpat Rai was apparently influenced by his conversations in jail with one Maulana Habib-ur-Rahman of Ludhiana, a known Khilafatist in Punjab who nevertheless was likely relatively unknown to the all-India Khilafat/ Congress leaders. When Lajpat Rai asked him about the limits within which, in strict conformity with Islamic injunctions, Muslims would cooperate with Hindus, Rahman had apparently replied that the cooperation could last till Christians were turned out of India but not after that.[69] There were indeed certain other maulvies in Punjab who also argued that the Quran prohibited them from befriending non-Muslims.[70] Equally, this reading of Islamic law and history by Rai, and such *maulanas* and maulvies, contrasted with the views of many top all-India Muslim leaders of the Khilafat/non-cooperation movement who were close to Gandhi and emerging as staunch Congressites.[71]

Men like Azad and Ansari invoked the Quran to argue that Indian Muslims had a religious duty to cooperate with Hindus who lived in peace with Muslims, and to unite with them as members of a plural Indian nation.[72] This principle was never limited to the end of British rule. Following his return from prison, as president of the special Congress session in Delhi in September 1923, Azad would declare: 'I would sacrifice swaraj rather than Hindu–Muslim unity.'[73] In the face of rising Hindu–Muslim tension and polarization, he would pledge, alongside Gandhi, to give up his life for Hindu–Muslim unity, and to be at the forefront of active efforts to bring Hindus and Muslims together.[74] He held that Hindus and Muslims needed to cooperate for the larger goal of communal harmony in free India.[75] Committed to his political ideal of a united and plural Indian nation, two decades later, in the 1940s, the same Azad would stand against Jinnah's demand for Pakistan. Mohamed Ali looked forward to a 'swaraj' which, to him, meant rule in which Sikhs, Hindus and Muslims were united, and 'treated like brothers and equals'.[76] Ajmal Khan and Ansari too valued Hindu–Muslim unity for its own sake, and envisioned an Indian national swaraj as predicated on this principle. In the coming years, Khan would become despondent at the deterioration in 'Hindu–Muslim relations' and his own inability to bring the communities together, even as he sponsored and participated in 'Unity Conferences' to resolve disputes, and sometimes rushed to riot-stricken areas to restore peace.[77] He would lament that communal strife was weakening the Indian nation, stress the need for tolerance and urge Muslims to give up everything for Hindu–Muslim unity.[78] Ansari too despaired at the rise in Hindu–Muslim discord, which he believed harmed the Indian nation.[79] His commitment to Hindu–Muslim unity was reflected in his decision a few years later to sever links with all 'sectional' organizations, which, he hoped, would help arrest polarization, and to work from within the Congress to strengthen it as a representative of a diverse and united Indian nation.[80]

In his letter to Das, Lajpat Rai overlooked several mainstream Khilafat/Congress leaders to focus on the words of the Maulana from Ludhiana. He also assumed that the thoughts and actions of Muslims must always be bound solely by the Quran. This was a curious assumption for a Hindu whose own thoughts and actions were not determined exclusively by Hindu scriptures. This presupposition also overlooked the fact that Indians with a Muslim identity were internally diverse, and not necessarily always guided by religious texts, or even religion alone. The politics of different Indian Muslims was informed by their different and shifting family, gender, village, locality, class, occupational, caste, regional, linguistic and sectarian identities/backgrounds, varying local customs, cultures and everyday practices, and a range of different, often conflicting ideas, world views and ideologies.[81]

British imperialism had reasserted its strength by clamping down on the anti-imperial, Pan-Islamic Khilafat/non-cooperation movement. As the movement's lost momentum resulted in increasing estrangement between embittered sections of Hindu and Muslim opinion, and was overshadowed by increased polarization and the riot in Multan, Lajpat Rai's buoyant Indian nationalist imagination threatened to unravel. The creeping atmosphere of mistrust and suspicion had finally sown in his mind seeds of doubt, and raised fears about whether India's Muslims wanted to unite with Hindus to establish democratic self-government in India.

To be sure, some prominent Muslims like the by-now-well-known poet–philosopher Muhammad Iqbal (1877–1938) did reject the idea of democracy, for what he considered its amoral, arbitrary emphasis on numbers (and numerical majorities) rather than religious ethics and character.[82] It was also in these years that Maulana Abul Ala Maududi—who in the 1940s would champion the Pakistan movement, and who had been a Khilafatist (and written laudatory biographies of Gandhi and Malaviya)—turned sceptical of the idea of a shared nationhood uniting Hindus and Muslims, and began to express the view that democracy was harmful for India's Muslims.[83] But, just as in 1909, and as evident in the 1916 Lucknow Pact, much of the Indian Muslim leadership of these years accepted democratic representation, but attempted to negotiate the *form* of this democracy, so as to ensure that Indian Muslims were granted what they thought was an adequate share of representation.[84] The Congress/Khilafat leaders close to Gandhi embraced the notion of democratic government in India, with some, most notably Azad, using Islamic arguments to build Indian Muslim support for the idea of pluralist democracy in India.[85] Azad emphasized the religious duty of Muslims to protest against any tyrannical and oppressive government, even an Islamic one.[86]

Still, general suspicions regarding the Muslim commitment to Hindu–Muslim cooperation and democratic principles swelled in Lajpat Rai's mind. In light of his new anxiety about the Quran compelling Muslims to maintain distance from Hindus, he also began to view Indian Muslim sympathies with the wider 'Muslim world' in a different light. He no longer saw these as necessarily strengthening the causes of Hindu–Muslim unity and Indian self-government. The Muslim world stopped appearing to him as the guardian ally of India, protecting India and its Hindus from European imperialism. In his mind, it transformed into a daunting force encircling India and its Hindus, potentially menacing both, especially if India's Muslims were passionately devoted to this world while maintaining—as he feared they would be compelled to by the Quran—their distance from Hindus.

In fact, nothing had changed in the Khilafat leaders close to Gandhi, whose Pan-Islamic sympathies remained compatible with their commitment to Hindu–Muslim unity and Indian nationalism. Mohamed Ali had called on Muslims to continue 'the fervour of their extraterritorial sympathies' and simultaneously contribute to 'territorial [Indian] nationalism'.[87] After his return from jail, speaking as Congress president in Kakinada in December 1923, he would question the need for separate Khilafat committees and Hindu sabhas, and insist on joint committees to promote harmony. He argued that 'if the Muslims or the Hindus attempt to achieve success in opposition to or even without cooperation with each other, they will not only fail, but fail ignominiously'.[88] Azad—who had fought for the Ottoman caliphate as a symbol of true Islam, which he in turn interpreted as a 'perfect system of democracy and freedom'—called for Hindu–Muslim cooperation for the sake of communal harmony as the basis of the plural Indian nation.[89] As noted above, Ansari and Khan continued to believe in Hindu–Muslim unity as the basis of Indian nationalism.[90]

What *had* changed by late 1922 was the fate of the Ottoman Empire. In 1920, Ottoman lands had already been divided by the victorious European powers into Greek, Armenian, Italian, French, British, Kurdish and Turkish zones.[91] In November 1922, a month before Rai wrote his letter to Das, Turkey's new nationalist government, led by Mustafa Kemal Atatürk, abolished the Ottoman dynasty and sultanate, deposed the Ottoman sultan and elected a new caliph. In stripping the caliphate of its temporal powers and confining it to spiritual affairs, the Turks did exactly what much of the Indian Muslim Khilafat leadership had been opposing in their protests against the British since 1919.[92] The 600-year-old Ottoman Empire, whose resurrection had been the aim of many Khilafat leaders, was gone. The already-fragmented Khilafat leadership had responded in different voices, with some ulema opposing this separation of the spiritual and worldly powers of the caliph, while others like Ansari and Khan welcoming the idea of an elected caliph.[93] At a historical juncture when its most potent symbol—the Ottoman caliphate—was severely weakened, Pan-Islamism, nonchalantly dismissed by Lajpat Rai in previous years as an imaginary 'ghost', was coming alive to haunt him. Nevertheless, Lajpat Rai's letter to C.R. Das contained more a series of open questions than final statements.

During the next eight months from December 1922 to August 1923, whilst Lajpat Rai remained in prison, Hindu–Muslim relations continued to deteriorate. Riots occurred with increasing frequency and intensity: in Multan (again), Amritsar and Panipat in the Punjab, and Agra and Saharanpur in the United Provinces.[94] Increasing polarization between 'Hindus' and 'Muslims' found expression in the competitive mirroring campaigns of shuddhi and sangathan among Hindus, and *tabligh* (propagation) and *tanzim* (organization) among Muslims.[95] In early 1923, the Arya Samaj, led by Swami Shraddhanand, launched an energetic shuddhi campaign to convert—or, as they put it, 'reclaim'—the Muslim Malkana Rajputs of UP.[96] These were Muslims on the edge of Islam who returned themselves as 'Muslim' in the census, and also followed certain beliefs and customs grounded in Hinduism.[97] During the campaign, there was talk of millions of Hindus mistakenly thinking of themselves as Muslims, and all of India's Muslims being products of forced conversion who needed to be 'reclaimed'.[98] This caused an uproar, with some Muslim leaders expressing the worry that Hindus wanted to enslave Muslims forever.[99] Others proclaimed that shuddhi showed that swaraj would mean the 'death of the Muslims' and the 'departure of Islam from India'.[100] The result was a Muslim counteraction in the form of the tabligh movement led, among others, by Abdul Bari and the Islamic scholar Khwaja Hasan Nizami.[101] Tabligh sought to counter shuddhi by urging Muslims to remain true to Islam.[102] Shuddhi and tabligh aimed to prevent conversions *out* of Hinduism and Islam, respectively, while simultaneously converting groups *into* their respective communities.[103] While a tract by Nizami called on all Muslims to counter Arya Samajists and protect and propagate Islam using various methods, Shraddhanand's response conjured the spectre of a pan-Muslim conspiracy against Hindus.[104] Some tabligh activists also did aim to spread Islam among Hindus as a way to counter shuddhi.[105] And some Arya Samajists stirred suspicions that every Muslim was out to convert Hindus by any means possible.[106] The hateful acrimony generated even manifested itself in threats to the lives of Swami Shraddhanand and Khwaja Nizami by the followers of the other.[107] Collectively, these developments further 'tipped the scales' against the spirit of alliance which had dominated the Khilafat/non-cooperation movement.[108]

Meanwhile, Shraddhanand and Malaviya linked the shuddhi campaign to the Hindu Mahasabha's new programme of Hindu sangathan started after the Mappila and Multan riots.[109] This coupling symbolized the new alliance between Sanatanist Hindus (who till now dominated the Hindu Mahasabha) and Arya Samajists (who now became prominent in it), which emerged to counter riot violence and tabligh.[110] Upon his return from prison in late 1923, Saifuddin Kitchlew had initially appealed for Muslims to be allowed to join the sangathan to attain swaraj, but after being rebuffed, he started tanzim as a Muslim counter to sangathan. He gave up on Hindu–Muslim amity to frequently target the Arya Samaj, shuddhi and sangathan.[111] These movements, partly a response to Hindu–Muslim violence, also severely exacerbated polarization and violence. The 1923 riots in Agra and Saharanpur were the direct consequence of shuddhi and tabligh activities.[112] Meanwhile, Hindu–Muslim tension also began to adversely impact the Lucknow Pact.[113] Hindu and Muslim leaders, unhappy with the Pact, manipulated and even encouraged fresh violence on the part of their co-religionists to press their demands and push for the Pact's revision. Bengali and Punjabi Muslims, who had been denied their demands for guaranteed representation as slim and insecure regional majorities, and the Hindus of UP and Punjab, who felt that they had been asked to concede too much, began to push for its renegotiation.

Lajpat Rai's province of Punjab was particularly in the grip of 'communal tension', and in urban areas, Hindu–Muslim relations became 'implacably hostile'.[114] In March 1923, whilst Rai was still in prison, C.R. Das, Motilal Nehru, Sarojini Naidu, Azad, Ajmal Khan and Ansari visited the province, and noted in their report that: 'we found that the relations between the Hindus and Mussulmans, both educated and uneducated, were so greatly strained that each community had practically arrayed itself in an armed camp against the other.'[115] In fact, Khan even held Punjab responsible for the vitiated, polarized atmosphere across India, and reminded Punjabi Hindus and Muslims of their duty to preserve Indian unity.[116] On the other hand, the British government commented that 'it is generally conceded by Congress and Khilafat leaders alike that political life in the Punjab is stagnant and that for the present, at all events, Hindu–Muslim unity is out of the question'.[117]

Punjab was hit by riots in Multan, Amritsar and Panipat in 1922–23, and matters made worse by the mushrooming of local Arya Samajist/Hindu Sabha activists and their counterparts in various Muslim anjumans. They viciously attacked, accused and abused each other's religions, and stressed the impossibility of Hindu–Muslim coexistence.[118] Swami Shraddhanand's zestful campaign to 'reclaim Hindus' who apparently mistakenly thought themselves Muslim played a pivotal role in further embittering Hindu–Muslim relations to an extraordinary degree.[119] Local Hindu Sabhas appealed for funds to bring Muslims into the fold of Hinduism, which provoked fears of conversion and Hindu Raj, and the formation of tabligh organizations.[120] Some Muslim pirs vowed to convert thirty-two crore Hindus to Islam.[121] Some Punjabi 'Hindu' newspapers expressed fears that Punjabi Muslims wished to crush Hindus and establish Muslim rule.[122] Elsewhere, some Arya Samajists made provocative statements about Muslims and their Prophet being originally Hindu, Mecca originally a Hindu temple, and Quran originally a Hindu book and of the need for Hindus to 'take Mecca back from Muslims'.[123] On the other hand, some local Muslims made provocative remarks about the need to increase cow sacrifice.[124] Matters were made worse by fierce religious debates between Arya Samajists and local maulvis. The rush to convert and reconvert severely strained Hindu–Muslim relations in Punjab, and members of the two communities began to economically and socially boycott the other.[125] In Punjab more than anywhere else, Hindu–Muslim (Indian) unity towards the goal of anti-colonial Indian nationalist swaraj was replaced by deep polarization represented by shuddhi/sangathan and tabligh/tanzim.[126] The all-India Indian nationalist leadership—Gandhi, the Ali brothers, Azad and Ajmal Khan—was attacked by certain local maulvies for harming Islam and deceiving Muslims, and by Arya Samajists, some of whom cited the Vedas to justify their opposition to the Hindu–Muslim unity preached by Gandhi.[127]

But there was yet another factor that damaged inter-community relations in Punjab. In 1919, the Montagu–Chelmsford Reforms had granted substantial power to British India's provinces, and within the provinces, to a pro-British rural landed elite that wished to enter legislative councils and cooperate with constitutional reforms.[128] In Punjab, by 1923, this led to the sharp political ascendancy of Fazl-i-Hussain (1877–1936) and his agriculturalist Unionist Party which worked closely with Hindu and Sikh agriculturalists but was dominated by Muslim zamindars.[129] As minister for education and local government, Fazl-i-Hussain introduced policies for all 'communities' but also attempted to consolidate the Muslim majority vote by extending communal representation to local bodies and educational institutions.[130] His Municipal Amendment Act of 1923 aimed to reorganize seats on Punjab's municipalities such that they better reflected the make-up of Punjab's population. In other words, it aimed to mitigate the potential dominance within municipalities of the educationally and economically much-better-off Punjabi Hindu minority (which, due to Delhi being considered separately, was now counted as 32 per cent). This meant that Punjab's majority Muslim population would get more seats in municipalities (in accordance with their greater numerical strength in the province) than Punjabi Hindus with their much greater educational and economic advantages.[131] Hussain had also instituted a policy that distributed places at the Lahore Medical College and Lahore Government College among Hindus, Muslims and Sikhs in the ratio 40:40:20. This was done to rectify abysmal Muslim representation in these institutions, which had stood at 15 per cent and lower, despite Muslims constituting a majority in Punjab.[132] Even so, it meant significant losses for urban Hindus, who were used to seats being open to 'merit' and therefore favourable to themselves, since they had made the switch to Western education generations earlier.[133] Similarly, Fazl-i-Hussain called for a redistribution of grants given to schools to ensure that meagre government funds would go towards advancing the educationally backward Muslim community. But this again would occur at the expense of schools operating under Hindu auspices.[134] Collectively, these measures caused deep anxiety among urban Punjabi Hindus about potential marginalization and rapidly and seriously embittered Hindu–Muslim relations throughout Punjab.[135] Many Punjabi Hindus now turned away from Gandhi and the Congress and towards the local Hindu Sabhas of Punjab.[136]

Several prominent Punjabi Hindu leaders like Shraddhanand and Bhai Parmanand (1876–1947)[137] had joined Malaviya's revitalized Mahasabha by 1923. But when the fifty-eight-year-old Lajpat Rai returned from prison in August 1923,[138] he kept away. Instead, although he did not formally join it, he focused on helping C.R. Das and Motilal Nehru's new Swaraj Party, choosing its candidates for the Punjab legislative council.[139] Disputing Gandhi, Lajpat Rai insisted that the Hindu–Muslim problem could not be solved through 'sentimental talk'. This referred to the Gandhian approach, which emphasized that conflict had to be resolved by Hindus and Muslims actively developing relations of mutual trust, understanding, friendship, respect, love, tolerance, self-sacrifice, self-restraint, mercy and kindness—rather than through what he considered cold-hearted contractual 'pacts' between Hindus and Muslims.[140] During the Khilafat/non-cooperation movement, in a manner similar to Gandhi—and perhaps even under his influence—Lajpat Rai had spoken of the need for Hindus to support the Khilafat cause to strengthen Hindu–Muslim unity and friendship, as 'trustees' of the honour of Islam, and out of considerations of mutual reciprocity.[141] Now, in the new context of 1922–23, he clearly thought differently.

On behalf of the Congress, and with the help of thirty-five-year-old Azad, he and M.A. Ansari, drafted an 'Indian National Pact' settling the principles on which different 'communities' would be represented in the future government. The National Pact was ultimately eclipsed by the bitter debate generated at the Congress's December session by C.R. Das's 'Bengal Pact', which was much more generous towards Muslim representation in Bengal.[142] Certainly less accommodating of Muslim claims to representation, the Ansari–Rai 'National Pact' reveals Rai's imagination of the Indian nation in 1923. It resolved the following.[143] First, that the principal objective of the 'communities' represented by the signatories would be to secure complete swaraj for India in the manner that 'every free and independent nation enjoys'. Second, that India would have a 'democratic', 'federal' form of self-government. Third, its national language would be Hindustani in the Urdu or Devanagari script. Fourth, 'full religious liberty, that is liberty of belief, worship, propaganda, association, and education' would be guaranteed to 'all communities forming the Indian nation and shall form a constitutional right which it shall never be lawful for any Government to annul, modify, suspend or otherwise interfere with'. Fifth, that 'to prevent any particular religious denomination being given any undue preference over any other, no Government funds or funds collected by local bodies from public revenues and public taxes including cesses shall be devoted to the promotion and furtherance of any denominational institutions or purposes'. Sixth, that there would be communal representation in proportion to numerical strength in state and federal legislatures. The electorate in all cases was to be joint. But one difference between Lajpat Rai and Ansari reflected the continuing political difference between many Hindus and Muslims:[144] while Ansari wished to extend communal representation to municipalities and local boards, Lajpat Rai wanted it to exist for a fixed (although as yet unspecified) time and then be abolished altogether.

Lajpat Rai's version of the Pact shows that in the post-Khilafat period marked by Hindu–Muslim tension and violence, he had begun to seriously reconsider his view of the Lucknow Pact and its sanction of separate electorates and communal representation. His National Pact also shows that in this new context, Lajpat Rai had begun to believe that rather than the consciousness of a shared culture or history, or any principle of mutual reciprocity, the unification of Hindus and Muslims as an Indian nation required the establishment of a particular kind of government in free India. This would be a democratic, federal government which would therefore give considerable autonomy to India's Muslim-majority provinces. It would also be a secular government. The government would keep itself quite strictly separated from religion, and disallow government funds to be used for the purpose of any religion. It would grant religious freedom to all communities as a constitutional right. Here, Rai's rudimentary conception of a secular government came close to the American ideal of secularism, which imagines a strict 'wall of separation' between state and religion. In this ideal, the state does not interfere with religion either negatively, to hinder or reform it, nor positively, to assist it. This strict non-interference by the state in the religious domain is seen as granting religious freedom.[145] Yet, Rai's fledgling conception of a secular government cannot be straightjacketed into the American ideal of secularism. This is because Rai was willing to grant Muslim reservations (according to population strength and alongside joint electorates) for a fixed time period.[146] Lajpat Rai's imagined secular government breached the strict 'wall of separation' by considering community-based reservations for minorities even if for a fixed time.

Lajpat Rai was not alone in searching for a cure for Hindu–Muslim trouble. Madan Mohan Malaviya, as the Mahasabha's sixty-two-year-old president, declared that Indian unity was possible only between two equally strong 'communities', and identified Hindu weakness as the primary cause of Hindu–Muslim disunity and Hindu sangathan as the cure.[147] This trope of Hindu weakness, and even effeminacy, had been part of British colonial discourses for a long time. Hindu men were portrayed as woman- or child-like, unmanly, weak and feeble, as opposed to strong, muscular and martial European men.[148] Such portrayals had to do with anxieties of British men about their own masculinity in the face of shifting gender roles in Britain and the need to justify to themselves and others their imperial rule over India. According to this masculine imperial logic, manly British heroes would create order out of the feminine chaos that was India, where even the men were emotional, irrational, lacked self-control and could not govern themselves.[149] Malaviya was only one more in the line of several colonized educated Indians who had partly internalized this theme of Hindu weakness since the nineteenth century. The Hindu–Muslim 'disunity' in the early 1920s was the outcome of several complex factors. Among others, these included: economic distress, urban overcrowding, and competition over jobs and housing; attempts by certain groups to use religion to assert control over public spaces and challenge local power structures; the display of outraged religious sentiments to communicate with the state and demand protection; the desire of some lower-caste groups to get involved in militant religious mobilization to portray themselves as defenders of their community and thus gain respectability vis-à-vis dominant castes; the tendency of some upper-caste groups to use religious mobilization to project their power and status; the desire of men to assert their masculinity and portray themselves as defenders of the symbols of their community and women; incendiary propaganda pamphlets published by tanzim/tabligh and shuddhi/sangathan organizations; increased newspaper circulation, biased and inflammatory reportage, and the spread of rumours; the proliferation of martial *akharas* (gymnasiums) which increased belligerence, and the desire to make quick gains in elections now taking place at the local and provincial level.[150] Based on British colonial discourse, Malaviya's anxieties about Hindu weakness had been triggered by the new context of polarization and violence in the early 1920s. Ignoring the complex factors behind 'Hindu–Muslim disunity', he identified Hindu weakness as its central cause. Overlooking how this itself was likely to worsen disunity, he urged a muscular Hindu sangathan to counter this perceived Hindu weakness and reinvigorate Hindu strength and masculinity.

M.R. Jayakar (1873–1959), the Bombay-based 'Liberal' Congressman who had opposed Gandhian non-cooperation, and soon to be Lajpat Rai's associate in the Hindu Mahasabha, concluded that Hindu–Muslim conflagrations were a consequence of the non-cooperation movement which had made people more conscious and assertive of their 'rights'. For him, the key to returning to Hindu–Muslim cooperation, which—interestingly for a man soon to join the revitalized Mahasabha—he considered a centuries-old phenomenon, was gleaning from both Hinduism and Islam principles which emphasized 'toleration' and goodwill.[151] A connoisseur of Indian classical music associated with the Gandharva Mahavidyalaya, Jayakar also announced that music showed him that the path to Hindu–Muslim unity required a schooling in 'national' education, which would teach the Hindu and Muslim 'masses' each other's contributions to the common culture and civilization of India.[152]

In May 1924, in his article 'Hindu–Muslim Tension: Causes and Cure',[153] Gandhi, now fifty-five, rejected the charges levelled at him by many Hindus and Muslims who blamed his Khilafat movement for injuring their communities.[154] He argued that the immediate and most potent cause of Hindu–Muslim trouble was that leaders from both had begun to find non-violence repugnant, the former possibly more than the latter (many Hindus had written to him claiming that the Gita justified violence in defence of one's faith).[155] Hindus and Muslims wished to force each other to respect each other's religious wishes. Hindus sought to kill Muslims to save the cow, and Muslims wished to force Hindus not to play music in front of mosques.[156] Other causes, Gandhi claimed, included Muslim 'bullying' and Hindu 'cowardice' which enabled the Muslim 'bully';[157] intense and growing distrust between the leaders of the two communities;[158] the Arya Samaj's shuddhi movement which repeatedly 'reviled other religions' and thus violated the principle of tolerance; and tabligh and 'Aga Khani' propaganda which did the same.[159]

As a cure, Gandhi argued that Hindus and Muslims needed to resolve to not use violence to force the other to respect their religious wishes—the Hindu wish to end cow slaughter or the Muslim desire to have music stopped around mosques.[160] He emphasized that the two communities had to trust each other and leave such decisions to the other's good sense.[161] Hindus needed to shed their 'cowardice' and, instead of running away, in the spirit of true non-violence learn to bravely suffer and even die while protecting their dear ones (although Gandhi clarified that even violence in self-defence was better than cowardly fleeing in the face of violence).[162] Although his disapproval of shuddhi and tabligh did not culminate in blanket repudiation, he strongly criticized them for attacking each other's religions, and called for mutual civility.[163] Regarding the issue of political representation, Gandhi suggested that Hindus, as the 'more powerful majority', should not bargain with politically 'weaker' Muslims but leave this question to a man like Hakim Ajmal Khan,[164] being conscious that Hindus would not lose anything even if 'minorities' were over-represented (granted political representation above their percentage in the population). This, according to Gandhi, was the only honourable and just solution. Ultimately, the key to the quandary lay with Hindus.[165] They had to shed their cowardice and 'have the courage to trust minorities' if they wanted Indian national 'unity'. This would in turn inspire the trust of minorities in the bona fides of Hindus.[166]

Gandhi had stereotyped both Hindus and Muslims, inadvertently drawing on long-standing colonial discourses about Hindu cowardice and Muslim aggressiveness.[167] His remark offended some Hindus, and simultaneously seemed to concede significant ground to that section of Hindus which was now increasingly using such stereotypes to justify muscular, aggressive Hindu communal organization. Hindu sangathan was necessary, they said, to overcome Hindu cowardice and counter Muslim aggression.[168] Gandhi's stereotyping of Muslims as bullies offended some Muslims, who worried it would 'excite the Hindus', giving them an excuse to initiate violence against Muslims.[169] Such stereotyping of Hindus and Muslims was problematic. Sweeping overgeneralizations left little room for individual variation, internal complexity and diversity within the categories of 'Hindus' and 'Muslims'.[170] Stereotyping was also problematic in its consequences, doing little to counter the preconceived beliefs among some Hindus that aggression always originated with Muslims and that Hindus were mostly always the victim. This potentially discouraged reflection among such Hindus about incidents where Hindus were the aggressors and Muslims the victims. Gandhi's overgeneralizations were not the most effective way to counter muscular consolidation occurring among Hindus, and may have even inadvertently encouraged it. Such stereotyping was not productive for reducing polarization. It caused some Muslims to feel that Gandhi was biased against Muslims and in favour of Hindus, and some Hindus to think he was biased against Hindus in favour of Muslims. Interestingly, both charges are levelled at the Mahatma by the Left and Right, respectively, even today.

To left-leaning critics who charge Gandhi with being biased against Muslims and with encouraging muscular Hindu consolidation, it might be pointed out that Gandhi, even as a deeply religious Hindu, aspired to impartiality, and longed for reconciliation with the religious other and for Indian national unity. This was why he had accorded more space in his article to more forthright criticism of both those Hindus who insisted that Hinduism sanctioned violence, and of Arya Samajist shuddhi for its role in the polarization and violence that was tearing apart Indian society—interpreted as his bias against Hindus by those who flocked to the Mahasabha. Gandhi's stereotypes of 'cowardly Hindus' and 'Muslim bullies' may have inadvertently provided another pretext to the Mahasabha's militant sangathan movement. Even so, crucial differences remained between the two intellectual stances. Sangathanists wished to counter 'Hindu cowardice' through physical training and militant communal organization (to perpetrate violence on others offensively or in defence). For Gandhi, resorting to violence and militant organization further vitiated Hindu–Muslim relations,[171] and itself only further reflected Hindu cowardice, weakness and emasculation.[172] He wished that Hindus overcome cowardice primarily by building their inner strength/courage to consciously do *tapasya* (suffer in self-discipline) and sacrifice even their lives for the sake of their morals.[173] Such non-violent bravery, he believed, would convert even a 'Muslim bully' encountered in a conflict into a respecting friend and facilitate unity. This was part of Gandhi's broader philosophy that conscious self-suffering can effectively expose the moral wretchedness of the violent other, change their hearts and enable resolution.[174] In the late 1930s, he would even advise Germany's Jews to meet Nazi violence with non-violent self-sacrifice, and thus convert both the Nazis and the German public to morality—which, interestingly, some researchers on non-violence/violence argue, was less preposterous and more practically reasonable than it sounds.[175]

Gandhi's philosophical permissiveness of violence, as preferable to cowardly flight, would indeed be used by some Hindus to justify militant sangathan. As we will see in Chapter 16, in less than a year, Lajpat Rai would point to this statement by Gandhi to justify sangathan as a preparation of Hindus for violence in self-defence; this was, as the Mahatma had said, better than cowardice. But for Gandhi the *primary* form of countering violence was always *non-violent* resistance via *self*-suffering and *self*-sacrifice. It was only in the minority of rare cases where this was absolutely impossible that he permitted violence in self-defence as preferable to 'cowardly' fleeing. Moreover, Gandhi imagined this violence in self-defence as an act of moral courage at the level of each *individual*. *Communal* consolidation (sangathan) by the Hindu majority for violent self-defence could only ever be cowardice. Relying on the greater *numbers* of Hindus only revealed lazy pusillanimity and timidity, since here strength was drawn not from moral claims and considerations but merely the random fact of possessing greater numbers. Only *individual* violence in self-defence, resulting from deep moral convictions rather than reliance on superior numbers, could ever count as real courage and bravery.[176] Gandhi's stance, even if idiosyncratic and problematic in some respects, was more complex than simply a bias against Muslims and abetment to Hindu communal organization. Indeed, he wished the Hindu majority to be magnanimous towards the much smaller Muslim minority, and was open towards Muslim representation even in excess of their numerical strength—a stance that also drew charges of bias from those Hindus who were turning to the Mahasabha.

Finally, while Gandhi's stereotyping of Muslims may make him appear as a biased Hindu, he consciously attempted to avoid bias in his daily practice—whether by justifying his ashram vows not only through Hindu scriptures but with references to all faiths, ensuring that hymns from different religions were recited in his daily prayer meetings, or by insisting that nationalist workers in his ashram dressed not in saffron (the colour of Hindu sanyasis) but white khadi (to signify their intent to serve the people in a non-sectarian manner).[177]

To Right-leaning critics who hold that the Mahatma was soft on Muslims and biased against Hindus, it might be acknowledged that Gandhi had indeed chosen to be slightly more critical of Hindus, going an extra step to criticize shuddhi for vitiating Hindu–Muslim relations.[178] He also more forthrightly criticized 'Hindus' for being increasingly seduced by violence, for their alleged 'cowardice' and lack of inner strength to sacrifice themselves or defend themselves individually. But this was because, as a Hindu, Gandhi felt more familiar with Hindus, and more comfortable criticizing members of his own religious community. Aware of the polarization and violence that resulted from Hindus and Muslims constantly criticizing each other, rather than self-reflecting, and as a Hindu seeking to bridge divides for the sake of Indian national unity, he chose to criticize Hindus a little more than Muslims. Yet, Gandhi had also criticized

Muslim aggressiveness, even causing anxiety and offence to some Muslims by his stereotyping of Muslims—a fact proffered by left-leaning critics as evidence of his Hindu bias even today. More importantly, Gandhi had criticized not just Arya shuddhi or Hindus, but also tabligh and Aga Khan propaganda, and blamed the leaders of *both* communities for their attraction to violence and their distrust of each other.

Gandhi's special appeal to Hindus as the majority to be magnanimous to the numerically smaller and therefore more vulnerable Muslim minority during negotiations over political representation was interpreted by some contemporary Hindus as too soft on Muslims and neglectful of Hindus. This was not the last time Gandhi faced this charge. In 1948, this would be one of the main reasons given by his assassin, Nathuram Godse, for why he killed Gandhi.[179] Gandhi's position derived from his consistent conviction that as the potentially more powerful majority community, it was ultimately more incumbent on Hindus to remove feelings of mistrust, inferiority and insecurity from the minds of the more vulnerable Muslim minority, facing prospects of political marginalization.[180] This was like a Muslim leader advising Muslims in a region where they constituted a majority (e.g., Muslim-majority Kashmir) that they must be more generous to the Hindus, who were, because of their much smaller numbers, susceptible to political marginalization.

Gandhi's use of stereotypes was problematic in its attribution of essential traits to Hindus and Muslims and its obscuring of individual variation and complexity. It was counterproductive to Gandhi's aim of reducing polarization and encouraging reconciliation and peace. At the same time, these stereotypes, and the charges of bias levelled at Gandhi from opposite sides can overshadow the importance of what he was primarily attempting to achieve through his article on Hindu–Muslim tension—to foster a politics of mutual *non-violence* and *trust, restraint* and *tolerance*. In an atmosphere of deep polarization and violence, Gandhi's article made important points about the need for Hindus and Muslims to disavow violence; to voluntarily respect each other's religious observances; to not use force to compel the other to respect one's religious observance but instead exercise self-restraint and actively develop trust in each other; to develop the courage to sacrifice the self for the sake of one's moral convictions rather than perpetrate violence on the other, and to practise mutual tolerance and not attack each other.

Often dismissed as unrealistic 'airy-fairy' idealism, such ideas stemmed from Gandhi's astute understanding of practical politics, both as a political thinker and as a skilled political leader/strategist.[181] He had a sharp grasp of the tendencies in modern politics towards conflict, escalation, domination, coercion, violence and ideological polarization.[182] Rather than an apolitical moral stance, Gandhi's suggestions were a set of strategic responses practically oriented towards constraining, countering and obstructing these tendencies, ever present in politics but now rapidly ascendant in India.[183] Though largely ignored by many Indian political actors in the 1920s,[184] and often even afterwards, Gandhi's approach—with its emphasis on non-violence, self-restraint, self-suffering, tolerance and trust-building—would resonate with Abdul Ghaffar Khan and his Khudai Khitmatgars ('Servants of God') in the North-West Frontier Province (today's Khyber Pakhtunkhwa province in Pakistan). Stereotyped as having a propensity for violence, these Pashtuns (or 'Pathans' as they were called[185]) stood up against reactionary clerics, joined the Congress and took an oath to abide by the Quran and non-violence, showing that Gandhian methods could triumph over narrow religious divides.[186] Gandhi's approach would soon inspire many generations of thinkers and activists who opposed or sought a path out of polarized ('us' vs 'them'), domineering, intolerant or violent politics, both in India and across the globe.[187] It still finds resonance with many who seek to do so today, both in India and abroad.

But for Lajpat Rai in 1924, Gandhi's analysis tackled merely the symptoms of the problem.[188] He was affronted by Gandhi's stereotyping of Hindus, and by his advice that they should bravely and non-violently suffer even in the face of grave injustice and be magnanimous on the question of Muslim representation. Lajpat Rai deemed Gandhi's analysis of the causes and solutions of 'Hindu–

Muslim' trouble as partial to Muslims and offensive to Hindus.[189] In September 1924, on his voyage back from a six-month-long trip to Europe and the Middle East,[190] Lajpat Rai began writing a series of thirteen articles on 'Hindu–Muslim unity', suggesting his own set of alternative solutions to the Hindu–Muslim problem.[191] These articles were published in the Lahore-based *Tribune* between 26 November and 17 December.

15

The Path to Hindu–Muslim Unity

In his series of articles on 'Hindu–Muslim Unity', the fifty-nine-year-old Lajpat Rai first identified some causes of the current suspicion, distrust and violence between Hindus and Muslims. One of these, he thought, was the notion that the 'communities' forming the nation possessed 'absolute rights'.[1] He argued that one community could not act in a manner that clashed with the just rights of another; the rights of each community must be limited by the equal rights of the other. He further emphasized that instead of self-interestedly insisting on their own rights, communities should be inspired by an ideal of 'duties and obligations' towards each other. They must readily 'adjust' or even 'sacrifice' their rights for each other. Putting duties before rights, which he stressed was also the teaching of 'Buddha, Christ and Gandhi', was essential for Indian national unity.

Lajpat Rai rejected the view that to be a good Hindu or Muslim required absolute freedom in the matter of 'strict and full observance of all their religious rituals and ceremonials'.[2] Some 'religious observances' of the communities conflicted, and absolute freedom to practise each would thwart Indian national unity. While private religious beliefs of individuals belonging to communities were inviolable, their more public 'religious observances'—rituals, rites, practices and ceremonies—were less sacrosanct. There could be no absolute freedom to practise all of these. Reflecting his reformist background, Lajpat Rai argued that numerous contemporary 'observances' were liable to be 'purged' as they were not sanctioned by scriptures and went against the 'spirit' of the faiths.[3] It was a small step from here to insist that those 'observances' of communities that caused 'social collision' had to be 'actively discouraged' for the sake of 'peace and neighbourly goodwill',[4] and for the 'political' aim of Indian national unity.

In Lajpat Rai's view, India's 'communities' had accumulated an excess of religious observances which only served as a 'solid wall' or 'barrier' that separated and estranged them.[5] This tendency, he held, had been encouraged by all religious reform movements including the Arya Samaj, an interesting view given his own erstwhile intimate association with the Samaj and the latter's general dislike of excessive rituals and ceremonies. Contrary to Gandhi who rejected these charges,[6] and moving closer to Jinnah's position on the question,[7] Lajpat Rai now proclaimed that this trend had been reinforced by Gandhi's Khilafat movement that had encouraged narrow-mindedness within each community, bolstering reactionaries who gave prominence to petty observances that divided communities.[8] From viewing the Khilafat movement as an opportunity for Hindus and Muslims to unite, Lajpat Rai began to regretfully see it as having deepened their disunity, in a manner 'antagonistic to the idea of a united India'.[9]

These 'observances' included the insistence by a Hindu of his right to carry an idol in a procession or play music before a mosque in a Muslim area, the Hindu practice of untouchability towards Muslims or the assertion by a Muslim of his right to sacrifice a cow in a Hindu area.[10] Although Lajpat Rai sometimes bluntly categorized these conflicting 'observances' as 'false' distortions of religion, he often admitted them as a part of religion but considered them as its 'petty' or 'non-essential' rather than its 'integral' portions.[11] These 'non-essential', peripheral 'observances' could be 'eliminated' for 'peace and neighbourly goodwill'.[12] Consequently, religions of both communities would be left with only their few 'essentials', which themselves created conditions for unity.[13] Therefore, declaring that 'Mazhab' (in the narrowest sense) was the 'curse of India',[14] Lajpat Rai recommended that such 'rationalisation' of religion by India's communities was essential for them to unite into an Indian nation.

For Lajpat Rai, the 'religion' of Hindus and Muslims was unproblematic as long as it was expressed in private, which he assumed would not cause conflict. Religion expressed in what he called public 'observances' too was acceptable as long as it was minimal, and did not conflict to harm prospects for 'national' unity. However, excessive public religious observances bred conflict between communities. Many of these only served to divide members of different religions. Perhaps an alarming thought for many believers and practitioners of Hinduism,[15] Lajpat Rai unhesitatingly suggested that religion had to be actively reconfigured—'rationalized'—for the political end of national unity.

Lajpat Rai's radically reformist attitude to religion reflects continuity from previous years. In the late nineteenth century, he had minimalized Arya Samajist theology and redefined Hinduism in terms of the Samaj's broadest tenet of Vedic monotheism. In the first decade of the century, he de-emphasized theology even more strongly to redefine Hinduism in terms of national spirit. By this increasing secularization of Hinduism he aimed to reshape and reform religion in the present, under the pretext of a 'revival' of a Hinduism that had purportedly existed in the past. Now, in the mid-1920s, Lajpat Rai's demand for religious reform for the sake of arriving at nationhood only became more direct and explicit.

Yet, this continuity eclipses an underlying change. Before the war years, Lajpat Rai had *equated* 'religious community' with the 'nation' (evident in the term 'Hindu nationality') and sought to re-fashion Hindu religion in order to construct the Hindu nation. Now, using the term 'nation' to signify only the single 'Indian' community encompassing different 'religious communities', Rai's reform demanded the *subordination* of religions and religious communities to this larger Indian nation. The nation, imagined as entirely separated from religion, had to now *supersede* it; religion, acceptable as long as it did not conflict with the nation, had to be deliberately, explicitly and unabashedly *curtailed* when conflict arose.

To be sure, Lajpat Rai believed that when it came to reforming religion in order to create a united nation, Islam needed more work than Hinduism.[16] Hinduism was described as the most 'tolerant' of all religions, allowing the fullest freedom to its own followers and respecting the religious freedoms of others.[17] Islam, on the other hand, was characterized as a faith of 'dogmas', with a history of 'religious intolerance' and still having retained its 'original violence'.[18] Lajpat Rai seemed to consider dogma, intolerance and violence as an important part of Islam.

In drawing a simplified dichotomy between a tolerant Hinduism and a dogmatic/intolerant/violent Islam, Lajpat Rai worked with stereotypes which need elaborate qualification, and revealed some of his own biases as a Hindu. Hinduism has indeed been internally characterized by diverse and strongly independent sectarian–religious communities, such as the Shaivites and Vaishnavites, with little evidence of sectarian warfare and violence.[19] As in all faiths, there has historically occurred everyday violence of inequality and coercion, as well as internal tension and competition. But these have often been resolved through the public and shared performance of plural religiosities. This was also supplemented by tolerance through the belief that all religions were one. Yet, Hinduism cannot simply be equated solely with pacifism as opposed to the violence supposedly inherent in other faiths. The absence of sectarian violence coexists with legitimization of war in ancient Hindu texts like the Rigveda, Ramayana and Mahabharata (particularly the Gita), of violence in the Manusmriti, and the real presence of violence in the politics of ancient and medieval Hindu kingdoms.[20] It also coexists with the legitimization of a deeply hierarchical and unequal caste-based social order, often experienced as intolerant, oppressive and degrading by lower castes and 'Untouchables', and which Lajpat Rai had himself vociferously attacked during 1909–13.

On Islam, Lajpat Rai was right to the extent that because Islam was born in a historical context where war was the normal state of affairs, between Arabian tribes on the one hand, and the Byzantine and Persian empires on the other, and because Islam faced persecution almost immediately, the notion of waging even violent jihad (struggle) as a means to survive, and guidance regarding the conduct of war, is found in the Quran.[21] Violent struggles were indeed part of the history of early Islam. Later developed by the ulema, the *sharia* (Islamic law) does mention the duty to wage war on polytheists, apostates and people of the Book (Christians and Jews) and later Zoroastrians, who refuse Muslim rule.[22] The Shia faith, born after Muhammad's death, and out of the experience of oppression, too waged jihads of liberation, expansion and conquest.[23] In the seventh century, the Kharijites, a pious and militant rebel group, waged wars against other Muslims and non-Muslims.[24] The eleventh to fourteenth centuries saw the Assassins terrorize the Umayyads, ulema, and Muslims and non-Muslims alike.[25] A radical and militant Islamic revivalism had also been preached by the medieval intellectual–activist Ibn Taymiyyah (1268–1328) who had called for jihad against the Mongols who had caused his family to flee from Baghdad to Damascus.[26] Taymiyyah called on a literalist interpretation of the Quran, and denounced saint worship and Sufism.[27] In the eighteenth century, the Wahhabi movement in Arabia was puritanical and iconoclastic to the extent of destroying the tombs of Prophet Mohammed and his Companions in Mecca and Medina, as well as the tomb of Hussein venerated by Shias (the source of the antipathy between Shias in both Iran and Saudi Arabia and Wahhabis in Saudi Arabia to this day).[28] Lajpat Rai's words therefore had some historical evidence backing them; violence and puritanical dogmatism have been a strand in the history of Islam.

Yet, Rai overlooked the fact that this is only *one* strand in a complex, multi-layered religion and its history. The Quran also contains injunctions such as 'Fight in the way of God those who fight you, *but aggress not. God loves not the aggressors*' (2:190), 'There is *no compulsion in religion*' (2:256), 'we believe what you believe, your God and our God is one' (29:46), 'If your enemy inclines towards peace then you should seek peace' (8:16), as well as injunctions against killing non-combatants.[29] Following his return from battle, Muhammad had said to his followers, 'We return from the lesser jihad to the greater jihad' i.e., from war to the more difficult struggle—the personal *spiritual* struggle against one's ego, selfishness, greed and evil.'[30] Following this, the majority of Muslims have seen militant jihad as limited to the particular historical context of early Islam, and interpreted jihad in terms of a non-violent, personal spiritual struggle.[31] The militant piety of the Kharijites and Assassins was marginalized by Islamic law, theology and practice.[32] Most Muslims took a broader, flexible view of Islam, enabling a vast variety of spiritual and cultural growths within the overarching framework of 'Islam'.[33] Historically, the ulema never exercised political power and no Islamic society has been governed only according to the sharia, which was often ignored and openly flouted.[34] Most Muslim scholars have agreed that it is not justified to wage war against non-Muslims simply because of their faith or to convert them.[35] Moreover, non-Muslims under Muslim rule were historically protected and allowed the right to retain their religion (although after paying a discriminatory poll tax).[36] Indeed, as scholars of Islam today have highlighted, it has been more tolerant historically than Christianity, provided greater religious freedom to non-Muslims and did not persecute heretics, which Imperial Christianity was known for.[37] Those who equate Islam and violence forget that the theme of war appears in the sacred texts of Christians and Jews, and in the Vedas, Mahabharata and Ramayana, and that violence, sectarian warfare, authoritarian absolutism and/or oppression have been carried out historically in the name of Judaism and Christianity. Violence and militancy have also been associated with the Sikh religion.[38]

The oversimplified view of Islam and its history as 'violent' also overlooks a rich history of religious and cultural exchange between Islam and other religions. For instance, in the 'age of translation' between the eighth and tenth centuries, Muslims collected great books on science, medicine, and philosophy from the West and East, and translated them into Arabic from Greek, Latin, Persian, Coptic,

Syriac and Sanskrit.[39] In this period of great creativity, Muslims also made their own contribution to learning in philosophy, medicine, algebra, optics, art and architecture, such that now Europeans learnt from Muslim advances. In straightforwardly associating Islam with violence and intolerance, Lajpat Rai made a common mistake of—in the words of one contemporary scholar of Islam—'exaggerating the militancy of a few over the quietism of the many',[40] viewing Islam in a way that contrasted with how most Muslims see their religion i.e., as no less peaceful than Christianity, Judaism, Hinduism or Buddhism.[41]

Interestingly, the stereotyping of the totality of Islam as backward and violent has long-standing roots in the threat Europe felt from Muslim military expansion in certain periods of history. Then, in Europe's encounter with Islam during the high noon of European colonialism, the image of violent, barbaric and backward Muslims was used by European colonizers to justify their colonial civilizing mission and domination over them in North Africa, the Middle East and Asia.[42] Today, the totalizing image of Islam as an uncompromising, violent religion has gained currency due to the spread of radical Muslim groups in many parts of the 'Muslim world' since the 1970s, and particularly the rise of terrorist groups that use Islam to justify attacks, symbolized best by Osama bin Laden and 9/11.[43] Yet, this image is also born out of selective media representations which focus on a terrorist minority to the exclusion of the beliefs and actions of the majority of peaceful and moderate Muslims.[44] The straight linkage of the Islamic faith with violence overlooks the fact that Islamist extremism is one side of the struggle between extremist and moderate Muslims,[45] as well as the complex historical, political and economic contexts which have encouraged radicalism. In the twentieth century, these have included European colonialism, repressive secular Muslim governments and American foreign policy vis-à-vis the Muslim world.[46]

As for the Indian subcontinent, Islam had spread in medieval times in large part through a spiritually oriented Sufism, which rejected dogma, ritualism and the use of force/violence or state

power to convert non-Muslims to Islam. Instead, Sufism preached
love for all of God's creations (and therefore for non-Muslims) and
peace with all. The Sufis were very much interested in the spread
of Islam but insisted that the best way to propagate faith was to be
a good, self-reflective Muslim and compassionate human being.
Politically and socially marginalized lower-caste and tribal groups
were attracted to Sufi Islam because of its emphasis on austerity,
charity, healing and blessings, and the supposed supernatural
powers of Sufi saints to perform miracles (which was particularly
important). They were also drawn to its emphasis on serving all of
humanity, preaching of love and tolerance, speaking in local idioms
and languages, borrowing from Hindu mystical traditions, its use of
music and dance, and embedding Islam in the local sociocultural
milieu of different regions. Thus, the history of Sufism in India
reveals an Islam grounded not in dogma, intolerance and violence,
but accommodation, inclusion, tolerance, love and peace.[47] As for
medieval Muslim rulers, they did invoke Islam to justify violent
conquest (which initially did involve the plunder and destruction
of temples, sometimes out of iconoclasm but mostly for wealth
and to signal the overthrow of the old regime). But when it came
to governance, these Muslim rulers realized that a non-Muslim
population could not be ruled according to a narrow interpretation
of the sharia, and evolved a secular state law (*zawabit-mulki*), ignored
the ulema who pressured them to forcibly convert non-Muslims, and
settled for principles of just and benevolent governance, regardless
of religion. The vast Hindu population were subjects of Islamic
supremacy and faced occasional hostility and intolerance, but were
not killed, forced to migrate or convert to Islam. Most lived in
peace, with considerable religious freedom, and many served in the
bureaucracy at lower and higher levels.[48]

Complexity notwithstanding, in his articles on 'Hindu–Muslim
Unity' in 1924, Lajpat Rai seemed to view dogma, intolerance and
violence as an important part of Islam. At the same time, interestingly,
he ultimately also appeared to construe dogmatism, intolerance and
violence as 'non-essentials' of the Islamic faith. This is suggested by

his praise for the Muslims of Turkey and Egypt who, he held, were marching with the times and discarding the 'inessentials' of Islam while retaining its 'essentials'.[49] This was a reference to secular, liberal–democratic constitutionalist currents being stirred in Turkey by Mustafa Kemal Atatürk and in Egypt by the Wafd Party among others. Rai declared that he preferred these so-called 'bad' Muslims of Turkey to those specific 'pious' Muslims of India who clung to 'insignificant' details of the 'Shara [sic]' and 'Hadis'.[50] Rai again straightforwardly equated Islamic piety and rigid intolerance, on the one hand, and less pious Muslims and flexible tolerance, on the other, ignoring the fact that religious individuals could be peaceful and non-religious people belligerent. Moreover, Hindu piety was not seen as producing intolerance, only Islamic piety was. And while overly pious Hindus were not compared with their secular, liberal co-religionists, pious Muslims were pushed to be more like secular, liberal Muslims in Turkey and Egypt. Even so, in conceptualizing secular, liberal Muslims as having retained the 'essentials' of Islam, Rai seemed to, in a circuitous way, concede that dogma and violence were after all peripheral and non-essential to Islam. India's Muslims were urged to move, like Turkish and Egyptian Muslims, towards the tolerance and liberalism at the heart of original Islam.

Lajpat Rai also began to believe that Indian Muslims should discard their Pan-Islamic concerns for the sake of Indian national unity. To show the dangers of Pan-Islamism to (Indian) 'nationalism', he contrasted Mohammad Iqbal's earlier poems to his later ones.[51] His earlier poems like *Tarana-i-Hindi* and *Chisti Ne Jis Zamin Mein* exemplified 'the height of nationalism'. From the first, Lajpat Rai quoted English translations of the following verses, part of which many Indians today know and sing as part of the patriotic song 'Saare Jahan Se Achha':

> Religion does not teach mutual animosity
> We are Indians; our country is Hindustan
> Greece, Egypt and Rome have all been effaced from the world,
> but our name and distinction is still living.[52]

(*Mazhab nahi sikhaata aapas mein bair rakhna*
Hindi hain hum watan hai Hindustan hamara
yunan-o-misr-o-roma sab mit gaye jahan se
ab tak magar hai baqi nam-o-nishan hamara[53])

He then quoted from the second:

The land in which Chisti delivered his message of truth;
the garden in which Nanak sang the song of theism;
the land which Tartars adopted as their home;
the land which made the people of Hijaz leave the desert of Arabia;
the same land is my native land, the same is my native land[54]

(*Chishti ne jis zamin mein paigham-e-haq sunaya*
Nanak ne jis chaman mein wahdat ka geet gaya
tatariyon ne jis ko apna watan banaya
jis ne hijaziyon se dasht-e-arab chhudaya
mera watan wahi hai mera watan wahi hai[55])

Lajpat Rai further wrote that Iqbal's *Naya Shivala* was 'full of the noblest possible sentiments of Hindu–Muslim unity'. His *Sada-i-Dard* and *Taswir-i-Dard* 'lamented Hindu–Muslim disunity'. But he then contrasted these with a quotation from one of Iqbal's later poems *Tarana-i-Milli*: 'China and Arabia are ours (and so) is India ours. We are Muslims, the whole world is our native land'. He also highlighted another poem which dwelt on the 'evils' of patriotism, and 'hinted that the Prophet cut the roots of the tree of patriotism'.[56] For Lajpat Rai, Iqbal's turn to Pan-Islamism and concomitant opposition to nationalism proved that Pan-Islamism necessarily conflicted with Indian nationalism.

Some scholars have indeed argued that with Iqbal's turn to Pan-Islamism in 1905–08, he transformed from an Indian nationalist advocating Hindu–Muslim unity to a man who opposed both the general principle of nationalism and the specific idea of Hindus and Muslims forming one Indian nation.[57] Yet, this view needs qualification.[58] Rai was right to the extent that Iqbal did not see Indian Muslims as part of a united Indian nation alongside Hindus, but instead part of a religiously defined, non-territorial global Muslim 'nation' of believers in Islam. He was also correct in understanding that Iqbal strongly opposed the ideology of nationalism. Viewing it as a Western ideology brought to India through colonialism, Iqbal disliked nationalism because he found it excessively focused on the state, believed it oppressively homogenized diverse individuals and societies into a single dominant culture, and was grounded in atheism and divorced from the ethical concerns of religion. It therefore stifled the development of individual personalities, which needed to develop according to their own religious precepts and religiously grounded cultures. For Iqbal, Indian nationalism, like all other territorial nationalisms, asked for the privatization of religion so that people could unite on a secular basis, and therefore conflicted with true Islam which he believed provided universal ethical principles and solutions to contemporary social, economic and political problems. Iqbal saw territorial nationalism as a product of Western history, which had fractured the universal ethics of Christianity, and now threatened the universal, humanistic ethics of Islam.

At the same time, Iqbal did not dream of an Islamic state either organized globally or in India. When he referred to the global Muslim community as a nation, he delinked the idea of a 'nation' (community) from the idea of territory or the state. His Islamic universalism and notion of Indian Muslims as part of a global Muslim nation–community coexisted alongside his imagination of India as a territory and state containing multiple nations inside it. Iqbal imagined the Indian state as a loose federation within which India's distinct Hindu and Muslim nations would be allowed full freedom to develop according to their own religious–national cultures. This, he believed, would promote unity and amity between India's Hindu and Muslim nations which, he acknowledged, did share significant linguistic and historical affinities.

Lajpat Rai's reading of Iqbal missed the fact that his Islamic universalism, and rejection of Indian nationalism, coexisted with a continued commitment to a loosely defined Indian political unity. Still, Lajpat Rai was right that Iqbal placed tremendous emphasis on belonging to a global Muslim nation, the religio-cultural separateness of Hindus and Muslims, and opposed the notion that all those inhabiting the territory of India formed a single Indian cultural and political nation. Here, Rai overlooked the fact that Iqbal's isolationist federal vision somewhat resembled his own political imagination in the first decade of the century. He potentially underplayed the fact that other Muslim leaders were contesting ideas that considered Islam and nationalism as irreconcilable extremes, and whose conception of Islam—as essentially emphasizing the equal worth of all humans (*insaniyat*)—led them to reject such separatism and advocate a united, diverse and inclusive Indian nation.[59]

Rai further substantiated his claim that Pan-Islamism conflicted with Indian nationalism by referring to 'the Fatwa of the Ulemas' during the Khilafat movement that had declared India to be 'Dar-ul-Harb' (place of war) and enjoined good Muslims to migrate to a Muslim country.[60] The issue of whether, given the British mistreatment of the Khilafat, India had become dar-ul-harb, and whether this made it a religious duty of Muslims to withdraw to a dar-ul-Islam until India once again becomes safe for Islam, had indeed been raised by some Khilafat leaders during the Khilafat movement. The fatwa Rai mentioned seemed to refer to the fatwa issued in April 1920 by Abul Kalam Azad which stated that an organized *hijrat* (emigration) by some Muslims was a legitimate alternative to non-cooperation as a means of protesting against the British undermining of Muslim religious freedoms (through their unjust policy towards the Khilafat) and the general oppressiveness of British rule in India. Between May and August 1920, religious protest, combined with anti-colonial protest based on socio-economic and political disaffection, had prompted thousands of mostly poor Indian Muslims from rural Punjab, Sindh, UP, and the North-West Frontier to migrate to Afghanistan.[61] Local maulvis too had played a role by raising the spectre of what would happen to Muslims in the afterlife if they did not flee British rule.[62] The Amir of Afghanistan had initially encouraged the hijrat and offered refuge to any Hindus and Muslims wishing to migrate. But this had only been a strategy to gain leverage in peace negotiations with the British following the 1919 Anglo–Afghan war.[63] Myths of Pan-Islamic unity notwithstanding, the vast majority of migrants were ultimately forced to return to India, now even more destitute than before.[64] Many died on the return journey.

While Azad and some other ulema had sanctioned hijrat, the majority of the prominent ulema had not authorized it. The Deobandi ulema had remained aloof, and others criticized the idea of hijrat and of India under the British having become dar-ul-harb. Hijrat had been strongly opposed by much of the top and middle ranking Khilafat leadership, including Bari, Mohani, Kitchlew, Khan and Ansari. Both the Jamiat al-Ulema-i-Hind, the organization of the Indian ulema, and the Central Khilafat Committee had opposed the idea of emigration en masse. Azad had clarified that it was not desirable for India's entire Muslim population to migrate. Moreover, while possibly a strange, outlandish and ultimately even irresponsible means of doing so, the fatwa legitimizing hijrat had been a way to register extreme protest against British colonialism.[65] However imprudent, the sanction of hijrat had not reflected a lack of Indian nationalism on the part of the leaders, like Azad, who urged it, and who—as we have noted—were committed to Indian national unity and freedom. That hijrat did not translate into a lack of commitment to Indian nationalism is also revealed by the trajectory of Ghaffar Khan who migrated to Kabul[66] and returned to join the Congress and espouse an Indian nationalism based in Hindu–Muslim unity. Be that as it may, Lajpat Rai understood the fatwa and hijrat as a reflection of Pan-Islamism that conflicted with Indian nationalism. While he held that Pan-Islamic sympathies were 'natural' and even necessary for Indian Muslims, he also concluded that they implied a 'love' for and 'allegiance' to Muslim countries which preceded and divided their love and loyalty to India.[67]

As we saw in Chapters 12 and 13, Muslim leaders sympathetic to events in Turkey had simultaneously spoken of India's Muslims as children of the soil and as proud inheritors of India, of Indian

Muslims' duty to the motherland; they had used Quranic arguments to encourage Muslim–Hindu unity, and made strong pleas for Indian freedom from British rule and for pluralist democratic Indian self-government.[68] But in Lajpat Rai's mind, 'sympathy' with Turkey and other Muslim countries (at a specific historical juncture where an important Islamic institution and symbol of prestige was being dismantled by European powers) was first seamlessly translated as 'allegiance', and then assumed to supersede allegiance to India.[69]

Lajpat Rai now also unsubscribed from the notion of a 'Muslim world' which he had, to some extent, espoused earlier. He argued that the Muslim world was mythical: Muslims around the world did not constitute a global unity but were divided by different nationalisms. He stressed that Indian Muslims were considered 'foreigners' in Muslim countries. And to substantiate his point, he pointed to the failure of the Hijrat movement when thousands of Indian Muslims were forced to return after the Afghan government refused to provide them refuge.[70] Lajpat Rai's recent visit to Turkey, Asia Minor, Syria, Palestine and Egypt had convinced him that these countries were unconcerned about Indian 'Mahajarins' and were instead embroiled in their own 'national' problems. He now declared his new-found respect for the late Sir Syed's insistence that rather than indulging in Pan-Islamic affairs, Indian Muslims should devote their attention to improving their conditions 'at home'.[71] Rai expected Indian Muslims to forgo what he now saw as their oddly unique devotion to this fictitious global community and devote their energies solely to Indian national unity and autonomy.[72]

In reality, Pan-Islamic fervour among Indian Muslims was already dissipating. In early 1924, the new Turkish nationalist government, under the staunchly secular and anti-traditional Atatürk, itself abolished the caliphate. While saddened by this event like many Muslims across the world,[73] most Indian Muslims accepted the fate of the caliphate, and began to turn away from Pan-Islamic affairs and precisely to affairs 'at home'.[74] This included the ulema, including the Jamiat, and the masses of ordinary Muslims who stopped taking interest in the Khilafat committees.[75] Lajpat Rai focused on those few Indian Muslim leaders who continued to express interest in Pan-Islamic affairs. He may have had foremost in mind the Ali brothers, whose popularity was now in sharp decline, but who continued to desperately speak about the need to resurrect a caliph.[76] With the Muslim world no longer conceptualized by Lajpat Rai as an ally, taking interest in Pan-Islamic affairs was no longer seen as a means of serving the Indian nation; the Pan-Islamism of Indian Muslims could now only be seen as working at cross purposes. Any sense of belonging to a global Muslim community, however loose, could no longer coexist with loyalty to the Indian nation.

In fact, even the Ali brothers, who continued to take a strong interest in Pan-Islamic affairs, simultaneously spoke of a 'composite Nation', and the need to sacrifice Muslim interests for the sake of Indian national unity.[77] Around the same time as Rai's article series, Mohamed Ali wrote newspaper articles denying that Islam required Muslims to foist a Muslim government on non-Muslims, reassuring Muslims that a self-governing Indian state would protect all religions, repudiating attacks by some Muslim-owned newspapers against Gandhi, rejecting the charge that Congress was a Hindu body and urging Muslims to join it.[78] Clarifying that the Hindu objection to Muslim sympathy with an Islamic world abroad flowed from a lack of understanding, and the lack of Hindu religious places like Kashi and Mathura outside India, he argued that Muslim feelings for the Muslim world outside coexisted with their commitment to Indian nationalism. But Lajpat Rai was sure that for most Muslims their community always trumped the (Indian) nation: 'most Muslim leaders say they are Muslims first and Indians afterwards'.[79] Between the concentric circles of the Indian Muslim religious community, the larger Indian nation, and the even wider global Muslim community, Muslim loyalty was seen by Rai as primarily lying with the first and the third circle, both detracting from the second.

On the other hand, Hindus were sometimes assumed to be devoted to the Indian nation by default. The possibility of Hindus being distracted by extraterritorial allegiances was foreclosed by the global absence of Hindu countries and, as Mohamed Ali pointed out, of Hindu places of worship outside India. The fact that the Hindu 'community' and India roughly shared the same geographical boundaries made 'Hinduism and Indianism . . . synonymous terms' for Lajpat Rai.[80] This automatic identification of India's Hindu 'community' with the 'national' ensured that questions of loyalty to their religious community *preceding* their loyalty to the Indian nation—of some Hindus acting as if they were 'Hindus first and Indians afterwards'—were not asked. Lajpat Rai conceded that Hindus were equally responsible for creating an 'aggressive communal feeling' through their 'militant' Hinduism.[81] He named Arya Samaj as one such practitioner of this militant Hinduism, and evaluated the Hindu Mahasabha's sangathan movement as being 'anti-Muslim' and estranging the two 'communities'.[82] Yet, this never led him to sweepingly assume that 'Hindus' prioritized their 'community' over the Indian 'nation'.

Thus, in Lajpat Rai's eyes, the Muslim 'community' needed more reform than the Hindu 'community' to facilitate Indian national unity. This was also evident in his suggestion that the creation of a 'united nation of communities' necessitated removing barriers to free social intercourse between them.[83] He insisted that Hindus must destroy their practice of untouchability against Muslims; this form of 'non-cooperation' might have been justified when Muslims were foreign conquerors and 'enemies of the people', but it was inexcusable to continue this prejudice today.[84] But he assumed that Muslims needed more reform when he stressed that they must destroy the allegedly widespread belief that Hindus were Kafirs because this caused violence during riots.[85] This overlooked the multiple, complex forces that caused riots in 1920s India—be they micro-level local factors, caste-related assertions, class-related distress and competition, masculine assertion, negotiations and assertions of control over public spaces, press reportage, inflammatory propaganda, rumour mongering, or the now-widened practice of elections. It ignored the fact that riots were variously provoked by the acts of members of both communities. It also glossed over the existence of prejudices among Hindus about Muslims. Lajpat Rai found it difficult to resist pinning riot violence on the stereotype about the supposed 'Muslim' belief that all Hindus were Kafirs.

In the immediate aftermath of the collapse of the Khilafat period, while proposing that religion and religious communities be reformed for the sake of Indian national unity, Lajpat Rai can be read as being partial to Hindus. This was most evident in his unquestioning, simplified claims about Hindus (by virtue of following the more tolerant Hinduism) being more tolerant and basically constituting the Indian nation, and of Muslims (by virtue of following the less tolerant Islam) being more intolerant and prioritizing the Muslim world and their religion over the Indian nation. It was also evident in his ultimate assumption that riots were mostly initiated by Muslims. However, in Rai's analysis, Hindus were not exempt from undertaking reform for the sake of a united Indian nation; the Arya Samaj was called out for its aggressive militancy and the Hindu Mahasabha's sangathan movement for its essentially 'anti-Muslim' bent and for worsening Hindu–Muslim estrangement. His biases notwithstanding, Lajpat Rai, significantly, still aimed at creating a united Indian nation. And he did so not on the basis of a cold contractual 'pact' or modus vivendi but on the principle of reciprocal obligation. This signified his refusal to view Hindus and Muslims as 'communities' with a significant distance between them; they could still share deeper ties of mutual respect and affection as members of the Indian nation.

Before turning to the next phase of Lajpat Rai's thought, it is worth pausing to briefly discuss a scheme he proposed in his eleventh article as a possible solution to the 'Hindu–Muslim' conundrum. This scheme is often misunderstood as propagating the two-nation theory, and the first proposal to partition India into separate nation-states.[86] True, Lajpat Rai proposed that Punjab be partitioned into two provinces: a Muslim-majority West Punjab, and a Hindu–Sikh majority East Punjab. Rai conjured a 'scheme' wherein 'Muslims would have four Muslim states: 1) the Pashtun province or the North-West Frontier Province, 2) Western Punjab, 3) Sindh, and 4) Eastern Bengal', adding that 'if there are any communities in any other part of India sufficiently large to form a *province*, they should be similarly constituted.'[87] But, as historian Ayesha Jalal—known for her criticism of Indian nationalist schools of history and their tendency to pin blame for partition solely on Jinnah—has pointed out, Lajpat Rai was not advocating India's partition into two separate nation–states.[88] First, Rai's proposal to divide Punjab into two separate Hindu–Sikh- and Muslim-majority *provinces*, and to politically organize India into Hindu-majority and Muslim-majority provinces, was part of an imagined *federal* solution to the 'communal problem'. This is also evident from his toying with the idea that Maulana Hasrat Mohani's scheme, which aimed at 'Muslim states in India, united with Hindu states, under a National Federal Government', might be the 'only workable proposition'.[89]

It has been rightly argued that Iqbal's call, six years later, in 1930, for an autonomous consolidated Muslim state in North-West India did not propose partition, but a loose federal political framework for India to allow fuller cultural autonomy to its Hindus and Muslims.[90] Not identically but somewhat similarly, Rai's scheme too dreamt up not the partition of India into separate nation–states, but a federal India consisting of different Hindu and Muslim states or provinces. Second, Rai did not seem particularly enamoured by his own suggestion of a partitioned Punjab and an India coldly divided into Hindu and Muslim states. He followed up his proposal with the words: 'But it should be distinctly understood that this is not a united India. It means a clear partition of India into a Muslim India and non-Muslim India'. A solution to the 'Hindu–Muslim' tangle that did *not* involve partitioning Punjab and segregating India's political framework along religious lines was more in line with Rai's idea of a 'united India', an ideal he clearly seemed to prefer. Lajpat Rai seemed to have floated his scheme almost in desperation, as something to perhaps consider in case all else failed. He did not mention it again after this juncture.

16

The Kohat Riot and Joining
the Hindu Mahasabha

As Lajpat Rai wrote his 'Hindu–Muslim Unity' articles, the cumulative impact of another event, and the response of prominent political leaders to it, made him further recalibrate his thoughts on nationhood: the Kohat riot of 9–10 September 1924. Historian Neeti Nair has diligently reconstructed the events leading up to this riot in the Kohat district of the North-West Frontier Province (NWFP). I draw heavily upon her research. The riot was triggered by a pamphlet of *bhajans* (devotional songs) written by Jivan Das, the secretary of Kohat's Sanatan Dharma Sabha, who, fed on ideas about sangathan, had made a call to spread the 'faith of Vishnu' all the way to Mecca, and promised to annihilate Muslims.[1]

Jivan Das's pamphlet had been read aloud in a congregation in late June, distributed on Janamashtami in August and approved for publication thereafter.[2] When the pamphlet came to the notice of Kohati Muslims, probably on 1 September, tensions rose.[3] On 3 September, a 'big mob' asked the assistant commissioner, Sardar Ahmad Khan, to arrest Das; they also burnt copies of the pamphlet. The title page of the pamphlet, with an image of Lord Krishna and the word *Om*, were also burnt.[4] This hurt the sentiments of some Sanatanist Hindus, who then observed a hartal to protest the pamphlet-burning and now also Das's arrest. They launched a prosecution against assistant commissioner Khan.[5] Their petition complained that Hindus felt insecure, and might be compelled to leave their houses and migrate to Punjab. Nair argues that Kohat's Hindus expected British protection as a matter of course. The assistant commissioner's meeting with Kohati Muslims had resulted in Das's arrest, and the case was scheduled for hearing on 11 September.[6] However, the British deputy commissioner, N.E. Reilly, secretly struck an agreement whereby Jivan Das was permitted to leave the district on 8 September.[7] Some Hindus had argued against Das's hasty and ill-considered release, as they knew it would anger Muslims. But they were overruled. As some Hindus later stated, 'the fate of Kohat was sealed as soon as the news of his release spread into the town'.[8] On the night of 8 September, large numbers of Muslims gathered at a mosque to angrily protest Das's release.[9] Reilly did not act on warnings from subordinate officials and Kohati Hindus about a possible 'breach of public peace'.[10]

On the morning of 9 September, a meeting of 250 Hindus and the Hindu Muhalla Panchayat (neighbourhood council) decided to collectively protect Hindu homes.[11] The Sanatan Dharm Sabha sent a telegram to Reilly asking for action to prevent the unlawful assembly of Muslims. Reilly, who received the telegram during a meeting with Muslims at Kohat's Town Hall, ordered the police to protect the Hindu Muhalla. Nair writes: 'When the meeting ended, groups of young [Muslim] boys wandered towards the Hindu Muhalla, while the larger portion of the crowd accompanied the assistant commissioner to launch proceedings against Jiwan Das. The groups of boys reached the Muhalla shouting they had won victory in the case; with their sticks they rattled closed shopfronts. This was apparently misconstrued by Hindus locked in their homes as an imminent attack. They began "panic firing".'[12] A Muslim boy was hit in the chest by a revolver bullet.

Fires started soon after, around noon. The military was called in. According to later statements by Reilly, the Hindu Muhalla was not touched on 9 September, and so additional troops were not called in that night.[13] Considering that the casualties on 9 September had been Muslim—ten, including one or two young boys,[14] retaliatory violence could be expected. Yet, reinforcements of troops were still not sought as a stronger precautionary measure to prevent further violence on 10 September.[15] Instead, it was assumed that 'the calm that descended on Kohat on the night of 9 September was permanent', and decided that the military under Col. Kirkpatrick would be stationed at the city's perimeter, outside the city's gates, to keep out the Fronter Province 'tribes'.[16] The next morning, on 10 September, Kirkpatrick awoke to thirteen holes cut into the city's walls overnight and 'a steadily increasing mass of intruders'.[17] It was then that reinforcements were sought.

But it was too late. The riots in Kohat saw thirteen Hindus and ten Muslims dead; thirteen Hindus and one Muslim missing or believed killed; twenty-four Hindus and six Muslims seriously wounded; and sixty-two Hindus and seventeen Muslims 'slightly wounded'.[18] Homes and shops were burnt—319 Hindu and 159 Muslim. As fires had spread, about 600 Hindus were protected by sympathetic Muslims.[19] Nair writes, 'as the fires spread and the large crowd of Muslims became harder to hold back, Hindus who had not yet taken refuge in the houses and mosques of friendly Muslims elsewhere in the city were escorted by members of the Khilafat Committee and troops to the police station and cantonment'.[20] According to Nair's analysis, the British authorities did not do nearly enough to protect the Hindu Muhalla, and instead, at their request, *evacuated* the Hindus out of Kohat [the emphasis is Nair's].[21]

Shaken by the riot, Gandhi decided on a twenty-one-day fast from 17 September, as a prayer to Hindus and Muslims to end their quarrels,[22] to teach both communities not to fight like cowards,[23] and as penance for not realizing that the non-cooperation offered by Hindus and Muslims had not been non-violent.[24] The fast was in line with Gandhi's belief that—in the words of Gandhi scholar Bhikhu Parekh—'individuals could not be shaken out of complacency on issues of vital moral importance by sermons and arguments alone';

'one had to touch their hearts and activate their consciences'.[25] For Gandhi, when all else had failed, fasting was the final, most effective weapon for a non-violent person seeking to achieve this.[26] As Parekh notes, Gandhi's ideas about fasting drew on Hindu notions of tapasya and the Christian idea of suffering love. The fast was an act of self-imposed suffering geared towards self-purification and vitalizing the conscience of others.[27] According to his secretary Mahadev Desai, Gandhi's Kohat fast was addressed in the first instance to Muslims.[28]

Lajpat Rai heard of the riot and Gandhi's fast just as he landed in Bombay from his trip to Europe and the Middle East, and as he finished writing the first of his thirteen articles on 'Hindu–Muslim Unity'.[29] At the end of this first article, he stated that Kohat's Hindus may have provoked Muslims into attacking them but also insisted that it was the government's duty to arrest and punish the guilty Hindus while protecting the rest from Muslims, to dissuade them from leaving Kohat and provide sufficient military security so they could stay in their homes. He interpreted Gandhi's fast as penance for mishandling the Hindu–Muslim situation, and for securing Hindu cooperation for the Muslim 'temple' of Khilafat only to see the desecration of Hindu temples in return.[30] He rightly also saw it as intended to create an atmosphere conducive to improving Hindu–Muslim relations.

In 1947, Gandhi's fast, in response to communal violence in Calcutta, would see several riotous Hindus and Muslims coming to Gandhi, begging for forgiveness, surrendering weapons and promising to lay down their lives to prevent further violence.[31] Considered one of Gandhi's most remarkable achievements, it would successfully end rioting in Calcutta and, more generally, in Bengal. In January 1948, his final fast before his death, this time in post-Partition Delhi, and in response to large-scale attacks on Muslims and their houses and shops, had a similar effect.[32] The demand to drive every Muslim out of Delhi lost its appeal. Representatives of the RSS, Hindu Mahasabha, Sikh and Muslim organizations as well as groups of government employees and the Delhi Police pledged to work for peace. The deputy commissioner would be inspired to take a group of Hindu and Sikh leaders to repair a desecrated shrine. Peace committees were formed and the people of Delhi began to return to living and rebuilding their lives.

Gandhi's 1924 fast resulted in a Unity Conference during 26–27 September, attended by Lajpat Rai alongside C. Raja, the Ali brothers, the Nehrus, Azad, Ajmal Khan and others. The conference passed resolutions condemning desecrations of places of worship, the persecution of individuals converting to any faith, forced attempts to convert and attempts to enforce one's own religious observances at the cost of the rights of others.[33] It was not so effective, however, in ending violence; riots occurred in Jabalpur and Allahabad just as Gandhi ended his fast.[34] Nor were Gandhi's repeated appeals to Hindus and Muslims to choose the godly and brave path of self-reform, self-restraint, self-sacrifice and non-violence over the irreligious and cowardly path of hate and violence and of grooming goondas to defend their faiths effective.[35] He pleaded for them to stop 'blaspheming God by fighting one another' only because they saw 'Him through different media' such as the Quran or the Gita.[36] But these pleas went unheard by many.

Writing as Gandhi embarked on his fast, and adopting an interesting stance for a Hindu about to join the newly revived Hindu Mahasabha, Lajpat Rai expressed scepticism about Gandhi's reliance on the Hindu practice of fasting to tackle Hindu–Muslim polarization and violence. He hoped Gandhi would adopt a 'scientific' approach to determine their root causes. Rai's subsequent twelve articles had represented his effort to arrive at these. Although these did not contain further references to Kohat, Lajpat Rai's statements elsewhere during the period of their publication suggest that this riot, and what he considered the inadequate reaction of other all-India leaders to it, deeply troubled him.

Upon breaking his fast in early October, Gandhi was keen to visit Rawalpindi and Kohat to generate peace between its Hindus and Muslims, and asked for permission from the viceroy to be permitted to travel to the region.[37] On 27 October, as he waited for the government's reply, Gandhi privately wrote to Lajpat Rai asking whether he would join him.[38] The next day, when Gandhi was denied permission by the viceroy, he wrote to Rai informing him of the government's decision, and stated the current pointlessness of his visit to Rawalpindi since he could presently bring no comfort to Kohati Hindu refugees.[39] Meanwhile, Gandhi grappled with the continuing, serious and acrimonious rift within the Congress between Swarajists like Motilal, who sought to depart from Gandhian-style non-cooperation and oppose the British after entering legislative councils, and No-Changers like Patel, who resisted change from Gandhian non-cooperation and followed Gandhi in advocating focus on constructive rural work as a way to strengthen the Indian nation.[40] Infighting threatened to break up the anti-colonial Indian nationalist movement, and was benefiting British imperial interests.[41] In the midst of communal rioting and polarization, which he believed was seriously weakening the Indian nation, Gandhi, as the mentor of No-Changers, was also propagating spinning and khadi as a way to unite Indians, rich and poor, dominant and marginal, Hindu and Muslim, in a tie of national kinship.[42] Incidentally, in these years, Gandhi's khadi and constructive work programme greatly inspired the forty-five-year-old Periyar, the radical anti-caste reformer in Madras, who believed it would help in the moral transformation of Indians, demolish hierarchical relations and create fraternal relations based on equality.[43]

On 12 November, presumably responding to another query by him, Gandhi wrote to Lajpat Rai again, expressing doubts about his usefulness in Rawalpindi given his present inability to get to the truth of what happened at Kohat, and given that he was 'powerless to do the one thing I can usefully do' i.e., to promote reconciliation between the Hindus and Muslims of Kohat.[44] Gandhi said he would go to Rawalpindi if Lajpat Rai asked him to, but this would have to be after a meeting he was committed to attending in Bombay. The meeting was an attempt to build a common political platform through which India's different political parties could present a united front to the British government.[45] After he had finished writing this letter, Gandhi received a letter from Lajpat Rai, dated

11 November, which asked him to go to Rawalpindi. Gandhi now quickly added the following below his already written letter, 'if after you have read the foregoing you think I should proceed to Rawalpindi before going to Bombay, please wire. I will start at once and if you join me at Lahore we can talk on the way. All this will on my present state of health [adversely affected by the twenty-one-day fast] be a great strain but it won't be unbearable if I must go through with it'.[46] On 14 November, Lajpat Rai wired, 'I think Rawalpindi visit necessary. But cannot strain your health for this purpose.'[47]

On 16 November, Gandhi publicly responded to statements in the press asking him to go to Rawalpindi.[48] He apologized that his present state of health did not permit continuous journeys, and clarified that he was unable to postpone his meeting in Bombay on the matter of the British government's pre-emptive repression of reviving revolutionary activity in Bengal.[49] As part of this, the British had raided Swaraj Party offices and arrested C.R. Das's lieutenant, the twenty-seven-year-old Subhas Chandra Bose, under false charges of organizing revolution and possessing links with Bolsheviks.[50] Gandhi said he hoped to proceed to Rawalpindi immediately on his return from Bombay. As a way of further explaining his decision to not immediately rush there, he said he knew Pandit Malaviya and other friends were already giving the refugees special attention. Gandhi reassured Kohati Hindus that they were in his mind and emphasized: 'the Kohat question is an all-India question. Both the Hindus and Muslims of India are interested in a proper, honourable and correct solution. Any settlement, therefore . . . must be from a national as distinguished from a parochial standpoint'.[51]

On 19 November, in a statement to the *Tribune*, Lajpat Rai apologized that 'so far illness had prevented him from taking an active interest in the misfortunes of the Hindus of Kohat'.[52] He severely criticized the British government for their inadequate security response despite awareness of brewing trouble, for failing to ensure the safety of Hindus and for arranging their evacuation from Kohat.[53] He fumed, 'Was it not the duty of the government to provide for their safety and to keep them in Kohat at all risks? Is this the

security which the government guarantees to its subjects in India? . . .
Is it for this for which they maintain such a huge army and expensive
police?'[54] Rai admitted the possibility that Kohati Hindus may have
'started the trouble' through the provocative pamphlet and criticized
the government for its failure to prevent violence and decision to
evacuate Hindus. But he simultaneously also wrote in a manner that
seemed to overlook the fact of Hindu firing and Muslim deaths and
losses during the riot. He also understated the government's primary
agency in evacuating Hindus, and the help several Muslims had
provided to Hindus: 'Here is a Hindu–Muslim trouble that results
in a whole Hindu community fleeing from their homes, to a place
several hundred miles away, from their enraged countrymen of
Muslim faith.'[55] Lajpat Rai then expressed disappointment with what
he considered the indifferent attitude of Gandhi and other all-India
Hindu and Muslim leaders (excluding Malaviya) towards the Kohati
Hindus.[56] He also criticized the 'Hindu' press outside Punjab for not
realizing the gravity of the situation.[57] For Rai, the events at Kohat
were a 'national disaster' without whose solution Hindu–Muslim
unity was impossible:

> Does anybody imagine that there is any possibility of this unity
> being achieved so long as the Kohat wounds are not healed? There
> may be unity in the south and the west. There may be unity in
> resolutions and conferences, but there will be no unity in hearts.
> What are the riots of Delhi, Gulbarga, Amethi and Lucknow as
> compared to Kohat? [58]

As noted, Gandhi too considered the Kohat tragedy an important
'all-India question', for which he had undertaken his longest ever fast
yet. As planned, he (alongside Shaukat Ali) visited the Kohati Hindu
refugees in Rawalpindi in early December.[59] In a speech to the Hindu
refugees at Rawalpindi on 9 December, Gandhi blamed Hindus,
Muslims and the government for the exodus (the government for
its failure to do its duty and for exacerbating conflict).[60] He asked
the Hindu minority to not rely on the government's help and

assurances, and return to Kohat only if Kohat's Muslims requested them to after assuring the preservation of their life and honour.[61] In an interview to the *Tribune* on 11 December, Gandhi expressed his hope that 'the Mussulmans of Kohat will see their way to meet the refugees and invite them to return under a promise of friendship and full security'.[62] For Gandhi, the onus was on Kohat's Muslim majority to give full assurance to the refugees and take them back to Kohat. He repeated his advice to Kohati Hindus to actively refuse to return to Kohat until Muslims had assured them full protection. This was the only path to a lasting peace; reliance on the British would only bring about a fragile, superficial and temporary peace. On 18 December, Gandhi once again castigated the government for its incompetence and criminal indifference during the Kohat riots.[63] He stated that Kohati Hindus could not accept the government's report on the Kohat riot, which he believed was more favourable to the Kohati Muslim narrative, and asked Muslims not to accept it either. Once more, Gandhi asked Kohat's Muslims to reassure and take back Kohati Hindus.

Although Lajpat Rai had criticized him for his alleged indifference towards Kohati Hindus, Gandhi refused to accept the government's report which had blamed the riot primarily on Hindu provocation. He had shown sympathy towards Kohat's Hindus in putting the onus on Kohat's Muslim majority to reassure the Hindu minority and create conditions for lasting peace. Some scholars like Nair criticize Gandhi for, like Rai, eventually speaking in a manner which underplayed the role of Jivan Das's pamphlet and Hindu firing, the government's responsibility for maintaining and restoring order and the government's primary agency in the evacuation of Hindus, thus promoting the misleading impression that Hindus were forced out of Kohat by Muslims.[64] Gandhi's insistence that the Hindu refugees return to Kohat only after they are invited and reassured by Kohat's Muslims may have indeed promoted a simplified impression that Kohat's Hindus were forced out by Muslims. Yet, a significant erosion of trust had occurred between Kohat's Hindus and Muslims. And Gandhi was consistent in believing that the onus of alleviating inter-community mistrust and violence in the long run ultimately always lay with the majority. As he stated in his presidential address to the Congress session at Belgaum (in what is now Karnataka) on 26 December, he believed that ultimately a Hindu minority could not peacefully live among an unwelcoming Muslim majority 'just as Mussulmans, if in a minority, must depend for honourable existence in the midst of a Hindu majority on the latter's friendliness'.[65] Either way, Lajpat Rai was unimpressed by Gandhi's response to Kohat.

As for other Hindu Congressmen, Motilal Nehru was dealing with the poor health of his daughter-in-law (Kamala Nehru), organizing the Swaraj Party's disciplined opposition to British policies in the legislatures, and actively promoting peace between Hindus and Muslims by personally visiting various muhallas in his city, Allahabad.[66] At the Belgaum Congress in December, he moved a resolution condemning the Kohat riots, the Hindu exodus and the failure of the government to protect them.[67] Thirty-five-year-old Jawaharlal who, as chief of the Allahabad Municipal Board, was attempting to make 'life a little more bearable, a little less painful' for Allahabad's inhabitants, by late 1924 was grappling with the loss of a newborn son and his wife's deteriorating health.[68] The Nehrus were not the only political actors whose preoccupations with other issues had made them pay relatively less attention to events in NWFP. C.R. Das was preoccupied with governing the Calcutta municipality,[69] reconciling Bengali Hindus and Muslims,[70] leading Swarajist opposition to the British in the Bengal Legislative Council, and with governmental raids on the Party in Bengal.[71] Twenty-seven-year-old Subhas Chandra Bose, secretary of the Swaraj Party in Bengal and chief executive officer of the Calcutta municipality, had been involved in local self-government of Calcutta until his arrest in late October 1924.[72] His retrospective account of the state of the Indian freedom struggle in 1924 remembers Gandhi's fast in response to 'Hindu–Moslem dissensions' but makes no specific mention of Kohat.[73] Sardar Patel, a dedicated follower of Gandhi, too remained busy with the Congress's constructive programme in Gujarat and with governing the Ahmedabad municipality.[74]

Among Muslim Congressmen, Hakim Ajmal Khan had sponsored the September 1924 Unity Conference, where he urged Hindus and Muslims to develop the spirit of toleration and end their conflicts which were weakening India in the face of European domination.[75] Muslims were specifically told that quarrelling in the name of religion was not a service to Islam, and to abjure all other work in favour of Hindu–Muslim unity.[76] Having travelled to Punjab twice the year before to restore peace after the Multan riots, and having donated to its Hindu victims from the Khilafat fund,[77] Khan now made the long journey to Rawalpindi to meet the Kohati Hindu refugees.[78] Mohamed Ali donated to the Kohat Hindu Relief Fund.[79] Azad spent 1923–24 challenging the ulema who argued that council entry was a religious sin, and attempting to prevent a split in the Congress by negotiating between Swarajists and No-changers.[80] He had also been involved in trying to promote peace and reconciliation between Hindus and Muslims. He had travelled to Punjab, alongside Motilal Nehru, Das, Khan and Patel, in 1923 for this reason.[81] At the September 1924 Unity Conference, he asked Hindus and Muslims not to take the law into their own hands, impressed on Hindus that they should not use force to get Muslims to stop cow slaughter, reminded them that many Muslims had never tasted beef, and equally told Muslims that cow sacrifice was not fundamental to Islam.[82] Even in 1926, Azad would be found moving around in riot-hit areas in Bengal, attempting to pacify crowds, even as abuses were hurled at him.[83]

But just as Gandhi would after May 1925,[84] Azad, by 1924, had begun to feel demoralized and withdrawn from politics. He was beginning to enter a period of intellectual and spiritual crisis and rethinking about Islam and politics, the latter also involving greater clarification of his growing opposition to the politics of the Muslim League.[85] In fact, helplessness and despondency, in the face of Hindu–Muslim polarization and violence, were now also affecting the mental and physical health of Hakim Ajmal Khan who, needing a break from India, would in a few months leave for Europe for treatment.[86] There thus existed several reasons for all-India Hindu and Muslim leaders not giving events in Kohat the kind of attention that Rai would have liked: personal tragedies and crises; preoccupation with fighting British imperialism through municipalities and councils and with preventing Hindu–Muslim polarization and violence in their own provinces; despondency at their lack of control in the face of Hindu–Muslim polarization, and sheer fatigue after attempting and failing to prevent riot after riot.

Be all that as it may, Lajpat Rai expected more from all-India Hindu and Muslim leaders. In late November of 1924, reacting to the lukewarm response to his appeal for contributions towards the relief of Kohati Hindus, Lajpat Rai had lamented the lack of 'corporate communal life among Hindus' and the 'hollowness of the Sangathan cry'.[87] By late December, he concluded that Hindus needed to organize a community-based politics through the Hindu Mahasabha.[88]

Some Hindu leaders from UP and Punjab had stuck with the Mahasabha even as it was politically marginalized by, first, the Tilak–Jinnah-engineered Lucknow Pact and then, the Gandhi-led Khilafat/non-cooperation movement. They stuck with it as it was rejuvenated by Malaviya in 1922. But, as we saw, after the Mappila and Multan riots, the Hindu Mahasabha had begun to gain significant support. Tilakites like the Swarajist Congressman N.C. Kelkar and the future co-founder of RSS, B.S. Moonje, were emerging as important Mahasabha leaders from Maharashtra and the Central Provinces (now, Madhya Pradesh).[89] More Punjabi Hindus had joined the Mahasabha in 1923 in the wake of Fazl-i-Hussain's policies.[90] Now, in 1924, Kohat pushed the fifty-nine-year-old Lajpat Rai towards the Hindu Mahasabha. The riot featured in speeches he gave at the Congress and Mahasabha sessions at Belgaum, revealing both the degree to which it disconcerted him and its role in nudging him towards the Mahasabha, leading him, after several years, to articulate a 'Hindu' politics.[91]

At the December 1924 Belgaum Congress session, Lajpat Rai had attempted to be fair. He stated: 'I am a Hindu, and as a Hindu I am ashamed to say that any Hindu should have penned that poem which was rightly objected to by the Mussulmans of Kohat. The defence of the writer was that it was written in response to an even more scurrilous attack on the Hindu religion by a Mohammedan scribe. That is no defence at all. I refuse to accept that defence . . . anything done in retaliation is worse than the original offence itself.'[92] He castigated the British government once again for its 'criminal negligence' and inaction despite being aware of escalating tensions, and forcefully argued that if the government had done its duty, no riot or exodus would have occurred.[93] He agreed with Gandhi's statement that the tiny Hindu minority of Kohat could not live without the goodwill and friendship of Muslims.[94] Arguing that Hindus and Muslims had on the whole lived peacefully, he hinted that the government may be the cause of the unfortunate change in their relations in Kohat. Rai ended with a desperate appeal: 'For God's sake, for Heaven's sake, for the sake of this Motherland . . . give up your feelings of retaliation, give up all ideas of anger and try to realise that every wound inflicted on a single Hindu or Mohammedan . . . is a wound inflicted on the breast of your mother.'[95]

At the Mahasabha session, Rai again mentioned government failures at Kohat. But that a sense of foreboding, and even paranoia, was seizing him is clear from his appeal to 'Gandhiji and others to save Hindus . . . from the death which threatened them'.[96] Despite attempts at fairness which acknowledged the wrongness of the pamphlet and the government's negligence, Lajpat Rai's view of Kohat ultimately tended to again understate the facts of Hindu firing and Muslim deaths and losses during the riots, the actions of those Kohat Muslims who had provided shelter to Hindus, and the government's agency in evacuating the Hindus. This promoted a simplified Muslim perpetrator vs Hindu victim binary, which fuelled paranoia and polarization. This was evident in the resolutions of the Hindu Mahasabha, which Rai does not seem to have disputed. These condemned the 'outrage committed by a larger number' of Kohat's Muslims on Kohat's Hindus, as well as the destruction of Hindu houses, shops and temples.[97] But they made no mention of Muslim deaths or the destruction of Muslim homes, shops and mosques. The image that Kohat had created in Lajpat Rai's mind—of Hindus besieged by intolerant, fanatical and violent Muslims—pushed him towards the Hindu Mahasabha, whose politics was now reinforcing that image.

A week after the Kohat riot, and a few days before he had embarked on his fast, Gandhi had once again touched upon the theme of Hindu cowardice. For Gandhi, the 'ceaseless fear' Hindus harboured of Muslims and their consequent reliance on physical strength— in the form of a Hindu sangathan that trained hooligans in akharas for violence—was a sign of cowardice and lack of faith in God. (He added that Islam too could not be truly defended by violence through goondas.)[98] Bravery lay, he said, in dying for the defence of Hinduism and one's loved ones. Gandhi had also repeated that fleeing and leaving behind loved ones was cowardly, unmanly and irreligious.

A day after he began his fast, Gandhi had, in *Young India*, responded to a Hindu correspondent who blamed Muslims exclusively for communal skirmishes in Nagpur. The correspondent had argued that Hindus were cowards and Muslims took advantage of this fact. The world had no place for the weak, and so Hindus needed to organize and become stronger. He had then praised B.S. Moonje for doing so. In this reply, Gandhi had agreed that the average Hindu was a coward, once again indulging in avoidable, even provocative stereotyping. Yet, he stressed that Hindu cowardice lay in educated Hindus relying on goondas to fight Muslims and protect Hinduism. This not only encouraged the militarization of Indian society, ruined Hinduism and made the Hindu community a slave to goondas, but also showed a lack of courage on the part of educated Hindus to themselves die in defence of Hinduism, which, in his view, alone constituted true bravery.[99]

Then, in December, Gandhi repeated his belief that the inability to trust the other, and resorting to killing and violence, only reflected cowardice and adharma; non-violent self-sacrifice to defend one's faith was bravery and dharma.[100] After meeting the Kohati Hindu refugees at Rawalpindi, he had also declared that 'history would have been . . . more honourably written if the Hindus had not sought the protection of officials, and had stuck to their homes and without offering any defence, or even in the act of forcibly defending themselves and their property and their dependents, had been reduced to cinders.'[101] As mentioned, he advised them to return to Kohat only if Frontier Muslims voluntarily called them back.[102] Without this invitation, he repeated, the Kohati 'Hindu minority' could not live amidst a 'Muslim majority' as their equal friends.[103]

Pondering over Gandhi's statements about Kohati Hindus, Lajpat Rai found himself disagreeing strongly. On 1 January 1925, he protested publicly in the *Tribune*:

> It seems that in Mahatmaji's opinion Kohat Hindus should have died defending their lives and temples, and that they were guilty of cowardice in not doing so. In my opinion, all the facts show that the Kohat Hindus, at any rate, did not exhibit cowardice, and that it was only circumstances that ultimately compelled them to desert their homes and temples. Man can fight against man and die in his own defence, but no one likes to be burnt to death, nor is there any merit in so dying . . . It was great cowardice to run away, as the Saharanpur Hindus did. But this stigma cannot be attached to the Hindus of Kohat. It is great injustice to lay this blame upon them, and I protest against this injustice.[104]

In fact, a statement made by Lajpat Rai five months later would reveal that Gandhi's references to Hindu cowardice had stuck in his mind, and were strengthening his belief in the need for Hindu consolidation.[105] But in January, Lajpat Rai rejected the charge of cowardice, and emphasized both the normalcy of Kohati Hindu fear and flight and the government's responsibility in their plight.[106] He also reiterated that Gandhi and other all-India leaders had neglected their duty towards Kohati Hindus.[107] In an interview to the *Bombay Chronicle* on 3 January 1925, he stated that 'some Muslim leaders' were using the initial provocation of the admittedly 'very indiscreet and foolish' pamphlet to justify what 'the Kohat Mohammedans have done—they have turned out practically a whole community', a tragedy 'unparalleled in the history of British rule in India'. [108]

It is unclear precisely which Muslim leaders Lajpat Rai was referring to. On 24 December, at the session of the All-India Khilafat Conference at Belgaum, its president Saifuddin Kitchlew had remarked, 'As for the Kohat riots, though they were due to Hindu firing, I hope that Kohat Muslims would welcome the Hindus back.'[109] In light of several Hindu-owned newspapers and Hindu leaders repeatedly leaving out the fact of initial Hindu firing and Muslim deaths and losses, Kitchlew attempted to set the record straight. The suggestion that Kohat's Muslims invite the Hindus back was meant in a spirit of generosity and reconciliation. But his brief statement did not condemn wrongdoings by a section of Kohat's Muslims. Nor did it sympathize enough with Kohat's Hindus to have a properly reconciliatory effect.

At the Muslim League session in Bombay on 30 December, its president Syed Reza Ali had suggested that Gandhi had been slightly biased against Kohat's Muslims. He questioned Gandhi's putting the onus on them for the return of the Hindu refugees to Kohat. He pointed out that Kohat's Muslims had not expelled Kohat's Hindus; 'their evacuation took place, according to the Government of India Resolution dated December 9, 1924, "at the earnest entreaty of the Hindus themselves"'. Nor, he stressed, had Kohat's Muslims opposed their return. Under these circumstances, Reza Ali questioned the soundness of Gandhi's advice to the refugees not to return to Kohat until Muslims give them full assurances. He stressed the duty of 'our countrymen, Hindu and Muslim, to keep in check the growing tendency in one community to provoke and the violent proclivity in the other to retaliate'.[110] Reza Ali's statements too attempted to rectify the impression potentially promoted by Gandhi's advice to Kohat's Hindus and Muslims, that Kohat's Muslims threw out its Hindus or were opposing their return. While speaking of Hindu provocation, he criticized what he called the Muslim tendency to violently retaliate. This was a condemnation of Muslim violence during the riots. His criticism of Gandhi's advice to Kohat's Hindus reveals his belief that Kohat's Hindus had the right to and should return. Reza Ali also donated money to Kohat's Hindus.[111]

At the same session, a Subjects Committee, with Jinnah as member, had drafted a resolution which accepted the government's account of the occurrences at Kohat. It also stated that the League, 'while expressing sympathy with the sufferers, Hindu and Mussulman, sees no justification for the refusal of Hindus to return to Kohat, and appeals to both communities to resume their old peaceful relations'.[112] This resolution attempted to promote reconciliation by expressing sympathy for both Hindu and Muslim sufferers and asking both communities to resume peaceful relations. It clearly asserted the right of Kohat's Hindus to return. But it fell short when it accepted the government's account of the Kohat riots which blamed them on Hindu provocation. Apart from this, the Punjabi Muslim journalist–politician Zafar Ali Khan had submitted his draft resolution stating that the Muslim League 'deplored' the tragedy, 'sympathised with both Hindu and Muslim sufferers' of the riot, and while placing on record its conviction that Hindus started the riots 'appealed to both communities to forget the past and resume their old peaceful relations'. It also hoped that Kohat's Muslims, 'being the predominant element in the population . . . will receive their Hindu neighbours with open arms'.[113] Khan's resolution, once again, attempted to rectify the picture that only Kohat's Muslims had been aggressors. It tried to promote reconciliation by not accepting the government's report, expressing sympathy with both communities and asking them to resume peaceful relations, and by suggesting that Kohat's Muslim majority welcome back its Hindu minority warmly. Yet, for the sake of reconciliation, and as Mohamed Ali would soon point out, it could have gone further in sympathizing with Hindu suffering and condemning Muslim violence following Hindu firing, and asking Kohat's Muslims to invite Hindus back to Kohat.[114]

But in any case, Mohamed and Shaukat Ali, along with some others, were not satisfied with this resolution.[115] Later in January, Mohamed Ali would try to clarify that this was because while Khan's resolution was an improvement because it did not certify the government's report which blamed Hindus, and did not criticize the Hindu refusal to return to Kohat (as advised by Gandhi and affirmed by the Ali brothers), it still fell short on the following points. It did not state that Hindu sufferings in Kohat were greater than those of Muslims, did not ask Muslims to invite Hindus to return to Kohat, and it accused Hindus of starting the riots but made no reference to the subsequent actions of Muslims. It also did not explicitly condemn the government's inaction. Mohamed Ali decided to draft his resolution on Kohat, supposedly intended to be an improvement on Khan's. However, according to his own account, Mohamed Ali tiredly and hastily wrote his own rough draft of a resolution on Kohat at the League session as it extended into the early hours of the morning of 31 December.[116] When the formal session restarted again at a reasonable hour, Mohamed Ali said, his hastily formulated rough draft was moved as a resolution by Khan and passed by the Muslim League. But as it turned out, Mohamed Ali's resolution, passed by the Muslim League on 31 December, ultimately read more uncharitably than he had supposedly intended.

It began by deploring the 'loss of life and property' in Kohat. It stated that 'the sufferings of the Hindus of Kohat are not unprovoked', that facts showed that 'gross provocation was offered to the religious sentiments of Musalmans, and the Hindus were the first to resort to violence'. It stated that though the sufferings of Kohat's Hindus were 'very great', and were 'deserving of the sympathy of all Mussulmans', 'it was not they alone that suffered'. The resolution ended by recommending that Kohat's Muslims 'invite the Hindu residents of Kohat to return to Kohat'.[117] As noted earlier, several Hindu newspapers and Mahasabha leaders tended to gloss over Jivan Das's pamphlet, Hindu firing, and Muslim deaths and losses during the Kohat riot. Mohamed Ali feared this promoted the mistaken impression that Muslims had resorted to violence against the unoffending Hindus without any provocation. He had understandably wished to set the record straight. In a spirit of reconciliation, the resolution acknowledged the 'very great' suffering of Kohat's Hindus and recommended that Kohat's Muslims invite Hindus back. But its overall formulation read more defensively and did not dwell enough on the grievances of Kohat's Hindus and on injustices committed by some of Kohat's Muslims to be considered properly reconciliatory. Gandhi would reprimand Mohamed Ali privately.[118]

The Khilafat Conference president, Kitchlew, had hoped that Kohat's Muslims would welcome the Hindus back. League president Reza Ali had condemned Muslim violence following Hindu firing. The Subjects Committee headed by Jinnah clearly wished that Kohat's Hindus return rather than refuse to do so in protest as Gandhi and the Ali brothers advised. Khan's resolution hoped that the Kohati Muslim majority would welcome the Hindus back. Mohamed Ali's resolution noted the suffering of Kohat's Hindus and explicitly asked Kohati Muslims to invite them back. Muslim attempts to rectify an oversimplified Muslim perpetrator vs Hindu victimhood binary that marked many Hindu narratives were understandable. But just as many Hindus underplayed the inflammatory pamphlet and Hindu firing on Muslims, these resolutions often did not dwell long enough on wrongdoings by some Kohati Muslims and the suffering of Kohat's Hindus.

It may have been the League resolution drafted by Mohamed Ali that alarmed Lajpat Rai. Ali meant to set the record straight in light of the general tendency of several Hindu newspapers and Mahasabha leaders to promote the impression that Muslims had resorted to violence against unoffending Hindus without any provocation. But his attempt at contextualization and his framing of the resolution was less than ideal. In the new atmosphere of violence, mistrust and polarization, it was interpreted by Lajpat Rai as a justification of Muslim violence. And Rai's answer was to urge Hindus to 'strengthen their organisation' and 'consolidate themselves'.[119]

But Lajpat Rai justified his turn to the Hindu Mahasabha in another manner. Between late December 1924 and early January 1925, he argued that Hindus had supported the Khilafat movement in the hope that in return, Muslims would give up their 'communal political organisation' and begin trusting the Congress for 'all political work'.[120] However, he regretted that all Muslim leaders, including 'nationalists', had rejected the Congress's claim to safeguard Muslim interests, and were strengthening their own 'communal' political organizations to safeguard themselves as a precondition for Swaraj.[121] In his view, Muslims were rejecting a common politics against the British, and persisting with their own politics of community to negotiate with the Hindu 'community' and the British government.[122] If Muslims insisted on being politically represented as a 'community' by the Muslim League and Khilafat Committee (rather than the Congress), on the assumption that Hindus and Muslims were 'two parties to a quarrel', Hindus too had to be represented by their own organization.

A degree of ambivalence about how far religion could be mixed with politics had marked Lajpat Rai's discourse during the wartime years he spent abroad and the post-war Khilafat movement. Whilst in America, in the *Self-Determination* pamphlet, he had welcomed the Lucknow Pact between the Congress and the League. In doing so, he had endorsed its imagination of the Indian nation as composed of smaller, distinct Hindu and Muslim political communities.[123] At the same time, in the *Problem of National Education*, he had longed for religion to be transcended completely at the political level.[124] During the Khilafat movement, Lajpat Rai had called for Hindu–Muslim unity and encouraged Muslims to discard the Aligarh policy of loyalism and aloofness and join the Congress in large numbers.[125] It is possible that Rai tacitly hoped that Muslims would abjure Muslim organizations entirely for the Indian National Congress. But it is equally likely that Lajpat Rai, who had welcomed the Lucknow Pact, had been, in those years, comfortable with Muslims joining the Congress and yet remaining members of Muslim political organizations like the Muslim League or Khilafat Committee (dual membership was allowed in these days), so long as the politics of Muslim organizations remained broadly oriented towards opposing the British and cooperating with the Congress.

When Lajpat Rai had asked Muslims to join the Congress in large numbers during the Khilafat movement, he had never expressed any expectation that they should abandon 'Muslim' organizations. In fact, he had urged Hindus to support Muslims in their fight to save the Khilafat unconditionally. Hindu support for the Khilafat was never intended to be conditional upon the dissolution of the Muslim League or the Khilafat Committee. Nor had any Muslim leaders promised this. Men like Azad, Syed Mahmud, Ajmal Khan and Ansari remained devoted to Congress and its kind of Indian nationalism. Some would soon break ties with Muslim political organizations entirely.[126] But the Ali brothers continued to try and lead the dying Khilafat organization and remained members of the Congress and the Muslim League. Moreover, several leaders in the Muslim League, whether Jinnah or the older guard, had disliked the Khilafat movement for its reliance on the ulema and its methods of mass mobilization.[127] As the Khilafat movement erupted, the Muslim League had waited in the wings. These Muslims, who had never endorsed the Khilafat movement, had certainly never promised to give up Muslim organizations in favour of the Congress.

Was it that Lajpat Rai's support for the Khilafat had not really been unconditional, and he had tacitly hoped that large numbers of Muslims would give up Muslim political organizations completely in favour of the Congress? Or had Rai's support been indeed unconditional, but now, in the new atmosphere of violence, polarization and mistrust, and particularly after Kohat, Rai was retrospectively remembering things differently? It is difficult to say. Either way, in the post-Kohat years, it was through these conditional terms that Lajpat Rai interpreted Hindu support for the Khilafat. And he seemed to see the continuation of Muslim organizations as a betrayal of these conditions. He may have been particularly troubled by Indian 'nationalists' like Mohamed Ali retaining their connections to the Muslim League, and Jinnah not returning to the Congress, despite its suspension of non-cooperation, and choosing to lead the League instead.[128]

But Lajpat Rai's belief that Muslims were strengthening their 'communal political organisation' needs qualification.[129] In 1919, the Montagu–Chelmsford reforms had granted no power to Indians at the centre but substantial power was given to them in the provinces. This had shifted the focus of politics from the centre to the provinces.[130] Political energies were drawn away from all-India confrontation with the British government to provincial political groups and, particularly, rural landed elites wishing to collaborate with the British.[131] This new centrifugal tendency not only adversely affected the Congress,[132] but also the Muslim League and Khilafat Committee. As the Khilafat movement subsided, the all-India Muslim leadership in these organizations had to suddenly contend with multiple new provincial political actors like Fazl-i-Husain's Unionist Party in Punjab, the Agriculturalist party of Hindu and Muslim landlords in the United Provinces and a new crop of rural Muslim politicians in Bengal.[133] Overshadowed by newly influential provincial forces working for their own causes and interests, the Muslim League, without any significant popular base, was greatly weakened and, for the first time since its foundation in 1906, was finding it difficult to consistently and cogently articulate Muslim demands at the all-India level.[134] In fact, according to some historians, the British would not take the Muslim League seriously for much of the 1920s.[135]

The shift of influence towards provincial rural forces had shifted the centre within Muslim politics.[136] Long dominated by upper-caste notables from the United Provinces, after 1919, the centre of Muslim politics shifted to Muslim-majority provinces, particularly to Punjab, where Hussain's Unionist Party was much more organized than the internally divided Bengal Muslim politicians. The Unionist Party was emerging as the most powerful Muslim party in British India. Jinnah had hoped that the decline of the Khilafat leadership would again give him the influence he had commanded at Lucknow in 1916 to articulate an all-India Muslim politics through the League. But with the 'provincialization' of Indian politics, he, a Bombay politician with no base in Muslim-majority provinces, found that this was more difficult than he had thought. Jinnah and the weakened Muslim League he was now trying to lead were forced to reckon with newly influential Punjabi Muslim voices suddenly asserting themselves strongly. In fact, differences would widen so much that Punjabi Muslim leaders would torpedo Jinnah's proposals in early 1927 and break away from the All-India Muslim League completely by the end of the year.[137] Fazl-i-

Hussain's decision to form the All-India Muslim Conference in late 1928 as the true voice of Indian Muslims would reflect continuing political differences. The Conference would continue to seriously challenge the political standing of Jinnah, his followers, and the Muslim League even in the 1930s.[138] The Khilafat Committee was wrecked by divisions *among* Western-educated Muslims (like the Ali brothers, Ansari and Ajmal Khan), and *between* them and the ulema, many of whom soon withdrew from politics.[139] Thoroughly weakened by the abolition of the caliphate by the Turks,[140] the Committee was also deeply divided between the Ali brothers, who desperately tried to keep alive the dead issue of the caliphate, and the many Muslims in the Swaraj Party who, increasingly frustrated with the Ali brothers' continued preoccupation with events in the Middle East, wished to repurpose the Khilafat organization towards the end of strengthening their 'pro-change' Party.[141] The all-India leadership of the Khilafat Committee, divided, was further weakened by the Montagu–Chelmsford Reform-induced provincialization of politics.[142]

Given this fragmentation, what explains Lajpat Rai's belief that Muslims were strengthening their political organization? Thanks to Jinnah's efforts, the Muslim League managed to cobble together two sessions in 1924 to define the Muslim position on a future scheme for self-government. The League resolved to work towards a federal government at the centre. This was a concession to the Punjabi Muslim vision of India. It reiterated its rejection of joint electorates as a 'source of discord' and as 'inadequate' for the 'effective' representation of 'communal groups'. It pressed for the *continuation of separate electorates* while explicitly leaving open the possibility of their abandonment in the future.[143] The Muslim position defined at this session sought a revision of the Lucknow Pact towards a further increase in communal representation by demanding guaranteed *Muslim majority representation* in the Muslim-majority provinces of Punjab and Bengal. This met the demands of Punjabi and Bengali Muslim leaders who were dissatisfied with the Lucknow Pact, which had not provided reservations for the Muslim majorities of Punjab and Bengal. Punjabi and Bengali Muslim leaders, worried that their slight majorities would be easily encroached upon by sizeable and socio-economically dominant Hindu and Sikh minorities, had been clamouring for guaranteed representation of their Muslim majority populations.[144]

The League also resolved that 'the mode of representation' shall 'guarantee adequate and effective representation for minorities in every province, subject, however, to the essential proviso that no majority shall be reduced to a minority or even an equality'. This left room for demanding the *extension of weightages in Muslim-minority provinces* beyond the level agreed at Lucknow, which accommodated the demands of Muslim leaders from Muslim-minority provinces (i.e., provinces where Muslims were a minority), particularly UP. Incidentally, these different Muslim leaders had not been alone in their attempts to revise the Lucknow Pact in their favour. Hindus from UP and Punjab, many represented by the Mahasabha, were doing so too. The Congress was seeking the abolition of separate electorates accepted at Lucknow.[145] Lajpat Rai's 'National Pact' had attempted to roll back the Lucknow Pact, and he had called for the abolition of separate electorates and proportionate representation for a fixed time. Additionally, the above-mentioned 'essential proviso' meant that even as the League sought to protect Muslim majorities in Muslim-majority provinces like Punjab and Bengal, and provide weightages to Muslim minorities in Muslim-minority provinces like UP, it also accepted Hindu majorities in Muslim-minority provinces, and protection for Hindu and Sikh minorities in Muslim-majority provinces as long as this did not nullify Muslim majorities.[146]

Significantly, the League also made noises about the need for adequate and possibly weighted representation for Muslims in *government services*.[147] This was not identical but broadly similar to the 'reservations' granted to Dalits in government jobs by the Indian constitution in 1950. At the bottom of the caste hierarchy and historically discriminated against by upper castes as 'untouchables', reservations aimed to rectify the 'backwardness' that resulted from this, compensate for past harm and injustice, and create effective equality of opportunity.[148] The origin of reservations in government services can in fact be traced to 1895 when the princely state of Mysore introduced reservations for non-Brahmin backward classes (including Muslims).[149] In 1902, the Maharaja of Kolhapur, a descendant of Shivaji, and an enthusiastic patron of Maharashtra's growing non-Brahmin movement, had decided to recruit only non-Brahmins into state service until they formed 50 per cent of the posts.[150] Reservations in services had been vociferously fought for by non-Brahmins in Madras since 1913, and in 1921 the ruling Justice Party had attempted to make government service more accessible to non-Brahmins by government order.[151] The objective was to rectify 'age-old inequality and injustice'.[152] In 1924, this demand by Muslims did not result from historic injustice but out of a sense of educational and economic weakness and the prospect of rapid marginalization as a vulnerable minority in Hindu-majority India.

In 1924, Jinnah negotiated with other provincial Muslim voices in a spirit of give-and-take, and succeeded in arriving at a united Muslim position, however fragile. Curious for a man who had so painstakingly struggled to engineer this hard-to-achieve political consensus in 1916, Jinnah was now committed to securing an improvement on the Lucknow Pact as a precondition for united action with the Congress,[153] with which, it might be emphasized, the League was still eager to cooperate politically to demand more power for Indians at the centre.[154] Jinnah considered 'political unity between Hindus and Muslims' as an 'essential condition for Swaraj'.[155] The League 'deplored' the 'bitterness' between Hindus and Muslims, and recommended the establishment of conciliatory boards in different districts to negotiate disputes and differences and reduce Hindu–Muslim polarization.[156] The supposedly united 'Muslim' position arrived at in Lahore was not just vague but also tenuous, as Jinnah soon realized when he faced the uncompromising attitude of Bengali Muslim politicians who wished not to concede weightage for the Bengali Hindu minority that Jinnah wished to grant.[157] In a resolution, the Muslim League had 'deplored the present scandalous state of disorganization existing among Muslims'.[158] Fragmentation and confusion would continue to plague Muslim politics in the years to come. And the 'Muslim position' arrived at by the Muslim League was opposed strongly by Muslim leaders such as Mohamed Ali, Ansari and the Swarajist Chaudhuri Khaliquzzaman.[159] Still, for Lajpat Rai, several influential Muslim leaders uniting in the League in 1924 to state a common position represented a strengthening of Muslim political organization. And this, Rai believed, necessitated a Hindu organization to articulate the 'Hindu' position.

For Lajpat Rai, the Congress could not serve as the organization of Hindus. The Muslim League rejected the Congress as a Hindu body which did not represent Muslim political interests.[160] But, interestingly, for Rai, this did not mean that the Congress represented the interests of the Hindu community. He gave three reasons why it could not do so. One, the Congress acted as a 'joint organisation of Hindus and Muslims' which had 'done more for Muslims than Hindus'.[161] Lajpat Rai was possibly referring to the Congress's approval of the Lucknow Pact, its support for the Khilafat movement, to Gandhi's criticism of the Arya Samaj and his appeals to the Hindu majority to show magnanimity towards the Muslim minority on the question of Muslim representation. A section of Hindu political leaders, particularly the urban Hindu minority in Punjab, had begun to suspect that the Congress was keen to win over Muslims at their expense.[162] In fact, Gandhi's recent offer of proportionate communal representation in the legislatures and government services in exchange for the abolition of separate electorates indicated the Congress's *unwillingness* to accept the League's terms.[163] But the offer of communal representation in services was possibly interpreted by individuals like Lajpat Rai as softness towards Muslims. Second, as a 'national' organization, the Congress could not partake in negotiations that Muslim 'communal' organizations wished to have with Hindus. Its constitution allowed three-fourths of the members of a 'community' to block a resolution, and so three-fourths of its Muslim members could prevent the Hindu majority from passing its resolutions.[164] Overlooked by both those Muslim and secular critics who straightforwardly view the 1920s Congress as a Hindu majoritarian organization, this mechanism sought to prevent a communal majority from passing decisions which would result in Hindu domination over religious minorities. Such a community 'veto' is considered by political scientists and theorists as an important element of multiculturalism and consociational democracy.[165] For Rai, it made the Congress an (Indian) 'national' organization, and prevented it from freely articulating and representing Hindu interests. Third, Rai believed that the fear of being accused of partiality, if they managed to pass their resolutions, had paralysed Hindus in the Congress. Therefore, the politics of the Hindu community could be represented in an unfettered manner only by a properly Hindu political organization: the Hindu Mahasabha.[166]

Although recent historical scholarship views Congress's Indian nationalism as compromised by the politics of the Hindu 'community',[167] Lajpat Rai saw it differently. For him, the Mahasabha needed to express the politics of the Hindu 'community' precisely because the Congress, by *continuing* to embody an Indian nationalism that stood above the politics of communities, could *not* represent a solely Hindu politics. According to his contemporary, Jayakar, Lajpat Rai played a pivotal role in pressing all major Hindu leaders to deeply consider this view before they assembled at the Congress and Mahasabha sessions in December 1924.[168] At the same time, Lajpat Rai now regretted the Congress's recognition of communal representation in the Lucknow Pact as a 'great blunder'[169] signifying its departure from its previous conduct along 'purely national lines'.[170] So, although the Congress was supposedly too 'national' to represent the politics of the 'Hindu community', he worried that it was letting its Indian nationalism be sullied by the politics of the 'Muslim community'. Rai was now espousing an Indian nationalism which tended to see demands for guaranteed political representation for Muslims as contaminating Indian nationalism. The Hindu Mahasabha had to prevent this from happening.

17

Serving Secular Indian Nationalism

By some accounts, Lajpat Rai's call to prominent Hindus across India's provinces to articulate their politics through the Hindu Mahasabha was what fuelled this organization's distinctly political turn at its 1924 Belgaum session.[1] Here, the Mahasabha appointed a committee under Lajpat Rai's chairmanship[2] to ascertain, crystallize and represent 'Hindu public opinion' on political questions in which Hindus were 'required to act as a community'.[3] In February 1925, Rai sent out a questionnaire to 'provincial Hindu leaders' to ascertain 'Hindu opinion' on communal representation.[4] The Mahasabha's secretary had reported in January that the organization was confined to larger cities and had few provincial and local branches.[5] Nine provincial branches had been formed by August and the Mahasabha's organization now included the majority of British Indian provinces and native states. But it was still strongest in the UP, Punjab, Delhi and Bihar, and attracted little more than 'casual support' outside Hindi-speaking regions of north India.[6] The *Leader* reported that the Mahasabha's eighth annual session at Calcutta in April 1925 was practically boycotted by Bengali Hindus of all hues.[7] Even so, presiding over that same session, the sixty-year-old Lajpat Rai announced, presumably after perusing responses of those prominent

Hindu leaders who did respond to his circular, that Hindus as a 'community' regarded the Lucknow Pact's sanction of communal representation as a mistake and were opposed to it 'in any shape or form'.[8] Henceforth, till the final years of his life, he, as a prominent Mahasabha leader, repeatedly advised Hindus to 'stoutly oppose' this principle and reiterated the Mahasabha's condemnation of it.[9]

In various articles and speeches between late 1924 and late 1926, Lajpat Rai identified 'communal representation' and separate electorates as the 'root cause' of Hindu–Muslim disunity.[10] Communal representation, he argued, was 'destructive and antagonistic to the idea of common nationhood', and separate electorates made 'this vicious principle immeasurably worse'.[11] By permanently institutionalizing a religion- or religious community-based politics, and politically dividing India's Hindus and Muslims into 'watertight compartments', they perpetuated religious differences and created conditions for 'a never-ending civil war'.[12] Hindering understanding between India's 'religious communities', they prevented the emergence of 'one national will in the political field'[13] and made it impossible to evolve a nation.[14] This, in turn, prevented Hindus and Muslims from standing together against the British, encouraged British denial of Indian self-government, and ensured India's 'perpetual bondage'.[15] Lajpat Rai wanted the Hindu Mahasabha to oppose communal representation because, for him, it prevented (Indian) national unity and (Indian) national autonomy (the former conceived as a prerequisite for the latter), and thus foreclosed the possibility of Indian nationalism.

But if Lajpat Rai held that the politics of the Muslim community was opposed to Indian nationalism, how did he justify his own championing of the politics of the Hindu community through the Mahasabha? How was Muslim politics unjustified but Hindu politics legitimate? Rai easily resolved what according to his own logic appeared contradictory. For him, the politics of the Muslim community was 'communalism'[16] because it sought to permanently institutionalize such a politics. But the politics of the Hindu community was not so because instead of affirming the separate political interests of Hindus,[17] it aimed to resist communal representation and eventually 'kill communalism in politics' altogether.[18] Indeed, Rai defined the 'communal' political interests of Hindus in terms of Indian 'nationalism'. He viewed the Hindu Mahasabha's 'communal' politics—what many then and today call his Hindu 'communalism'—as geared towards abolishing a nationalism-negating communal representation, and thus as serving, rather than abandoning, Indian nationalism.

For many Muslim leaders, their demands for guaranteed Muslim 'communal representation' were the outcome of fears that Indian national democratic self-government would easily result in the domination of India's Muslim minority by the Hindu majority. As Mohamed Ali once tried to explain, 'Hindus who profess to think that separate representation, if once permitted, will never disappear, must know that it is the child of the minorities' mistrust, and will go the day the Hindu majority proves not just by its words, with which it is ever free, but by its acts, that it is not only Hindu, but Indian also.'[19] As one Muslim organization would state in later years, there was a sense that 'real [Hindu] communalism masquerades as [Indian] "nationalism" while safeguards against communalism itself are called "communalism"'.[20] Many Muslims, Jinnah most prominent among them, considered their demands in a context where Hindus formed the overwhelming majority, in line with both justice and Indian nationalism. They rejected the offensive charge of 'communalism'.[21] Additionally, as members of a majority, it was easier for Hindus *not* to organize a Hindu politics demanding separate communal representation. The language of pure 'Indian national' democratic self-government could be relied on, given the overwhelming probability of the easy election and representation of Hindus without special safeguards. The charge of 'communalism' was thus more easily avoided by Hindus. Nevertheless, to Lajpat Rai, Muslim demands for communal representation, especially when accompanied by separate electorates (an important detail), were sure to cleave India into two halves and prevent the forging of a strong and united Indian nation. Demands for it reflected a 'communalism' which was opposed to (Indian) 'nationalism'.

Historian Gyanendra Pandey was among the first to analyse the historically 'constructed'[22] nature of the discourses of Indian 'nationalism' and 'communalism' in modern India. He has argued that before the 1920s, 'nationalists' easily saw the politics of religious communities as compatible with, and even serving, Indian nationalism. However, the violent turmoil of the post-Khilafat period led (Indian) 'nationalists' to redefine the politics of the religious community as a backward, 'distorted and distorting tendency', and to its exclusion from the conception of the nation.[23] A new 'pure' Indian nationalism now emerged, and was defined in opposition to community-based politics, which was now pejoratively labelled 'communalism'. As Pandey recognizes, by 1924, Lajpat Rai too was articulating this vision of 'pure' nationalism unsullied by the politics of 'community'. By 1925, he was using the term 'communalism' as the *other* of 'nationalism'. But while Pandey presents him as adopting this language only fleetingly in 1924,[24] as you may have noticed, Lajpat Rai had intermittently elaborated a version of this 'pure' Indian nationalism in previous years. This had been evident in his engagement with Sir Syed in 1888, his intervention in the separate electorates debate in 1909, and during his years in America. Moreover, although Pandey interprets it as a transient thought experiment nullified by his participation in the Hindu Mahasabha,[25] Rai's Mahasabhaite politics in fact reflected a forceful intensification of his renewed belief in a 'pure' Indian nation.

In fact, Lajpat Rai opposed communal representation because he saw it as violating what he saw as the 'secular' preconditions necessary to forge an Indian nation. He had already expressed his discomfort with it in the following terms in his Hindu–Muslim Unity article series in late 1924:

The history of several European countries shows that . . . what helped them to become nations was a decisive refusal to give in to the claims of religion. As a fundamental principle of their policy, they recognised the supremacy of the state over religion, and gradually removed all religious distinctions so far as they affected

the constitution of the state, including services under the state . . .
In India . . . the acceptance of communal representation was a
concession to religion . . . The supremacy of religion over the state
has thus been enthroned.[26]

What Lajpat Rai meant here is clarified by placing these remarks
in the context of scattered statements he made in two other articles
over the next two years. A year later, in November 1925, he wrote:

> In ancient times, all systems of religion insisted on the unity of life
> and hence politics were only a department of religion. But those
> were more or less days of isolation. A single religion held sway
> in large areas and often men of one race, speaking one language
> and following one religion were the sole occupants of the soil of
> a country . . . Hence, we find that every system of religious law
> professes to be a complete code for its followers, dealing almost
> exhaustively with every department and phase of individual and
> collective life. No one ever imagined a condition of things which
> would involve a variety of religions . . . a variety of languages
> or a variety of races in one country . . . The conditions of life
> throughout the world have now been so completely changed that
> any insistence on sticking to the letter of the old laws is out of the
> question. Modern Europe and America have practically banished
> religion from the orbit of their political activities.[27]

For Rai, the conflation of religious and political domains was possibly
suitable in ancient times which, he assumed, were characterized by
religiously homogenous societies. However, such conflation was
'out of the question' for 'modern' times, supposedly marked by
unprecedented levels of religious diversity. In this reading, it was in
response to this new religious diversity—and the injustice and conflict
presumably generated by religious politics under such conditions—
that 'modern Europe and modern America' had 'practically banished
religion from the orbit of their political activities'.

In fact, the modern age of industrialism and nationalism had
produced much greater levels of homogenization than had existed

in pre-modern, pre-industrial societies.[28] In much of Europe, the notion of separating religion from politics arose, not as a response to religious diversity, but in predominantly single-religion, often even single-denomination societies. After the Reformation in the sixteenth century, Christian sectarian diversity provoked terrible religious warfare in Europe for more than a century. These wars were ended in the mid-seventeenth century, not by the establishment of secular states, but by the reaffirmation of 'confessional states' i.e., states with strong links to particular denominational churches (or 'confessions'). In many places, these alliances between European states and their churches translated into various forms of intolerance, homogenization, migration, expulsion, forced conversion and legal sanctions against minorities.[29] Over the next two centuries, the tremendous power of established churches was felt to be disproportionate and meddlesome by various social actors in these European states, as well as by the states themselves, as they sought to increase their own power over their societies. This culminated in the separation of church and state.[30] Secular states therefore emerged in European countries which possessed a high degree of religious homogeneity, and which had tended to meet sectarian diversity with homogenization. The notion that politics must be separated from religion, having gained wider currency in Europe only from the mid-nineteenth century,[31] also emerged within this context. When Lajpat Rai stated that Europe separated religion from politics as a response to religious diversity and conflict, he overlooked the extent to which diversity had already been ironed out in European societies by the time secular states and the notion of secular politics emerged. He also failed to sufficiently consider that this politics was often the result of political objectives other than the management of religious diversity and conflict. Nevertheless, Rai understood European history differently, believing the idea of religious–political separation to be a response to religious diversity and conflict. So, in an article in 1926 titled 'Religion and Politics', he went on:

> Europe eventually decided to divorce religion from politics . . .
> Thus religion has become an affair of the individual . . . religion has

been completely relegated to its proper and legitimate function of
forming and regulating the inner consciousness of each individual
in matters spiritual. As a result, Europe has been completely rid of
all religious influences in the political and economic fields. Men
can freely join in political and economic organisations in spite of
all religious differences.[32]

Clearly, Lajpat Rai believed that the *differentiation* of separate religious
and political spheres and what scholars/theorists of 'secularisation'
today call the *privatization* of religion (i.e., its relegation to the
non-public, individual, private sphere) was how 'modern Europe
and modern America' had transcended differences of religion to—
as stated in his first quotation from 1924—'become nations'. Rai
did not explicitly use these terms while articulating this specific
reasoning, but he evidently saw secularism and secularization[33] as
the West's answer to religious conflict, and as a precondition for the
transformation of Western countries into modern nations.[34]

As for India, Lajpat Rai wrote that ancient Hindu lawmakers,
assuming that India would always be inhabited by Sanskrit-
speaking, Veda-worshipping Hindus, had not conceived of a body
politic containing non-Hindus.[35] But, with the presence of non-
Hindus in the modern body politic, sticking to old Hindu laws
was out of the question. Rai evidently considered the idea of a
Hindu theocratic state, or even a state with Hinduism as its official,
'established' religion, to be inappropriate for India's religiously
diverse society. Yet, he believed this modern-day religious diversity
was causing conflict, particularly as religions were mixed with
politics, and preventing India from emerging as an 'effective'
nation.[36] Retrospectively distancing himself from the Khilafat
movement which he had supported, Rai argued that Gandhi and
Khilafatist leaders had worsened the situation by bringing 'religion
into such prominence in connection with a movement which was,
really and more fundamentally, more political than religious'.[37]
Instead, the ideal remedy for this religious conflict was to follow
the modern West by divorcing religion from politics and ending
all religious distinctions in politics.[38] Thus, Lajpat Rai saw the

separation of religion from politics and, as we saw above, the privatization of religion as the ideal means for members of India's religious communities to unite into an Indian nation. His vision went beyond the establishment of a state free of religion to advocate that all politics be entirely free of religious markers; political organizations intending to control or influence the state also had to be free of religious markers, with Rai even dreaming of the privatization of religion as a means of facilitating this. Therefore, he saw a radically secularized state and politics as essential preconditions for Hindus and Muslims to unite as members of an Indian nation. A political actor thickly embedded in the dynamic and charged political atmosphere of the mid-1920s, Lajpat Rai did not elaborate on the nuances of what he meant precisely by such 'unity'. But, given his political–intellectual bent, he likely meant their existence and conduct—despite differences, divisions and friction—as a relatively harmonious, conflict-free and broadly cooperative political community or nation. The imperative of functioning in this manner was likely felt more urgently in the context of British colonial rule and the desire to fight it.

Interestingly, Lajpat Rai's opposition to the politics of religious communities was also driven by another purpose. He considered the victory of 'secular power'—the removal of religion from political and economic domains—as directly linked to Europe's global ascendancy:

> Europe decided to divorce religion from politics. Churches protest and contest, rebel and resist but eventually secular power wins . . . This has directly led to Europe's ascendancy in the world. Europe is today the master of the world, in fact practically of the whole world, as America is only a child of Europe . . .[39]

Lajpat Rai argued that once religion was divorced from politics, as it had been in Europe and America:

> Racial and credal prejudices may still prevail but the real determining factor in the governance of every body-politic is [now] economic. Every nation recognises that its place and

position in the council of nations depends on the efficiency of its
people, [which is] determined by its intellectual and economic
potentialities. It is the latter that determine the power of a body-
politic and not its religious faiths. We have yet to realise that
politics must be divorced from religion if the Indian nation is ever
to be efficient in the modern sense.[40]

Lajpat Rai had joined the Independent Labour Party of Britain in
April 1924 and attended the eighth International Labour Conference
at Geneva in the spring of 1926.[41] Possibly partly reflecting his
continuing association with left-wing circles, Lajpat Rai believed that
once religion had been divorced from politics, the real determining
factor in the governance of Western nations had become economic.
Unshackled by religion, they became free to reach their economic
potential, and became 'efficient in the modern sense', which in turn
determined their position in the international council of nations. The
strict separation of religion from politics was considered necessary
for the future Indian nation to attain a respectable international
status in the council of nations, to attain a respectable position
internationally. As Lajpat Rai felt the resilient strength of Western
global hegemony in the post-war years, and as his Pan-Asianism and
Pan-Islamism faded, he ceased talk of the superiority of 'the East' or
'the Orient', and instead returned to viewing Europe and the United
States as superior models that India had to emulate. Identifying their
'secular' character as the most important factor in their emergence
as modern, successful self-governing nations, he wished India to
emulate this feature.

Lajpat Rai explicitly used the term 'secular power' only in late
1926, 'secularism' in late 1927 and called for a 'secular government'
in early 1928.[42] But in conceptualizing a political domain *entirely
free* of markers of religion, he was already elaborating the conceptual
blocks of what may be called a hard-line secularism from late 1924
onwards. Like many other Indian nationalists, Lajpat Rai mostly
contrasted the term 'communal' with the term 'national' because he
saw the politics of religious communities as violating the national.

But, for him, the 'communal' violated the 'national' precisely because it mixed religion with politics, and thus defied ideas of a 'secular' state and politics, which he considered crucial for the foundation of a united Indian nation.[43] It was this vision of secularism and secular Indian nationalism that propelled his retrospective opposition to the Lucknow Pact and communal representation as well as his agenda of Hindu political consolidation through the Hindu Mahasabha.

Compromising with Muslim 'Communalism'?

Lajpat Rai clearly dreamt of a hard-line secularism, entailing even the 'privatization' of religion—the removal of religion from the political and even public domain, and its confinement to the private domain. But his stance softened as he faced multiple challenges and overall was even more complex than elaborated thus far. He sometimes claimed that if electorates were joint, Hindus would agree to a 'compromise' or 'reasonable settlement'. As we saw in Chapter 14, in the 1923 'National Pact' he drafted with M.A. Ansari, along with the assistance of the young Abul Kalam Azad, he had imagined a democratic, federal Indian government that would guarantee 'full religious liberty, that is liberty of belief, worship, propaganda, association, and education to all communities forming the Indian nation and shall form a constitutional right which it shall never be lawful for any Government to annul, modify, suspend or otherwise interfere with'.[44] Moreover, it had stated that 'to prevent any particular religious denomination being given any undue preference over any other, no Government funds or funds collected by local bodies from public revenues and public taxes including cesses shall be devoted to the promotion and furtherance of any denominational institutions or purposes'. As mentioned in Chapter 14, this came close to the US conception of secularism:[45] a strict separation of the state and religion, such that the state interfered in religion neither *negatively* to hinder or reform it, nor *positively* to assist it (with this strict non-interference being conceived as guaranteeing religious freedom). At the same time, as we have seen—again, in Chapter

14—this National Pact also accepted for a limited, although as yet unspecified, time, proportional communal representation in state and central legislature (alongside strictly joint/territorial rather than separate/communal electorates).[46]

In his Hindu–Muslim Unity articles, he had conceded that proportionate communal representation was a 'perfectly reasonable' principle, without insisting on it being temporary.[47] In an article in late 1925, he seemed reluctantly willing, if only as a necessary evil, to even consider the continuation of the level of Muslim weightage provided in the Lucknow Pact. 'Even if communal representation is to continue in the form sanctioned at Lucknow', he said, 'it is nothing but suicidal to extend it further.'[48] In a speech in October 1926, he said he 'stood for just rights', and 'offered the Mussulman the choice of the principle of representation applicable to the whole of India—population, education or taxation'. Stating his strong objection to Muslims having both guaranteed majority representation in Punjab and Bengal *and* the weightages in Muslim-minority provinces granted by the Lucknow Pact, he declared that he 'stood by the pact that had been drafted by Dr. Ansari and himself in collaboration with Maulana Abdul Kalam Azad in 1923'.[49] This was a declaration that he stood by proportionate communal representation (reservations in proportion to population strength).

Even as a Mahasabha leader, instead of rigidly sticking to his ideal of strict separation between religion on the one hand, and the state and politics on the other, Lajpat Rai displayed a willingness to depart from his ideal of a hard-line secularism and secular Indian nationalism to accept a certain level of community-based representation for Muslims. Rai's Indian nationalism, and what is often viewed as his Hindu 'communalism', seemed to occasionally admit, however reluctantly, the following possibility. That what he often pejoratively labelled as Muslim 'communalism' (i.e., the politics of the Muslim community) might just be compatible with Indian nationalism, even if it repudiated a purely secularized politics. Lajpat Rai was willing to depart from his hard-line 'secular' vision for the sake of Indian national unity.

Many of the Muslim League leaders, like Jinnah, had shunned a 'purely national' politics in favour of a 'Muslim' politics at least partly to safeguard against domination of the Muslim minority community by the Hindu majority community. For them, safeguards for the Muslim minority were not contrary to Indian nationalism but compatible with and necessary for it. Jinnah rejected the charge of 'separatism' against Muslims, and saw the Muslim League as a 'great communal organisation' functioning as 'a powerful factor in the birth of a United India'.[50] Dubbed by poet–nationalist Sarojini Naidu as the 'ambassador of Hindu–Muslim unity' a few years back,[51] and speaking for the currently weakened Muslim League, he repeated his long held stance that Hindu–Muslim unity was the 'one essential requisite condition' for Indian self-government.[52] Yet he held that 'majorities are apt to be oppressive and tyrannical' and 'minorities always dread and fear that their interests and rights . . . would suffer'.[53] Jinnah therefore considered safeguards for Muslims an essential prerequisite for Indian national unity. He believed that, given its much smaller numbers and vulnerable status, 'a minority must, above everything else, have a complete sense of security before its broader political sense can be evoked for co-operation and united endeavour in the national tasks'.[54] Jinnah here aligned with broader Muslim political discourse which, by the 1910s, had ceased demanding separate and weighted political representation and avoiding Muslim marginalization by referencing their 'historical and political importance'.[55] These were now demanded by referencing fears of majoritarian tyranny and oppression. Unlike Lajpat Rai who once said that the retention of communal representation would lead to civil war, for Jinnah, its obliteration and the consequent insecurity among minorities was a sure path to civil war. By accepting communal representation (in a certain form) for Muslims, Rai was able to admit, however reluctantly and tacitly, that the Muslim League's demand for communal representation—and what he saw as its 'communalism'— was the consequence of possibly legitimate fears of Hindu majority domination, and that such safeguards (in specific, limited forms) could be legitimately construed by the Muslim minority as essential for Indian national unity. That Rai was aware of such fears is indicated by his statement that 'The Hindus . . . form the majority and the Muslims are afraid of not receiving justice at their hands without the necessary guarantees for projection and safeguarding of their communal or minority interests'.[56]

Opposing the Extension of Communal Representation

If Lajpat Rai was able to grasp this logic of Muslim leaders, what precisely perturbed him about their politics? While he could assent to what he called Muslim 'communalism' up to a point, he held that by rejecting joint electorates and demanding a revision of the Lucknow Pact to *extend* Muslim representation both within legislatures, and beyond legislatures to government services, 'Muslims' were 'pushing forward their communalism to an extent injurious to the interests of the whole nation and certainly disastrous to those of the Hindu community'.[57] Lajpat Rai alarmingly noted that 'Muslim leaders' wanted communal representation with separate electorates extended beyond legislatures, 'all along the political line' to local bodies, government services, universities and 'other official or semi-official bodies'.[58] As we saw in Chapter 14, in his own province, to rectify the under-representation of educationally and economically worse-off Punjabi Muslims, Unionist Party leader Fazl-i-Hussain had in 1923 already extended communal representation to local bodies and educational institutions.[59] In March 1925, a month before Lajpat Rai became the president of the Mahasabha, the government announced one-third reservation for Muslims in public services.[60]

For Lajpat Rai, the extension of communal representation with separate electorates within legislatures and even beyond them would 'completely divide' India into 'a Muslim India and a non-Muslim India'. In the previous chapter, we saw that at the two Muslim League sessions in 1924, Jinnah had come to some sort of a temporary, fragile agreement with provincial Muslim leaders on a united Muslim political position as he sought to negotiate politically with the Congress. This position had included the continuation of *separate electorates, guaranteed majorities in Punjab and Bengal,* the *extension of weightages in Muslim-minority provinces,* and *weighted representation in government services.* Piqued at Jinnah for becoming the 'latest recruit' to the party that was pushing what, from his point of view, was an excessive, divisive 'communalism', Lajpat Rai proclaimed that Jinnah must confess that he did not believe in 'nationalism or a united India'.[61] In his presidential address to the Bombay Hindu Mahasabha Conference in December 1925, Lajpat Rai also argued that government recognition of a separate politics of the Muslim community in the form of communal representation was responsible for inflating the 'ego' of the 'Muslim community' to an extent that it might 'devour' other communities.[62] The demands for the extension of communal representation by spokespersons of the Muslim minority community were often viewed by Rai as stemming from the desire to become the 'dominating communal entity' in India.[63]

The united Muslim position had indeed demanded weighted representation in legislatures and government services, in excess of their numbers in the population. But it had also stated in an 'essential proviso' that 'no majority shall be turned into a minority or even an equality [sic]'.[64] This meant where Muslims were a minority, they could not, for example, demand 60 per cent reservation, reducing the Hindu majority to a political minority. They could also not demand 50 per cent reservation, reducing the Hindu majority to 'an equality [sic]' having an equal number of political representatives as the Muslim minority. The 'proviso' represented a broad agreement among Jinnah and provincial Muslim leaders, and was intended to reassure Hindu leaders. Nevertheless, it left room for Muslim spokespersons of different provinces to negotiate the extent of Muslim weightages in each province, technically leaving room for small Muslim minorities in Muslim minority-provinces like Bombay, UP or Madras to demand up to 49 per cent reservation. In the polarized, unstable and deeply uncertain political context of the mid-1920s, which often also involved multiple reasonable and unreasonable political players, this ambiguity was enough to raise Lajpat Rai's suspicions that Muslim demands for extension of communal representation were in fact attempts by the Muslim minority to achieve political dominance.

And, as he saw it, with the politics of the Muslim community having become avaricious, Hindus had no alternative but to get organized to prevent this outcome by 'fighting out the disease of communal representation'.[65] At times, in frustration, Lajpat Rai wished that the 'Hindu community' go beyond opposing the extension of communal representation to oppose the entire principle itself. While open to diverging from his hard-line secular nationalist vision, Lajpat Rai's fear of a covetous Muslim 'communalism' aimed at domination could sometimes make him assume an unbending position and return to wanting Hindu politics to seek a complete rollback of communal representation and realize his dream of a hard-line 'secular' Indian nationhood.[66]

A month after the Muslim League's December 1925 session at Aligarh, where it reiterated its demands for the extension of communal representation, Lajpat Rai insinuated that Jinnah's attempt to portray the revised Muslim demands as 'the best things for Indian nationalism' was 'camouflage (conscious or unconscious)'.[67] He bitterly stated that Jinnah best follow the candour of Sir Abdur Rahim. Rai was referring to the firebrand and communally divisive Bengali politician who had been catapulted to greater prominence by the provincial autonomy promoted by the 1919 Montagu–Chelmsford reforms. As president of the Muslim League at Aligarh, Rahim had justified separate Muslim and Hindu organizations by asserting that the differences that separated India's Hindus and Muslims were so absolute that they prevented their constitution into a single nation:

> Their respective attitude towards their life, their distinctive culture, civilization and social habits, their traditions and history, no less than their religion divide them so completely that the fact that they have lived in the same country for nearly a thousand years has contributed hardly anything to their fusion into a nation.[68]

Rahim had clarified that the Muslim League was very much concerned about the good of the country as a whole, and dismissed claims that India belonged solely to Hindus.[69] He also despaired at the 'wide gulf separating the two communities', and envisioned the 'substantial fusion of the two peoples', even if many years into the future.[70] But, as the quote above reveals, Rahim saw Hindus and Muslims as two completely separate people who did not constitute one Indian nation. He had also begun to attack Muslims in Bengal's Swarajist Party for allying with Hindus and thereby internally dividing the Muslim community, and to encourage the polarization of Bengali politics along community lines.[71] It was presumably his extreme politics, which saw Muslims as radically separate from Hindus, to which Lajpat Rai referred when he caustically asked Jinnah to follow Abdur Rahim's candour.

Rahim and Jinnah were in fact different kinds of politicians. Rather than articulating a Muslim politics which emphasized radical differences between Hindus and Muslims and deny their common Indian nationhood, Jinnah saw safeguards for Muslim representation as a means for strengthening the Indian nation. The two men had clashed recently, with Rahim assuming an inflexible stance and throwing a spoke in Jinnah's attempts to offer a reasonable weightage to the Bengali Hindu minority in negotiations with the Congress.[72] But because Lajpat Rai was so affronted by Jinnah's demand for the extension of communal representation above the level of the Lucknow Pact, he conflated Jinnah with the more extreme Abdur Rahim, reducing his Indian nationalism to nothing but camouflage, and interestingly even stating his preference for the supposedly more candid, if more extreme, isolationist and divisive Rahim. Rahim's extremist dismissal of Indian nationalism was accepted as the more authentic, even preferred Muslim voice, and Jinnah's relative moderation and Indian nationalism dismissed as deceit.

Still, the differences between Rahim and Jinnah remained irrelevant to the reasoning behind Lajpat Rai's stance. He was willing to grant, even if somewhat begrudgingly, that a reasonably limited 'communalism'—in the form of proportionate reservations, or even the weighted representation granted in the Lucknow Pact—could be compatible with Indian nationalism. But, to him, its *extension* beyond this limit was bound to encourage an unchecked isolationist communalism, which rode roughshod over and completely wrecked the entire Indian nation. Hindus had to organize a Hindu community-based politics to, if not inaugurate a hard-line 'secular' Indian nation, at least confine Muslim 'communalism' to a limit still broadly compatible with Indian nationalism.

Apart from arguments based on the defence of the Indian nation, Lajpat Rai also considered the extension of communal representation a serious encroachment on the rights and interests of the Hindu community.[73] In early 1926, he railed against Jinnah for what he believed was his role in drafting the Muslim League resolution demanding 'adequate and effective representation of minorities' in all elected bodies as a necessary precondition for Swaraj.[74] Lajpat Rai suspected the resolution was designed to make Muslim minorities 'effective' by winning over some members of the Hindu majority and by combining with 'government blocs' to render it ineffective.[75] At its 1924 Lahore session, the Muslim League had also resolved to ensure that in any constitutional scheme 'no bill or resolution . . . affecting any community' would be passed in any legislature or elected body if three-fourths of that community's elected members opposed it.[76] The clause was meant for measures concerning 'communities'. At Aligarh, a resolution affirming such a community-based veto was reiterated.[77] Although this clause was reciprocal, giving Hindu and Sikh minorities in Muslim-majority provinces the same right in legislatures and elected bodies, it exacerbated Lajpat Rai's suspicions about the intentions of Jinnah and the Muslim League. For him, such a veto would institute government by the 'consent of the minority' and, he asked, if this was the case, what was the need for Muslim weightage?[78]

Lajpat Rai suspected that Jinnah wanted a periodic revision of the Lucknow Pact to make Muslim representation in all provinces 'adequate and effective'.[79] Dismissing as 'self-deception' Jinnah's assertions that he intended a revision towards the eventual abolition of communal representation, Lajpat Rai proclaimed that Jinnah's objective was to get an extension of Muslim representation with each constitutional advance on the pretext that there could be no advance towards Swaraj without a Hindu–Muslim agreement, and no Hindu–Muslim agreement without a revision of the Pact in favour of Muslims.[80]

Lajpat Rai clarified that Hindus were open to a reasonable settlement, presumably one based on proportionate representation with joint electorates, as granted in the National Pact which he continued to stand by. But Hindu agreement to a further *extension* of communal representation would amount to committing 'political harakiri'.[81] Men like Abdur Rahim attributed successive communal riots to the 'propaganda' of the Mahasabha, shuddhi and sangathan, even naming Lajpat Rai and Shraddhanand as leaders of these movements.[82] Lajpat Rai insinuated that riots were being used to 'coerce Hindus' into conceding an extension of communal representation, and he declared that Hindus would not tolerate this.[83] Much of the force of Lajpat Rai's calls to Hindus to organize a politics of 'community' was directed towards urgently and resolutely opposing the *extension* of communal representation which he considered beyond 'reasonable' limits, and as a serious encroachment upon 'Hindu' rights and interests. If it must be retained at all, communal representation confined to 'very narrow limits'[84] alone was consistent with the political interests of Hindus. Arguments for extension began to appear to Lajpat Rai not as legitimate safeguards for the minority against Hindu majority domination, but artful attempts by the Muslim minority to dominate the Hindu majority. An organized politics of the Hindu 'community' aimed at pushing back Muslim 'communalism' to reasonable limits was thus also imagined as protecting the Hindu 'community' from perceived threats of Muslim domination. It was essential for Hindus to organize to prevent their 'merging' into or 'subordination' to the Muslim community.[85]

It is interesting to compare Lajpat Rai's rejection of the extension of communal representation with Gandhi's attitude towards it.

Reflecting the Congress's retreat from the Lucknow Pact, in late 1924, Gandhi had asked Muslims to abjure separate electorates and offered them proportionate representation in legislatures and government services.[86] He was now willing to compromise a little more to reach a settlement and once again revive a common nationalist fight against the British colonial government. By early 1925, Gandhi had shifted his stance slightly, not an uncommon occurrence in the politics of this time as evident from Lajpat Rai's own political fluidity. He now considered the demand for statutory majorities in Punjab and Bengal as 'irresistible'.[87] Gandhi argued that the extension or even retention of the Lucknow Pact was fraught with danger as this could encourage similar demands by various groups and delay Swaraj. But he believed that Muslim demands were driven by the fear of potential mistreatment by the Hindu majority, and that ignoring Muslim fears, as if they were not felt, also postponed Swaraj.[88] He asked Hindus to set aside their fears of Muslims while considering their just claims and to 'have the courage to trust the minorities' if they wanted unity and Swaraj.[89] Unlike Lajpat Rai, Gandhi harboured no suspicion that the extension of the Lucknow Pact was aimed at Muslim political domination. Such suspicions were also absent in a range of other political figures—whether Motilal and Jawaharlal Nehru, or Sarojini Naidu and Srinivas Iyengar (Congress presidents in 1925–26), or Subhas Chandra Bose and, it seems, also Sardar Patel.[90] This was true even in cases where these individuals (for example, the younger Nehru) were not particularly enamoured with communal representation.

Contrary to Lajpat Rai's fears, instead of progressively escalating demands, Jinnah would climb down in March 1927. In the 'Delhi proposals', he would go against several provincial Muslim leaders to offer to give up both *separate electorates*, the central demand insisted on by various Muslim spokespersons since 1906, and also *weightages* in Muslim minority-provinces, which had been conceded in the Lucknow Pact.[91] A community veto would not be mentioned either. But in 1924–25, Jinnah and other Muslim spokespersons in the Muslim League together demanding 'adequate and effective' representation, conjured up in Lajpat Rai fears of disproportionately weighted Muslim political representation, despite the 'essential proviso' that no majority could be reduced to a minority or even 'an equality'. This arrangement may have translated to, say, 36 per cent reservations in Bombay where Muslims constituted 20 per cent of the population, or 14 per cent in Central Provinces where they constituted 4 per cent. However, Lajpat Rai imagined the possibility of 40 or even 49 per cent Muslim reservation in provinces where they constituted a minority of 5 per cent.[92] The 'proviso' granted that Hindus would remain political majorities in Hindu-majority provinces despite weightages for Muslim minorities. Still, the prospect of increased weightages for minorities provoked anxieties about the political power and influence of 'Hindu' majorities being severely reduced. These in turn produced fears of 'Muslim' domination.

Lajpat Rai feared that the resolution for 'adequate and effective representation' was designed to make Muslim minorities 'effective' by *winning over some members of the Hindu majority* and by *combining with 'government blocs'* to render it ineffective.[93] So, apart from a lack of fixity and broad vagueness in the extent of weightages demanded, fears of Muslim domination were heightened by the following two factors. First, the tacit assumption that Hindu representatives allying with Muslims was not a potentially worthy act of mutual accommodation, in which even Muslims would have to compromise on their political aims; instead, such alliances were only a means to undercut the power of Hindu representatives supposedly speaking in the real interests of the Hindu majority. This charge was similar to that levelled by Abdur Rahim at Swaraj Party Muslims. By allying with Bengali Hindus, such Muslims took away Muslim support from those voices supposedly speaking in the Muslim community's real interests. In both cases, inter-community cooperation was seen to diminish the authentic voice of the community, although Rahim saw it as internally dividing and reducing the political influence of the Muslim community, while Rai saw it as internally dividing and reducing the political influence of the Hindu community.

The second factor which intensified Lajpat Rai's fears of Muslim domination was the British colonial presence. Jinnah seemed to have drafted constitutional schemes keeping in mind a future self-governing India without British presence. The Muslim League's resolution about adequate and effective representation, with its promise not to encroach on Hindu majorities in Muslim-minority provinces, may have perhaps appeared a little less daunting if the future context was seriously imagined, without British rule and where Hindus had substantial access to political power. But Lajpat Rai seemed to remain tied to the immediate context where he worried about Muslim minorities combining with 'government blocs' to render Hindu majorities ineffective, admittedly a real possibility in the mid-1920s. The current context of British colonial rule and the general lack of political power of Hindus exacerbated Rai's fears about the domination of Hindus by Muslims in alliance with the British. Incidentally, the same general lack of political power held true for, and deeply worried, Muslim spokespersons too. Their anxieties were aggravated by their much smaller numbers and prospective political marginalization, and drove Muslim demands for what they considered an adequate and fair share of Muslim representation. But in the context of British colonial domination, British preference for loyalists like Fazl-i-Hussain and Abdur Rahim, and the polarized and violence-ridden atmosphere of the mid-1920s, Lajpat Rai remained focused on the Hindu community, and was seized by fears that increased weightages would result in Muslim domination of Hindus. These were likely aggravated not only by the current context of instability and uncertainty but also Lajpat Rai's position as a member of the Hindu minority in Muslim-majority Punjab, and more specifically a member of the urban Hindu middle class who was more likely to feel disempowered than a rural Hindu Jat agriculturalist in Hussain's Punjab. (Unlike urban Hindus, Punjab's Jat Hindu peasantry felt more represented in Punjab's government thanks both to the Unionist Party's agriculturalist ideology and Chhotu Ram (1881–1945), the top Unionist leader, who was a Jat lawyer from Rohtak and a spokesman for Punjabi Hindu agricultural interests).[94]

Lajpat Rai feared the combination of *weightage* and the *community veto* as instruments to institute Muslim minority domination. According to the Muslim League's vision, both these measures would be reciprocally granted to the small Hindu minority in NWFP, with its overwhelming Muslim majority and small Hindu minority, once it was elevated to full provincial status, a current demand of the League. In short, the small Hindu minority there would have weightage and the same veto power on a bill that three-fourths of its members in a legislature decided was injurious to it. This would presumably have the potential to substantially undercut the political influence of the Frontier Muslim majority too. But British India was presently constituted by a much greater number of Hindu-majority provinces, where Hindus were numerically and, therefore, potentially politically stronger, and Muslims numerically and, therefore, potentially politically weaker. Because of this, the prospect of weightages and vetoes reducing the political influence of the Hindu majorities and augmenting the political influence of Muslim minorities was greater.

Moreover, in the only two currently properly existing Muslim-majority provinces, Punjab and Bengal, Muslims had very *slight* majorities (around 55 per cent in Punjab and 53 per cent in Bengal), and Hindus *large* minorities (around 32 per cent in Punjab and 45 per cent in Bengal).[95] Scared of easily losing these slight political majorities, especially in the face of socio-economically and educationally more advanced Hindus, Muslim spokespersons of these provinces demanded their guaranteed representation.[96] This left room only for *slight* or *no* weightages for Hindus and Sikhs in Punjab, and Hindus in Bengal, although it was precisely the larger size of these Hindu minorities that made them politically more secure and less deserving of weightages.

Whatever the case, guaranteed political majorities for Muslims in Punjab and Bengal *plus* the possibility of increased weightages and community vetoes for Muslim minorities in the majority of British India's Hindu-majority provinces was too much for Lajpat Rai to accept. In the context of general powerlessness under British colonial rule, in the polarized, turbulent and violent mid-1920s context, and from his position as a Punjabi Hindu minority, talk of such arrangements produced fears of domination of Hindu majorities by Muslim minorities. Rai's mention of Hindu weakness in the face of Muslim invaders in a different context in another article during the same period suggests that a revived and reductive image of medieval 'Muslim rule' likely also played its part in heightening these fears.[97]

Lajpat Rai's anxieties about the 'Muslim' desire for political dominance were further reinforced by certain statements appearing in some Punjabi 'Muslim' newspapers. Contrary to much of Indian Muslim opinion, one such newspaper had apparently expressed the hope of establishing 'Muslim Raj' in India. In December 1925, Lajpat Rai refuted statements by 'a few self-styled responsible leaders' that only a few 'irresponsible' Muslim leaders dreamt of Muslim Raj.[98] He exclaimed that *Muslim Outlook*, 'a responsible Muslim paper of Lahore', widely read by educated Muslims of Punjab and UP, had openly advocated for Muslim Raj in India, which in turn had supposedly only drawn the 'mildest rebuke' from one 'responsible' Muslim leader that Muslims in India should work instead for Islamic Raj in which the administration was shared by Hindus. This, he held, gave insight into 'the Muslim mentality'.[99]

Of course, Muslim spokespersons also highlighted instances of some Hindu leaders speaking about driving Muslims out of India as the Spaniards had expelled the Moors unless they underwent shuddhi, and about enslaving Muslims.[100] Calls by some Hindu leaders for all to adopt the 'Hindu mode of living' sparked fears of Hindu domination.[101] Such extreme statements by extremist Hindu leaders showed as much about the 'Hindu mentality' as extreme statements of extremist Muslims did about the 'Muslim mentality'. As is almost always the case, these represented certain individuals and sections rather than the whole community. Moderate leaders championed pluralist democracy and refuted the claim that Islam required Muslims to force their government on non-Muslims.[102] The Muslim League may not have responded to every stray statement that it did not endorse, from every corner of India, but it made no pronouncements about Muslim or Islamic Raj in India. It aimed for greater political Muslim parity with Hindus, rather than Muslim rule over them. The majority of Muslims in British India were poor, low-caste and too economically hard-pressed to have such tall dreams. Nevertheless, such statements appearing in some Punjabi Muslim newspapers,[103] along with what he considered as Fazl-i-Hussain's attempt to 'monopolise political power' in the Punjab, at times persuaded Lajpat Rai that 'Muslims' as a whole desired domination. Thus, Rai could, in the same speech, acknowledge 'communal' safeguards as measures demanded by an insecure minority fearful of Hindu majority domination, and also articulate his belief that the Muslim 'community' itself was driven by a desire for domination.[104]

At times, Lajpat Rai acknowledged that not all Muslims wanted 'Muslim Raj' but expressed doubts about whether those of North-Western India were of the same view.[105] He found sincere the reassurances of Muslim leaders that they were as interested as Hindus in keeping India free from foreign Muslim control, but suspected that Muslims of the Frontier Province, Punjab and Sindh were impelled by a Pan-Islamism whose aim was to keep Indian Muslims separate from Hindus, and combine with Muslim powers beyond the Frontier to establish 'Muslim dominions in India'. As proof, he cited a statement made before the North-West Frontier Enquiry Committee in 1923 by Sardar Muhammad Gul Khan, president of the Islamia Anjuman, Dera Ismail Khan District, whom he considered 'a very important Mohammedan leader'. Responding to the question of whether the Frontier Province, created out of the Punjab province in 1901, should be 're-amalgamated' or re-unified with Punjab, the Sardar declared that Muslims would:

> . . . much rather see the separation of Hindus and Muslims, 23 crores of Hindus to the South, and 8 crores of Muslims to the North. Give the whole portion from Raskumari to Agra to the Hindus and from Agra to Peshawar to the Mohammedans. I mean transmigration from one place to another. This is an idea of exchange. It is not an idea of annihilation.[106]

Gul Khan had further announced that Muslims wanted the Frontier Province to remain separate and function as a link between an

'Islamic League of Nations' and the 'Britannic commonwealth'. Khan's scheme resembled proposals advanced at the time by the likes of Bhai Parmanand, the Punjabi Hindu Mahasabhaite, who was advocating the 'complete severance of the two [Hindu and Muslim] peoples. India could be partitioned in such a manner as to secure the supremacy of Islam in one zone and that of Hinduism in the other'.[107] Its 'Islamic League of Nations' dream of a global conglomerate of Muslim countries was similar to the fantasies harboured by Hindutva exponents about a Hindu India (presided over by the Hindu king of Nepal) forming a geopolitical conglomerate with Buddhist nations of South-East Asia.[108] Moreover, many Frontier Muslims, presenting their views to the same Committee, articulated neither Pan-Islamist nor separatist ideas, and even wanted re-amalgamation with Punjab.[109] As mentioned in Chapter 14, many Pashtuns of the Frontier Province would soon become followers of Ghaffar Khan, and ally with Gandhi and the Congress. They would champion Hindu–Muslim unity and Indian nationalism, and oppose the Muslim League as it would turn increasingly separatist.[110] But Lajpat Rai believed that the view expressed by Gul Khan was shared by large numbers of North-West Indian Muslims, and remarked that this proved that 'Hindu' apprehensions were not unfounded.

Once more, the stances of more reasonable, moderate Indian Muslims were brushed aside in favour of more extreme voices. And again, this likely resulted from Lajpat Rai's own sense of belonging to the Hindu minority in Muslim-majority Punjab, neighbouring another Muslim-majority region, the Frontier Province, which was also conceived as a potential link with Muslim powers outside India. In the post-Khilafat period, Lajpat Rai's Pan-Asian/Pan-Islamic internationalist vision collapsed to narrowly focus on India and still further on the north-western region from which he hailed. From this angle, and in the context of suspicion, hostility and violence in 1925, the Pan-Islamist dreams of some Frontier Muslims about a global Muslim conglomerate appeared particularly threatening. As we saw in Chapters 14 and 15, between late 1922 and 1924, Lajpat Rai had already started viewing the Muslim world beyond India as a threat to Hindus[111] and the Pan-Islamic sentiments of Indian

Muslims as diminishing their commitment to India.[112] Now, he linked Pan-Islamic expressions with the belief that some Indian Muslims wanted Muslim domination in India. The extension of communal representation was the main vehicle through which he believed Muslim domination was being attempted. Hindus had to organize a Hindu politics through the Hindu Mahasabha to resist this extension.

Here, Lajpat Rai was unlike Gandhi who dismissed Hindu fears of Pan-Islamism as illegitimate grounds to oppose Muslim demands: 'So long as we fear the outside world, we must cease to think of Swaraj. But Swaraj we must have. I would therefore rule out the Hindu fear in considering the just claim of the Mussulmans.'[113] The thirty-eight-year-old Jawaharlal Nehru would dismiss as 'pure fancy' the threat of Pan-Islamism, arguing that Islamic countries were developing along 'intensely national lines' with 'absolutely no room' for 'an external policy based on religion'.[114] Although not enamoured with Muslim demands for communal representation, the young Nehru considered these as evidence of backward, pre-modern thinking rather than as attempts to achieve domination. The lack of fear about both Pan-Islamism and Muslim attempts to achieve domination was also evident in the young Subhas Chandra Bose, who praised his mentor C.R. Das's Bengal Pact, which had generously conceded substantial communal representation to Muslims.[115] When criticized by some Bengali Hindus for implementing Das's pact in the Calcutta Corporation, Bose had retorted that Hindus had so far enjoyed 'a sort of monopoly' when it came to appointments, and that he would support the 'just claims' of Muslims, Christians, and members of the Depressed Classes even if this caused 'heart burning' among Hindus.[116] In the absence of fears about Pan-Islamism and Muslim domination, these figures did not view the political demands of Muslim spokespersons as attempts to achieve domination, and did not involve themselves in the organization of a Hindu politics to oppose Muslim demands.

In Lajpat Rai's case, several factors came together to produce in him fears of Muslim domination: the new atmosphere of polarization and violence; various Muslim leaders demanding increased levels of communal representation; Lajpat Rai's position as an urban middle-class Hindu and member of Punjab's Hindu minority; isolationist or extreme statements by certain Muslim individuals (focused on at the expense of reasonable ones); and the likely appearance in his mind—in this new turbulent context—of a particular image of medieval 'Muslim' rule. Together, these factors ensured that Lajpat Rai interpreted Muslim proposals for increased communal representation as attempts by the Muslim minority to attain political dominance. He therefore championed a Hindu politics aimed at strongly resisting increases in communal representation for Muslims.

Regardless of how his Hindu politics appeared to Muslims or even some other Hindus, Lajpat Rai did not see his organization of a Hindu community-based politics through the Hindu Mahasabha as a *belligerent* attempt to politically dominate Muslims. Instead, he saw it as a legitimate *defence* of the Hindu majority community (and other communities of India) against the perceived threat of Muslim domination, and a justified attempt to ensure that communal representation was kept within 'reasonable' limits. As we have seen, however, Muslim minority demands for the extension of communal representation were also driven by fears of Hindu domination rather than an aggressive intent to dominate Hindus and, just like Lajpat Rai, many Muslim leaders saw their community-based politics as a legitimate defence of their 'community' against perceived threats of Hindu majority domination.[117] In these strange times, sections of both the minority and majority communities construed the politics of the other as aggressive and domineering, and justified their own politics as legitimate self-defence.

18

Hindu Sangathan: Organizing Hindus outside 'Politics'

The previous chapter showed that, for Lajpat Rai, the Hindu Mahasabha's main purpose was to organize a Hindu politics to oppose, through a complete or limited rollback of, what he considered the excessive and divisive 'communal' politics of Muslims. But he often also conceived the 'organization' of the Hindu community, which he urgently called for, as occurring *outside* the 'political'— or at least strictly political—realm.[1] In this supposedly non-political or sub-political[2] realm, Hindus were to 'organize'—or strive for 'sangathan'—to protect themselves against perceived 'attacks' from 'others', by whom he meant Muslims, often with the tacit backing of the British.[3] Attacks on 'Hindus' in this purportedly sub-political realm were perceived as taking two forms: violent aggression and attempts at forcible conversion.

In January 1925, Lajpat Rai had justified his first calls for Hindu 'organization' by pointing to the alleged justification of the violence in Kohat by some Muslim leaders. We had seen in Chapter 16 that, in light of the glossing over of some facts by certain Hindu leaders and certain Hindu-owned newspapers, various Muslim leaders had attempted to set the record straight. The president of the 1924

Khilafat Conference, Saifuddin Kitchlew, had highlighted the role of Hindu firing in initiating the Kohat riots. But even as he hoped that Kohat's Muslims would call its Hindus back, he had failed to mention wrongdoings by a section of Kohat's Muslims or express much overt sympathy for Kohat's Hindus. Reza Ali, the president of the Muslim League in 1924, had reminded the public of the role of the provocative sangathan pamphlet and of the fact that Kohat's Hindus were evacuated by the British government at their own insistence, and that things were more complex than that 'Muslims had expelled Hindus from Kohat'. He had also condemned the violent 'retaliation' by Kohat's Muslims and believed that Kohat's Hindus had the right to return. A committee formed by the Muslim League, and involving Jinnah, had accepted the government's report which attributed riots to Hindu provocation. The same committee had also expressed sympathy for both Hindu and Muslim sufferers in the riot, and wished that Kohat's Hindus return to Kohat, and that both communities resume their erstwhile peaceful relations. The influential Punjabi Muslim journalist-politician Zafar Ali Khan had submitted a draft resolution that placed on record that Hindus had started the riots. This resolution also sympathized with both Hindu and Muslim sufferers in Kohat, appealed to both communities to resume their peaceful relations, and expressed the hope that Kohat's Muslims would receive their Hindu neighbours with open arms. As Mohamed Ali pointed out, it failed to condemn Muslim violence following Hindu firing. But Ali's own hastily drafted resolution seemed to blame the fate of Kohat's Hindus on the provocative pamphlet and Hindu panic firing. Acknowledging the suffering of Kohati Hindus, it pointed out that they alone had not suffered, and ended by recommending that Kohat's Muslims invite its Hindus back.

While one Muslim leader or another had wished for the return of Kohat's Hindus, acknowledged Hindu suffering and condemned violence on part of some Kohati Muslims, they had also attempted to counter Hindu narratives which often glossed over the role of the sangathan pamphlet, Hindu firing, Muslim deaths and losses, and the government-led evacuation. In doing so, they ended up not dwelling long enough on wrongdoings by some of Kohat's Muslims and on the plight of Kohat's Hindus as was expected by leaders like Lajpat Rai. This attempt to set the record straight and counter a simple 'the Muslims threw out the Hindus' narrative prompted them to highlight wrongdoings by 'Hindus' and not condemn violence by 'Muslims' strongly enough publicly. This was interpreted by Lajpat Rai as a justification of violence against Kohat's Hindus.

Some Hindus, like one Raj Indro Lal Sahni, had responded to the Kohat riot by speaking of culprits on both sides and stressing the need for mutual love over suspicion and hatred.[4] Another, Dr Satyapal, pleaded that British rulers were reaping the benefits of communal polarization. There were several such Hindu voices. But for several other Hindus like Lajpat Rai, the Kohat riot became a symbol of Hindu vulnerability in the face of a violent and domineering Muslim community,[5] even as this image simplified a more complex episode—involving an incendiary sangathan pamphlet, gunfire by some Hindus, violence by some Kohati Muslims which filled Hindus with fear, violence by some Hindus, losses incurred by a number of Kohati Muslims, several Kohati Muslims providing help and refuge to Hindus in the face of violence by other Kohati Muslims, and the government's failures and decision to evacuate Hindus.[6] Several Punjabi Hindus like Lajpat Rai saw in Kohat's Hindus their own predicament as a minority community in a Muslim-majority province.[7] Lajpat Rai's specific position as a Hindu in North-West India, particularly in the post-Kohat context, influenced his perception of the threat of Muslim violence, which in turn drove his calls to Hindus to 'organize' themselves in what he believed was self-defence.

The psychological function that the Kohat riot performed for Lajpat Rai in 1924 was performed in subsequent years by other riots. 1925–26 saw riots in Panipat and Rawalpindi in Punjab, and in several places in UP, Delhi, Bombay, Bihar and Bengal. In April 1926, Calcutta saw arguably the most widespread and longest riots India had ever seen, spanning a whole month.[8] Each riot had its own complex causes, with victims and aggressors on both sides, besides people who tried to stem the violence and work for peace and harmony. And for every riot in a village or neighbourhood, there were hundreds of villages and neighbourhoods where no clashes occurred. Peaceful living and accommodation remained the norm.[9] But the unprecedented wave of rioting, and the concomitant polarized atmosphere, that embroiled parts of north India in these years heightened Lajpat Rai's perception—particularly as a member of the Punjabi Hindu minority—of the nature of the threat faced by Hindus. In the immediate aftermath of the Lahore riot of May 1927, Rai imagined the Muslim 'community' as a super-coordinated, conspiratorial entity, with its various 'organs' quickly entering 'deliberate or unconscious' cooperation to act jointly in times of crisis, with hooligans doing the 'stabbing' and its leaders 'cajoling' and talking about the 'helplessness of Muslims'.[10]

Such an image of Indian Muslims as a single sociopolitical body with its 'hooligan' limbs engaging in violence and 'leader' limbs camouflaging it with narratives of Muslim vulnerability gave a hyper-exaggerated unity to Indian Muslims that did not exist. India's Muslims were as internally divided as India's Hindus along lines of village, locality, class, education, occupation, caste, sect, region, language, ideology and politics. To give a broad, if still very simplified, picture: the politics of Congress Muslims differed from that of Jinnah and the Muslim League, whose politics was strongly challenged by Punjabi Muslim Unionists and Bihari Muslims, both of whose politics in turn remained distinct from that of Bengali Muslims, whose politics itself was divided along lines of loyalist aristocrats and peasants opposing the British government.[11] In UP, Muslim politics was divided along lines of Muslim landlords and tenants.[12] The politics of Western-educated Muslims diverged from that of the ulema. The Momin Ansari community articulated the politics of low-caste artisans and weavers through the All-India Jamiat-ul-Ansar (also known as the All-India Momin Conference), and the All-India Jamiat-ul-Quresh represented the low-caste politics of the Muslim butcher caste, with both vehemently challenging the politics of the upper-caste-led Muslim League.[13] The All-India Shia Political Conference, formed in 1925, opposed the perceived Sunni dominance of the Muslim League.[14] Different Muslim individuals and groups—from different villages, classes, castes and regions—in different parts of India often did not know each other, or engaged in disparate political activities which had little connection to each other and were frequently even mutually conflicting; these could not be encompassed under one umbrella simplistically. For any Muslim who wished to see it this way, the Hindu community could similarly appear as one social organism with Hindu hooligans doing the stabbing, Gandhi the cajoling and Hindu Mahasabha leaders like Lajpat Rai conjuring images of the helplessness of Hindus. Of course, this massively simplified and distorted the thoroughly complex reality of the disparate and often mutually conflicting world views and politics of different Hindus. It is interesting to note parenthetically that non-Brahmin leaders like 'Periyar' E.V.R. Naicker sometimes saw 'Brahmins' in similarly conspiratorial terms, writing of the countless creative and devious strategies they used to dupe non-Brahmins, deprive them of their rights and subjugate them.[15] Nevertheless, in the wake of the riot in Lahore, it was the above-mentioned conspiratorial image of Indian Muslims that was in Lajpat Rai's mind as he called on the Hindu 'community' to urgently 'organize' in the face of threats to its very 'existence'.[16]

Lajpat Rai's sense that the Hindu community was under threat of violence was fuelled by another development. Khwaja Hasan Nizami's 1923 tabligh pamphlet, *Da'i-i-Islam* (Missionary of Islam), had elaborated different ways in which Muslims could counter shuddhi and preach Islam among Malkana Rajputs and non-Muslims (as well as among *jahil* or ignorant Muslims), and called on all Muslims to involve themselves in the effort to protect Islam and counter Arya Samajists.[17] Swami Shraddhanand had in turn responded with a tract which raised the spectre of a great pan-Muslim conspiracy against Hinduism.[18] This had prompted suspicions among other Arya Samajists that every Muslim was involved in a secret conspiracy to convert Hindus by any means possible, including by abducting Hindu women and children.[19] This in turn made Swami

Shraddhanand an object of suspicion and resentment among some Muslims. Shraddhanand had also exhorted Hindus to bring into the Hindu fold '65 million Indian Muslims'.[20] His shuddhi of a Muslim woman in early 1926 had resulted in a legal case and, although he was acquitted in December, some 'Muslim' newspapers continued their strong condemnation of the Swami.[21] Just as Shraddhanand had appealed to his followers not to resort to violence, Nizami had counselled his followers to not attack the leaders of shuddhi but only to fight their ideas.[22] But by December 1926 the atmosphere of mutual suspicion generated by shuddhi and tabligh had led one Abdul Rashid to fire two bullets into Shraddhanand's chest.[23]

Gandhi had called the assassination a 'monstrous act', and expressed that it 'pained him to imagine the feeling this will evoke among the Hindus. Without doubt it will create ill feeling for Mussulmans among the Hindus'. Concerned about the lack of love and trust between the two communities, which could not 'live together in perpetual conflict', and had no choice but to live like brothers, Gandhi worried that this act would further polarize Hindus and Muslims into antagonistic camps, and provoke a violent reaction from some Hindus. He argued that it was unsurprising that Muslims and Hindus were now killing each other, considering individuals on both sides were engaging in inflammatory speech and writing. He called on Hindus to refrain from seeking violent revenge, and from perpetuating polarizing tendencies that were ripping apart Indian national unity. He also proclaimed that any Muslim who thinks that the assassin did well would be disgracing his religion.[24] In another statement, Gandhi noted: 'We see from the newspapers that the assassination of Swamiji has evoked grief and horror throughout the land.' Expressing his 'horror' at the circumstances in which Swami Shraddhanand was killed, Gandhi argued that the Quran nowhere sanctions such murders. The murder, he argued, was made possible because the two communities had begun to look at each other with feelings of hatred and enmity. Many Muslims saw 'Swamiji' and 'Lalaji and Malaviyaji' as sworn enemies of Islam, and many Hindus saw 'Sir Abdur Rahim and others' as enemies of Hinduism. But, Gandhi emphasized, even if one deeply disagreed with such leaders and their politics, 'no one may excite feelings of hatred against them'. He appealed for a removal of the atmosphere of 'mutual hatred and calumny' by boycotting newspapers that spread misinformation and hatred.[25] In another statement, he said that 'an evil deed done by a Mussulman hurts me as much as that done by a Hindu', and that he 'deeply regretted the event'. He asked Hindus not to 'disgrace Hinduism', to show self-restraint worthy of the Upanishads and of Yudhistir, 'the embodiment of forgiveness'. 'Let us not ascribe the crime of an individual to the whole community. Let us not harbour the spirit of retaliation'. Then, he turned to Muslims:

> Mussalmans have an ordeal to pass through. There can be no doubt that they are too free with the knife and the pistol. The sword is no emblem of Islam. But Islam was born in an environment where the sword was and still remains the supreme law. The message of Jesus has proved ineffective because the environment was unready to receive it. So with the message of the Prophet. The sword is yet too much in evidence among Mussalmans. It must be sheathed if Islam is to be what it means—peace. There is danger of Mussalmans secretly endorsing the mad deed. It will be a calamity for them and the world. For ours is after all a world problem. Reliance upon the sword is wholly inconsistent with reliance upon God. There should be, on their part, unequivocal mass condemnation of the atrocity.[26]

Gandhi ended by stating that only Abdul Rashid was not to blame. His actions were the result of the incendiary press, as well as the educated and semi-educated leaders, who were collectively spreading slanderous and false or exaggerated propaganda.[27]

At the Muslim League's Delhi session, Muhammad Hussain, chairman of the reception committee, had expressed his 'grief at the sudden loss of Swami Shraddhanand, a very old friend of mine. The dastardly manner in which he was assassinated by a maniac must excite feelings of abhorrence.'[28] The League's president in 1926, Sheikh Abdul Qadir, ended his speech by stating that:

> The mean outrage, of which the late Swami Shraddhanand was the victim, deserves to be denounced in the most unmistakable terms by every right-thinking Indian, whether he is a Hindu or Mussulman, and I do so emphatically on behalf of you all as well as my own behalf. We have assembled here under the shadow of this serious tragedy which must act as a damper on the spirits of even the optimists among us. The first impression made on one's mind by an occurrence like this is that of despondence, but while deeply regretting the dastardly murder of the Swami, I venture to all my countrymen and particularly the members of the Hindu community to control their feelings and to keep the general question of relations between the communities separate from this cowardly deed of a misguided individual. There were many Mussulmans who had differences with Swami Shraddhanand over his religious propaganda, but I am sure they will be as sorry as others to find that a co-religionist of theirs should take into his head to put an end to his life. The man could not render a greater disservice to Islam or lend a stronger impetus to the Shuddhi propaganda than he has done by this foul deed.[29]

The *Aligarh Mail* reported that it was glad that Qadir, as League president, had 'unequivocally condemned the murder of Swamiji by a Muslim fanatic', and had given a 'correct lead to the Muslim community'.[30] Later, while allowing that the assassination was bound to cause some turmoil among Hindus, the paper warned that the Sangathanist press were conducting themselves in a manner bound to lead to disturbances. It reminded its intended readership that 'on the murder of Swami Shradhhanandji a wave of universal resentment against the assassin swept over the entire length and breadth of India. Mussulmans, one and all, denounced the deed as cowardly and despicable and sympathised with the Hindus for the great loss which they had suffered.' But it regretted that the event was being used to now fan 'communal fanaticism' among Hindus and to vilify all Muslims and Islam as a whole.[31]

Interestingly, Gandhi's statements and the above-mentioned Muslim voices complicate certain impressions, promoted by Savarkar, writing from house arrest in Ratnagiri in 1927, and most recently by Savarkar's biographer, Vikram Sampath. These are that Gandhi 'rationalized' the crime and remained 'ambivalent', harsher on Hindus and softer on Muslims, not asking Muslims to condemn the violent act, and also that Muslim voices did not strongly condemn the assassination.[32] In fact, Lajpat Rai was careful to note the condemnation by Muslims: 'The Muslim community have condemned the crime. They have felt the blow that the assassin has struck at their religion and the good name of their community. I have no reason to doubt their sincerity.'[33] He also attempted to stem the tide of further polarization: 'Hindus and Mohammedans are so intermingled and interwoven with one another that it is impossible to segregate any one section from another. The idea is grotesque and absurd . . . I strongly deprecate anything that is likely to have an appearance of a mutual boycott . . .'[34]

But, as Gandhi predicted, Swami Shraddhanand's assassination would further vitiate the atmosphere and exacerbate polarization. While Hindus like Savarkar criticized Gandhi for not being strong enough on 'Muslims', Gandhi's statement that Muslims were 'too free with the knife and pistol' alienated even Mazharul Haq,[35] the strong advocate of Hindu–Muslim unity whose presidential speech to the Muslim League Rai had lauded in 1915, and who was considered pro-Hindu by several Muslims.[36] Haq presumably felt Gandhi's statement unfairly promoted the stereotypical view that Muslims were more prone to violence than Hindus at a time when many Muslims were already vulnerable to belligerent sections of the Hindu community. Lajpat Rai had appealed for calm and mutual understanding. He showed nuance in noting that a violent act by one individual did not represent an entire community, and in taking Muslim condemnations seriously. But Shraddhanand's assassination ultimately still entered his mind, as it did the minds of several other Hindus, as symptomatic of wider attacks on the Hindu community by 'Muslims'. It became a reason why Hindus must continue to organize in Hindu sangathan in 'self-defence'.[37]

In some cases, communal organization or sangathan purportedly in 'self-defence' slid into or was already a cover for belligerence against Muslims. Muslim voices which strongly condemned the assassin and believed that 'some allowance should be made for the excitement of the Hindus caused by the assassination' complained that some 'demagogues' among Hindus and the Sangathanist press were using the horrible incident to fan the communal fanaticism of Hindus and carry out a campaign to vilify all Muslims.[38] These sangathan activities were then responded to by some Muslims with calls for organization in 'self-defence', which then either slipped into belligerence or what was already a cover for it.[39] Lajpat Rai's own fears about Muslim violence might have been aggravated by newspaper reports of threats to his own life in response to his often militant calls for Hindu sangathan. Some newspapers reported that Shraddhanand's assassin had confessed to plotting to kill Madan Mohan Malaviya and Lajpat Rai.[40] Rai publicly stated that he 'decline[d] to believe that my life is in danger or anybody has been planning my murder', chided the press for publishing this 'alleged confession' which was 'likely to cause undesirable alarm', and declined police protection.[41] But, according to his biographer Feroz Chand, in close contact with him in these days, Lalaji 'acquired a new habit in these circumstances—of going about with a revolver in his pocket'.[42] This personal sense of threat to his life may have further fuelled his calls to Hindus to organize under the banner of Hindu sangathan.

Lajpat Rai's sense that the Hindu community was under assault was further exacerbated by newspaper reports about kidnappings of Hindu women. As historian Charu Gupta has argued, certain Hindu circles had, since the late nineteenth century, resorted to falsifying historical narratives and promoting myths about the medieval Muslim rapist, with the legend of Padmini and Allauddin Khilji being a prominent example.[43] While this image of the 'sexually charged, lustful Muslim male' served to construct a 'bad' medieval past, in the

1920s, it 'became a discourse about contemporary realities'.[44] From being a thing of the past, abductions were portrayed as happening here and now, provoking immediate fears and anxieties. The year 1923 saw a sudden proliferation of supposed cases of abductions of Hindu women in the local papers of UP.[45] Gupta argues that 'inflammatory and demagogic appeals were based on atrocity stories about women, ranging from allegations of rape, to abduction, forced marriage and luring women by males of the 'other' community'.[46] A series of pamphlets and tracts began appearing which spoke of a grand Muslim conspiracy to take away Hindu women, make them Muslim, and increase Muslim numbers.[47] During 1924–25, rumours about Muslims kidnapping women and children for conversion were pervasive in Kanpur, Benares and Allahabad, following propaganda by the Hindu Sabha.[48]

Gupta notes that these rumours denied the agency of Hindu women, who were very much capable of exercising control over their own bodies and minds.[49] It was not conceived that many women had fallen in love and eloped voluntarily.[50] In one case, a Hindu woman eloped with a Muslim man. A charge of abduction was brought by the father, with the case fought and won by an Arya Samajist lawyer.[51] The parents secured custody of the young woman who was married off to a 'suitable' Hindu man. But the woman had never been allowed to appear in court. The biases of local newspapers were sometimes evident in instances like the following. A prominent news item would categorically state that a Hindu woman was kidnapped by a Muslim. Ten days later, a small item would appear stating that the words 'alleged to have been' had been omitted in the report by mistake.[52] Sweeping and irresponsible generalizations were made and statements published in the local press without any substantiation or evidence.[53]

Gupta argues that stories branding Muslim men as predatory and Hindu women as victims also consciously or subconsciously served two purposes. They glossed over uncomfortable differences of class and caste within the Hindu community. And they helped establish and strengthen control over Hindu women, their movement and their sexuality.[54] Equally, the stereotype of the lustful, rowdy, forceful Muslim male, preying on vulnerable Hindu women, served to justify masculine, muscular Hindu consolidation through sangathan.[55] Hindus had to organize, the logic went, to protect their women. The abducted Hindu woman became the symbol of the victimization of the Hindu community, and the justification for why heightened militant Hindu sangathan was urgently needed. The Hindu woman's honour had to be defended, and sangathan needed to prove the virility and masculinity of the Hindu community.[56]

As P.K. Datta has shown, since 1923, Bengali newspapers had also been circulating stories about alleged abductions by Muslim goondas in East Bengal.[57] Newspapers, often organized along communal lines, sometimes not only directly incited violence but also used subtler methods of biased reporting, exaggeration and sensational editorializing against 'the other'.[58] While abduction cases were registered mostly in Rangpur district, newspapers suggested a province-wide occurrence.[59] Stories about abductions derived their power partly from lawyers from Rangpur, who were 'particularly communalized', and worked for Hindu zamindars resentful of the assertion of Muslim peasants.[60] Rural litigants picked up news and ideas from the court and spread them in their villages and newspapers made them an everyday concern.[61] Sometimes, a story with the headline 'Woeful Story of a Girl', on closer inspection, turned out to be one about the acquittal of a Muslim for abduction.[62] Sometimes, propagandists spoke about eleven reported cases of 'abductions' by Muslims, whereas the official investigation revealed one case, which in fact involved Hindu men and women, and still propagandists stuck to a discourse about a Muslim abductor.[63]

To be clear, there were indeed instances of abductions of (mostly low-caste) Hindu women by (low-caste) Muslim men.[64] But, often, alleged abductions of women involved men of all communities, or the complicity of the woman's own family members, or a Hindu police officer, or cases which suggested that women left of their own accord due to mistreatment in their marital homes. These were still reported as cases of Muslim abductions of Hindu women.[65]

In the case of Sovana who eloped with Moinuddin, there was no outrage on the woman to justify the headline 'Sovana Abduction Case'.[66] In instances where Hindu women were assaulted by Muslim men, the facts of help provided to these women by Muslims and condemnations by Muslims were drowned out by dogged 'Muslim vs. Hindu' propaganda determined to keep all focus only on the atrocity.[67] Additionally, more Muslim women were 'abducted' than Hindu women, and Hindu and Muslim males preferred to abduct women from their own communities, 'although such divisions did not prove an insuperable bar'.[68] Muslim men did 'outrage' Hindu women, but Hindu men also 'outraged' Muslim women; more Hindu men 'outraged' Hindu women than Muslim women, and more Muslim men 'outraged' Muslim women than Hindu women.[69] Interestingly, over time, with the decline in communal polarization, 'abductions' would be reported in a non-communal manner, and the same organizations which had spawned a communalized discourse on 'abductions', would speak of family complicity or women exercising their choice to leave their homes because of domestic oppression, dowry demands or abandonment.[70]

All this notwithstanding, in the early- and mid-1920s Bengal, a communalized discourse about 'abductions' was engaged in and fuelled by multiple actors with different motivations. Elites from a 'low-caste' community known as the Rajbansis, wished to gain higher caste status and acceptance in the eyes of upper castes, and to reform their unusually flexible marital customs that were looked upon with revulsion by upper castes. They used the discourse of 'abductions' by lustful Muslim males to control the movement, freedoms and relationships of their poorer woman folk.[71] An alliance with the Hindu Mahasabha helped turn a local issue into a national one.[72] This discourse also helped upper-caste zamindars, at a time when their power was being challenged by the lower classes and legislations supporting them. Violent economic revolts against zamindars were sometimes represented by them as threats to Hindu women, and provided zamindars with the opportunity to project themselves as vital defenders of Hindu women against the threatening Muslim male, and thus reassert their social position.[73] The 'abductions' charge was also utilized by the political alliance of zamindars and middle-class professionals to attack the increasing Muslim political clout in Bengal's institutions of local self-government as well as C.R. Das's Bengal Pact, which had agreed to weighted Muslim political representation in Bengal.[74]

Stirring up 'sexual anxiety' regarding 'the other' has been a common mark of particular political groups throughout modern history and across the world. At the same time as the 'abductions' discourse emerged in north India in the mid-1920s, various groups in Germany were stirring up mass hysteria about the supposed mass rapes of German women by African soldiers serving in World War I alongside French troops.[75] The Nazis portrayed Jews as being behind a conspiracy to use black soldiers to rape Aryan women and 'destroy' the 'white race'.[76] Meanwhile, in the United States, the Ku Klux Klan was portraying Jews as conspiring to ensure the mass rape of white women by black men to undermine the white race in America.[77] The image of the sexual threat of black men to white women was used to mobilize whites against blacks, often leading to the mass lynching of black men, and provided justification for it.[78] In South Africa, Afrikaner nationalists imagined the sexual threat to white Afrikaner women as coming from Indian males, who were accused of seducing white women and forcing them into marriage.[79] Researchers have noted how such expressions of sexual anxiety often have other real and unaddressed anxieties behind them, sometimes to do with loss of status, sometimes with economic uncertainty and sometimes with a challenge to traditional gender roles.[80]

Whatever the multiple complexities and motivations behind the newly emergent newspaper reports about 'abductions' in the early 1920s, these quickly became a 'commonsensical' reference point for Hindu political players urging communal organization.[81] In his 1923 presidential speech to the Hindu Mahasabha in Benaras, Madan Mohan Malaviya had referred to these alleged abductions while emphasizing the urgent imperative for Hindu organization.[82] While these had not been a concern for Lajpat Rai before this year, in 1927, reports about abductions in Bengal were finally also adduced by him to justify his continued calls for Hindu sangathan. [83]

In these polarized times, a siege mentality was also found among certain sections of India's Muslims, who frequently experienced themselves as constituting the threatened and vulnerable minority. As we saw in the previous chapter, Muslim leaders referred to instances of some Hindus speaking about driving Muslims out of India, and about wanting to convert and enslave them.[84] Calls by some Hindu leaders for everyone to Hinduize sparked fears of Hindu domination.[85] One tabligh activist wrote that a book outlining various strategies for converting the many 'neo-Muslim' groups in the Indian subcontinent to Hinduism had been secretly circulating among leading Hindus.[86] The organized and successful shuddhi campaign to convert thousands of Muslim Malkana Rajputs sparked fears of an upper-caste Hindu plot to permanently enslave Muslims by turning them to Shudras at the bottom of the Hindu social hierarchy.[87] Tablighi literature saw in the shuddhi movement a conspiracy to bring all Muslims into the fold of Hinduism, and as launching heinous assaults on Islam and its Prophet.[88]

Conferences of Muslim leaders saw mentions of how violence similar to what occurred at Kohat had occurred at Arrah and Katarpur, with large numbers of Muslim victims; of Hindu organizations jeopardizing the existence of Islam and pushing Muslims into the 'ditch of communalism', and of prominent Hindu leaders openly inciting Hindus against Muslims even as they spoke of national unity. Shuddhi, funded by native princely states like Kashmir and Baroda, was aimed at 'dragging back Moslems who were progressing forward for the attainment of Swaraj'.[89] Hindus could 'not tolerate to see the Muslims free'. Sangathan and shuddhi were meant to divert Muslims from swaraj and enchain them for years to come.[90] Complaints were made about how while 'Muslims were advocates of Indian Swaraj, and not of the Afghan rule in India', the latter allegation was repeatedly made by Hindus.[91] Mentions were made of anti-Muslim literature and victimization of Muslims by the government and Hindus.[92] All this justified the efforts to organize and consolidate the Muslim community through tanzim.

It must be remembered that world views that were extremist and communally polarized, however loud, were representative of only sections of both communities. Even if currently overshadowed, strong voices, urging dialogue, reconciliation and the recognition of commonality and shared humanity, remained in both. Many Hindus and Muslims remained engaged in affairs relating to their own village, locality, class, occupation, caste, sect and region. Tribal and peasant activists in different parts of India were protesting against forest laws and exploitation by moneylenders, and for rent reduction and the abolition of zamindari.[93] Thousands of workers, across community lines, were organizing strikes against their employers.[94] Emergent communist groups, with Hindu and Muslim members, many of them erstwhile Yugantar, Khilafatist and Ghadar revolutionaries, were trying to organize a politics centred on peasants and workers.[95] A new network of revolutionaries, under the banner of the Hindustan Republican Association, included Hindus and Muslim members, and attempted to raise money for an armed rebellion against the British through dacoities which seized government funds.[96] The eighteen-year-old Bhagat Singh (1907–31), studying at the Lajpat Rai-founded National College at Lahore, had recently founded the Naujawan Bharat Sabha, which actively sought to unite and galvanize the Hindus, Muslims and Sikhs of Punjab, even organizing inter-communal dinners to this end.[97] In various parts of India, including the Bombay and Madras Presidencies, the UP, and Lajpat Rai's Punjab, 'Untouchable' and 'low-caste' Hindus and Muslims were organizing against upper-caste Hindus and upper-caste ashraf Muslims, the latter being the main targets of their political narratives.[98] Shuddhi and sangathan, and tabligh and tanzim were one part of a multi-layered, complex web of different types of politics witnessed by 1920s India. Nevertheless, sidestepping the various other parts of this complex web, Lajpat Rai viewed Indian politics through a particular, 'Hindu–Muslim' lens. Viewing the world through this prism, he perceived a threat of Muslim violence and called for Hindu sangathan to counter it.

Of Ahimsa and Gymnasiums

For Lajpat Rai, one major aspect of organizing Hindus in the purportedly non- or sub-political realm was to equip them with the means to defend themselves against 'attacks' by 'Muslims', allegedly occurring in the form of violence and coercion. This required Hindus to raise their voices against 'false' ideas of ahimsa which Rai believed encouraged others to 'humiliate' and 'crush' them.[99] This of course patently alluded to Gandhi. Lajpat Rai agreed that ahimsa was an integral part of Hinduism. But for him, this 'most tolerant of all religions' did not impose 'its principles or *dharma* on everyone' but instead let 'everyone's *dharma* grow out of them'.[100] In a curious manoeuvre, Lajpat Rai seemed to argue that Hinduism's 'tolerance' allowed even for the conditional use of violence. Unlike Gandhi who believed that ahimsa could be practised by all Hindus, he argued that while ahimsa was the highest religion for a *sanyasi*, Hinduism opposed the imposition of the dharma of sanyasis on *grhasthas* (householders).[101] A grhastha's dharma was to defend his life and that of his loved ones, his country and people; and violence, if necessary to 'protect' these, was permitted.[102] The attempt by ordinary grhasthas to practise the high religion of sanyasis—ahimsa 'at all costs and under all circumstances'—led them to use it as an excuse to shun 'manly' deeds, resulting in cowardice.

In Brahminical theology around the ashrama system, no equation is made between the sanyasi mode of life and non-violence, and the grhastha mode of life and violence. The married householder's supreme duty is to perform daily ritual sacrifices (to gods, forefathers, human and non-human beings) and procreate.[103] Beyond raising a family, a householder's duties are to engage in productive caste-based economic activity and be a responsible member of society.[104] Lajpat Rai's innovation was to link the grhastha mode of life with the defence of community and country through violence, if required. Returning to the trope of Hindu decline after many years, he linked the political 'downfall' of Hindus to the wrong application of the doctrine of ahimsa which, he argued, led to a loss of 'virility' and military discipline.[105] He lamented that now ahimsa was again making Hindus unworldly, falsely content, unambitious, fatalistic, slavish, cowardly and unmanly.[106] This was a complete inversion of the Gandhian view of ahimsa as the 'virtue of the manly' (since it involved mature self-restraint).[107] Thus, Lajpat Rai's calls for the 'organization' of the Hindu community in the non-political realm involved appeals to Hindus to protest against the propagation of ahimsa as a principle requiring unconditional adherence. As we saw in Chapter 14, Gandhian ahimsa permitted conditional violence in self-defence for *individuals* facing violence if they lacked the courage to non-violently sacrifice themselves.[108] Nevertheless, it of course promoted non-violent action above all else as the brave answer to immoral violence, and discouraged communal organization as not just cowardly but also encouraging inter-community violence. Gandhian ahimsa made Lajpat Rai uneasy because he saw it as blunting the collective Hindu capacity for violence in 'self-defence'. The retention of this ability, he believed, was crucial for Hindus to change their mentality and act in an assertive, supposedly more masculine manner.

Lajpat Rai's exhortations to Hindus to disavow non-violence might not have involved explicit calls for violence and remained limited to demands for the active disavowal of the principle of unconditional ahimsa. A charitable reading would be that merely the retention of the Hindu *capacity* for violence was seen by Lajpat Rai as endowing Hindus with capacity to act more assertively vis-à-vis Muslims. A less charitable one would be that calling on Hindus to disavow ahimsa entailed a tacit call for violence when required. Either way, such calls were made in the context of the Hindu Mahasabha's promotion of Mahabir Dals (Groups of the Brave), consisting of 'volunteers' physically trained to 'defend' Hindus when needed.[109] In some parts of India, the Mahasabha had also been encouraging martial akharas, centres of physical culture and wrestling, club- and sword-wielding and lathi-fighting.[110] Whether or not this was known to Lajpat Rai, these institutions, proliferating in various neighbourhoods, sometimes 'formed the basis of marauding gangs during communal clashes'.[111]

In May 1925, Lajpat Rai toured eastern India for purposes of sangathan,[112] during which he penned a series of articles in which he returned to the theme of the ascetic–renunciatory tradition within Hinduism, which he had first addressed almost two decades ago in his 1907 commentary on the Gita.[113] He argued that the Hindu ideals of renunciation and *vairagya* (detachment) had endowed Hindus with a 'mentality' characterized by general 'pusillanimity'. Historically, they had undermined the Hindu will to resist 'Muslim invaders', by either promoting a fatalism about eventual Muslim supremacy or an other-worldliness which trivialized the significance of worldly rule. In 1907, Lajpat Rai had utilized the Gita to argue that Hinduism taught action over renunciation. Now, he emphasized that Hinduism's ideal of renunciation produced paralytic doubt, adversely affecting the Hindu capacity to act. Hindu mentality, dominated by doubt and fear, needed to be revolutionized by de-emphasizing renunciation and introducing 'virility' in thought. This in turn would inform Hindu action, making the 'Hindu community' capable of 'fighting its own battles manfully' and defending itself against the aggression of others.[114] During his sangathan tours in mid-1927, Lajpat Rai again goaded Hindus to substitute their 'mild', 'submissive' mentality, characterized by 'tolerance to a sinful extent', with a more 'militant' attitude: militancy in defence of one's rights, he declared, was no crime.[115] The difference between Lajpat Rai's exhortations to Hindus to abandon 'renunciation' for militant and possibly violent action in 1907 and 1927 was that its imagined target was now Muslims rather than the British. As always, he, like many Mahasabhaites, including Malaviya,[116] conceived his own sanction of sangthanist violence not as 'aggression' but as 'self-defence' against violence perceived as always originating with 'Muslims'. And once again, unsurprisingly, those Muslims who stressed the need for Muslim consolidation also conceived it as necessary 'self-defence' of their 'community' against the attacks of belligerent Hindu leaders, and the 'mischievous' and 'menacing' activities of shuddhi, sangathan and the Hindu Mahasabha, as led by Lajpat Rai and others.[117]

Along with wilfully forgetting the religious ideals of ahimsa and renunciation, Hindus also had to bolster their capacity for confrontational action vis-à-vis Muslims through secular/non-religious means. Reflecting the increased prominence of akharas as a feature of politics in the 1920s,[118] Lajpat Rai, like other Mahasabhaites, exhorted Hindus to establish gymnasiums to build a strong and healthy physique. Yet, unlike Malaviya and, when he was alive, Shraddhanand, who sought to build the physical strength of Hindus through the self-denying practice of *brahmacharya* (disciplined celibacy),[119] Lajpat Rai enjoined Hindus to build 'pleasure resorts' to 'enjoy innocent pleasures' to instil in them ambition and determination.[120] Thus, both strengthening Hindu bodies and hedonism, a principle far from the strict disciplinary regimens of traditional akharas,[121] were conceptualized as tools for refashioning Hindu 'mentality' and buttressing capacity for 'manly' action against the perceived Muslim threat. But, as we have seen, the lines between revolutionizing Hindu mentality to make it capable of meeting a potential threat from Muslims, on the one hand, and violent belligerence on the other, were difficult to maintain. Several akharas were developing as centres not just of bodybuilding and wrestling but also sword- and club-wielding and lathi-fighting.[122] They were engaging in displays of arms and swordsmanship, emerging as basic units of mobilization for collective militant action by volunteer corps such as the various Mahabir Dals, Bhimsen Dal and Abhimanyu Dal. Akharas were involved in neighbourhood conflicts over jobs or land, and gang violence during communal clashes.[123]

In the 1890s, Lajpat Rai had seen 'Hindu decline' as caused by Brahmin priestcraft and Buddhist encouragement of ritualism and idolatry.[124] This, incidentally, contrasted with the fact that Buddhism was born precisely as a counter to the Vedic ritual tradition. Now, almost three decades later, linking Hindu decline with ahimsa, he overlapped with Savarkar, the founder of Hindutva eighteen years younger than him. Having internalized British colonial discourses about Hindu effeminacy, Savarkar insisted that the decline of a once great and virile Hindu masculinity and martial spirit was caused by Ashoka's embrace of Buddhist ahimsa.[125] Lajpat Rai was similar in viewing ahimsa as having effeminized Hindus (i.e., made them more effeminate), making them historically vulnerable to Muslim invasions.[126] Both men believed that resisting Gandhian pressure for a politics of non-violence was crucial to resurrecting a confident, masculine Hindu politics. The difference was that Savarkar dreamt of turning Hindus into a permanent masculine, militarized national brotherhood, and saw warfare, militarism, aggression, assassination and violence as central and absolutely essential features and modes of politics.[127] Indeed, some scholars who have studied Savarkar's ideology closely argue that, for him, engaging in violence was necessary to forge, express and sustain a Hindu nationalist brotherhood, which could in turn establish its primary claim of belonging to India.[128] On the other hand, even as he believed that a militant Hindu politics was urgently required in the current moment of violence-ridden uncertainty, Lajpat Rai did not valorize and eulogize violence, warfare and militarism as Savarkar did. For him, violence was not an exhilarating, essential or even primary mode of politics by which Hindus had to be transformed into and be sustained as a national fraternity, or by which they had to establish their superior claim over the territory of India. Instead, it was a last resort, distasteful mode of politics to be used only in 'self-defence' and only temporarily, in the short term, so as to ensure the survival of both the Hindu community and a harmonious 'Indian' national fraternity in the long term. As we will be reminded again in the next chapter, Lajpat Rai continued to believe in a secular democratic Indian nation–state that respected India's diversity, and could consider a measure of communal representation for Muslims.

We already saw in Chapters 14 and 16 that Gandhi disapproved of Hindu sangathan as preached by Lajpat Rai and other Mahasabha leaders.[129] He believed sangathan's obsessive focus on 'muscular development' through akharas involved the organization of hooligans to violently fight Muslims, and was wrong for three reasons. First, it further polarized the Hindu and Muslim communities which formed the Indian nation, and which had no choice but to learn to coexist and live together. Second, militant organization encouraged a dangerous, potentially uncontrollable militarization of Indian society. And third, it ruined Hinduism and made the Hindu community a slave to goondas. In addition, Gandhi considered the training of goondas in akharas to fight Muslims as a sign of cowardice and emasculation. The reliance on the physical strength of goondas reflected a lack of conviction in oneself, in one's morals and one's religion, and a lack of courage to suffer and die for the sake of Hinduism. Instead of training hooligans, he challenged the educated Brahmin and Bania leaders of the Hindu 'community' to end their cowardice and show themselves to be brave enough to die to defend Hinduism.[130] Gandhi wanted Hindus to overcome cowardice by developing the inner strength to suffer (tapasya) and die for the sake of their morals.[131]

Such calls to the Hindu community to train in self-sacrifice held little appeal for Lajpat Rai, whose efforts were aimed at overcoming these very self-effacing attitudes, which he believed were the bane of the Hindu community. For Gandhi, a belligerent other had to be met with non-violent but clear-headed, assertive and fearless *actions* of resistance. Such brave non-violent actions in response to provocation had the potential to reduce polarization, de-escalate conflict and produce reconciliation between groups comprising the Indian nation. These not only increased the moral standing and strength of the community, but were also a mark of true manliness. But for Lajpat Rai, Gandhian non-violence represented sanyasa, other-worldliness, doubt, fear, timidity, complacency, passivity, inactivity and femininity. He wished to activate what he saw as a masculine, militant Hindu politics through sangathan. Interestingly, Gandhi and Rai shared the belief that regulating and disciplining the body was crucial for collective regeneration. Physical culture was central to Gandhi's political vision. But it was seen as essential for creating a disciplined, controllable, and physically and mentally trained body of non-violent *satyagrahi*[132] agitators for anti-colonial Indian nationalism.[133] The 1928 Bardoli Satyagraha would soon emerge as a watershed event where, among others, Sardar Patel actualized this bio-political[134] vision of his guru, Gandhi, for the first time. On the other hand, Lajpat Rai's sangathanist vision of building strong bodies aimed to create Hindu agents capable of mobilizing to militantly 'defend' Hindus from 'Muslims', using violence, if necessary.

Hindu Unity: The Problem of Sect and Caste

In Lajpat Rai's view, apart from violence, another threat faced by Hindus in the sub-political realm was the attempt by Christian and particularly Muslim 'proselytism' to 'submerge' the 'power' of Hindus.[135] By the mid-1920s, he finally joined those Hindu spokespersons who had expressed such fears after the forced conversions during the Mappila rebellion. As we saw in Chapter 14, these had propelled the Arya Samaj to revive shuddhi to 'reclaim' the converted.[136] In early 1923, Swami Shraddhanand had launched the shuddhi campaign among Muslim Malkana Rajputs.[137] The successful shuddhi campaign among the Malkanas shocked some Muslim individuals and organizations into launching tabligh.[138] Reflecting the mutually reinforcing nature of these campaigns, tabligh, itself conceived as a defensive movement against the threat of shuddhi, had begun to function, for some Hindus, as a threat against which their 'community' had to defend itself.

Tabligh included drives to convert Hindus, particularly low castes, to Islam. But, in fact, its success remained confined to preventing more 'neo-Muslims' from being converted by the Arya Samaj, and preaching to them a scriptural Islam (to replace the centuries-old syncretic beliefs and practices of such groups).[139] Much of tabligh consisted of spreading awareness of basic Islamic beliefs and practices not just among 'neo-Muslims' but also among 'jahil' Muslims. Proper knowledge of and loyalty to the faith among ordinary (often low-caste) Muslims came to be seen as a vital test of whether Islam would survive in an India where Muslims no longer held political power.[140] Despite hyperbolic propagation rhetoric, which called on Hindus to turn to Islam and predicted that India will turn Muslim,[141] the tablighi drive to convert Hindus to Islam has been deemed by Yoginder Sikand, a historian who pioneered research on tablighi propagation, as 'for the most part, a failure'.[142]

Be that as it may, fears of tabligh had, by the early 1920s, led the avowedly 'orthodox' Sanatanist Hindus to support the Arya Samajist shuddhi campaign.[143] Long having represented mostly sections of Sanatanist Hindus from UP and Punjab, in these years the Hindu Mahasabha had finally begun to function as a political organization representing *both* Sanatanist and Arya Samajist Hindus, who began to cooperate with each other much more than before. The endorsement of Arya Samajist shuddhi in 1922 by the Mahasabha and its Sanatanist founder and then president, Malaviya, reflected this new collaboration. It appeared as if 'orthodox' Sanatanist and reformist Arya Samajist Hindus had united in the common cause of Hindu sangathan, agreeing on shuddhi as the path to it.

But this had merely elided deeper tensions soon revealed at the Hindu Mahasabha's August 1923 Benaras session. When Swami Shraddhanand had tabled his shuddhi programme, the Mahasabha accepted only the part that endorsed shuddhi for the 'reclamation' of the Malkana Rajputs. The Malkanas, who had no social contact with caste Rajputs but followed many Hindu practices and had purportedly not intermarried with other communities, were to be reclaimed back into their *original caste*. Decisions regarding two other shuddhi resolutions—one concerning the principle of accepting into Vedic practice converts from other religions, and the other the access of the so-called 'Untouchables' to wells, temples and schools—had been deferred. At its Allahabad special session in February 1924, although concessions were made for Untouchables in that their access to wells, temples, schools was generally encouraged, the Mahasabha rejected shuddhi amongst them, stating that to give 'Untouchables' the sacred thread, to teach them the Vedas and interdine with them was 'against scriptures and tradition'.[144] The other resolution came with conditions attached—any non-Hindu was welcome within the Hindu fold, but not into *any* (read: twice-born/upper) caste. So, shuddhi conversions could be conducted but without changing the existing hierarchical caste structure.[145] Put differently, Muslims and Christians could be converted into Hinduism but not be invested with twice-born status by rising in the caste hierarchy through 'merit'.[146] Swami Shraddhanand's efforts to have a 'vertical', equality-based approach to Hindu sangathan through the shuddhi of 'Untouchables' i.e., through a radical dismantling of the caste hierarchy, had regularly produced tensions with the Sanatanist Mahasabhaites. The latter preferred a 'horizontal', hierarchy-preserving approach to Hindu sangathan, which sought to sidestep issues of caste-based inequality and caste reform.[147]

Tabligh drives to convert Hindus may have remained confined largely to rhetoric, and on the ground tabligh may have concentrated on keeping neo-Muslims within the Islamic fold and making better Muslims of Muslims. But, like other Mahasabha leaders, Lajpat Rai responded to what he considered 'Christian' and 'Muslim' attempts to 'take away' members of the Hindu 'community' by emphasizing the need for Hindu sangathan. In his April 1925 presidential speech to the Hindu Mahasabha,[148] he argued that Hindus needed to overcome 'divisions' within their 'community' to facilitate 'unity of action' in what he thought were 'critical times'. Yet, he wished the Hindu Mahasabha to achieve Hindu unity by avoiding religious, sectarian and doctrinal controversies, suggesting his preference for a symbolic, 'horizonal' approach. Although he stated his personal preference for the removal of untouchability, in urging unity between the Arya Samajists and Sanatanists, he publicly took a conservative stance on caste, and did not urge the Mahasabha to go beyond 'the minimum' laid down at its 1924 Allahabad session.[149] This referred to the decision to allow 'Untouchables' access to temples, wells and schools, but to reject their shuddhi via the grant of the sacred thread, their access to teachings of the Vedas, and interdining with them. In what must have been deeply disappointing for Swami Shraddhanand, Lajpat Rai asked Arya Samajists in the Mahasabha to limit their caste reform with the admitted objective of conciliating Sanatanists. He did not push for the Hindu Mahasabha's recognition of shuddhi of 'low' castes and 'Untouchables'. To achieve Hindu sangathan, he supported shuddhi 're-conversions' of Muslims and Christians, but spoke of 'bringing lost sheep back into the fold of their *respective biradaries*'.[150] His shuddhi reconversions did not involve caste reform whereby these 'reconverted' low caste groups could be considered equal to high-caste Hindus. Lajpat Rai thereby succumbed to the increasingly popular 'horizontal' approach to Hindu sangathan propagated by many Mahasabhites.

As president of the Bombay Hindu Mahasabha conference in December 1925, Lajpat Rai castigated Sanatanists for raising the 'most mischievous' cry of 'religion in danger' and denouncing Hindu 'social reformers' at a time when Hindu unity was urgently need.[151] He now blamed Sanatanist opposition, rather than Arya Samajist attempts at caste reform, for exacerbating sectarian dissensions within the Hindu 'community'. Lajpat Rai's criticism of Sanatanist alarmism regarding reform shows his continued sympathy with the Arya Samaj's chosen, anti-hierarchical means of achieving Hindu sangathan. He declared that untouchability could no longer be allowed to disfigure the face of Hinduism, that a nation with a subjugated shudra majority was doomed to fail, and that in ancient times shudras were 'allowed, by proved fitness' to 'rise to higher castes'.[152] He appealed to the 'orthodox' Hindus to change with changing times.

Lajpat Rai then turned to what he called a 'war' between non-Brahmins and Brahmins in Southern and Western India.[153] This statement requires some contextualization. South India and Maharashtra were marked by stark Brahmin predominance and great caste rigidity.[154] Equally, it was also these regions which had seen the steady growth of non-Brahmin and Untouchable movements and organizations since the late nineteenth and early twentieth centuries. These had become a lot more socially and politically prominent by the 1920s. In Madras Presidency, Brahmins, only 3 per cent of the population, held a disproportionate majority of administrative posts open to Indians as of 1912. The Brahmin-led Home Rule agitation of Annie Besant had sparked fears of British rule being replaced by Brahmin rule oppressive to non-Brahmins.[155] In response, the Justice movement was launched in 1915–16 on behalf of these 'intermediate castes', including the Tamil Vellalas, Mudaliars and Chettiars, the Telugu Reddis, Kammas and Balija Naidus, and the Malayali Nairs. The newly formed Justice Party then began its agitation for communal representation for non-Brahmins in legislatures and government services as safeguards against Brahmin domination. The 1919 Montagu–Chelmsford Reforms had granted reserved seats for non-Brahmins, despite virulent opposition from Brahmin Congressmen.[156] By the mid-1920s, Periyar had started the much more radical 'Self-Respect' movement which launched vehement attacks on Brahmin privilege and the caste hierarchy on behalf of shudra non-Brahmins.[157] In the princely state of Mysore, Brahmins, less than 4 per cent of the population, had held 65 per cent of gazetted posts in 1918. Here, the Praja Mithra Mandal had been established as an anti-Brahmin organization.[158] In Travancore state, Nambudiri Brahmins monopolized land and non-Malayali Brahmins enjoyed privileged access to state administration. Here, anti-Brahmin movements were led by non-Brahmin Nairs and the lower-caste Ezhavas. The latter also challenged Brahmin dominance through the religious leadership of Sri Narayan Guru[159] and pushed for forcible entry into temples.[160] In Maharashtra, the movement against Brahminical dominance and caste hierarchy was led by the Satyashodhak Samaj and the Non-Brahmin Party led by Bhaskarrao Jadhav.[161]

This was the context for Lajpat Rai's reference in his 1925 Bombay Mahasabha speech to the war between Brahmins and non-Brahmins in Southern and Western India. Rai argued that Hindu shastras made no distinction between Brahmins and non-Brahmins, and urged the Brahmins of these regions to readmit 'at least' those non-Brahmins to *dwija* (twice-born) rights (of wearing the sacred thread and performing *yajnas* or ritual sacrifices) who were dwija and not shudra by occupation.[162] He therefore did occasionally veer towards some limited form of caste reform—towards a 'vertical', anti-hierarchical approach to Hindu sangathan. Equality between Brahmins and non-Brahmins was argued for, and an appeal made to grant twice-born rights to those non-Brahmins, including even born shudras and 'Untouchables' engaged in upper-caste occupations. But the lower hierarchical position of the vast numbers of shudras and 'Untouchables' engaged in labour stigmatized as lowly and impure—which included agricultural and artisanal labour, hair-cutting (*nais*), clothes-washing (*dhobis*), gardening (*malis*), alongside 'coolie'-

work, leather-work, cremation-work, sweeping, and sanitation-work—was ultimately left largely intact. B.S. Moonje also records the attempts made by Lajpat Rai to persuade a prominent Mahar (an 'Untouchable' caste of village servants)[163] leader attending a Hindu Sabha conference in 1927 to withdraw his resolution calling for the abolition of caste, as 'it is against the present policy of the Hindu Mahasabha which holds in itself all shades of thought and opinion though the conference has fully sympathy with the resolution'.[164] The deliberate restrictions Lajpat Rai ultimately put on attempts at radical caste reform reveal his deference to the horizontal, hierarchy-conserving approach to Hindu sangathan.

Gone were the charged principled appeals Lajpat Rai had used in the 1910s to rebuke upper castes for their 'shockingly unjust', 'cruel', 'immoral', 'undemocratic' and 'inhuman' treatment of the Depressed Classes. Dropped now were exhortations to break caste taboos regarding food, residential living, social interaction and marriage. Although the backwardness and illegitimacy of the caste hierarchy was alluded to, Lajpat Rai, contrary to his own personal beliefs, aimed at Hindu sangathan at the expense of vertical caste reform. In the context of the unprecedented Hindu–Muslim tension in the mid-1920s, his fears that alienating Sanatanist Hindus would have detrimental consequences for the urgently needed Hindu sangathan led him to support a conservative programme of horizontal sangathan through the Hindu Mahasabha. In overlooking caste reform in his pursuit of Hindu sangathan, Lajpat Rai's public position was very different from Shraddhanand whose pamphlet 'Hindu Sangathan: Saviour of a Dying Race' (1926) had criticized the Mahasabha for forbidding shuddhi among 'Untouchables' and thus hindering real sangathan. Unlike Lajpat Rai, Shraddhanand had resigned from the Mahasabha in 1926 to pursue this very end.[165] In retreating from caste radicalism, Lajpat Rai also differed from Savarkar. Released from jail but still restricted by the British to Ratnagiri (Bombay Presidency), Savarkar in these years was leading the Ratnagiri Hindu Sabha, thorough which he sought to more radically challenge caste-based hierarchy as a path to achieve Hindu unity.[166]

Political Implications of Hindu Sangathan in the 'Social' Realm

Although Lajpat Rai often spoke of Hindu sangathan as lying outside the political realm, he must have been aware of its political implications. This is especially likely given his belief that Muslim conversions had a 'substantial political bearing' because the numerical strength of 'communities' currently determined the extent of their political representation.[167] It is also very probable, given his belief, noted in Chapter 17, that Muslims were using violence in the non-political realm to 'coerce' Hindus into making concessions on the question of communal representation.[168] Lajpat Rai explicitly expressed concerns about the political consequences of 'Muslim' actions in the non-political realm. He must have therefore been aware that Hindu activities in this purportedly social realm—such as a disavowal of the principle of unconditional violence—also had political implications. In fact, despite his occasional insistence on the non-political nature of sangathan, his appeals to Hindus to cease their internal dissensions in favour of sangathan were accompanied with an explicit objective of maintaining Hindu 'numerical preponderance' or 'majority', and unapologetic proclamations that numbers were important determinants of 'political strength' and 'political influence'.[169] The maintenance and display of the Hindu majority through sangathan was conceptualized by Lajpat Rai as an important means of ensuring that both the British and Muslims appreciated Hindu strength.[170] This, he felt, was needed in a context where efforts were afoot to renegotiate the extent of political representation for each community in India's future constitution. Lajpat Rai argued that there could be no 'friendship' between the weak and the strong, and by strengthening the Hindus, sangathan would ensure a permanent political pact with Muslims that was fair to the Hindu community.[171]

In viewing Hindus as weaker than Muslims, Lajpat Rai shared ground with Savarkar—and several other Hindu nationalists historically and today—who conceptualized 'Muslims' as stronger by virtue of their supposedly stronger religious fervour and internal solidarity, which Hindus were seen to lack.[172] Such a view overlooked multiple internal dissensions within 'Muslims', which many Muslims experienced and frequently lamented. It also elided the fact that in the context of the gradual devolution of democratic power wherein, as Rai himself noted, numbers determined political power, 'Hindus' formed an overwhelming numerical majority in India and therefore the potentially politically stronger community. In contrast, 'Muslims' constituted a significantly smaller numerical minority and therefore a potentially politically weaker community. This conceptualization of the Muslim minority as stronger and Hindu majority as weaker created a felt need to rectify this imagined imbalance in the comparative strengths of the two communities, and the space to imagine Hindu sangathan as necessary for establishing 'equality' between a 'weaker' Hindu majority and 'stronger' Muslim minority.

For Savarkar, Hindu sangathan was necessary for enacting Hindu violence. Fear-inducing, 'super-atrocious' Hindu violence would be righteous retribution for what he considered Muslim historical wrongs.[173] Violence, in the form of a civil war, was also imagined as a necessary condition for transforming Hindus into a Hindutva national brotherhood, and to establish its claim over the land of India.[174] Hindutva violence was also seen as crucial for proving Hindu strength, in turn imagined as a prerequisite for establishing future equality and any friendship with Muslims.[175]

For Lajpat Rai, militant communal consolidation of the Hindu community through a social sangathan was necessary to secure a political pact with Muslims over the question of political representation which was fair to Hindus, at a time when constitutional negotiations were underway. The Hindu majority's sangathan in the non-political realm was conceptualized by Rai as a prerequisite for and supplement to the organization of the Hindu community in the overtly political realm, whose aim was to resist, what he considered, the divisive and domineering 'communal' politics of the Muslim community. It aimed at fortifying an overt Hindu politics geared towards opposing, to the furthest extent possible, an excessively 'communal' politics insisted upon by Muslims and encouraged by the British.

The political aim of maintaining and displaying a Hindu majority for this same purpose also caused Lajpat Rai to conceive Hindu sangathan as a refutation of the new politics of the so-called Untouchable and low castes. In fact, 'Untouchable' activists had begun to organize in various regions of India much before the 1920s. In Maharashtra, a regional movement had arisen among Mahars in the late nineteenth century.[176] Mahar activists had founded the first organization of 'Untouchables' in the Bombay Presidency by the 1890s, with more organizations and conferences coming up in the early years of the twentieth century.[177] Following the non-Brahmin anti-caste activist Jotirao Phule, their sense of history was founded on the idea that through trickery, the Aryan invaders, the ancestors of Brahmin Hindus, had subjugated, marginalized and exploited the original Dravidian Kshatriya inhabitants of the Indian subcontinent, and reduced them to shudras and Untouchables. These were the ancestors of present-day shudras and Untouchables.[178] These nineteenth-century activists had petitioned against caste-based discrimination, exclusion and humiliation, and fought the denial of their access to the military, schools, temples, roads, public transport and public water tanks.[179] In Madras Presidency, two organizations of Untouchables, the Dravida Mahajana Sangam and Pariar Mahajanasabha, had been formed by the 1890s. They contested practices of untouchability and aimed to secure concessions in education and government services.[180] The first was formed by the 'Untouchable' activist Iyothee Thass (1845–1914) who, having announced that Untouchables were not Hindu, called on them to identify as casteless Dravidians.[181] By 1907, Thass had begun using the press to popularize his ideas—similar to Maharashtrian activists—about Aryan–Brahmin–Hindu invaders, who had conquered and subjugated the original, glorious and inclusive Tamil–Dravidian–Buddhist inhabitants of India through cunning and force, reduced them to lower castes, and even falsified religious texts to justify their tyrannical domination and exclusivism.[182] Thass attacked various forms of caste-based discrimination, exploitation and exclusion practised by Brahmins.[183] In UP, from the start of the twentieth century, well-off sections of the Chamar caste[184] had begun establishing organizations to claim 'superior' Kshatriya status and assert equality with high castes. Poorer Chamars had also begun to attack caste inequality by relying on the *nirguna bhakti* protest tradition, which worshipped poet–saints like Kabir and Ravi Das, opposed caste hierarchy and emphasized equality.[185]

These earlier efforts notwithstanding, it was only after 1918–19 that a more organized and assertive politics gained ground among larger numbers of 'Untouchables'—or Dalits, as many such groups prefer to be called today.[186] A more energized and strongly organized 'Adi Dravida' movement had taken root among Madras's Untouchables by 1918, led by M.C. Rajah, their chief spokesman, and the most famous 'Untouchable' in India at the time.[187] This movement popularized, now even more widely, the idea that it was the 'Untouchables' (from among all other 'low' castes) who were the descendants of the original ('adi') inhabitants of India, and had been conquered and subjugated by the Aryan invaders, the ancestors of upper-caste Hindus, in the Vedic times.[188] Adi Dravidas used the liberal language of the rule of law and rights to challenge caste-based discrimination and humiliation.[189] More importantly, in anticipation of the Montagu–Chelmsford reforms, they had advanced a claim about their distinctive social and political identity by demanding separate political representation through a separate electorate.[190] In the 1920s, Adi Dravidas stepped up their efforts to establish their separate political identity.[191] They had also inspired the organization of a similarly energetic and radical 'Adi-Andhra' movement among Dalits of the coastal Andhra region of the Madras Presidency, and the 'Adi-Karnataka' movement among Dalits in Karnataka.[192]

In UP, the Arya Samaj had been aiding the so-called 'Untouchable' Chamar castes in their efforts to acquire higher caste status and gain access to temples, public wells and education.[193] But by the mid-1920s, many Chamars had begun to suspect that Arya Samajist caste reform was an insincere, merely instrumental effort to boost Hindus numbers vis-à-vis Muslims. They dissociated themselves from the Arya Samaj.[194] The new 'Adi Hindu' movement, spearheaded by the Adi–Hindu Mahasabha, spread among large numbers of them.[195] Similar to the Adi Dravidas of Madras, its leaders, such as Swami Acchutanand[196] (1879–1933), now vociferously proclaimed that 'Untouchables' were the original, pre-Aryan *bhakti*-following inhabitants and rulers of India. These original natives had been deprived of their bhakti religion, and forcibly reduced to servile 'untouchable' labourers by Aryan invaders, who followed Vedic Hinduism and created religious texts and laws to justify their oppression.[197] They now sought to challenge caste-based hierarchy, discrimination and exclusion, and claim what they considered their original rights and political power.[198] In anticipation of the next round of political reforms in the late 1920s, Adi–Hindus too had begun agitating for separate electorates for Untouchables and reservations in government services and education.[199]

In Punjab, several 'Untouchables' of the Chamar caste, educated through Arya Samaj schools and colleges in previous decades, had, by the mid-1920s, emerged as activists who broke with the Samaj to start the 'Ad Dharm' movement.[200] Ad Dharm leaders like Swami Shudranand and the charismatic Mangoo Ram argued that Untouchables constituted a separate 'Ad Dharm' religious community or nation—a 'qaum'—similar and equal to the Hindus, Muslims and Sikhs.[201] Inspired by other 'Adi' movements, the Ad Dharmis too advanced the notion that those now considered Untouchable were in fact the original people and rulers of India, whose religion was Ad Dharm, which venerated Kabir, and particularly Ravi Das, and taught equality. The original Ad Dharm natives were subjugated and enslaved by the foreign Aryan Hindu qaum, which turned itself into 'upper castes'.[202] In the mid-1920s, Ad Dharmis adopted the red colour, as the symbol of the original Ad Dharm people of India, to mark themselves out as a separate 'qaum'.[203] The latter half of the 1920s saw regular Ad Dharm meetings and rallies in Punjab, with masses in attendance.

In Maharashtra, B.R. Ambedkar had called for separate electorates for the 'dehumanised' Untouchables in 1919.[204] He had also formed the Bahishkrut Hitakarni Sabha (Association for the Amelioration of the Boycotted; hereafter, BHS) in 1924, to promote, among other

things, education among the so-called 'Untouchables'.[205] A critical
juncture in Maharashtrian Dalit politics arrived in 1926–27 when
Mahar leaders organized, for the first time, mass satyagrahas to
demand their 'civil rights' of equal access to temples and water
tanks.[206] This included the famous 1927 Mahad satyagraha in
which thousands would gather to non-violently take water from a
public tank as a test of whether 'Untouchables' were equal to other
Hindus (the violent resistance of upper castes was interpreted as a
'resounding no').[207] It was as part of this satyagraha, that its organizers,
including thirty-six-year-old (now Dr) Ambedkar, publicly burnt the
Manusmriti, a Brahminical text that defined lower castes as polluting
and sanctioned their punishment and social exclusion.[208] In mid-
1927, in his journal *Bahishkrut Bharat* (Outcaste India), Ambedkar
equivocated over 'whether the Hindu religion was our own or not'
and contemplated conversion to Islam.[209] The journal also criticized
the shuddhi movement for moving away from its original goal of
destroying caste towards a focus on bringing in more and more
numbers into the Hindu fold.[210] Ambedkar, as leader of the BHS, had
acquired a significant mass base, and was moving towards demanding
separate representation for Dalits via reservations in legislatures,
government services and educational institutions (which he did in
1928).[211] While Ambedkar and other Maharashtrian Mahar leaders
did not articulate an 'Adi' politics, their new assertion was evident
in their mass satyagrahas and their demand for a political status for
Dalits separate from the general electorate of Hindus.

Collectively taken, by the mid-1920s, Dalits in different parts of
India had begun to mobilize on a much larger scale than before. Dalit
movements arising in different parts of India were also beginning
to make their first (but not always successful) attempts to develop
broader regional and all-India coalitions.[212] Many had begun to
assert an 'Adi' identity separate from Hindus and, in anticipation of
the next round of constitutional reforms, to organize politically to
secure separate political representation.[213]

As mentioned earlier, apart from Dalits, an overt caste politics
was also visible among 'non-Brahmins', the designated 'shudra'

caste. In Maharashtra, radical non-Brahmin politics was represented by the Satyashodhak Samaj (Truth Seeking Society), founded by Phule six decades ago in 1873. Its ideology and activism of radical anti-casteism and equality, which had inspired generations of non-Brahmins and Dalits, continued to do so in the 1920s.[214] Now some Maharashtrian non-Brahmins also organized themselves politically in the new 'Non-Brahmin Party'.[215] In Madras Presidency, political non-Brahminism was represented by the Justice Party. During the war years, it was the Justice Party which had widely popularized the idea—which had in turn influenced subsequent Dalit 'Adi' movements—that 'non-Brahmins' were the descendants of the original 'Dravidian' inhabitants of India, and Brahmins of the Aryan invaders.[216] As noted earlier, the Party's demand for separate non-Brahmin communal representation had been granted by the 1919 Reforms, which reserved seats for non-Brahmins in the Madras Legislative Council.[217] The Justice Party's victory in the 1920 elections had facilitated the formation of the first non-Brahmin ministry, which held office till 1926.[218] While in power, it attempted, not very successfully, to rectify Brahmin over-representation in government services through preferential appointments of non-Brahmins, which caused resentment among Brahmin Congressmen.[219] Apart from the Justice Party, a much more militant and mass-oriented Non-Brahminism rose to prominence in Madras by the late 1920s under Periyar and his 'Self-Respect Movement'.[220] It not only vehemently attacked the Congress, but set out to destroy Brahmin privilege and the caste system, as well as Hinduism and religion itself, while insisting on increased political representation for non-Brahmins.[221]

Such complexity notwithstanding, Lajpat Rai saw this more radically assertive caste politics straightforwardly as the product of British and Muslim machinations to politically fracture the Hindu community. He pointed to the suggestion by the Aga Khan, the spiritual head of Shia Ismailis, to have separate representation for every caste, and by the Punjabi Muslim leader Mohammad Shafi to have 'Depressed Classes' represented separately from Hindus.[222] He further insinuated that the 'supposed representatives of the depressed classes', B.R. Ambedkar and M.C. Rajah,[223] were at worst 'hired agents' of either the British or such Muslims, or at best naively playing into the hands of the British policy of 'divide and rule' and Muslim attempts to politically divide Hindus to secure an advantage for themselves.[224]

There was of course a grain of truth in Lajpat Rai's suggestion. The British government, on the defensive in the face of rising nationalism, had an interest in keeping 'lower castes' loyal and away from nationalism by hearing out and meeting their demands, if only partially.[225] Similarly, upper-caste Muslims had occasionally argued that the creation of the Hindu political majority depended on what they believed was an unjustified classification of lower castes as 'Hindu', which then turned 'Muslims' into a vulnerable and marginalized political minority.[226] It is not hard to imagine that Dalit mobilization for separate political representation would be seen as a positive development, and even encouraged, by some Muslim leaders wishing for a future political arrangement in which 'Muslims' were not the lone, permanently beleaguered political minority. Yet, neither the grievances nor the political demands of 'low' castes were simply the manufactured creations of the British or of Muslims. To view Non-Brahmin and Dalit politics—from Phule to Thass, from Mangoo Ram to Swami Acchutanand, from M.C. Rajah, the Justice Party and Periyar to Ambedkar—as simply the product of British and Muslim machinations hugely reduced the tremendous complexity that produced and composed this politics, and was dismissive of its integrity.

Nevertheless, this is how Lajpat Rai understood the more radically assertive caste politics of the 1920s. His exhortations, as part of his call for Hindu sangathan, to the Brahmins of South and West India to readmit all non-Brahmins not engaged in shudra occupations into the 'twice-born' fold was openly conceived as a means of 'destroying' the non-Brahmin movement for 'separate political existence'—or their 'separatist tendencies', as he sometimes called them.[227] Lajpat Rai's Hindu sangathan was conceptualized as a means to counter perceived attempts by others to encourage a divisive caste politics within the Hindu community and thus reduce its political power.[228] Refusing to see the overt politics of Dalits and lower castes as a legitimate vehicle of emancipation, his sangathan opposed such politics because it thwarted attempts to consolidate a politics of the majority Hindu community.

* * *

Let us pause to summarize what we have learnt so far in the previous and present chapters. We saw in the previous chapter that for Lajpat Rai, the Hindu Mahasabha's main purpose was to organize a Hindu politics to oppose, through a complete or limited rollback, what he considered the excessively 'communal' politics of Muslims. But as we learnt at the start of this chapter, he often also conceived the 'organization' of the Hindu community as occurring outside the political realm. Here, this Hindu sangathan was imagined as needed to counter perceived threats in the form of violence and conversions. As part of his vision for Hindu sangathan, Lajpat Rai exhorted Hindus to oppose the Gandhian ideal of ahimsa and retain the capacity for violence, considered necessary to endow Hindus with a more assertive, 'masculine', and action-ready character. Hindus were also encouraged to establish akharas to build their bodies. Made in a context of periodic rioting, and the proliferation of akharas and volunteer groups which often engaged in violence, these suggestions came close to an explicit sanction of Hindu violence. Lajpat Rai wished to engineer a muscular, even violence-ready consolidation of the Hindu community. Hindu sangathan was also believed to be needed to counter the perceived threat of tabligh conversions, seen as reducing the power of Hindus. Lajpat Rai's Hindu sangathan demanded that Hindus temporarily retreat from potentially fracturing projects of anti-hierarchical caste reform, and instead symbolically unite as a Hindu community. Yet, although Lajpat Rai frequently spoke of Hindu sangathan as lying outside the political realm, his awareness of the political consequences of Muslim actions in the non-political realm suggests that he must have been equally aware of the political implications of Hindu actions in this realm. Indeed, Lajpat Rai was often explicit about his objective of maintaining a Hindu majority in a context where numbers determined political power. The consolidation and display of a Hindu majority through Hindu sangathan in the supposedly non-political realm was considered vital at a time when the question of the political representation of different communities in India's future constitution was still open. The Hindu majority's sangathan in the purportedly non-political realm was aimed at fortifying Hindu consolidation in the political realm, which in turn was geared towards opposing what Rai considered a divisive and potentially domineering Muslim politics. Hindu sangathan would, Rai believed, ensure a political pact that was fair not just to Muslims but also to Hindus. The aim of consolidating a Hindu majority for this political purpose also drove Lajpat Rai to conceive a Hindu sangathan which strongly opposed the emergent political separatism of Dalits and non-Brahmins.

To be clear, Lajpat Rai's sangathanist politics of consolidating the Hindu majority was more complex than consisting of a majoritarian[229] desire to dominate India's Muslim minority. It must be understood in light of his fears about Muslim domination. As we saw in the previous and present chapter, these fears were likely fuelled by a combination of factors: the current atmosphere of suspicion, polarization and recurrent violence; the lack of resolution over the question of representation and Muslim demands for increased communal representation; British colonial presence and felt Hindu powerlessness; stray statements by some extremist Muslim voices (focused on at the cost of other reasonable ones); Rai's position as a member of the Hindu minority in Muslim-majority Punjab; and, in this turbulent context, the likely revival of a particular reductive mental image of medieval 'Muslim' rule.[230] Put differently, the tumultuous context of polarization and violence converged with an uncertain context where the British colonial rulers held a large measure of power over Indians, where Hindus (like Muslims) held little political power, and where the question of how political power and influence would be distributed among different communities was still open and unsettling. These contexts merged with Lajpat Rai's belonging to the Punjabi Hindu minority. From this position, Rai seemed to conflate the Hindu–Muslim equation in Punjab with the all-India level. Possibly legitimate fears of Muslim majority domination over the Hindu minority in Punjab were transferred onto the all-India level, where the Hindu–Muslim equation was the reverse of Punjab—where Hindus formed the majority, and Muslims the minority. Despite Hindus constituting an all-India majority, Lajpat Rai's fears of Muslim domination in Punjab produced in him fears about Muslim domination over Hindus at the all-India level. His subconscious impression of medieval 'Muslim' rule fed these fears. Together, these factors combined to encourage Lajpat Rai's fears that, at the all-India level, the Muslim minority's demands for increased levels of communal representation were designed to secure untrammelled dominance, rather than—as its spokespersons insisted—simply adequate, meaningful political representation and protection against Hindu majority domination. As we saw, he could even see Dalit and non-Brahmin politics as part of a Muslim political ploy to attain political dominance.

In this context, Lajpat Rai believed that Hindus needed to harness their greatest strength—their numerical majority—to protect themselves from potential Muslim domination. Moreover, he held that the consolidation of the Hindu majority was needed to ensure that communal representation was kept within reasonable limits, and did not spoil Lajpat Rai's political dream of a 'secular' Indian nation–state. Because he aimed to engineer a united Hindu politics to limit the Muslim politics of communal representation, Lajpat Rai was obviously alarmed by the emerging politics of caste. An even narrower politics of caste thwarted efforts at Hindu sangathan, and went against the grain of organizing a consolidated Hindu politics that would either ideally inaugurate a 'pure', hard-line secular Indian nationalism or, at most, a secular Indian nationalism which confined communal representation to narrow limits. Whatever the legitimacy or rationality of Rai's view, he believed that if 'Muslims' were scheming to splinter and dominate the Hindu community, 'Hindus' could harness their political power as a majority to counter this attempt and realize a 'secular' Indian nationalist vision. Thus, Lajpat Rai's insistence on consolidating a Hindu majority was often a consequence of his fears of Muslim domination. In the absence of the context of the mid-1920s, and the fears it generated in him, Lajpat Rai might have articulated a 'secular' Indian nationalist vision devoid of such pronounced emphasis on a majority, as he had indeed done before. As mentioned at the end of Chapter 17, his fears of potential Muslim domination, however their reasonableness is evaluated, were also what made Lajpat Rai conceive the Hindu Mahasabha's politics of consolidating a Hindu majority not as a belligerent attempt to dominate the Muslim minority, but as a legitimate 'defence' of the Hindu majority against possible domination by the Muslim minority, and a legitimate means by which to ensure that communal representation was kept within a 'reasonable' limit.

Yet, we also saw in Chapter 17 that it was *proportionate* communal representation that Lajpat Rai regarded as a 'perfectly reasonable' principle. The National Pact, which Rai had drafted with Ansari in 1923, and continued to stand by, granted proportionate communal representation in the central and state legislatures for a fixed (but unspecified) time.[231] Therefore, the reasonable limit of communal representation for Muslims—beyond which Muslim political demands provoked, for Rai, fears of domination—was often defined by him in terms of Muslim representation in the legislatures in proportion to their *numbers* in India's population. Lajpat Rai of course never explicitly clarified why he defined the limit of a community's reasonable representation to be that which was proportionate to that community's numerical strength in the population. But his belief very likely stemmed from the emergent and increasingly dominant modern democratic conviction that there must be an integral connection between numbers and share of political power and representation.[232] Any Muslim representation over and above their numbers was seen as a serious encroachment on the rights and interests of Hindus, whose acceptance of such a political arrangement would amount to committing 'political hara-kiri'.[233] As Lajpat Rai would make quite clear once in 1928, for him, a just political arrangement was one where communal representation for the Muslim minority did not impinge on the Hindu majority's 'rightful place' in the future government of India.[234] For Lajpat Rai, the purpose of the Mahasabha's Hindu sangathan was therefore to organize and consolidate the Hindu majority to defend its supposedly rightful place in India's future polity. Lajpat Rai's militant Hindu mobilization aimed at realizing either his ideal of a more hard-line secular state with no communal representation, or the secular state he envisioned in his National Pact, which permitted proportionate communal representation, and was more sensitive to the Muslim minority. Both these secular visions sought to put a break on the expansion of political representation for Muslims,[235] and were unwilling to relinquish India's Hindu majority, which was to be defended even violently, if necessary.

At the same time, while Lajpat Rai wished Hindus to benefit from the advantage that would accrue to them under 'democratic raj', he did not want them to misuse their numerical strength to dominate other religious communities. Even as he turned to the Hindu Mahasabha, nothing in his political speeches and writings indicate that he had moved away from what he had written in one of his articles on 'Hindu–Muslim Unity' in late 1924:

> To the Hindus, I will say, if there are any among you who still dream of a Hindu Raj in this country, who think they can crush the Mussulmans and be the supreme power in this land, tell them that they are fools or, to be more accurate, that they are insane, and that their insanity will ruin their Hinduism along with their country . . .[236]

The absence of a desire for Hindu domination was evident in Lajpat Rai's vision as reflected in his National Pact which he continued to support.[237] As we saw in Chapters 14 and 17, he imagined a state that did not privilege Hinduism as its official religion, abstained from funding any religion, and granted religious freedom. He still advocated for Hindustani, a language with a more or less equal number of Sanskrit and Perso-Arabic words, in both the Sanskrit Devanagari and Persian scripts, as India's national language.[238] His desire for a federal government meant substantial autonomy for India's Muslim majority provinces like Punjab, Bengal and North-West Frontier Province (whose full provincial status Lajpat Rai had argued for in the Central Assembly in 1926).[239] Finally, in conceding proportionate communal representation for a limited time, Lajpat Rai implicitly acknowledged, even if a little grudgingly, Muslim fears of Hindu domination. Lajpat Rai's secular Indian nationalism was predicated on a clear awareness of, and even insistence on, a *democratic advantage* for the Hindu majority (in the sense of putting Hindus in a favourable position). But he did not wish this advantage to translate into *domination* (that is, untrammelled power and influence) over minorities. He was therefore ultimately open to political arrangements and mechanisms, such as proportionate reservations for Muslims in the legislatures, to prevent the degeneration of Hindu democratic advantage into Hindu majority domination.

19

Temporary Communalism for a Future Secular Indian Nation

As we saw in the previous chapter, despite the political aims of sangathan, Lajpat Rai had felt it necessary to insist that it was mostly being conducted in another non-political realm. Because he had frequently branded 'community'-based politics as illegitimate and divisive, he felt compelled to emphasize that much of Hindu 'organisation' was being conducted in this apparently more legitimate arena for such action. But interestingly, Lajpat Rai also insisted on the *limited* nature of the Hindu Mahasabha's 'direct' politics:[1] the Mahasabha would take an interest in politics only to the extent of guarding Hindu interests in 'communal' matters and leave the rest of the political programme to the 'purely political' Congress.[2] Here, he was like Madan Mohan Malaviya. Despite their promotion and leadership of the Hindu Mahasabha, these men never meant it to displace the Congress.[3] Lajpat Rai wished to preserve the sanctity of Congress which, as the only 'national' organization, alone had the capacity to unite the different 'communities' of India and collectively represent them in the political sphere.[4] The Mahasabha was almost imagined as a temporary organization that could even cease to function when it had done its job of preventing the

Congress from giving in to 'communalism' (fears about Congress softness towards Muslim demands persisted despite its opposition to separate electorates and weightages for Muslims).[5] As M.R. Jayakar noted, there was a feeling of being in the midst of 'an era, however short, of intense communal organisation'.[6] The Mahasabha had an essential role to play in this short but critical period. This notion of the Mahasabha's temporariness was evident in Lajpat Rai's opposition, in early 1926, to the suggestion of some leaders of the Hindu Mahasabha, including Bhai Parmanand, that the Mahasabha should field its own candidates in the upcoming elections to the Central Legislative Assembly and councils.[7] For Lajpat Rai, the Mahasabha's entry into electoral politics would indicate that Hindus were forsaking the Congress and turning to political separatism. He declared, 'I do not favour the idea of the Hindus setting up a separate political existence of their own.'[8] To thus perpetuate 'communal distinctions' in politics was precisely the opposite of what Lajpat Rai believed was the purpose of Hindu politics.

That Lajpat Rai saw the Hindu Mahasabha as a 'temporary remedy' necessary only while Hindu–Muslim riots lasted was suspected by Parmanand. He read Lajpat Rai's strong opposition to his insistence on the Mahasabha fielding candidates in this light. In his autobiography published in 1934, he would write: 'I also came to realise that the founders of the Hindu Mahasabha had been moved by Hindu–Muslim riots, and had looked upon the movement, more or less, as a temporary remedy. On the other hand, the conviction grew in me that the Hindus were so weak that Hindu Sangathan as a temporary movement could be of no use whatsoever . . . As I took my stand on this fundamental principle, my differences with Lala Lajpat Rai grew still more marked. An annual session of the Hindu Mahasabha was held at Delhi . . . where I insisted with all the force at my command that the Mahasabha should set up staunch Hindu candidates for election to the councils . . . Lalaji was strongly opposed to this view.'[9]

Of course, things were never quite that simple when it came to Lalaji. In line with the capacity he had displayed through his political career of being radically fluid in politics,[10] in September 1926, along with the erstwhile 'moderate' Malaviya, the sixty-one-year-old erstwhile 'extremist' Lajpat Rai established the Independent Congress Party (ICP) to send Hindus to councils. The ICP was, for all practical purposes, the electoral front of the Mahasabha.[11] Lajpat Rai did a volte-face on his earlier opposition to the Mahasabha entering electoral politics. But, as we shall see, even this decision, to send Hindus to councils through Mahasabha and via the ICP, did not mean Rai had changed his views about the undesirability of Hindus establishing a permanently separate politics from the Congress, its ideal of Indian nationalism, and from the other religious communities of India.

But before coming to that, we must quickly take stock of what had changed in the context that led Lajpat Rai to suddenly switch to accept taking the politics of Hindu Mahasabha into the electoral arena. The Swaraj Party had gained official control of the Congress by August 1925.[12] This meant control of Congress organization, funds, machinery and acquiring the prestige associated with the Congress.[13] The Swaraj Party was also functioning as the Congress's electoral wing.[14] Having joined the party in January 1926, Lajpat Rai resigned seven months later in August on the ground that its good 'neutral' Indian nationalism was harming the interests of the Hindu community and therefore had to be challenged *electorally*. He argued that the Swarajists' policy of non-cooperation through 'obstruction' within legislatures could only be successful if Hindus and Muslims supported it unitedly. In the face of the Muslim community's cooperation with the government, the Hindu community's non-cooperation would ultimately lead only to its 'subordination'.[15] Lajpat Rai may have been referring to the Muslim group in the assembly led by one Sir Abdul Qaiyum; this group had assumed a pro-government position, and as a nationalist working for Indian self-government, even Jinnah was finding it difficult to work with them.[16]

Additionally, Lajpat Rai believed that the resolution passed by the All-India Congress Committee, that no 'communal' matter could be made a 'party question' if three-fourths of either community in the legislature was opposed to it, made Swarajist Congressmen less capable of representing Hindus.[17] Although it applied to both communities, Rai found Congress's internal community-based veto unfair to Hindus. Considering the following years critical for negotiating a settlement regarding the constitutional question, Lajpat Rai concluded that such Congressmen could not negotiate as *Hindu* representatives, a condition necessitated by 'Muslim' insistence on having their own representatives. The question of the Swarajists' anti-colonial obstructionism undermining the ability of 'Hindus' to voice their concerns and interests in legislative debates, and of the importance of Hindus voicing their community-based concerns, were especially relevant for urban Punjabi Hindus like Lajpat Rai. A numerical minority in their province, they felt themselves vulnerable to potential Muslim majority domination. At the same time, Rai considered the Congress's community veto relevant to all-India questions. Hindus constituted a majority and Muslims a minority at the all-India level. Several Muslim spokespersons viewed the Congress as an essentially Hindu organization and Congress's 'Indian' nationalism as ultimately reflecting only the notions and interests of the Hindu majority. Nevertheless, Lajpat Rai seems to have remained concerned that the Congress Swarajists' anti-colonial Indian nationalism was inadequate for protecting the Hindu majority's interests and rights in a context where the Muslim minority's interests were being represented in constitutional negotiations by the Muslim League. He therefore resigned from the Swaraj Party and, along with Malaviya, formed the ICP to send to the councils Hindus who, apparently unlike the Swarajists, did not compromise the rights of the Hindu community.[18]

Clearly, when anxious that the 'national' Congress was sacrificing the rights of the Hindu community, Lajpat Rai was ultimately willing to take his Hindu politics even into the electoral arena. This was thought necessary to protect the Hindu community. But entering the electoral arena still did not imply the will to institute a 'separate political existence' in opposition to the (Indian) 'national' Congress and the Muslim community. Rather, like the Swaraj Party, the ICP was conceptualized as a faction existing within the Congress, as a temporary unit whose existence was necessitated by the Swarajist dominance of the Congress.[19] For Rai, the Hindu politics of the ICP in the electoral arena continued to represent the older attempt to safeguard the Hindu community from perceived encroachments from an Indian nationalism supposedly naive about Muslim 'communalism', but without disavowing commitment to a united and diverse 'Indian nation' itself. As Lajpat Rai had resigned from the Swaraj Party, he distanced himself not just from Motilal Nehru's self-proclaimed 'constitutional unfitness to think communally' but also those 'Hindus who think that the reconversion of the whole Muslim community and the establishment of an all-prevailing all-absorbing Hindu policy is not only desirable but feasible'.[20] He still saw himself as pursuing an Indian nationalism consistent with 'justice to the Hindu community'.[21]

Lajpat Rai had emphasized the *limited* nature of the Mahasabha's politics also because he himself realized the dangers that arose from organizing politics on 'community' lines. He sometimes regretfully claimed that in the face of what he considered 'Muslim' intransigence and Congress naivety, Hindus had no choice but to organize a politics of 'community' despite admitting that this was 'antagonistic to the growth of national feeling' or 'harmful for political evolution along national lines'.[22] Whether one sees this as stemming from sound or mistaken reasoning, or a sincere or subconsciously self-serving and self-perpetuating one, Lajpat Rai saw himself as reluctantly assuming a Hindu 'communal' politics. In surrendering to the mode of politics he thought was (wrongly) preferred by 'Muslims', Lajpat Rai curiously not only let 'Muslims' define his own politics to a significant extent, but also appropriated a mode of politics which he found intensely distasteful. Despite yearning for what he considered the ideal of radically 'secular' Indian nationalism, he was willing to step down from his ideal and assume this 'communal' mode of politics if he thought circumstances demanded it. But recognizing that such a politics could become 'rabid' and thus needed to be kept within 'proper limits', Lajpat Rai appealed to Congressmen to join the Mahasabha to prevent it from mistakenly becoming 'aggressive' towards other communities.[23] While repudiating Congresswoman Sarojini Naidu's insinuation that he had abandoned Indian nationalism in favour of 'narrow communal considerations',[24] he had admitted the importance of 'minimising the evil' and argued that the only way to do so was to keep the Mahasabha under the guidance of (Indian) 'nationalist' leaders, a role he evidently saw himself as playing.[25]

Gyanendra Pandey, a historian we have encountered in previous chapters, who was one of the first to study how Indian nationalists broadly defined the relationship between the religious community and the Indian nation, has argued that while before the Khilafat movement Indians saw religious community-based politics as compatible with the Indian nation, the post-Khilafat period in the mid-1920s saw the emergence of a *new* secular Indian nationalism which defined itself in opposition to community-based politics, which it labelled pejoratively as 'communalism'. Yet, Pandey argued that the likes of Lajpat Rai who, in the mid-1920s, turned to the Hindu Mahasabha, represented a *continuation* of the pre-Khilafat lens that saw religious community-based politics as compatible with and serving the Indian nation.[26] There is certainly truth in this analysis. As we have seen, Lajpat Rai saw the Hindu politics he engineered through the Hindu Mahasabha as compatible with, and serving, the ideal of secular Indian nationalism. But Lajpat Rai's thought on Hindu 'communal' politics and the Indian nation in the post-Khilafat period was more nuanced in its recognition of the possible tension, even 'antagonism', between the two. Much of historical scholarship over the past three decades has highlighted how the overlap between the personnel of the Congress and 'Hindu communal organisations' like the Mahasabha often compromised the Congress's institutional–ideological ideal of secular Indian nationalism.[27] But interestingly, Lajpat Rai's own intention behind persuading Hindu Congressmen to participate in the Hindu Mahasabha was not only to facilitate the Mahasabha's influence over the Congress, but also to enable the Congress's Indian nationalism to check the 'communalism' of the Mahasabha.

Perhaps this is why hard-line Hindu Mahasabha leaders like B.S. Moonje (1872–1948), N.C. Kelkar (1872–1947), Bhai Parmanand and Raja Narendra Nath (1864–1942) distrusted moderates like Lajpat Rai and Malaviya, as being in the 'pocket' of the Congress.[28] By 1927, these hard-liners would marginalize Rai and Malaviya and capture the Mahasabha organization.[29] Unlike Rai and Malaviya, this more militant group saw the Mahasabha as an outright rival of the Congress and strongly opposed the Congress and its ideological vision of a strongly anti-colonial, diversity-respecting Indian nationalism.[30] Believing India to be inhabited by and belonging exclusively to the 'Hindu nation', their vision was to establish in India a brazenly and strongly majoritarian, homogenous 'Hindu state' with 'one language, one religion, one culture'.[31] It is this kind of Hindu politics, found among some Hindu Mahasabha leaders, that Lajpat Rai had wanted to limit by keeping the Mahasabha's Hindu politics subordinated to Congress's Indian nationalism.

The storm of violence and competitive organization in the post-Khilafat period had convinced the sexagenarian Lajpat Rai that India's two main 'communities' were locked into a relationship of 'friction', 'competition' and 'rivalry',[32] and now rendered him ambivalent about whether or not they formed a nation. Gone were the confident reiterations of the 'essential', 'fundamental' unity of Indians, as well as elucidations of their common racial or cultural distinctiveness. His reasoning for why the diverse people of India constituted a nation, so carefully constructed in his years in America, unravelled in the turbulent post-Khilafat period. Instead, this crisis period rekindled historical themes of 'Hindu' downfall and 'Muslim' conquest, invasion and violence. The history of relative harmony, concord and peace that Lajpat Rai had publicly avowed seemed to have, at least for now, vanished from his mind. He declared that 'the statement that India is not a nation is neither true nor false'[33] and, alluding to Congress rhetoric, asserted the pointlessness of repeating that India was one nation in the face of present antagonism between Hindus and Muslims.[34] Yet, as we saw, it was because Rai still aimed at creating precisely such a united Indian nation in the *future* that he both required the temporary 'communal' politics of the Hindu Mahasabha, and simultaneously wished to limit it.

As we saw in the previous chapter, Lajpat Rai's envisioned 'secular' Indian nation rested on the notion of a Hindu majority.[35] Much of the animus of his Hindu 'communalism' targeted what he considered the Muslim League's ploy to encroach upon the Hindu majority. Yet, he did not desire Hindu domination. As president of the Mahasabha, Lajpat Rai had wished Hindus to strive for a 'national', 'democratic' Raj in which 'Hindus, Muslims and the other communities' would participate 'as Indians, and not as followers of any particular religion'. It would be founded on 'justice to all communities, all classes and all interests'.[36] Such apparently benign rhetoric has often constituted mere sophistry and disguised ulterior motives of majoritarian domination. But that this was not the case with Lajpat Rai is evident by his reference, as we saw in Chapter 18, to the idea of Hindu Raj—that is, Hindu majority domination—as constituting an 'insanity' that would ruin Hinduism and India.[37] It is demonstrated by his continued support for his National Pact which, as we have seen, envisioned a secular state which did not privilege Hinduism, granted religious freedom to all communities, and advocated Hindustani rather than Hindi as the national language, and a federal government with substantial autonomy for Muslim majority provinces.[38] It was further evident in Lajpat Rai's willingness to concede proportionate communal representation to Muslims. Therefore, as mentioned in the previous chapter, while Lala Lajpat Rai's secular Indian nationalism was predicated on a clear awareness of, and even insistence on, a democratic advantage for the Hindu majority, it did not wish this advantage to translate into domination over minorities. He was ultimately open to political arrangements and mechanisms, such as proportionate reservations for Muslims in legislatures, to prevent the slide of Hindu democratic advantage into Hindu majoritarian domination.

This was also evident in Lajpat Rai's willingness by January 1928, despite initial intransigence,[39] to support Jinnah's 'Delhi Proposals' of March 1927.[40] Jinnah's claim to speak for Indian

Muslims had been under challenge from provincial forces and was made difficult by his predicament as a spokesperson for Muslims without a significant Muslim following. Yet, as a prominent Muslim politician taken seriously by both the British and Indian leaders, Jinnah attempted once again to arrive at a common national front.[41] Alongside a group of other Muslim spokespersons,[42] and on behalf of the Muslim League and 'Muslims' more broadly, he offered to give up separate electorates—the keystone of Muslim politics since 1909 and a mechanism from which Jinnah himself had personally benefited greatly. Separate electorates would be abandoned in favour of joint electorates, if the following four proposals were accepted: the carving out of a new Muslim-majority province of *Sind* (Sindh) out of Bombay Presidency,[43] the extension of full provincial status and democratic reforms to *NWFP and Baluchistan*,[44] representation in proportion to the population in *Punjab and Bengal*, and *one-third Muslim representation* in the Central Assembly.[45] The proposals made no mention of weightages for Muslims in provinces like UP where they constituted a minority.[46] Weightages in Muslim-minority provinces had been granted in the Lucknow Pact and insisted on in Muslim League resolutions till now. Jinnah's plan was to concede to joint electorates with Hindus while still securing Muslims against Hindu majority domination through assured Muslim democratic advantage in five Muslim majority-provinces, and via weighted representation at the centre.[47] Lajpat Rai's consideration of Jinnah's Delhi proposals—involving their vision of assured Muslim regional dominance in five provinces and even one-third reservation for Muslims at the centre—reveals his willingness to conciliate vulnerable minorities and his openness towards political mechanisms which checked Hindu majoritarian domination.

By January 1928, Lajpat Rai was openly arguing that Muslims like Jinnah, who wished to safeguard their 'community', could simultaneously be 'nationalist':

> . . . there are Muslims who although very anxious to protect
> and safeguard the interests of their community in any future

constitution, that may be evolved for India, are also true nationalist [*sic*]. They may be at times communalists, but their outlook is essentially nationalistic. To this class belongs Mr. Jinnah.[48]

Jinnah had been elected to the Central Assembly in 1923, and Lajpat Rai in 1925.[49] Fellow-members of the Assembly, Lajpat Rai and Jinnah shared a free and informal working relationship, cooperated with each other over many assembly matters, and were often seen engrossed in discussions about 'the broader aspects of the Hindu–Muslim relationship'. This was despite continuing political disagreements which sometimes took the form of sharp public criticism of each other.[50] Lajpat Rai had come to appreciate Jinnah's painstaking, issue-by-issue fight in the assembly against British colonialism.[51] He seems to have come to respect Jinnah for not just working narrowly for the Muslim community, but for the welfare of a broader 'Indian nation' composed of Muslims and Hindus. Rai was also once again able to view the Pan-Islamism of the Ali brothers as wholly compatible with 'nationalism'. While Jinnah and the Ali brothers cared for their community, the latter even on an extraterritorial plane, neither put their 'community' above the 'nation'; their concern for their community *coexisted* with their commitment to national unity with Hindus and (Indian) national self-government.[52] These 'genuine Muslim patriots' were willing to join Hindus in boycotting the all-white Simon Commission, the appointment of which in November 1927 signified the British intention to delay Indian self-government.[53] Lajpat Rai argued that these 'Muslim nationalists' differed from 'communalists' like the Punjabi Muslim leader Mohammad Shafi who sought to protect the Muslim 'community' at the expense of 'national' unity with Hindus and, as their desire to cooperate with the Commission revealed, at the expense of India's national freedom.[54]

The year 1928 saw the emergence of widespread political agreement among various political parties over an all-India boycott of the Simon Commission. These included the Swarajist Congress, the ICP, Jinnah's group in the Muslim League, and the Hindu

Mahasabha. By calling for cooperation with the Commission, Lajpat Rai believed that Shafi's group in the Muslim League was willing to sacrifice Indian nationalism (Indian national unity and freedom) out of what Rai considered narrow 'communal' considerations. In fact, in various speeches and writings in 1928, Lajpat Rai also vehemently opposed the Punjab Hindu Sabha whose leaders, Raja Narendra Nath and Parmanand, too had called for cooperation with the Commission.[55]

Indeed, by early February 1928, Lajpat Rai was distinguishing between different types of Hindus. 'Hindu nationalists'[56] like himself strove to protect the interests of the Hindu community while simultaneously striving for Hindu–Muslim (Indian national) unity, Indian self-government and freedom from foreign rule.[57] On the other hand, Hindus like the Punjab Hindu Sabha leader Narendra Nath, for the sake of protecting the Hindu 'community', were willing to forsake the struggle for unity with Muslims, cooperate with the British and relinquish the fight for Indian self-government. These were not 'nationalists'[58], but 'communalists'.[59]

So, now, among both Muslims and Hindus, Lajpat Rai identified a 'communalism' that negated Indian nationalism, and one that was compatible with it. He now clearly saw in Jinnah his own reflection. Just as Lajpat Rai's own 'communal' politics existed alongside his Indian nationalism, so did Jinnah's demand for communal representation in his Delhi proposals exist alongside his 'nationalist' opposition to the Simon Commission and desire for 'national' unity with Hindus. In accepting Jinnah's communalism as compatible with (Indian) nationalism, Lajpat Rai once more revealed his willingness to give up his ideal of a radically secularized political domain, if this is what alleviated the anxieties of India's Muslim minority, and if this was required to forge and stabilize a united Indian nation. He could now see structurally sanctioned Muslim regional dominance in five of India's provinces, and even *weighted* communal representation for Muslims at the centre as compatible with Indian nationalism.

But nothing came of Lajpat Rai's conciliatory stance towards Jinnah's Delhi proposals in the face of continued opposition to them from other quarters. The Congress had reiterated its acceptance of these at various junctures in 1927.[60] Contrary to what is often assumed, this indicates continued efforts at reconciliation and significant political and ideological convergence, even in the polarized context of the late 1920s, between the Congress and Jinnah, who would make his demand for Pakistan in the 1940s. But political agreement based on the Proposals was wrecked by continuous opposition from the Hindu Mahasabha, now led by the hard-liner Moonje, with support from the provincial Punjab Hindu Sabha.[61] Chances of an all-India settlement were equally ruined by provincial Muslim leaders, particularly from Punjab.[62]

The accommodative stance Lajpat Rai had assumed in early 1928 towards the Delhi Proposals was then more firmly disrupted by the Congress's Nehru Report of August 1928. Two All-Parties Conferences had been convened by the Congress in early 1928 to settle continuing differences over the question of representation and together draft a constitution for India,[63] at a time when the British insisted that Indians were incapable of drafting a constitution for themselves.[64] At the second conference in May, a ten-member committee was appointed for this purpose, with Motilal Nehru as chairman and Jawaharlal Nehru as secretary. Its other members consisted of individuals offering the 'Muslim', 'Mahasabha', 'non-Brahmin', 'Sikh', 'Liberal' and 'Labour' points of view.[65] Subhas Chandra Bose represented 'Bengal'. The catch was that because he had convinced neither the Hindu Mahasabha, nor the Congress, nor the several Muslim spokespersons who mattered, about his Delhi Proposals, a dispirited Jinnah had pulled the Muslim League out of the All-Parties Conferences by March 1928.[66] The 'Nehru committee' had been formed, had conducted its deliberations, and produced the 'Nehru Report' in August in the absence of Jinnah and other major Muslim leaders.[67]

To recall, the Delhi Proposals of March 1927 had been willing to relinquish separate electorates in exchange for four demands: 1) the separation of Sind, 2) the extension of full provincial status and democratic reforms to NWFP and Baluchistan 3) guaranteed representation according to their numbers in the population in

Punjab and Bengal, and 4) weighted representation of one-third seats in the central legislature for Muslims. They had also kept silent on weightages in Muslim minority provinces as granted in the 1916 Lucknow Pact. The plan was to concede joint electorates and give up safeguards for Muslim minorities in Hindu majority-provinces but protect Muslims from Hindu domination via a new route of assured Muslim democratic advantage in five Muslim majority-provinces alongside weighted Muslim representation at the centre. The Nehru Report of August 1928 proposed joint, instead of separate, electorates.[68] It recommended the separation of Sind and reforms in NWFP but rejected reservation for Muslim majorities in Punjab and Bengal. This dismissed Punjabi and Bengali Muslim fears of being swamped by an economically and educationally privileged and, especially in the case of Punjab, numerically still quite substantial Hindu minority.[69] In a harsh repudiation of Jinnah, the Report also rejected the demand for one-third (weighted) reservation for Muslims at the centre. It further rejected weightages in Muslim-minority provinces.

The Nehru Report therefore dismissed two of the four demands embodied in Jinnah's Delhi Proposals (pertaining to Muslim majority reservations in Punjab and Bengal and weighted Muslim representation at the centre). This was even as it advanced what may be broadly considered 'Hindu' political preferences of joint electorates and the end of weightages for minorities in minority-provinces, conceded more than ten years ago in the Lucknow Pact. Reservations were permitted at the centre and in Muslim-minority provinces alone, and only in 'strict proportion' to (and not in excess of) their numbers in the population.[70] This amounted to a reservation of one-fourth seats in the central legislature for Muslims, in proportion to their forming nearly 24 per cent of British India's population. Joint electorates with communal representation were recommended for ten years as a halfway compromise between joint and separate electorates.[71]

The Nehru Report is considered 'the most radical statement of Indian nationalist aspirations to date [till 1928]', 'one of the most important Congress documents on constitutional reform', and a 'giant leap in terms of settling the constitutional question for a [future] divided [post-partitioned] India'.[72] But it had ignored the opinion of the majority of India's Muslim leaders, including even of the few hand-picked to help Motilal Nehru produce the Report.[73] The Report found support among Congressmen like Ansari and Azad, Punjabi Khilafatists like Saifuddin Kitchlew, Zafar Ali Khan, Habib-ur-Rahman (and others), and among radical young Muslim college students of Lahore.[74] But it failed to satisfy most prominent Muslim leaders and organizations,[75] and finally completely alienated even the Ali brothers from the Congress.[76]

For Lajpat Rai, the Nehru Report granted precisely what he had ideally wanted: it undid the 'wrong' of the Lucknow Pact and restricted communal representation to very narrow limits. It paved, what he considered, the best way for the emergence of a united, 'secular' Indian nation.[77] As we have seen, Rai's secular Indian nationalism rested on the assumption that Hindus, as the numerical majority, must have their democratic advantage. But it could equally accept proportionate communal representation for Muslims—i.e., 'reservations' for Muslims similar to what Dalits have in Parliament today—as compatible with itself. His sincere ideological commitment to this vision is evident in his ardent defence of the Nehru Report in the weeks and days before he was gravely injured in a police-led lathi-charge at an Anti-Simon Commission demonstration on 30 October 1928. This defence was directed against a group of Punjabi Hindus led by Bhai Parmanand, who fulminated against the Report for not granting separate electorates and communal representation to the sizeable Hindu minority in Punjab.[78] For Lajpat Rai, this was a flagrant volte-face which sought to perpetuate that which prevented the emergence of a common Indian nationality.[79] He explained that reservations had been conceded to Muslim minorities where they were small minorities of less than 15 per cent of the population; Punjabi Hindus, 32 per cent of Punjab's population, constituted a large minority not warranting reservation.[80] Defending the Report's recommendation of communal representation according to numerical strength for minorities for a ten-year period,[81] he urged Hindus to accept the Report 'out of a profound necessity of reconciling Mohammedan sentiment'.[82] Unlike Parmanand who announced the futility of Hindu–Muslim unity[83] and soon proclaimed that Hindus and Muslims were two separate nations,[84] Lajpat Rai remained committed to a united Indian nation till the last days of his life.

On 17 November 1928, Lala Lajpat Rai succumbed to the injuries he had suffered during the brutal lathi charge on 30 October.[85] Till the end, he remained not just committed to a united Indian nation, but was also anxious about Jinnah's politics and the Congress's ability to fight what he considered excessive Muslim 'communalism'. This is evident in a private letter he wrote to his friend, G.D. Birla, just a day before his death. Here, he expressed his suspicion that Jinnah would try to 'kill' the Nehru Report and that Motilal Nehru was already yielding to him.[86]

Lajpat Rai would turn out to be right about Jinnah. Given that it ignored major Muslim demands and the fears from which they stemmed, Jinnah would contest the Nehru Report in December 1928, a month after Lajpat Rai's death. He would repeat his demand for one-third reservation at the centre and reservations for Muslim majorities in Punjab and Bengal.[87] In fact, as previously stated, the Nehru Report would be opposed not just by Jinnah but by the majority of Muslim leaders and organizations, including the Ali brothers and, most notably, the powerful Punjabi Muslim leadership.[88] Because it had rejected most Muslim demands, some Muslim spokespersons would even view the Report as a 'Hindu document' reflecting Mahasabha influence and the desire to establish Hindu Raj.[89] All in all, the Report's attempt to draft a constitution for India without regard for most major Muslim leaders would further increase their distance from the Congress, and bring them closer together to one another than they had hitherto been.[90] As the Congress would ignore his entreaties in response to pressure from Mahasabha leaders like Jayakar, Jinnah would reunite with Mohammad Shafi's League, with whom he had split a year ago over separate electorates and cooperation with the Simon Commission. Four months after Lajpat

Rai's death, in March 1929, Jinnah would unveil his 'Fourteen Points' on behalf of the Muslim League. Having been conceded little in return for what he considered his generous offer of renouncing separate electorates and weightages for minorities, Jinnah's Fourteen Points would repeat old demands and now also reintroduce the demand for separate electorates until the Hindus were willing to consider the other Muslim demands.[91] Some scholars see these events as marking the beginning of Jinnah's disillusionment with Indian nationalism.[92]

Lajpat Rai may have been right in foreseeing Jinnah's rejection of the Nehru Report, but he was wrong in predicting that Motilal Nehru would yield to Jinnah. Instead, by the end of 1929, a full year after Rai's demise, the father of independent India's first prime minister would conclude that the 'only way to reach a compromise with the truly nationalist Muslims is to ignore Mr. Jinnah and the Ali brothers altogether'.[93] A notion would therefore begin taking root within the Congress that an Indian nationalist political consensus perhaps required the exclusion of Muslim leaders who diverged by too many degrees from the Congress's position on communal representation, and from its definitions of 'Indian nationalism' and 'communalism'.[94] In subsequent years, rather than yielding to Muslim demands, the Congress would become much more resistant to departing from a position of what it considered 'pure' Indian nationalism.[95] Even if posthumously, Lajpat Rai would get what he had ideally wanted: the Congress leaning more strongly towards a harder line secular Indian nationalism.

20

Understanding Lajpat Rai's Hindu Politics and Secularism

We have encountered Savarkar's Hindutva in the chapters of this book which cover Lajpat Rai's life before the 1920s. But there it frequently appeared as a comparative foil to better understand the nuances and distinctiveness of Lajpat Rai's thought in these earlier years. It was really in the 1920s that the distinct and more extreme form of Hindu nationalism, represented and inspired by Savarkar's Hindutva ideology, rose in popularity.[1] After being deeply influenced by Savarkar's *Hindutva* tract, Keshav Baliram Hedgewar formed the RSS in 1925.[2] Scholars have highlighted that the Hindu Mahasabha acquired 'a more clearly Hindu nationalist orientation in the 1920s' when it adopted Hindutva as its creed.[3] Because of Lajpat Rai's close association with the leadership of the Hindu Mahasabha, he too is often assumed to have espoused, in these years, either Hindutva or the 'stage' of Hindu nationalism immediately preceding it.[4] But we have seen that even as he sought to use the Hindu Mahasabha to engineer a sociopolitical consolidation of Hindus, Lajpat Rai did so to establish a 'secular' Indian nation–state, which—we will soon see—was based on a basic level of respect for India's religio-cultural diversity.

To be sure, Lajpat Rai's ideas and politics in the 1920s did intersect with Savarkar's in significant ways. As we saw in Chapter 15, Rai was capable of occasionally expressing the belief that the Pan-Islamic concerns of Indian Muslims relating to key Islamic symbols or institutions (like the office of the caliphate) or holy sites (like Mecca and Medina) outside India, and the accidental fact of the existence of a significant number of Muslim countries on the world map (such as Afghanistan or Turkey), divided Muslim love and loyalty to India.[5] Here, he indeed overlapped with Savarkar. An overlap was also evident in Lajpat Rai's assumption that the mere accidental fact of the absence of similar Hindu symbols, institutions or holy sites outside India, and of the virtual absence of Hindu countries in the world automatically made them more loyal to India. Such assumptions by both Rai and Savarkar seamlessly sidestepped repeated expressions of 'loyal attachment' to the Kingdom of Nepal on behalf of India's Hindus by Hindus like Savarkar, and raised no questions about divided loyalties. The assumption of both men that Indian Muslim commitment to Islam detracted from their commitment to India was problematic. It drew hasty conclusions about the personal identities of countless Muslims simply on the basis of Islam's links to lands outside India, a fact beyond the control of Muslims. These conclusions also overlooked Islam's centuries-old, deep historical links to the Indian subcontinent.[6] According to this surface-level, exclusionary and punishing logic, being born into a Muslim family in India, a fact dependent on mere chance, halved your love and loyalty to India. Savarkar's recent biographer Vikram Sampath has called his 'broad generalization' about Indian Muslims' 'extraterritorial allegiance' overriding their commitment to India as 'worrisome' and 'alienating' for Muslims.[7] Nevertheless, Rai could occasionally veer towards such reasoning, and in doing so overlapped with Savarkar. He also did so when, as we saw in Chapters 14 and 17, he occasionally expressed fears that the Pan-Islamism of Muslims in North-West India, if not all Indian Muslims, was linked to a desire to establish 'Muslim dominions' in India.[8]

As revealed in Chapter 18, similarity with Savarkar is also visible in Lajpat Rai's espousal, in the mid-1920s, of a view of 'history' in which Hindu political decline and vulnerability was attributed to their adoption of non-violence, and in Rai's opposition to Gandhian non-violence in favour of a masculine, violence-ready politics of Hindu sangathan.[9] The two men further converged when Lajpat Rai, at times and in certain contexts, viewed India's Muslim minority, despite their significantly smaller numbers, as stronger than India's Hindu majority.[10] These convergences were significant. They meant that at least once Lajpat Rai fleetingly wondered, although with a sense of despair and foreboding, whether the Savarkarite way was perhaps not the only option left.[11] They also meant that Rai could be impressed with certain aspects of Savarkar's *Hindutva* tract when he reviewed it in 1926.[12] This included its expansive yet precise definition of 'Hindu-ness' as constituting something broader than simply following Hindu religion, and of Hindus being united by common blood and culture.[13] The intellectual convergences between the two men potentially meant that Lajpat Rai could occasionally overlook what distinguished his political world view from Savarkarite Hindutva nationalism, which in turn diminished his capacity to publicly criticize it. This in turn may have prevented observers from clearly distinguishing his political–intellectual world view from that of Hindu nationalists like Savarkar, encouraging them to gloss over meaningful distinctions between Lajpat Rai's politics and the politics of Savarkar, and others—like Parmanand, Kelkar, Moonje and Hedgewar—who shared a much closer ideological affinity with him.[14]

Regardless of genuine intellectual overlaps, and his own fleeting seduction by aspects of *Hindutva* when he read it, Lajpat Rai's views remained distinct from Savarkar's. Firstly, Rai's expression of discomfort about 'Pan-Islamism' itself does not make him a Hindu nationalist of a Hindutva or any other variety. Whether one evaluates this position as problematic or not, such unease has sometimes also accompanied certain types of secular Indian nationalism that substantially respected India's religio-cultural diversity. Additionally,

in Rai's case, fears about Pan-Islamism, Muslim strength, and
Muslim domination were at least partly also the result of his position
as a member of a Hindu minority in Muslim-majority Punjab.
His consideration of democratic reforms for Muslim-majority
NWFP, and support for the Delhi Proposals and the Nehru Report
illustrate that Lajpat Rai was able to overcome his anxieties about
Pan-Islamism and Muslim domination, and grant Muslims their
democratic advantage where they were majorities and constitutional
protections where they constituted minorities. But fears about
Muslim domination relentlessly gripped Savarkar, despite his hailing
from Bombay Presidency with an overwhelming Hindu majority
of 80 per cent. Savarkar's politics remained predominantly and
systematically guided by the belief that Indian Muslims were 'anti-
national', more moved by Pan-Islamic concerns abroad than Indian
concerns, and conspiring with Muslim nations to establish Muslim
rule over Hindus in India.[15] Unlike Lajpat Rai, Savarkar supported
neither the Delhi Proposals nor the Nehru Report, apparently unable
to bring himself to sanction constitutional protections for India's
religious minorities in the ways these proposals sought.

A second difference, which we have already encountered, was
that throughout his life, as both an anti-colonial revolutionary
and Hindutva proponent, Savarkar valorized violence, warfare,
assassination, militarization and aggression as integral to politics.[16]
For him, Hindu sangathan was a vehicle to turn India's Hindu
majority into a permanent masculine and militarized Hindutva
national brotherhood capable of violence. This was to take revenge
on India's Muslims for what he believed were historical wrongs
committed by 'them', show Hindu majoritarian national strength and
claim that India belonged primarily to Hindus.[17] Lajpat Rai viewed
Hindu violence in communal 'self-defence' as legitimate, but was far
from seeing militarism, aggression and violence as essential to any
and all Hindu politics. While this constituted potentially perilous
reasoning, considering there was no explicitly defined end to this
temporariness, Lajpat Rai viewed militant Hindu sangathan as a
temporary measure to demonstrate Hindu strength at a time when

constitutional negotiations were underway. Hindu sangathan was conceptualized as an urgent but temporary and instrumental means by which to secure a constitutional pact with India's Muslims that was 'fair' to the Hindu majority and in consonance with a secular democratic Indian nation–state, which respected diversity and could even consider reservations for Muslims. Aware of the potentially harmful effects of a 'rapidly' aggressive Hindu communal politics, Lajpat Rai sought to deliberately limit such politics by keeping it under the wing of Congress's Indian nationalism.

As for Lajpat Rai's praise for Savarkar's definition of 'Hindu-ness' as constituting something broader than Hindu religiosity, and of 'Hindus' being united by common blood and culture, in the unsettling, violent context of the 1920s, Lajpat Rai had read this as providing a robust definition to a Hindu 'community' rather than a Hindu 'nation'. Despite his praise, he had also hinted that he did 'not agree with all his [Savarkar's] views'.[18] Even if we disregard Rai's cursory, vague allusion to some intellectual disagreement, we can discern from his writings and speeches, key differences between Rai's nationalism and Savarkar's Hindutva nationalism. As we have seen, first in Chapter 5 and then subsequently, for Savarkar, a 'Hindu', a member of the Hindutva nation, was one who: 1) was born in India and loved it as their fatherland, 2) possessed 'Hindu blood', 3a) had inherited Hindu culture and felt a loving attachment to it, and 3b) whose holy lands lay within the territory of India. The first two 'essentials' of Hindutva were necessary to be considered part of the Hindu nation, but not sufficient. Both parts of the third 'essential' were key: claiming 'Hindu culture' as one's own and considering India alone as one's holy land.

For him, the followers of different sects of Hinduism as well as Sikhs, Buddhists and Jains met all these criteria, and were part of the Hindu/Hindutva national fold. India's Muslims and Christians met the first two criteria, but not the third. They had disowned their original Hindu culture and by converting to Islam and Christianity, respectively, had adopted different cultures entirely. Their religion, with their origin in and inextricable links to geographical spaces outside the territory of India, had endowed them with alien, 'foreign' cultures and a primary love for and loyalty towards their extraterritorial holy lands over and above their Indian fatherland. In later years, while charging Muslims with extraterritorial loyalties to Muslims outside India, Savarkar would compare them to the 'Jews of Germany', echoing the Nazi view of Jewish treachery to Germany.[19] 'Hindus', on the other hand, not only loved the land of India as their fatherland, but were attached to the 'Hindu culture' (the cultural essence of India), and belonged to religions which had their origin in, and intimate, inextricable links with, the territory of India. This in turn endowed them with a supreme love and loyalty to India as both fatherland and holy land. Savarkar linked the territory of India exclusively with Hindus, and claimed that because India was loved and revered most loyally and monogamously by Hindus, it belonged solely to 'Hindus' (a category in which he included Sikhs, Buddhists and Jains).[20]

As mentioned, Savarkar himself consistently expressed, on behalf of 'all Hindudom', extraterritorial sympathy, 'attachment' and 'loyalty' towards the 'independent Hindu kingdom of Nepal'.[21] Under Savarkar's leadership, the Ratnagiri Hindu Sabha had paid 'loyal homage' to the King of Nepal, 'the cultural head of Hindudom'.[22] But this never prompted him to conclude that Hindu love and loyalty for India was bigamous and divided. While Muslim reverence for the extraterritorial holy site of Mecca supposedly rendered them less committed to India, Hindu 'loyal attachment' to extraterritorial Nepal apparently did not have the same effect on Hindus. Savarkar continued to view Hindus as monogamously devoted to India, and therefore possessing a supreme claim over it. The *Hindutva* tract asserted that the Hindus were a 'nation' and that the 'Hindu nation' had a supreme claim over India. In 1938, Savarkar would explicitly proclaim that Hindus constituted the *only* nation in India, with Muslims constituting only a minority 'community'.[23] He would also insist that 'India must be a Hindu land, reserved for the Hindus', and ecstatically approved of the slogan 'Hindusthan Hinduon Ka' (India belongs to Hindus).[24] For Savarkar, Muslims and Christians could only become members of the Hindutva nation, with its special and inextricable links to India, if they displayed the same monogamous love for India as fatherland and holy land, which could only be done by renouncing their religions, along with their inextricable links to extraterritorial, 'alien' and 'foreign' holy places and cultures. In short, India's Muslims and Christians could only become part of the nation by abandoning their religions and assimilating into 'Hindu culture'.[25]

As Savarkar's ideology of Hindutva nationalism began gaining popularity in India in the mid-1920s, Lajpat Rai did not embrace it. Nowhere did he argue that Hindus constituted a separate 'nation' by virtue of their sharing common Hindu blood, inheriting and loving a common Hindu culture, and because their holy lands lay within the territory of India. He did not define nationhood in a manner that excluded Indian Muslims and Christians because they had supposedly disowned India's essential, indigenous Hindu culture, and adopted supposedly foreign religions and cultures. True, in the aftermath of the Khilafat movement, Lajpat Rai overlapped with Savarkar in espousing beliefs that Pan-Islamic concerns of India's Muslims and the mere existence of Muslim countries could divide Indian Muslim love and loyalty to India. Such generalizations about Indian Muslims' divided love and loyalty for India were problematic; they called into question the personal identities, and the commitments to their homeland, of millions of individuals that Rai did not know, simply on the basis of their religion. Yet, unlike Savarkar, Lajpat Rai neither insisted on equating Hindu culture with India, nor saw Islam and Christianity or Muslim and Christian cultures as essentially alien and foreign to India. He was neither driven by a desire to link India exclusively with Hindu religion and culture nor sought to claim that the territory of India exclusively or specially belonged to Hindus. In other words, unlike Savarkar, Lajpat Rai did not consistently labour to appropriate the territory of India solely for Hindus by linking it exclusively to them. He did not believe that India was a Hindu land to be reserved only for Hindus. And significantly, nowhere did Lajpat Rai express or endorse the expectation that India's Muslims and Christians needed to actively repudiate their religions and cultures, and assimilate into 'Hindu culture'. Expressing reverence for and assimilating into 'Hindu culture' was not an essential requirement for Indian Muslims and Christians to be included in Lajpat Rai's definition of the Indian nation. The Savarkarite Hindutva logic of 'exclusion from the nation unless you assimilate into Hindu culture' never entered his thinking. Even as a prominent leader of the Hindu Mahasabha—and as one who advocated a militant Hindu politics— Lajpat Rai had not espoused a diversity-averse, exclusionary and forcefully assimilationist Hindu nationalism.

As a Mahasabha leader, Lajpat Rai had aimed at a militant sociopolitical consolidation of Hindus. But this Hindu consolidation coexisted with, and was guided by, a secular Indian nationalism, which sought to still respect India's religious and cultural diversity. Some would argue that Savarkar was like Rai in his apparent openness towards granting 'equal' citizenship rights to India's religious minorities. As president of the Hindu Mahasabha in 1937, Savarkar spoke of 'equal rights of free citizenship' for all, irrespective of religion, 'as long as everyone discharged the common obligations and duties which one owes the Indian nation as a whole'. He also stated: 'let all citizens of the Indian state be treated according to their individual worth irrespective of religious or racial parentage in the general population'.[26] However, Savarkar's ostensible willingness to grant equal citizenship rights to Muslims and Christians needs to be read alongside an analysis of his exclusivist–assimilationist Hindutva nationalist ideology as elaborated in his 1923 *Hindutva* tract, which he never renounced, and continued to champion. As we have seen, Hindutva held that Muslims and Christians could be full members of India's Hindu nation only by assimilating into India's Hindu culture (as defined by Savarkar). Savarkar's willingness to grant equal citizenship rights was also conditional upon duties and obligations owed to the nation.[27] This he could never bring himself to see Indian Muslims as fulfilling. In his 1937–38 speeches, Indian Muslims were, as always, inevitably seen as guided by 'anti-Indian', 'Pan-Islamic' and 'extraterritorial allegiances'.[28] Moreover, his statement on citizenship rights for religious minorities in 1937 needs to be read alongside his attacks in 1938 on 'territorial patriots' in the Congress who allegedly wanted Hindus to cease to be 'a national and political unit'.[29] He attacked the Congress's concept of a territorially-based common Indian nationhood which, he believed, failed to understand that 'in the formation of a nation–state, religious, racial, cultural and historical affinities count more than territorial unity or common habitant'.[30] That Savarkar privileged Hindus in his imagined future 'Indian state' is evinced by his expressed beliefs in a 'Hindu nation', and in this Hindu nation constituting *the* nation in India.[31] It was evident in Savarkar's slogan '*Hindusthan Hinduon ka*', and his desire that Hindi in the Devanagari script be this Hindu *rashtra*'s national language. While Rai was comfortable with Hindustani in both scripts as India's national language, Savarkar considered this proposal as 'perverse hybridism'.[32] That Savarkarite Hindutva wanted to 'give the Hindus an empire over Muslims', and desired a 'constitution' which would give 'the Hindu nation' a 'predominant position' and have the 'Muslim nation' live in a 'position of subordinate cooperation with the Hindu nation' was also Ambedkar's view.[33] Therefore, Savarkar's statements apparently granting rights to Muslims need to be read alongside his other statements that were exclusionary, and undercut their belonging to India's nationhood.

Between the two men, only Lajpat Rai was willing to unconditionally consider religious minorities members of the national community, despite their religious and cultural differences with Hindus. Savarkar was willing to have Indian Muslims and Christians live in India as 'citizens', but his exclusivist–assimilationist definition of Hindutva nationhood ensured they could only ever exist as second-class citizens of India.[34] In contrast, regardless of religio-cultural differences, Lajpat Rai imagined Hindus, Muslims, Christians and others as members of the Indian national community, and thus as equal citizens of a future pluralist secular Indian nation–state. To belong to the Indian nation, India's Muslims and Christians were not required to abandon their religions and assimilate into 'Hindu culture', imagined as the essence of the Indian nation. They were already envisioned as belonging to it, irrespective of their religious and cultural differences with Hindus. For Rai, India belonged not just to its Hindu majority, which adhered to Hindu culture, but also to its religious minorities which (alongside significant cultural overlaps)[35] possessed their own cultures distinctive from Hindus.

In the mid-1920s, Lajpat Rai did not return to the 'Hindu nationalism' he had frequently expressed before 1915. That is, he did not return to the vision of India as inhabited by different 'religious nationalities' largely isolated from one another. Nor did he turn to newly ascendant Hindutva nationalism. Instead, he stuck to the concept of an 'Indian' nation to which he had shifted in 1915. Even as the turbulent mid-1920s shook his confidence in whether such a nation currently existed, Lajpat Rai wished to realize precisely such an 'Indian' nation, composed of India's different religious communities, all of whom had a claim upon India.

With his faith in the current existence of an 'Indian nation' shaken, Lajpat Rai now ceased to elaborate the cultural identity of the Indian nation. Instead, he focused his energies on opposing separate electorates and communal representation. It is possible that, as during his wartime years in America, he could still oscillate between two kinds of 'Indian' nationalisms. Perhaps Lajpat Rai's Indian nationalism could sometimes still veer towards endorsing the idea that the people of India were united by India's Hindu culture and common descent from an ancient Aryan race. While this had been his way of endowing India's Hindus and Muslims with a sense of common belonging, such Hindu cultural assumptions could make this Indian nationalism insensitive to Muslim religious and cultural differences. Nevertheless, despite alienating Hindu assumptions, this Indian nationalism remained non-assimilationist and practically respectful of diversity. More importantly, Lajpat Rai's continued comfort with the idea of Hindustani, in both scripts, as India's national language[36] suggests that he continued to be guided by that other broader, more pluralist Indian nationalism he had also articulated whilst in the United States. This had entailed the notion of Hindus and Muslims belonging to a common 'Aryan–Mongolian' mixed race, and had attempted to craft a pluralist public national culture for

India that celebrated the best elements of Islam and Hinduism, and of Hindu and Muslim cultures. While in the mid-1920s, Lajpat Rai had ceased to elaborate a cultural identity for his 'Indian nation', the same above-mentioned cultural imaginations of the Indian nation likely still guided his opposition to separate electorates and excessive communal representation. These, he now firmly believed, were sure to undermine the possibility of a united Indian national community ever emerging. In political terms, Rai's Indian nationalism was consistently firm in its explicit willingness to grant equal citizenship rights to all individuals, and religious liberty, equality and justice to all religious groups. It was also willing to countenance community-specific political rights (in the form of reservations) for religious minorities. As shown by his support for the Nehru Report, and as you will see, Rai's cultural imaginations of the Indian nation coexisted with, and were tempered by, his imagination of a civic nationalism in the political domain. The latter aimed to achieve a united Indian nation by granting individuals equal political rights and freedoms. This—as much as his cultural imaginations—gives insight into the nature of Lajpat Rai's secular Indian nationalism.

But what should we make of Lajpat Rai's sanction of a militant, violence-ready Hindu politics? Rai's sanction of Hindu violence in 'self-defence' aimed at protecting the Hindu majority from perceived threats of Muslim violence and designs of domination. The sanction of potential Hindu violence was performed not through an appeal to intellectual resources within Hinduism, analogous to the manner that the concept of jihad is appealed to in Islam. Nor was this done through an appeal to the Bhagavad Gita which is how many Hindus, including the younger Lajpat Rai himself, had previously justified political violence, predominantly against the British. Instead, as we saw in Chapter 18, violence was rendered permissible mainly by undermining the concept of ahimsa which Gandhi sought to make central to Hinduism. Hinduism was defined to stress its compatibility with violence. This constituted religious justification for political violence, guided by a 'religiously' defined political end: to protect a 'religiously' defined majority from the perceived threat of Muslim domination.[37]

But Lajpat Rai's militant Hindu consolidation, and even violence, ultimately aimed to realize not a Hindu state guided by the anti-secular goal of Hindu domination but instead a secular Indian nation–state. Lajpat Rai flouted conceptual dichotomies by permitting 'religious' violence for the sake of realizing a secular Indian nation. Much of violent modern religious politics has historically been a revolt against the oppressiveness of certain harsh forms of secularism.[38] But Lajpat Rai's permissiveness towards Hindu violence was not guided by a desire to establish a Hindu state and to criticize and replace secular nationalism.[39] Instead, Hindu political violence was intended to serve the ideology of secular nationalism. Lajpat Rai neither sanctioned Hindu violence to establish a Hindu state, not secular violence against religious authorities and institutions for the sake of secular Indian nationalism.[40] What was distinctive about Rai was his permissiveness of 'religion'-related violence for the sake of secular Indian nationalism. Violence was permitted not to generate unbridled Hindu domination over Muslims or to eliminate diversity, but to realize a secular Indian nationalism that respected diversity and granted minority rights, even as it protected Hindu democratic advantage.

Lajpat Rai articulated both a militant Hindu politics and a secular Indian nationalism, flouting long held assumptions among many that these two stances cannot be articulated by the same individual. However, it is not as if Rai's militant Hindu politics had no bearing on his secular nationalism. The implications of his decision to champion a militant Hindu communal politics for his secular Indian nationalism cannot be ignored. Lajpat Rai did not hold these stances together easily. Rather than a stable, seamless intellectual position, Rai's simultaneous articulation of a militant Hindu politics and a secular Indian nationalism constituted a complex, dynamic and precarious balancing act between sets of ideas in deep tension. He brought together secular Indian nationalism and Hindu communalism into an internally combustible relationship, in which, over time, one was bound to destroy the other. Lajpat Rai may have considered it an instrumental and temporary means to actualize his secular Indian nation–state, but his adoption of a militant Hindu communal politics heightened mistrust, estrangement, polarization and perhaps even violence between Hindus and Muslims. This perilous path threatened to undermine the very secular Indian nation that Lajpat Rai longed to realize. His consciousness about this danger had impelled him to occasionally try and deliberately limit the Hindu Mahasabha's politics. At the same time, he continued to spearhead a Hindu politics that threatened to sabotage his secular vision. Rai's complex intellectual position—what may be called his 'secular-communal complex' or 'secular-communal' combine—was marked by internal tension, friction and risk. And his turn towards a militant Hindu politics rendered his secular Indian nationalism rickety and unstable.

Equally importantly, Lajpat Rai's Hindu communal politics did not invalidate the intellectual significance of his secular Indian nationalism. For more than three decades now, 'revisionist' scholarship[41] has been challenging the oppositional binary long drawn between 'secular Indian nationalism' and 'Hindu communalism' by older generations of Indian nationalist historians. Ayesha Jalal has argued that, historically, secular Indian nationalism often 'compromised' with Hindu majoritarianism, while proponents of Hindu majoritarianism comfortably claimed the mantle of secular Indian nationalism and secularism.[42] More recently, scholars like Shabnum Tejani and C.S. Adcock have shown that secular Indian nationalism and Indian secularism rest on a history of a Hindu majority having first been manufactured by opposing the political separatism of 'low' castes. This history was also complicit in denying Muslim demands for political representation.[43] The historically-minded political anthropologist Partha Chatterjee has argued that the Hindu right approves of the secular idea of religion–state separation and easily uses the ideological resources of the secular state to promote its own homogenizing and domineering political and cultural agenda.[44] Sometimes deliberately, sometimes inadvertently, such revisionist scholarship has collectively promoted the misconception that secular Indian nationalism/secularism and Hindu communalism/ majoritarianism can be comfortably championed together, and that secular Indian nationalism or Indian secularism are, therefore, ideals compromised by Hindu majoritarian communalism. Some scholars have argued, and some have been understood as arguing, that secular Indian nationalism and Indian secularism have in fact consisted of little more than Hindu majoritarianism—merely 'Hindu confessionalism by another name', as one scholar put it.[45]

This body of scholarship has rightly corrected previously held mistaken assumptions about a neat and complete mutual exclusivity between secular Indian nationalism and Hindu communal politics. Lajpat Rai's political thought and actions in the mid-1920s certainly reveal that these two positions are not mutually exclusive; they can be held simultaneously by the same individual. Rai's secular Indian nationalism was articulated alongside a militant politics of Hindu consolidation, which aimed, by force, if necessary, to safeguard a Hindu majority and restrict separate Muslim representation. As a politician advocating a politics of Hindu consolidation, Rai did not oppose the secular state, but rather approved of the idea of separating religion and the state/politics for the sake of certain political and moral values. An examination of Rai's simultaneous articulation of a militant Hindu politics and a secular Indian nationalism appears to align with the above-mentioned revisionist scholarship. It seems to suggest that Lajpat Rai's secular Indian nationalism was deceptive or empty at worst, and contaminated and compromised at best.

But as mentioned earlier, Lajpat Rai's complex intellectual position was marked by internal tension, friction and instability. To recognize this tension is to recognize the analytical and conceptual tension, contrast and even incompatibility that continues to exist between 'secular Indian nationalism' and 'Hindu communalism'. It reminds us to retain and respect the meaningful analytical distinctions that still exist between these categories, even as we discard assumptions about absolute mutual exclusivity. Lajpat Rai's adoption of a militant Hindu politics may have threatened to undermine it and render it unstable, but his vision of secular Indian nationalism continued to hold integrity and sincerity. As we will see in a little more detail below, it continued to possess positive, multi-layered content and meaning. While Rai engineered a politics of Hindu consolidation and sought to safeguard a Hindu majority, he aimed to separate religion from the state and from politics for the sake of values like inter-religious peace, religious freedom, equality and equal citizenship irrespective of religion. Moreover, rather than seeking Hindu domination over religious minorities, he was open to establishing certain institutional measures to prevent Hindu majoritarian domination. In short, his secular Indian nationalism cannot be reduced to Hindu communalism or Hindu majoritarianism. Rather than being dismissed as a mere cover for his underlying and supposedly more deeply held Hindu communalism, Lajpat Rai's secular Indian nationalism has to be taken seriously.

To be sure, another reason why some revisionist scholars view secular Indian nationalism as compromised by Hindu majoritarian communalism is due to a conceptual overlap between them, at least in the case of some proponents of secular Indian nationalism. Here, the two concepts share the assumption of, and in some cases even attachment to, the notion of a Hindu majority. This overlap, an important revelation of revisionist historiography, cannot be ignored. But this has then tended to also slip into a mistaken tendency to conflate the two concepts, suggesting that due to it resting on a notion of Hindu majority, secular Indian nationalism is deceptive or compromised. This overlap between secular Indian nationalism and Hindu majoritarian communalism—with both sitting on notions of a Hindu majority—needs to be admitted, while remembering the meaningful differences that still exist between them.

This overlap is clearly evident in Lajpat Rai's thought in the mid-1920s. Both his secular Indian nationalism and his Hindu politics rested on an attachment to the existence of a Hindu majority in India. Yet, Lajpat Rai's attachment to the idea of a Hindu majority was not equivalent to a desire to establish Hindu cultural–political domination over India's religious minorities. In other words, it was not equivalent to a desire for Hindu majoritarian domination. We may note and even critique Rai's fervent attachment to the idea of a Hindu majority. Indeed, it went against Rai's own vision of a future politics for India, where democratic decision-making, and majorities and minorities, would be based on, and continuously shift according to, a mathematical aggregation of political preferences. In such a future, religious identities would not matter in politics, and political majorities and minorities would not be determined by them.[46] Yet, a critique of Rai's attachment to the notion of a Hindu majority does not have to end in the notion that his secular Indian nationalism had little substance. However limited it might appear from the viewpoint of our best ideal of secularism, Lajpat Rai's secular nationalism was still conceived as an attempt to establish a secular Indian nation–state grounded in inter-religious peace, religious freedom, equal citizenship and respect for diversity. He remained comfortable with certain political arrangements to prevent Hindu domination. Rai's attempt to secure democratic advantage for the Hindu majority coexisted with his opposition to any fantasies of Hindu domination over Muslims or others. Therefore, Lajpat Rai's secular Indian nationalism remained opposed to 'inter-religious domination', which the political theorist Rajeev Bhargava considers one of secularism's core aims.[47] For Rai, Hindu majoritarianism was to be checked not by dissolving the majority but by granting certain constitutional guarantees to the minority. Bhargava has argued that a 'majority–minority framework' offsets majoritarianism—another name for the domination of the minority by the majority—and that secularism is compatible with notions of majority and minority.[48] Rai's attachment to the majority–minority framework itself therefore does not turn his secular Indian nationalism or his secularism into a mere cover for Hindu majoritarianism.

Lajpat Rai considered the separation of religion from the state and broader politics as an essential condition for building a secular Indian nation. Put differently, for him, secularism was a prerequisite for building his secular Indian nation. Lajpat Rai's secular Indian nationalism envisioned that his imagined secular Indian nation, inclusive of all of India's religious communities, would politically rule itself in a future Indian state, which would have all members of these communities as its citizens. But what was the precise nature of Lajpat Rai's secularism? Theorists of secularism have argued that secularism may well be a universal doctrine, but its internal elements are interpreted and related to each other in different ways, adding up to different conceptions of secularism.[49] Each conception defines 'separation' (between religion and the state) differently, chooses different political and moral values as the point of this separation, or places different weight on the same values. As a Hindu 'communal' politician', Lajpat Rai arranged the basic conceptual elements of secularism in a particular way.

How, then, did he conceptualize 'separation'? We saw in Chapter 17 briefly that Lajpat Rai did not conceive India as a Hindu theocracy.[50] Certainly, he did not envision the future Indian state as having a union or alliance with a Hindu religious order, as being guided by religious ends and purposes, or being directly administered by a priestly order or other religious authority. But rejecting theocracy does not make one a champion of secularism. Apart from rejecting theocracy, proponents of secularism also do not allow a state to have an 'established' religion—one official, privileged, dominant religion of the state.[51] Though such 'established' states entail a degree of religion–state separation—they are *not* governed by a priestly order or other religious authority—they still grant one religion official, legal recognition. Such a state's goals, and its laws and policies privilege this one religion over others. Lajpat Rai did not wish the Indian state to have Hinduism as its established religion. Lajpat Rai endorsed a secular state with goals entirely separate from the divine ends of religion, a state whose institutions were conceived as being distinct from the institutions of religion, and one which did not privilege Hinduism.

But, as Bhargava argues, secular states need to determine their relation with religion not just at the levels of goals and institutions, but also at a third level of law and public policy.[52] He argues that while secularism must have religion–state separation at the levels of goals and institutions, it can permit some religion–state connection at the level of law and public policy. Secular states across the world have related state and religion at this level in different ways. This is what has produced different varieties of secularism in different countries. As stated in his 'National Pact', 'to prevent any particular denomination being given undue preference over any other', Rai envisioned that 'no Government funds' should be devoted to the 'promotion and furtherance of any denominational institutions or purposes'. In his belief that the state must not actively fund any religious institution or purpose, Rai's secularism resembled, as noted already, the 'wall of separation' ideal of secularism cherished in the United States. This is also evident in his granting 'full religious liberty', including 'liberty of belief, worship, propaganda, association, and education to all communities forming the Indian nation' as a 'constitutional right'. It is further shown in his desire to abolish communal political representation altogether. But Rai's secularism cannot be straightjacketed into the America-style strictly separationist ideal of secularism. This is suggested by his willingness to grant community-specific political rights (communal representation) in a certain form and for a limited time. Rather than being indifferent to religious communities, Rai's secularism breached the wall of separation to consider political reservations for vulnerable religious communities in the form of reservations.

What were the political and moral *values* for which Lajpat Rai desired a substantial separation of religion from the state (and broader politics)?[53] Clearly, the unrelenting waves of Hindu–Muslim violence that ravaged Indian society were a cause behind his stressing the importance of such separation. This inter-religious violence undergirded his discomfort with excessive community-based political representation, at least beyond 'reasonable' limits. One of the values his secularism therefore sought to achieve was *peace*, i.e., the prevention of what he called a 'never-ending civil war', arising out of a clash of politicized religious identities. Secondly, the secular state he envisioned would guarantee the constitutional right to *religious liberty* to all religious communities in India. A person would have the freedom to worship any god(s)/goddess(es) he/she wanted, or refuse allegiance to all. Religious freedom would be granted not just to the numerically stronger religious community of Hindus, but to all religious communities in India. And the prohibition of government funding for any religious purpose, to prevent preferential treatment for any particular religion, reflected a concern for impartial state treatment. Therefore, Rai's secularism was guided by values of *equality* and *justice*. Moreover, belonging to one particular religion would not determine the rights and freedoms the state would grant to individuals. Lajpat Rai sought *equal citizenship* for all individuals in India. In Chapter 10, we saw that in 1918 he had argued that 'every human being born in India, or of Indian parents, or who has made India his or her home, is a compatriot, a brother or a sister, regardless of colour, creed, caste or vocation'.[54] Then, in 1928, he championed the Nehru Report which granted universal suffrage and defined a citizen as 'every person who was born, and whose father was either born or naturalised within the territorial limits of the Commonwealth'.[55] He took for granted that every such Indian would possess what may be called passive citizenship rights, by which they would claim entitlements from the state, without discrimination on grounds of religion. His endorsement of the Nehru Report, which granted the right to vote to every citizen above the age of twenty-one, reveals his acceptance of equal citizenship rights for all Indians, irrespective of religion. All persons, irrespective of religion, were recognized as active citizens i.e., equal participants in the political domain.[56]

Yet, it is true that the value that remained supremely important for Lajpat Rai was *nationalism*—the principle that the people of India must form a relatively harmonious and self-ruling political community. Rai opposed separate electorates and communal representation, believing that dividing India into two compartmentalized religio-political communities would inevitably cause religious division and strife, which would, in turn, thwart the unity and autonomy of the Indian national–political community. His secularism aimed at inter-community peace, precisely because peace was indispensable for Indian national unity and autonomy. It could also be argued, however, that Rai's granting of religious liberty,

equality and justice to all religious groups, equal citizenship for all
individuals, and even limited community-based political rights to
religious minorities, intended to promote a *particular* kind of Indian
nation. In this sense, while his secularism remained supremely
concerned with national unity, its other goals—peace, liberty,
and equality for individuals and religious communities—while
appearing as subordinate, less significant political–moral values, in
fact give insight into the ways in which Lajpat Rai attempted to forge
an inclusive national community, and therefore into the *nature* of
his secular Indian nationalism. Additionally, as we saw in Chapter
17, Rai also believed in secularism's vital importance for the Indian
nation to achieve economic *prosperity* and *international status*
after gaining independence from the British.[57] National prosperity,
recognition and respect also constitute values, which coexisted
with other liberal, egalitarian and communitarian[58] moral values
that guided Rai's secularism and nationalism. It is because of this
layered, multi-value[59] nature of Rai's secularism that it cannot be
reduced merely to a cynical, valueless Hindu majoritarian grab for
power. Rather than a farcical secularism that existed only to veil
an ulterior motive of securing Hindu majority domination, Rai's
secularism possessed positive content, was guided by multiple values
and attempted to accommodate, and do justice to, India's religious
diversity. This remained true even as his adoption of a militant
Hindu politics rendered his secularism unstable, threatening to
undercut the very ideal that he wished to establish—particularly
through its permissiveness towards violence, which undermined
inter-community peace.

* * *

On 17 November 1928, sixty-three-year-old Lala Lajpat Rai
succumbed to injuries he suffered after being hit by police lathis.[60]
Exactly a month later, the twenty-one-year-old Bhagat Singh
avenged his death by assassinating Saunders, an act for which he
would be sent to the gallows in 1931.[61] A militant atheist inspired

by Marx and Lenin,[62] and recently involved in organizing inter-community dinners, avenged the death of a Hindu Mahasabha leader who had been involved in organizing a militant Hindu sangathan to guard against perceived threats from Muslims. It was with Rai that Bhagat's uncle, the radically anti-colonial Ajit Singh, was deported to Burma in 1907, the year Bhagat was born. Although a Jat Sikh, Bhagat's upbringing had been Arya Samajist,[63] with the Samaj laying the ground for his radicalism.[64] The knowledge of Lajpat Rai's association and contribution to the Samaj must have formed part of his childhood. It was the radically anti-colonial National College founded by Lajpat Rai and Rai's book collection that had inspired the young Bhagat into revolutionary anti-colonialism.[65] Despite these connections, however, by the mid-1920s, Bhagat had come to vehemently disagree with Lajpat Rai's Hindu Mahasabha politics.[66] More than personal indebtedness or ideological convergence, it was Lajpat Rai's lifelong service to anti-colonial nationalism, and his stature as a symbol of this anti-colonial nationalism, that had prompted Bhagat Singh to avenge his death.

The anti-colonial Indian nationalist fight for which both Lajpat Rai and Bhagat Singh lost their lives would be won nineteen years after Rai's death. In the days before his death, Lajpat Rai had not been entirely right in his predictions about the direction that Congress nationalism would take. The Congress would become more, rather than less, inclined towards a stricter secular Indian nationalism which it wished to remain unspoiled by communal representation. Still, Lajpat Rai had been right in foreseeing that things would be complicated. Because the Nehru Report had failed to resolve political differences between Hindu and Muslim leaders, and was rejected by the majority of Muslim leadership, it would be temporarily shelved as a possible, consensus-based constitutional framework for a future, independent India.[67] In the subsequent years, right up till Partition, attempts to negotiate would continue, come close to a solution, but fail for some reason or the other.[68] This was ultimately a failure to resolve the following conundrum. The ideal of a 'pure' or hard-line secular Indian nationalism unsullied by the politics of 'communities'

was attractive in its apparent progressiveness. But it produced fears
that in an India with an overwhelming Hindu majority, such a
stricter secular Indian nationalism without political safeguards for
religious minorities would inevitably culminate in Hindu majority
domination. On the other hand, demands for safeguards in the form
of separate electorates, 'weightages' or reservations may have been
conceived as mechanisms to ensure effective equality, freedom,
justice and solidarity. But they produced fears about division and
fragmentation and, among the Hindu right, even about Muslim
minority domination.

The reluctance to grant Muslims many of the political safeguards
their spokespersons demanded was met by Jinnah, in the late
1930s, with an attempt at a radically new solution to this intractable
problem. Having denied this notion his whole life, Jinnah would now
declare that India's Muslims were not merely a 'community', but a
'nation'.[69] This was a way to offset the permanent reduction of India's
Muslims, the world's largest Muslim population, to a 'minority'
forever dependent on the goodwill of the Hindu 'majority'.[70] Jinnah
now held that as part of one 'Indian nation', Hindus would form a
dominant 'majority' and Muslims a weak 'minority'. As two distinct
'nations', he hoped they could arrive at a multinational, consociational
power-sharing settlement based on political parity between Hindus
and Muslims.[71] But rather than a multinational solution within one
strongly federal state, his new 'two-nation theory', and danger-ridden
rhetoric about a Muslim 'homeland', would eventually culminate in
the Partition of British India, mutual massacres and the uprooting of
millions, and the creation of two separate nation–states of India and
Pakistan.[72] In a key sense, the Partition was the result of the failure, of
all parties involved, to arrive at a political and constitutional solution
that resolved a difficult quandary and substantially allayed fears
and promoted trust on both sides. Or, seen differently, the failure
to resolve the 'Hindu–Muslim' quandary within the framework of
a *single* (Indian) nation and a *single* state resulted in the Partition,
which itself represented a particular *kind* of political solution. With
this two-state solution, which conjured into being India and Pakistan,

British India's overwhelming Hindu majority became dominant in the Indian nation–state, which included a minority of Muslims. And a huge section of the erstwhile Muslim population of British India was transformed from a minority into a dominant majority in the new nation–state of Pakistan.[73]

India's constitution was drafted between 1946 and 1950, amidst a boycott by the Muslim League, and the violent massacres and large-scale migration of millions that accompanied Partition.[74] The world's longest political document laid out the fundamental laws, structures, principles and values by which newly Independent India was to be governed and by which the rights and duties of Indian citizens were to be defined.[75] Once the subcontinent had been partitioned, India's constitution did away with not only separate electorates and weightages, but also proportionate communal representations or 'reservations' for Muslims and other religious minorities.[76] Two decades before, Lala Lajpat Rai had been willing to accept weighted communal representation of one-third seats in the central legislature for Muslims as demanded in Jinnah's 1927 Delhi proposals. A year later, he had enthusiastically welcomed the Nehru Report, which guaranteed reservations to minorities both at the state level and at the centre (the latter amounting to one-fourth reserved seats in Parliament, in proportion to their constituting one-fourth of British India's population). The Indian constitution represented a cutback on the restricted level of communal representation granted even by the Nehru Report, which was itself a cutback on the 1916 Lucknow Pact which Rai too had once gladly accepted.[77] Although India's constitution refused to concede any religious community-based political representation, it granted religious minorities community-based rights in religious, cultural and educational matters.[78] As we saw in Chapter 17, Lajpat Rai had frequently dreamt of precisely such a secular constitution as the *ideal* way of ensuring a secular, united and harmonious Indian nation.

But his ideal had been achieved in the midst of, and even at the cost of, the terrible, violence-inducing partition of both his Punjab and India. Had he lived on, it is difficult to imagine him as feeling happy at the achievement of his ideal at the cost of these bloody upheavals. Yet, one can also imagine him lending his wholehearted support to the process of drafting India's constitution. In line with his ideal vision of a harder line secular Indian nationalism, we can visualize him supporting the Indian constitution's total rollback on reservations for the religious minorities left behind in India, seeing them, as many did, as partly the cause of Partition, and therefore unjustifiable after it.[79] However, equally, and as always, one can envision him resonating with the group in the Constituent Assembly that, up to Partition, was willing to depart from their ideal of a 'pure', harder line secular Indian nationalism to concede reservations for religious minorities.[80]

Much like Lajpat Rai's vision, India's constitution established India as a secular state. Unlike the Pakistani state's relationship to Islam, India did not establish Hinduism as India's official, privileged and dominant religion. Out of considerations of equality, freedom and justice, the Indian state was not meant to favour Hinduism only because of the coincidental fact that its followers happened to be in a numerically stronger position of being a majority in India. As Rai wanted, India's secular constitution granted religious liberty and equal citizenship to all individuals, irrespective of religion, and granted community-specific rights to India's religious minorities.[81] A difference lay in India's constitution committing the Indian state to providing aid for certain religious institutions and purposes, something Rai had refrained from doing.[82] His National Pact suggests that Lajpat Rai envisioned a relatively strict wall of separation between the state and religion, granting religious communities full freedom (from state intervention) to manage their internal affairs. Yet, in Chapter 15 we saw that he was in favour of reforming, rationalizing and even purging religious observances which caused religious conflict and thwarted Indian national unity.[83] Therefore, the Indian constitution's permission to the Indian state to actively intervene in religious communities to make them more liberal and egalitarian may well have been supported by Lajpat Rai.[84] India's constitution predominantly rested, and rests, on a history of rejecting militant communal political consolidation—whether Muslim or Hindu—as a means to achieve a secular Indian nation-state. As a document that enshrined not just laws and procedures but also particular political–moral values, it instituted a version of secularism which sought to, through its emphasis on individual rights, discourage militant 'communal' politics via non-violent, democratic and institutional means. Certainly, Indian constitutional secularism did not sanction militant Hindu or Muslim consolidation for its own sake. India's constitution discourages the kind of temporary, instrumental communal politics Lajpat Rai felt compelled to adopt for the sake of his dream of a secular Indian nation–state. Equally, it implements Rai's dream of discouraging communal politics such that all individuals, substantially (though not always) act politically as individual citizens of India rather than primarily as members of different religious communities.

By not letting Lajpat Rai's Hindu politics nullify the significance of his secularism, and taking the latter seriously, we can arrive at a more nuanced understanding of the historical and conceptual relationship between India's constitutional secularism and the 'Hindu right'.[85] Some sections of the latter, however small, historically articulated what can be recognized as a genuine secularism, and played a role in shaping India's secular constitution. One aspect of this history relates to the curbing of community-based political rights such as 'weightages' and eventually even reservations for minorities. This tendency to limit community-rights, alongside the creation of Pakistan, culminated in a constitutional secularism which has failed to prevent the severe under-representation of India's Muslims in virtually all of its power-holding institutions.[86] Yet, another relates to the rejection of separate electorates, which had the potential to freeze and institutionalize polarization, lock individuals into particular identity-groups and constrain their political choices. Importantly, yet another aspect of this same history involving the Hindu right and India's constitution relates to figures like Lajpat Rai agreeing on a secular state which does not officially privilege India's Hindus, being willing to grant community-based rights to India's religious minorities, and respecting India's religious, cultural and linguistic diversity. This challenges assumptions of both some 'secularists' and some within the Hindu right today that the Hindu right has had little historical relation to India's constitutional secularism and its grant of minority rights, which they associate only with Jawaharlal Nehru and the Congress.[87] While much of the Hindu right indeed opposed the Indian constitution, this ideological family constituted a spectrum, and some within it, like Lajpat Rai, today claimed by the Hindu right as an icon and ancestor, articulated certain ideas of secularism which found their way into India's secular constitution. Rather than undermine or resent it, the Right can choose to claim and uphold this legacy.

Acknowledging Rai's secularism opens the theoretical possibility of legitimate secularisms existing among some sections of the Hindu right. It also allows us to analytically differentiate between the different 'secularisms' emanating from within the Hindu right. Some of its sections, however small, articulate a version of secularism but one which is harsher and more minority-insensitive than the one enshrined in India's constitution. These sections mistakenly consider the Indian constitution's grant of sociocultural community-based rights for religious minorities as 'pseudo-secular' or 'anti-secular'.[88] This fails to understand that secularism can allow a measure of religion–state connection at the level of law and public policy in order to promote equality and justice. This secularism is also more uncompromising and minority-insensitive than the one championed by Lajpat Rai, who was happy to grant minorities community-based rights in the sociocultural domain.[89] Acknowledging and understanding Lajpat Rai' s secularism allows us to clearly see how the harsher secularism of some within the Right departs from the more minority-sensitive version championed by its one of its claimed icons. More importantly, Rai's secularism throws into relief the nature of the self-proclaimed 'secularism' promoted by several others within the Hindu Right. While many among the Right champion the separation of religion and state, this does not automatically make them champions of secularism, if they are not genuinely guided by values such as peace, tolerance, religious liberty, respect for religio-cultural diversity, equal citizenship and non-domination. Those who talk of the separation of state and religion, but use this language of separation to oppressively assimilate India's religious minorities into their own homogenized notion of Hindu/Indian national culture do not count as proponents of secularism. The instrumental use of the language of separation and of secularism to actually usher in a disguised privileging of Hinduism or Hindu culture, and to establish Hindu cultural and political domination, does not amount to secularism, and in fact severely undercuts the core values of secularism in all its varieties.[90] Any such dreams of Hindu supremacy and domination also violate the core values that guided Lajpat Rai's secularism.[91] Those among the Hindu right today who link questions of Indian citizenship to religion,[92] and overtly or covertly dream of having hierarchically arranged citizenship rights on the basis of religion, with Hindus as first-class citizens and Muslims as subordinate, second-class ones, may be aligned with Savarkar. But they violate the vision of secularism held dear by Lala Lajpat Rai. Of course, it goes without saying that this holds even more true for those among the Hindu right who dream of stripping India's Muslims of their voting and other basic citizenship rights.[93]

Conclusion

This book has undertaken the first systematic intellectual study of Lala Lajpat Rai's nationalist thought. It has attempted to show that the dominant historiographical assumption that his thought embodied a 'Hindu nationalism' and constituted an antecedent of Hindutva is much too simplistic. Through a fine-grained, contextualized analysis, it has shed light on the distinct nationalist narratives Lajpat Rai articulated in the four broad historical phases of his intellectual life. In the first two phases, Lajpat Rai's narratives contained conceptions of both Hindu and Indian nationhood, while in the latter two Lajpat Rai abandoned his conception of the Hindu nation and firmly shifted to Indian nationhood. These narratives were distinguishable from the other by the strength or weakness of Lajpat Rai's conceptions of the 'Hindu' and/or 'Indian' nation, by how he related one to the other, by whether these conceptions were predominantly cultural (even if not apolitical) or political–statist or both, and by their specific, complex internal texture.

By a cultural conception of the 'nation', I mean one that imagines a large community with its own distinctive culture, and whose members are seen as alike in the aspects in which they differ from others. A cultural conception of the 'nation' can be political (and mobilize to have the cultural nation's imagined political interests addressed by an overarching state not owned exclusively by it), but not political–statist, i.e., seeking political expression through self-government in a state. By a political–statist conception of the 'nation', I mean one which imagines a large community which has something in common and which wishes that this community either have partial political self-rule or total political self-government in the form of a full-blown state of its own.

If this is so, then, a conception of a Hindu cultural nation emerges when 'Hindus' are imagined as constituting a community with a distinctive identity, an individuality that sets them apart from others, when attempts are made to define their unique cultural character, and to arrive at Hindu unity in sociocultural terms.[1] This conception becomes political–statist when Hindus are imagined as a community that must have collective political self-rule in the sense of having a measure of political power to determine and realize their cultural, economic and political interests. The most robust conception of political–statist Hindu nationalism entails efforts to ensure that the 'Hindu nation' has total political self-rule in the form of a full state of its own. Likewise, a cultural conception of the Indian nation transpires when all inhabitants of India are imagined as constituting a community with a distinctive culture which goes beyond 'Hindu culture' to include other diverse cultures of India, when efforts are made to define the contours of this culture, preserve its autonomy, and to crystallize an Indian sociocultural unity. A conception of Indian nation in the political–statist sense arises when the same Indian people are imagined as ideally possessing a share in political power to realize all their interests or have the whole state at their disposal to realize their common interests.

With these senses clarified, we can now see that in the first phase of his intellectual life, lived in the 1880s and 1890s, Lajpat Rai articulated the notion of a 'Hindu nation' in a cultural sense and a notion of the 'Indian nation' in its nascent political–statist sense. All things considered, his second phase spanning 1900–15 was marked by robust conceptions of a cultural, semi-political 'Hindu nation' alongside a weak conception of an 'Indian nation' in the political–statist sense. The third intellectual phase of his life, lasting from 1915 to roughly 1923, saw Lajpat Rai shift to a robust conception of an 'Indian nation' in both the cultural and political–statist senses. In his fourth and final phase, lived from 1924 to 1928, Lajpat Rai ceased to dwell explicitly on the cultural identity of his imagined nation but articulated a robust political–statist conception of the 'Indian nation'.

The nationalist narratives articulated by Lajpat Rai unfolded in engagement with evolving political and intellectual contexts. The four parts of this book, arranged chronologically, uncovered the narratives articulated by Lajpat Rai in each of the four distinguishable phases of his intellectual life. Part 1 explored the nationalist narratives expressed by him in the first two decades of his political life, the 1880s and 1890s. Rai's open letters to Sir Syed Ahmad Khan illustrate that in the late 1880s, Lajpat Rai had begun to imagine democratic–political self-rule by an 'Indian nation' constituted by different religious 'communities'. This part of the book also showed that in the 1890s, when Lajpat Rai expressed his ideas, outside the overtly political context, as an Arya Samajist, he attempted to forge a Hindu unity. His effort to reconcile the Arya Samaj with a broader 'Hindu' identity resulted in de-emphasizing Arya tenets, setting aside the definition of Hinduism as simple Vedic monotheism, and turning from theology to secular categories like Hindu culture and history. Part 1 ended by highlighting that, by the 1890s, Lajpat Rai had begun to explore the concept of a 'Hindu nation', but he used this term in the imperial context to refer to a cultural community, without political–statist connotations. His Hindu cultural nation was imagined alongside a Muslim (cultural) 'nation'. Lajpat Rai's construction of India's history demonstrated that in the nineteenth century, his Hindu cultural nationalism primarily aimed to impart a sense of pride to the 'Hindu nation', not to demonize Muslims. This aligned with Lajpat Rai's ability to see Muslims as a group with whom Hindus could work within a common Indian polity.

Part 2 unveiled the nationalist narratives Lajpat Rai expressed between 1900 and 1915. At the turn of the century, Lajpat Rai rejected the Congress's notion of a common 'Indian nation' to elaborate a 'Hindu nationality', although imagined alongside other 'religious nationalities'. For Lajpat Rai, strengthening India's different nationalities was a prerequisite for building a future 'Indian nation'. To prove the existence of Hindu nationality, Rai now constructed a history of Hindu 'national' resistance to 'foreign' Muslim rule. By 1904, Lajpat Rai also 'found' resources to build a Hindu nation within Hinduism. He dropped Arya Samajist tenets and embraced Hinduism's multiple non-Vedic texts, moving towards a more broad-based definition of Hinduism as nationalism itself. Lajpat Rai's writings around 1907 show that Hinduism's internal diversity continued to hinder his project of proving the existence of a 'Hindu nationality'. Rai insisted that just as the internal diversity of Islam and Christianity did not nullify their existence as a nation, just so Hindu diversity did not. Yet, without insisting on monotheism or any other theological belief, he continued to retain the Vedas as a surface-level rallying point for Hindu unity.

This part of the book then examined how Lajpat Rai's thought as articulated after the Swadeshi agitation (1906–08) opened up possibilities for more confrontational politics. Rai now turned to the Gita to prove that Hinduism contained resources for militant political action to reclaim a measure of power for the nation. Part 2 further explored Lajpat Rai's ideas of nationhood in the context of Muslim League demands for separate electorates and 'weightage' in 1908–09. His opposition to separate electorates shows that when thinking in unambiguously political terms about self-government and representation, Lajpat Rai returned to the conception of the 'Indian nation' he first articulated in 1888. Rai's opposition to separate electorates and 'weightage' reflected his belief that the 'Indian nation' would work best within the dominant liberal–individualist democratic framework. Yet, his openness towards proportionate Muslim representation showed his ultimate willingness to grant a particular form of community-based political rights within this framework.

The final chapter of Part 2 illustrated how following the 1909 Morley–Minto reforms, Lajpat Rai articulated his most robust 'Hindu nationalism'. Abandoning his attempt to find Hindu nationality in the

Hindu religion and locating it instead in Hindu culture, he provided his most catholic definition of the Hindu nation to now include even Sikhs, Jains and Buddhists. This most strident claim on the notion of a Hindu majority excluded Muslims and Christians from his 'Hindu nation'. Yet, despite appearances, Lajpat Rai's Hindu nationalism remained distinct from Savarkar's Hindutva ideology elaborated more than a decade later. This was evident in its non-insistence on cultural assimilation, imagination of a coexisting Muslim nation, and their future union into a greater 'Indian nation'. The rest of this chapter showed that, between 1909 and 1914, Lajpat Rai adopted a radical attitude toward caste reform as a path to building a more egalitarian, stronger Hindu nation. This was imagined as an essential prerequisite for building the future Indian nation.

Part 3 analysed Lajpat Rai's nationalist thought between 1915 and 1922. During his exile from 1915 to 1919, and in response to various political developments (within and outside India), Lajpat Rai permanently eschewed the notion of India being inhabited by separate 'religious nationalities'. Separating religion from the idea of nationhood, he now used the term 'nation' to firmly signify only a single larger 'Indian' community encompassing both Hindus and Muslims. The Indian nation would be built not by strengthening smaller 'religious nationalities' but by individuals transcending 'religious communities' to unite in this single 'Indian nation'. It is this nation that had to strive for self-government. Put differently, from 1915 onwards, Lajpat Rai decisively discarded the idea that there existed in India two main Hindu and Muslim (cultural) 'nations', which could in the future unite into a larger self-governing 'Indian nation'. Instead, there was only one (cultural) 'Indian nation' which deserved and needed to struggle for self-government. The First World War, and the anti-imperial wave that followed, empowered Lajpat Rai to seriously challenge the given-ness of the imperial–hierarchical world order and instead envision an egalitarian one consisting of self-governing nation–states. Interestingly, as he moved towards articulating a robust political–statist conception of nationhood, he decided that there was only one (cultural) nation which needed to find political expression in a self-governing state. For the first time, he began elaborating in detail a conception of an 'Indian nation' in the cultural sense.

Lajpat Rai asserted the existence of this Indian nation by arguing that Hindus and Muslims shared an Aryan ancestry and a Hindu culture. 'Hindu culture', defined as India's national essence, now also served to include Muslims and Christians. Yet, Lajpat Rai's imagined 'Indian nation', although sometimes grounded in such potentially alienating Hindu assumptions, practically respected India's religio-cultural diversity. That Rai evoked an Aryan ancestry to establish the indigeneity of Muslims and unite them with Hindus is corroborated by his assertion elsewhere that Hindus and Muslims belonged to an Aryan–Mongolian mixed race. His disinterest in cultural homogeneity is attested by his abandonment of the notion that 'Hindu culture' was India's national essence, and by his desire that Indian national culture be a pluralist blend of Hindu and Muslim cultures. This cultural pluralism was manifest in his suggestion that Hindustani in two scripts be India's national language. Lajpat Rai also attempted to accommodate India's diversity by asserting that Hindus and Muslims constituted a nation simply because they intensely desired to be one. Inspired by America, where he spent most of his years in exile, he also suggested federalism as a solution to India's religio-cultural diversity.

Part 3 further demonstrated that Lajpat Rai's new 'Indian' nationalism was also evident in his rewriting of India's history. The 'Muslim' period was presented as an age not of conquest and domination by foreigners, but as one in which Muslim rulers became indigenous and ruled as Indians. Lajpat Rai's historical narrative de-emphasized both the violence frequently associated with Muslim rule and the religious conflict often assumed between Hindus and Muslims. Instead, he highlighted the relative peace, tolerance and stability of India's 'Muslim' period.

The final chapters of Part 3 focused on Lajpat Rai's ideas on nationhood during the Khilafat agitation of 1920–21. For the first time, Lajpat Rai proclaimed that Hindu–Muslim unity was crucial for

Indian national identity and self-government. He exhorted Hindus
to support the Khilafat cause of Indian Muslims, for the sake of
strengthening Hindu–Muslim (Indian national) unity. Hindus also
had to join India's Muslims in their struggle to restore the Ottoman
caliphate in order to protect the world from European imperialism
and inaugurate an egalitarian world order based on nation–states.
Pan-Islamism was viewed as crucial to protect India from European
imperialism and to achieve Indian self-government. Conversely,
India's autonomy was seen as vital for the autonomy of Islam and the
Muslim world. Contrary to what might be assumed about a so-called
precursor of Savarkar, Lajpat Rai saw Pan-Islamism as compatible
with and even necessary for the Indian nation.

Part 4 concentrated on Lajpat Rai's ideas of nationhood in the
turbulent and violent context of the post-Khilafat period. It showed
that Lajpat Rai first responded to this new context by asking that
Hindus and Muslims subordinate their religions and religious
communities to the Indian nation. Lajpat Rai was partial to Hindus,
but continued to dream of forging an Indian nation and to see
Hindus and Muslims not as estranged communities but as potentially
sharing ties of mutual respect and affection.

It then demonstrated how by late 1924 the Kohat riot drove
Lajpat Rai into the Hindu Mahasabha. From now until his death
in 1928, Lajpat Rai played a leading role in spearheading what
may be called a Hindu communal politics. Another justification
Rai gave for his turn to the Mahasabha was that the persistence of
Muslim political organization to state the 'Muslim' position on
communal representation necessitated a mirroring Hindu political
organization to state the 'Hindu' position. Lajpat Rai's Hindu politics
opposed Muslim demands for separate electorates and communal
representation which, he felt, foreclosed the emergence of a united, self-
governing Indian nation. Muslim demands may have sought to check
Hindu majority domination. But since they would institutionalize a
religious community-based politics, Lajpat Rai tended to see them
as 'communal' and against (Indian) 'nationalism'. For him, since
his own Hindu politics opposed such institutionalization, it was

not 'communal' but served Indian nationalism. Moreover, since Lajpat Rai opposed communal representation because he believed it defied ideas of a radically 'secular' state and politics (which he now considered crucial to realize a united Indian nation), Rai saw his Hindu politics as serving a 'secular' Indian nationalism.

If we see Lajpat Rai's hard-line secular Indian nationalism as insensitive to Muslim fears, he was willing to shift to a minority-sensitive secular Indian nationalism which conceded proportionate Muslim representation and, at times, even 'weightage', and admitted that such 'communalism' could be compatible with Indian nationalism. This was evident in his National Pact (1923), and openness towards Jinnah's Delhi proposals (1927) and the Nehru Report (1928). Lajpat Rai's secular Indian nationalism was ultimately willing to acknowledge Muslim fears of Hindu domination and see a limited Muslim 'communalism' as reconcilable with Indian nationalism. Much of Lajpat Rai's Hindu politics aimed at opposing the extension of communal representation, which he feared would institute Muslim domination and preclude the realization of a secular, united Indian nation.

Part 4 also showed that perceived threats from Muslims led Lajpat Rai to call for a Hindu sangathan which opposed Gandhian ahimsa and discouraged radical caste reform. Despite Rai's insistence that sangathan was being organized in a 'non-political' realm, its aim to consolidate a Hindu majority during constitutional negotiations with Muslims revealed political intent. This made him vulnerable to the charge of Hindu communalism/majoritarianism, and certainly threatened to undermine his secular nationalism. Still, Rai's Hindu sangathan aimed to establish a secular Indian nation–state that rejected Hindu Raj and considered political mechanisms to check it. Lajpat Rai's insistence on the non-political nature of sangathan, and the limited nature of the Hindu Mahasabha's politics, results from his conceptualization of Hindu politics as a temporary requirement to make the Congress adhere to a secular nationalism which was firm against apparently excessive Muslim communalism and fair to Hindus. The Mahasabha's politics had to be limited by the Congress's

Indian nationalism to prevent its degeneration into rabid aggression, majoritarian domination or a Hindu nationalism that was unfair to others.

In the 1920s, a period known for the popularization of extreme forms of Hindu nationalism inspired by Savarkar's Hindutva, Lajpat Rai did not articulate any form of Hindu nationalism. As a Mahasabha leader, his Hindu politics aimed to realize a secular Indian nation, which was attached to a Hindu majority but also respected India's religio-cultural diversity, granted minority rights and considered Muslim reservations. It desired neither assimilation nor Hindu domination, unconditionally viewing Muslims and Christians as equal members of the Indian nation. Rai's militant Hindu politics seriously threatened his secularism, which nevertheless retained its integrity and significance for minorities.

Lajpat Rai's intellectual trajectory from espousing an incipient idea of a nation in its political sense to a robust idea of it in its full-fledged political–statist sense coincided with his move from espousing Hindu nationalist conceptions to a robust Indian nationalist conception. Culturally, he moved from envisioning robust Hindu and Muslim cultural nations existing within a political Indian nation to imagining a single Indian nation with a pluralist culture. There was no linear movement from an incipient cultural Hindu nationalism to Hindutva or a robust Hindu nationalism in the political–statist sense. Nor was there a simple move from an incipient to a robust Indian nationalism. For a large part of his life, Lajpat Rai articulated narratives containing both conceptions, and he could have gone in either direction. He placed his different narratives in the public domain, which others possibly took forward or reworked in their own ways. But his own choice to move in the direction of Indian nationalism strongly challenges any teleological assumption that articulations of a 'Hindu nation' or 'Hindu nationalism' necessarily culminate in Hindutva. His own certainly did not.

While later Hindu nationalists like Savarkar may have drawn upon and added their own ideas to his conceptions of 'Hindu nationalism', a reading of Lajpat Rai from the perspective of its possible retrospective significance, blocks an understanding of what he himself intended to achieve through his nationalist narratives. By highlighting the distinct internal texture of his 'Hindu nationalist' positions, this book has sought to challenge the teleological tying of all Hindu nationalist conceptions to Hindutva and open up spaces to explore the internal complexity within 'Hindu nationalism'. In throwing into relief his 'Indian nationalist' narratives articulated in the latter two phases of his life, it further serves as a warning about how labels like 'Hindu nationalist' or 'Indian nationalist' for an individual's entire body of thought can sometimes obscure its tremendous fluidity and complexity.

Additionally, through a textured analysis of Lajpat Rai's 'Indian nationalist' narratives, my study hopes to shed light on the distinct ways in which 'Indian nationalism' can be internally configured. For instance, Lajpat Rai's Indian nationalist thought was unlike Gandhi's which based its vision of Indian nationality on a respect for absolute differences between Hindus and Muslims and therefore rarely sought to overcome these by emphasizing their shared history and culture.[2] To give another example, it was also unlike that of Nehru whose historical narrative was more deliberate in its attempt to avoid imposing Hindu assumptions on India's minorities.[3] The distinctness of Lajpat Rai's narrative was evident in the specific ways in which he attempted to unite Hindus and Muslims via notions of a common ancestry and shared pluralist culture, and a reinterpreted history of India's 'Muslim' period, and in the specific reasoning he furnished for viewing Indian Muslim reverence for extraterritorial Islamic holy places or broad concerns about the fate of a wider Muslim world as compatible with Indian nationalism. It was evident much more starkly later in the mid-1920s, when he engineered a militant 'communal' politics in service of his 'secular' Indian nationalism even while showing a willingness to resist his fears and prejudices to concede weighted representation for Muslims out of considerations of justice. The secular Indian nationalism Rai articulated in the final phase of his life respected diversity and countenanced Muslim reservations, but had also been predicated on fear and suspicion of Muslim intentions. Being served by Hindu militancy which undermined inter-community trust and peace, it was rendered weaker than the secular Indian nationalisms of Gandhi and Nehru, which were devoid of fears about Muslim minority domination over a Hindu majority, and aimed to promote inter-community trust, non-violence, and peace. By highlighting this, this book seeks to encourage space to take seriously the internally differentiated nature of 'Indian nationalism'.

My research also illustrates that Lajpat Rai, as an important leader of the Hindu Mahasabha, did not intend to use it to establish a Hindu nation (in the Hindutva or any other mould), or even Hindu supremacy within an 'Indian' nation, but instead wished to give it a different direction. He imagined the Mahasabha's politics as geared towards establishing a 'secular' Indian nation which fundamentally respected India's religio-cultural diversity. In illuminating this fact, it brought to light the complex reasoning that can undergird an intellectual position which can imagine 'communal' politics as an instrument to establish a 'secular' Indian nation, however risky this may be. While this interpretation is disputed, some have read Jinnah's speech to Pakistan's Constituent Assembly on 11 August 1947, three days before Pakistan was founded, as suggesting that he envisioned Pakistan as a land over which a Muslim majority would create a secular democratic state with equal rights for all. If Jinnah indeed thought that his eventually fervent Muslim politics would end in (a Muslim majority-based and still) secular democratic Pakistani state, in this limited respect of viewing militant community-based politics as a path to an ultimately secular state, Lajpat Rai's reasoning prefigured Jinnah's, which ironically reveals the poverty of the Hindu–Muslim binary that these figures themselves often created. The difference, if such an interpretation of Jinnah's 1940s politics is indeed true, is that his instrumental and hazardous use of Muslim politics quickly resulted in the complete ruination of his larger vision. On the other hand, the internal risk and tension in Lajpat Rai's politics remained till his death in 1928, and a (Hindu majority-based and still) secular Indian nation–state was ultimately successfully created in India, buttressed as it was by other individuals and forces which took less perilous paths to establish a secular Indian nation–state.

Lajpat Rai's fervent championing of a 'secular' Indian nation as a Mahasabha leader points to the variety of thinking within the Hindu Mahasabha (even if only for the short period when it was led by Lajpat Rai and Malaviya). While many or even most may have, not all of its members turned to Hindutva or Hindu nationalism. Even as they engaged in Hindu politics with damaging effects on inter-community relations and the Indian nation, and even as they sought to strongly limit separate Muslim political representation, some championed a secular Indian nationalism that, while more hostile to Muslim demands than Congress's nationalism, was still genuine rather than disingenuous in granting equal citizenship and respecting India's religio-cultural diversity. However indirectly, the secular nationalism of such actors played a part in shaping India's secular constitution, not only in its containment of separate Muslim representation, but also in its grant of equal citizenship and minority rights, and its basic respect for India's diversity. This challenges the assumptions of some within the Hindu right that they have had no historical relationship with India's constitution, which they consider an anti-Hindu document imposed by Nehru and the Congress. Lajpat Rai's secular Indian nationalism also allows us to explore the possibility of a similar intellectual strand existing among supporters of the Hindu right historically and today.

Indeed, that Lajpat Rai often saw himself as championing a truly 'secular' state and politics and the Congress as diverting from these ideals might help us make more sense of the claim of some within the contemporary Hindu right that they are the true champions of 'secularism' while others are 'pseudo-secular'. Instead of dismissing this claim as a bizarre distortion by 'communal' individuals, we need to consider the possibility that some among the Hindu right have indeed articulated, and are possibly still articulating, a form of 'secularism'. This does not equal succumbing to the claim that there is only one 'true' form of secularism championed by the Hindu right, but instead allows us to explore the possibility that India is partly witnessing a contestation between different conceptions of secularism.[4] Acknowledging that secularism and secular nationalism have been articulated from within the Hindu right by figures like Lajpat Rai allows us to better understand the differences between the 'secularisms' of the Congress/the Left/Indian constitution, on the one hand, and the Hindu right, on the other. We need to decide which version of secularism is better and most fair not just to India's Hindu majority but also to those of India's nationals/citizens who form religious minorities, and due to their significantly smaller numbers are disadvantaged and now severely under-represented in all of India's power-holding institutions.[5]

Acknowledging Rai's secularism and secular nationalism also opens space to explore the different 'secularisms' articulated from *within* what is perceived as the 'Hindu right'. Some among the Hindu right articulate a secularism which is even more hard-line and minority-insensitive than Rai's, viewing any grant of sociocultural rights or any policies specifically meant for religious minorities as 'pseudo-secular' and 'anti-secular', missing the point that a sophisticated secularism allows a religion–state connection at the level of law and policy if this promotes equality and justice. Importantly, grasping Rai's position allows us to better understand the true nature of the so-called 'secularism' of many others, who may deploy the term and insist on a secular-sounding separation of religion and politics, but are in fact—unlike him—driven by ulterior aims of cultural and political supremacy and domination. Guided by the desire for inter-religious domination, these supposedly truer champions of secularism, in fact, oppose the core values of secularism and therefore need to be plainly recognized as anti-secular. I hope Lajpat Rai can serve as an entry point through which readers can equip themselves with analytical tools to distinguish between better and worse secularisms, and between genuine secularisms and disingenuous, instrumental uses of this word to cover what are actually designs of majoritarian domination.

Methodologically, I hope this book serves as a reminder to any historian who wishes to study ideas to seriously consider the broader and more proximate political and intellectual contexts out of which they arise. This is relevant for high theorists, thinkers with a high degree of abstraction, but even more so for more thickly politically embedded, contextual, organic and everyday political activist–thinkers like Lajpat Rai. I hope to have created space for other scholars to undertake similar, much-needed contextualized intellectual biographies of political thinkers in India. Through my study, I also hope to discourage the tendency to conflate the retrospective historical effect of an individual's ideas with what he or she himself may have intended in articulating them.[6] Finally, I hope to inspire intellectual histories that respect the efforts, confusion, struggle and change in an individual's thought, and do not attempt to iron out its fluidity and complexity to impute an exaggerated level of uniformity and coherence. Indeed, as Quentin Skinner has argued, historians who try to forcefully find such levels of 'inner coherence' in their subject's thought often end up providing mythological rather than historical accounts of what they actually thought.[7] My research on Lajpat Rai's thought is a call to intellectual historians to take seriously Skinner's warning about this 'mythology of coherence'.

By undertaking this fine-grained, textured study of how Lajpat Rai's nationalist thought developed and shifted through time, in response to changing political and intellectual contexts, this book builds on scholarship that emphasizes that there is no homogenous or fixed way of imagining the nation for all individuals and for all times. Different political actor–thinkers imagine the nation differently at the same time, and the same actor–thinkers imagine the nation differently over time. In other words, different individuals imagined the 'Hindu nation' and 'Indian nation' differently at the same time, and imagined these concepts differently over time. These nationalisms might possess several concepts and tropes in common— for instance, 'Hindu culture', 'Hindu resistance', 'Hindu decline', 'Muslim rule', 'Hindu majority', 'Indian nation', and so on. But the different meanings attributed to these tropes and the specific ways in which these are configured in relation to each other distinguish one nationalism from another.

Public debates positing Gandhi as a nationalist and Savarkar as a loyalist collaborator, and expressing alarm at the Hindu right calling Nathuram Godse a patriot miss the point. Godse, Savarkar, Lajpat Rai, Gandhi and Nehru were all nationalists. The point is that they were different *kinds* of nationalists, espousing different *kinds* of nationalisms. Surface-level debates which paint one side as nationalist and the other as less national or even as 'anti-national' distract us from asking the deeper, critical question of 'what is the precise difference in their nationalisms?' We need to, in a non-partisan manner and with genuine curiosity and good faith, ask: Do some nationalisms only talk of inclusion, equality and 'unity in diversity' but in reality favour some groups in India while neglecting, marginalizing or excluding others, making them feel as if they don't belong? Do some treat all humans as equally worthy of freedoms, rights, respect and dignity, while others hierarchize human worth on the basis of their different religions and cultures? Do some misguidedly promote mistrust, polarization and strife between groups, and therefore instability, while others foster peace, dialogue and understanding between groups, and therefore greater stability? Do some immaturely promote blind, uncritical pride towards India's traditions, cultures, histories and knowledges (thus preventing honest evaluation and future improvement), while others promote a mature and healthy combination of pride, conservation, critical appraisal, reform and improvement? Do some feel the need to childishly claim that India is the most superior nation in the world, while others maturely accept that all nations have elements, its members should be very proud of and others which should be critiqued and discarded? While most nationalisms are based on myths and simplified histories, are some closer to complex biological and historical truths than others? These questions need to be asked of our 'nationalist' heroes and icons who existed in the past.

These questions must also be asked of all self-proclaimed 'nationalists' and 'patriots' in India today. Decades of research on nations and nationalism has revealed that nations and nationalisms are not an unmitigated good. 'Nations' are the dominant way in which human beings have defined and organized themselves for the last two centuries.[8] They have provided humans across the world with a strong sense of identity, community, belonging and even stability, and people in the global South (the 'third world') freedom from colonization. However, the creation of nation–states and their man-made borders has often involved violence, displacement, loss, pain and suffering. (*This occurred in Israel/Palestine, India and Pakistan, Ireland, and the nationalism-inspired breakup of Yugoslavia which created Serbia, Croatia and Bosnia and other Balkan states, to give only a few examples*).[9] Many nationalisms have involved claims of racial, religious or cultural supremacy, and have resulted in internal oppression, forced assimilation, expulsion, extermination and even genocide. (*Take, for example, Nazi nationalism vis-à-vis Jews, Serbian nationalism vis-à-vis Bosnian Muslims and Kosovo Albanians, Burmese nationalism vis-à-vis Rohingyas, Chinese nationalism vis-à-vis Tibetans and Uigurs, Turkish nationalism vis-à-vis Armenians and Greeks, Greek nationalism vis-à-vis Turks, Sri Lankan Sinhalese nationalism vis-à-vis Tamils, Pakistani nationalism vis-à-vis Ahmediyas, Iraqi and Turkish nationalism vis-à-vis Kurds, Russian nationalism vis-à-vis Chechens and Georgians, and American White nationalism vis-à-vis Blacks*).[10] Nationalisms have led to belligerence, imperialist expansion and bloody wars (*e.g., nationalism-inspired European imperialist expansion and world wars, Nazi nationalism, Fascist Italian nationalism, Japanese militarized nationalism, Greek and Turkish nationalism, the nationalism-inspired Yugoslav wars, Serbian and Kosovo Albanian nationalisms, and recent Russian nationalism vis-à-vis Ukraine*).[11] Many malevolent intentions and actions can pass under what is often noble-sounding rhetoric about 'national' glory, 'national' interests or 'national' unity.[12]

Awareness about this unsavoury history and potential of 'nationalism' has led a small section of Indians to renounce it altogether. Some dream of a world without nations. But human beings are inescapably social and have always lived in some form of a community. Nations are only the modern form of such community living, with no foreseeable practical alternative in sight. This is precisely why deeper self-reflection by those who speak of a world without nations would quickly reveal such individuals as nationalists, according to broad working definitions of nation and nationalism. They have a fiercely cherished (constitutional, democratic, pluralist, cosmopolitan, egalitarian) vision of India's national *identity*. They sincerely care for *unity* among Indians, and for India's integrity and stability, and certainly would not like India's *autonomy* to be encroached upon by a foreign power such as America, China or Pakistan. They possess deep attachments to India, to various things Indian, consider India as a home where they belong, and are terribly pained by Indian society and politics taking a turn in a direction opposite to the ideals they wish it to follow. Such people function within a narrower Indian national frame, even as they emphasize their broader internationalist and humanitarian ideals. Some people who are aware of the unsavoury potential of nationalism have tried to analytically distinguish between (malevolent) 'nationalism' and (benign) 'patriotism', proclaiming that they are against nationalism while still being patriots. This has not made a mark politically and only enabled their political opponents to label them as 'anti-national', appropriate the language of nationalism entirely and portray their own *version* of nationalism as the *only* possible nationalism. This has not helped illuminate the intellectual–political possibility of different kinds of nationalisms.

The language of nationalism (over patriotism) is pervasive in India and globally. Despite globalization and internationalism, the world remains organized according to nation–state lines. So does each country's political system and constitution. Nations are real and long-lasting, even if they are constructs which are contingent, fragile, internally contested and open to critique. Feelings of attachment and belonging to nations is a pervasive political reality. Given these facts, and the rise in extremist, authoritarian–populist, illiberal, anti-democratic and domineering nationalisms across the globe, it becomes important to emphasize the fact that there exist different—worse and better, less and more humane—nationalisms. Not doing so allows extremists to pass off their harmful nationalisms as the only way of being 'national', while de-legitimizing alternatives as 'anti-national' and treacherous. Some nationalisms are more mature, quietist, easy-going, open-minded, scientific, honest, reflective, democratic, inclusionary, respectful of human diversity, cosmopolitan, stability-promoting, law-abiding and ethical than others. Conversely, some nationalisms are more immature, chest-thumping, muscular, rigid, narrow-minded, unscientific, dishonest, unreflective, anti-democratic, exclusionary, chauvinist, supremacist, instability-promoting, illegal and unethical than others. As a people, we Indians need to much more seriously, deeply and urgently ask ourselves: what kind of nationalists/patriots do we really want to be? What kind of nation do we want India to be? And which ideological, cultural and political resources from within and outside, and from our past and present, can help us achieve this?

Timeline*

1757		**Battle of Plassey; British conquest of Bengal**
1803		Conquest of Delhi
1818		Defeat of Marathas; British virtually control whole subcontinent except the north-west
1828		**Rammohun Roy founds Brahmo Samaj**
1849		**Conquest of Punjab**
1856		Annexation of Awadh (Oudh)
1857		**Revolt throughout north India against East India Company rule**
1858		**Company rule abolished; last Mughal ruler exiled; Crown rule instituted**
1860s–1880s		
1865	28 January	Lajpat Rai born at Dhudike village in Ferozepore district in Punjab
1874		Admission to District Board School, Rupar

---

* This timeline merges the chronology provided in *The Collected Works of Lala Lajpat Rai* with broader political and intellectual developments relevant to the history this book seeks to convey.

1875		**Syed Ahmed Khan establishes Muhammadan Anglo-Oriental College at Aligarh; Dayanand Saraswati founds Arya Samaj in Bombay**
1876		Jotirao Phule founds Satyashodhak Samaj
1877		Lajpat Rai marries Radha Devi
		Lahore Arya Samaj established
1880		Joins Mission High School, Ludhiana
1881		Passes entrance examinations of Calcutta and Punjab Universities
	February	Joins Government College, Lahore
		Joins Law School, Lahore
1882		Joins Brahmo Samaj
		Qualifies as *mukhtar* (junior pleader)
	December	Joins Arya Samaj
1883	January	Starts legal practice as mukhtar at Jagraon
	October	Addresses condolence meeting in Lahore on Swami Dayanand's death
1884		Moves to Rohtak and continues legal practice as mukhtar
		Elected secretary of Rohtak Arya Samaj
1885		**Indian National Congress founded**
		Passes law examination and starts practising law as a *vakil* (lawyer) in Rohtak
1886		Shifts to Hissar and continues legal practice there till 1892
		Associated with founding of DAV School in Lahore which became a college in 1889
1888	October–December	Writes open letters to Syed Ahmed Khan
	December	Attends Congress for the first time in Allahabad as delegate from Hissar

1889		Attends Congress session at Bombay and supports resolution in favour of separate and proportional representation of minorities
1890s		
1891		Elected corresponding secretary of DAV College Managing Committee, Lahore
1892		Moves to Lahore and starts legal practice at Chief Court
		Elected honorary secretary of DAV College Managing Committee, Lahore
		Supports College Faction against Gurukul Faction in the Lahore Arya Samaj conflict
1893		**Split in Arya Samaj**
		Elected president of Anarkali Arya Samaj founded after Lahore Arya Samaj split
	December	Member of Reception Committee of Lahore Congress
		Develops contact with B.G. Tilak and G.K. Gokhale
1895		Founds Punjab National Bank in Lahore along with Lala Harkishen Lal
		Princely state of Mysore establishes reservations for non-Brahmins (eleven years before the Muslim League demands separate electorates and weightages for Muslims)
1896		Lajpat Rai publishes three books in his Great Men of the World series—on Shivaji, Giuseppe Mazzini and Giuseppe Garibaldi
1897		Starts Hindu Orphan Relief Movement in Central Provinces
1898		Lajpat Rai's biography of Swami Dayanand published as part of the Great Men of the World series

		Elected director of Punjab National Bank
	June	Curtails work at the Bar and devotes more time to public work
1899		Takes active part in famine relief work in Rajputana, Kathiawar and Central Provinces
1900s		
1900		Publishes book on Krishna as part of the Great Men of the World series
	December	Attends Lahore Congress and is elected member of the Industrial and Educational Committees
1901	November	Writes 'Defects of the Congress and Remedies' in the *Hindustan Review and Kayastha Samachar*, where he rejects the Congress's notion of 'Indian nationality'
		Elected member of All India Congress Committee; attends Calcutta Congress
1902	September	Writes article on Hindu nationalism in *Hindustan Review and Kayastha Samachar*
		Maharaja of Kolhapur introduces quotas for non-Brahmins
1904	April	Lajpat Rai writes 'The Social Genius of Hinduism' in *Hindustan Review and Kayastha Samachar*
		Writes article titled 'Reform or Revival?' in *Hindustan Review and Kayastha Samachar*
	October	Starts the *Panjabee*, a Lahore-based weekly
		Attends Bombay Congress; selected along with Gokhale to be a part of the Congress deputation to England
1905	January	Visits Ceylon (Sri Lanka) and south India
	February	Meets Gokhale in Calcutta
	13 May	Leaves for England as Congress delegate

27 July	Addresses meeting at Stockport Labour Church, Lancashire
August	Stays at Shyamji Krishnavarma's newly founded India House
September	Visits America and delivers lectures in New York, Philadelphia and Boston
October	In London
	Makes contact with prominent members of Britain's newly formed Labour Party and British socialist intellectuals
	Outbreak of Swadeshi movement of Bengal in response to Bengal's partition
1 November	Leaves England for India
22 November	Arrives in Lahore
26 November	Delivers speech on the anniversary of Anarkali Arya Samaj, Lahore, which was used to arrest and deport him in May 1907 to Mandalay, Burma (Myanmar)
29 December	Attends Benaras Congress and supports resolution against repressive measures in Bengal
1906	Participates in agitation against the partition of Bengal (alongside Tilak and other radicals); Surendranath Banerji arrested during Swadeshi movement
	All India Muslim League founded; demands separate electorates and weightages for Muslims
	Attends Calcutta Congress, where sharp divisions arise between 'extremists' and 'moderates'
1907	Swadeshi movement in Bengal continues; Maharashtra witnesses 'extremist' fervour;

	Lajpat Rai takes part in agitation against Punjab Colonisation of Government Lands Bill and Punjab Alienation Act (Amendment) Bill
9 May	Arrested under Regulation III of 1818 and deported to Mandalay
16 May	Lodged in Mandalay Fort Prison
19 June	Lajpat Rai sends memorial to the governor-general protesting his arrest
September	B.C. Pal imprisoned for six months
22 September	Lajpat Rai sends memorial to secretary of state for India
11 November	Taken from Mandalay Fort prison to Lahore Central Jail
18 November	Released in Lahore
26 December	Attends Surat Congress and withdraws his nomination for presidentship
27 December	Attends National Convention convened by Moderates in Surat
30 December	Presides over All India Swadeshi Conference in Surat
	Muslim League's agitation for separate electorates continues through the year
1908 March	Lajpat Rai's 'Message of the Bhagwad Gita' published in *Modern Review*
April	Khudiram Bose and Prafulla Chaki attempt to assassinate Douglas Kingsford, Calcutta's district magistrate, in 'Muzaffarpur Conspiracy Case'
May	Government crackdown; Aurobindo Ghose arrested in connection with Muzaffarpur Conspiracy (aka Alipur Bomb Case)

	July	Tilak arrested for sedition and sentenced to six years' hard labour
	29 August	Lajpat Rai sails for England
		League's agitation for separate electorates occurs through the year
	November	**Secretary of state Lord Morley proposes scheme of mixed electorates and proportionate representation**
1909		Lajpat Rai attends dinner thrown by Indian Majlis at Cambridge and meets Indian students, including Jawaharlal Nehru
	February	Intervenes in controversy over separate electorates and weightages
	March	Returns to India
		Government grants separate electorates and weightages to Muslims under the Morley–Minto Reforms
	July	Lajpat Rai urges Congress not to hold session in Lahore
		Publishes 'Urgency of Improving the Lot of Depressed Classes' in *Modern Review*, the first of his many articles between 1909 and 1914 on 'Depressed Classes'
	October	Attends first Hindu conference of Punjab Hindu Sabha; delivers 'Hindu nationalism' speech
	December	Madan Mohan Malaviya presides over Lahore Congress; Lajpat Rai stays away
		V.D. Savarkar's 'Indian War of Independence' is published
1910s		
1910	March	Lajpat Rai's third visit to England

	June	Attends Conference on Nationalities and Subject Races in London
	September	Returns to India
		Congress begins overtures to the Muslim League
1911		**Partition of Bengal revoked**
		Elected to Lahore Municipal Committee
		Italy invades Muslim-dominated Libya province of the Ottoman Empire; Britain refuses to support the Ottomans
		Younger-generation Muslims begin questioning Muslim League's old policy of loyalism and express desire to cooperate with Hindus
1912		**British government refuses to accept Muslim University in Aligarh without government control**
		Lajpat Rai attends Bankimpur (Patna) Congress and advocates the cause of Indians in South Africa
		Azad expresses anti-imperial and pro-Ottoman rhetoric as editor of Calcutta-based *Al-Hilal* (the Crescent) through the year
1913	May	Presides over Depressed Classes Conference at Gurukul Kangri
	December	Attends Karachi Congress and speaks on 'Indian nationals in South Africa'
		Kanpur Mosque incident; anti-colonial sentiments among younger-generation Muslims surge; Azad and Ali brothers emerge as important political voices

1912–13		**Balkan wars against the Ottoman Empire; Britain tacitly approves; pan-Islamic fears and sympathies surge**
		Ali brothers and M.A. Ansari lead campaign to protect holy places of Islam
1914	April	Lajpat Rai leaves for England as Congress delegate
	17 May	Reaches London
		Interacts with British labour, socialist and trade union circles
	July	**First World War begins**
	October–November	**Ottomans enter war on the side of Central Powers; Britain declares war on the Ottoman Empire**
		British government clamps down on 'pan-Islamic' press
	14 November	Lajpat Rai leaves England for New York
	21 November	Reaches New York
		Interacts with liberal–progressive and university intellectual circles; begins tour of the United States (which lasts till June 1915)
		Tilak is released from jail and indicates acceptance of separate electorates
1915	April	Lajpat Rai reaches San Francisco
		Meets Ghadar revolutionaries on the West Coast
		Annie Besant urges need for joint scheme by Congress and the League
		All-India Hindu Sabha (later, Hindu Mahasabha) founded in Hardwar, UP
	3 July	Lajpat Rai leaves for Japan
	19 July	Reaches Yokohama, Japan

	Meets Japanese prime minister Count Okuma, Chinese leader Sun Yat-sen and Indian revolutionary Rash Behari Bose
	Lajpat Rai exposed to pan-Asian thought
September	Annie Besant announces plans to form a Home Rule League in India
12 December	Lajpat Rai leaves Yokohama for San Francisco
27 December	Reaches San Francisco; meets Ghadar revolutionaries
	Lajpat Rai's book *The Arya Samaj: An Account of its Origins, Doctrines and Activities* is published
	Ali brothers interned for their pan-Islamic writings
	Gandhi returns from South Africa to India
	Gokhale and Aga Khan draft joint constitutional scheme
	Congress and League begin cooperation to produce joint constitutional scheme
	Lajpat Rai makes decisive shift to 'Indian nationalism'
1916	Lajpat Rai's book *The United States of America: A Hindu's Impressions and a Study* is published
March	Lajpat Rai in Santa Barbara, California
April	Tilak forms his Home Rule League
May	Lajpat Rai returns to New York after more travels within the US; re-establishes connections with liberal, socialist and radical intellectuals and activists
June	Meets Ambedkar in New York
December	**Congress and Muslim League join hands in the Lucknow Pact**

Lajpat Rai's book *Young India: An Interpretation and a History of the Nationalist Movement from Within* is published

The British encourage Sharif Hussain's Arab revolt against the Ottoman Empire; Ottomans lose Mecca and are besieged in Medina

Meets M.N. Roy in New York

1917	March	**Start of Bolshevik rhetoric on liberation of colonies following the Russian Revolution**
	April	**The United States enters First World War**
		Gandhi starts Champaran peasant struggle in Bihar
	22 October	Lajpat Rai establishes India Home Rule League of America in New York
	December	**The Ottoman Empire loses Jerusalem**
		Tilak and Annie Besant's Home Rule agitations continue through the year
1918	January	Lajpat Rai starts *Young India*, a monthly journal of the Home Rule League of America
	February	Attends conference of radical, socialist and labour organizations; refers to Bolshevik rhetoric on egalitarian world order
		Beginnings of Woodrow Wilson's rhetoric of self-determination
	March	Gandhi starts Kheda peasant struggle in Gujarat with the help of Vallabhbhai Patel
	July	Lajpat Rai's review of Vincent Smith's book *Akbar, the Great Mogul* is published in *Young India*
	November	**Armistice signed; First World War ends; Allies defeat Central Powers, including the Ottomans**

Lajpat Rai refers to Wilsonian self-
determination rhetoric through the year

Lajpat Rai's book *Problem of National
Education in India* and pamphlet *Self
Determination for India* are published

Tilak and Besant's Home Rule
agitations continue

Adi Dravida movement takes firm root among
Madras 'Untouchables'

1919	January	**Paris Peace Conference to deliberate on peace terms; fears about dismantling of the Ottoman Empire and caliphate peak**
	March	**Rowlatt Bills turned into law**
		Khilafat organizations are formed and Khilafat campaign starts
	March–April	**Gandhi leads all-India Rowlatt Satyagraha; Swami Shraddhanand delivers speech at Delhi's Jama Masjid on 4 April; Jallianwala Bagh massacre on 13 April; Brutal government crackdown in Punjab**
		Hindu–Muslim cooperation surges
		Montagu–Chelmsford reforms begin 'provincialization' of politics, grant reserved seats for non-Brahmins and begin to spark new political consciousness among non-Brahmins and 'Untouchables'
		B.R. Ambedkar calls for separate electorates for 'Untouchables'
	24 December	Lajpat Rai leaves New York for London on the way to India
1920s		
1920	20 February	Reaches Bombay
	May	Starts *Bande Mataram* (Urdu daily) in Lahore

		Hunter Commission Report made public; does not go far enough in condemning Punjab atrocities
		Terms of Treaty of Sevres published; confirms fears about dismemberment of the Ottoman Empire
	1 August	**Launch of Khilafat/non-cooperation mass movement**
	10 August	**Turks sign Treaty of Sevres**
	4 September	Presides over special session of the Congress in Calcutta
	7 November	Presides over first All India Trade Union Congress in Bombay
	December	Founds the Tilak School of Politics in Lahore
		Attends Nagpur Congress and supports Gandhi's resolution on non-cooperation
		Founds Dwarka Das Library in Lahore (later shifted to Chandigarh)
		Year Justice Party comes to power in elections in Madras Presidency. First non-Brahmin ministry formed (which holds office till 1926)
1921	March	Founds Servants of the People Society
	April	Mohamed Ali's speech on Afghan invasion; sparks fear among some Hindu leaders
	May	On Gandhi's insistence, Ali brothers apologize publicly for pronouncements that may be considered violent
		Lajpat Rai intervenes in Afghan invasion controversy
	August	**Mappila rebellion; Arya Samaj revives shuddhi campaign**
	3 December	Arrested for taking part in Khilafat/non-cooperation movement and sentenced to eighteen months' imprisonment

1922	31 January	Lajpat Rai released and re-arrested
	4 February	**Chauri Chaura killings**
	12 February	**Gandhi calls off non-cooperation movement**
	20 February	Lajpat Rai sentenced to two years' rigorous imprisonment
	10 March	Gandhi arrested under Section 124A and soon sentenced to six years' imprisonment
	September	**Multan riot in Punjab**
	November	**Ottoman Sultanate abolished by Nationalist Turkey; Ottoman Empire ceases to exist**
	December	**Congress split between 'No Changers' and Swarajists**
		Factionalism splits Khilafat leadership
		Lajpat Rai writes private letter to C.R. Das
		Hindu Mahasabha, sidelined by Khilafat/ non-cooperation movement, is revived; Arya Samaj's shuddhi campaign linked to newly launched Hindu sangathan movement
1923		Fazl-i-Hussain's Municipal Amendment Act aims to reorganize seats on Punjab's municipalities to reflect the make-up of Punjab's population
		Arya Samaj launches shuddhi movement to 'reclaim' Muslim Malkana Rajputs of UP
		Tabligh movement launched
		Riots in Multan, Amritsar and Panipat in Punjab
		Tanzim movement starts
	August	**Riots in Agra and Saharanpur in UP**
	16 August	Released from Lahore Central Jail
		Drafts National Pact with M.A. Ansari and Azad

		V.D. Savarkar's *Hindutva: Who Is a Hindu?* **is published**
		Year Adi-Hindu Mahasabha founded by Swami Achhutanand
1924	January	Visits Gandhi in hospital in Poona
	March	**Turks abolish caliphate**
	9 April	Leaves Bombay for England
	May	Gandhi publishes 'Hindu-Muslim Tension: Causes and Cure'
	June	Lajpat Rai visits Switzerland
	July	Riots in Delhi
	August–September	Lajpat Rai visits Constantinople (Istanbul), Syria, Palestine and Egypt
	9–10 September	**Kohat riot**
	17 September	Gandhi embarks on twenty-one-day fast in response to Kohat riot
	20 September	Lajpat Rai returns to India
	26-27 September	Unity Conference
	November-December	Lajpat Rai's thirteen articles on 'Hindu–Muslim Unity' published in the Lahore-based *Tribune*
	December	Attends Belgaum Congress
		Attends Belgaum session of the Hindu Mahasabha
		Year Lajpat Rai turns to Hindu Mahasabha and starts to articulate conceptual blocks of a hard-line secular Indian nationalism and secularism
		Ambedkar forms the Bahishkrut Hitakarni Sabha
1925	11 April	Presides over Calcutta session of the Hindu Mahasabha

July	Starts the *People*, a weekly, at Lahore
August	Riots in Panipat
5 December	Presides over Bombay Provincial Hindu Conference
25 December	Attends Kanpur Congress
December	Elected to Central Legislative Assembly

Rashtriya Swayamsevak Sangh is founded by K.B. Hedgewar (along with V.D. Savarkar's brother Babarao and B.S. Moonje)

Adi-Hindu movement of UP in full swing; Mangoo Ram's Ad Dharm movement takes off in Punjab

Year Periyar (E.V. Ramasamy) leaves Congress to start Self-Respect Movement

1926 January	Lajpat Rai joins Swaraj Party and is elected its deputy leader in the Central Legislative Assembly
April	Major riots in Calcutta
May	Leaves for Europe
7 May	Arrives in Marseille and leaves for Paris
	Visits London for a week
26 May	Attends Eighth International Labour Conference in Geneva
2 June	Speaks at International Labour Conference
	Meets Jawaharlal Nehru, who is in Switzerland at the time
	Meets Romain Rolland in Geneva
	Attends World Parliaments Union in Geneva
	Returns to London and addresses World Migration Congress
June	Riot in Rawalpindi
13 August	Returns to India

	24 August	Resigns from Swaraj Party
	14 September	Founds the Independent Congress Party (ICP) alongside Madan Mohan Malaviya
	December	Shraddhanand is assassinated
		Elected to Central Legislative Assembly from two constituencies
1927	9 January	Presides over first session of Burma Provincial Hindu Sabha in Rangoon (now Yangon)
	March	Jinnah gives up demand for separate electorates in his Delhi proposals
	May	Riots in Lahore and Multan
		Leaves for Europe
	19 August	Returns to India
	December	Attends Madras Congress and supports resolution advocating boycott of the all-white Simon Commission
		The Mahad Satyagraha, led by Dalit leaders including Ambedkar
1928	16 February	Moves resolution in Central Legislative Assembly refusing cooperation with Simon Commission
	28–30 August	Attends All Parties Conference in Lucknow at which the Nehru Report is adopted
	27–28 October	Presides over Agra Provincial Hindu Conference at Etawah, UP
	30 October	Leads demonstration against the Simon Commission in Lahore; injured in police-led *lathi* charge
	3–4 November	Attends All India Congress Committee meeting in Delhi
	17 November	Lajpat Rai dies at Lahore
	17 December	**Bhagat Singh and Rajguru gun down J.P. Saunders to avenge Lajpat Rai's death**

1931 23 March   Bhagat Singh, Rajguru and Sukhdev
                       are hanged

1946 9 December   **Indian Constituent Assembly convenes
                       without the Muslim League; deliberations
                       continue till 1949**

1947   **India wins independence from Britain but
                       is partitioned, creating the new Indian and
                       Pakistani nation states; up to a million lives
                       lost; 12 million people displaced**

1948 30 January   **Gandhi is assassinated by Godse**

1949   Indian Constituent Assembly
                       votes against reservations
                       for minorities; Constitution passed

1950   **Indian Constitution adopted; India becomes
                       a secular republic**

Acknowledgements

I owe a debt of gratitude to several people without whom this book would not have been possible. First and foremost, Faisal Devji, who first encouraged me to pursue intellectual history as an undergraduate at Oxford, to open-mindedly follow seemingly counterintuitive lines of thought and challenge historiographical or ideological orthodoxies that I found myself disagreeing with, no matter how influential they had become and how daunting it felt to contest them. As my DPhil supervisor at Oxford, Faisal patiently read through several patchy pre-drafts, drafts and post-drafts, and goaded me to push my intellectual limits to extents I never knew possible. He taught me to see the familiar in the strange and the strange in the familiar. To Sudipta Kaviraj, whose confidence in the importance of this research and the validity of my chosen approach helped me endure self-doubt and imposter syndrome during my doctorate. Conversations with him, however infrequent, have always deepened my understanding of my own scholarship. I am extremely thankful to Amar Sohal for being a wonderful friend and brilliant intellectual peer, for the ritual meetings at the Lamb and Flag (and the Wine Café!), where we obsessively discussed our ideas, for reading the early drafts of my chapters and giving comments and encouragement. To Priya Atwal, for leading the way during our doctorates. I am deeply grateful to my friends Nicole Beardsworth, Jessie Barton-Hronesova, Claudia

Stoicescu and Ana Budimir, for being my Oxford family, for helping me tread the exhilarating and agonizing path of research, and for always being there for me to lean on. To Andrew and Peggotty, who were like foster parents and provided crucial emotional support at the excruciating last stage of writing and refining my doctoral research thesis. To my DPhil thesis examiners, William Gould and Yasmin Khan, for their probing questions during the viva and constructive feedback in the examiners' report.

To Aditya Sarkar, for his effusive enthusiasm for my research, approach and arguments, and for immediately understanding exactly what I was trying to achieve through this project. To Christophe Jaffrelot and the anonymous reviewers at *Studies in Indian Politics* (*SIP*), for their comments on my research on Lajpat Rai's ideas on caste, which helped improve it. To Taushif Kara, Farzana Shaikh and the anonymous reviewers at *Global Intellectual History* (*GIH*), for their comments on my research on Lajpat Rai's letters to Sir Syed. To Margrit Pernau, whose relentlessly critical and forensic eye has sharpened my scholarship. To the scholars at her colloquium (Rukmini Barua, Soheb Niazi and Fredrik Schröer, among others), who critically engaged with a journal article I wrote on Lajpat Rai's ideas during his stay in America and helped refine it. To the first two anonymous reviewers at *Modern Asian Studies* whose positive reviews on this article gave me confidence as an early-career academic researcher regularly plagued by self-doubt and whose constructive comments improved my arguments. To Neeladri Bhattacharya and Shruti Kapila, for their support to me as an early-career researcher, particularly in the face of one puzzling episode of petty academic hostility. To Vinayak Chaturvedi, Joseph Alter and the editorial board at the *Journal of Asian Studies* (*JAS*), for their encouragement at a critical time and for the anonymous reviewers at *JAS* whose feedback sharpened my argument on Lajpat Rai's ideas during the Khilafat movement. Versions of the contents of Chapter 2, Chapter 9 and Chapters 12–13 have appeared in *Global Intellectual History* (2021), 7(6), 974–993; *Studies in Indian Politics* (2018), 6(1), 15–26; and *Journal of Asian Studies* (2022), 81(4), 689–705. I am grateful to these journals for their permission to draw on them here. I am thankful to Sushmita Nath for being an excellent interlocutor during my postdoctoral fellowship at the 'Multiple Secularities Research Group' at the University of Leipzig in Germany. To Monika Wohlrab-Sahr, for her support and encouragement of and engagement with my research, and the scholars who engaged with my presentations at the Multiple Secularities research colloquium. Thanks are due to the anonymous reviewer of the article I wrote for the Working Paper Series of the centre, whose comments helped nuance my argument about Lajpat Rai's co-articulation of a Hindu politics and secularism. Many thanks to Wolfgang Höpken for providing me with references to hone my arguments about the context for the emergence of secular states in Europe. To Hubert Seiwert, Rinku Lamba, Isabella Schwaderer and Amiya P. Sen, and the anonymous reviewers at *Interdisziplinäre Zeitschrift für Südasienforschung* and *Religions*, for their constructive engagement with my research on Rai's ideas on religion, culture and Hindu nationalism. I am deeply grateful to Vasudha Dalmia, A.G. Noorani, Eve Tignol, C.M. Naim, Pratap Bhanu Mehta, Arudra Burra, Aishwary Kumar, P.K. Datta, Cemil Aydin, Gudrun Kramer, SherAli Tareen, Lajwanti Chatwani, Jack Hawley, Markus Dressler, Judith Zimmerman, Johannes Duschka, Maria Framke, Kama Maclean, Dermot Killingley, J. Barton Scott, Shaunna Rodrigues, Chris Moffat, Vikram Visana, Duncan Kelly, Dhananjay Rai, Sundeep Dougal and Sonja Hegasy, for their engagement with and appreciation of different aspects of my research, and/or for encouragement in general. Upinder Singh and Suraj Yengde very kindly took the time and effort to look over certain passages related to ancient Indian history and caste. This alleviated some of my neurosis about whether I had dealt with these themes in a sufficiently accurate and ethical manner.

I am thankful for each and every institution and individual whose cooperation and hard work are behind the publication of *The Collected Works of Lala Lajpat Rai*, 2003–2010. Without this collection, this book would not exist. A special thank you to Satya Paul of the Servants of the People Society. I also owe deep gratitude to the scholars whose research I have learnt from and built upon. I have often worried about what may happen should a shrill, intolerant minority choose to be offended by the arguments and conclusions of the scholarship I have relied upon and cited. I have done so in the faith that the citizens of the world's largest democracy will remain committed to scientific temper, open to different interpretations, and will engage in democratic dialogue and disagreement rather than anti-intellectual 'mobocracy' (to use one of Gandhi's terms).

A special thank you to Richa Burman for noticing my article on Lajpat Rai in the *Indian Express*, believing I had something meaningful to say to a wider audience beyond academics and students of history, and for giving me the opportunity to fulfil my dream of writing history for the public, and for periodically being my publishing anxiety-related therapist. The final edits of this book were conducted during my fellowship at the M.S. Merian – R. Tagore International Centre of Advanced Studies: 'Metamorphoses of the Political: Comparative Perspectives on the Long Twentieth Century' (ICAS: MP), an Indo–German research cooperation funded by the German Federal Ministry of Education and Research (BMBF). I am grateful for the support of my colleagues and the entire ICAS: MP family. Thanks to Karthik Venkatesh, my editor at Penguin Random House India, for his edits, reassurances and for bringing this book out into the world. I am also deeply grateful to Tripti Negi, whose diligence is the sole reason why this book managed to have photographs.

Trishna Agarwala reminded me to recognize the multiple challenges I took on when I chose to undertake this project in the way I did and be less harsh to myself. I am thankful to my in-laws, Gita and Ramesh Bamezai, for their constant support and encouragement. To Tata, Sunita Didi and Charan Singh, for providing support in so many ways that should never go unrecognized. To Amira, for the thoughtful Lajpat Rai-related gift she gave me recently. To Miran, for bringing joy and making me smile as I revised the manuscript. I am grateful to my extended family and friends, for being a source of stability and well-being more generally.

Finally, thank you to my husband, Shiva Bamezai, for patiently listening to my endless ramblings about Lajpat Rai even after a hard day at the lab, for knowing how to deal with a person who could be neurotically obsessive about the bottlenecks and lows of research, and for always believing in me much more than I believe in myself. Thank you for always encouraging my dream to write history for the public. To my father, Rajeev Bhargava, whom I cannot adequately thank in words, for helping me detangle several knots in my brain, including emotional ones that often overwhelmed me during my doctorate and made me doubt whether I was worthy of this project. Thank you for trying to teach me about perseverance through your cricket analogies. I feel privileged to have learnt from him about the importance of making conceptual distinctions, the need to be as imaginative as rigorous, to balance theory and empiricism, rationality with feeling, and to resist the urge to conform to a group or label, even one that you broadly see yourself as belonging to. To my mother and father collectively, for teaching me early on to care about humanity, ethics, morality, citizenship and the common good. This book on Hindu and Indian nationalism would not exist without your early education. To my mother, Tani Bhargava, specifically, for standing as an example of selfless generosity and sincerity. And to my sister, Aranyani, for a lifetime of unconditional support, love and care.

Endnotes

Introduction

1 Rakeysh Omprakash Mehra, *Rang De Basanti*, 2006.; Rajkumar Santoshi, *The Legend of Bhagat Singh*, 2002; Guddu Dhanoa, *23rd March 1931: Shaheed*, 2002; Also see S. Ram Sharma, *Shaheed*, 1965, https://www.youtube.com/watch?v=9k6-3XlAU7s&ab_channel=FILMISONGfilmoraSUBSCRIBNOW.

2 For a quick survey, search #LalaLajpatRai on Twitter.

3 The Press Trust of India, 'Kiran Bedi Puts BJP Scarf around Lala Lajpat Rai's Statue; Spare the Freedom Fighter, Says Kejriwal', *The Indian Express (Online)*, 21 January 2015, http://indianexpress.com/article/cities/delhi/kiran-bedi-puts-bjp-scarf-around-lala-lajpat-rais-statue-spare-the-freedom-fighter-says-arvind-kejriwal/.

4 'Dr Mahesh Sharma Inaugurates an Exhibition on Lala Lajpat Rai at a Function to Commemorate His 150th Birth Anniversary', *Press Information Bureau, Government of India, Ministry of Culture*, 13 January 2016, https://pib.gov.in/newsite/PrintRelease.aspx?relid=134433.

5 Ajay Mittal, 'Homage: 150th Birth Anniversary on January 28', *The Organiser*, 31 January 2016, http://organiser.org//

487

Encyc/2016/1/25/Homage---150th-Birth-Anniversary-on-
January-28.aspx.

6 'Tweet by The Aryavarth Express', 17 May 2022, https://twitter.
com/AryavarthThe/status/1526368199511396352.

7 'When Lala Lajpat Rai Bombed Mohandas Gandhi's Politics
of Ahimsa', *The Dharma Dispatch*, n.d., https://www.
dharmadispatch.in/history/when-lala-lajpat-rai-bombed-
mohandas-gandhis-politics-of-ahimsa.

8 Gyanendra Pandey, 'Hindus and Others: The Militant Hindu
Construction', *Economic and Political Weekly* 26, no. 52
(1991): 2997–3009; Christophe Jaffrelot, *The Hindu Nationalist
Movement and Indian Politics: 1925 to the 1990s* (New Delhi:
Penguin Books, 1999).

9 Jaffrelot, *Hindu Nationalist Movement*, 11, 18.

10 Christophe Jaffrelot, 'Genesis and Development of Hindu
Nationalism in the Punjab: From the Arya Samaj to the Hindu
Sabha (1875–1910)', in *Religion, Caste, and Politics in India*
(London: Hurst, 2011), 113.

11 Chetan Bhatt, *Hindu Nationalism: Origins, Ideologies and
Modern Myths* (Oxford: Berg, 2001), 2–4, 42–44, 48–55, 59.

12 C.S. Adcock's sophisticated study of the relationship between the
Arya Samaj, with which Lajpat Rai was associated, and Hindu
nationalism problematizes the Samaj's links with Hindutva
nationalism. But while she complicates the links between the
Samaj's 'Gurukul' faction and Hindutva, she maintains them
between the Samaj's 'College' faction, the Hindu Mahasabha
and Hindutva. While Lajpat Rai is not the focus of Adcock's
research, he appears as articulating the notion of a 'Hindu nation'
in the early twentieth century and as a member of the College
faction. Due to her association of College faction Arya Samajists
and the Hindu Mahasabha with Hindutva, we are left with the
impression that Lajpat Rai too very likely subscribed to Hindutva
nationalism. See *The Limits of Tolerance: Indian Secularism and
the Politics of Religious Freedom* (New York: Oxford University
Press, 2013), 92–99, 129–32, 149–55. Another scholar, William

Gould, who has researched Hindu nationalism in the United Provinces (now, Uttar Pradesh) in the 1930s and 1940s, very briefly mentions Lajpat Rai as embodying an earlier, nascent 'stage' of Hindu nationalism when it was not 'exclusivist' (i.e., not exclusionary towards non-Hindus). While Gould alludes to a distinction between Lajpat Rai's nationalism and Hindutva, this remains unanalysed and obscured by its teleological linkage to Hindutva—in short, by the assumption that Rai articulated an earlier 'stage' of the Hindu nationalist ideology that flowered more fully in the 1920s into Hindutva nationalism. See *Hindu Nationalism and the Language of Politics in Late Colonial India* (Cambridge: Cambridge University Press, 2004), 38–39. This is also how Lajpat Rai appears in older, general histories of colonial-era India. See Sumit Sarkar, *Modern India: 1886–1947* (Delhi: Macmillian, 1983), 127, 233.

13 Lala Lajpat Rai, *The Collected Works of Lala Lajpat Rai*, ed. B.R. Nanda (New Delhi: Manohar) [hereafter *CWLLR*]. The fifteen volumes were published between 2003 and 2010.

14 Jaffrelot, *Hindu Nationalist Movement*, 19.

15 Adcock, *Limits of Tolerance*, 151.

16 Jaffrelot, 'Genesis and Development', 106–07, 108–09.

17 Jaffrelot, 78–86.

18 Jaffrelot, 88–89.

19 Deriving from the Greek word 'telos', meaning purpose or goal, a teleology refers to the understanding of phenomena in terms of a supposed purpose they are assumed to serve, rather than in their own right. For instance, Lajpat Rai's nationalism is understood by reference to its supposed purpose of creating conditions for Savarkarite Hindutva, rather than in its own right and on its own terms.

20 Bhatt, *Origins*, 61.

21 Bhatt, 50–55.

22 Bhatt, 2.

23 Bhatt, 2.

24 Bhatt, 70.

25 Gould, *Language of Politics*, 38–39.
26 Bipan Chandra, *Modern India* (New Delhi: National Council of Educational Research and Training, 1971), 252–53; *India's Struggle for Independence* (New Delhi: Penguin, 2000), 248, 402, 441; Gyanendra Pandey, *The Construction of Communalism in Colonial North India* (New Delhi: Oxford University Press, 2006), 204–12.
27 Pandey, *Construction of Communalism*, 204–12.
28 John Zavos, *The Emergence of Hindu Nationalism in India* (Oxford: Oxford University Press, 2000), 9.
29 Neeti Nair, *Changing Homelands: Hindu Politics and the Partition of India* (Cambridge, MA: Harvard University Press, 2011), 16–19; chap. 2.
30 I use 'Hindu' and 'Muslim' throughout this book without taking these as 'given' categories, and with awareness that these blanket terms can problematically elide caste, sectarian, linguistic, regional, class and other distinctions. I use such terms because of the lack of a proper academic language which can capture these complex distinctions. I also do so because my primary task is to capture the political thought of a man who often *did* think of politics in predominantly Hindu–Muslim terms, however reductive this was in its sociological assumptions. Similarly, I use terms such as 'Hinduism', 'Islam', 'Hindu culture', 'Muslim culture', 'religion' and 'community' while unveiling Lajpat Rai's thought, remaining aware of the socially constructed, evolving and contested nature of these concepts.
31 Several elements were important for Savarkar's Hindutva nationalism. One was birth in and love for the Indian fatherland. A second was possessing 'Hindu blood'. But these were insufficient to belong to the Hindu nation. The third element of Hindutva was key: partaking in and revering 'Hindu culture'. For Savarkar, because the majority of Muslims and Christians had disowned 'Hindu culture', they could not be included in the Hindu nation. It was only after 'Hindu culture' had first excluded the majority of Muslims and Christians from Hindu national belonging that

Savarkarite Hindutva turned to his final criterion: belonging to religions that had the territory of India as their birthplace and considered India their holy land. This final criterion then decisively excluded from Hindu nationhood even that supposed minority of Muslims and Christians which still partook in Hindu culture, defined as the essence of nationhood in India. Vinayak Damodar Savarkar, *Hindutva: Who Is a Hindu?* (Bombay: Veer Savarkar Prakashan, 1969), 83–92, 99–102, 110–15.

32 Savarkar, *Hindutva*, 84, 115, 130; Pandey, 'Hindus and Others', 3000; Bhatt, *Origins*, 98; Janaki Bakhle, 'Country First? Vinayak Damodar Savarkar (1883–1966) and the Writing of Essentials of Hindutva', *Public Culture* 22, no. 1 (2010): 178, 180.

33 I will elaborate this argument, with relevant sources, in the last quarter of the book.

34 I do not mean to draw a necessary oppositional binary between Congress's secular Indian nationalism and Hindu communalism/ nationalism. I am cognizant of research, such as that by William Gould, which points to Hindu nationalist idioms emanating from within the Congress (See Gould, *Language of Politics*.).

35 Gould, chaps 1, 8. Zavos, *Emergence of Hindu Nationalism*, 4, 9, 218–19.

36 Ayesha Jalal, 'Exploding Communalism: The Politics of Muslim Identity in South Asia', in *Nationalism, Democracy and Development: State and Politics in India*, ed. Sugata Bose and Ayesha Jalal (Delhi: Oxford University Press, 1999), 78, 89, 100, 102; Shabnum Tejani, *Indian Secularism: A Social and Intellectual History, 1890–1950* (Bloomington: Indiana University Press, 2008), 236, 255–56; Adcock, *Limits of Tolerance*. Jalal was among the first to suggest complicity between secular Indian nationalism and Hindu majoritarian communalism. Building on Jalal's research, Shubnum Tejani and C.S. Adcock have argued that secular Indian nationalism and Indian secularism rest on the manufacturing of a Hindu political majority.

37 Gould, *Language of Politics*, chaps 1, 8. Unearthing a *particular* form of Hindu nationalism originating from within the

Congress at local levels (which he clarifies was distinct from the harder, exclusivist Hindu nationalism of the Sangh Parivar), Gould rightly questions assumptions of mutual exclusivity between Congress's secular nationalism and Hindu nationalism. However, this revelation has obscured a simple fact Gould himself acknowledges in scattered statements: that the Congress continued to simultaneously and sincerely espouse secular Indian nationalism at provincial and all-India levels. While acknowledging overlaps, slippage and conflation in some cases, an analytical distinction can and should be retained between Hindutva/Hindu nationalism and Indian nationalism.

38 This view is most starkly represented by Perry Anderson, *The Indian Ideology* (Verso Books, 2013); Also see Jalal, 'Exploding Communalism: The Politics of Muslim Identity in South Asia'. This is also how Tejani's argument about secular Indian nationalism and Indian secularism has been read. See Nandini Chatterjee, *The Making of Indian Secularism: Empire, Law and Christianity, 1830–1960*, Cambridge Imperial and Post-Colonial Studies Series (Basingstoke, Hampshire; New York: Palgrave Macmillan, 2011), 4–5.

39 See Chapters 1 and 3 in this book.

40 See Chapter 6 in this book.

41 See Chapters 3, 6 and 9 in this book.

42 I use 'theology' broadly, to refer simply to a network or set of religious beliefs. 'Secular' is used here simply to mean broadly non-religious, and not as a derivative of 'secular*ism*' (i.e., an ideological project seeking to separate religion and politics for the sake of political–moral values like freedom, non-domination, equal citizenship, peace or respect for diversity). Throughout the book, this is how I use the term 'secular' when I use it alongside 'culture' or contrast it with theology. Moreover, by using the term 'secular Hindu culture', I do not mean to suggest any clear-cut empirical distinction between 'religion' and 'culture', and between Hinduism and Hindu culture. Still, I use it as a heuristic shorthand for phenomena which are predominantly decoupled

from belief and observance and seen as largely non-religious, secular and cultural. For instance, for many, Christmas or Diwali are not faith-related but cultural celebrations.

43 See Chapter 10 in this book.

44 By this I mean 'religion' when conceived as de-linked from belief and observance, and only as a marker of community identity. Avi Astor and Damon Mayrl, 'Culturalized Religion: A Synthetic Review and Agenda for Research', *Journal for the Scientific Study of Religion* 59, no. 2 (2020): 2, 5.

45 See Chapters 14 and 16 in this book.

46 Throughout this book, when I use the term 'secular' alongside the concepts of the nation, nationalism, the state (e.g., 'secular Indian nation', 'secular Indian nationalism', 'secular state'), I use it as a derivative of secular*ism* (and not to mean simply non-religious). For more clarity, see n. 42.

47 This theme is most stark in Chapter 2, but also flickers in Chapters 8–9 and 17–20 of this book.

48 The simple act of granting each person a vote in elections does not amount to democracy in its full, substantive sense. Respect for liberty/freedom (to speak, assemble and organize), equality, disagreement, plurality and political uncertainty are central to it. Conflict and disagreement (even to the point of rudeness) are part of democracy. What violates it is treating some citizens as if they are second-class citizens or do not really belong to the 'the demos' (the people). See Jan-Werner Müller, *Democracy Rules* (London: Allen Lane, 2021).

49 See Chapter 6.

50 See Chapter 9.

51 See Chapter 18.

52 See Chapters 1 and 3.

53 See Chapter 4.

54 A historian of ideas and thought.

55 Lecture by Quentin Skinner, 'Belief, Truth and Interpretation', YouTube, (recorded 18 November 2014, uploaded 1 December

2014), https://www.youtube.com/watch?v=VJYsTJt8vxg (21 January 2017)

56 Quentin Skinner, *Visions of Politics*, vol. 1 (Cambridge: Cambridge University Press, 2002), 2–4.

57 Skinner, 1:2–4, 56, 70–71.

58 By 'radical contextuality', I mean a trait of political thinking where it is strongly influenced by its contexts, surroundings and settings.

59 That the absence of self-conscious theorizing requires methods different from Skinner's methodology has also been briefly noted by the respected scholar of Indian political thought, Sudipta Kaviraj. See his 'Ideas of Freedom in Modern India', in *The Idea of Freedom in Asia and Africa*, ed. Robert H. Taylor, *The Making of Modern Freedom* (Stanford, Calif: Stanford University Press, 2002), 99.

60 I adopt a chronological narrative or storytelling style against trends in the discipline in the knowledge that we humans yearn for and resonate with stories, and that stories can be a powerful vehicle to convey ideas, knowledge and understanding. For more on the importance of crafting our understanding into a narrative, see Matthew d'Ancona, *Post-Truth: The New War on Truth and How to Fight Back* (London: Ebury Press, 2017), chap. 5.

Chapter 1

1 Barbara Daly Metcalf and Thomas R. Metcalf, *A Concise History of Modern India* (Cambridge [England]; New York: Cambridge University Press, 2012), 68–90.

2 Persian had become the most widely used language of governance across South Asia by the fourteenth century. It was also a prestigious literary language and the main language for inter-regional diplomacy along the Silk Road between Anatolia and East China. Richard Eaton, *India in the Persianate Age: 1000–1765*, 2019, 36, 41. Unlike Arabic, Persian was not tied

to scriptural Islam, and was viewed in India as an everyday language of correspondence, literary expression and social mobility (Francesca Orsini and Samira Sheikh as cited in Eaton, 705.). The language would experience a steep drop in patronage after the formal end of the Mughal Empire in 1858, and with the rise of Indian nationalism. Eaton, 726.

3 Lala Lajpat Rai, *Autobiographical Writings*, ed. V.C. Joshi (Delhi: University Publishers, 1965), 12–13.

4 Lajpat Rai, 13.

5 Lajpat Rai, 13.

6 Christophe Jaffrelot, 'Genesis and Development of Hindu Nationalism in the Punjab: From the Arya Samaj to the Hindu Sabha (1875–1910)', in *Religion, Caste, and Politics in India* (London: Hurst, 2011), 81.

7 Gulab Devi's family worshipped the Guru Granth Sahib, and by Lajpat Rai's own account 'hated' Muslims and Islam. Lajpat Rai, *Autobiographical Writings*, 14.

8 Lajpat Rai, 15; Kenneth Jones, *Arya Dharm: Hindu Consciousness in Nineteenth Century Punjab* (Delhi: Manohar, 1976), 53.

9 As historian of medieval India Richard Eaton argues, the Persianate world was a cultural zone primarily grounded not in religion but in 'a prestige language and culture that conferred elite status on its users'. It embraced within itself peoples of varied ethnic and religious backgrounds. Eaton, *India in the Persianate Age*, 33.

10 Jones, *Arya Dharm*, 1–2.

11 Jones, *Arya Dharm*, 50–51.

12 The 1881 census would reveal that Hindus constituted 40.7 per cent of the population of Punjab, Muslims 51.3 per cent, and Sikhs 7.5 per cent. Jaffrelot, 'Genesis and Development', 78.

13 Jaffrelot, 98–99.

14 Jaffrelot, 98.

15 Sumit Sarkar, *Modern Times: 1880s–1950* (Ranikhet: Permanent Black, 2014), 38.

16 Jones, *Arya Dharm*, 56, 60.

17 Feroz Chand, *Lajpat Rai: Life and Work* (New Delhi: Publications Division, Ministry of Information and Broadcasting, Government of India, 1978), 8–9, 11.

18 This was the title Lajpat Rai later gave to the chapter in his autobiography that focused on his early education, which was regularly interrupted by malaria, an enlarged spleen, an abscess and fever. Lajpat Rai, *Autobiographical Writings*, 17–18.

19 Kenneth Jones, *Arya Dharm: Hindu Consciousness in Nineteenth Century Punjab* (Delhi: Manohar, 1976), 30–32.

20 Lajpat Rai, 26; Jones, *Arya Dharm*, 44.

21 Lajpat Rai, *Autobiographical Writings*, 32.

22 Lajpat Rai, 36.

23 Lajpat Rai, 33; Jones, *Arya Dharm*, 67–72, 158.

24 Lajpat Rai, *Autobiographical Writings*, 35–40; Chand, *Lajpat Rai*, 45.

25 David Lorenzen, 'Who Invented Hinduism?', *Comparative Studies in Society and History* 41, no. 04 (1999): 631, 651–52; Andrew J. Nicholson, *Unifying Hinduism: Philosophy and Identity in Indian Intellectual History* (New York: Columbia University Press, 2010), 199–200; Rajeev Bhargava, 'Secularism: A Search for Conceptual Spaces', in *Brill's Encyclopedia of Hinduism*, ed. Knut A. Jacobsen et al., vol. 6 (Leiden; Boston: Brill, 2009), 4. The use of the term 'Hindu' to refer to a group united by certain cultural practices such as cremating the dead and veneration of the cow, arose in the fifteenth–sixteenth century, although it was not commonly used at the time. See Bhargava, 4. A growing body of scholarship now rejects the argument that Hinduism was a modern colonial invention and pushes for a serious exploration of pre-colonial iterations of a common Hindu religious identity, however fuzzy or different from its modern form. See, for example, Brian K. Pennington, *Was Hinduism Invented? Britons, Indians, and Colonial Construction of Religion* (Oxford; New York: Oxford University Press, 2005), chaps 1, 6. These scholars of Hinduism assert that Hinduism as we know it today, like all other religions, is the culmination of continuous

historical processes which cannot just be reduced to a British colonial intervention. Yet, they equally insist that Hinduism, again like other religions, cannot be seen as a pristine growth of ideas and principles; it has been shaped by a messy history of numerous external influences. Pennington, 6–7.

26 The term 'religion' came to India with British colonialism and was subsequently deployed by the Indian intelligentsia. In this encounter, not only did Hindu beliefs and practices transform as they were reinterpreted in light of this novel Western category, but the term itself evolved beyond its narrow, Christian range of meaning. Pennington, *Was Hinduism Invented?*, 176–77; Will Sweetman, 'Unity and Plurality: Hinduism and the Religions of India in Early European Scholarship', *Religion* 31, no. 3 (2001): 218.

27 Gauri Vishwanathan, 'Colonialism and the Construction of Hinduism', in *The Blackwell Companion to Hinduism*, ed. Gavin Flood (Oxford: Blackwell, 2008), 29; John Zavos, *The Emergence of Hindu Nationalism in India* (Oxford: Oxford University Press, 2000), 40–41; Dermot Killingley, 'Modernity, Reform, and Revival', in *The Blackwell Companion to Hinduism*, ed. Gavin Flood (Malden, MA: Blackwell, 2003), 509–11. As will be clear from the rest of the chapter, I use the term 'Hinduism' recognizing that it does not refer to a homogenous whole with given, fixed and timeless characteristics (what among researchers is called 'essentialism', and is considered problematic and unscientific). Instead, 'Hinduism' was, and is, a dynamic, internally differentiated and contested entity, with multiple meanings and forms. The same applies for my use of categories such as 'Hindu', 'Punjabi Hindu', 'Christianity'/'Christian', 'British', 'the West', 'Islam'/'Muslim' and so on.

28 Sarkar, *Modern Times*, 33.; C.S. Adcock, *The Limits of Tolerance: Indian Secularism and the Politics of Religious Freedom* (New York: Oxford University Press, 2013), 25–26.

29 Sarkar, *Modern Times*, 27–28.

30 Sarkar, 28.

31 Sarkar, 32–34.

32 Thomas Metcalf, *Ideologies of the Raj* (Cambridge: Cambridge University Press, 1994), 137.

33 Kenneth Jones, 'Religious Identity and the Indian Census', in *The Census in British India: New Perspectives*, ed. N.G. Barrier, 1981, 74–84.

34 Vishwanathan, 'Construction of Hinduism', 28; Zavos, *Emergence of Hindu Nationalism*, 43.

35 Vishwanathan, 'Construction of Hinduism', 25. While the British had built 'a rich descriptive tradition' for Islam since medieval times, British understanding of Hinduism really began only in the eighteenth century. Thomas Metcalf, *Ideologies of the Raj* (Cambridge: Cambridge University Press, 1994), 134.

36 Zavos, *Emergence of Hindu Nationalism*, 32; Vishwanathan, 'Construction of Hinduism', 25.

37 For such 'Indo-mania' among British orientalists from the mid-eighteenth century to the early nineteenth century, see Thomas R. Trautmann, *Aryans and British India* (New Delhi: Vistaar, 2006), chap. 3. As Trautmann argues, early British enthusiasm was above all an enthusiasm for Hinduism. It manifested in a keen interest in Sanskrit, saw ancient Hindu scriptures as completing Biblical revelation, and considered India's ancient civilization a living repository of ancient wisdom. In contrast, this British Indo-mania was hostile to Islam, viewed Muslims as foreigners to India, and attributed most of India's evils to Muslim conquest and rule. Early orientalists like William Jones, Europe's foremost Orientalist scholar in the eighteenth century, also posited the theory about the kinship between Sanskrit and European languages, and between Europeans and Hindus.

38 Idolatry and the worship of the 'one and the many' had puzzled European travellers to India even in the sixteenth century. Conceiving of monotheism as a precious gift bestowed by God to Adam, they had either sought to discover the monotheism they believed was concealed behind pagan worship or declared such religiosity as the worship of false gods. See Partha Mitter,

'Rammohun Roy and the New Language of Monotheism', *History and Anthropology* 3, no. 1 (1987): 181–85. Interestingly, attacks on Hindu idolatry reflected the rampant anti-Catholic fervour of Protestant missionaries and informed even atheist British administrators. Pennington, *Was Hinduism Invented?*, 19, 65–69; J. Barton Scott, *Spiritual Despots: Modern Hinduism and the Genealogies of Self-Rule* (Chicago; London: The University of Chicago Press, 2016), 17, 36–38.

39 Amiya P. Sen, ed., *Social and Religious Reform: The Hindus of British India* (Delhi; Oxford: Oxford University Press, 2003), 3, 47–48; Vishwanathan, 'Construction of Hinduism', 27; Pennington, *Was Hinduism Invented?*, 3.

40 Gauri Vishwanathan, 'Colonialism and the Construction of Hinduism', in Gavin Flood (ed.), *The Blackwell Companion to Hinduism* (Oxford: Blackwell Publishing, 2008).

41 Pennington, *Was Hinduism Invented?*, 4.

42 For the argument regarding what has been called the 'Semiticisation' of Hinduism, see Romila Thapar, 'Imagined Religious Communities? Ancient History and the Modern Search for a Hindu Identity', *Modern Asian Studies* 23, no. 2 (1989): 218; 'Syndicated Hinduism', in *Hinduism Reconsidered*, ed. Gunther-Dietz Sontheimer and Hermann Kulke (New Delhi: Manohar, 1997), 66; Robert Frykenberg, 'The Emergence of Modern "Hinduism" as a Concept and as an Institution: A Reappraisal with Special Reference to South India', in *Hinduism Reconsidered*, ed. Hermann Kulke and Gunther-Dietz Sontheimer, 1989, 82–107. For a lucid summary and critique, see C.S. Adcock, *The Limits of Tolerance: Indian Secularism and the Politics of Religious Freedom* (New York: Oxford University Press, 2013), 11.

43 Scott, *Spiritual Despots*, 152–55; Pennington, *Was Hinduism Invented?*, 4. It was not just Hinduism that was transformed as a result of the colonial encounter with Britain. While colonialism involved a massive asymmetry of power, and rested on violence and dehumanizing subordination, it did not constitute a one-

way flow of influence. It established an entire milieu, a complex web of encounters, interactions and relationships, which also transformed Britain itself in multiple ways. Pennington, 10, 12–13, 17.

44 Zavos, *Emergence of Hindu Nationalism*, 44–45.

45 While some Hindus deployed the European language of 'religion' to emphasize the infallible truth of their doctrines, others used alternative European discourses of 'religion' to insist on the truth of all religions. As religious studies scholar C.S. Adcock argues, one must not draw a false dichotomy between exclusivist/intolerant Semitic religion vs inclusive/universalist indigenous religion. Yet, as Adcock admits, formulations of 'religion' based on Christian theological notions insisted on the exclusive truth of their God and text, and often charged alternative European discourses of religion insisting on the universal truth underlying all religions, with blasphemy or infidelity. Adcock, *Limits of Tolerance*, 67–68, 72–79.

46 Philosophic texts composed between 500 and 100 BCE. Wendy Doniger, *On Hinduism*, 2016, 12.

47 Encyclopaedic Sanskrit (and later vernacular) texts dating between 250 CE and 1700 CE that expound the myths, rituals and philosophies of sectarian Hinduism, especially of the Shaivite and Vaishnavite traditions. Doniger, xix–xx, 14.

48 For details of this culture of controversy, see Kenneth Jones, *Socio-Religious Reform Movements in British India* (Cambridge and New York: Cambridge University Press, 1989), vol. 1.

49 To recognize this internal diversity, evident in Hinduism even today, is not to highlight a weakness but to acknowledge a sociological fact that characterizes all religions. For similar internal debate and contestation within Islam, see Shahab Ahmed, *What Is Islam? The Importance of Being Islamic* (Princeton; Oxford: Princeton University Press, 2016).

50 Jaffrelot, 'Genesis and Development', 75.

51 Roy's dislike of Brahmins reflected the influence upon him of European Enlightenment anticlerical thought. For instance, the

On his tour of the US in 1915, Lajpat Rai visited the Tuskegee Institute (founded in 1881 to provide higher education to African–Americans); Rai also met its founder and first principal, the African–American educator Booker T. Washington (*front row, centre*)

A rare photograph of Lala Lajpat Rai

Lajpat Rai, undated photo

Gandhi (1869–1948) in 1920, the year he launched the Khilafat/ non-cooperation movement; here, he is sitting next to Rabindranath Tagore (1861–1941)

Shaukat Ali (1873–1938) in 1932, elder of the Ali brothers with whom Lajpat Rai toured parts of India during the Khilafat/non-cooperation movement

Seen here in his later years, A.K. Azad (1888–1958) rose to political prominence as a young man during the Khilafat agitation, when he called on Muslims to fight British rule, and cooperate with Hindus and the Congress; Azad soon became part of Gandhi's inner circle, which included Patel and Nehru

Lajpat Rai in a Gandhi-style topi, undated photo

Photographed here with Gandhi in 1930, Sarojini Naidu (1879–1949) was Congress president in 1925; by this time, Lajpat Rai was demonstrating a deep discomfort with the politics of Gandhi and the Congress, and had joined the Hindu Mahasabha

Wikipedia

A young Mohammad Ali Jinnah (1876–1948) in 1910; in the 1920s, Lajpat Rai opposed Jinnah's politics through the Hindu Mahasabha but also cooperated with him in the Central Legislative Assembly

NMML

Lajpat Rai

Madan Mohan Malaviya (seated next to Gandhi), with whom Lajpat Rai formed the Independent Congress Party in 1926; this photograph is from the Round Table Conference in London in 1931

Lajpat Rai with Jawaharlal and Kamala Nehru, and nine-year-old Indira, in Switzerland in 1926

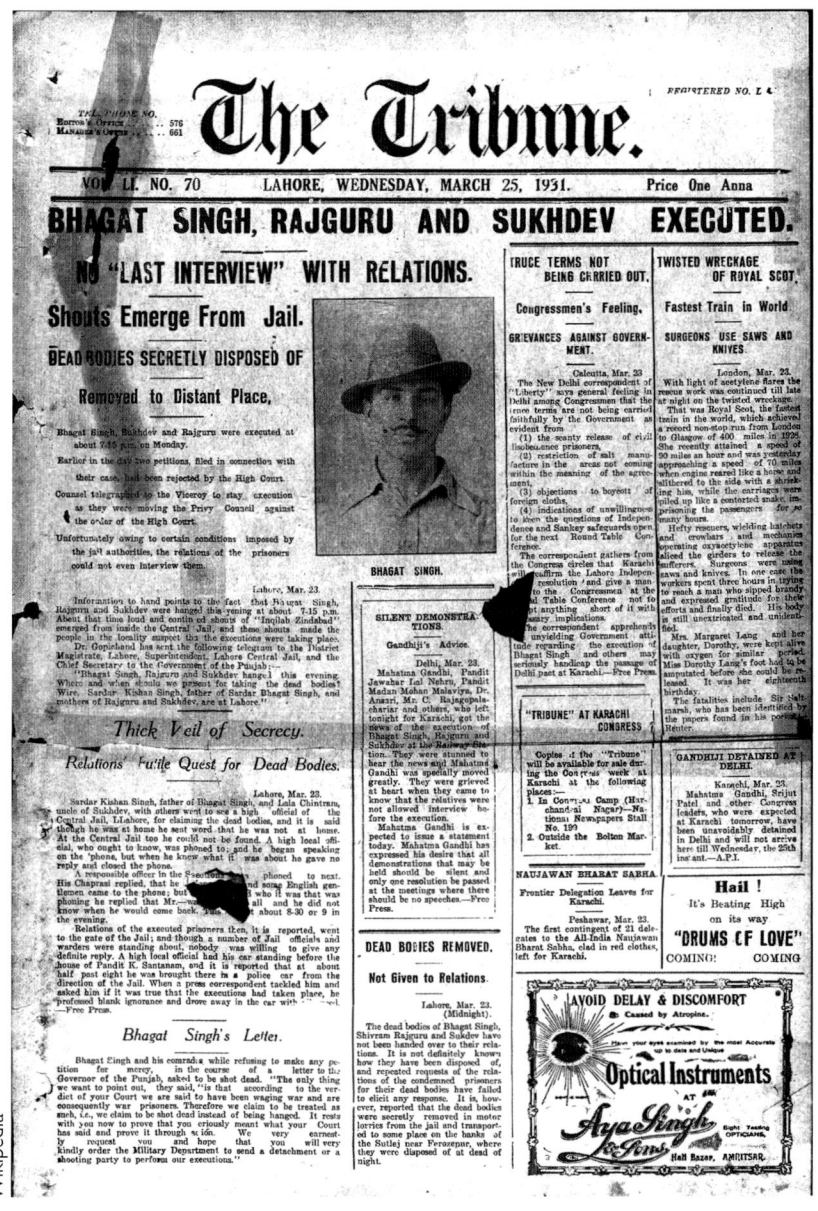

On 17 December 1928, Bhagat Singh and Rajguru gunned down J.P. Saunders to avenge Lajpat Rai's death, an act for which they were hanged; this front page of the *Tribune*, from 25 March 1931, reports the hanging of Bhagat Singh (1907–1931), Rajguru (1908–1931) and Sukhdev (1907–1931)

Lala Lajpat Rai in his quintessential turban, as he is most
often depicted and remembered

French Enlightenment philosopher Voltaire had similarly held organized priesthood responsible for the decline of the innate rational monotheism of the golden age of human history. Similar anticlerical beliefs also marked the thought of eighteenth-century European Orientalist scholars of India. Mitter, 'Rammohun Roy', 186–88, 193.

52 For more on Rammohun Roy, see Andrew Sartori, *Bengal in Global Concept History: Culturalism in the Age of Capital* (Chicago: University of Chicago Press, 2008), 79–80; Killingley, 'Modernity, Reform, and Revival', 515–16; Mitter, 'Rammohun Roy'.

53 Sen, *Social and Religious Reform*, 32.

54 Killingley, 'Modernity, Reform, and Revival', 517–18; Scott, *Spiritual Despots*, 53. Roy died in 1833.

55 Killingley, 'Modernity, Reform, and Revival', 517.

56 Jones, *Arya Dharm*, 16–17.

57 These earliest Sanskrit texts were composed between 1500–900 BCE.

58 Lala Lajpat Rai, 'Swami Dayanand, 1898', in *CWLLR*, vol. 1, 2003, 375, 377; Lala Lajpat Rai, 'The Arya Samaj: An Account of Its Origin, Doctrines, and Activities, with a Biographical Sketch of the Founder, 1915', in *CWLLR*, vol. 5, 2004, 221.

59 Lajpat Rai, 'Swami Dayanand', 377–78.

60 A large body of texts, composed between about 650–1800 CE, which proposed transgressive ritual actions, violating all the taboos of conventional Hinduism, such as drinking wine and menstrual blood, eating meat and engaging in sexual activity with forbidden women.

61 Adcock, *Limits of Tolerance*, 43–44.

62 Lajpat Rai, 'Swami Dayanand', 409.

63 Lajpat Rai, 378, 383, 410.

64 Lajpat Rai, 409.

65 Adcock, *Limits of Tolerance*, 10–11. For Ramakrishna, see Sumit Sarkar, 'Kaliyuga, Chakri and Bhakti: Ramakrishna and His Times', *Economic and Political Weekly*, 1992, 1543–66.

66 Kenneth Jones, *Arya Dharm: Hindu Consciousness in Nineteenth Century Punjab* (Delhi: Manohar, 1976), 31.
67 Jones, *Arya Dharm, 32, 95*
68 Jones, *Arya Dharm*, 95–96.
69 Lajpat Rai, 'Swami Dayanand', 378.
70 Michael Witzel, 'Vedas and Upanisads', in *The Blackwell Companion to Hinduism*, ed. Gavin Flood (Malden, MA: Blackwell, 2003), 68–101; Killingley, 'Modernity, Reform, and Revival', 517.
71 Lajpat Rai, 'Swami Dayanand', 378–79.
72 Lajpat Rai, 380.
73 Jones, *Socio-Religious Reform Movements*, 107.
74 Vasudha Dalmia, 'The Only Real Religion of the Hindus: Vaisnava Self-Representation in the Late Nineteenth Century', in *Representing Hinduism: The Construction of Religious Traditions and National Identity*, ed. Vasudha Dalmia and Heinrich von Stietencron (New Delhi; London: SAGE, 1995), 180–90.
75 Lajpat Rai, 'Swami Dayanand', 412–13, 415.
76 Lajpat Rai, 378–79.
77 Jones, *Arya Dharm*, 36.
78 Lajpat Rai, 'Arya Samaj', 227.
79 Witzel, 'Vedas and Upanisads'.
80 Scott, *Spiritual Despots*, 155–57. The term *lila*, closely associated with Krishna devotion and Vaishnava thought, denotes God's mischievous play in the world of creation, through miracles or the assumption of avatars. The Arya Samajist equation of lila with craftiness and deceit signalled its rejection of this rich devotional tradition. Scott, 157–58.
81 In rejecting bhakti as a form of worship, the Arya Samaj followed in the footsteps of Rammohun Roy who had seen mystical bhakti movements around Shiva and Visnu as a form of corrupted Hinduism. Mitter, 'Rammohun Roy', 179–80.
82 Jones, *Arya Dharm*, 109.
83 For more on Christian missionary activity in the Punjab, see Jaffrelot, 'Genesis and Development', 80. Christian missionaries

were never a homogenous bloc. In some parts of India, they followed a more tolerant, syncretic approach which sought to build bridges between Christianity and Brahminical ideas, customs and norms. Moreover, many colonial officials often feared proselytization (religious conversion) as unnecessary provocation, and after the 1857 rebellion recommended distance between the state and missionaries. For the complex, shifting relations between the colonial state and missionaries, see Sarkar, *Modern Times*, 45–53; Robert Frykenberg, *Christianity in India: From Beginnings to the Present* (Oxford; New York: Oxford University Press, 2008). Mark Juergensmeyer has also pointed out that colonial administrators often viewed Christian missionaries as threatening the new secular ideology that they wished to present as the characteristic of the West. 'Rethinking the Secular and Religious Aspects of Violence', in *Rethinking Secularism*, ed. Craig J. Calhoun, Mark Juergensmeyer, and Jonathan Van Antwerpen (Oxford, NY: Oxford University Press, 2011), 189.

84 Jones, *Arya Dharm*, 25, 71.

85 Jaffrelot, 'Genesis and Development', 80; Jones, *Arya Dharm*, 41. For more on Brahmo eclecticism and syncretism, see Scott, *Spiritual Despots*, 87. Rather than turning to Christianity, Keshub Chandra Sen repudiated the particular dogma of Christianity to align himself with the ethical content of its 'spirit' of ascetic self-sacrifice, and even claimed Christ as an Asiatic yogi. He even demanded the renunciation of the name of Christianity in order to realize its spiritual potential. At the same time, Sen required that Hinduism too discard its name to acquire this 'spirit', which he termed the 'New Dispensation' (the true religion). Such projects of syncretism, as Scott points out, ran into problems since syncretism sometimes reifies and sharpens the very boundaries (between different 'religions') that it seeks to erase or transgress. Scott, 87, 106–9.

86 Jones, *Arya Dharm*, 41–42.

87 In doing so, Roy abandoned the relativist conception of divinity embodied in the Upanishadic notion of the Supreme Being, or Brahman, which allowed both the merger of the soul or Atman with it as well as the worship of other gods. This was replaced by a more rigid monotheism drawn from Abrahamic traditions, which conceived God as the ultimate other. Mitter, 'Rammohun Roy', 181–83, 197.

88 Jaffrelot, 'Genesis and Development', 76; Mitter, 'Rammohun Roy', 195. Roy had sparred with Christian missionaries and, while interested in Christianity, had also been careful not to identify too closely with it lest he be labelled a Christian convert. Scott, *Spiritual Despots*, 53, 86.

89 Killingley, 'Modernity, Reform, and Revival', 517.

90 Adcock, *Limits of Tolerance*, 76; Killingley, 'Modernity, Reform, and Revival', 515.

91 As a whole, the Arya Samaj's formulation of Hinduism, as Scott eloquently puts it, was neither wholly derivative nor pristinely Hindu. Having a clear affinity for Protestant Christianity, it was also imbued with Hindu tradition. Scott, *Spiritual Despots*, 155–56.

Chapter 2

1 Much of the content of this chapter has been previously published as Vanya Vaidehi Bhargav, 'Letters to Sir Syed: Lajpat Rai's Response to the Muslim Refusal of Minorityhood', *Global Intellectual History*, 2021, 1–20, https://doi.org/10.1080/238018 83.2021.1939501. The journal can be accessed at: https://www.tandfonline.com/journals/rgih20

2 Christopher Bayly, *Origins of Nationality in South Asia: Patriotism and Ethical Government in the Making of Modern India* (Delhi; New York: Oxford University Press, 1998), 79; Rajat Kanta Ray, *The Felt Community: Commonalty and Mentality before the Emergence of Indian Nationalism* (New Delhi: Oxford University Press, 2003), 6.

3 The first telegraph line was laid in 1852, and the first 200 miles of railway lines were built in 1853–56. Dermot Killingley, 'Modernity, Reform, and Revival', in *The Blackwell Companion to Hinduism*, ed. Gavin Flood (Malden, MA: Blackwell, 2003), 511.

4 Partha Chatterjee, 'Whose Imagined Community?', in *The Nationalist Movement in India: A Reader*, ed. Sekhar Bandyopadhyay (New Delhi: Oxford University Press, 2009), 4–8.

5 The historian Manan Asif has argued that Hindustan, as a concept conveying the geographic–territorial and even loose political integrity of the subcontinent (including all its diverse faith communities), had existed in medieval times. However, this political concept had been seen as encompassing multiple countries and polities. Manan Ahmed Asif, *The Loss of Hindustan: The Invention of India* (Cambridge, Massachusetts: Harvard University Press, 2020), 3, 103–04. The idea of the 'Indian nation' as a more strongly cohesive political community whose members were thickly united by a common political purpose was a wholly modern concept.

6 Daniel Argov, *Moderates and Extremists in the Indian National Movement, 1883–1920: With Special Reference to Surendranath Banerjea and Lajpat Rai* (London: Asia Publishing House, 1967), 14. For example, in 1878, Banerjea was arguing that the people of India, despite their linguistic and religious differences, were being regenerated and moulded into a single Indian national unity, with the British Empire—not least through its introduction of Western education and railways—providing the impetus. Surendranath Banerjea, 'Indian Unity, Speech at Student's Association, Calcutta, 1878', in *Speeches and Writings of Hon. Surendranath Banerjea* (GA Natesan and Co., n.d.), 214–24.

7 Sekhar Bandyopadhyay, *From Plassey to Partition: A History of Modern India* (New Delhi: Orient Longman, 2004), 221; John R.

McLane, *Indian Nationalism and the Early Congress* (Princeton: Princeton University Press, 1977), 44–47.

8 Anil Seal, *The Emergence of Indian Nationalism: Competition and Collaboration in the Later Nineteenth Century* (Cambridge: Cambridge University Press, 1971), 247.

9 Seal, 277.

10 Seal, 277.

11 Seal, 277.

12 The Congress promoted interaction between different regions of British India at a time when it was still rare. This indeed contributed to a novel sense of pan-Indian identity and unity. McLane, *Indian Nationalism and the Early Congress*, 103–04.

13 One exception was the armed revolt organized in 1879 by Vasudev Balwant Phadke, a Chitpavan Brahmin, in parts of the Bombay Presidency to overthrow British rule. Yet, this remained a small, isolated revolt, and was quickly crushed. Ideas about expelling the British from India would take root among some radical nationalists only from the late 1890s. The revolutionary societies aiming to overthrow British rule through armed struggle (such as Aurobindo Ghose's Anushilan Samiti and Savarkar's Abhinav Bharat) were established only in the early years of the next century. That twenty-three-year-old Tilak was inspired by Phadke in 1879 suggests that such ideas excited some minds even early on. However, in 1885, even Tilak would still be found stating that the top posts in the civil service must be kept for Englishmen. Similarly, B.C. Pal who, by the turn of the century, would be identified as an 'Extremist', presently proclaimed loyalty to the British government. Vikram Sampath, *Savarkar: Echoes from a Forgotten Past, 1883–1924* (Gurgaon: Viking, 2019), 15–19; Bal Ram Nanda, *Gokhale: The Indian Moderates and the British Raj* (Delhi: OUP, 1977), 11–12, 154–55; Dhananjay Keer, *Lokmanya Tilak: Father of the Indian Freedom Struggle* (Bombay: SB Kangutkar, 1959), 19; Seal, *Emergence of Indian Nationalism*, 281.

14 Seal, *Emergence of Indian Nationalism*, 190–91; McLane, *Indian Nationalism and the Early Congress*, 26–27.

15 Argov, *Moderates and Extremists in the Indian National Movement, 1883–1920: With Special Reference to Surendranath Banerjea and Lajpat Rai*, 37. The denial of Indian national sentiment would persist for many decades. One British official would remark in 1899, 'India is wanting in the one qualification essential to independence, inasmuch as she possesses no sentiment of nationality'. See Sikata Banerjee, *Make Me a Man!: Masculinity, Hinduism, and Nationalism in India*, SUNY Series in Religious Studies (Albany, NY: State University of New York Press, 2005), 40.

16 Argov, *Moderates and Extremists in the Indian National Movement, 1883–1920: With Special Reference to Surendranath Banerjea and Lajpat Rai*, 36.

17 The college would become the Aligarh Muslim University in 1920.

18 Christophe Jaffrelot, *The Pakistan Paradox: Instability and Resilience* (Oxford: Oxford University Press, 2015), 26–27; Peter Hardy, *The Muslims of British India* (Cambridge: Cambridge University Press, 1972), 61–68.

19 David Lelyveld, *Aligarh's First Generation: Muslim Solidarity in India* (Princeton: Princeton University Press, 1978), 130–34.

20 Jaffrelot, *Pakistan Paradox*, 31–32; Faisal Devji, 'Apologetic Modernity', *Modern Intellectual History* 4, no. 1 (2007): 67–68.

21 Devji, 'Apologetic Modernity', 66.

22 Lelyveld, *Aligarh's First Generation*, 102.

23 Lelyveld, 309.

24 McLane, *Indian Nationalism and the Early Congress*, 113; Hardy, *Muslims of British India*, 254.

25 Lelyveld, *Aligarh's First Generation*, 309.

26 J.P. Misra, *Madan Mohan Malaviya and the Indian Freedom Movement* (New Delhi: Oxford University Press, 2016), 6–7.

27 Seal, *Emergence of Indian Nationalism*, 334.

28 Kenneth Jones, *Arya Dharm: Hindu Consciousness in Nineteenth Century Punjab* (Delhi: Manohar, 1976), 244.

29 Lala Lajpat Rai, *Autobiographical Writings*, ed. V.C. Joshi (Delhi: University Publishers, 1965), 85.

30 Lajpat Rai, 85.

31 Lelyveld, *Aligarh's First Generation*, 305–06, 311.

32 Sir Syed Ahmed Khan, *Causes of the Indian Revolt*, ed. Frances W. Pritchett, 2005, http://www.columbia.edu/itc/mealac/pritchett/00urdu/asbab/translation1873.html.

33 Farzana Shaikh, *Community and Consensus in Islam: Muslim Representation in Colonial India, 1860–1947* (Delhi: Imprint One, 2012), 84–85, 88.

34 For a quick overview of the imperial structure, see Sumit Sarkar, *Modern India: 1886–1947* (Delhi: Macmillian, 1983), 12–13.

35 Shaikh, *Community and Consensus*, 91.

36 Sir Syed's grandfather was a *wazir* (minister) of the Grand Mughal.

37 David Lelyveld cited in Shaikh, *Community and Consensus*, 93–94.

38 Plural of *rais* or *raees*.

39 Syed Ahmad Khan, 'On Muslim Attitude to the Congress and the British Government, Speech at Lucknow, 28 December 1887', in Shan Mohammad (ed.), *Writings and Speeches of Sir Syed Ahmad Khan* (Bombay: Nachiketa Publications, 1972) [hereafter cited as 'On Muslim Attitude'], 204–05.

40 Ahmad Khan, 204, 209.

41 Indian Patriotic Association, *Showing the Seditious Character of the Indian National Congress and the Opinions Held by Eminent Natives of India Who Are Opposed to the Movement* (Allahabad: Pioneer Press, 1888), 45–46.

42 William Doyle, *Aristocracy: A Very Short Introduction* (Oxford; New York: Oxford University Press, 2010), chap. 5.

43 For a subtle account of the continuities and discontinuities between ancient and modern forms of democracy, see Melissa Lane, *The Birth of Politics: Eight Greek and Roman Political Ideas and Why They Matter* (Princeton, NJ: Princeton University Press, 2015), https://doi.org/10.1515/9781400865543.

44 David Lelyveld, 'Next Year, If Grain Is Dear, I Shall Be a Sayyid: Sayyid Ahmed Khan, Colonial Constructions, and Muslim

Self-Definitions', *Journal of the Royal Asiatic Society 30*, no. 3 (2020), 1, 13.

45 Shaikh, *Community and Consensus*, 114–16.

46 Ahmad Khan, 'On Muslim Attitude', 212–13; 'The Indian National Congress, Speech at Meerut, 16 March 1888', in Shan Mohammad (ed.) *Writings and Speeches of Sir Syed Ahmed Khan* (Bombay: Nachiketa Publications, 1972) [Hereafter cited as 'Meerut Speech'], 191.

47 As cited in Shaikh, *Community and Consensus*, 116.

48 Jaffrelot, *Pakistan Paradox*, 38.

49 Jaffrelot, 38–39.

50 Cited in Lelyveld, *Aligarh's First Generation*, 311.

51 Lelyveld, 86, 112; Hardy, *Muslims of British India*, 31.

52 Ahmad Khan, 'On Muslim Attitude', 208.

53 Jaffrelot, *Pakistan Paradox*, 30.

54 Jaffrelot, 33.

55 Lelyveld, *Aligarh's First Generation*, 83–95; Jaffrelot, *Pakistan Paradox*, 34–36. Most contemporary commentators agreed that 'Muslims' had fallen behind in education. It must be remembered, however, that even among the Hindus, the student population was overwhelmingly Brahmin and Kayastha, with barely any presence of Rajputs, Jats and Banyas. More importantly, the vast majority of Indians, whether Hindu or Muslim, had no access to English education. Even among the Kayasthas of the North-Western Provinces, the overwhelming majority never received any English education.

56 In 1857, out of the total number of clerks in subordinate executive and judicial services, 24.1 per cent had been Hindu and 63.9 per cent Muslim. By 1887, the share of the former had risen to 50.3 per cent, while that of the latter had dropped to 45.1 per cent. Jaffrelot, *Pakistan Paradox*, 36.

57 Jaffrelot, 36; Lelyveld, *Aligarh's First Generation*, 98.

58 Ahmad Khan, 'On Muslim Attitude', 209–10. America was the first large-scale popular democracy in the history of the world, abolishing property qualifications by the 1830s, and

establishing de jure universal adult male franchise by the 1880s. Of course, the late nineteenth century also saw growing attempts by southern whites to deprive black Americans of their voting rights by both law and brute force. Nevertheless, America was seen by many around the world as the vanguard of democracy. Donald Ratcliffe, 'The Right to Vote and the Rise of Democracy, 1787–1828', *Journal of the Early Republic* 33, no. 2 (2013): 219, 254; Jill Lepore, *These Truths: A History of the United States* (New York: W.W. Norton & Company, 2018), 365, 370, 631, 661, 707; Christopher Hobson, *The Rise of Democracy: Revolution, War and Transformations in International Politics since 1776* (Edinburgh: Edinburgh University Press, 2015), 133.

59 Syed Ahmad Khan, 'Speech at Gurdaspur, 27 January 1884', in Shan Mohammad (ed.), *Writings and Speeches of Sir Syed Ahmad Khan* (Bombay: Nachiketa Publications, 1972), 266.

60 Ahmad Khan, 265.

61 For another example, see Syed Ahmad Khan, 'On Hindu–Muslim Relations, Speech at Patna, 27 January 1883', in *Writings and Speeches of Sir Syed Ahmad Khan*, ed. Shan Mohammad (Bombay: Nachiketa Publications, 1972), 157–58.

62 In fact, till the mid-1880s, this was the sense in which the term 'nation' was used around the world. See Eric Hobsbawm, *Nations and Nationalism since 1780: Programme, Myth, Reality* (Cambridge [England]; New York: Cambridge University Press, 1990), 14–15.

63 Ahmad Khan, 'Meerut Speech', 184–87.

64 Ahmad Khan, 'On Muslim Attitude', 204, 208. Interestingly, the Congress stalwart Surendranath Banerjea had once cited examples of Switzerland, Belgium, Germany and Italy to argue that Indians, like the peoples of these countries, could be moulded into a national unity despite deep linguistic and religious differences. Banerjea, 'Indian Unity', 218–19.

65 Ahmad Khan, 'Meerut Speech', 208.

66 'Clarification of Sir Syed's Earlier Speech at Lucknow', Ahmad Khan, 218–19.

67 Sir Syed often used the word 'nation' and 'community' interchangeably. See Syed Ahmad Khan, 'Lecture at Jullundar, 4 February 1884', in Shan Mohammad (ed.), *Writings and Speeches of Sir Syed Ahmad Khan* (Bombay: Nachiketa Publications, 1972), 260; 'On Muslim Attitude', 203.

68 Lala Lajpat Rai, 'Open Letter to Sir Syed Ahmed Khan—I, The Tribune, 27 October 1888', in *CWLLR*, vol. 1, 2003, 4.

69 Lala Lajpat Rai, 'Open Letter to Sir Syed Ahmed Khan—II, The Tribune, 17 November 1888', in *CWLLR*, vol. 1, 2003, 10.

70 Lajpat Rai, 8–10.

71 Sanjay Seth, 'Rewriting Histories of Nationalism: The Politics of "Moderate Nationalism" in India, 1870–1905', *American Historical Review*, 1999, 101.

72 Pattabhi Sitaramayya, *The History of the Indian National Congress*, vol. 1 (Bombay: Padma Publications, 1947), 24; Sarvepalli Gopal, *British Policy in India, 1858–1905* (Cambridge: Cambridge University Press, 1965), 166; Bandyopadhyay, *From Plassey to Partition: A History of Modern India*, 228; Nanda, *Gokhale*, 46–47; Argov, *Moderates and Extremists in the Indian National Movement, 1883–1920: With Special Reference to Surendranath Banerjea and Lajpat Rai*, 23–34. Tilak and Gokhale attended their first Congress session in 1889.

73 Seth, 'Rewriting Histories', 107–08; McLane, *Indian Nationalism and the Early Congress*, 97.

74 Sarkar, *Modern India*, 40; Bernard Crick, *Democracy: A Very Short Introduction* (Oxford: Oxford University Press, 2002), 72–73; Seth, 'Rewriting Histories', 108–13.

75 Raja Shiva Prasad and Raja Peary Mohan Mukherjee were both landholders who had served on councils, the latter a member of the BIA. McLane, *Indian Nationalism and the Early Congress*, 108.

76 Lala Lajpat Rai, 'On Sir Syed's Opposition to Congress Demands, The Tribune, 10 March 1888', in *CWLLR*, vol. 1, 2003 [hereafter cited as 'On Sir Syed's Opposition'], 32.

77 Lajpat Rai, 32.

78 Lajpat Rai, 31–32.

79 Ahmad Khan, 'On Muslim Attitude', 208–10.

80 Syed Ahmad Khan, 'Clarification of Sir Syed's Earlier Speech at Lucknow', in Shan Mohammad (ed.), *Writings and Speeches of Sir Syed Ahmad Khan* (Bombay: Nachiketa Publications, 1972), 219.

81 Ahmad Khan, 'On Muslim Attitude', 208.

82 Lala Lajpat Rai, 'Open Letter to Sir Syed Ahmed Khan—IV, The Tribune, 19 December 1888', in *CWLLR*, vol. 1, 2003, 22–23.

83 Lajpat Rai, 22.

84 Lajpat Rai, 23. Emphasis his. For the original, see Syed Ahmad Khan, 'Reply to Address Presented by the Indian Association, Lahore', in Shan Mohammad (ed.), *Writings and Speeches of Sir Syed Ahmad Khan* (Bombay: Nachiketa Publications, 1972), 163.

85 Nanda, *Gokhale*, 321.

86 Lajpat Rai, 'On Sir Syed's Opposition', 32–33.

87 Lajpat Rai, 31.

88 Surendranath Banerjea, 'An Appeal to the Mohammedan Community, Speech at Congress Meeting, Dacca, 1 October 1888', in *Speeches and Writings of Hon. Surendranath Banerjea* (GA Natesan and Co., n.d.), 265–72.

89 For more on the concept of descriptive representation, see Shaikh, *Community and Consensus*, 73, 90, 137; Rajeev Bhargava, *The Promise of India's Secular Democracy* (Oxford: Oxford University Press, 2010), 200, 209.

90 Lala Lajpat Rai, 'Representation of Minorities in Legislative Councils, Report of the Indian National Congress, Fifth Session, 1889', in *CWLLR*, vol. 1, 2003, 38.

91 Lajpat Rai, 37–38.

92 Lajpat Rai, 37–38. 'Report of the Proceedings of the Fifth Indian National Congress, Bombay, 1889', in Mushirul Hasan (ed.), *Proceedings of the Indian National Congress* (New Delhi: Niyogi Books, 2012), 23. The measure would apply to 'Parsis, Christians, Muhammadans, or Hindus' wherever they were in a minority. For the text of this scheme, see Hasan, 14.

93 Parmananda, *Mahamana Madan Mohan Malaviya: An Historical Biography*, vol. 1 (Varanasi: Malaviya Adhyayan Sansthan: Banaras Hindu University, 1985), 81.

Chapter 3

1 Kenneth Jones, *Arya Dharm: Hindu Consciousness in Nineteenth Century Punjab* (Delhi: Manohar, 1976), 168–73; C.S. Adcock, *The Limits of Tolerance: Indian Secularism and the Politics of Religious Freedom* (New York: Oxford University Press, 2013), 90–99.

2 Adcock, *Limits of Tolerance*, 97–99.

3 Jones, *Arya Dharm*, 170.

4 Adcock, *Limits of Tolerance*, 97.

5 Adcock, 97.

6 Lala Lajpat Rai, 'The Arya Samaj: An Account of Its Origin, Doctrines, and Activities, with a Biographical Sketch of the Founder, 1915', in *CWLLR*, vol. 5, 2004 [hereafter cited as 'Arya Samaj'], 221.

7 Jones, *Arya Dharm*, 171.

8 Lajpat Rai, 'Arya Samaj', 224.

9 I owe this point to Adcock, *Limits of Tolerance*, 97–98.

10 Lala Lajpat Rai, 'Swami Dayanand, 1898', in *CWLLR*, vol. 1, 2003, 413; Lajpat Rai, 'Arya Samaj', 217.

11 Lajpat Rai, 'Arya Samaj', 201.

12 Amiya P. Sen, *Hindu Revivalism in Bengal, 1872–1905: Some Essays in Interpretation* (Delhi; New York: Oxford University Press, 1993), 9–10; Dorothy Figueira, *Aryans, Jews, Brahmins: Theorizing Authority through Myths of Identity* (Albany: State University of New York Press, 2002), 123.

13 Lajpat Rai, 'Arya Samaj', 266.

14 In elaborating the 'history' of how Islam arrived in India, Rai stated that Pauranic Hindus were vanquished because, having become idol worshippers who followed countless gods, they had been unable to stand up to Muslims who were united by

the monotheistic belief in 'One God, One Prophet'. Lajpat Rai, 'Swami Dayanand', 393–94.

15 The supposedly 'rigorous monotheism' of Islam sometimes drew the envy of even British colonial officials. The Arya Samajist definition of Hinduism as a simple creed shorn of idolatry and ceremonial excess was likely partly also formulated in engagement with Islam. That features of Islam, including its abstract monotheism, served as an inspiration for nineteenth-century Hindu reform movements has also been suggested by others. See Partha Mitter, 'Rammohun Roy and the New Language of Monotheism', *History and Anthropology* 3, no. 1 (1987): 190. Romila Thapar, 'Syndicated Hinduism', in Gunther-Dietz Sontheimer and Hermann Kulke (ed.), *Hinduism Reconsidered* (New Delhi: Manohar, 1997), 54–81. Once again, of course, this was not a simple process of wholesale derivation but a complex one involving active, creative engagement by Hindus and where the end product had a legitimate claim to be called 'Hindu'.

16 See Gauri Vishwanathan, 'Colonialism and the Construction of Hinduism', in *The Blackwell Companion to Hinduism*, ed. Gavin Flood (Oxford: Blackwell, 2008), 23–44.; Adcock, *Limits of Tolerance*, 11.

17 Vasudha Dalmia, 'The Only Real Religion of the Hindus: Vaisnava Self-Representation in the Late Nineteenth Century', in *Representing Hinduism: The Construction of Religious Traditions and National Identity*, ed. Vasudha Dalmia and Heinrich von Stietencron (New Delhi; London: SAGE, 1995), 189–90.

18 Richard Cashman, *The Myth of the Lokmanya: Tilak and Mass Politics in Maharashtra* (Berkeley: University of California Press, 1975), 77–79.

19 These Urdu-medium schools had replaced Persian-language ones attended in pre-colonial times by a cultural elite comprising Muslims and Hindu Khatris. Jeffrey M. Diamond, '"Calculated to Be Offensive to Hindoos"? Vernacular Education, History Textbooks and the Waqiat Controversy of the 1860s in Colonial

North India', *Journal of the Royal Asiatic Society* 24, no. 1 (2014): 77–78.

20 Diamond, 78–79; Ali Usman Qasmi, 'Textbooks for History and Urdu in Punjab: Transiting from the Colonial to the Post-Colonial Period', *Südasien-Chronik - South Asia Chronicle, Südasien-Seminar Der Humboldt-Universität Zu Berlin* 6 (2016): 231–41.

21 Qasmi, 'Textbooks for History', 231–41. For a further discussion of school history textbooks in Punjab, see Diamond, '"Calculated to Be Offensive to Hindoos"? Vernacular Education, History Textbooks and the Waqi'at Controversy of the 1860s in Colonial North India'.

22 Thomas R. Trautmann, *Aryans and British India* (New Delhi: Vistaar, 2006), 113; Sanjay Seth, *Subject Lessons: The Western Education of Colonial India* (New Delhi; New York: Oxford University Press, 2008), 1.

23 Sumit Sarkar, *Modern Times: 1880s–1950* (Ranikhet: Permanent Black, 2014), 39; Seth, *Subject Lessons*, 1. As Sarkar points out, this had defeated Rammohun Roy who had intervened in the debate demanding English education with a scientific emphasis.

24 Trautmann, *Aryans and British India*, 111; Sarkar, *Modern Times*, 3.

25 Sarkar, *Modern Times*, 41. Interestingly, Sanjay Seth argues that the aim of Western education may well have also been to demonstrate the inability of Indians to acquire it. *Subject Lessons*, 27.

26 Ellen E. McDonald, 'English Education and Social Reform in Late Nineteenth Century Bombay: A Case Study in the Transmission of a Cultural Ideal', *The Journal of Asian Studies* 25, no. 3 (1966): 456, 462.

27 Partha Chatterjee, 'History and the Nationalisation of Hinduism', in *Representing Hinduism: The Construction of Religious Traditions and National Identity*, ed. Vasudha Dalmia and Heinrich von Stietencron (London: SAGE, 1995), 117–21.

28 McDonald, 'English Education and Social Reform in Late Nineteenth Century Bombay: A Case Study in the Transmission of a Cultural Ideal', 456; Seth, *Subject Lessons*, 173–74. As Sarkar points out, the rapid spread of print from 1800 onwards also contributed to the advance of Indian vernacular literatures during the colonial era, building on the substantial development of vernacular languages in pre-colonial times following the 'Muslim invasions'. For more details, see *Modern Times*, 327–45.

29 Lala Lajpat Rai, *Autobiographical Writings*, ed. V.C. Joshi (Delhi: University Publishers, 1965), 79; Feroz Chand, *Lajpat Rai: Life and Work* (New Delhi: Publications Division, Ministry of Information and Broadcasting, Government of India, 1978), 23. By his own admission, Rai learnt 'precious little of Sanskrit'.

30 Seth, *Subject Lessons*, 1.

31 Sanjay Seth, 'Rewriting Histories of Nationalism: The Politics of "Moderate Nationalism" in India, 1870–1905', *American Historical Review*, 1999, 112–13; John R. McLane, *Indian Nationalism and the Early Congress* (Princeton: Princeton University Press, 1977), 68. This was as much the view of 'moderates' such as Banerjea, Ranade, Gokhale as it was of Tilak who, Western-educated himself, had started the New English School in 1880 in Poona to impart English education to the people. As we saw in Chapter 2, Sir Syed's Aligarh college similarly aimed to provide English education to the Muslim gentry.

32 Sarkar, *Modern Times*, 44; Christophe Jaffrelot, *The Pakistan Paradox: Instability and Resilience* (Oxford: Oxford University Press, 2015), 34.

33 Lala Lajpat Rai, 'A Historical Glance at Sanskrit Education in the Dayanand Anglo–Vedic College, 1893', in *CWLLR*, vol. 1, 2003 [Hereafter cited as 'Historical Glance'], 104.

34 Jones, *Arya Dharm*, 85–86; Harald Fischer-Tiné, 'The Only Hope for Fallen India: The Gurukul Kangri as an Experiment in National Education (1902–1922)', ed. Georg Berkemer et al., *Explorations in the History of South Asia: Essays in Honour of Dietmar Rothermund*, 2001, 283.

35 Lajpat Rai, 'Historical Glance', 104.
36 Lajpat Rai, 104.
37 Lajpat Rai, 98.
38 Lajpat Rai, 98, 100–101.
39 Vasudha Dalmia, *The Nationalization of Hindu Traditions: Bhāratendu Hariśchandra and Nineteenth-Century Banaras* (Delhi: Oxford University Press, 2001), 146–52. Also see Alok Rai, *Hindi Nationalism* (Delhi: Orient Longman, 2000).
40 Dalmia, 192, 219–20.
41 J.P. Misra, *Madan Mohan Malaviya and the Indian Freedom Movement* (New Delhi: Oxford University Press, 2016), 11; Parmananda, *Mahamana Madan Mohan Malaviya: An Historical Biography*, vol. 1 (Varanasi: Malaviya Adhyayan Sansthan: Banaras Hindu University, 1985), 98; Christopher Bayly, *The Local Roots of Indian Politics: Allahabad, 1880–1920* (Oxford: Clarendon Press, 1975), 108–09.
42 Dalmia, *Nationalization of Hindu Traditions*, 146–52, 219–20.
43 When a government-appointed commission toured the Punjab in 1881–82 to review its education policy, it opened, for the first time, the question of which language—Hindi or Urdu—was the true language of Punjab. Punjabi Hindus demanded that Urdu be replaced by Hindi as the language of secondary schools and the courts, sparking mobilization and counter-mobilization by supporters of Hindi and Urdu, respectively. Jones, *Arya Dharm*, 65; Norman Barrier, 'The Punjab Government and Communal Politics, 1870–1908', *Journal of Asian Studies* 27, no. 3 (1968): 532; Christophe Jaffrelot, 'Genesis and Development of Hindu Nationalism in the Punjab: From the Arya Samaj to the Hindu Sabha (1875–1910)', in *Religion, Caste, and Politics in India* (London: Hurst, 2011), 102. The Arya Samaj devoted itself to the cause of Hindi in the Devanagari script in the early 1880s. See Jones, *Arya Dharm*, 65, 72. Rai began his public career with the Hindi movement, delivering his first public speech on the issue in 1882 in Ambala city. It was this movement that had, in large measure, brought him closer to his Arya Samajist college mates, and made him turn away from Islam to 'develop a love for

the ancient Hindu culture'. *Autobiographical Writings*, 26–27, 79; Chand, *Lajpat Rai*, 22–25.

44 Lala Lajpat Rai, 'Giuseppe Mazzini—A Biography, 1896', in *CWLLR*, vol. 1, 2003, 291.

45 English was taught but accorded lesser priority. Fischer-Tiné, ''The Only Hope for Fallen India': The Gurukul Kangri as an Experiment in National Education (1902–1922)', 391; 'Arya Samaj', in *Brill's Encyclopedia of Hinduism*, ed. Knut A. Jacobsen et al., vol. 5, Handbuch Der Orientalistik Zweite Abteilung Indien (Leiden: Brill, 2013), 283.

46 This hybrid Anglo–vernacular approach also seemed to underline Tilak's New English School in Poona. Dhananjay Keer, *Lokmanya Tilak—Father of the Indian Freedom Struggle* (Bombay: SB Kangutkar, 1959), 26–27.

47 Lajpat Rai, 'Historical Glance', 98; 'On Opening of a New School at Rawalpindi, The Tribune, 31 April 1899', in *CWLLR*, vol. 1, 2003, 86.

48 Lajpat Rai, 'Historical Glance', 97.

49 Lajpat Rai, 'Opening of a New School', 86.

50 For the argument about how English education intended to further Western cultural hegemony, see Gauri Viswanathan, *Masks of Conquest: Literary Study and British Rule in India*, 25th anniversary edition (New York: Columbia University Press, 2015). Other scholars suggest that both the small numbers of Indians that actually received this education and the sorts of themes it included complicate the view that English education was a means of imperial thought control. See Sarkar, *Modern Times*, 38–41.

51 This supports scholarship which argues that the effects of colonial education went beyond the intentions with which it was introduced. Sarkar, *Modern Times*, 41. Indeed, historian Dipesh Chakravarty suggests that Western education introduced Indians to concepts such as citizenship, the state, civil society, public sphere, human rights, equality before the law, the individual, the subject, democracy, popular sovereignty, social justice, scientific rationality and so on. See as cited in Sekhar Bandyopadhyay,

From Plassey to Partition: A History of Modern India (New Delhi: Orient Longman, 2004), 211.

52 Lala Lajpat Rai, 'On Opening of a New School at Rawalpindi, The Tribune, 31 April 1899', in *CWLLR*, vol. 1, 2003, 86.

53 The historical writings of W.W. Hunter, Mountstuart Elphinstone, Max Muller, Alexander Cunningham, R.W. Fraser and James Todd were among those with which Rai was familiar. Lala Lajpat Rai, 'Preface to "A History of India"', 1898', in *CWLLR*, vol. 1, 2003, 117–18.

54 Diamond, '"Calculated to Be Offensive to Hindoos"? Vernacular Education, History Textbooks and the Waqi'at Controversy of the 1860s in Colonial North India', 81.

55 Nicholas B. Dirks, 'History as a Sign of the Modern', *Public Culture* 2, no. 2 (1990): 25.

56 Chatterjee, 'History and the Nationalisation of Hinduism'; Diamond, '"Calculated to Be Offensive to Hindoos"? Vernacular Education, History Textbooks and the Waqi'at Controversy of the 1860s in Colonial North India', 93.

57 Lala Lajpat Rai, *Autobiographical Writings*, ed. V.C. Joshi (Delhi: University Publishers, 1965), p.77

58 Lajpat Rai, 'History of India', 115.

59 Lajpat Rai, 'History of India', 115–16.

60 Lajpat Rai, 115–16.

61 Terry Eagleton, *The Idea of Culture*, Blackwell Manifestos (Malden, MA: Blackwell, 2000), 51; Raymond Williams, *Keywords: A Vocabulary of Culture and Society*, 3479 (London: Fontana/Croom Helm, 1977), 14, 17.

62 Eagleton, *The Idea of Culture*, 14–18; Williams, *Keywords*, 49–53. Also see Andrew Sartori, 'The Resonance of "Culture": Framing a Problem in Global Concept History', *Comparative Studies in Society and History* 47, no. 4 (2005): 676–99.

63 Terry Eagleton, *The Idea of Culture*, Blackwell Manifestos (Malden, MA: Blackwell, 2000), 17.

64 Andrew Sartori, *Bengal in Global Concept History: Culturalism in the Age of Capital* (Chicago: University of Chicago Press, 2008), chap. 4.

65 Fischer-Tiné, 'The Only Hope for Fallen India: The Gurukul
    Kangri as an Experiment in National Education (1902–1922)',
    284–92.

66 For more on the culturalization of religion, and the different
    forms 'culturalised religion' assumes, see Avi Astor and Damon
    Mayrl, 'Culturalized Religion: A Synthetic Review and Agenda
    for Research', *Journal for the Scientific Study of Religion* 59, no. 2
    (2020): 3, 7–10.

67 I do not mean to overstate the differences between Lajpat
    Rai and his College Party, on the one hand, and the Gurukul
    Party, on the other. Like Rai and his faction, the Gurukul Party
    would attempt to transcend internal diversity among Hindus
    and forge a Hindu unity by emphasizing their common Hindi
    language, Hindu history and Aryan Hindu culture. Fischer-
    Tiné, 'The Only Hope for Fallen India: The Gurukul Kangri as
    an Experiment in National Education (1902–1922)', 284–92. It
    too evidently engaged in the civilization of Hinduism as a means
    to unite Hindus. But Lajpat Rai (and his faction) diverged from
    the Gurukul Party in that to build a Hindu unity he defined
    Hinduism in terms of minimalist theology and de-emphasized
    theology in favour of non-religious instruction in what he
    considered 'Hindu' language, history and culture. On the other
    hand, the Gurukul's emphasis on theological details (Adcock,
    Limits of Tolerance, 97–99; Fischer-Tiné, 'Arya Samaj', 391.)
    simultaneously ran counter to its projects of Hindu unity.

Chapter 4

1   Kenneth Jones, *Arya Dharm: Hindu Consciousness in Nineteenth
    Century Punjab* (Delhi: Manohar, 1976), 236–37; See Lala Lajpat
    Rai, 'Appeal to Hindus for Famine Relief and Help to Orphans,
    Letter to the Editor, The Tribune, 24 October 1899', in *CWLLR*,
    vol. 1, 2003, 122; 'Call to Hindus to Excel Christian Missionaries
    in Relief Work, Letter to the Editor, The Tribune, 22 March 1900',
    in *CWLLR*, vol. 1, 2003 [hereafter cited as 'Call to Hindus'], 132.

2 Lajpat Rai, 'A Historical Glance at Sanskrit Education in the Dayanand Anglo–Vedic College, 1893', in *CWLLR*, vol. 1, 2003, 98, 100–101.

3 Lala Lajpat Rai, 'A Historical Glance at Sanskrit Education in the Dayanand Anglo-Vedic College, 1893', in *CWLLR*, vol. 1, 2003, 97–98.

4 Lala Lajpat Rai, 'On Opening of a New School at Rawalpindi, The Tribune, 31 April 1899', in *CWLLR*, vol. 1, 2003, 86.

5 Lala Lajpat Rai, 'Shivaji—Extracts from Shivaji, The Great Patriot, Lahore, 1896', in *CWLLR*, vol. 1, 2003, 336–37.

6 Lala Lajpat Rai, 'Giuseppe Mazzini—A Biography, 1896', in *CWLLR*, vol. 1, 2003, 285.

7 Lajpat Rai, 292–93.

8 Lajpat Rai, 'Call to Hindus', 130.

9 Lala Lajpat Rai, 'On Munshi Abdul Aziz's Conversion to Hinduism and Comments of the Editor of "Rafiq-i-Hind", The Regenerator of Aryavarta, 5 May 1884', in *CWLLR*, vol. 1, 2003, 268.

10 Richard Cashman, *The Myth of the Lokmanya: Tilak and Mass Politics in Maharashtra* (Berkeley: University of California Press, 1975), 105–06; Stanley Wolpert, *Tilak and Gokhale: Revolution and Reform in the Making of Modern India* (Berkeley: University of California Press, 1962), 80.

11 J.P. Misra, *Madan Mohan Malaviya and the Indian Freedom Movement* (New Delhi: Oxford University Press, 2016), 5; Christopher Bayly, *The Local Roots of Indian Politics: Allahabad, 1880–1920* (Oxford: Clarendon Press, 1975), 108.

12 Vasudha Dalmia, 'The Only Real Religion of the Hindus: Vaisnava Self-Representation in the Late Nineteenth Century', in *Representing Hinduism: The Construction of Religious Traditions and National Identity*, ed. Vasudha Dalmia and Heinrich von Stietencron (New Delhi; London: SAGE, 1995), 188–89; *The Nationalization of Hindu Traditions: Bhāratendu Hariśchandra and Nineteenth-Century Banaras* (Delhi: Oxford University Press, 2001), 26.

13 Partha Chatterjee, 'Whose Imagined Community?', in Sekhar Bandyopadhyay (ed.), *The Nationalist Movement in India: A Reader* (Oxford University Press, 2009); Vasudha Dalmia and Heinrich von Stietencron, 'Introduction', in Vasudha Dalmia and Heinrich von Stietencron (eds.), *Representing Hinduism: The Construction of Religious Traditions and National Identity* (SAGE Publications Pvt. Limited, 1995), 19; Michael Freeden, 'Is Nationalism a Distinct Ideology?', *Political Studies* 46, no. 4 (1998): 755.

14 Max Muller was German but lived in Oxford (England) for most of his life. His scholarship on India was hugely influential among both the British and the Indian intelligentsia.

15 Dorothy Figueira, *Aryans, Jews, Brahmins: Theorizing Authority through Myths of Identity* (Albany: State University of New York Press, 2002), 23–25, 39–40.

16 Ronald Inden, *Imagining India* (Bloomington: Indiana University Press, 2000), 45.

17 John Zavos, *The Emergence of Hindu Nationalism in India* (Oxford: Oxford University Press, 2000), 33; J. Barton Scott, *Spiritual Despots: Modern Hinduism and the Genealogies of Self-Rule* (Chicago; London: The University of Chicago Press, 2016), 32. Mill (1773–1836) had never been to India and was ignorant of Indian languages. Yet he was widely considered an expert on India after writing the *History of India*, which had gone into its fifth edition by 1858, and was the prescribed text for young British lads training to become civil servants in India. Interestingly, Mill's assessment of Indian civilization was disliked by the likes of H.H. Wilson, professor of Sanskrit at Oxford, and the leading Orientalist in the generation after Colebrooke. Thomas R. Trautmann, *Aryans and British India* (New Delhi: Vistaar, 2006), 117–18, 123–24.

18 Trautmann, *Aryans and British India*, 129.

19 Zavos, *Emergence of Hindu Nationalism*, 30; Mrinalini Sinha, *Colonial Masculinity: The 'Manly Englishman' and the 'Effeminate Bengali' in the Late Nineteenth Century* (Manchester; New York:

Manchester University Press, 1995), 15, 101; Thomas Metcalf, *Ideologies of the Raj* (Cambridge: Cambridge University Press, 1994), 133.

20 C.S. Adcock, *The Limits of Tolerance: Indian Secularism and the Politics of Religious Freedom* (New York: Oxford University Press, 2013), 94–95.

21 Ronald Inden, 'Orientalist Constructions of India', *Modern Asian Studies* 20, no. 03 (1986): 3, 28.

22 Inden, 25–28.

23 Metcalf, *Ideologies*, 8–9, 133. English prejudices about the Ottomans were a historically recent phenomenon. In the sixteenth century, in an effort to challenge Spain and Portugal, England spent considerable effort to forge closer relations with the Ottoman Empire. The Ottoman sultan was courted with warm letters of friendship and gifts from the court of Queen Elizabeth. English merchants, in turn, were given special privileges in the Ottoman Empire. Positive views about the Ottomans and the Muslim world pervaded mainstream culture in England. See Peter Frankopan, *The Silk Roads: A New History of the World* (London: Bloomsbury, 2016), 245–47.

24 Metcalf, 8–9, 133.

25 Metcalf, 89, 143–44.

26 Partha Chatterjee, 'History and the Nationalisation of Hinduism', in Vasudha Dalmia and Heinrich von Stietencron (eds.), *Representing Hinduism: The Construction of Religious Traditions and National Identity* (London: SAGE, 1995), 121–22; John Zavos, *The Emergence of Hindu Nationalism in India* (Oxford: Oxford University Press, 2000), 34; C.S. Adcock, *The Limits of Tolerance: Indian Secularism and the Politics of Religious Freedom* (New York: Oxford University Press, 2013), 93–94.

27 Figueira, *Aryans, Jews, Brahmins*, 23–25.

28 Sinha, *Colonial Masculinity*, 44.

29 Here, I am inspired by the concept of the 'epistemic injustice of colonialism' as elaborated by Indian political theorist Rajeev

Bhargava. Bhargava argues that colonialism involved not only political subjugation and economic extraction but also a conquest of the mind and culture of the colonized. Colonization involved epistemic injustice (a form of cultural injustice) wherein the ways in which Indians understood themselves and their world were replaced or at least adversely affected by the knowledges produced by the colonizer. Indians were not victims of the kind of grave cultural injustice faced by the native American population in the United States, whereby their culture or systems of meaning and significance were completely destroyed and no longer accessible (also called 'natal alienation'). Yet, they still faced a variety of systematic injustices in that colonialism interfered with and altered their culture(s) and systems of epistemic frameworks largely (though not wholly) without their consent and in the context of deeply asymmetric power relations. This resulted in a significant degree of loss in their intellectual and cultural autonomy. An important facet of this epistemic and cultural injustice was a loss of self-esteem and self-confidence. Here, the role of colonial representations of Indian society and history were important, encouraging the belief in the inferiority of large parts of their own cultures and traditions. The discomfort of Hindus like Lajpat Rai with forms of contemporary Hinduism and their adoption of the narrative of Hindu degeneracy was a manifestation of such cultural colonialism. See 'Overcoming the Epistemic Injustice of Colonialism', *Global Policy* 4, no. 4 (2013): 413–15; *What Is Political Theory and Why Do We Need It?* (New Delhi: Oxford University Press, 2013), 157–61, 168–71. Importantly, Bhargava warns against post-colonial revenge, reactive anti-Westernism, the 'pitfalls of a naïve and dangerous nativism or an intellectually impoverished cultural nationalism', and against denials of how elites among the formerly colonized often played an active role in the neglect or inferiorization of their fellow citizens and of their own cultures and traditions (192.). For the different cultural injustices under colonialism, and appropriate moral responses to these, see 193–95.

30 J.T.F. Jordens, *Dayānanda Sarasvatī: His Life and Ideas* (Delhi: Oxford University Press, 1997), 110; Zavos, *Emergence of Hindu Nationalism*, 32–33. Modern degenerationist narratives were also partly built on pre-colonial Sanskrit texts that painted a narrative of cyclical decline, culminating in the present *kali yuga*. Interestingly, a few Hindus such as Ramachandra Ghosha (close friend of Surendranath Banerjea and a scholar–member of the Royal Asiatic Society) challenged narratives of Hindu degeneration, arguing that Indo-Aryans were savages and that Hindus were gradually developing a purer monotheistic religious conception. The British mission in India was aiding the evolution of the Hindu mind towards monotheism. Tony Ballantyne, *Orientalism and Race: Aryanism in the British Empire*, Cambridge Imperial and Post-Colonial Studies Series (Houndmills, Basingstoke, Hampshire; New York: Palgrave, 2002), 175.

31 Lala Lajpat Rai, 'Swami Dayanand, 1898', in *CWLLR*, vol. 1, 2003, 382.

32 Lajpat Rai, 382.

33 Vedic priests were ritual specialists, indispensable to their patron's ritual performance. They recited and sang Vedic mantras, supervised the entire ritual, and expected material rewards and *dakshina* (priestly gift) in return. Michael Witzel, 'Vedas and Upanisads', in *The Blackwell Companion to Hinduism*, ed. Gavin Flood (Malden, MA: Blackwell, 2003), 75. 79–80; Romila Thapar, 'Syndicated Hinduism', in *Hinduism Reconsidered*, ed. Gunther-Dietz Sontheimer and Hermann Kulke (New Delhi: Manohar, 1997), 57.

34 Historian–theorist of religion J. Barton Scott has argued that the attack by nineteenth-century Hindu reform movements such as the Brahmo Samaj and the Arya Samaj on priesthood gave rise to the notion of a spiritually self-governing subject. This in turn laid the foundations for the rise of the liberal ideal of the politically self-ruling subject, which became important for later nationalist thought. See Scott, *Spiritual Despots*. In the

1890s, Lajpat Rai's Arya Samajist anticlericalism played into his fashioning of a Vedic past wherein Aryan resistance to religious tutelage (and insistence on spiritual self-rule) was advanced as the cause of their political independence.

35 Lajpat Rai, 'Swami Dayanand', 383.

36 Lajpat Rai, 383.

37 For more details, see Figueira, *Aryans, Jews, Brahmins*, chaps 1–2.

38 Jordens, *Dayānanda Sarasvatī*, 110; Zavos, *Emergence of Hindu Nationalism*, 32–33.

39 Figueira, *Aryans, Jews, Brahmins*, chaps 1–2.

40 Figueira, 157, 160; Bal Gangadhar Tilak, *The Orion, or, Researches into the Antiquity of the Vedas* (Rádhábái Átmárám Sagoon, 1893); Wolpert, *Tilak and Gokhale*, 63–64.

41 Figueira, *Aryans, Jews, Brahmins*, 95, 99.

42 Surendranath Banerjea, *Speeches and Writings of Hon. Surendranath Banerjea* (GA Natesan and Co., n.d.), 4–9.

43 Figueira, *Aryans, Jews, Brahmins*, 141.

44 Figueira, 105–15.

45 Figueira, 132. Along with European Orientalist knowledge, Tilak also utilized older indigenous astrological and geographical traditions while advancing his claims about the Aryan past. Ballantyne, *Orientalism and Race*, 181.

46 Ballantyne, *Orientalism and Race*, 181.

47 African theorists of colonialism such as Frantz Fanon have argued that colonialism led to the loss of self-respect and basic self-confidence, causing dehumanization to 'enter the psyche and subjectivity of the colonised people'. Hindus like Lajpat Rai were victims of this effect of colonialism. Yet, they simultaneously deployed European colonial discourse for their own purposes of overcoming this very cultural victimizing effect of colonialism. See Bhargava, *What Is Political Theory*, 159–60.

48 Lajpat Rai, 'Swami Dayanand', 373.

49 Lajpat Rai, 375.

50 Lajpat Rai, 'Shivaji', 343. The comparison is with the medieval Ottoman Empire which, by the early sixteenth century, had

expanded into South East Europe, conquering Serbia, Bulgaria, Constantinople (now, Istanbul), and then Greece, Bosnia, Albania, Herzegovina, modern Romania and Hungary. The Ottomans had ruled over millions of Eastern European Christian subjects just as the majority of the world's Muslims would soon be governed by European Christians. Christian (and Jewish) populations had been reconciled by conceding some form of communal autonomy. See John Darwin, *After Tamerlane: The Rise and Fall of Global Empires, 1400–2000* (London: Penguin Books, 2008), 39, 73, 76; Cemil Aydin, *The Idea of the Muslim World: A Global Intellectual History* (Cambridge, Massachusetts: Harvard University Press, 2017), 66.

51 Lajpat Rai, 'Giuseppe Mazzini', 290–91.

52 Lajpat Rai, 'Shivaji', 343–44. Rajput Rajas had over time entered into alliances with the Mughals, accepting their sovereignty and paying tribute, but remaining autonomous and collecting revenue within their own domains. Although the Mughals faced periodic opposition from some Rajputs, they were largely incorporated into the Mughal ruling elite. This arrangement continued until the late seventeenth century, when the two most important Rajput houses rebelled, inaugurating a period of extended conflict which alienated these long-standing erstwhile allies. Barbara Daly Metcalf and Thomas R. Metcalf, *A Concise History of Modern India* (Cambridge [England]; New York: Cambridge University Press, 2012), 16–17, 23, 30–31; Stewart Gordon, *The Marathas, 1600–1818*, The New Cambridge History of India, II, 4 (Cambridge [England]; New York: Cambridge University Press, 1993), 104; Audrey Truschke, *Aurangzeb: The Life and Legacy of India's Most Controversial King* (Stanford: Stanford University Press, 2017), 93.

53 Lala Lajpat Rai, *Chattrapati Shivaji*, ed. and tr. Bhawanilal Bharatiya (Delhi: Vijaykumar Govindpuram Hasananad, 2012), 73, https://www.hindustanbooks.com/books/shivaji/shivaji.pdf. Shivaji had been the pivotal player in the Maratha insurgency that raged against Aurangzeb in the Deccan, and founded the Maratha polity. This laid the ground for the establishment of the

Maratha confederacy under the Peshwas (the chief ministers of Shivaji's descendants) in 1713, which lasted till their defeat at the hands of the British in 1818. Interestingly, Shivaji had allied with numerous 'Muslim' sultanates, including Bijapur and Golkonda, and even the Mughals when it suited him (while allying against Hindu powers such as the Nayakas of the Carnatic). He welcomed Muslims in his army, employed Muslim *qazis* (judges) as well as commanders. Later Peshwa rule saw a predominance of Brahmins in administration and the army, but continued the practices of 'Muslim' kingdoms and the recruitment of Muslims into the army. For more on the sort of polity Shivaji sought to create, see Gordon, *The Marathas, 1600–1818*, 66, 81; Truschke, *Aurangzeb*, 93–99. For more on the Peshwas, see Gordon, *The Marathas, 1600–1818*, 185–86, 192.

54 Wolpert, *Tilak and Gokhale*, 80, 82; Cashman, *Myth of Lokmanya*, 101, 103, 105–07. Although Ranade's book, *The Rise of Maratha Power* (1900) had not yet been published, Lajpat Rai had consulted its manuscript to write his own 1896 tract on Shivaji. Feroz Chand, *Lajpat Rai: Life and Work* (New Delhi: Publications Division, Ministry of Information and Broadcasting, Government of India, 1978), 82–83. With Lajpat Rai having already met Tilak at the 1893 Congress session, he was likely influenced by the latter's efforts to popularize the Shivaji memorial fund in 1895–96. Dhananjay Keer, *Lokmanya Tilak— Father of the Indian Freedom Struggle* (Bombay: SB Kangutkar, 1959), 51. This has indeed been suggested by Rai's biographer. See Chand, *Lajpat Rai*, 410.

55 Sikh warrior clans had consolidated and governed portions of Punjab during the eighteenth century, eventually laying the ground for the establishment of Ranjit Singh's Sikh Empire in the early nineteenth century, which for some time would rival that of the English East India Company. Although Lajpat Rai presented the Sikh Empire as an example of Hindu rule, it had been established in opposition to both the Mughals as well as local Hindu rulers in the Pahari region. Moreover, Ranjit Singh

ran his government as a *Sarkar-i-Khalsa* (Khalsa being the model of Sikh divine sovereignty). At the same time, it was a cosmopolitan administration and court. Sikh courtly culture creatively deployed the 'grammar' of the Mughal court, its rituals, symbols and ceremonies, to convey power and authority as it was understood in early modern times. The Maharaja had not refrained from marrying Muslim and Hindu women, his most famous 'love marriages' being with two Muslim dancing girls, Moran and Gul Begum. He had also keenly supported and engaged with religious scholars and institutions of all faiths in Punjab, lavishly celebrating many of the festivals observed (jointly) by Sikhs, Muslims and Hindus. See Priya Atwal, *Royals and Rebels: The Rise and Fall of the Sikh Empire* (London: Hurst and Company, 2020), chaps 1–2.

56 Jones, *Arya Dharm*, 136, 207. Arya Samajists attacked Sikh ideas about the infallibility of Guru Nanak in the 1880s, resulting in a loss of Sikh support for the Samaj, and seriously embittering Sikh–Arya relations. In the late 1890s, Arya attempts to portray Sikhism as part of the Hindu fold were resisted by Sikhs through pamphlets with titles like '*Hum Hindu Nahin*' (We Are Not Hindu). Harnik Deol, *Religion and Nationalism in India: The Case of the Punjab* (London; New York: Routledge, 2003), 70, 74; Harjot Oberoi, 'From Ritual to Counter Ritual: Rethinking the Hindu–Sikh Question', in *Sikh History and Religion in the Twentieth Century*, ed. Joseph O'Connell, Milton Israel, and Willard Oxtoby (The Centre for South Asian Studies: Toronto: University of Toronto, 1988); Mark Juergensmeyer, *Religious Rebels in the Punjab: The Ad Dharm Challenge to Caste*, New Delhi (Berkeley: Navayana Publishing, 2009), 27–28.

57 Lajpat Rai, 'Shivaji', 345. Rai seems to have been alluding to the Chalukyas (973–1189 CE), Hoysalas and Yadavas (12th–14th century), the Cholas (907–1300 CE) and the Kakatiyas (12th century). The reference is also to the Vijayanagara Empire that ruled from 1336 to the late seventeenth century, existing alongside the Deccan sultanates.

58 Lajpat Rai, 345. Rajputs (including a few non-Hindu Rajputs) were indeed part of Mughal administrative and military elite under Akbar. For more, see John F. Richards, *The Mughal Empire*, The New Cambridge History of India, I, 5 (Cambridge; New York, NY: Cambridge University Press, 1993), 21–24.
Later, under Jahangir and Aurangzeb, Marathas and Brahmins too were attached to the Mughal administration.

59 Interestingly, some like W.C. Bonnerji and Dadabhai Naoroji, looking past the Hindu–Muslim binary, seemed to view all former polities as examples of 'Asiatic despotism', together inferior to the British imperial polity which introduced to them Western political ideas of representative government, equality before law, and freedom of speech and press. Daniel Argov, *Moderates and Extremists in the Indian National Movement, 1883–1920: With Special Reference to Surendranath Banerjea and Lajpat Rai* (London: Asia Publishing House, 1967), 32.

60 Chatterjee, 'History and the Nationalisation of Hinduism', 115.

61 In the early medieval period, these included rulers like the Katehariya Rajputs, the Chauhans of Ranthambore, the Chaulukyas of Gujarat, Paramaras of Malwa, Chandelas and Baghelas. After the fifteenth century, important Rajput houses encompassed the rulers of Marwar, and the Sishodias of Mewar. These states were able to maintain autonomous control for significant periods of time and, often, even when subdued, paid tribute to and served the Delhi sultans or Mughals while keeping authority within their compact domains. For more, see Satish Chandra, *History of Medieval India: 800–1700* (New Delhi: Orient Longman, 2007).

62 This periodization of Indian history, according to the religion, into 'Hindu' and 'Muslim' periods was also a legacy of European history-writing.

63 Chatterjee, 'History and the Nationalisation of Hinduism', 108–09.

64 Lajpat Rai, 'Giuseppe Mazzini', 290.

65 Lajpat Rai, 'Swami Dayanand', 383.

66 Lajpat Rai, 387.

67 Lajpat Rai, 389.

68 The idea that followers of the Vedic religion, under influence from Buddhism, began to depict Rama and Krishna as incarnations of God is also seen in Lala Lajpat Rai, 'Sri Krishna, Extracts from Yogiraj Shri Krishna, Lahore, 1900', in *CWLLR*, vol. 1, 2003, 426.

69 The majority of the Puranas were composed between the third and the eighth centuries, before the arrival of Islam.

70 Lajpat Rai, 'Swami Dayanand', 390–91.

71 Lajpat Rai, 'Swami Dayanand', 391–92.

72 Here, Lajpat Rai differed from Dayanand Saraswati who regarded Sankaracharya as a Vedic reformer who combated anti-Vedic teachings and set the model for future Vedic reformers including Dayanand himself. Pandit Lekh Ram of the Gurukul Party similarly extolled Sankara for defeating Jain and Buddhist heterodoxies. Adcock, *Limits of Tolerance*, 43, 118.

73 Lajpat Rai, 'Swami Dayanand', 393.

74 Lajpat Rai, 'Swami Dayanand', 393.

75 Lajpat Rai, 'Swami Dayanand', 393.

76 Metcalf, *Ideologies*, 8–9, 133.

77 Lajpat Rai, 'Swami Dayanand', 393–94. The spread of early Islam was not simply an outcome of violent conquest. It was enabled by alliances with Jews and Christians (who were often given guarantees of protection), religious tolerance and the theological common ground between these Abrahamic faiths. For details, see Peter Frankopan, *The Silk Roads: A New History of the World* (Bloomsbury, 2016), 79–87.

78 Lajpat Rai, 'Swami Dayanand', 393–94.

79 Lajpat Rai, 'Swami Dayanand', 393.

80 Tilak, *Orion*, 199, 206; Dermot Killingley, 'Modernity, Reform, and Revival', in *The Blackwell Companion to Hinduism*, ed. Gavin Flood (Malden, MA: Blackwell, 2003).

81 Figueira, *Aryans, Jews, Brahmins*, 125.

82 Daniel Argov, *Moderates and Extremists in the Indian National Movement, 1883–1920: With Special Reference to Surendranath*

Banerjea and Lajpat Rai (London: Asia Publishing House, 1967), 32.

83 Jordens, *Dayānanda Sarasvatī*, 103; Jones, *Arya Dharm*, 32–33.

84 Christophe Jaffrelot, *Religion, Caste, and Politics in India* (London: Hurst, 2011), 88.

85 Jaffrelot, 88.

86 Tanika Sarkar, *Hindu Wife, Hindu Nation, Community, Religion, and Cultural Nationalism* (Bloomington: Indiana University Press, 2001), 182.

87 Chatterjee, 'History and the Nationalisation of Hinduism', 114.

88 Dalmia, 'Vaisnava Self-Representation', 191, 202.

89 M.B. Kolaskar, ed., *Religious and Social Reform* (Bombay: Gopal Narayen and Co., 1902), 98–100, 190; Figueira, *Aryans, Jews, Brahmins*, 125.

90 Chatterjee, 'History and the Nationalisation of Hinduism', 117.

91 Interestingly, Banerjea evoked the notion of Hindu degradation and pre-colonial anarchy but, as we saw in Chapter 2, rather than dwelling on Hindu rule, Hindu defeat and decline, he construed the medieval period as embodying the 'history of 800 years of goodwill and amity' between India's Hindus and Muslims, 'which but for the fanaticism of Aurangzeb would have lasted another 800 years'. For him, the cordiality, love and trust between Hindus and Muslims had even survived the wreck of the Mughal Empire to pervade rural India till today. Surendranath Banerjea, 'An Appeal to the Mohammedan Community, Speech at Congress Meeting, Dacca, 1 October 1888', in *Speeches and Writings of Hon. Surendranath Banerjea* (G.A. Natesan and Co., n.d.), 268–70; 'Indian Unity, Speech at Student's Association, Calcutta, 1878', in *Speeches and Writings of Hon. Surendranath Banerjea* (GA Natesan and Co., n.d.), 215.

92 Rai, *Chattrapati Shivaji*, 73–74. Interestingly, by the early 1920s, Rai would acquire an attitude of critical respect towards Shivaji, viewing him as an empire builder (rather than a nation-builder), who did not champion the people's swaraj or freedom, but

whose bureaucratic machinery was despotic in its exploitation of ordinary cultivators. Chand, *Lajpat Rai*, 410–11.

Chapter 5

1 Lala Lajpat Rai, *Autobiographical Writings*, ed. V.C. Joshi (Delhi: University Publishers, 1965), 87–88.

2 Lajpat Rai, 89; Feroz Chand, *Lajpat Rai: Life and Work* (New Delhi: Publications Division, Ministry of Information and Broadcasting, Government of India, 1978), 79.

3 Daniel Argov, *Moderates and Extremists in the Indian National Movement, 1883–1920: With Special Reference to Surendranath Banerjea and Lajpat Rai* (London: Asia Publishing House, 1967), 86.

4 Reasons for the Congress's loss of vitality included lack of full-time leadership and organization, financial troubles, anxieties about its narrow social base, factionalism among provincial delegates and their involvement in local and provincial politics and controversies which consumed their time. Interestingly, another reason was that the top Congress leaders, often also social reformers, faced deeply strained domestic lives and hostility from society, which limited their ability to devote their time to all-India 'national' issues. A final reason was also the tendency of the Congress oligarchy to concentrate their efforts in England, stemming from the belief that hope for political advancement lay in appealing directly to the British parliament and the British public. See John R. McLane, *Indian Nationalism and the Early Congress* (Princeton: Princeton University Press, 1977), 69–83, 91, 132–47.

5 Dhananjay Keer, *Lokmanya Tilak—Father of the Indian Freedom Struggle* (Bombay: SB Kangutkar, 1959), 175.

6 David Hardiman, *The Nonviolent Struggle for Indian Freedom, 1905–19*, 2018, 33–34.

7 Argov, *Moderates and Extremists in the Indian National Movement, 1883–1920: With Special Reference to Surendranath*

Banerjea and Lajpat Rai, 85; Hardiman, *The Nonviolent Struggle for Indian Freedom, 1905–19*, 33; Keer, *Lokmanya Tilak*, 76; McLane, *Indian Nationalism and the Early Congress*, 67.

8　Lala Lajpat Rai, 'Defects of the Congress and Remedies, Kayastha Samachar, November 1901', in *CWLLR*, vol. 2, 2003 [Hereafter cited as 'Defects of the Congress'], 9.

9　Lajpat Rai, 4, 6.

10　Lajpat Rai, 7–8.

11　Lajpat Rai, 'Defects of the Congress', 8.

12　Farzana Shaikh, *Community and Consensus in Islam: Muslim Representation in Colonial India, 1860–1947* (Delhi: Imprint One, 2012), 104–09.

13　Shaikh, 114–18.

14　For more details, see Shaikh, 129–31.

15　Shaikh, 104–09, 115, 129, 132.

16　The image of the bigoted *julaha* was born as weavers in the nineteenth century protested (sometimes violently) against the loss of livelihood, honour and identity in the wake of the new economic realities of colonialism and industrialism. Weavers often reacted against the loss of their status as independent craftsmen and their new dependence on Hindu moneylenders and merchants, who gained an unprecedented hold on both the trade and weavers themselves. Just as with low-caste Hindus and 'Sanskritization' (the adoption of upper-caste norms and practices), increased Islamicization was a means for julahas to gain self-respect. Anxieties related to socio-economic dislocation and attempts to gain social standing underlay the julaha concern to preserve and defend their religious festivals and places of worship. All this social, political and economic context was left out of unchanging stereotypes about the fanatical julaha produced by colonial knowledge, and upon which Rai now unconsciously drew. Gyanendra Pandey, *The Construction of Communalism in Colonial North India* (New Delhi: Oxford University Press, 2006), chap. 3.

17　Lajpat Rai, 'Defects of the Congress', 6–7.

18 McLane, *Indian Nationalism and the Early Congress*, 112–14.
19 Argov, *Moderates and Extremists in the Indian National Movement, 1883–1920: With Special Reference to Surendranath Banerjea and Lajpat Rai*, 72.
20 Lajpat Rai, 'Defects of the Congress', 9.
21 Lajpat Rai, 8.
22 Lajpat Rai, 6.
23 Lajpat Rai, 9.
24 Lajpat Rai, 6.
25 Christophe Jaffrelot, 'Genesis and Development of Hindu Nationalism in the Punjab: From the Arya Samaj to the Hindu Sabha (1875–1910)', in *Religion, Caste, and Politics in India* (London: Hurst, 2011), 102.
26 See Gopal Krishna Gokhale, 'Budget Speech as Member of the Imperial Legislative Council, 1902', in John Hoyland (ed.), *Gopal Krishna Gokhale: His Life and Speeches* (YMCA Publishing: Calcutta, 1933), 89–98.
27 Gopal Krishna Gokhale, 'Speech Delivered at a Farewell Meeting for A.O. Hume, Poona, 1894', in *Speeches of Gopal Krishna Gokhale* (Madras: GA Natesan and Co., 1920), 554–56.
28 Gopal Krishna Gokhale, 'The Servants of India Society', in *Speeches and Writings of Gopal Krishna Gokhale*, ed. D.G. Karve and D.V. Ambedkar, vol. 2 (Bombay: Asia Publishing House, 1966).
29 Cited in Bal Ram Nanda, *Gokhale: The Indian Moderates and the British Raj* (Delhi: Oxford UP, 1977), 58.
30 Surendranath Banerjea, *Speeches and Writings of Hon. Surendranath Banerjea* (GA Natesan and Co., n.d.), 265.
31 Mahadev Govind Ranade, 'Inaugural Address at Thirteenth Social Conference, Lucknow, 1899', in *The Miscellaneous Writings of the Late Hon'ble Mr. Justice MG Ranade* (New Delhi: Sahitya Akademi, 1915) [hereafter cited as 'Inaugural Address], 214–29.
32 Madan Mohan Malaviya, 'Representation of Indians in Parliament, Speech at Twentieth Indian National Congress,

Bombay, 1904', in *The Hon. Pundit Madan Mohan Malaviya: His Life and Speeches* (Madras: Ganesh and Co., 1910), 47–48.

33 Bal Gangadhar Tilak, 'Speech at Bharat Dharma Mahamandal, Benaras, 3 January 1906', in *Balgangadhar Tilak: His Speeches and Writings*, 1918, 12–20.

34 Norman Barrier, 'The Arya Samaj and Congress Politics in the Punjab, 1894–1908', *The Journal of Asian Studies* 26, no. 03 (1967): 378–79; Prabhu Bapu, *Hindu Mahasabha in Colonial North India, 1915–1930: Constructing Nation and History* (London: Routledge, 2013), 20.

35 Lajpat Rai, 'Defects of the Congress', 6.

36 Lajpat Rai, 6.

37 Lajpat Rai, 6.

38 Lajpat Rai, 10.

39 Lala Lajpat Rai, 'Progress of D.A.V. College Not Satisfactory, Indian Social Reformer, 30 August 1903', in *CWLLR*, vol. 2, 2003, 233–34.

40 Bal Gangadhar Tilak, 'Is Shivaji Not a National Hero?, Mahratta, 24 June 1906', in *Balgangadhar Tilak: His Speeches and Writings*, 1918, 29–30.

41 Lala Lajpat Rai, 'The Lesson That India Should Learn from the United States, Evening Post, 2 October 1905', in *CWLLR*, vol. 2, 2003, 187.

42 Pandey, *Construction of Communalism*, 210–18.

43 Ranade, 'Inaugural Address', 226–27.

44 Lajpat Rai, 'Defects of the Congress', 8.

45 Lala Lajpat Rai, 'Hindu Nationalism, Hindustan Review and Kayastha Samachar, September–October 1902', in *CWLLR*, vol. 2, 2003, 295–96; Chetan Bhatt, *Hindu Nationalism: Origins, Ideologies and Modern Myths* (Oxford: Berg, 2001), 50. Most contemporary theorists of nationalism would agree with the 'anonymous Hindu nationalist' in arguing for the modern origins of the ideology of nationalism. See Benedict Anderson, *Imagined Communities: Reflections on the Origin and Spread of Nationalism* (London: Verso, 1983); Ernest Gellner, *Nations*

and Nationalism (Ithaca, New York: Cornell University Press, 1983); Eric Hobsbawm, *Nations and Nationalism since 1780: Programme, Myth, Reality* (Cambridge [England]; New York: Cambridge University Press, 1990).

46 This encyclopaedic Sanskrit epic was composed in different stages over many centuries, between 400 BCE and 400 CE. The core story revolves around a great war fought between two sets of cousins, the Pandavas and Kauravas, in Kurukshetra. Archaeologists and historians of ancient India argue that the historicity of events and characters in a literary epic like the Mahabharata cannot be proved from archaeological evidence. It is possible that a small-scale conflict occurred around 1000 BCE, which was then transformed into a gigantic epic war by bards and poets. Upinder Singh, *A History of Ancient and Early Medieval India: From the Stone Age to the 12th Century* (New Delhi; Upper Saddle River, NJ: Pearson Education, 2008), 114–18.

47 Romila Thapar, *The Penguin History of Early India: From the Origins to AD 1300* (London: Penguin, 2003), 285–86; Singh, *Ancient and Early Medieval India*, 1674. Less likely, this may be a reference to the eleventh-century Paramara king of Malwa, Central India. Thapar, *Penguin History*, 420; Satish Chandra, *History of Medieval India: 800–1700* (New Delhi: Orient Longman, 2007), 61–63.

48 Bhatt, *Origins*, 91.

49 Lajpat Rai, 'Swami Dayanand', 389–90.

50 Thapar, *Penguin History*, 409–11; Singh, *Ancient and Early Medieval India*, 1747.

51 Lajpat Rai, 'Hindu Nationalism', 295.

52 Lajpat Rai, 'Hindu Nationalism', 296.

53 Chandra, *History of Medieval India: 800–1700*, 61–70.

54 Lajpat Rai, 'Hindu Nationalism', 296–97.

55 Ranade, 'Inaugural Address', 219–24.

56 Gopal Krishna Gokhale, 'The Swadeshi Movement, 9 February 1907', in *Speeches and Writings of Gopal Krishna Gokhale*, ed.

D.G. Karve and D.V. Ambedkar, vol. 2 (Bombay: Asia Publishing House, 1966), 225.

57 Jyotirmaya Sharma, *Hindutva: Exploring the Idea of Hindu Nationalism* (New Delhi: Viking, 2003), 150–51.

58 Lajpat Rai, 'Hindu Nationalism', 299.

59 Lajpat Rai, 299.

60 Lajpat Rai, 299.

61 Lajpat Rai, 299.

62 Lajpat Rai, 299.

63 Lajpat Rai, 299.

64 Vinayak Damodar Savarkar, *Hindutva: Who Is a Hindu?* (Bombay: Veer Savarkar Prakashan, 1969) [hereafter cited as *Hindutva*], 44–45.

65 According to some accounts, Savarkar finished writing the treatise by 1907, but since the government proscribed the book even before it was finished, he found it difficult to find publishers for two years. The book was eventually published in 1909. Vinayak Chaturvedi, 'Rethinking Knowledge with Action: V.D. Savarkar, the Bhagavad Gita, and Histories of Warfare', *Modern Intellectual History* 7, no. 02 (2010): 425. Banned in India, it would be smuggled to India, interestingly, with the help of a certain Sikandar Hayat Khan. Vikram Sampath, *Savarkar: Echoes from a Forgotten Past, 1883–1924* (Gurgaon: Viking, 2019), 130.

66 Janaki Bakhle, 'Country First? Vinayak Damodar Savarkar (1883–1966) and the Writing of Essentials of Hindutva', *Public Culture* 22, no. 1 (2010): 153–70; Sharma, *Hindutva*, 156.

67 Bakhle, 'Country First'; Chaturvedi, 'Rethinking Knowledge', 429–30.

68 Bakhle, 'Country First', 169; Sharma, *Hindutva*, 169–70.

69 Chaturvedi, 'Rethinking Knowledge', 431–32; Bhatt, *Origins*, 89–90. Savarkar would hold negative views about Ashoka's Buddhist non-violence till the end of his life, with this theme reappearing in his final book, *Six Glorious Epochs of Indian History*, completed three years before his suicide in 1966. Shruti

Kapila, *Violent Fraternity: Indian Political Thought in the Global Age* (Princeton: Princeton University Press, 2021), 98, 109.

70 Chaturvedi, 'Rethinking Knowledge', 432–33.

71 Gyanendra Pandey, 'Hindus and Others: The Militant Hindu Construction', *Economic and Political Weekly* 26, no. 52 (1991): 2997, n. 7; Bakhle, 'Country First', 169; Bhatt, *Origins*, 92; Manan Ahmed Asif, *The Loss of Hindustan: The Invention of India* (Cambridge, Massachusetts: Harvard University Press, 2020), 11; For more on Savarkar's 'war on' India's history, and his radical re-presentation of it as a history of warfare, see Kapila, *Violent Fraternity*, 101, 103–05, 108, 111, 113.

72 See Aamir Mufti, *Enlightenment in the Colony: The Jewish Question and the Crisis of Postcolonial Culture* (Princeton: Princeton University Press, 2007), 161–64.

73 Savarkar, *Hindutva*, 83–84.

74 Savarkar, 84, 100, 110.

75 Savarkar, 91.

76 Savarkar, 84, 100, 110.

77 Savarkar, 91.

78 Savarkar, 92, 100, 101–02.

79 Savarkar, 100.

80 Savarkar, 100–101.

81 Savarkar, 100–101.

82 Savarkar, 101.

83 Savarkar, 100.

84 Savarkar, *Hindutva*, 101.

85 Savarkar, 102.

86 Savarkar, 111.

87 Savarkar, 111–13.

88 Savarkar, 113.

89 Savarkar, 113.

90 Savarkar, 113.

91 Savarkar, 113.

92 Savarkar, 115.

93 Savarkar, 84, 92, 100–101, 113, 130, 135.

94 Bhatt, *Origins*, 52.

95 Bhatt, 52.

96 Peter Heehs, *Nationalism, Terrorism, Communalism: Essays in Modern Indian History* (Delhi: Oxford University Press, 1998), 98, 109–11.

97 Heehs, *Nationalism, Terrorism, Communalism*, 110–11.

98 Heehs, *Nationalism, Terrorism, Communalism*, 109–11.

99 Heehs, *Nationalism, Terrorism, Communalism*, 111–12.

100 For Aurobindo's and B.C. Pal's nationalism, see Peter Heehs, *Nationalism, Terrorism, Communalism: Essays in Modern Indian History* (Delhi: Oxford University Press, 1998), 98–118; Semanti Ghosh, *Different Nationalisms: Bengal, 1905–1947* (New Delhi: Oxford University Press, 2017), 12, 54–55.

Chapter 6

1 Lala Lajpat Rai, 'Hindu Nationalism, Hindustan Review and Kayastha Samachar, September–October 1902', in *CWLLR*, vol. 2, 2003, 298.

2 Lala Lajpat Rai, 'The Social Genius of Hinduism, The Hindustan Review and Kayastha Samachar, April 1904', in *CWLLR*, vol. 2, 2003, 302, 307.

3 Lajpat Rai, 301–02.

4 Daniel Pick, 'The Politics of Nature: Science and Religion in the Age of Darwin', in *The Cambridge History of Nineteenth-Century Political Thought*, ed. Gareth Stedman Jones and Gregory Claeys (Cambridge University Press, 2011), 649–58.

5 Pick, 657; Lawrence Goldman, 'Conservative Political Thought from the Revolutions of 1848 until the Fin de Siècle', in *The Cambridge History of Nineteenth-Century Political Thought*, ed. Gareth Stedman Jones and Gregory Claeys (Cambridge University Press, 2011), 713.

6 Pick, 'Politics of Nature', 677.

7 Pick, 678; Christopher Bayly, 'European Political Thought and the Wider World during the Nineteenth Century', in *The Cambridge History of Nineteenth-Century Political Thought*,

ed. Gareth Stedman Jones and Gregory Claeys (Cambridge: Cambridge University Press, 2011), 851.

8 Shruti Kapila, 'Self, Spencer and Swaraj: Nationalist Thought and Critiques of Liberalism, 1890–1920', *Modern Intellectual History* 4, no. 1 (2007): 115.

9 Kapila, 113.

10 A.M. Shah, 'The Indian Sociologist, 1905–14, 1920–22', *Economic and Political Weekly* 41, no. 31 (5–11 August 2006): 3438.

11 Lala Lajpat Rai, *Autobiographical Writings*, ed. V.C. Joshi (Delhi: University Publishers, 1965), 105–07.

12 Harald Fischer-Tiné, *Shyamji Krishnavarma: Sanskrit, Sociology and Anti-Imperialism* (New Delhi: Routledge, 2015), chap. 2.

13 Kapila, 'Self, Spencer and Swaraj', 114–16.

14 Lala Lajpat Rai, 'The Social Genius of Hinduism, The Hindustan Review and Kayastha Samachar, April 1904', in *CWLLR*, vol. 2, 2003 [Hereafter cited as 'Social Genius'].

15 Lajpat Rai, 'Social Genius', 303.

16 Thomas Dixon, *The Invention of Altruism: Making Moral Meanings in Victorian Britain* (Oxford: Oxford University Press, 2008), 184, 198–99.

17 Dixon, 8.

18 Dixon, 193.

19 Dixon, 195–200.

20 Dixon, 207–08.

21 Dixon, 198–99.

22 Ibid.

23 Dixon, 303–06.

24 For Kidd's views, see Thomas Dixon, *The Invention of Altruism: Making Moral Meanings in Victorian Britain* (Oxford: Oxford University Press, 2008), 304–12.

25 Upinder Singh, *A History of Ancient and Early Medieval India: From the Stone Age to the 12th Century* (New Delhi; Upper Saddle River, NJ: Pearson Education, 2008), 793–96, 815–16.

26 Some scholars point out that there is no indication in the Rig Veda that membership in these four strata was determined by birth and suggest the possibility of social mobility. Singh, 816.

27 Lajpat Rai, 'Social Genius', 308.

28 Lajpat Rai, 308–09.

29 Lajpat Rai, 308.

30 Lajpat Rai, 309.

31 Lajpat Rai, 313–17.

32 Constance Jones and James Ryan, *Encyclopedia of Hinduism* (Infobase publishing, 2006), 259.

33 Lajpat Rai, 'Social Genius', 313–16.

34 Lajpat Rai, 319.

35 Lajpat Rai, 319–22. The Atharva Veda mainly consists of spells and charms to ward off diseases and influence events. It is considered the origin of the system of Ayurveda. Jones and Ryan, *Encyclopedia of Hinduism*, xix.

36 Lajpat Rai, 'Social Genius', 321.

37 Lajpat Rai, 322.

38 Lajpat Rai, 322.

39 Lajpat Rai, 301–02.

40 Lajpat Rai, 'Hindu Nationalism', 298.

41 Lajpat Rai, 'Social Genius', 301–02, 319.

42 The phrase is Ranade's. Charles Heimsath, *Indian Nationalism and Hindu Social Reform* (Princeton: Princeton University Press, 1964), 180.

43 Heimsath, 183.

44 Heimsath, 200–04; Swaminath Natarajan, *A Century of Social Reforms in India* (London: Asia Publishing House, 1959), 86.

45 Lajpat Rai, 'Social Genius', 301, 306.

46 Lajpat Rai, 306.

47 Dixon, *Invention of Altruism*, 311–12.

48 For more see, Adam Swift, *Political Philosophy: A Beginners' Guide for Students and Politicians* (Polity Press, 2014), 198.

49 Lala Lajpat Rai, 'Reform or Revival?, The Hindustan Review and Kayastha Samachar, 1904', in *CWLLR*, vol. 2, 2003 [hereafter cited as 'Reform or Revival?'], 327.

50 Mahadev Govind Ranade, *The Miscellaneous Writings of the Late Hon'ble Mr. Justice MG Ranade* (New Delhi: Sahitya Akademi, 1915), 71.

51 Dixon, *Invention of Altruism*, 200.

52 Lala Lajpat Rai, 'Reform or Revival?, 328.

53 Kenneth Jones, *Arya Dharm: Hindu Consciousness in Nineteenth Century Punjab* (Delhi: Manohar, 1976), 251.

54 C.S. Adcock, *The Limits of Tolerance: Indian Secularism and the Politics of Religious Freedom* (New York: Oxford University Press, 2013), 44–45, 120–21.

55 Lala Lajpat Rai, 'Hinduism and Common Nationality, before 1907', in *CWLLR*, vol. 2, 2003, 331.

56 Lajpat Rai, 332.

57 Lajpat Rai, 333–34; Theodore Goldstücker, 'Religious Difficulties of India', in *Literary Remains of the Late Professor Theodore Goldstücker*, vol. 2 (London: W.H. Allen and Co., 1879), 41.

58 Lajpat Rai, 'Hinduism and Common Nationality', 332.

59 See Christophe Jaffrelot, *The Hindu Nationalist Movement and Indian Politics: 1925 to the 1990s* (New Delhi: Penguin Books, 1999), 20.

60 Lajpat Rai, 'Hinduism and Common Nationality', 332.

61 Lajpat Rai, 331.

62 Lajpat Rai, 332.

63 Lajpat Rai, 332.

64 For more on belonging without believing, see Avi Astor and Damon Mayrl, 'Culturalized Religion: A Synthetic Review and Agenda for Research', *Journal for the Scientific Study of Religion* 59, no. 2 (2020): 9.

65 Vinayak Damodar Savarkar, *Hindutva: Who Is a Hindu?* (Bombay: Veer Savarkar Prakashan, 1969), 3–4.

66 Having touched upon these in the previous chapter, I revisit them again in Chapter 9.

67 Lajpat Rai, 'Hinduism and Common Nationality', 335.

68 Dhananjay Keer, *Lokmanya Tilak–Father of the Indian Freedom Struggle* (Bombay: SB Kangutkar, 1959), 201.

69 Bal Gangadhar Tilak, 'Speech at Bharat Dharma Mahamandal, Benaras, 3 January 1906', in *Balgangadhar Tilak: His Speeches and Writings*, 1918, 13–15.

Chapter 7

1 Feroz Chand, *Lajpat Rai: Life and Work* (New Delhi: Publications Division, Ministry of Information and Broadcasting, Government of India, 1978), 105; N.G. Barrier, *The Arya Samaj and Congress Politics in the Punjab, 1894–1908*, 368.
2 Surendranath Banerjea and Jinnah were the other two members of the Congress deputation.
3 Sumit Sarkar, *Modern Times: 1880s–1950* (Ranikhet: Permanent Black, 2014), 5.
4 Sarkar, 5.
5 Sarkar, 5.
6 Sarkar, 6. Sarkar, 7.
7 Gregory Claeys, 'Non-Marxian Socialism 1815–1914', in *The Cambridge History of Nineteenth-Century Political Thought*, ed. Gareth Stedman Jones and Lawrence Goldman (Cambridge University Press, 2011), 523.
8 Lala Lajpat Rai, *Autobiographical Writings*, ed. V.C. Joshi (Delhi: University Publishers, 1965), 100–108; Chand, *Lajpat Rai*, 105–11; Bal Ram Nanda, *Gokhale: The Indian Moderates and the British Raj* (Delhi: Oxford UP, 1977), 190; Daniel Argov, *Moderates and Extremists in the Indian National Movement, 1883–1920: With Special Reference to Surendranath Banerjea and Lajpat Rai* (London: Asia Publishing House, 1967), 106–08.
9 David Hardiman, *The Nonviolent Struggle for Indian Freedom, 1905–19*, 2018, 23–24.
10 The following description of the Swadeshi movement is largely drawn from Hardiman, *The Nonviolent Struggle for Indian Freedom, 1905–19*, 24–37.
11 I of course do not use the term 'extremist' in a pejorative sense, but follow standard academic language used to refer to the

political faction of the Congress which urged more radical anti-colonial politics than the milder 'moderates'. These categories are also used in works such as Vikram Sampath, *Savarkar: A Contested Legacy, 1924–66* (Gurugram: Viking, 2021), 194–95, 219.

12 Nanda, *Gokhale*, 204–05.

13 Nanda, 208–09.

14 Lajpat Rai, *Autobiographical Writings*, 111; Nanda, *Gokhale*, 210.

15 Nanda, *Gokhale*, 211.

16 Lajpat Rai, *Autobiographical Writings*, 113.

17 Hardiman, *The Nonviolent Struggle for Indian Freedom, 1905–19*, 30.

18 Hardiman, *The Nonviolent Struggle for Indian Freedom, 1905–19*, 29.

19 Hardiman, 29; Sekhar Bandyopadhyay, *From Plassey to Partition: A History of Modern India* (New Delhi: Orient Longman, 2004), 232.

20 Nanda, *Gokhale*, 264. A similar criticism of Swadeshi and boycott was advanced by Rabindranath Tagore, initially an enthusiastic participant in the movement. Hardiman, *The Nonviolent Struggle for Indian Freedom, 1905–19*, 64.

21 Bandyopadhyay, *From Plassey to Partition: A History of Modern India*, 249.

22 Hardiman, *The Nonviolent Struggle for Indian Freedom, 1905–19*, 30; Bandyopadhyay, *From Plassey to Partition: A History of Modern India*, 250.

23 Hardiman, *The Nonviolent Struggle for Indian Freedom, 1905–19*, 30. Also see Lajpat Rai, *Autobiographical Writings*, 113.

24 Hardiman, *The Nonviolent Struggle for Indian Freedom, 1905–19*, 30.

25 Hardiman, 60.

26 Sumit Sarkar, *Modern India: 1886–1947* (Delhi: Macmillian, 1983), 132. Already in 1905, the twenty-two-year-old Savarkar was expelled from his Fergusson college residence for organizing

a bonfire of British goods in Poona. Vikram Sampath, *Savarkar: Echoes from a Forgotten Past, 1883–1924* (Gurgaon: Viking, 2019), 74.

27 The following details about the events in Punjab and Rai's deportation are drawn from Lajpat Rai, *Autobiographical Writings*, 111–13, 123–25, 186–88; Hardiman, *The Nonviolent Struggle for Indian Freedom, 1905–19*, 64–65; Nanda, *Gokhale*, 269. Also see C.S. Adcock, *The Limits of Tolerance: Indian Secularism and the Politics of Religious Freedom* (New York: Oxford University Press, 2013), 87–88.

28 Hardiman, *The Nonviolent Struggle for Indian Freedom, 1905–19*, 64–65, 76–77.

29 Hardiman, 65.

30 Hardiman, 66.

31 Adcock, *Limits of Tolerance*, 87–88; Also see Norman Barrier, 'The Punjab Disturbances of 1907: The Response of the British Government in India to Agrarian Unrest', *Modern Asian Studies* 1, no. 4 (1967): 14–21. Rai was deported along with Ajit Singh, a much more radical leader–organizer of the 1907 rural movement (and uncle of Bhagat Singh). See Lajpat Rai, *Autobiographical Writings*, 118–23; Hardiman, *The Nonviolent Struggle for Indian Freedom, 1905–19*, 66–67; Neeti Nair, *Changing Homelands: Hindu Politics and the Partition of India* (Cambridge, MA: Harvard University Press, 2011), 18–20.

32 Rai would later sue *The Englishman* for insinuating that he had tampered with the loyalty of troops, and was awarded fifteen thousand rupees in damages by a court. Nair, *Changing Homelands*, 44–45.

33 Scholarship on modern commentaries of the Gita generally give prominence to Gandhi, Tilak and Aurobindo Ghose while ignoring Lajpat Rai. An exception that acknowledges Rai's intervention, although without extended analysis, is Richard Davis, *The Bhagavad Gita: A Biography* (Princeton: Princeton University Press, 2014), 124–25.

34 This move interestingly resembled some British Protestants who portrayed the Gita as the Hindu bible, glossing over other Hindu

texts and even the rest of the Mahabharata, as well as Hindu gods like Shiva or Ram mentioned therein. See Wendy Doniger, *On Hinduism*, 2016, 16.

35 Mishka Sinha, 'Corrigibility, Allegory, Universality: A History of the Gita's Transnational Reception, 1785–1945', *Modern Intellectual History* 7, no. 2 (2010): 299, 304–06. Prior to the 1880s, the frolicsome Krishna of the Puranas was more popular than the charioteer–god of the Gita. Dipesh Chakrabarty and Rochona Majumdar, 'Gandhi's Gita and Politics as Such', *Modern Intellectual History* 7, no. 2 (2010): 339; Davis, *Bhagavad Gita*, 43–45.

36 In Hinduism, a *sampradaya* is an institutionalized order or tradition, marked by a guru–pupil lineage, and often traced to a historical or mythical founder, or to God (however identified). Sampradaya is often also translated as sect, denomination, school or community.

37 Lala Lajpat Rai, 'Message of the Bhagwad Gita, Modern Review, March 1908', in *CWLLR*, vol. 3, 2004, 329–30.

38 Already in 1900, Lajpat Rai had shown his ingenuity in claiming the post-'Vedic' Gita even as an Arya Samajist. He did this by denying Vaishnava claims of Krishna's divinity as a false distortion of Puranas like the Bhagavata Purana, and instead recasting Krishna as a historical figure, a model human being and hero of the Vedic period. For Rai, while the Puranas had distorted Krishna's personality, turning him into a vulgar figure prone to childish self-indulgence and sensual frivolity, the real Krishna was the solemn adult Krishna of the historically earlier Gita. This Krishna was depicted as a model ancient Aryan warrior–hero, whose teachings were consistent with the Vedic religion. Lala Lajpat Rai, 'Sri Krishna, *Extracts from Yogiraj Shri Krishna,* Lahore, 1900', in *CWLLR*, vol. 1, 2003, 425–40.

39 Christopher Bayly, 'India, The Bhagavad Gita and the World', *Modern Intellectual History* 7, no. 02 (2010): 286.

40 The following brief summary of the Gita's content is drawn from Davis, *Bhagavad Gita*, 18–20.

41 Davis, 54–64.

42 Lajpat Rai, 'Message of the Bhagwad Gita', 335.

43 Lajpat Rai, 335.

44 Lajpat Rai, 350; Annie Besant, trans., *The Bhagavad-Gîtâ: Or the Lord's Song* (Theosophical Publishing Society, 1903), 63; Barbara Stoler Miller, *The Bhagavad-Gita: Krishna's Counsel in Time of War* (New York: Bantam Classics, 2004), 59.

45 Lajpat Rai, 'Message of the Bhagwad Gita', 344–47.

46 Lajpat Rai, 347–48. Theosophy was a late-nineteenth-century spiritual philosophy, blending European thought with elements of Hindu and Buddhist philosophy. Unlike the many unsavoury colonial and Christian views of Hinduism, Theosophists saw Hinduism as a basis from which to build a peaceful world order founded on universal brotherhood. Theosophical readings of the Gita from the 1880s played a crucial role in its emergence as a trans-nationally influential text of universal spiritual significance. Annie Besant, who would rise to become Congress president in 1917, had arrived in India in the 1890s on a mission to awaken Indians to their own religious wisdom and spiritual leadership of the world. Contrary to the dominant colonial denigration of Hinduism, she had established the Central Hindu College in Benaras to establish the teaching of Sanskrit, ancient Indian history and philosophy. Her translation of the Gita symbolically interpreted the war in the Mahabharata as possessing parallels with India's national struggle for a greater measure of self-government. See Sunil Khilnani, 'Annie Besant: An Indian Tomtom', podcast, Incarnations: India in 50 Lives (BBC Radio 4, 25 February 2016); Sinha, 'Corrigibility, Allegory, Universality', 312–13.

47 Lajpat Rai, 'Message of the Bhagwad Gita', 348; Besant, *The Bhagavad-Gîtâ: Or the Lord's Song*, 44.

48 Lajpat Rai, 'Message of the Bhagwad Gita', 348; Besant, *The Bhagavad-Gîtâ: Or the Lord's Song*, 11. For a more recent translation of this verse, see Miller, *Bhagavad-Gita*, 44.

49 Andrew Sartori, *Bengal in Global Concept History: Culturalism in the Age of Capital* (Chicago: University of Chicago Press, 2008), 119–20.

50 Sinha, 'Corrigibility, Allegory, Universality', 312–13; Annie Besant, *The Bhagavad-Gita: Or the Lord's Song*, vol. 2 (London: Theosophical Publishing Society, 1895), v–vi.

51 Sanjay Seth, 'The Critique of Renunciation: Bal Gangadhar Tilak's Hindu Nationalism', *Postcolonial Studies* 9, no. 2 (2006): 142.

52 Davis, *Bhagavad Gita*, 128–29.

53 Having first read the Gita in 1889 as a twenty-year-old in London, Gandhi would remain dedicated to it throughout his life. He too criticized those who followed the paths of renunciation and devotion to the exclusion of worldly social duties, and viewed *karmayoga* as the Gita's most central teaching. For Gandhi, the Gita enjoined not renunciation of action, but self-control in order to perform social duties without attachment. Davis, 137–40.

54 Robert E. Upton, '"Take out a Thorn with a Thorn": B.G. Tilak's Legitimization of Political Violence', *Global Intellectual History* 2, no. 3 (2017): 337; Seth, 'Critique of Renunciation', 139; Davis, *Bhagavad Gita*, 130.

55 Sugata Bose, 'The Spirit and Form of an Ethical Polity: A Meditation on Aurobindo's Thought', *Modern Intellectual History* 4, no. 01 (2007): 136. Davis, *Bhagavad Gita*, 128–30, 149–52; Hardiman, *The Nonviolent Struggle for Indian Freedom, 1905–19*, 38.

56 Lajpat Rai, 'Message of the Bhagwad Gita', 336.

57 Lajpat Rai, 337.

58 Lajpat Rai, 337.

59 Lajpat Rai, 337.

60 Lajpat Rai, 337.

61 Lajpat Rai, 336–38.

62 Lajpat Rai, 336, 347.

63 Lajpat Rai, 347.

64 Lajpat Rai, 337.

65 Davis, *Bhagavad Gita*, 139–42. Explicitly differing with the literalist readings of Tilak, Savarkar and Krishnavarma, in his sustained commentary on the Gita in the mid-1920s, Gandhi

deployed its message of disinterested action to articulate a theory of non-violent political action. See Chakrabarty and Majumdar, 'Gandhi's Gita', 335, 347–49. Several years later, after India's partition and the terrible violence that accompanied it, in January 1948, Gandhi would be shot dead at one of his daily public prayer meetings, which included recitations of the Gita and the Quran. His assassin, Nathuram Godse, would draw an analogy between himself and Lord Krishna of the Gita: as Krishna had killed many influential persons for the betterment of the world, so too had he assassinated Gandhi for the same purpose. On the day of his hanging, he would carry with himself a copy of the Bhagavad Gita. Davis, *Bhagavad Gita*, 143–45.

66 Lajpat Rai, 'Message of the Bhagwad Gita', 341.

67 Lajpat Rai, 343–44.

68 Lajpat Rai, 352.

69 Lajpat Rai, 332, 339.

70 Lajpat Rai, 333.

71 Lajpat Rai, 353.

72 Lala Lajpat Rai, 'Need for Reform in the System of Government of India, The Panjabee, 4 September 1905', in *CWLLR*, vol. 2, 2003, 150; 'Punjab's Sympathy with Bengal, The Panjabee, 11 December 1905', in *CWLLR*, vol. 2, 2003, 37–40; 'Repressive Measures in Bengal, Report of 21st Session of the Indian National Congress, 1905', in *CWLLR*, vol. 2, 2003, 24; 'British Misrule in India, The Panjabee, 4 December 1905', in *CWLLR*, vol. 2, 2003, 158–61.

73 Interestingly, it was the 'moderate' Jinnah who was employed by Tilak to plead for his release pending trial. Although the British Empire had made up its mind regarding Tilak, Jinnah argued passionately. In 1916, he would once again defend Tilak in another charge of sedition, earning Tilak's gratitude and admiration.

74 Upton, 'Take out a Thorn', 333–34.

75 Shruti Kapila, 'A History of Violence', *Modern Intellectual History* 7, no. 2 (2010): 437–40, 453.

76 Upton, 'Take out a Thorn', 330, 340–41.

77 Lajpat Rai, *Autobiographical Writings*, 119–22.

78 Lajpat Rai, 138.

79 Lajpat Rai, 161.

80 Chand, *Lajpat Rai*, 139.

81 Lajpat Rai, *Autobiographical Writings*, 136–37.

82 Lajpat Rai, 149.

83 In a broad sense, Rai continued a long tradition of Hindu ambivalence towards violence. Violence and non-violence have been debated throughout Hinduism's long existence, but mostly in relation to the ritual sacrifice of animals. For long, violent sacrifice and the consumption of animals coexisted with rituals meant to alleviate guilt regarding such violence. In response to Buddhism and Jainism, post-Vedic Hinduism—as represented by the Upanishads, Manusmriti, the renunciatory and the bhakti tradition—grew more uncomfortable with the killing of animals, but ultimately often still remained ambivalent about Ahimsa. (See Doniger, *On Hinduism*, 410–17.) Lajpat Rai continued this ambivalence into the modern period and took it into the human and political domain.

84 Davis, *Bhagavad Gita*, 126; Chakrabarty and Majumdar, 'Gandhi's Gita', 342; Vinayak Chaturvedi, 'Rethinking Knowledge with Action: V.D. Savarkar, the Bhagavad Gita, and Histories of Warfare', *Modern Intellectual History* 7, no. 02 (2010): 427. Writing his *Indian War of Independence* at about the same time as Rai's commentary on the Gita, Savarkar praised what he called the spirit of jihad among Indian Muslims who had revolted against the British in 1857. Unlike Rai and Tilak, Savarkar valorized violence as essential to anti-colonial politics, arguing that passive resistance was futile without the backing of arms. From 1907, he and his associates at India House in London began to train in the use of guns, and smuggle guns and bomb manuals to India, with Savarkar even manufacturing bombs himself. During his meeting with Gandhi in London in 1909, he invoked Durga as the symbol of war as well as

Rama's slaying of Ravana to justify political violence. It was of course Savarkar's eagerness for violence—his manufacture of bombs, his pivotal role in the assassination of a British official in London, and his supply of pistols used in the assassination of another in India—that would lead to his arrest in 1910 on five separate charges, and his subsequent fifty-year sentence in Cellular Prison on the Andaman islands. Sampath, *Savarkar: Echoes from a Forgotten Past*, 126, 139–42, 150–51, 160–61, 180, 192, 244–45; Vinayak Chaturvedi, 'A Revolutionary's Biography: The Case of VD Savarkar', *Postcolonial Studies* 16, no. 2 (2013): 131.

Chapter 8

1 Most of the men who led the Muslim League in its early years have been forgotten from popular memory. For a list of names, see Syed Razi Wasti, *Lord Minto and the Indian Nationalist Movement, 1905 to 1910* (Oxford: Clarendon Press, 1964), 225. Contrary to popular belief, Jinnah did not found the Muslim League. Associated with the Congress at least since 1904, the young Khoja barrister from Bombay idolized Dadabhai Naoroji, Pherozeshah Mehta and Gokhale, and would join the League only in 1913 (while remaining a Congressman) at the insistence of the Muslim Leaguers Wazir Hasan and Maulana Mohamed Ali. Stanley Wolpert, *Jinnah of Pakistan* (New York: Oxford University Press, 1984), 18–26, 34.

2 There were large numbers of such Muslims, both 'traditional', like Maulana Abul Kalam Azad, and 'modern', like Congressman Dr Sayyid Mahmud. See Farzana Shaikh, *Community and Consensus in Islam: Muslim Representation in Colonial India, 1860–1947* (Delhi: Imprint One, 2012), 141.

3 Shaikh, 150.

4 For more details on the Congress split, see Bal Ram Nanda, *Gokhale: The Indian Moderates and the British Raj* (Delhi: Oxford

University Press, 1977), 282–88; Daniel Argov, *Moderates and Extremists in the Indian National Movement, 1883–1920: With Special Reference to Surendranath Banerjea and Lajpat Rai* (London: Asia Publishing House, 1967), 118–35.

5 Nanda, *Gokhale*, 291.

6 Lala Lajpat Rai, 'Unity in Congress Despite Internal Quarrels, Speech at Meeting Convened by Moderates, Surat, 28 December 1907', in *CWLLR*, vol. 3, 2004; Nanda, *Gokhale*, 284, 290.

7 The Muzaffarpur Conspiracy Case wherein Bose and Prafulla Chaki attempted to assassinate the magistrate of Calcutta, Douglas Kingsford. Aurobindo Ghose and other members of the Anushilan Samiti were tried at the Alipur court for the same conspiracy in what became known as the 'Alipur Bomb Case'.

8 David Hardiman, *The Nonviolent Struggle for Indian Freedom, 1905–19*, 2018, 71.

9 Hardiman, 72. Tilak was sentenced to six years hard labour. Ghose's arrest set him on a path that would have him flee British India for the French territory of Pondicherry, where he would live in an ashram for the rest of his life, never again playing an active part in Indian nationalist politics. Hardiman, 73.

10 Amalendu Prasad Mookerjee, *Social and Political Ideas of Bipin Chandra Pal* (Calcutta: Minerva Publications, 1974), 82.

11 In Punjab, the agrarian agitation of 1907 had been followed by a spate of prosecutions against journalists and restrictions on public meetings. The Arya Samajist background of Lajpat Rai and Ajit Singh meant that the Punjab government suspected the Samaj of having engineered the 'disloyal' political agitation. Despite the common Hindu, Muslim and Sikh participation in the rural agitation, the educated Hindu middle class was held responsible. Prominent sections of the Arya Samaj and the larger Punjabi Hindu community soon distanced themselves from anti-colonial politics and from Lajpat Rai,

instead emphasizing their loyalty to British rule. Neeti Nair, *Changing Homelands: Hindu Politics and the Partition of India* (Cambridge, MA: Harvard University Press, 2011), 20–27. For details of British official suspicion and harassment of Arya Samajists on charges of sedition and conspiracy between 1907 and 1910, and the subsequent, at least part-strategic, presentation of the Samaj by both its factions as a non-political, purely religious organization, see C.S. Adcock, *The Limits of Tolerance: Indian Secularism and the Politics of Religious Freedom* (New York: Oxford University Press, 2013), 88–90, 111. The government would come to accept this Arya Samajist self-representation by 1911.

12 Feroz Chand, *Lajpat Rai: Life and Work* (New Delhi: Publications Division, Ministry of Information and Broadcasting, Government of India, 1978), 232.

13 Shabnum Tejani, *Indian Secularism: A Social and Intellectual History, 1890–1950* (Bloomington: Indiana University Press, 2008), 118–20.

14 Shaikh, *Community and Consensus*, 136–37, 142.

15 'Amir Ali on Simla Deputation', in Shan Muhammad (ed.), *The Indian Muslims: A Documentary Record (1900–1947)*, vol. 1 (Meerut: Meenakshi Prakashan, 1980), 236.

16 'First Draft of the Memorial of the Simla Deputation', Appendix I', in Matiur Rahman, *From Consultation to Confrontation: A Study of the Muslim League in British Indian Politics, 1906–1912* (London: Luzac, 1970), 295.

17 Shaikh, *Community and Consensus*, 137; 'Memorial of Simla Deputation', 295, 297.

18 'Memorial of Simla Deputation', 295–97.

19 The belief that any born Muslim was not automatically an authentic representative of Muslims was also a view expressed by important colonial officials like Viceroy Minto. According to this logic, a born Muslim could have views which were more 'Hindu' than 'Muslim'. To be considered a true Muslim

representative, a Muslim had to live in an 'absolutely separate' way from Hindus. Tejani, *Indian Secularism*, 124.

20 While Ambedkar would argue against separate electorates for 'Untouchables' in his testimony to the Simon Commission in 1928, he would demand these in 1919 and famously again in 1932, prompting Gandhi's fast and the 'Poona Pact'. The latter was a compromise in which Ambedkar accepted joint electorates, and Gandhi accepted reservations in proportion to the population of 'Untouchables' in India. It would form the basis of the reservations granted to Dalits by the Indian Constitution in 1950. Gail Omvedt, *Ambedkar: Towards an Enlightened India* (London: Penguin UK, 2008), 26, 36, 41–48; Vinay Sitapati, 'The Dalit Contract with India', *Seminar*, November 2010, https://www.india-seminar.com/2010/615/615_vinay_satapati.htm. Separate electorates were also demanded for Sikhs by the Chief Khalsa Diwan from 1911 onwards. See Chhanda Chatterjee, *The Sikh Minority and the Partition of the Punjab 1920–1947* (Routledge, 2018), 113.

21 Francis Robinson, *Separatism among Indian Muslims: The Politics of the United Provinces' Muslims, 1860–1923* (Cambridge: Cambridge University Press, 2007), 154.

22 Matiur Rahman, *From Consultation to Confrontation: A Study of the Muslim League in British Indian Politics, 1906–1912* (London: Luzac, 1970), 99.

23 'Aga Khan's Views on the Reform Scheme, The Times, 15 February 1909', in Shan Muhammad (ed.), *The Indian Muslims: A Documentary Record (1900–1947)*, vol. 2 (Meerut: Meenakshi Prakashan, 1980), 151–52. The view of Hindus and Muslims constituting discrete and mutually exclusive communities was encouraged by British officials. For instance, Viceroy Minto declared that Muslims formed 'an absolutely separate community, distinct by marriage, food and custom, and claiming in many cases to belong to a different race from the Hindus'. See Tejani, *Indian Secularism*, 124.

24 'Presidential Address of Sayyid Ali Imam to All-India Muslim League, 1908', in Shan Muhammad (ed.), *The Indian Muslims: A Documentary Record (1900–1947)*, vol. 2 (Meerut: Meenakshi Prakashan, 1980), 55.

25 'Presidential Address of Sayyid Ali Imam to All-India Muslim League, 1908', in Shan Muhammad (ed.), *The Indian Muslims: A Documentary Record (1900–1947)*, vol. 2 (Meerut: Meenakshi Prakashan, 1980), 55.

26 'Mian Mohammad Shafi's Letter to Dunlop Smith, 13 January 1909', in Shan Muhammad (ed.), *The Indian Muslims: A Documentary Record (1900–1947)*, vol. 2 (Meerut: Meenakshi Prakashan, 1980), 108–09.

27 Shaikh, *Community and Consensus*, 146–47. Other Muslims like Dr Sayyid Mahmud opposed the League's notion of exclusive Muslim representation by declaring, 'We can elect as our representative even a Hindu if he is fit for our purpose'. 147.

28 Shaikh, *Community and Consensus*, 145–46.

29 'Morley's Speech on the Second Reading of the Indian Council Bill', 23 Febuary 1909', in Shan Muhammad (ed.), *The Indian Muslims: A Documentary Record (1900–1947)*, vol. 2 (Meerut: Meenakshi Prakashan, 1980), 158.

30 Pieter Judson, *Exclusive Revolutionaries: Liberal Politics, Social Experience, and National Identity in the Austrian Empire, 1848–1914* (Ann Arbor: University of Michigan Press, 1996), 263; Pieter Judson and Marsha Rozenblit, *Constructing Nationalities in East Central Europe*, vol. 6 (New York: Berghahn Books, 2004), 70.

31 The 1909 reforms enlarged the imperial and provincial councils. While they conceded elections for the first time to these councils, the majority of British officials was of course retained in the Imperial Legislative Council. The provincial councils were allowed majorities of non-official Indians, but the importance of this non-official majority was undercut

by the fact that many of these non-official Indians were still nominated by the government rather than elected by Indians. The power of provincial councils was in any case limited and further subjected to the government's veto. The franchise, limited by high property qualifications, still remained severely restricted. Nanda, *Gokhale*, 312–19; Sekhar Bandyopadhyay, *From Plassey to Partition: A History of Modern India* (New Delhi: Orient Longman, 2004), 281–82; Benjamin Zachariah, *Nehru* (London ; New York: Routledge, 2004), 22. It must be remembered, therefore, that the entire debate on minority representation was occurring within highly constrained democratic conditions. Rochana Bajpai, *Debating Difference: Group Rights and Liberal Democracy in India* (Oxford: Oxford University Press, 2011), 37.

32 Shaikh, *Community and Consensus*, 140, 153.

33 'Memorial of Simla Deputation', 294–95.

34 'Memorial of Simla Deputation', 294.

35 'Amir Ali on Simla Deputation', 236.

36 Khushwant Singh, *A History of the Sikhs*, 2nd ed (New Delhi: Oxford University Press, 2004), 221; J.S. Grewal, *The Sikhs of the Punjab*, The New Cambridge History of India, II, 3 (Cambridge [England]; New York: Cambridge University Press, 1990), 152.

37 Farzana Shaikh, *Community and Consensus in Islam: Muslim Representation in Colonial India, 1860–1947* (Delhi: Imprint One, 2012), 151; 'Mian Mohammad Shafi's Letter to Dunlop Smith, 13 January 1909', in Shan Muhammad (ed.), *The Indian Muslims: A Documentary Record (1900–1947)*, vol. 2 (Meerut: Meenakshi Prakashan, 1980), 110.

38 'Presidential Address of Sayyid Ali Imam', 54.

39 'Simla Deputation: Presentation of Address to Lord Minto', in Shan Muhammad (ed.), *The Indian Muslims: A Documentary Record (1900–1947)*, vol. 1 (Meerut: Meenakshi Prakashan, 1980), 194.

40 'Deputation of the London Muslim League to the Secretary of State for India on the Proposed Reform, 27 January 1909', in Shan Muhammad (ed.), *The Indian Muslims: A Documentary Record (1900–1947)*, vol. 2 (Meerut: Meenakshi Prakashan, 1980), 116.

41 Bajpai, *Debating Difference*, 116.

42 See 'Dr. Ambedkar with the Simon Commission (Indian Statutory Commission)', in Vasant Moon (ed.), *Dr. Babasaheb Ambedkar Writings and Speeches*, vol. 2 (Bombay: Education Department, Government of Maharashtra, 1989), 362–63.

43 In these early years, Jinnah broadly subscribed to the Congress's view of the Indian nation, and opposed separate electorates. Interestingly, according to Jinnah's biographer, historian Stanley Wolpert, it was separate electorates that increased Jinnah's personal consciousness of Muslim identity. Jinnah would indeed eventually soften up to separate electorates. But, even so, in 1910, he would strongly oppose their expansion to local bodies. Jinnah would also continue to espouse the notion of a common Indian nation, albeit one diverging from the Congress's conception, until the late 1930s. Stanley Wolpert, *Jinnah of Pakistan* (New York: Oxford University Press, 1984), 94.

44 This was also true of certain prominent Muslims in Punjab. Nair, *Changing Homelands*, 32.

45 For details, see Tejani, *Indian Secularism*, 132.

46 For a brief overview of the features of consociationalism, see Arend Lijphart, 'The Puzzle of Indian Democracy: A Consociational Interpretation', *American Political Science Review* 90, no. 2 (1996): 258; Lijphart as summarized in Roberto Belloni, 'Peacebuilding and Consociational Electoral Engineering in Bosnia and Herzegovina', *International Peacekeeping* 11, no. 2 (2004): 336.

47 Lijphart, 'The Puzzle of Indian Democracy: A Consociational Interpretation', 259.

48 Lijphart, 259; Allison McCulloch, 'Consociational Settlements in Deeply Divided Societies: The Liberal–Corporate Distinction', *Democratization* 21, no. 3 (2014): 505.

49 Note the use of the word softening rather than eliminating.
50 McCulloch, 'Consociational Settlements in Deeply Divided Societies: The Liberal–Corporate Distinction', 504–05; Belloni, 'Peacebuilding and Consociational Electoral Engineering in Bosnia and Herzegovina', 336–37. Also see Rajeev Bhargava, *The Promise of India's Secular Democracy* (Oxford: Oxford University Press, 2010), 104–5, 158, 195–97.
51 For a comprehensive survey of the campaign see Rahman, *From Consultation to Confrontation*, 101–02.
52 Dhananjay Keer, *Lokmanya Tilak—Father of the Indian Freedom Struggle* (Bombay: SB Kangutkar, 1959), 290–91, 297, 314–19.
53 Lala Lajpat Rai, 'Muslim Representation in Legislative Councils, Mahratta, 21 February 1909', in *CWLLR*, vol. 3, 2004 [hereafter cited as 'Muslim Representation], 195.
54 Lala Lajpat Rai, 'The Ideals of the Aga Khan, India, 26 February 1909', in *CWLLR*, vol. 3, 2003, 197.
55 Aga Khan, 'The Problem of Minorities in India', in K. K. Aziz (ed.) *Aga Khan III: Selected Speeches and Writings of Sir Sultan Muhammad Shah* (Kegan Paul International: London and New York, 1998), 288–89.
56 Lala Lajpat Rai, 'The Mahomedan Demand, India, 12 March 1909', in *CWLLR*, vol. 3, 2003, 199.
57 Madan Mohan Malaviya, 'The Minto–Morley Reforms, Indian Review, December 1908', in *The Hon. Pundit Madan Mohan Malaviya: His Life and Speeches* (Madras: Ganesh and Co., 1910), 35.
58 Madan Mohan Malaviya, 'Lahore Congress Presidential Address, 1909', in *The Hon. Pundit Madan Mohan Malaviya: His Life and Speeches* (Madras: Ganesh and Co., 1910), 47, 53.
59 Malaviya, 115.
60 Gopal Krishna Gokhale, 'Budget Speech in Imperial Legislative Council, 29 March 1909', in *Speeches of Gopal Krishna Gokhale* (Madras: GA Natesan and Co., 1920), 177–78. At its 1909 Lahore session, however, the Congress passed resolutions expressing its 'strong sense of disapproval of the creation of

separate electorates on the basis of religion', disgruntlement
with 'the excessive and unfairly preponderant representation
given to the followers of one religion' and 'the unjust, invidious
and humiliating distinctions made between Moslem and non-
Moslem subjects of his Majesty in the matter of electorates, the
franchise and the qualification of candidates'. 'Resolutions—
Twenty-Fifth Congress, Lahore, 1909', in *The Indian National
Congress Presidential Addresses* (Indian National Congress,
n.d.), 175.

61 Lajpat Rai, 'The Mohamedan Demand', 199.

62 Bajpai, *Debating Difference*, 91–92. Political scientist Rochana
Bajpai stresses that the individualist interpretation of democracy,
grounded in one-man–one-vote and territorial electorates, is
a *particular* conception of democracy. At the same time, this
particular conception, upon which Lajpat Rai drew, has been its
dominant conception historically and globally.

63 Rochana Bajpai's research, focusing on Indian nationalist
discourse during the process of constitution-making in the
1940s, rightly draws our attention to its liberal democratic bias
towards individualism and hostility to group rights. But she
stops short of providing a persuasive answer to the question
of whether group-based representation through a mechanism
like *separate electorates* is indeed compatible with the ideals of
liberalism, democracy or secularism, and—if not—whether it
is still a normatively defensible consociational mechanism. See
Bajpai, *Debating Difference*.

64 Lajpat Rai, 'The Mohamedan Demand', 198–99.

65 Raziuddin Aquil, *Lovers of God: Sufism and the Politics of Islam
in Medieval India* (New Delhi: Oxford University Press, 2020),
32.

66 Lajpat Rai, 'Muslim Representation', 195.

67 Lajpat Rai, 196.

68 Lajpat Rai, 196. Emphasis mine.

69 Gopal Krishna Gokhale, 'The Hindu–Mahomedan Question, 4
July 1909', in *Speeches of Gopal Krishna Gokhale* (Madras: GA
Natesan and Co., 1920), 998–99.

70 J.P. Misra, *Madan Mohan Malaviya and the Indian Freedom Movement* (New Delhi: Oxford University Press, 2016), 24; Parmananda, *Mahamana Madan Mohan Malaviya: An Historical Biography*, vol. 1 (Varanasi: Malaviya Adhyayan Sansthan: Banaras Hindu University, 1985), 163–64.

71 Parmananda, *Mahamana Malaviya*, 1:180.

72 Gokhale, 'Hindu–Mahomedan Question', 998–99.

73 Lajpat Rai, 'The Mohamedan Demand', 199.

74 'Expectations from the British Government', India, 20 November 1908, Lala Lajpat Rai, *The Collected Works of Lala Lajpat Rai*, ed. B.R. Nanda (New Delhi: Manohar, 2004), vol. 3, p. 172.

75 Lala Lajpat Rai, 'Hindu Nationalism, The Punjabee, 23 October 1909', in *CWLLR*, vol. 4, 2004, 167.

Chapter 9

1 Christophe Jaffrelot, 'Genesis and Development of Hindu Nationalism in the Punjab: From the Arya Samaj to the Hindu Sabha (1875–1910)', in *Religion, Caste, and Politics in India* (London: Hurst, 2011), 105.

2 'Resolutions—Twenty-Fifth Congress, Lahore, 1909', in *The Indian National Congress Presidential Addresses* (Indian National Congress, n.d.), 174–75.

3 Neeti Nair, *Changing Homelands: Hindu Politics and the Partition of India* (Cambridge, MA: Harvard University Press, 2011), 17.

4 Elena Valdameri, *Foundations of Gokhale's Nationalism: Between Nation and Empire* (Milan, State University of Milan, 2016), 188–89.

5 Nair, *Changing Homelands*, 30–36.

6 Lala Lajpat Rai, 'Plea Not to Increase Differences in the Congress, The Panjabee, 15 July 1909', in *CWLLR*, vol. 4, 2004, 9–10.

7 Lala Lajpat Rai, 'Hindu Nationalism, The Punjabee, 23 October 1909', in *CWLLR*, vol. 4, 2004, 158–59.

8 Christophe Jaffrelot, *The Hindu Nationalist Movement and Indian Politics: 1925 to the 1990s* (New Delhi: Penguin Books, 1999), 32, 53–54.

9 Lajpat Rai, 'Hindu Nationalism', 159; Johann Caspar Bluntschli, *The Theory of the State* (Kitchener, Ontario: Batoche, 2000), 79–80.

10 Lajpat Rai, 'Hindu Nationalism', 159–60; Bluntschli, *Theory of the State*, 81.

11 Lajpat Rai, 'Hindu Nationalism', 157.

12 Dorothy Figueira, *Aryans, Jews, Brahmins: Theorizing Authority through Myths of Identity* (Albany: State University of New York Press, 2002), 42–43, 46, 58. According to Figueira, a scholar of religion, myth theory and literature, Nietzsche, who would posthumously inspire the Nazis despite his own condemnation of anti-Semitism and even encouragement of 'Aryan'–Jewish intermixing, interestingly portrayed India's ancient Brahmins, the products of caste-based breeding regulations, as exemplars of the pure Aryan master-race. Interestingly, Nietzsche equated Judaism and Christianity as promoting anti-Aryan, *chandala* ('outcaste', 'lower strata', 'mixed caste') values. See chap. 3.

13 Lajpat Rai, 'Hindu Nationalism', 160.

14 Lajpat Rai, 162.

15 Lajpat Rai, 163.

16 Lajpat Rai, 155–58.

17 Lajpat Rai, 155–58.

18 Dhananjay Keer, *Lokmanya Tilak: Father of the Indian Freedom Struggle* (Bombay: SB Kangutkar, 1959), 171.

19 Vikram Sampath, *Savarkar: Echoes from a Forgotten Past, 1883–1924* (Gurgaon: Viking, 2019), 126, 139–42, 150–51, 160–61, 180, 192.

20 Bakhle, 'Country First', 169; Sharma, *Hindutva*, 169–70.

21 Vinayak Damodar Savarkar, *Hindutva: Who Is a Hindu?* (Bombay: Veer Savarkar Prakashan, 1969), 92, 99–100. Savarkar's definition of 'Hindu religion' was itself extremely broad, including the Sikh, Jain and Buddhist religions. But his tract quickly asserted that Hindutva or Hindu-ness was broader than Hinduism. The first two essentials of Hindutva included living in and loving India as a Fatherland, but these were

insufficient for Hindu national belonging. What was key was adherence to the third essential of Hindutva—Hindu culture. In Savarkar's view, the majority of India's Muslims and Christians met the first two criteria of Hindutva, but not the third. To be sure, it was the 'religious aspect' of 'Hindu culture' that decisively excluded Muslims and Christians from the Hindu nation. This entailed belonging to any of the schools of Hindu religion which had India as their birthplace and considered it their holy land, a criteria which Savarkar believed all Muslims and Christians failed. So, alongside culture, religion and geography were key to Savarkar's definition of Hindu nationhood, and to excluding Muslims and Christians from it. But it was really 'Hindu culture', and their assumed disinheritance of it, which already excluded the majority of them. Religion surfaced in Hindutva not to emphasize belief but to tie 'Hindus' to the Indian homeland, while questioning the ties of Muslims and Christians to it. In Savarkar's view, their religions, by drawing them to alien, non-Hindu cultures, excluded Muslims and Christians from Hindu nationhood. To be included, they had to abandon their religions, with their links to foreign holy lands and cultures. Yet, Muslims and Christians were ultimately required not to convert to Hindu religion but assimilate into *Hindu culture*. This demonstrates the vital importance of 'Hindu culture' in Savarkar's Hindutva ideology. Vanya Vaidehi Bhargav, 'From Theology to Culture: Secularisation in Lajpat Rai's "Hindu Nationalism", 1880s–1915', *Interdisciplinary Journal of South Asian Studies*, no. 7 (2022), 91–127.

22 Chetan Bhatt, *Hindu Nationalism: Origins, Ideologies and Modern Myths* (Oxford: Berg, 2001), 59.

23 Jaffrelot, *Hindu Nationalist Movement*, 19; 'Genesis and Development', 113.

24 Lajpat Rai, 'Hindu Nationalism', 165–66, 168.

25 For these features of Savarkarite Hindutva, see Savarkar, *Hindutva*, 104–08, 92, 99–100, 110–15.

26 Lajpat Rai, 'Hindu Nationalism', 165–67.

27 Lajpat Rai, 165.

28 Lajpat Rai, 165.

29 Lajpat Rai, 167.

30 Lajpat Rai, 165–66.

31 Lala Lajpat Rai, 'The Mahomedan Demand, India, 12 March 1909', in *CWLLR*, vol. 3, 2004, 199.

32 Lala Lal Chand, 'Self-Abnegation in Politics', in Christophe Jaffrelot (ed.), *Hindu Nationalism: A Reader* (Princeton: Princeton University Press, 2007), 4, 20, 22–23.

33 Madan Mohan Malaviya, 'Lahore Congress Presidential Address, 1909', in *Speeches and Writings of Pandit Madan Mohan Malaviya* (Madras: GA Natesan and Co., 1918), 116–18.

34 Valdameri, 'Gokhale's Nationalism', 166–68.

35 Valdameri, 86–87, 205–06.

36 Bal Ram Nanda, *Gokhale: The Indian Moderates and the British Raj* (Delhi: Oxford U.P., 1977), 379–401.

37 See n. 535 in Valdameri, 'Gokhale's Nationalism', 193–94.

38 The content of the rest of this section, focusing on Lajpat Rai's ideas on caste, has been previously published as Vanya Bhargav, 'Lala Lajpat Rai's Ideas on Caste: Conservative or Radical?', *Studies in Indian Politics* 6, no. 1 (3 April 2018): 15–26, https://doi.org/10.1177/2321023018762672.

39 Shan Muhammad, ed., 'Simla Deputation: Presentation of Address to Lord Minto', in *The Indian Muslims: A Documentary Record (1900–1947)*, vol. 1 (Meerut: Meenakshi Prakashan, 1980), 193; 'Presidential Address of Sayyid Ali Imam to All-India Muslim League, 1908', in *The Indian Muslims: A Documentary Record (1900–1947)*, vol. 2 (Meerut: Meenakshi Prakashan, 1980), 59; Farzana Shaikh, *Community and Consensus in Islam: Muslim Representation in Colonial India, 1860-1947* (Delhi: Imprint One, 2012), 153.

40 Today, the term commonly used to refer to the supposedly 'untouchable' castes at the bottom of the caste hierarchy is 'Dalit' (derived from the Sanskrit *dalita,* which means broken, crushed or destroyed). The Indian Constitution refers to Dalit or

'untouchable' groups as 'Scheduled Castes', signifying the special list or 'schedule' in which they were put to grant them separate representative quotas. In the early twentieth century, these caste groups were referred to as 'Untouchables' or 'Depressed Classes'. In this chapter, I use the term 'Untouchable' in line with Lajpat Rai's occasional use of it, and in the knowledge that it has historically been the most commonly used term to describe the castes in question, including by those caste groups themselves. I use the term with the awareness that many 'lower' castes have often referred to themselves as *achhut* ('untouchable'), with their leaders insisting on using the term because they believe euphemisms obfuscate the harsh truth of the Hindu caste order, which regards these groups as literally beyond bodily touch. See Mark Juergensmeyer, *Religious Rebels in the Punjab: The Ad Dharm Challenge to Caste* (New Delhi: Navayana Publishing, 2009), viii, 13, 16–18. My use of this term follows standard academic practice. See C. S. Adcock, *The Limits of Tolerance: Indian Secularism and the Politics of Religious Freedom* (New York: Oxford University Press, 2013); Anupama Rao, *The Caste Question: Dalits and the Politics of Modern India* (Berkeley: University of California Press, 2009); Gail Omvedt, *Ambedkar: Towards an Enlightened India* (London: Penguin UK, 2008). It is not meant to endorse the treatment of such groups as socially inferior but instead plainly acknowledge the depth of prejudice that they have faced. For the origins of caste, see Constance Jones and James Ryan, *Encyclopedia of Hinduism* (Infobase publishing, 2006), xxii, 100, 471; K.M. Sen, *Hinduism* (London: Penguin Books, 1969), chap. 4; Brian K. Smith, *Classifying the Universe: The Ancient Indian Varna System and the Origins of Caste* (New York ; Oxford: Oxford University Press, 1994).

41 Lala Lajpat Rai, 'Urgency of Improving the Lot of the "Depressed Classes"', The Modern Review, July 1909', in *CWLLR*, vol. 4, 2004 [hereafter cited as 'Urgency'], 270.

42 Rai retrospectively insisted that he was apprehensive about the possibility of a premature political agitation by agricultural

classes. Even so, when the house of Bhai Parmanand, Arya Samajist and professor at DAV college, Lahore, was raided in late 1909, the British police found letters from Lajpat Rai, written during the 1907 agitation to Bhai Parmanand in London, asking him to further ask Shyamji Krishnavarma to send some revolutionary political novels. This was one reason why Rai was under surveillance by the British, and also why he was asked to step down from the Arya Samaj Managing Committee. Interestingly, the heightened fervour that infused the network of anti-colonial revolutionaries spanning parts of Europe, North America and East Asia (of which Savarkar had been a part until his arrest in 1910) was having an impact on how the British colonial regime was treating Lajpat Rai in Punjab. Feroz Chand, *Lajpat Rai: Life and Work* (New Delhi: Publications Division, Ministry of Information and Broadcasting, Government of India, 1978), 243–45; Nair, *Changing Homelands*, 21–28, 40. A copy of a bomb manual was found in Parmamand's house. In 1915, he was sentenced to transportation for life, to be released in 1920 on the condition of abstention from 'seditious agitation'. Nair, 41–42.

43 Lala Lajpat Rai, 'Swami Dayanand, 1898', in *CWLLR*, vol. 1, 2003, 408.

44 C.S. Adcock, *The Limits of Tolerance: Indian Secularism and the Politics of Religious Freedom* (New York: Oxford University Press, 2013), 11, 45; John Zavos, *The Emergence of Hindu Nationalism in India* (Oxford: Oxford University Press, 2000), 46.

45 Believing in or based on the principle of equality.

46 Despite his forceful articulation of the notion of a Hindu nation in 1909, Rai continued to fluctuate between the terms 'Hindu nation' and 'Hindu community' during the subsequent five years, revealing his continuing inner intellectual and moral struggle regarding how best to relate Hindu identity to the idea of nationhood. Did Hindus form a nation by themselves, or were they a religio-cultural community within the Indian nation? Rai remained unsure.

47 Lala Lajpat Rai, 'The Arya Samaj: An Account of Its Origin, Doctrines, and Activities, with a Biographical Sketch of the Founder, 1915', in *CWLLR*, vol. 5, 2004 [hereafter cited as 'Arya Samaj'], 214.

48 Lajpat Rai, 211.

49 Lajpat Rai, 227.

50 Lajpat Rai, 'Urgency', 271.

51 Lajpat Rai, 'Urgency', 271.

52 Lajpat Rai, 'Arya Samaj', 213–14.

53 Lajpat Rai, 'Urgency', 272.

54 This point, with reference to the general Arya Samaj understanding of shuddhi, has also been made by Adcock, *Limits of Tolerance*, 122–23.

55 In Arya Samaj usage, shuddhi referred to a reformed variation on the Brahminical ritual of *prayaschit*, which was a form of purification or expiation for deviations from prescribed practice. Literally, shuddhi referred to a state of purification associated with the individual who was free from error because of observing dharma, and to the pure state that was required for performing dharma. But since the Vedas were restricted to upper castes, shuddhi was a 'state of purity' that only upper castes could attain. The shastras prescribed prayaschit rituals for the shuddhi of upper castes who had deviated from correct practice. In a major departure, the Arya Samaj reinvented shuddhi as a ritual to prepare Hindu low castes, Muslims and Christians for Vedic practice. In the context of the Arya Samaj, shuddhi has been understood as a procedure to 'purify', to 'admit'/'readmit' individuals into Vedic practice, or to 'convert'/'reconvert' them. However, it was also a means for some upper and lower castes to assert the place of low castes within Hindu society. Here I draw heavily from Adcock, 117–20.

56 Lala Lajpat Rai, 'Untouchability—the Bane of the Hindu Community', Zamana, October 1913', in *CWLLR*, vol. 4, 2004 [hereafter cited as 'Untouchability'], 305–06; 'Our Duty to the "Depressed Classes"', The Tribune, 21–22 May 1913', in *CWLLR*, vol. 4, 2004 [hereafter cited as 'Our Duty'], 297–98.

57 Lajpat Rai, 'Our Duty', 298.

58 For this argument see Jaffrelot, 'Genesis and Development', 75–121.

59 Adcock, *Limits of Tolerance*, 127–28.

60 Lala Lajpat Rai, 'Service of the "Depressed Classes"—the Greatest Duty of Hindus, December 1913', in *CWLLR*, vol. 4, 2004, 313. Shuddhi had also been the vehicle by which 36,000 Meghs from Sialkot, Punjab, had become Arya Samajist by 1910. Juergensmeyer, *Religious Rebels*, 27. Even before this, in Multan, many leaders of the Od community had approached the Samaj to secure shuddhi for hundreds of families. Adcock, *Limits of Tolerance*, 121.

61 Lajpat Rai, 'Untouchability', 305–06.

62 Lajpat Rai, 'Service of the Depressed Classes', 313.

63 Lajpat Rai, 'Urgency', 272.

64 Twenty-five-year-old Ambedkar would voice this view in a paper read at Columbia University in 1916. B.R. Ambedkar, 'Castes in India', in Vasant Moon (ed.), *Dr. Babasaheb Ambedkar Writings and Speeches*, vol. 1 (Bombay: Education Department, Government of Maharashtra, 1989), 8. For the role of sexual regulation in reproducing the caste hierarchy, see Anupama Rao, *The Caste Question: Dalits and the Politics of Modern India* (Berkeley: University of California Press, 2009), 232–33. I use the term Dalit in quotes only to highlight that it was not as commonly used during these years as it was after the 1920s. Jyotirao Phule had, however, used the term as early as the nineteenth century to refer to 'outcastes' and 'untouchables' as the 'oppressed and crushed victims of the caste system'. See Badri Narayan, *Women Heroes and Dalit Assertion in North India: Culture, Identity, and Politics*, Cultural Subordination and the Dalit Challenge, v. 5 (New Delhi; Thousand Oaks, Calif.: SAGE Publications, 2006), 34.

65 Lala Lajpat Rai, 'Education of the "Depressed Classes", The Tribune, 31 August 1912', in *CWLLR*, vol. 4, 2004 [hereafter cited as 'Education of Depressed Classes'], 284.

66 Lala Lajpat Rai, 'The "Depressed Classes", The Indian Review, May 1910', in *CWLLR*, vol. 4, 2004 [hereafter cited as 'The Depressed Classes'], 282. Arya Samajist DAV schools and colleges (along with Christian and government institutions) were already playing an important role in creating a new generation of educated Scheduled Caste youth. Many future lower-caste leaders of the Ad Dharm movement that would arise in 1920s Punjab would come from Arya Samaj-sponsored schools and social reform organizations. For this reason, many Ad Dharm activists retained a measure of sympathy for the Samaj, and many, fearing separation from Hindu society, would ultimately return to it. Juergensmeyer, *Religious Rebels*, 27, 37, 67–68.

67 Lala Lajpat Rai, 'Appeal to Help to Establish Schools for Untouchables, The Tribune, 20 February 1914', in *CWLLR*, vol. 4, 2004 [hereafter cited as 'Appeal to Help'], 314.

68 Lajpat Rai, 'Education of Depressed Classes', 285.

69 Lajpat Rai, 286.

70 Rosalind O'Hanlon, *Caste, Conflict, and Ideology: Mahatma Jotirao Phule and Low Caste Protest in Nineteenth-Century Western India* (Cambridge and New York: Cambridge University Press, 1985), 234.

71 Rao, *Caste Question*, 70.

72 Lajpat Rai, 'The Depressed Classes', 280; Lajpat Rai, 'Our Duty', 290–93.

73 Rao, *Caste Question*, 39, 47; O'Hanlon, *Caste, Conflict, and Ideology*, 193–99. This discourse of humanity and human rights, used only very sparingly in the late nineteenth and early twentieth century, was of course distinct from the human rights discourse that gained widespread currency in the 1970s and is still used today. While the former attempted to protect individuals by asserting their full-fledged membership/citizenship *to* a nation or state, the latter is an internationalist language that emerged to protect all individuals *from* nation–states. Samuel Moyn, *The Last Utopia: Human Rights in History* (Cambridge, Mass.: Belknap Press of Harvard University Press, 2012), 1–43.

Nevertheless, there is a broad overlap between Rai's invocation of humanity and human rights and contemporary human rights discourse: the invocation of the right of every human being to full dignity and respect.

74 For instance, British socialists (and left liberals) argued that all individuals were 'equally entitled as human beings to consideration and respect' because they possessed an underlying common humanity that should trump inequalities of talent or wealth. Ben Jackson, *Equality and the British Left: A Study in Progressive Political Thought, 1900–64* (Manchester: Manchester University Press, 2007), 20–21.

75 Lala Lajpat Rai, 'India and English Party Politics, The Panjabee, 11 December 1905', in *CWLLR*, vol. 2, 2003, 203–05. On his 1905 trip to England, Lajpat Rai, along with Gokhale, addressed several meetings organized by the infant Labour Party, and among others, made contact with British socialist writer and founder of Marx-inspired Social Democratic Federation, H.M. Hyndman. See Lala Lajpat Rai, *Autobiographical Writings*, ed. V.C. Joshi (Delhi: University Publishers, 1965), 108. Rai was in close touch with the key Labour Party politician (and future British Prime Minister) Ramsay MacDonald in 1909–11. See Lala Lajpat Rai, *The Collected Works of Lala Lajpat Rai*, ed. B.R. Nanda (New Delhi: Manohar, 2003), vol. 4. Although there remains no evidence of any of these exchanges, Rai also befriended Fabian socialist intellectuals Beatrice and Sydney Webb (who would write the preface to his 1914 book on the Arya Samaj) and prominent Labour Party politician Keir Hardie. Rai also met the famous Fabian socialist author, George Bernard Shaw, and the prominent Socialist academic, G.D.H. Cole. See Chand, *Lajpat Rai*, 259–61.

76 Lajpat Rai, 'Urgency', 270; 'Our Duty', 291.

77 O'Hanlon, *Caste, Conflict, and Ideology*, 111.

78 Lajpat Rai, 'Our Duty', 293–94.

79 Lajpat Rai, 'Urgency', 306.

80 During this period, socialists and left liberals in Britain, with whom Lajpat Rai interacted, were articulating a strongly

egalitarian view of social justice (Conservatives, by contrast, attempted to delink justice from equality, arguing that justice only requires that no one be injured or cheated). They articulated strong critiques of class-based inequality, arguing that it resulted in an unequal distribution of individual freedoms and of the ability to exercise democratic citizenship rights. Class inequality violated the basic ideal of equal respect for all human beings. Seeing Right-wing and Centrist Liberal arguments in favour of a meritocratic notion of equality of opportunity as falling short of their understanding of social justice, socialists and left liberals together countered these by arguing that equality of opportunity could not be realized as long as the privilege of richer classes (in terms of their inherited wealth and access to education) gave them a massive head start. Apart from creating a truly level playing field for all individuals, the socialist and left liberal ideal of social justice emphasized the need to radically reduce the economic and social distance between social classes, which they believed was necessary to create a properly equal society or community. Jackson, *Equality and the British Left*, chap. 1, and p. 48. Lajpat Rai's use of a strongly egalitarian (or equality-based) notion of social justice while arguing for greater equality between lower and upper castes may well have drawn on British Left discourses with which he was familiar.

81 Lajpat Rai, 'Education of Depressed Classes', 285.

82 Lajpat Rai, 'Untouchability', 303.

83 Rao, *Caste Question*, 69.

84 Lajpat Rai, 'Urgency', 273–74; 'Our Duty', 296; 'Appeal to Help', 314–15; 'Need to Check Conversion of the "Depressed Classes"', *Tribune*, 12 December 1913', in *CWLLR*, vol. 4, 2004 [hereafter cited as 'Need to Check Conversion'], 306–07.

85 Kenneth Jones, *Arya Dharm: Hindu Consciousness in Nineteenth Century Punjab* (Delhi: Manohar, 1976), 288.

86 For more details, see Pradip Kumar Datta, *Carving Blocs: Communal Ideology in Early Twentieth-Century Bengal* (New Delhi: Oxford University Press, 1999), 23–24.

87 Datta, 22, 39.

88　Lajpat Rai, 'Urgency', 276.

89　Lajpat Rai, 276.

90　Lajpat Rai, 'Our Duty', 296.

91　Lajpat Rai, 'Appeal to Help', 315.

92　Lajpat Rai, 'Urgency', 276.

93　Lajpat Rai, 276–77.

94　Lajpat Rai, 'Need to Check Conversion', 307.

95　Lajpat Rai, 307.

96　Lajpat Rai, 'The Depressed Classes', 280.

97　Datta, *Carving Blocs*, 27, 33.

98　Datta, 30–31.

99　Lajpat Rai, 'Urgency', 270, 273.

100　Lajpat Rai, 'Need to Check Conversion', 307.

101　Lajpat Rai, 'Urgency', 270.

102　Zavos, *Emergence of Hindu Nationalism*, 111.

103　Cited in John Zavos, 'The Ārya Samāj and the Antecedents of Hindu Nationalism', *International Journal of Hindu Studies* 3, no. 1 (1999): 70.

104　Zavos, 70–71; Adcock, *Limits of Tolerance*, 131.

105　Lajpat Rai, 'The Depressed Classes', 282. Rai's short-lived interest in the Punjab Hindu Sabha has also been noted by his biographer. Chand, *Lajpat Rai*, 491.

106　Datta, *Carving Blocs*, 35–36; Pradip Kumar Datta, '"Dying Hindus": Production of Hindu Communal Common Sense in Early 20th Century Bengal', *Economic and Political Weekly* 28, No., no. 25 (1993): 1310.

107　Lajpat Rai, 'Service of the Depressed Classes', 311.

108　Adcock, *Limits of Tolerance*, 130–31; Zavos, *Emergence of Hindu Nationalism*, 70.

109　Adcock, *Limits of Tolerance*, 131.

110　During these years, 'Untouchable' or Dalit social and political organization was relatively scarce. The first independent Dalit political movements were apparently launched in 1910, when the All-India Depressed Classes Association and All-India Depressed Classes Federation were established under the auspices of the Bombay Presidency Social Reform Association. Their initial purpose was to pressure the Congress to include the removal of untouchability as one of its main planks, an aim it succeeded in achieving in 1917. Things would change by the early 1920s, when Dalits would begin to separately and politically organize much more, as manifest in Adi-Hindu politics in the UP and the Ad-Dharm movement in Punjab. Juergensmeyer, *Religious Rebels*, 23; Adcock, *Limits of Tolerance*, 52, 155. I elaborate more on this in Chapter 18.

Chapter 10

1 Feroz Chand, *Lajpat Rai: Life and Work* (New Delhi: Publications Division, Ministry of Information and Broadcasting, Government of India, 1978), 250–51; Also see, Neeti Nair, *Changing Homelands: Hindu Politics and the Partition of India* (Cambridge, MA: Harvard University Press, 2011), 38.
2 Nair, *Changing Homelands*, 38.
3 Stanley Wolpert, *Jinnah of Pakistan* (New York: Oxford University Press, 1984), 36.
4 Chand, *Lajpat Rai*, 259–61. Unfortunately, little evidence remains of these exchanges.
5 Rai's autobiography covers his life from his childhood to 1907.
6 Naeem Gul Rathore, 'Indian Nationalist Agitation in the United States: A Study of Lala Lajpat Rai and the India Home Rule League of America, 1914–1920' (PhD diss., Columbia University, 1965), 46.
7 Rathore, 47–48; Erez Manela, *The Wilsonian Moment: Self-Determination and the International Origins of Anticolonial Nationalism* (Oxford: Oxford University Press, 2007), 89.
8 Manela, *Wilsonian Moment*, 87; Alan Raucher, 'American Anti-Imperialists and the pro-India Movement, 1900–1932', *Pacific Historical Review* 43, no. 1 (1974): 92–93.
9 Chand, *Lajpat Rai*, 272; Rathore, 'Indian Nationalist Agitation', 68.

10 Lala Lajpat Rai, 'The United States of America: A Hindu's Impression and a Study', in *CWLLR*, vol. 5, 2004 [hereafter cited as 'United States'], 95–96; Raucher, 'American Anti-Imperialists', 92–93; Rathore, 'Indian Nationalist Agitation', 47–48, 75.

11 Lajpat Rai, 'United States', 160.

12 Lajpat Rai, 'United States'.

13 Rathore, 'Indian Nationalist Agitation', 49, 66–67; Manela, *Wilsonian Moment*, 85, 88–89. The Ghadar revolutionaries sought to organize armed rebellions against the British Empire while the latter was embroiled in the First World War. In 1917, Lajpat Rai would be questioned by the US Justice Department and the Military intelligence service due to his occasional meetings with Ghadarites. He, however, rejected revolutionary methods, and was critical of most Ghadarites, particularly their efforts to seek help from Germans to organize resistance against British rule. Lala Lajpat Rai, *Autobiographical Writings*, ed. V.C. Joshi (Delhi: University Publishers, 1965), 199, 218–20.

14 Lajpat Rai, *Autobiographical Writings*, 216. In his memoirs, Roy records Lajpat Rai as having purchased the collected works of Marx, and as taking Roy along to meetings of socialist groups in New York as part of his efforts to understand the American Left. See Chris Moffat, 'The Itinerant Library of Lala Lajpat Rai', *History Workshop Journal*, no. 89 (Spring 2020): 126.

15 Gail Omvedt, *Ambedkar: Towards an Enlightened India* (London: Penguin UK, 2008), 8.

16 Rathore, 'Indian Nationalist Agitation', 68.

17 Raucher, 'American Anti-Imperialists', 92–96; Rathore, 'Indian Nationalist Agitation', 107–08.

18 Manela, *Wilsonian Moment*, 89.

19 Lala Lajpat Rai, 'Defects of the Congress and Remedies, Kayastha Samachar, November 1901', in *CWLLR*, vol. 2, 2003, 4–9.

20 Lala Lajpat Rai, 'Hindu Nationalism, The Punjabee, 23 October 1909', in *CWLLR*, vol. 4, 2004, 165.

21 Lala Lajpat Rai, 'Problem of National Education in India, 1918', in *CWLLR*, vol. 7, 2005, 184.

22 Lala Lajpat Rai, 'The Arya Samaj: An Account of Its Origin, Doctrines, and Activities, with a Biographical Sketch of the Founder, 1915', in *CWLLR*, vol. 5, 2004, 271.

23 For these and the following details, see Chapter 8, pp. 128–34.

24 The 'Ali brothers', as they were called, had graduated from Aligarh in the mid-1890s. Having joined government service in UP, the elder brother Shaukat financed Mohamed's BA in History at Oxford in 1898, after which Mohamed joined the service of the State of Baroda in 1902. The brothers remained immersed in Aligarh affairs, and popular with the students and alumni. They had been founder–members of the Muslim League and, believing that Indian society was organized primarily along religious lines, supported its demand for separate electorates. In fact, Mohamed had urged his co-religionists to work for unity but to not join the Congress. In 1910, Mohamed Ali had left Baroda to become a journalist and full-time politician. Now, British policies within and outside India had the brothers leading public campaigns on behalf of a younger generation of Western-educated Muslims against the British. They also caused a shift in their political stance vis-à-vis the Congress and Hindus. David Hardiman, *Noncooperation in India: Nonviolent Strategy and Protest, 1920–22* (Oxford University Press, USA, 2021), 6–7; Rakhahari Chatterji, *Gandhi and the Ali Brothers: Biography of a Friendship* (New Delhi: SAGE, 2013), 52–68.

25 Azad would go on to become the most famous 'secular' Muslim politician in the Congress leadership in late colonial India, well-known for his resolute opposition in the 1940s to Jinnah, the Muslim League, the Pakistan movement and Partition. He would serve as independent India's first Education Minister until his death. Young Azad had received a traditional Islamic education at his home in Calcutta under the supervision of his father, an Islamic scholar. His home-schooling and self-study made him a polyglot and erudite *alim* (religious scholar),

taught him to reject *taqliq* or the tradition of conformity and embrace *tajdid* or innovation, criticize the existing ulema, and reinterpret the Quran and Hadis. Azad was inspired by the anti-imperialism of nationalists he met in Turkey, Egypt and Iraq during his travels to West Asia in 1908–09, and by Bengal-based revolutionary groups such as Jugantar and Anushilan Samiti. He emerged as an enigmatic and influential journalist after he started his Calcutta-based weekly journal *Âl Hilal* (The Crescent) in 1912 at age twenty-four. Through it, Azad sought to revive in India's Muslims the true spirit of Quranic Islam as the solution to India's problems, and to urge them into anti-imperialism via the Congress. This theoretician of Islamic law and ethics, journalist and writer–poet would join the Congress in 1920. Most biographical accounts of Azad seem to suggest that he never joined the Muslim League even in the early years of his political career. See Christian W. Troll, 'Āzād, Abū al-Kalām', in *The Oxford Encyclopedia of Islam and Politics [Electronic Resource]*, ed. Emad Eldin Shahin, Oxford Reference (Oxford: Oxford University Press, 2014); David Hardiman, *Noncooperation in India: Nonviolent Strategy and Protest, 1920–22* (Oxford University Press, USA, 2021), 9–10.

26 Farzana Shaikh, *Community and Consensus in Islam: Muslim Representation in Colonial India, 1860–1947* (Delhi: Imprint One, 2012), 167.

27 Shaikh, 167.

28 Shaikh, 167; Francis Robinson, *Separatism Among Indian Muslims: The Politics of the United Provinces' Muslims, 1860–1923* (Cambridge: Cambridge University Press, 2007), 212–15; Gail Minault, *The Khilafat Movement: Religious Symbolism and Political Mobilization in India* (Delhi: Columbia University Press, 1982), 46–48.

29 Hugh Owen, 'Negotiating the Lucknow Pact', *The Journal of Asian Studies* 31, no. 03 (1972): 568–70.

30 Cemil Aydin, *The Idea of the Muslim World: A Global Intellectual History* (Cambridge, Massachusetts: Harvard University Press, 2017), 8.

31 This is also suggested by Minault, *Khilafat Movement*, 7.

32 Owen, 'Lucknow Pact', 570; Minault, *Khilafat Movement*, 44. For the Pan-Islamic politics of the Aligarhite Ali brothers, and their increased willingness to cooperate with the Congress, see Minault, *Khilafat Movement*, 24, 35, 46, 50–56, 66. For the Pan-Islamic, anti-imperial rhetoric of Azad during these years, see Ayesha Jalal, 'Striking a Just Balance: Maulana Azad as a Theorist of Trans-National Jihad', *Modern Intellectual History* 4, no. 01 (2007): 95–107; David Hardiman, *Noncooperation in India: Nonviolent Strategy and Protest, 1920–22* (Oxford University Press, USA, 2021), 10.

33 Owen, 'Lucknow Pact', 568; Minault, *Khilafat Movement*, 48. Jinnah and Haq were members of both the Congress and the League.

34 Owen, 'Lucknow Pact', 572; Wolpert, *Jinnah*, 38–41.

35 Gopal Krishna Gokhale, 'Budget Speech in Imperial Legislative Council, 29 March 1909', in *Speeches of Gopal Krishna Gokhale* (Madras: GA Natesan and Co., 1920), 209.

36 Owen, 'Lucknow Pact', 567.

37 Owen, 570, 572–73; Sumit Sarkar, *Modern India: 1886–1947* (Delhi: Macmillian, 1983), 150. For Besant's background, see Chapter 7, p. 548, n. 46.

38 Owen, 'Lucknow Pact', 571.

39 Dhananjay Keer, *Lokmanya Tilak: Father of the Indian Freedom Struggle* (Bombay: SB Kangutkar, 1959), 329.

40 Cited in Owen, 'Lucknow Pact', 575.

41 Bal Gangadhar Tilak, 'Mr. Tilak's Second Speech at Ahmednagar, 1 June 1918', in *Balgangadhar Tilak: His Speeches and Writings* (Madras: Ganesh and Co., 1918), 217–18; Owen, 'Lucknow Pact', 573; Sarkar, *Modern India*, 150.

42 Lala Lajpat Rai, 'Young India: An Interpretation and a History of the Nationalist Movement from Within, 1916', in *CWLLR*, vol. 6, 2005, 226.

43 Lajpat Rai, 319, 321.

44 There of course existed several reasons for anti-Muslim sentiment among Hindus. In Punjab, these ranged from readings of Indian

history as involving Muslim oppression of Hindus to resentment against perceived or, in some cases, real discrimination by the British in favour of Muslims to competition with Muslims for government jobs. Christophe Jaffrelot, 'Genesis and Development of Hindu Nationalism in the Punjab: From the Arya Samaj to the Hindu Sabha (1875–1910)', in *Religion, Caste, and Politics in India* (London: Hurst, 2011), 92–110.

45 Ian Douglas, '"Abul Kalam Azad and Pakistan" A Post-Bangladesh Reconsideration of an Indian Muslim's Opposition to Partition', *Journal of the American Academy of Religion* 40, no. 4 (1972): 473; Mohammad Ali Jinnah, *Mohammad Ali Jinnah An Ambassador of Unity: His Speeches and Writings (1912–1917)*, ed. Sarojini Naidu (Madras: GA Natesan and Co., 1918), 36–49.

46 Shan Mohammad, ed., 'Comrade on the Creed of Muslim League, 4 January 1913', in *The Indian Muslims: A Documentary Record (1900–1947)*, vol. 3 (Meerut: Meenakshi Prakashan, 1980), 222–24.

47 This was also true for Maulana Shibli Nomani (1857–1914), the anti-Aligarh Islamic scholar–poet, and friend of Azad, who wrote poems for Azad's newspaper lamenting the fate of the Ottoman empire–caliphate. Mushirul Hasan, *M.A. Ansari* (New Delhi: Publications Division Ministry of Information & Broadcasting, 1995), 27; Jalal, 'Striking a Just Balance', 96; Minault, *Khilafat Movement*, 43–44.

48 This language was reflected in the League's newly amended 1913 constitution. Shan Mohammad, ed., 'Amended Draft Constitution and Rules of the All-India Muslim League, February 1913', in *The Indian Muslims: A Documentary Record (1900–1947)*, vol. 3 (Meerut: Meenakshi Prakashan, 1980).

49 That there was emerging a new discourse on the Indian nation to which India's Hindus and Muslims were contributing has been briefly noted by historian Ayesha Jalal in 'Striking a Just Balance', 96.

50 See Chapter 5, pp. 78–80.

51 Owen, 'Lucknow Pact', 561.

52 Richard Cashman, *The Myth of the Lokmanya: Tilak and Mass Politics in Maharashtra* (Berkeley: University of California Press, 1975), 214; Owen, 'Lucknow Pact', 575. Tilak and the 'extremists' had been readmitted into the Congress by 1916.

53 Sarkar, *Modern India*, 150. The League accepted 50 per cent representation for Muslims in Punjab (where they formed 55 per cent of the population) and 40 per cent representation for Muslims in Bengal (where they formed 53 per cent of the population). Apart from separate electorates, the Congress accepted the following level of weightages for Muslims in Muslim minority-provinces: 33 per cent representation in United Provinces (where Muslims constituted 14 per cent of the population), 33.3 per cent representation in Bombay (where they constituted 20 per cent of the population), 10 per cent in Central Provinces (4 per cent of the population), 25 per cent in Bihar (13 per cent of the population), 15 per cent in Madras (7 per cent of the population). Owen, 'Lucknow Pact', 577.

54 Owen, 'Lucknow Pact', 578.

55 Lala Lajpat Rai, 'Self-Determination for India, 1918', in *CWLLR*, vol. 7, 2005 [hereafter cited as 'Self-Determination for India'], 245.

56 See Chapter 8, pp. 137–41.

57 Lajpat Rai, 'Young India', 319, 321.

58 Lala Lajpat Rai, 'East and West, *The Tribune*, 19 December 1914', vol. 5, 2004, 55–56. Interestingly, in the decades preceding the First World War, Europeans had increasingly regarded war as something only less advanced and less civilized parts of the world engaged in. They had even viewed the American Civil War as evidence that Americans had not yet advanced in civilization as far as the Europeans had. Margaret MacMillan, *War: How Conflict Shaped Us*, 2020, 201.

59 Lajpat Rai, 'East and West', 55–56; 'An Asiatic View of the Japanese Question, The Outlook, 18 October 1916', in *CWLLR*, vol. 6, 2005, 111–12; 'The Dilemma of Asia, The Independent, 2 October 1916', in *CWLLR*, vol. 6, 2005, 125.

60 Unlike the period before when prospects for empire had looked uncertain, the decades between the 1880s and 1914 had seen Europe's rapid territorial and economic expansion in Afro-Asia, entrenching a Eurocentric global order which imposed, for the first time in world history, a global hierarchy of physical, economic and cultural power. The scale of Europe's physical dominance over Afro-Asia and the Pacific reinforced the belief in Europe's cultural primacy, which in turn sustained its global colonialism. John Darwin, *After Tamerlane: The Rise and Fall of Global Empires, 1400–2000* (London: Penguin Books, 2008), chap. 6.

61 Lala Lajpat Rai, 'Asia and the War, The Masses, September 1916', in *CWLLR*, vol. 6, 2005, 104–05; 'Why India Is in Revolt Against British Rule?, February 1916', in *CWLLR*, vol. 6, 2005, 195.

62 Lala Lajpat Rai, 'Need for Reform in the System of Government of India, The Panjabee, 4 September 1905', in *CWLLR*, vol. 2, 2003, 150; 'Punjab's Sympathy with Bengal, The Panjabee, 11 December 1905', in *CWLLR*, vol. 2, 2003, 37–40; 'Repressive Measures in Bengal, Report of 21st Session of the Indian National Congress, 1905', in *CWLLR*, vol. 2, 2003, 24; 'British Misrule in India, The Panjabee, 4 December 1905', in *CWLLR*, vol. 2, 2003, 158–61. See Chapter 7, p. 121.

63 Lajpat Rai, 'East and West', 55–56; 'Is Not The East a Unity as Compared with the West?, Modern Review, December 1916', in *CWLLR*, vol. 6, 2005, 45–47; 'Asia and the War', 2003, 103–05; 'An Asiatic View', 106–12. As would be revealed more clearly in the post-war years, Lajpat Rai's new understanding of an 'Asia' united by colonial suffering also underlay his acceptance of the Pan-Islamism of Indian Muslims as compatible with Indian nationalism. By challenging British encroachment in Muslim Asia, Pan-Islamism weakened European colonialism abroad and in India and thus served Indian nationalism. See Chapters 12 and 13.

64 Lala Lajpat Rai, 'Reflections on the Political Situation in India, Pamphlet Written in Japan, December 1916', in *CWLLR*, vol. 6, 2005, 166.

65 Lajpat Rai, 'Why India Is in Revolt', 194–96.

66 Lala Lajpat Rai, 'Appeal to People of Punjab to Close Ranks, The Tribune, 20 October 1915', in *CWLLR*, vol. 6, 2005, 3.

67 Manela, *Wilsonian Moment*, 82.

68 Lala Lajpat Rai, 'An Indian View of the Great European War, The New York Times, 21 February 1916', vol. 5, 2005, 77–78; 'Asia and the War', 2005, 166.

69 Lajpat Rai, 'Young India', 327.

70 Although little is known about this interaction, whilst in Japan, Rai developed a friendship with the exiled Chinese nationalist leader Sun Yat-Sen. See Chand, *Lajpat Rai*, 277.

71 Japan had entered the war as Britain's ally but simultaneously saw a surge of anti-Western Pan-Asian ideas. Shumei, its leading theoretician, had himself turned to Pan-Asianism in 1913 after reading about India's plight under British rule convinced him of Japan's moral mission to liberate Asia. Cemil Aydin, *The Politics of Anti-Westernism in Asia: Visions of World Order in Pan-Islamic and Pan-Asian Thought* (New York: Columbia University Press, 2007), 113.

72 Lajpat Rai, 'Asia and the War', 2005, 104–05. After spending two weeks in Hawaii, Rai had landed in Japan. Here he visited Tokyo and Yokohama, lectured at Keio and Waseda universities, wrote in Japanese newspapers, met Premier Okuma Shigenobu and his cabinet, and came in contact with Indian revolutionaries such as Rash Behari Bose. Chand, *Lajpat Rai*, 274–77; Rathore, 'Indian Nationalist Agitation', 55–56.

73 Aydin, *Politics of Anti-Westernism*, 115.

74 Lajpat Rai, 'Asia and the War', 2003, 104–05.

75 Aydin, *Politics of Anti-Westernism*, 236.

76 Lajpat Rai, 'An Asiatic View', 111; 'Why India Is in Revolt', 195.

77 Aydin, *Politics of Anti-Westernism*, 120.

78 Lala Lajpat Rai, 'Asia Protests, The New Republic, 3 November 1917', in *CWLLR*, vol. 7, 2005, 21.

79 Lala Lajpat Rai, 'The New Internationalism, Young India, April 1918', in *CWLLR*, vol. 7, 2005, 25–28. The Bolsheviks had challenged the European colonial order by making a sweeping call

for the dismantling of colonial empires and the liberation of all colonies. As evident in his major work, *Imperialism: The Highest Stage of Capitalism* (1916), Lenin considered colonial liberation as crucial for undermining the capitalist–imperialist world order. In December 1917, in their radical peace plan, Trotsky, the new commissar for foreign affairs, had denounced as hypocritical the Allied claims of fighting for the freedom of small nations in Europe even as these imperial powers oppressed nations within their own empires. Manela, *Wilsonian Moment*, 37–41.

80 Manela, *Wilsonian Moment*, 36, 90.

81 Lajpat Rai, 'Self-Determination for India', 239.

82 Lajpat Rai, 'Young India', 319–20.

83 Lajpat Rai, 319–20.

84 Lala Lajpat Rai, 'The Constitution of the India Home Rule League for America, October 1917', in *CWLLR*, vol. 7, 2005, 85. For more on the League, see Rathore, 'Indian Nationalist Agitation'; Raucher, 'American Anti-Imperialists', 83–110. Although Rai's Home Rule League would be unsuccessful in impacting American foreign policy, it attracted the support of several Irish–Americans who opposed British imperialism, left–liberal intellectuals who believed economic imperialism provoked war, protestant pacifists like John Haynes and radical activists like Agnes Smedley. See Raucher, 92–97. After the United States joined the war, a few other Indian political figures such as Annie Besant's ally Subramanya Aiyar and the Ghadarite activist Ram Chandra had similarly appealed to America to recognize India's claims. Manela, *Wilsonian Moment*, 78–84.

85 Lajpat Rai represented a broader intellectual trend crystallizing in this historical moment among a section of Indian nationalists seeking to influence the opinion of the world's most powerful Western countries. To ensure that India, despite its diversity, qualified for self-determination, they were rejecting Wilson's culturally homogenous definition of nationhood (which would have meant India's balkanization) to define its nationhood in territorial terms. See Itty Abraham, *How India Became Territorial: Foreign Policy, Diaspora, Geopolitics*, 2014, 59–60.

86 Chand, *Lajpat Rai*, 272.

87 Lala Lajpat Rai, *The United States of America: A Hindu's Impression and a Study* (Calcutta: R. Chatterjee, 1916), 368, https://archive.org/details/in.ernet.dli.2015.278375/mode/2up. An ever-increasing flow of European migrants to America since the 1850s meant its population now included Germans, Irishmen, Italians, Hungarians, Poles, Russians and Jews, among other nationalities. Darwin, *After Tamerlane*, 319; Jill Lepore, *These Truths: A History of the United States* (New York: W.W. Norton & Company, 2018), 602–736.

88 Lala Lajpat Rai, 'Importance of India to Human Progress, Young India, February 1920', in *CWLLR*, vol. 8, 2006, 63. In the same speech, Rai spoke of America as 'the freest of all the countries of the world' and a place 'where equality, liberty and fraternity reigned and where people were inspired by goodwill and friendship for all peoples of the earth without distinction of colour, creed and caste'.

89 For an overview of the American intellectuals Rai interacted with, see Manela, *Wilsonian Moment*, 87–89, 172; Raucher, 'American Anti-Imperialists', 92–96; Rathore, 'Indian Nationalist Agitation', 75, 107–08, 115–16.

90 Lajpat Rai, 'United States', 77, 128. In drawing parallels between America's mistreatment of blacks to the mistreatment of India's lower castes, between American race relations and Indian caste relations, Rai inserted himself into a line of comparative thought contributed to, through the years, by many public intellectuals, including the famous abolitionist Fredrick Douglass (1818–1895), B.R. Ambedkar and then, more than a century later, and much more recently, Isabel Wilkerson's *Caste: The Origins of Our Discontents* (New York: Random House, 2020). For a quick overview of Wilkerson's argument, see Kwame Anthony Appiah, 'What Do America's Racial Problems Have in Common With India and Nazi Germany?', *New York Times*, 4 August 2020, https://www.nytimes.com/2020/08/04/books/review/caste-isabel-wilkerson.html.

91 Lajpat Rai may have encountered this discourse during his interactions with academics, particularly at Columbia University, where anthropologist Franz Boas, who had spearheaded such rethinking, was a professor. For this and more on American progressive thinking on race and environment/culture-based models of human nature, see Herbert Hovenkamp, 'The Progressives: Racism and Public Law', *Arizona Law Review* 59 (2017): 947–1001.

92 Lajpat Rai, 'Problem of National Education', 132–33, 136.

93 Lala Lajpat Rai, 'Open Letter to David Lloyd George, 13 June 1917', in *CWLLR*, vol. 7, 2005, 54.

94 Lajpat Rai, 'Problem of National Education', 185.

95 Lajpat Rai, 185.

96 'Open Letter', 54. This of course was an old imperial tune. See Anil Seal, 'Imperialism and Nationalism in India', *Modern Asian Studies* 7, no. 3 (1973): 322; Sikata Banerjee, *Make Me a Man!: Masculinity, Hinduism, and Nationalism in India*, SUNY Series in Religious Studies (Albany, NY: State University of New York Press, 2005), 40.

97 Lajpat Rai, 'Self-Determination for India', 243. According to his secretary in America, N.S. Hardikar, and biographer Feroz Chand, Lajpat Rai authored this pamphlet. See N.S. Hardikar, *Lala Lajpat Rai in America* (Servants of the People Society, n.d.), 18; Chand, *Lajpat Rai*, 315; Lala Lajpat Rai, *The Collected Works of Lala Lajpat Rai*, ed. B.R. Nanda (New Delhi: Manohar, 2003), vol. 7, p. xx. Interestingly, an identical pamphlet, published by the India Home Rule League's London Office at the same time, was used by Tilak in his international propaganda. See Manela, *Wilsonian Moment*, 163–64; Abraham, *How India Became Territorial*, 57. This raises questions about the pamphlet's precise authorship. Given they were in close touch during these years (see Chand, *Lajpat Rai*, 293–94; Manela, *Wilsonian Moment*, 167.), it is possible that Tilak coordinated with Lajpat Rai to have the pamphlet published in the US through his Home Rule League. See 'To N.S. Hardiker, 21 February 1919',

in *CWLLR*, vol. 8, 2006, 108. Importantly, Tilak's biographer does not mention him as the author of the pamphlet. See Keer, *Lokmanya Tilak*, 396. This leaves open the possibility that Lajpat Rai penned it and allowed Tilak to use it for his propaganda in London. The pamphlet's reference, as we shall see, to America and its federalism, a form of government which continued to attract Lajpat Rai in later years, indicates likewise. Either way, even if Lajpat Rai published a pamphlet authored by Tilak or indeed other persons, his publication of it reflected his endorsement of its content.

98 Ronald Inden, *Imagining India* (Bloomington: Indiana University Press, 2000), 45–46.

99 Lajpat Rai, 'Self-Determination for India', 243–44. These quotations seem to have been reproduced from a new, influential book by historian Radha Kumud Mookerji, which Lajpat Rai had just read. See Lala Lajpat Rai, 'Review of "Footfalls of Indian History", Modern Review, September 1915', in *CWLLR*, vol. 5, 2004, 375. For the original, see Radha Kumud Mookerji, *The Fundamental Unity of India* (London, New York, Bombay and Calcutta: Longmans, Greens and Co., 1914), 5.

100 Gyanendra Pandey, *The Construction of Communalism in Colonial North India* (New Delhi: Oxford University Press, 2006), 2.

101 Lajpat Rai, 'Self-Determination for India', 244.

102 Lajpat Rai, 'Self-Determination for India', 244.

103 See Sir Herbert Risley, *The People of India* (London: W. Thacker and Co., 1915), 299.

104 The assumption about the existence of a pre-modern nation by twentieth-century nationalists like Rai is at odds with contemporary scholarship on nationhood, which emphasizes that the nations are a modern phenomenon. See Benedict Anderson, *Imagined Communities: Reflections on the Origin and Spread of Nationalism* (London: Verso, 1983); Ernest Gellner, *Nations and Nationalism* (Ithaca, New York: Cornell University Press, 1983); Eric Hobsbawm, *Nations and Nationalism since*

1780: Programme, Myth, Reality (Cambridge [England]; New York: Cambridge University Press, 1990).

105 Lajpat Rai, 'Young India', 229; Syed Sharifuddin Pirzada, ed., 'Presidential Address of Mazhar Ul Haq', in *Foundations of Pakistan: All-India Muslim League Documents, 1906–1947*, vol. 2 (Karachi: National Publishing House, 1970), 332.

106 Soheb Niazi, 'Sayyids and Social Stratification of Muslims in Colonial India: Genealogy and Narration of the Past in Amroha', *Journal of the Royal Asiatic Society*, 3, 2020.

107 Amar Sohal, *The Muslim Secular: Parity and the Politics of India's Partition* (Oxford: Oxford University Press, 2023), 274–75.

108 Contemporary theorists of nationalism consider myths of ancestral relation as extremely important for nationalism. See Anthony Smith, *The Nation in History: Historiographical Debates about Ethnicity and Nationalism* (Oxford: Polity Press, 2000), 67.

109 Gyanendra Pandey, 'Hindus and Others: The Militant Hindu Construction', *Economic and Political Weekly* 26, no. 52 (1991): 2999; Vinayak Damodar Savarkar, *Hindutva: Who Is a Hindu?* (Bombay: Veer Savarkar Prakashan, 1969), v–vi.

110 Vikram Sampath, *Savarkar: Echoes from a Forgotten Past, 1883-1924* (Gurgaon: Viking, 2019), 126, 139–42, 150–51, 160–61, 180, 192, 199, 244–45.

111 Vinayak Chaturvedi, *Hindutva and Violence: VD Savarkar and the Politics of History* (State University of New York Press, 2022), 42; Sampath, *Savarkar: Echoes from a Forgotten Past*, 332–33.

112 Vinayak Chaturvedi, *Hindutva and Violence: VD Savarkar and the Politics of History* (State University of New York Press, 2022), 43.

113 Sampath, *Savarkar: Echoes from a Forgotten Past*, 324–25.

114 Sampath, *Savarkar: Echoes from a Forgotten Past*, 325.

115 Savarkar, 84, 92, 100–101, 113, 130, 135. Also see Pandey, 'Hindus and Others', 3000; Chetan Bhatt, *Hindu Nationalism:*

Origins, Ideologies and Modern Myths (Oxford: Berg, 2001), 98; Janaki Bakhle, 'Country First? Vinayak Damodar Savarkar (1883–1966) and the Writing of Essentials of Hindutva', *Public Culture* 22, no. 1 (2010): 178, 180.

116 Lajpat Rai, 'Young India', 319, 321.

117 By an 'assimilationist' Hindu nationalism, I mean one that requires that non-Hindus give up their religious and cultural beliefs and practices and adopt Hindu culture or *assimilate* into it. By a 'non-assimilationist' Hindu nationalism, I mean one that does not demand such assimilation from non-Hindus, and respects India's religious and cultural diversity.

118 Lajpat Rai, 'Problem of National Education', 183–84. Emphasis original.

119 Lala Lajpat Rai, 'Problem of National Education in India, 1918', in *CWLLR*, vol. 7, 2005, 183. Emphasis original; Charles Waldstein, *Patriotism, National and International: An Essay* (London; New York: Longmans, Green and Company, 1917), 97.

120 Grace Brockington, *Internationalism and the Arts in Britain and Europe at the Fin de Siècle*, 4 (Oxford: Peter Lang, 2009), 169.

121 Waldstein, *Patriotism*, 96–97.

122 Darwinian biology and anthropology, harnessed since the 1850s to give race theories a new modern, 'scientific' basis, were indeed sleeping partners of rising anti-Semitism across Europe and the United States in the early twentieth century.

123 Ali Rattansi, *Racism: A Very Short Introduction*, 161 (Oxford: Oxford University Press, 2007), chap. 4. For the role of race theories in British imperialism in India, see Thomas Metcalf, *Ideologies of the Raj* (Cambridge: Cambridge University Press, 1994), 69–84; Sumit Sarkar, *Modern Times: 1880s-1950* (Ranikhet: Permanent Black, 2014), 60.

124 Lajpat Rai, 'Review of Footfalls', 374; Sister Nivedita, *Footfalls of Indian History* (Calcutta: Longmans, Green and Company, 1915), 17. Sister Nivedita had for long held that India's diversity

itself was proof of its complex, organic unity, and constitutive of Indian nationhood. See Sister Nivedita, 'Unity of Life and Type in India, 1909', vol. 4 (Calcutta: Advaita Ashram, 1996), 269–70; 'Indian Nationality: A Mode of Thought, Undated', vol. 4 (Calcutta: Advaita Ashram, 1996), 288–94.

125 Lajpat Rai, 'Review of Footfalls', 374; Nivedita, *Footfalls*, 19.

126 Lajpat Rai, 'Review of Footfalls', 376; Nivedita, *Footfalls*, 20–21.

127 Lajpat Rai, 'Review of Footfalls', 373.

128 Maulana Altaf Hussain Hali.

129 Hasrat Mohani.

130 The Bengali nationalist poet Dwijendralal Roy.

131 Bharatendu Harishchandra of Benaras.

132 Lajpat Rai, 'Problem of National Education', 186.

133 Lala Lajpat Rai, 'William Archer's "India and the Future", Modern Review, June–October 1919', in *CWLLR*, vol. 7, 2005, 220. Interestingly, in spite of his many imperial prejudices, including refusing India's status as a civilization and its readiness for self-government, Archer denied that religious difference between Hindus and Muslims prevented the political unity of India, noted that the two communities were labouring to improve their relations and forecast that they would resolve their differences as time became ripe for self-government. William Archer, *India and the Future* (New York: Alfred Knopf, 1917), 48–49.

134 Lajpat Rai, 'Young India', 229.

135 Lala Lajpat Rai, 'Akbar, The Great Mogul, Young India, July 1918', in *CWLLR*, vol. 7, 2003, 287. Emphasis mine.

136 Lajpat Rai, 'Self-Determination for India', 244.

137 Lajpat Rai, 'Problem of National Education', 198–99.

138 For his advocacy of Hindustani, also see 'Claims of the Nationalists of India, The Evening Post, 7 September 1916', in *CWLLR*, vol. 6, 2003, 101–02.

139 Anthony Smith, *Nationalism: Key Concepts* (Cambridge: Polity Press, 2001), 45.

140 Lajpat Rai, 'Self-Determination for India', 245; Lord Acton, 'Nationality', in *Essays on Freedom and Power* (Boston: The Beacon Press, 1949), 187.

141 Lajpat Rai, 'Self-Determination for India', 245.

142 Lajpat Rai, 245.

143 Lajpat Rai, 245.

144 As we have seen, the Muslim League's old guard remained uncomfortable with the idea of an 'Indian nation', frequently referring to Hindus and Muslims, just as Lajpat Rai had in earlier years, as distinct 'nationalities'. Just as it had not for Rai, this did not mean that these individuals believed that these separate 'nationalities' could not live together under one state.

145 Lajpat Rai, 'Problem of National Education', 183.

146 Lajpat Rai, 'Review of Footfalls', 372.

147 Lajpat Rai, 'Problem of National Education', 185.

148 This point is inspired by Pandey, *Construction of Communalism*, 249.

149 Lajpat Rai, 'Review of Footfalls', 375.

150 Lajpat Rai, 'Self-Determination for India', 245.

151 Lajpat Rai would remain committed to the idea of a federal India in subsequent years. More on this in Chapters 14–15 and 17–19.

152 Now part of Pakistan, the North-West Frontier Province (NWFP) and Baluchistan were kept by the British under direct, military rule. They were considered too backward, tribal and turbulent to be granted democratic reforms. In 1926–28, Lajpat Rai supported the extension of full democratic reforms to NWFP and Baluchistan (See Chapters 18–19). In 1918, Rai's imagination of a future Indian federalism in independent India quite possibly imagined substantial autonomy for these four existing Muslim majority provinces (Punjab, Bengal, NWFP and Baluchistan).

The Muslim-majority region of Sindh, also with Pakistan since Partition, was currently part of Bombay Presidency. Demands for carving it out as a separate province were not yet as widely influential as they would become in the 1920s. Therefore, in

1918, Rai likely did not include Sindh in his imagination of a federal India.

153 By a 'sub-national' identity, I mean a group identity imagined as existing *below* the national level. Today, the Maharashtrian or Bengali identity is often conceptualized as a 'sub-national' identity (existing *below* the Indian national identity).

154 Lajpat Rai, 'Problem of National Education', 185.

Chapter 11

1 Chapter 5, pp. 85–6.

2 Jyotirmaya Sharma, *Hindutva: Exploring the Idea of Hindu Nationalism* (New Delhi: Viking, 2003), 149–67; Vinayak Chaturvedi, 'Rethinking Knowledge with Action: V.D. Savarkar, the Bhagavad Gita, and Histories of Warfare', *Modern Intellectual History* 7, no. 02 (2010): 430–34; Manan Ahmed Asif, *The Loss of Hindustan: The Invention of India* (Cambridge, Massachusetts: Harvard University Press, 2020), 11.

3 British imperial discourses portrayed India's medieval period as one in which Muslims exercised tyranny over Hindus. This served to justify the Raj on grounds that the British had introduced India to an enlightened era of sound and just government. As we will see, during these years, Lajpat Rai countered this British portrayal of India's medieval period. At the same time, he would leave unchallenged the British colonial periodization of Indian history into 'Hindu', 'Muslim' and 'British' periods. For problems with this anachronistic, religion-based view of India's pre-colonial history, see Richard Eaton, *India in the Persianate Age: 1000–1765*, 2020, 19–30. Instead of the 'Muslim period', historians of medieval India, like Eaton, suggest the use of the term 'Persianate age' to describe South Asian history between the eleventh and nineteenth centuries. The concept of the Persianate world conveys a broad cultural zone, covering West, Central and South Asia, grounded not in religion but in 'a prestige language

and literature that conferred elite status on its users'. This world embraced within it peoples of varied ethnic and religious backgrounds who readily subscribed to the prestige of the Persian language, architecture, dress, music, aesthetics, cuisine and so on. As Eaton emphasizes, rulers during this period did not base their political power in Islam but instead a Persianate political ideology grounded in the principle of universal justice and an accommodation of religio-cultural diversity. Eaton, 31–33, 39–41. I use the terms 'Muslim period' and 'Muslim rule' in this chapter only to reflect the historical imagination of Lajpat Rai and others like him, and while being aware of its problematic nature. As mentioned in Chapter 8, one problem with terms such as 'Muslim rule' is that they obscure the fact that the majority of Muslims in medieval India were indigenous converts from lower caste and tribal groups. They had no access to political power, were politically marginalized and were not rulers of India. In medieval India, a tiny minority of Muslim elites held power alongside their Hindu collaborators. See Raziuddin Aquil, *Lovers of God: Sufism and the Politics of Islam in Medieval India* (New Delhi: Oxford University Press, 2020), 32.

4 Lala Lajpat Rai, 'Young India: An Interpretation and a History of the Nationalist Movement from Within, 1916', in *CWLLR*, vol. 6, 2005 [hereafter cited as 'Young India'], 237–39.

5 Lala Lajpat Rai, 'Young India', 236–37.

6 Lala Lajpat Rai, 'Young India', 239.

7 Lala Lajpat Rai, 'Young India', 238–39.

8 Lajpat Rai, 239. Emphasis mine; Also see Lala Lajpat Rai, 'An Indian View of the Great European War, The New York Times, 21 February 1916', vol. 5, 2004, 77.

9 Eaton, *India in the Persianate Age*, 191–97, 653–54, 667–68.

10 Eaton, 713–14; Asif, *The Loss of Hindustan*, 104.

11 Asif, *The Loss of Hindustan*, 125, 129, 164.

12 For the colonial legacy of the term 'Muslim conquest' and why it is problematic, see Eaton, *India in the Persianate Age*, 19–30.

13 Michel Foucault, *'Society Must Be Defended': Lectures at the Collège de France, 1975-76*, ed. Mauro Bertani and Alessandro Fontana (New York: Picador, 2003), 103–05.
14 Foucault, 105.
15 Lala Lajpat Rai, 'Akbar, The Great Mogul, Young India, July 1918', in *CWLLR*, vol. 7, 2005 [hereafter cited as 'Akbar'], 287.
16 Lajpat Rai, 'Young India', 240.
17 Lala Lajpat Rai, 'Problem of National Education in India, 1918', in *CWLLR*, vol. 7, 2005, 282.
18 Lajpat Rai, 'Akbar', 282.
19 Eaton, *India in the Persianate Age*, 525.
20 Eaton, 432.
21 Lajpat Rai, 'Young India', 240.
22 Lajpat Rai, 239–41.
23 Lajpat Rai, 240–41.
24 Interestingly, for historian Jadunath Sarkar, writing a decade later, the Mughal empire represented a tragedy in its failure to successfully create a modern nation–state. Dipesh Chakrabarty, *The Calling of History: Sir Jadunath Sarkar and His Empire of Truth* (Chicago; London: The University of Chicago Press, 2015), 191–92.
25 Eaton, *India in the Persianate Age*, 23–27.
26 Partha Chatterjee, 'History and the Nationalisation of Hinduism', in *Representing Hinduism: The Construction of Religious Traditions and National Identity*, (eds) Vasudha Dalmia and Heinrich von Stietencron (London: SAGE, 1995), 122–25.
27 Lajpat Rai, 'Problem of National Education', 185.
28 Lajpat Rai, 'Akbar', 282.
29 For Smith's account of Akbar's 'tortuous' diplomacy and barbaric punishments, see Vincent Arthur Smith, *Akbar the Great Mogul, 1542-1605* (London: Clarendon Press, 1917), 342–45. Lajpat Rai's impression that Smith was uncharitable to Akbar is shared by professional historians. See Peter Hardy, *The Muslims of British India* (Cambridge: Cambridge University Press, 1972), 263.

30 Lajpat Rai, 'Problem of National Education', 185. Here, Rai's assessment aligned with twenty-first century historians of Aurangzeb's reign who similarly argue that historical evidence does not support the widely held belief that Aurangzeb massacred millions of Hindus. Audrey Truschke, *Aurangzeb: The Life and Legacy of India's Most Controversial King* (Stanford: Stanford University Press, 2017), 28.

31 Probably a reference to Muhammad bin Qasim who, in 711 CE, was sent by the Ummayid Caliphs to extend control into Sindh.

32 Lajpat Rai, 'Problem of National Education', 185.

33 Lajpat Rai, 'Akbar', 282. Akbar had publicly stressed equality before the law, regardless of religion, and actively supported Hindu institutions such as the Govinda Deva temple at Vrindavan. The *Ibadat Khana* or House of Worship at his court had conducted formal inter-religious debates between Muslims, Brahmins, Jains, Zoroastrians and Christians, which convinced him that all faiths were either equally true or equally false. Inspired by strands of mystical and Sufi Islam, as well as aspects of Hinduism, Akbar had seen himself as obliged to protect his non-Muslim subjects, and insisted that all should be free to follow their religions. His policy of *sulh-i-kul* (translated variously as 'perfect reconciliation', 'universal toleration', 'peace with all' or 'compete civility') acknowledged India's cultural diversity and challenged his subjects to engage with new sources of knowledge even if they conflicted with their own traditions. Eaton, *India in the Persianate Age*, 433–41.

34 Lajpat Rai, 'Problem of National Education', 185. Some present-day medieval historians have highlighted that Aurangzeb projected himself as a strict Muslim, cut back on many courtly functions which he considered as conflicting with Islam, and did proclaim certain discriminatory policies. But they also argue that he did not always enforce these policies strictly; that French and English travellers to India during his reign noted that non-Muslims were allowed the free exercise of their religion (with one English traveller contrasting this official tolerance with

the intolerance then prevailing in his own country); and that Aurangzeb largely refused to associate religion with political affairs. These scholars argue that Aurangzeb had continued the Hindustani kingly tradition of attacking temples of enemy kings or anti-state rebels, but that he had supported several temples with cash and land grants. For more details, see Eaton, *India in the Persianate Age*, 607–13; Truschke, *Aurangzeb*, 35, 146–47, 155–85.

35 Lajpat Rai, 'Akbar', 283. Indeed, much to the chagrin of conservative Muslim thinkers such as Ziauddin Barani, Hindu religious practices flourished under the Delhi sultans, who prioritized socio-political stability over religious-based domination, and adopted 'a pragmatic live-and-let-live policy' with regard to India's religious plurality. Eaton, *India in the Persianate Age*, 105–07.

36 Lajpat Rai, 'Problem of National Education', 184.

37 Lajpat Rai, 'Young India', 228. Lajpat Rai's revised interpretation of Aurangzeb diverged from dominant understandings of him (as a religious bigot who persecuted Hindus) current both in popular imagination and historical scholarship of his time. Chakrabarty, *The Calling of History*, 13, 15. Lajpat Rai's interpretation anticipated, by a century, the recent academic appraisal of Aurangzeb. Truschke, *Aurangzeb*.

38 Gyanendra Pandey, *The Construction of Communalism in Colonial North India* (New Delhi: Oxford University Press, 2006), 23.

39 Thomas Metcalf, *Ideologies of the Raj* (Cambridge: Cambridge University Press, 1994), 4.

40 Lajpat Rai, 'Akbar', 283.

41 Lajpat Rai, 'Young India', 282–87. Here, Lajpat Rai's views again broadly align with contemporary historians who argue that Akbar's reign exhibited an almost obsessive preoccupation with rational order and efficiency, particularly in the spheres of governance and administration, making it a harbinger of what we today call modernity. Eaton, *India in the Persianate Age*, 727–29,

733. Scholars of world empires have also noted that the Mughals, and especially Akbar, presided over a larger and wealthier economy than the Ottomans, and that India's manufacturing capacities at the time dwarfed those of Europe. A major trading power, India exported large quantities of foodstuffs, cotton textiles, tobacco, sugar and indigo to its Ottoman, Iranian and Uzbek neighbours. The Mughals had encouraged both internal and foreign trade, and their efficient revenue system had created a privileged aristocratic class of revenue holders (the *jagirdars* or *mansabdars*). John Darwin, *After Tamerlane: The Rise and Fall of Global Empires, 1400–2000* (London: Penguin Books, 2008), 86.

42 Chatterjee, 'History and the Nationalisation of Hinduism', 121.

43 Lajpat Rai, 'Young India', 227–28.

44 Lajpat Rai, 227–28.

45 Lajpat Rai, 'Problem of National Education', 185–86.

46 Stephanie Barczewski, *Myth and National Identity in Nineteenth-Century Britain: The Legends of King Arthur and Robin Hood* (Oxford: Oxford University Press, 2000), 35–38.

47 Barczewski, 129.

48 See Eaton, *India in the Persianate Age: 1000–1765*, 2020; Mukhia in Romila Thapar, Harbans Mukhia, and Bipan Chandra, *Communalism and the Writing of Indian History* (People's Publishing House (1969), 2017); Muzaffar Alam, *Languages of Political Islam in India 1200–1800* (Orient Blackswan, 2004); Satish Chandra, *Essays on Medieval Indian History* (New Delhi: Oxford University Press, 2003). Of course, Rai's remained a more unselfconsciously Indian nationalist reading of history, driven by the primary aim of buttressing the Indian nation. Professional historians have undertaken much deeper conceptual thinking and applied historical methods much more rigorously in their efforts to arrive at the most accurate and nuanced interpretation of India's medieval past.

49 Lala Lajpat Rai, 'Faiths of India, The New Republic, 16 August 1916', in *CWLLR*, vol. 6, 2005, 123.

50 Lajpat Rai, 'Akbar', 284. The trope of India's stagnation under 'Muslim' rule was a colonial stereotype which served to portray British rule as emancipatory. See Eaton, *India in the Persianate Age*, 17, 27.

51 Lajpat Rai, 287.

52 Asif, *The Loss of Hindustan*, 221. For the textures of this colonial discourse about India's history, see Asif, 13–21, 28–47.

53 In his efforts to challenge the British colonial account of India's medieval past, Rai's efforts broadly prefigured the efforts of a significant line of colonial-era and post-independent medievalist historians. Asif, *The Loss of Hindustan*, 220; Bhargava, *Promise*, 120; Also see Richard Eaton, *India in the Persianate Age: 1000–1765*, 2020.

54 Asif, *The Loss of Hindustan*, 221–22.

55 By 'separatism', I mean the tendency of an identity-based (Hindu, Muslim, non-Brahmin, or 'Untouchable') political and/ or social organization to focus exclusively on the realization of its interests even at the expense of cooperation with other communities. This book often uses the terms 'separatism' and 'isolationism' inter-changeably.

56 Asif, 221, 223.

57 Sushmita Nath, 'Jawaharlal Nehru and the Question of Indian Secularity' (KFG Conference, Secularities—Patterns of Distinction, Paths of Differentiation, Multiple Secularities, Leipzig University, October 2018), 5.

58 Neeladri Bhattacharya, 'Predicaments of Secular Histories', *Public Culture* 20, no. 1 (2008): 58–59. Rather than uncritically defending secular histories of Indian history, however, Bhattacharya, locating himself within secular historiography, urges a re-examination of some of its framings and narrativizations.

59 Bhattacharya, 68. Relatively more sensitive to the alienating effects of doing so, in *Discovery*, Nehru would explicitly refuse to name the Indian nation's cultural essence as 'Hindu'. He would argue

more deliberately than Rai that Indian national culture was a sum of its multiple historical layers, with each layer progressively enriching it. In his view, Indian culture, continuously evolving since the time of the Indus Valley civilization, had always been a product of cultural intermixing and was therefore marked by an essential tolerance for plurality. This Indian national culture—to which Hinduism had copiously contributed—was only further revitalized by the encounter with Islam. As Islam was 'absorbed' by Indian culture, it 'rejuvenated' the latter, producing 'new blooms of culture' and a 'new synthesis'. This pluralist Indian national culture reached its peak under Emperor Akbar, seen as embodying the Indian national ideal of synthesis, and contributing significantly to strengthening the diversity-respecting foundations of the Indian nation. Jawaharlal Nehru, *Discovery of India* (Calcutta: Signet Press, 1946), 74–75; Nath, 'Nehru and Indian Secularity', 6–8; Pandey, *Construction of Communalism*, 247–48.

Chapter 12

1   Aydin, *Idea of the Muslim World*, 19.

2   Aydin, *Idea of the Muslim World*, 20.

3   Aydin, *Idea of the Muslim World*, 20, Hugh Kennedy, *The Caliphate: The History of an Idea* (Penguin UK, 2016), 53, 72; also see Part 1 of the Aljazeera documentary: *The Caliph*, Aljazeera Documentaries, 2016, https://interactive.aljazeera.com/aje/2016/the-caliph-islamic-history/index.html.

4   Hugh Kennedy, *The Caliphate: The History of an Idea* (Penguin UK, 2016), 72.

5   Aydin, *Idea of the Muslim World*, 20.

6   Aydin, *Idea of the Muslim World*, 20.

7   Aydin, *Idea of the Muslim World*, 20.

8   Hugh Kennedy, *The Caliphate: The History of an Idea* (Penguin UK, 2016), 17, 169–210.

9   Aydin, *Idea of the Muslim World*, 20.

10 Aydin, *Idea of the Muslim World*, 20.
11 Aydin, *Idea of the Muslim World*, 20.
12 Aydin, *Idea of the Muslim World*, 20.
13 Aydin, *Idea of the Muslim World*, 20.
14 Aydin, *Idea of the Muslim World*, 22.
15 Aydin, *Idea of the Muslim World*, 22–23.
16 Aydin, *Idea of the Muslim World*, 23.
17 Aydin, *Idea of the Muslim World*, 23.
18 Aydin, *Idea of the Muslim World*, 24.
19 Aydin, *Idea of the Muslim World*, 24.
20 Aydin, *Idea of the Muslim World*, 24.
21 Aydin, *Idea of the Muslim World*, 24.
22 Aydin, *Idea of the Muslim World*, 24. The history of the caliphate until here draws heavily on Aydin, *Idea of the Muslim World*, 19–24. For the different manifestations of the caliphate from the advent of Islam to the modern era, see Hugh Kennedy, *The Caliphate: The History of an Idea* (Penguin UK, 2016). For an introduction to the topic, also see the three-part Aljazeera documentary: *The Caliph*, Aljazeera Documentaries, 2016, https://interactive.aljazeera.com/aje/2016/the-caliph-islamic-history/index.html.
23 Aydin, *Idea of the Muslim World*, 26–28.
24 Gail Minault, *The Khilafat Movement: Religious Symbolism and Political Mobilization in India* (Delhi: Columbia University Press, 1982), 4.
25 Minault, 4; Rakhahari Chatterji, *Gandhi and the Ali Brothers: Biography of a Friendship* (New Delhi: SAGE, 2013), 27.
26 Aydin, *Idea of the Muslim World*, 38–49.
27 Aydin, 59.
28 Aydin, 54–55.
29 Aydin, 60–61.
30 Aydin, 49–54, 61–62.
31 Minault, *Khilafat Movement*, 4–7; Aydin, *Idea of the Muslim World*, 58, 67–68, 95, 97; Mona Hassan, *Longing for the Lost Caliphate: A Transregional History* (Princeton; Oxford: Princeton University Press, 2016), 149.

32 Aydin, *Idea of the Muslim World*, 49, 65, 68. Seventy per cent of the world's Muslims were ruled by European powers. 66.

33 Aydin, *Idea of the Muslim World*, 49, 57, 68, 70–71. For details of the major themes in this transnational Pan-Islamist thought, see Aydin, 71–82.

34 Aydin, *Idea of the Muslim World*, 57–58, 63, 69–71. For an illustration of the absence of this idea before the nineteenth century, see Aydin, 25–36.

35 Aydin, *Idea of the Muslim World*, 65–68, 90. Of course, not everyone accepted the legitimacy of the Ottoman caliphate. Some Muslims in the Arab provinces of the Ottoman Empire sought separation of the office of the caliphate from the Ottoman sultanate, and dreamt of establishing an independent Arab caliphate. Kennedy, *The Caliphate: The History of an Idea*, 402.

36 Aydin, *Idea of the Muslim World*, 67, 97.

37 Aydin, 82.

38 Aydin, *Idea of the Muslim World*, 100, 104.

39 Aydin, 82, 85.

40 Aydin, 68, 82, 84.

41 Aydin, *Idea of the Muslim World*, 84, 89–90. Among the eminent Muslim personalities who never supported Pan-Islamism or Ottoman claims to the caliphate even amidst the late nineteenth century upsurge was Sir Syed Ahmed Khan. Mushirul Hasan, 'Nationalism and Communal Politics in India, 1885–1930', in *The Mushirul Hasan Omnibus* (New Delhi: Oxford University Press, 2010), 114–15.

42 Aydin, *Idea of the Muslim World*, 106–07. Most of the following details are from Aydin, chap. 4.

43 Aydin, *Idea of the Muslim World*, 107.

44 Aydin, 107.

45 Aydin, 105, 107.

46 Aydin, 108.

47 Even so, before the First World War (1914–18), non-Muslim revolutionaries abroad, like Madam Cama and Virendranath Chattopadhyay, often struggled to use Pan-Islamism as a gateway to goad India's Muslims into the anti-colonial movement. They

wondered why India's Muslims were indifferent to European interference in Muslim countries like Iran. See Maia Ramnath, *Haj to Utopia: How the Ghadar Movement Charted Global Radicalism and Attempted to Overthrow the British Empire*, The California World History Library, no. 19 (University of California Press: Berkeley, 2011), 156–57.

48 Aydin, *Idea of the Muslim World*, 108–19.

49 Chatterji, *Gandhi and the Ali Brothers*, 71.

50 Aydin, *Idea of the Muslim World*, 121–22.

51 It was this event, and subsequent British support for the idea of a Jewish homeland in predominantly Arab Muslim Palestine, that laid the foundation for the creation of Israel in 1948 and the still-continuing Israel–Palestine conflict.

52 David Hardiman, *Noncooperation in India: Nonviolent Strategy and Protest, 1920–22* (Oxford University Press, USA, 2021), 11. During the war, the new Muslim leadership in India was not alone in expressing Pan-Islamic ideas. Ghadar revolutionaries abroad expressed concern for the fate of the Ottoman Empire, working with Pan-Islamists, and simultaneously articulating Pan-Islamic and radical anti-colonial narratives. See Ramnath, *Haj to Utopia*, 155–59.

53 Ansari (1880–1936), a Britain-trained doctor who practised Western medicine in Delhi, had emerged as a prominent Khilafat activist by 1913. Beginning to deeply admire Gandhi by 1918, he would soon throw his weight behind his satyagraha campaign against the British government. Hardiman, *Noncooperation in India*, 9; Mushirul Hasan, 'A Nationalist Conscience: M.A. Ansari, the Congress and The Raj', in *The Mushirul Hasan Omnibus* (New Delhi: Oxford University Press, 2010), 58–61.

54 Khan (1863–1928) was a pious, cosmopolitan, Delhi-based medical practitioner heavily involved in the revival of traditional Unani and Ayurvedic medicine. Disillusioned with British rule during the early 1910s, for the same reasons as several younger Muslims, he emerged as a major figure in the new Khilafat and anti-imperial campaigns. Having always cooperated with Hindus

in his profession, he steadily grew close to Gandhi and the Congress, and was committed to Hindu–Muslim cooperation and evolving a common 'national' culture. Barbara Daly Metcalf, 'Nationalist Muslims in British India: The Case of Hakim Ajmal Khan', *Modern Asian Studies* 19, no. 1 (1985): 3, 13, 19.

55 In the context of colonial India, a 'constitutionalist' was a politician who believed in conducting politics—including a politics opposing the British—*within* the framework of the constitutional structure established by the British, i.e., through the legislative councils. Constitutionalists were often wary of mass-based political movements.

56 Jinnah, a major player in the crystallization of the Lucknow Pact, had supported and worked for Hindu–Muslim cooperation over the demand of self-government. He strongly opposed numerous colonial injustices. However, he was committed to achieving Home Rule for India through constitutional means, and was apprehensive of mass politics. He was also less interested in the cause of the caliphate. Stanley Wolpert, *Jinnah of Pakistan* (New York: Oxford University Press, 1984), 52, 64–72.

57 A sign of the differences in the political contexts and world views of Muslims across the 'Muslim world', the Indian Muslim Khilafat movement to preserve the Ottoman caliphate–empire ran counter to the 1916 Arab revolt against Ottoman rule, to dreams among some Arab Muslim intellectuals about a revived Arab caliphate, and also to the indifference of many Arab Muslims to the caliphate question. Still, Indian Muslims were not alone in their continued respect for the Ottoman caliphate–empire. Despite the revolt, many Arabs had remained loyal to Ottoman rule until its end, even as they asked for greater decentralization, viewing it as an obstacle to European occupation. Guided by their own dreams and motivations, some Arab Muslims still wished to preserve the Ottoman caliphate. Driven by a different set of dreams and motives, the Turks would wage their War of Independence (from Greek and European occupation) in 1919 in the name of preserving the integrity of the Ottoman sultanate

and caliphate. And for many Muslims living under European rule in North Africa, Egypt and Indonesia, the Ottoman caliphate-empire symbolized the last independent Muslim state in a world dominated by European imperialism. Hassan, *Longing for the Lost Caliphate*, 12, 149–50, 153; Bruce Masters, *The Arabs of the Ottoman Empire, 1516–1918: A Social and Cultural History* (Cambridge University Press, 2013), chap. 4.

58 Faisal Devji, *The Impossible Indian: Gandhi and the Temptation of Violence* (London: Harvard University Press, 2012), 73; Minault, *Khilafat Movement*, 5.

59 This was currently Azad's position. See Faisal Devji, 'Escaping the Global Event' (2022), 25. Also Minault, *Khilafat Movement*, 94.

60 Devji, 'Escaping the Global Event', 9–12, 24; Aydin, *Idea of the Muslim World*, 125.

61 Farzana Shaikh, *Community and Consensus in Islam: Muslim Representation in Colonial India, 1860–1947* (Delhi: Imprint One, 2012), 180, n. 80.

62 Devji, 'Escaping the Global Event', 24, 26; John Willis, 'Debating the Caliphate: Islam and Nation in the Work of Rashid Rida and Abul Kalam Azad', *The International History Review* 32, no. 4 (2010): 723, 726. As intellectual historian Faisal Devji argues, despite his concern for Islam's sacred sites, Azad was not particularly attached to them as objects of devotion and ritual practice. He saw Mecca as a city meant to 'join humanity's scattered hearts and dejected souls' and thus embody what he considered Islam's teaching of universalism and human equality. 'Escaping the Global Event', 28–29.

63 Aydin, *Idea of the Muslim World*, chaps 1, 3–4.

64 Also see Minault, *Khilafat Movement*, 7.

65 Devji, *Impossible Indian*, 73; Aydin, *Idea of the Muslim World*, 120–25; Hasan, 'Nationalism and Communal Politics', 121. M.A. Ansari, for instance, saw the Khilafat movement as a campaign against Western imperialist oppression of India and Asia in general. 121.

66 Minault, *Khilafat Movement*; Hardiman, *Noncooperation in India*, 177; Hasan, 'Nationalism and Communal Politics', 105.

67 Ayesha Jalal, 'Striking a Just Balance: Maulana Azad as a Theorist of Trans-National Jihad', *Modern Intellectual History* 4, no. 01 (2007): 96–97, 106; Willis, 'Debating the Caliphate', 713, 724–26, 729; Minault, *Khilafat Movement*, 42–43; Shaunna Rodrigues, 'Abul Kalam Azad and the Right to an Islamic Justification of the Indian Constitution', in *Dimensions of Constitutional Democracy*, ed. A. Roy and M. Becker (Springer, 2020), 126–30, 132, 136. Azad's anti-colonialism had been partly inspired by Bengali revolutionary groups. His idea of a common Indian nation was partly inspired by Mustafa Kemal Pasha's attempts to organize Muslims and non-Muslims in a common anti-colonial nationalist cause. Willis, 'Debating the Caliphate', 723; Hasan, 'Nationalism and Communal Politics', 120. In his attempt to build a Muslim–Hindu alliance, Azad also drew on Hindu tradition. Rodrigues, 'Azad and the Right to an Islamic Justification', 133.

68 Hasan, 'Nationalism and Communal Politics', 119, 121–22; Shan Muhammad, ed., 'Presidential Address by Hakim Ajmal Khan, All-India Muslim League, Amritsar, 30 December 1919', in *The Indian Muslims: A Documentary Record (1900–1947)*, vol. 6 (Meerut: Meenakshi Prakashan, 1980), 95. Like Azad, Ansari gave Islamic arguments to urge Muslims to unite with Hindus in anti-colonial 'national' struggle. Apart from these more 'well-born' Muslims, the Khilafat movement also saw many Muslim peasants and workers come out in anti-colonial protest against the British government for a range of grievances, from rising prices to its handling of cholera and influenza epidemics, to horrible working conditions in the railways. Hasan, 'Nationalism and Communal Politics', 125.

69 This broad alliance should not lead us to forget the differences which remained among Indian Muslims. For instance, Azad was critical of both the ulema for their obscurantism and Aligarh-based Western-educated leaders (like the Ali brothers)

for their imitation of the West. Hardiman, *Noncooperation in India*, 9–10; Minault, *Khilafat Movement*, 39–42. Divisions also persisted within the ulema. During these years, some members of the ulema, especially the Deobandis, were involved in a Ghadar-like attempt to foment a revolutionary struggle for India's liberation from abroad. See Faridah Zaman, 'Revolutionary History and the Post-Colonial Muslim: Re-Writing the "Silk Letters Conspiracy" of 1916', *South Asia: Journal of South Asian Studies* 39, no. 3 (2016): 626–32. Other Deobandi ulema condemned these politically-oriented ulema as infidels, complaining to the British government of their 'seditious' activities. Minault, *Khilafat Movement*, 29–31. Similarly, Abdul Bari, a prominent *alim* from Firangi Mahal (a Lucknow-based centre of Islamic learning with a longer history than Deoband), who emerged as a prominent activist for the Khilafat cause, was opposed by other pro-British, apolitical ulema at Lucknow. Minault, 32–34.

70 In Champaran, Gandhi helped organize a peasant boycott movement against exploitative white Indigo 'planters', taking their complaints to the British government, which was eventually compelled to legally abolish the indigo system which forced peasants to grow indigo on deeply unfavourable terms. In Kheda, Gandhi, with Vallabhbhai Patel's help, organized a peasant agitation of widespread tax-refusal to the British government, which had regularly used high degrees of extra-legal coercion to collect this land tax even in difficult times. The struggle succeeded in making the British conform to their own laws. For more details, see Hardiman, *Noncooperation in India*, 110–56.

71 Gandhi's method of satyagraha was objected to by moderate nationalists as well as Annie Besant who feared that law-breaking would open the floodgates to uncontrollable turmoil. David Hardiman, *The Nonviolent Struggle for Indian Freedom, 1905–19*, 2018, 176–77.

72 The draconian acts were passed despite the British government having already crushed the Ghadar movement, in which Punjabi émigrés and some extremist nationalists from Bengal and

Maharashtra had tried to seek German help to foment a revolt in India.

73 Hardiman, *The Nonviolent Struggle for Indian Freedom, 1905–19*, 179–84.

74 Minault, *Khilafat Movement*, 70. For more details on Shraddhanand's involvement in the Rowlatt Satyagraha and his Jama Masjid speech, see Neeti Nair, *Changing Homelands: Hindu Politics and the Partition of India* (Cambridge, MA: Harvard University Press, 2011), 96–101.

75 These details have been drawn from Hardiman, *The Nonviolent Struggle for Indian Freedom, 1905–19*, 181–93.

76 Minault, *Khilafat Movement*, 68.

77 Devji, *Impossible Indian*, 75–82.

78 Shabnum Tejani, *Indian Secularism: A Social and Intellectual History, 1890–1950* (Bloomington: Indiana University Press, 2008), 171–78.

79 Devji, *Impossible Indian*, 44, 68–84; Judith Brown, *Gandhi's Rise to Power, Indian Politics 1915–1922* (Cambridge: Cambridge University Press, 1972), 9, 190; Hasan, 'Nationalism and Communal Politics', 127–28; Tejani, *Indian Secularism*, 155, 177–78; Minault, *Khilafat Movement*, 68.

80 Devji, *Impossible Indian*, 50.

81 Devji, 51–53.

82 Devji, 51, 53, 64, 68–84, 88–89; Ajay Skaria, 'Gandhi's Politics: Liberalism and the Question of the Ashram', *The South Atlantic Quarterly* 101, no. 4 (2003): 955–86.

83 Brown, *Gandhi's Rise to Power, Indian Politics 1915-1922*, 47, 151–53, 190.

84 Hasan, 'Nationalist Conscience', 59–62. See Muhammad, 'Hakim Ajmal Khan's Presidential Address', 81–96.

85 As cited in Metcalf, 'Nationalist Muslims', 25.

86 Hasan, 'Nationalist Conscience', 90–91.

87 Minault, *Khilafat Movement*, 70–71, 77–78; Hardiman, *Noncooperation in India*, 14; Hasan, 'Nationalist Conscience', 71.

88 Hardiman, *Noncooperation in India*, 16.

89 Minault, *Khilafat Movement*, 86–98.
90 Francis Robinson, *Separatism Among Indian Muslims: The Politics of the United Provinces' Muslims, 1860–1923* (Cambridge: Cambridge University Press, 2007), 311; Minault, *Khilafat Movement*, 90; Aydin, *Idea of the Muslim World*, 123.
91 Minault, *Khilafat Movement*, 99.
92 Minault, 108. Council boycott as a form of non-cooperation was initially suggested by a section of the Muslim Khilafat leaders. Gandhi had remained open to elections, and the boycott of council elections was opposed by most Congressmen who wished to fight elections. Interestingly, it was Lajpat Rai's decision in June 1920 not to stand for election that encouraged Gandhi to include council boycott as part of his non-cooperation programme. Several Congressmen in UP (including Motilal Nehru), Bombay, Gujarat, Sindh and Bihar came around to Gandhi's position by September. Even then, council boycott was opposed by Tilakites in Bombay Presidency and by the Congress leaders of Madras and Bengal (led by Bengal's now-foremost nationalist leader, C.R. Das, and B.C. Pal). The leaders of Bengal also opposed the boycott of schools and courts. They instead demanded the economic boycott of foreign goods (which some Khilafat leaders had initially proposed but Gandhi opposed). While Gandhi eventually won on council boycott, he had to compromise with Bengal's leaders by giving into the boycott of foreign goods, and emphasizing a *gradual* boycott of schools and courts in his programme. Hardiman, *Noncooperation in India*, 20–27.
93 This moment, which signified the height of Gandhi's popularity, saw Jinnah resign from the Congress, ending a sixteen-year-long association. Jinnah opposed the method of non-cooperation and mass politics, but also denounced the participation of the ulema in politics. Minault, *Khilafat Movement*, 125; Shaikh, *Community and Consensus*, 182. Several Congressmen who feared Gandhi's movements of mass mobilization similarly resigned from the Congress forever, now forming the National Liberal Federation.

They were henceforth known in Indian politics as the 'Liberals'. Hardiman, *Noncooperation in India*, 28.

94 In England since 1905 for his high school and secondary education, Jawaharlal Nehru had watched the 1905 Swadeshi movement with great interest. Disagreeing with his 'moderate' father, he shared sympathies with the 'extremists', and was impressed with Lajpat Rai's talk on his trip to Cambridge in 1909. After returning to India in 1912, the young Nehru had first worked for Annie Besant's Home Rule League and then for Gandhi's Rowlatt Satyagraha. Part of the Congress team that investigated the Jallianwala Bagh massacre, he had attended Khilafat conferences before participating in the non-cooperation movement. Jawaharlal Nehru, *An Autobiography* (London: Bodley Head, 1936), 18–24, 34, 45–49; Benjamin Zachariah, *Nehru* (London; New York: Routledge, 2004), 34–42.

95 Das had been involved in anti-colonial activities since the Swadeshi days, and had been close to B.C. Pal and Aurobindo Ghose. He was catapulted to fame in Calcutta by his legal defence of Ghose in the 1910 Alipur bomb case. Hardiman, *Noncooperation in India*, 30.

96 C. Raja, or 'Rajaji' as he was ultimately called, would go on to become the first chief minister of Madras Presidency in 1937, the first governor of West Bengal in 1947–48, and India's first Indian-origin governor-general in 1948–50. E.V.R, or 'Periyar' (Great leader) as he would soon be called, would get disillusioned with the Congress by 1925, growing frustrated over what he considered its evasion of the issue of caste-based inequalities and its reluctance to concede communal representation for non-Brahmins.

97 For more on Patel's dedication to Gandhi during the non-cooperation movement, see Hindol Sengupta, *The Man Who Saved India: Sardar Patel and His Idea of India* (Gurgaon: Penguin/Viking, 2018), chap. 3.

98 See Chapter 10.

99 Rai was particularly unsure about the proposed boycott of government-funded educational institutions. V.C. Joshi, *Lala Lajpat Rai: Writings and Speeches*, ed. V.C. Joshi, vol. 1 (Delhi: University Publishers, 1966), xlvii; Feroz Chand, *Lajpat Rai: Life and Work* (New Delhi: Publications Division, Ministry of Information and Broadcasting, Government of India, 1978), 340, 347.

100 Chand, *Lajpat Rai*, 336; Joshi, *Lala Lajpat Rai: Writings and Speeches*, 1:xlvii. Lajpat Rai had followed Gandhi's struggle in South Africa at least since 1908, and in 1913 had issued appeals to raise funds for it. Lala Lajpat Rai, 'Treatment of Indians in South Africa, India, 23 October 1908', in *CWLLR*, vol. 3, 2004, 163–64; 'Appeal for Help to Indians in South Africa, The Tribune, 13 November 1913', in *CWLLR*, vol. 4, 2004, 67–68. In mid-1919, he directly corresponded with Gandhi, conveying his sympathy with the broader principle underlying his Rowlatt agitation i.e., collective suffering and sacrifice for the sake of national freedom. See Lala Lajpat Rai, 'To Mahatma Gandhi, 20 June 1919', in *CWLLR*, vol. 8, 2006, 77–78. M.K. Gandhi, 'Letter to Lala Lajpat Rai, 20 August 1919', in *Collected Works of Mahatma Gandhi* [hereafter cited as *CWMG*], vol. 16 (Ahmedabad: Navajivan Trust, 1965), 52–53.

101 Lajpat Rai's biographer, Feroz Chand, has noted his support for the Khilafat cause, donation to the Khilafat fund and tours with Shaukat Ali during the Khilafat-non-cooperation movement. *Lajpat Rai*, 477–78.

102 Christophe Jaffrelot, *The Hindu Nationalist Movement and Indian Politics: 1925 to the 1990s* (New Delhi: Penguin Books, 1999), 25; Chetan Bhatt, *Hindu Nationalism: Origins, Ideologies and Modern Myths* (Oxford: Berg, 2001), 47.

103 Gyanendra Pandey, *The Construction of Communalism in Colonial North India* (New Delhi: Oxford University Press, 2006), 234; Jaffrelot, *Hindu Nationalist Movement*, 25; Bhatt, *Origins*, 47.

104 John Zavos, *The Emergence of Hindu Nationalism in India* (Oxford: Oxford University Press, 2000), 145; Minault, *Khilafat*

Movement, 70–71; Hasan, 'Nationalism and Communal Politics', 127–28.

105 Minault, *Khilafat Movement*, 70, 77–78, 83; Hasan, 'Nationalism and Communal Politics', 132–33; Also see Shraddhanand's biography, J.T.F. Jordens, *Swāmī Shraddhānanda: His Life and Causes* (Delhi: Oxford University Press, 1981), 124.

106 Tejani, *Indian Secularism*, 178.

107 Minault, *Khilafat Movement*, 68; Tejani, *Indian Secularism*, 155, 171–78; Hasan, 'Nationalism and Communal Politics', 127–28; Devji, *Impossible Indian*, 68–84; Vikram Sampath, *Savarkar: Echoes from a Forgotten Past, 1883–1924* (Gurgaon: Viking, 2019), 370–77. Of these, Devji's is the only work that undertakes a proper intellectual analysis of the texture of Gandhi's reasons for supporting the Khilafat cause. Historian Maia Ramnath has shown that Hindu Ghadar revolutionaries expressed sympathies with the Ottoman Empire. Gandhi was clearly not the only Hindu sympathetic to Pan-Islamism.

108 Content from this and the subsequent chapter has previously appeared in Vanya Vaidehi Bhargav, 'A Hindu Champion of Pan-Islamism: Lajpat Rai and the Khilafat Movement', *The Journal of Asian Studies*, 2022, 1–17, https://doi.org/10.1017/S0021911822000511.

109 Swaraj was still variously conceived by Indian political actors, with some like the Ali brothers and Azad translating it as complete independence and others like Gandhi and Lajpat Rai countenancing Indian freedom and self-government within the British Empire or, as Rai called it, the 'British commonwealth', in the manner of South Africa, Canada and Australia. Hardiman, *The Nonviolent Struggle for Indian Freedom, 1905–19*, 27, 33; Lala Lajpat Rai, 'Presidential Address, Calcutta Congress, 4 September 1920', in *CWLLR*, vol. 9, 2007 [hereafter cited as 'Congress Presidential Address'], 124.

110 Lala Lajpat Rai, 'Amritsar—Place of Political Pilgrimage, The Tribune, 16 March 1920', in *CWLLR*, vol. 9, 2007 [hereafter cited as 'Amritsar'], 28–29.

111 Lala Lajpat Rai, 'Unity, the Foundation of Liberty, The Tribune, 26 February 1920', in *CWLLR*, vol. 9, 2007, 3.

112 Lala Lajpat Rai, 'Unity, the Price of Liberty, The Tribune, 28 February 1920', in *CWLLR*, vol. 9, 2007, 25; 'Amritsar', 26–28.

113 Sikhs may have been, once again, included by Lajpat Rai in his definition of 'Hindu'.

114 The trope of establishing a memorial at Jallianwala Bagh to cement Hindu–Muslim unity was also expressed by Hindu leaders like Malaviya. See *The Leader*, 16 May 1921; *The Leader*, 10 January 1920.

115 Lala Lajpat Rai, 'Towards Freedom, 20 February 1920', in *CWLLR*, vol. 8, 2006, 152. The meeting had been presided by Jinnah who hailed Lajpat Rai as one of India's greatest sons. Among others who had paid tributes were Tilak and Annie Besant. See Lala Lajpat Rai, *The Collected Works of Lala Lajpat Rai*, ed. B.R. Nanda (New Delhi: Manohar, 2006), vol. 8, 151.

116 M.K. Gandhi, 'Hindu–Muslim Unity, Young India, 6 October 1920', in *Communal Unity* (Ahmedabad: Navajivan Publishing House), 1949, 3; 'Why I Have Joined the Home Rule League, Navajivan, 2 May 1920', in *CWMG*, vol. 17, 1958, 369–71; 'How to Protect the Cow, Navajivan, 23 November 1919', in *CWMG*, vol. 16, 1965, 305–06; 'Speech at Khilafat Conference, Delhi, Bombay Chronicle, 6 December 1919', in *CWMG*, vol. 16, 1965, 307–12; 'Punjab Letter, Navajivan, 7 December 1919', in *CWMG*, vol. 16, 1965, 318–26; 'Cow Protection, Young India, 4 August 1920', in *CWMG*, vol. 18, 1965, 117–19; Faisal Devji, *The Impossible Indian: Gandhi and the Temptation of Violence* (London: Harvard University Press, 2012), 83, 88.

117 Lajpat Rai, 'Amritsar', 29.

118 Lajpat Rai, 'Congress Presidential Address', 131.

119 Lajpat Rai, 128–30; 'Khilafat, Bande Mataram, 9–10 June 1920', in *CWLLR*, vol. 9, 2007 [hereafter cited as 'Khilafat'], 202.

120 Lajpat Rai, 'Congress Presidential Address', 129–30.

121 Lajpat Rai, 129.

122 Peter Hardy, *The Muslims of British India* (Cambridge: Cambridge University Press, 1972), 191; Shaikh, *Community and Consensus*, 180, n. 80.

123 'Mohamed Ali to Lord Chelmsford, 24 April 1919', in Mushirul Hasan (ed.), *Mohamed Ali in Indian Politics: Select Writings*, vol. 2 (New Delhi: Atlantic Publishers and Distributors, 1983), 224; Mushirul Hasan, 'Secular and Communitarian Representations of Indian Nationalism: Ideology and Praxis of Azad and Mohamed Ali', in Mushirul Hasan (ed.), *Islam and Indian Nationalism Reflections on Abul Kalam Azad* (New Delhi: Manohar, 1992), 86.

124 'Khilafat Deputation to Viceroy, 19 January 1920' in Shan Muhammad (ed.), *The Indian Muslims: A Documentary Record (1900–1947)*, vol. 6 (Meerut: Meenakshi Prakashan, 1980), 129; 'Mohamed Ali to Lord Chelmsford, 24 April 1919', in Mushirul Hasan (ed.), *Mohamed Ali in Indian Politics: Select Writings*, vol. 2 (New Delhi: Atlantic Publishers and Distributors, 1983), 226–27, 237; Ali Ashraf, 'Appraisal of Azad's Religio-Political Trajectory', in Mushirul Hasan (ed.), *Islam and Indian Nationalism Reflections on Abul Kalam Azad* (New Delhi: Manohar, 1992), 110–11.

125 Muhammad, 'Khilafat Deputation to Viceroy', 132.

126 Minault, *Khilafat Movement*, 5–8; Shaikh, *Community and Consensus*, 176–79; Devji, 'Escaping the Global Event'.

127 B.G. Tilak, M.M. Malaviya, B.C. Pal and Motilal Nehru had also sympathized with these beliefs. See *The Leader*, 11 April 1920; 2 May 1920; 2 July 1920; 1 September 1920; 11 September 1920.

128 Minault, *Khilafat Movement*, 91.

129 Lajpat Rai, 'Unity, the Price', 25.

130 Devji, *Impossible Indian*, 52.

131 William Bain, *Between Anarchy and Society: Trusteeship and the Obligations of Power* (Oxford: Oxford University Press, 2003), 17–21.

132 Susan Pedersen, *The Guardians: The League of Nations and the Crisis of Empire* (Oxford: Oxford University Press, 2015), 24.

133 M.K. Gandhi, 'Speech at Amritsar Congress, 29 December 1919', in *CWMG*, vol. 16 (Ahmedabad: Navajivan Trust, 1965); M.K. Gandhi, 'General Dyer, 14 July 1920', in *CWMG*, vol. 18 (Ahmedabad: Navajivan Trust, 1965); M.K. Gandhi, 'Congress Report on the Punjab Disorders', in *CWMG*, vol. 17 (Ahmedabad: Navajivan Trust, 1965).

134 Lajpat Rai, 'Khilafat', 203.

135 Lajpat Rai, 'Congress Presidential Address', 131. Emphasis mine.

136 M.K. Gandhi, 'Turkey, Navajivan, 7 September 1919', in *CWMG*, vol. 16 (Ahmedabad: Navajivan Trust, 1965), 104; 'Punjab Letter', 318–20.

137 Aydin, *Idea of the Muslim World*, 116–17.

138 M.K. Gandhi, 'Pledges Broken, Young India, 19 May 1920', in *CWMG*, vol. 17 (Ahmedabad: Navajivan Trust, 1965), 434–36; 'Letter to Viceroy, 22 June 1920', in *CWMG*, vol. 17 (Ahmedabad: Navajivan Trust, 1965), 502–05; 'Speech on Non-Cooperation, Madras, The Hindu, 13 August 1920', in *CWMG*, vol. 18 (Ahmedabad: Navajivan Trust, 1965), 144.

139 Lajpat Rai, 'Congress Presidential Address', 131.

140 M.K. Gandhi, 'Speech at Subjects Committee Meeting, Calcutta, The Hindu, 8 September 1920', in *Communal Unity* (Ahmedabad: Navajivan Publishing House), 1949.

141 Lajpat Rai, 'Khilafat', 204–05.

142 Lajpat Rai, 'Khilafat', 205.

143 Aydin, *Idea of the Muslim World*.

144 Aydin, 66–79, 98.

145 Aydin, 62; Devji, *Impossible Indian*, 74.

146 Lajpat Rai, 'Khilafat', 204. While not in the same way as Lajpat Rai, Pan-Islamism was also deployed by Muslims outside India to ensure better treatment for colonial peoples. Aydin, *Idea of the Muslim World*, 79, 98.

Chapter 13

1 Lajpat Rai, 'Congress Presidential Address', 133.
2 Lajpat Rai, 133.
3 Lajpat Rai, 'Khilafat', 203.
4 For a glimpse of British and wider European anti-Ottoman propaganda, see Aydin, *Idea of the Muslim World*, 60–61, 100–103, 117. British historian Arnold Toynbee especially contributed to crafting anti-Turkish propaganda for the British empire during the war. See 152, 192, 272.
5 Lajpat Rai, 'Khilafat', 204.
6 Lajpat Rai, 'Congress Presidential Address', 130.
7 See Chapter 10, pp. 177–78.
8 Lajpat Rai, 'Congress Presidential Address'; 'Role of the Muslim National University, 15 December 1920', in *CWLLR*, vol. 9, 2007.
9 Lajpat Rai, 'Congress Presidential Address', 130.
10 Lajpat Rai, 130.
11 Lajpat Rai, 133.
12 Lajpat Rai, 130–31.
13 Lajpat Rai, 'Khilafat', 204.
14 Cited in Devji, *Impossible Indian*, 80.
15 Semanti Ghosh, *Different Nationalisms: Bengal, 1905–1947* (New Delhi: Oxford University Press, 2017), 129–30.
16 See Chapter 5, pp. 92–3.
17 *The Leader*, 11 April 1920.
18 Devji, *Impossible Indian*, 82; *The Leader*, 11 April 1920.
19 Devji, *Impossible Indian*, 82.
20 *The Leader*, 11 April 1920.
21 Lajpat Rai, 'Khilafat', 206.
22 Lala Lajpat Rai, 'Hindu–Muslim Unity and Non-Cooperation, The Tribune, 13 November 1920', in *CWLLR*, vol. 9, 2007, 243.

23 Lala Lajpat Rai, 'Apprehension of Afghan Invasion of India, Bande Mataram, 17–19 May 1921', in *CWLLR*, vol. 10, 2008 [hereafter cited as 'Apprehension of Afghan Invasion'], 273–74.

24 Lajpat Rai, 273–74.

25 Lajpat Rai, 'Congress Presidential Address', 133.

26 Minault, *Khilafat Movement*, 117; Hasan, 'Nationalist Conscience', 99–103. Jamia would eventually emerge as an anti-thesis of Aligarh, stand by Congress's Indian nationalism while opposing the 'two-nation theory' in the 1940s. Zakir Hussain (1897–1969), a student at the time of the Khilafat/non-cooperation movement, would serve as President of India in 1967–69.

27 Lajpat Rai, 'Role of the Muslim National University', 297–98.

28 Faisal Devji, 'Apologetic Modernity', *Modern Intellectual History* 4, no. 1 (2007): 61–76; David Lelyveld, *Aligarh's First Generation: Muslim Solidarity in India* (Princeton: Princeton University Press, 1978), 110; Christophe Jaffrelot, *The Pakistan Paradox: Instability and Resilience* (Oxford: Oxford University Press, 2015), 25, 31–32.

29 By 'minoritization', I mean the transformation of a community into a political minority which is vulnerable and marginalized.

30 Nair, *Changing Homelands*, 13, 26, 28, 39, 46.

31 Bhatt, *Origins*, 60; Prabhu Bapu, *Hindu Mahasabha in Colonial North India, 1915–1930: Constructing Nation and History*, Routledge Studies in South Asian History (London: Routledge, 2013), 20.

32 V. Geetha and S.V. Rajadurai, *Towards a Non-Brahmin Millennium: From Iyothee Thass to Periyar* (Calcutta: Bhatkal & Sen, 1998), 141; Sumit Sarkar, *Modern India: 1886–1947* (Delhi: Macmillian, 1983), 242.

33 Lajpat Rai, 'Apprehension of Afghan Invasion', 274–75.

34 Hasan, 'Secular and Communitarian Representations of Indian Nationalism: Ideology and Praxis of Azad and Mohamed Ali', 84–85.

35 Jalal, 'Striking a Just Balance', 96, 98–104, 106; Rodrigues, 'Azad and the Right to an Islamic Justification', 124–25.

36 Rodrigues, 'Azad and the Right to an Islamic Justification', 134–35. Azad would drop the notion of jihad from his political discourse by the end of the movement. But for the time that he used it, jihad, for Azad, meant any struggle against oppression and injustice and to establish truth, justice, peace and freedom. This struggle could assume non-violent verbal and written and organizational forms but, if required, also violent forms. Jalal, 'Striking a Just Balance', 96, 98–104, 106. Such use of religious language was unexceptional, as indicated by Swami Shraddhanand's reference to the Rowlatt Satyagraha as a 'Dharma Yuddha' (religious war). See Jordens, *Swāmī Shraddhānanda*, 110. As you may recall from Chapter 7, Lajpat Rai had himself used the Bhagavad Gita's concept of karmayoga and dharma to justify more confrontational, even potentially violent modes of anti-colonial politics in previous years. Moreover, willingness to depart from Gandhian non-violence was also not limited to Muslim leaders. C.R. Das of Bengal had been prepared to accept a degree of violence, and even wanted to use Bengal's revolutionary network to instigate mass protests and bring the government to its knees. See Hardiman, *Noncooperation in India*, 31–32. Sardar Patel too was never convinced about unqualified non-violence. See Sengupta, *The Man Who Saved India*, 124.

37 *The Leader*, 20 May 1920.

38 As quoted in Ashraf, 'Azad's Religio-Political Trajectory', 118.

39 Jalal, 'Striking a Just Balance', 106; Ian Douglas, '"Abul Kalam Azad and Pakistan": A Post-Bangladesh Reconsideration of an Indian Muslim's Opposition to Partition', *Journal of the American Academy of Religion* 40, no. 4 (1972): 471–73; Rodrigues, 'Azad and the Right to an Islamic Justification', 132, 135–36.

40 Aydin, *Idea of the Muslim World*.

41 Lajpat Rai, 'Congress Presidential Address', 133.

42 Lajpat Rai, 'Khilafat', 203.

43 It was then smuggled out of prison to be finally published in
    1923. Gyanendra Pandey, 'Hindus and Others: The Militant
    Hindu Construction', *Economic and Political Weekly* 26, no. 52
    (1991): 2999; Vinayak Damodar Savarkar, *Hindutva: Who Is a
    Hindu?* (Bombay: Veer Savarkar Prakashan, 1969), v–vi.

44 Shruti Kapila, *Violent Fraternity: Indian Political Thought in
    the Global Age* (Princeton: Princeton University Press, 2021),
    101; Janaki Bakhle, 'Country First? Vinayak Damodar Savarkar
    (1883–1966) and the Writing of Essentials of Hindutva', *Public
    Culture* 22, no. 1 (2010): 170.

45 Cited in Bakhle, 'Country First', 170.

46 See Chapter 10, p. 188.

47 Savarkar, *Hindutva*, 113.

48 Savarkar, 135, 140.

49 Bhatt, *Origins*, 99.

50 Devji, 'Escaping the Global Event', 28.

51 Minault, *Khilafat Movement*, 131.

52 Sneh Mahajan, 'The Foreign Policy of the Raj and Its Legacy',
    in *The Oxford Handbook of Indian Foreign Policy*, ed. David
    Malone, C. Raja Mohan, and Srinath Raghavan (OUP Oxford,
    2015), 190–91.

53 Zaman, 'Silk Letters Conspiracy', 631. Kabul-based anti-colonial
    Indian revolutionaries were part of wider wartime revolutionary
    efforts to seek foreign assistance and use other countries,
    including 'Muslim' ones, as bases to foment a revolution for
    India's liberation. Ramnath, *Haj to Utopia*, chap. 6.

54 With Pratap as president and Barakatullah as prime minister,
    the Provisional Government was meant to represent a deliberate
    attempt at Hindu–Muslim rapprochement. Ramnath, *Haj to
    Utopia*, 172.

55 Zaman, 'Silk Letters Conspiracy', 631–32; Minault, *Khilafat
    Movement*, 32. The allies of these revolutionaries in Hijaz were
    unsuccessful in securing Turkish help, were arrested by the
    Sharif of Mecca, Britain's new Arab ally, and interned at Malta.

56 Mahajan, 'Foreign Policy of the Raj', 192.

57 Ayesha Jalal, *Self and Sovereignty: Individual and Community in South Asian Islam since 1850* (London: Routledge, 2002), 207.

58 Jalal, 207.

59 Hasan, 'Nationalist Conscience', 66.

60 Jalal, *Self and Sovereignty*, 219.

61 The rest of the details of this paragraph are drawn from Ramnath, *Haj to Utopia*, chap. 6.

62 Ramnath, 161.

63 Vikram Sampath, *Savarkar: A Contested Legacy, 1924–66* (Gurugram: Viking, 2021), 158–59.

64 As cited in Tejani, *Indian Secularism*, 163.

65 *The Leader*, 25 April 1921.

66 *The Leader*, 12 May 1920; 16 May 1921.

67 *The Leader*, 18 May 1920.

68 16 May 1921.

69 *The Leader*, 8, 9, and 11 May 1921.

70 Jordens, *Swāmī Shraddhānanda*, 126.

71 Hasan, 'Nationalism and Communal Politics', 167. 'Militant' is also the adjective used for Moonje by sympathetic chroniclers of the Mahasabha's history. See Sampath, *Savarkar: A Contested Legacy*, 106.

72 *The Leader*, 23 May 1921.

73 Lajpat Rai, 'Apprehension of Afghan Invasion', 275–76.

74 Gandhi had similarly argued that the British forces were too well-organized for a successful Afghan invasion.

75 Lajpat Rai, 'Apprehension of Afghan Invasion', 275.

76 Lajpat Rai, 'Congress Presidential Address', 132.

77 Lajpat Rai, 'Apprehension of Afghan Invasion', 271, 276.

78 Lajpat Rai, 275–76.

79 Lajpat Rai, 274.

80 Minault, *Khilafat Movement*, 132.

81 Devji, *Impossible Indian*, 83–88; Skaria, 'Gandhi's Politics', 955–86; Tejani, *Indian Secularism*, 171.

82 Gandhi's nationalist and religious imagination was complex. Like Rai, he defined Indian national identity in secular terms in

that he did not associate it with any *one* religion. Yet, Gandhi believed that all politics should be informed by 'Religion' in the sense of the universal Truth or morality that underlay all religions. He was comfortable with the overarching secular Indian national identity being informed by 'Religion'/Truth or by multiple religious truths (and the religious idioms expressing these). His imagination of the Indian national identity may be seen as simultaneously secular and (multi-)religious. For him, to support an organized politics for the Khilafat was to support a politics of Religion/Truth as embodied by both Islam and a politics of ahimsa-based respect and empathy for the Other. Gandhi saw the overarching secular and religious Indian national identity as being strengthened by this religious politics. He also seemed comfortable with the existence of religious-based politics by Hindus and Muslims as long as they broadly worked in tandem. This was unlike Rai who articulated the Indian national identity in purely non-religious terms, occasionally expressed the notion that this national identity was to be strengthened by completely transcending religion, and mostly clearly permitted a religious politics which sought to save a threatened religion but within a basically secularised political framework.

Chapter 14

1 Liquor was the most important tax-earner for the British government, and its boycott hit the government hard. It was during the non-cooperation movement that Gandhi, as a corollary to the foreign cloth boycott, also encouraged Indians to take up spinning cotton thread on *charkhas* (spinning wheels) and give thread to weavers to turn into khadi cloth. Spinning and khadi-wearing became a sign of demonstrating commitment to the Indian national movement. David Hardiman, *Noncooperation in India: Nonviolent Strategy and Protest, 1920–22* (Oxford University Press, USA, 2021), 44–45.

2 Hardiman, 49–52; Gail Minault, *The Khilafat Movement: Religious Symbolism and Political Mobilization in India* (Delhi: Columbia University Press, 1982), 140.

3 Lajpat Rai was among the seventeen signatories to the statement for which the Ali brothers were being prosecuted. Feroz Chand, *Lajpat Rai: Life and Work* (New Delhi: Publications Division, Ministry of Information and Broadcasting, Government of India, 1978), 478.

4 Hardiman, *Noncooperation in India*, 54.

5 Hardiman, 56–57.

6 Hardiman, 55.

7 Minault, *Khilafat Movement*, 167, 179.

8 Chand, *Lajpat Rai*, 364; Minault, *Khilafat Movement*, 178.

9 Minault, *Khilafat Movement*, 179.

10 The following description is largely based on Minault, 143–83.

11 Minault, 141. In using phrases such as 'Hindu' or 'Muslim' newspapers and 'Hindu'- or 'Muslim'-owned newspapers, I follow current academic norms. See Margrit Pernau, 'Riots, Masculinity, and the Desire for Passions: North India 1917–1946', *South Asian History and Culture* 12, no. 2–3 (2021): 253; J Barton Scott, *Slandering the Sacred: Blasphemy Law and Religious Affect in Colonial India* (Chicago: University of Chicago Press, 2023), 33, 37–38; Markus Daechsel, *The Politics of Self-Expression: The Urdu Middle-Class Milieu in Mid-Twentieth Century India and Pakistan* (London ; New York: Routledge, 2006), 14, 118.

12 Minault, 142.

13 Minault, 142–45.

14 Minault, 138.

15 Minault, 138–39.

16 Minault, 140; Hardiman, *Noncooperation in India*, 49.

17 Lala Lajpat Rai, 'Moplah Riots and Relief Work by the Congress', The Tribune, 25 October 1921', in *CWLLR*, vol. 10, 2008, 251–53; 'Appeal for Funds for Relief Work in Malabar, The Tribune, 28 October 1921', in *CWLLR*, vol. 10, 2008, 254.

18 Minault, *Khilafat Movement*, 145–47; Shabnum Tejani, *Indian Secularism: A Social and Intellectual History, 1890–1950* (Bloomington: Indiana University Press, 2008), 165. After the rebellion, which took six months to quell, 2400 Mappillas were killed, 6000 captured and 40,000 persuaded to surrender. Manu Pillai, 'The Mapilla Rebellion of Malabar', 7 September 2018, https://www.livemint.com/Leisure/rjzd8IKbbcDUEjkJS7uq4M/ The-Mapilla-rebellion-of-Malabar.html.

19 Minault, *Khilafat Movement*, 147. To listen to a quick summary and analysis of the history of the Mappilas and 1921 Mappila rebellion, see Siddarth Bhatia, 'Religion as Politics Does Not Work in Kerala Feat. Manu Pillai', podcast, The Wire Talks, 31 August 2021.

20 Minault, *Khilafat Movement*, 148.

21 Also see Ayesha Jalal, *Self and Sovereignty: Individual and Community in South Asian Islam since 1850* (London: Routledge, 2002), 231.

22 Zafar Ahmad Nizami, *Hakim Ajmal Khan* (Publications Division Ministry of Information & Broadcasting, 1988), 148, 195–96, 199.

23 Minault, *Khilafat Movement*, 148; Hardiman, *Noncooperation in India*, 50–51.

24 Minault, *Khilafat Movement*, 149.

25 Jalal, *Self and Sovereignty*, 231.

26 Gyanendra Pandey, 'Hindus and Others: The Militant Hindu Construction', *Economic and Political Weekly* 26, no. 52 (1991): 2998; Charu Gupta, 'Articulating Hindu Masculinity and Femininity: "Shuddhi" and "Sangathan" Movements in United Provinces in the 1920s', *Economic and Political Weekly*, 1998, 728; Mushirul Hasan, 'Nationalism and Communal Politics in India, 1885–1930', in *The Mushirul Hasan Omnibus* (New Delhi: Oxford University Press, 2010), 168.

27 Hardiman, *Noncooperation in India*, 52.

28 Minault, *Khilafat Movement*, 172, 178.

29 Jalal, *Self and Sovereignty*, 231.

30 Minault, *Khilafat Movement*, 175–76; Jalal, *Self and Sovereignty*, 231–32.

31 Hardiman, *Noncooperation in India*, 54; Minault, *Khilafat Movement*, 177.

32 Hardiman, *Noncooperation in India*, 52; Minault, *Khilafat Movement*, 177.

33 Hardiman, *Noncooperation in India*, 57–58; Minault, *Khilafat Movement*, 181–82.

34 Minault, *Khilafat Movement*, 182.

35 Minault, 184.

36 Minault, 184–85. The long list of leaders who were taken aback by Gandhi's decision included Das, Patel, the Nehrus, Bose, Azad and Lajpat Rai himself. Hindol Sengupta, *The Man Who Saved India: Sardar Patel and His Idea of India* (Gurgaon: Penguin/Viking, 2018), 154–56; Chand, *Lajpat Rai*, 385–88.

37 Minault, *Khilafat Movement*, 185–86.

38 Minault, 168, 186.

39 Minault, 186.

40 Minault, 186; Jalal, *Self and Sovereignty*, 237.

41 Minault, *Khilafat Movement*, 188.

42 Differences had existed from the beginning between individuals, Hindu or Muslim, who favoured moderate and more radical forms of non-cooperation, and between those who were more and less committed to Gandhian non-violence.

43 Minault, *Khilafat Movement*, 188.

44 Minault, 188.

45 Sengupta, *The Man Who Saved India*, 162–63.

46 Minault, *Khilafat Movement*, 191; Hasan, 'Nationalism and Communal Politics', 187. Jawaharlal Nehru, unlike his father, disagreed with council entry at this juncture. Benjamin Zachariah, *Nehru* (London; New York: Routledge, 2004), 53.

47 David Page, *Prelude to Partition: The Indian Muslims and the Imperial System of Control, 1920–1932* (New Delhi: Oxford University Press, 1982), 98–99; Minault, *Khilafat Movement*, 191.

48 Jalal, *Self and Sovereignty*, 245–46, 260; Minault, *Khilafat Movement*, 191.

49 Yoginder Sikand, 'Arya Shuddhi and Muslim Tabligh: Muslim Reactions to Arya Samaj Proselytization (1923–30)', in *Religious Conversion in India: Modes, Motivations, and Meanings*, ed. Rowena Robinson and Sathianathan Clarke (New Delhi: Oxford University Press, 2003); C.S. Adcock, *The Limits of Tolerance: Indian Secularism and the Politics of Religious Freedom* (New York: Oxford University Press, 2013), 147; John Zavos, *The Emergence of Hindu Nationalism in India* (Oxford: Oxford University Press, 2000), 173; Pradip Kumar Datta, 'War over Music: The Riots of 1926 in Bengal', *Social Scientist*, no. No. 6/7 (1990): 39.

50 Sikand, 'Arya Shuddhi and Muslim Tabligh'; Adcock, *Limits of Tolerance*, 147.

51 One Arya Samaj journal later remarked that half the Hindus forcibly converted by Mappilas chose to remain Muslim because as Hindus they had been considered Untouchable. Adcock, *Limits of Tolerance*, 153.

52 Sikand, 'Arya Shuddhi and Muslim Tabligh'.

53 Minault, *Khilafat Movement*, 193; Sikand, 'Arya Shuddhi and Muslim Tabligh'.

54 The immediate trigger for the Multan riot was the stoning of a Muharram procession. Scholars of conflict and violence warn that attempts to identify the causes of riots can be difficult and misleading. This is because what is usually documented is only the immediate trigger of the cause and not the several other silent factors that invisibly converge to produce the violence we see. There is also a danger of introducing our own biases when we attempt to identify the causes of riots. However, scholars researching 'Hindu–Muslim riots' do insist on one thing: that they were/are never the straightforward result of a clash of two opposing religious identities. Religious mobilizations are often entangled with issues of caste, class, social status and local cultural identities, and violence is often better explained in

terms of local factors. See William Gould, *Religion and Conflict in Modern South Asia* (Cambridge University Press, 2011), 7–23; Arafaat Valiani, *Militant Publics in India: Physical Culture and Violence in the Making of a Modern Polity* (Palgrave Macmillan, 2011), 29–32; Suranjan Das, 'Communal Violence in Twentieth Century Colonial Bengal: An Analytical Framework', *Social Scientist* 18, no. 6/7 (June–July 1990): 23–26. It has also been demonstrated that 'Hindu–Muslim violence' is rarely impulsive and spontaneous, and that presenting it as such detaches violence from those who perpetrated it and from the socio-economic and political contexts that produce it. See Philippa Williams, *Everyday Peace? Politics, Citizenship and Muslim Lives in India*, RGS-IBG Book Series (Chichester, UK; Malden, MA: Wiley Blackwell, 2015), 21. The notion that riots are simply an outcome of spontaneous clashes motivated by irrational religious fanaticism and religious hurt misrecognizes the complex forces behind violence, and actually builds on British colonial prejudices and stereotypes about Indians. Valiani, *Militant Publics*, 29–30. The Khilafat movement is sometimes straightforwardly blamed for arousing religious passions that soon found violent outlets. Certainly, like any mass movement, the Khilafat movement drew participants whose emotions and actions were outside the control of its main leaders, sometimes even contravening their messages and values. Even so, the forces behind 'Hindu–Muslim riots' in the early 1920s were more complex. These included attempts to assert or negotiate control over public spaces and challenge power structures at the local level; the felt need to display outraged hurt sentiments to communicate with the state and demand its protection; the marginalized, lower-caste poor participating in riot violence to assert their social status and respectability vis-à-vis dominant castes and classes, and staking their claim as defenders of their religious community; economic distress, overcrowding of cities, and competition over jobs and housing; peasants protesting against landlords; militant religious mobilization as a way in which dominant castes and classes tried to project their power and status; incendiary propaganda pamphlets by certain religious and political organizations; and rumours spread through print culture. Participation in riots was sometimes driven by a desire to experience and display certain emotions like *josh* (fervour), seen as a sign of manliness at the personal level, and of the vitality of one's community; men wishing to display masculinity and show that they can protect sacred symbols of the community, including the cow, mosques, temples, holy texts, idols, and even women; the simply felt need to protect one's own family and survive, and rational decisions arising out of fears of excommunication by the local village community, and so on. See Margrit Pernau, 'Riots, Masculinity, and the Desire for Passions: North India 1917–1946', *South Asian History and Culture* 12, no. 2–3 (2021): 244–60; Margrit Pernau, 'Anger, Hurt and Enthusiasm: Mobilising for Violence, 1870–1920', in *Emotions, Mobilisations and South Asian Politics*, ed. Amélie Blom and Stéphanie Tawa Lama-Rewal (Taylor & Francis, 2019), 99, 106; Gould, *Religion and Conflict in Modern South Asia*, 70, 88–89, 93, 117; Datta, 'War over Music: The Riots of 1926 in Bengal', 47; Gupta, 'Articulating Hindu Masculinity', 730–31; Nandini Gooptu, 'The Urban Poor and Militant Hinduism in Early Twentieth-Century Uttar Pradesh', *Modern Asian Studies* 31, no. 4 (1997): 879–918. It also must be remembered that for every riot in a village or neighbourhood, there were hundreds of villages and neighbourhoods where no clashes occurred. Peaceful living and accommodation remained the norm. Pernau, 'Riots, Masculinity'; Gould, *Religion and Conflict in Modern South Asia*, 69.

55 Jalal, *Self and Sovereignty*, 247.

56 Richard Gordon, 'The Hindu Mahasabha and the Indian National Congress, 1915–26', *Modern Asian Studies* 9, no. 2 (1975): 168; J.P. Misra, *Madan Mohan Malaviya and the Indian Freedom Movement* (New Delhi: Oxford University Press, 2016), 145–48. In 1921, Malaviya had cooperated with Jinnah to chalk out an alternative approach to pressure the British

government to redress the Khilafat and Punjab wrongs and discuss further constitutional reforms. This was an alternative to Gandhi's agitational, mass politics-based programme of non-cooperation. Minault, *Khilafat Movement*, 180–81; Hardiman, *Noncooperation in India*, 55.

57 Gordon, 'Hindu Mahasabha', 150–56.

58 Gordon, 157–59.

59 Gordon, 158–60.

60 Gordon, 161.

61 Prabhu Bapu, *Hindu Mahasabha in Colonial North India, 1915–1930: Constructing Nation and History*, Routledge Studies in South Asian History (London: Routledge, 2013), 22–23. The Mahasabha was not the only political force which disagreed with Gandhian non-cooperation. The non-Brahmin Justice Party of Madras did too but for different reasons. Like cautious constitutionalists such as Jinnah and Malaviya, the Party was sceptical of mass-based agitational politics. Moreover, having formed the ministry in 1920, it aimed to use political power to alleviate the disabilities of non-Brahmins, and saw noncooperators as a Brahmin-led, disruptive political force. V. Geetha and S.V. Rajadurai, *Towards a Non-Brahmin Millennium: From Iyothee Thass to Periyar* (Calcutta: Bhatkal & Sen, 1998), 217–18.

62 Gordon, 'Hindu Mahasabha', 162.

63 Gordon, 170. After 1923, the Mahasabha would be reorganized along a Congress-like pattern and would function as an all-India organization. It extended its organization to include most British Indian provinces, the princely states and some colonies of Indians overseas. However, its growth remained sporadic and strongest where riots occurred. Its provincial branches were loose and confined to large cities. And its growth was most stark in Hindi-speaking areas, especially Delhi and Bihar. UP, Punjab, Delhi and Bihar sent an overwhelming majority of delegates, while Madras, Bengal and Bombay sent a minuscule number. Though it tried to spread its network, the Mahasabha remained

confined to the Hindi-speaking tracts of north India. Gordon, 173–76. Swarajists like Motilal Nehru publicly opposed the revival of the Hindu Mahasabha. Nehru also criticized 'Muslims' for allowing the ulema too much leeway in politics. Gordon, 180.

64 Gordon, 'Hindu Mahasabha', 154–55, 170.

65 Bapu, *Hindu Mahasabha in Colonial North India, 1915–1930*, 48–49. Scholars of violence and riots emphasize the critical role riots played in sparking off communal mobilization and polarization. See Datta, 'War over Music: The Riots of 1926 in Bengal', 39–41. Several historians view the Mappila riot as the main event which gave birth to Hindu sangathan. See Sumit Sarkar, *Modern India: 1886–1947* (Delhi: Macmillian, 1983), 236; Datta, 'War over Music: The Riots of 1926 in Bengal', 39; Gupta, 'Articulating Hindu Masculinity', 728. Others have pointed to the critical role played by the Multan riot. See Minault, *Khilafat Movement*, 194; Bapu, *Hindu Mahasabha in Colonial North India, 1915–1930*, 48–49; Adcock, *Limits of Tolerance*, 147. Yet it has also been argued that Hindu sangathan was partly developed to counter Muslim mobilization during the Khilafat movement and Gandhi's politics of ahimsa or non-violence. See Gould, *Religion and Conflict in Modern South Asia*, 92–93; Gupta, 'Articulating Hindu Masculinity', 728; Pandey, 'Hindus and Others', 2998.

66 Gupta, 'Articulating Hindu Masculinity', 729.

67 Chand, *Lajpat Rai*, 392, 425.

68 'To C.R. Das', Dec 1922, Lala Lajpat Rai, *The Collected Works of Lala Lajpat Rai*, ed. B.R. Nanda (New Delhi: Manohar, 2003), vol. 10, pp. 163–64. Das had remained uninterested in these aspects of Lajpat Rai's confidential letter but used other portions of it to bolster his view that Congress needed to rethink its position on council boycott. Chand, *Lajpat Rai*, 479. Interestingly, eighteen years later, and more than a decade after Lajpat Rai's death in 1928, in 1940, this letter would be quoted by Jinnah in his presidential address to the Muslim League at its Lahore session, at which he first demanded the right to self-determination for

the Muslim 'nation'. For Jinnah, Lajpat Rai's letter was evidence that 'you cannot get away from being a Hindu if you're a Hindu'. He cited it to argue that Rai had correctly recognized years ago the Indian Muslim belief that India indeed could not be ruled along 'British', 'democratic lines'. But Jinnah would ridicule what he considered Lajpat Rai's absurdly fantastical fears of Pan-Islamism. He would also proclaim that Rai's view that the Indian Muslim position on democracy stemmed from their reading of Islamic Law was indeed incorrect—just as Rai had hoped it was in 1922. Jinnah argued that Indian Muslims considered British-style democracy inapplicable to India not because Islamic law opposed it, but because democracy would lead to Hindu majority rule over India's substantial Muslim minority. 'Mahomed Ali Jinnah's Presidential Address, All-India Muslim League, Lahore Session, March 1940', in Jamiluddin Ahmad (ed.), *Some Recent Speeches and Writings of Mr. Jinnah*, vol. 1 (Lahore: S. M. Ashraf, 1942), 150–51.

69 Chand, *Lajpat Rai*, 478–79. Rahman espoused similar-sounding, radically isolationist views in 1928 but, counter-intuitively, then proceeded to support the Nehru Report, which recommended the elimination of separate electorates and the substantial limitation of separate Muslim representation. See Jalal, *Self and Sovereignty*, 304.

70 Jalal, *Self and Sovereignty*, 252.

71 Jalal, 237. Among those who joined Lajpat Rai in jail was the thirty-two-year-old Abdul Ghaffar Khan, who too had participated in the Rowlatt Satyagraha and Khilafat-non-cooperation movements. Already a votary of non-violence by 1921, Khan would soon become known among mainland Indian Hindus as 'Frontier Gandhi' for his advocacy of non-violence among the Pashtun Khuda'i Khitmatgars ('Servants of God') in the North-West Frontier Province. He would ally with Gandhi and the Congress, champion Hindu–Muslim unity and Indian nationalism, and oppose Jinnah's demand for Pakistan in the 1940s. Rajmohan Gandhi, *Ghaffar Khan: Nonviolent Badshah of*

the Pakhtuns, Penguin Lives (New Delhi; New York: Penguin Viking, 2004), 93–94, 101, 107. Perhaps partly because the two men did not interact at length and partly because Khan had not yet sharply and publicly expressed his key ideas, these had eluded Lajpat Rai despite their meeting in jail.

72 Minault, *Khilafat Movement*, 176; also see Chapter 12, p. 221 and n. 68 (p. 603); Hasan, 'Nationalism and Communal Politics', 119.

73 Hasan, 'Nationalism and Communal Politics', 120–21.

74 Mahadev Desai, *Maulana Abul Kalam Azad: The President of the Indian National Congress* (London: G. Allen and Unwin limited, 1941), 94–96.

75 Minault, *Khilafat Movement*, 197.

76 Tejani, *Indian Secularism*, 163.

77 Nizami, *Hakim Ajmal Khan*, 218–21; Pernau, 'Riots, Masculinity', 250.

78 Nizami, *Hakim Ajmal Khan*, 222–24.

79 Mushirul Hasan, *M.A. Ansari* (New Delhi: Publications Division Ministry of Information & Broadcasting, 1995), 90.

80 Mushirul Hasan, 'A Nationalist Conscience: M.A. Ansari, the Congress and The Raj', in *The Mushirul Hasan Omnibus* (New Delhi: Oxford University Press, 2010), 104–05, 114–15, 121.

81 Gould, *Religion and Conflict in Modern South Asia*, 4–10; Gyanendra Pandey, *The Construction of Communalism in Colonial North India* (New Delhi: Oxford University Press, 2006), 13; Jalal, *Self and Sovereignty*, 41, 57, 64, 137, 185; Gooptu, 'The Urban Poor and Militant Hinduism in Early Twentieth-Century Uttar Pradesh'; Peter Gottschalk, *Beyond Hindu and Muslim: Multiple Identity in Narratives from Village India* (New Delhi: Oxford Univ. Press, 2001), chap. 1. Historical and anthropological research has shown that Indian Muslims are far from homogenous, engage in different religious practices at the local level, and have different social structures and kinship systems [see Imtiaz Ahmad, ed., *Family, Kinship, and Marriage among Muslims in India* (New Delhi: Manohar, 1976); Imtiaz Ahmad, ed., *Caste and Social Stratification among the Muslims*

in India (New Delhi: Manohar, 1978); Imtiaz Ahmad, ed., *Ritual and Religion among Muslims in India* (New Delhi: Manohar, 1981); T.N. Madan, ed., *Muslim Communities of South Asia: Culture, Society, and Power* (New Delhi: Manohar, 1976).]. On caste among Muslims, see Syed Ali, 'Collective and Elective Ethnicity: Caste among Urban Muslims in India', in *Sociological Forum*, vol. 17 (Springer, 2002), 593–620; Douglas Goodfried, 'Changing Concepts of Caste and Status among Old Delhi Muslims', in *Modernization and Social Change among Muslims in India*, ed. Imtiaz Ahmad (Delhi: Manohar, 1983); Charles Lindholm, 'Caste in Islam and the Problem of Deviant Systems: A Critique of Recent Theory', in *Muslim Communities of South Asia: Culture, Society and Power*, ed. T.N. Madan (Delhi: Manohar, 1986), 61–73; E.A. Mann, *Boundaries and Identities: Muslims, Work, and Status in Aligarh*, vol. 31 (New Delhi: SAGE Publications, 1992); Mattison Mines, 'Social Stratification among Muslim Tamils in Tamil Nadu, South India', in *Caste and Social Stratification among Muslims in India*, ed. Imtiaz Ahmad (Delhi: Manohar, 1978), 159–69. Research demonstrates that individuals hold multiple identities and often do not see their religious identity as their primary identity. See Gottschalk, *Beyond Hindu and Muslim*, chap. 1; Nida Kirmani, *Questioning the 'Muslim Woman': Identity and Insecurity in an Urban Indian Locality* (New York: Routledge, 2013), 12–13, 17. For research questioning the assumption that Muslims—detached from their social, economic and political contexts, as well as other sources of ideas and values—are only guided by Islamic texts or Islam in general, see Kirmani, 10–13; Gottschalk, *Beyond Hindu and Muslim*, 4; Jalal, *Self and Sovereignty*, 57; Mushirul Hasan, *Legacy of a Divided Nation: India's Muslims since Independence* (London: Hurst, 1997), 8–9. Ethnographic research has also shown that, despite tendencies to focus on violence and divisive politics, Indians with Muslim and Hindu identities have often actively chosen to negotiate an 'everyday peace' with each other. See Williams, *Everyday Peace?*, chap. 1.

82 Iqbal Singh Sevea, *The Political Philosophy of Muhammad Iqbal: Islam and Nationalism in Late Colonial India* (Cambridge; New York: Cambridge University Press, 2012), 144, 170.

83 Cemil Aydin, *The Idea of the Muslim World: A Global Intellectual History* (Cambridge, Massachusetts: Harvard University Press, 2017), 153.

84 See Chapter 8, pp. 135–36.

85 Shaunna Rodrigues, 'Abul Kalam Azad and the Right to an Islamic Justification of the Indian Constitution', in *Dimensions of Constitutional Democracy*, ed. A. Roy and M. Becker (Springer, 2020), 125–43; Desai, *Azad*, 77. The argument that democracy originated with Islam, and that Islam was congruent with democracy, had been made by various Indian Muslim politician–thinkers since the late nineteenth century, and would continue to be made after the 1920s. Among such individuals were the scholar Maulvi Chirag Ali (1844–95), leading Islamic scholar and Muslim Leaguer Amir Ali (1849–1928), and Abdullah Yusuf Ali (1872–1953). See Sevea, *Muhammad Iqbal*, 56, 134.

86 Desai, *Azad*, 78.

87 Mushirul Hasan, 'Secular and Communitarian Representations of Indian Nationalism: Ideology and Praxis of Azad and Mohamed Ali', in *Islam and Indian Nationalism Reflections on Abul Kalam Azad*, ed. Mushirul Hasan (New Delhi: Manohar, 1992), 85.

88 Minault, *Khilafat Movement*, 198; Hasan, 'Secular and Communitarian Representations of Indian Nationalism: Ideology and Praxis of Azad and Mohamed Ali', 85.

89 Minault, *Khilafat Movement*, 176, 197; Hasan, 'Nationalism and Communal Politics', 119.

90 Hasan, *M.A. Ansari*, 90; Nizami, *Hakim Ajmal Khan*, 220–21.

91 Aydin, *Idea of the Muslim World*, 123.

92 Minault, *Khilafat Movement*, 201; Aydin, *Idea of the Muslim World*, 127.

93 Minault, *Khilafat Movement*, 201–02.

94 Minault, 194–95. Many of the complex factors mentioned in n. 54 played a role in such riots. What was new for the 1920s was greater political and economic instability; the migration of rural poor into cities where they faced economic distress and humiliation, and came into contact with the propaganda of shuddhi/sangathan and tabligh/tanzim organizations, which often provoked conflict and violence. The rapid growth of martial akharas (wrestling gymnasiums)—with their culture of wrestling, sword and club-wielding—too played their role. Increased newspaper circulation and extensive coverage of riots, which blurred lines between local and national causes, raised emotional tones across the country. Various 'Hindu' and 'Muslim' newspapers also indulged in biased and inflammatory press reportage, which normalized and even incited violence. Some riots were inflamed by political actors seeking to make quick gains in elections now taking place at the local and provincial level. The felt need by sangathanists to counter Gandhi and his politics of non-violence also played its role. Pernau, 'Riots, Masculinity'; Gooptu, 'The Urban Poor and Militant Hinduism in Early Twentieth-Century Uttar Pradesh'; Gould, *Religion and Conflict in Modern South Asia*, 82–93, 117; Gupta, 'Articulating Hindu Masculinity', 731; Tejani, *Indian Secularism*, 167–68.

95 Minault, *Khilafat Movement*, 193–94.

96 Some scholars view the revival of shuddhi as a direct response to Pan-Islamic mobilization during the Khilafat movement. *Self and Sovereignty*, 245.

97 Minault, *Khilafat Movement*, 193; Adcock, *Limits of Tolerance*, 149, 154; Gupta, 'Articulating Hindu Masculinity', 728; Tejani, *Indian Secularism*, 166; Sikand, 'Arya Shuddhi and Muslim Tabligh', 102–09; Jalal, *Self and Sovereignty*, 245.

98 Jalal, *Self and Sovereignty*, 248.

99 Sikand, 'Arya Shuddhi and Muslim Tabligh', 104.

100 Jalal, *Self and Sovereignty*, 246.

101 Adcock, *Limits of Tolerance*, 147.

102 Minault, *Khilafat Movement*, 193; Sikand, 'Arya Shuddhi
and Muslim Tabligh', 99, 104, 109–10. Many tabligh activists
believed that the way to prevent neo-Muslims like the Malkanas
from leaving the Muslim fold was to combat their 'Hinduistic'
beliefs and customs, thought to make them susceptible to Arya
shuddhi, and to spread among them knowledge of the Islamic
scripturalist tradition. Sikand, 104.

103 Sikand, 'Arya Shuddhi and Muslim Tabligh'; Jalal, *Self and
Sovereignty*, 258; Adcock, *Limits of Tolerance*, 152.

104 Sikand, 'Arya Shuddhi and Muslim Tabligh', 106–07. Here,
Shraddhanand conflated the words of one individual, which
may well have represented a sliver of the Muslim community,
with that of all Muslims.

105 Sikand, 109–15. Tabligh's focus was often on low-caste Hindus.
Sufis who engaged in tabligh accepted Hindu scriptures as
divine and legitimate, but reinterpreted them to suggest that
they predicted the arrival of Prophet Mohammad as 'World
Teacher', whom Hindus should accept and whose community
they should join. See Sikand, 105, 113–14. However, the bulk of
the ulema engaged in tabligh disagreed with such 'un-Islamic'
methods, and insisted that the way to counter shuddhi and
lead tabligh was to preach the basics of Islam and the *shariat*
(divine law) among the population. Sikand, 114. In the wake of
the shuddhi campaign, the Jamiat-i-Ulama-i-Hind, the largest
body of reformist Deobandi ulema, was established in mid-
1923, 'The Department for the Propagation and Protection
of Islam'. Sikand, 114. It despatched ulema to areas inhabited
by 'neo-Muslims' like the Malkanas, where they established
mosques and schools. Here, they aimed to counter what they
saw as Arya attempts to take advantage of the poverty of neo-
Muslims by offering them monetary inducements. Sikand,
114–15. Interestingly, the Tablighi Jama'at, which over time
became the largest Islamic movement in the world, active in
200 countries, was also formed in the wake of the shuddhi
movement and as a means to counter it. Sikand, 115.

106 Adcock, *Limits of Tolerance*, 148.

107 Minault, *Khilafat Movement*, 194.

108 Adcock, *Limits of Tolerance*, 147; Jalal, *Self and Sovereignty*, 245, 260.

109 Bapu, *Hindu Mahasabha in Colonial North India, 1915–1930*, 50.

110 Adcock, *Limits of Tolerance*, 150; Gordon, 'Hindu Mahasabha', 154–56, 171.

111 Minault, *Khilafat Movement*, 194; Jalal, *Self and Sovereignty*, 254. The Ali brothers, deeply critical of tanzim, soon fell out with Kitchlew over it. *Khilafat Movement*, 199.

112 Minault, *Khilafat Movement*, 194–95. Shuddhi/sangathan and tabligh/tanzim would also play a significant role in the 1924 Delhi riots and 1931 Kanpur riots. See Pernau, 'Riots, Masculinity', 246, 250.

113 Hugh Owen, 'Negotiating the Lucknow Pact', *The Journal of Asian Studies* 31, no. 03 (1972): 586.

114 Page, *Prelude to Partition*, 85.

115 Page, 85.

116 Nizami, *Hakim Ajmal Khan*, 219–20.

117 Page, *Prelude to Partition*, 85.

118 Jalal, *Self and Sovereignty*, 247–49, 251.

119 Jalal, 248, 260.

120 Jalal, 248–49.

121 Jalal, 251.

122 Jalal, 259.

123 Jalal, 248–50.

124 Jalal, 249.

125 Jalal, 250–51, 259.

126 Jalal, 250, 258.

127 Jalal, 251–53. There was also much infighting among Hindus and among Muslims, with Aryas attacking Gandhians, Sanatanists quarrelling with Aryas over the purification of 'untouchables', and some Muslims attacking the Muslim leaders of Khilafat and non-cooperation.

128 These new reforms did not grant power to Indians at the level of the central government. They involved only a very minor extension of the electorate, which remained limited by property and less than 5 per cent of the population, a stark contrast to Britain where universal male franchise had been introduced in 1918. They did, however, transfer subjects such as education and local government to ministers nominated by the provincial government. This tilted Indian politics away from an all-India politics of anti-colonial Indian nationalism towards province-focused politics loyal to the British. The new provincial councils were organized such that they were dominated by Indians loyal to the British, so that the British could retain control with help from a small elected minority. Gould, *Religion and Conflict in Modern South Asia*, 95; Neeti Nair, *Changing Homelands: Hindu Politics and the Partition of India* (Cambridge, MA: Harvard University Press, 2011), 71; Page, *Prelude to Partition*, 30.

129 Page, *Prelude to Partition*, 63. A Congressman who had initially participated in the protests in Punjab against the Rowlatt Acts during Gandhi's Satyagraha in 1919, Fazl-i-Hussain, by the end of the year, diverged from Punjabi Muslims like Kitchlew to withdraw from protests and remain aloof from Gandhian non-cooperation. In 1920, Hussain announced his decision to enter the new legislative councils to cooperate with the British government. Alongside him, the Unionist Party was led Chhotu Ram, a Jat Hindu lawyer and spokesperson for Punjabi Jat Hindu landed interests. The Unionist Party genuinely strove to represent landed elites across religious communities. This was why it was criticized by Muhammad Iqbal for encouraging class- and caste-based divisions among Muslims. At the same time, the cross-communal alliance at the heart of the Party remained dominated by Muslim zamindars. Rajmohan Gandhi, *Punjab: A History from Aurangzeb to Mountbatten* (New Delhi: Aleph Book Company, 2013), 533, 558–59, 568–74; Sevea, *Muhammad Iqbal*, 182. The weight given to the rural

electorate by the Montague–Chelmsford Reforms marginalized the urban-based, and already-quite-small Congress in Punjab politics, and alongside it virtually all political opposition to the British in Punjab. Nair, *Changing Homelands*, 71.

130 Ayesha Jalal and Anil Seal, 'Alternative to Partition: Muslim Politics between the Wars', *Modern Asian Studies* 15, no. 03 (1981): 426; Nair, *Changing Homelands*, 72.

131 Nair, *Changing Homelands*, 72.

132 Gandhi, *Punjab*, 570.

133 Nair, *Changing Homelands*, 72.

134 Nair, 72.

135 Page, *Prelude to Partition*, 86–87.

136 Nair, *Changing Homelands*, 71–72; Also see Gandhi, *Punjab*, 569–72.

137 Bhai Parmanand, *The Story of My Life* (New Delhi: S. Chand and Company Ltd., 1982), 166. Eleven years younger than Lajpat Rai, Parmanand had been a noted Arya Samaj preacher who, in 1907, had collected funds in London to avenge Rai's deportation to Burma. In 1910, it was in Parmanand's premises, being searched by the British in connection with a sedition case, that a letter from Rai (alongside a Bomb Manual of Bengali revolutionaries!) had been found. This had made Rai's interest in revolutionary literature clear. Following this, Rai had had to resign from the Managing Committee of the Arya Samaj and Arya Samaj Pratinidhi Sabha, and Parmanand from DAV College. Travelling through Europe and America in 1910–13, Parmanand interacted with Ghadar revolutionaries, before returning to India in 1913. During the Ghadar trial, Parmanand insisted he was not guilty, even as several young leaders of the movement claimed he was a key Ghadar leader. Parmanand was convicted of transportation for life in 1915, when he joined his old friend from London, Savarkar, in jail in the Andamans. He was released in 1920 on the condition of abstention from sedition. By the 1920s, his politics had shifted towards Hindu sangathan, and he called for the shuddhi of all

Muslims. By 1929, Parmamand would be articulating a Hindu nationalism strikingly similar to Savarkar's Hindutva. He saw Hindus as a nation, and Muslims and Christians as having alienated themselves from their country by adopting a 'foreign' religion. Hindus and Muslims, he argued, possessed different histories and different heroes, and did not form a common nationality. Nair, *Changing Homelands*, 22, 28, 41–42, 280 n. 119, 90–91; Chetan Bhatt, *Hindu Nationalism: Origins, Ideologies and Modern Myths* (Oxford: Berg, 2001), 76.

138 Chand, *Lajpat Rai*, 403.

139 Chand, 388, 414–15, 451. Rai's association with the Swaraj Party in 1923 has also been noted in Bhatt, *Origins*, 69.

140 Faisal Devji, *The Impossible Indian: Gandhi and the Temptation of Violence* (London: Harvard University Press, 2012), 68–70, 83, 88; Rinku Lamba, 'Gandhi's Response to Religious Conflict', *Studies in Religion/Sciences Religieuses* 45, no. 4 (2016): 470–75.

141 See Chapter 12, pp. 230–32.

142 Hasan, 'Nationalist Conscience', 117. According to Das's Pact, Bengali Muslims were allowed to retain separate electorates and given representation in Bengal's assembly according to their population strength. While the Lucknow Pact had accorded them 40 per cent of seats in Bengal's assembly (while they constituted almost 53 per cent of Bengal's population), they were now granted 55 per cent seats. In local bodies, it promised 60 per cent seats to the Muslim majority, and 40 per cent to the Hindu minority. Fifty-five per cent of all government appointments were fixed for Muslims and 45 per cent for other communities. For the sake of communal harmony, the Pact prohibited the playing of music before mosques, and granted Muslims the right to slaughter cows for religious purposes, terms which were favourable to Muslims. See Hasan, 'Nationalism and Communal Politics', 188; 'Nationalist Conscience', 116. The Congress rejected Das's Pact at its December 1923 session, but the Bengal Provincial Congress ratified the Pact in May 1924. In Bengal, Das's Pact achieved precisely the kind of

Hindu–Muslim reconciliation it aimed at. Bengali Muslims joined the Swaraj Party in huge numbers, turning it into an effective political force against the British. Das's efforts towards Hindu–Muslim unity were lauded by Subhas Chandra Bose. Hasan, 'Nationalism and Communal Politics', 188; Subhas Chandra Bose, *Subhas Chandra Bose Netaji: Collected Works*, ed. Sisir Kumar Bose, vol. 2 (Calcutta: Netaji Research Bureau, 1994), 129. Many Muslim-owned newspapers in other parts of India also praised Das's Pact. However, from the start, it was also deeply resented by many Bengali Hindus, who did not want a cut in their share of representation, and several Hindu-owned newspapers in Bengal and elsewhere raised fears of India's Islamicization. Jalal, *Self and Sovereignty*, 255–56; Mushirul Hasan, *Nationalism and Communal Politics in India, 1885–1930* (New Delhi: Manohar, 1994), 189. Das's death in 1925 and the revocation of his Bengal Pact in 1926 by the Swaraj Party would also severely strain Hindu–Muslim relations in Bengal. Das, 'Communal Violence', 30; Datta, 'War over Music: The Riots of 1926 in Bengal', 42.

143 'Report of the Indian National Pact Committee, All-India Muslim League, Fifteenth Session', in A.M. Zaidi (ed.), *Evolution of Muslim Political Thought in India*, vol. 2 (New Delhi: Michiko and Panjathan, 1975), 463–67.

144 Page, *Prelude to Partition*, 113.

145 For more on the American ideal of secularism, see Rajeev Bhargava, 'Is European Secularism Secular Enough?', in *Religion, Secularism, and Constitutional Democracy*, ed. Jean Cohen and Cecil Laborde (New York: Columbia University Press, 2016), 165–67. Also see Leonard Levy, *The Establishment Clause: Religion and the First Amendment* (New York: Macmillan, 1986).

146 The Rai–Ansari Pact was decried by several 'Muslim' newspapers, which raised fears of Hindu Raj and the extinction of Muslims and Islam from the subcontinent. Some accused Congress Muslims like Ansari and Azad of injuring Muslim

interests. Jalal, *Self and Sovereignty*, 256–57. The Pact was opposed by the All-India Muslim League, Khilafat Conference and Jamiat-ul-Ulama. It was also rejected by the Hindu Dharma Sangh of Calcutta and other Hindu opponents of communal representation. Hasan, 'Nationalist Conscience', 117 n. 12, 118.

147 'Madan Mohan Malaviya', in Christophe Jaffrelot (ed.), *Hindu Nationalism: A Reader* (Princeton: Princeton University Press, 2007), 39.

148 Sikata Banerjee, *Make Me a Man!: Masculinity, Hinduism, and Nationalism in India*, SUNY Series in Religious Studies (Albany, NY: State University of New York Press, 2005), 22, 28–29.

149 Banerjee, 22–26, 30–33.

150 Gooptu, 'The Urban Poor and Militant Hinduism in Early Twentieth-Century Uttar Pradesh'; Pernau, 'Riots, Masculinity'; 'Anger, Hurt and Enthusiasm: Mobilising for Violence, 1870–1920'; Gould, *Religion and Conflict in Modern South Asia*; Datta, 'War over Music: The Riots of 1926 in Bengal'; Gupta, 'Articulating Hindu Masculinity'.

151 M.R. Jayakar, *The Story of My Life*, vol. 2 (Bombay: Asia Publishing House, 1959), 466–67.

152 Jayakar, 2: 464–65.

153 M.K. Gandhi, 'Hindu–Muslim Tension: Causes and Cure, Young India, 29 May 1924', in *CWMG*, vol. 24 (Ahmedabad: Navajivan Trust, 1965), 136–54; 'Hindu–Muslim Unity, Young India, 5 June 1924', in *CWMG*, vol. 24 (Ahmedabad: Navajivan Trust, 1965), 188–90.

154 Some Muslims had always warned their co-religionists that Gandhi was not their well-wisher, and was undermining Muslim interests while actually working for Hindu Raj. Similarly, some Hindus had always disliked Gandhi for giving prominence to Pan-Islamic or indeed any Muslim voices, which they charged were secretly working for jihad against Hindus. The end of the Khilafat/non-cooperation movement brought to prominence some Muslim voices which declared

Gandhi a 'fake' (who did not really care about the Khilafat cause), and his movement a grand ploy which had fooled Muslims into believing in Hindu–Muslim unity while Hindus actually wished to convert Muslims, establish their absolute dominance over Muslims whom they hated, or expel them from India. Congress Muslims were accused of being closet Hindus or Hindu appeasers. Similarly, Hindu voices now arose which faulted Gandhi for taking up the Khilafat issue, being soft on the Ali brothers, and encouraging Muslims who, as they saw it, continued to slaughter cows considered holy by Hindus, and aggressively convert Hindus. Various 'Hindu' and 'Muslim' newspapers also blamed Gandhi's Khilafat movement for bringing religion into politics, and as the root cause of Hindu–Muslim polarization and all incidents of Hindu-Muslim violence. Jalal, *Self and Sovereignty*, 230–31, 237–38, 246, 249–51, 260; Rakhahari Chatterji, *Gandhi and the Ali Brothers: Biography of a Friendship* (New Delhi: SAGE, 2013), 157–58, 160, 162; David Hardiman, *Gandhi in His Time and Ours: The Global Legacy of His Ideas* (Ranikhet: Permanent Black, 2003), 233. The sense of helplessness felt by the Congress Muslim leaders close to Gandhi and within the Congress was captured by Mohamed Ali who complained: 'we are abused by men of our own communities and hit by men of opposite communities . . . We of the Congress are worse than useless just now, the object of everyone's wrath—for no reason other than preaching restraint'. See Chatterji, *Gandhi and the Ali Brothers*, 157.

155 Gandhi, 'Hindu–Muslim Tension', 139; Gandhi, 'Hindu–Muslim Unity, 5 June 1924', 188; Hardiman, *Gandhi in His Time and Ours: The Global Legacy of His Ideas*, 233.
156 Gandhi, 'Hindu–Muslim Tension', 140.
157 Gandhi, 141–42; 'Hindu–Muslim Unity, 5 June 1924', 188.
158 Gandhi, 'Hindu–Muslim Tension', 144–49.
159 Gandhi, 148–50; 'Hindu–Muslim Unity, 5 June 1924', 188.
160 Gandhi, 'Hindu–Muslim Tension', 140–41.

161 Gandhi, 150; 'Hindu–Muslim Unity, 5 June 1924', 189. Gandhi
      also pointed out that Hindus routinely mistreated cows and
      sold them to Muslim butchers. Hardiman, *Gandhi in His Time
      and Ours: The Global Legacy of His Ideas*, 235.

162 Gandhi, 'Hindu–Muslim Tension', 142.

163 Gandhi, 149–50; 'Hindu–Muslim Unity, 5 June 1924', 189.

164 Gandhi, 'Hindu–Muslim Tension', 152; 'Hindu–Muslim Unity,
      5 June 1924', 189–90.

165 Gandhi, 'Hindu–Muslim Tension', 153; 'Hindu–Muslim Unity,
      5 June 1924', 189.

166 Gandhi, 'Hindu–Muslim Tension', 152–53.

167 This statement of Gandhi's has drawn criticism from scholars,
      including Gandhi's grandson, Rajmohan Gandhi. See Chatterji,
      Gandhi and the Ali Brothers, 163; Gould, *Religion and Conflict
      in Modern South Asia*, 116–17; Nair, *Changing Homelands*, 52.
      For more on the British discourse regarding Hindu cowardice,
      see Banerjee, *Make Me a Man*, 24.

168 Gould, *Religion and Conflict in Modern South Asia*, 117.

169 Chatterji, *Gandhi and the Ali Brothers*, 164.

170 There exists a vast research literature on stereotypes, which
      are traits viewed as characteristic of social groups and their
      individual members. While they are a natural cognitive
      tendency, part of how human brains make sense of a complex
      world, stereotypes are often considered problematic since
      most are over-generalizations which are negative, inaccurate
      (statistically erroneous) and unfair. They often leave little
      room for individual variation, discourage thinking about
      individuals, create biases, support prejudice, and do real
      damage to members of stereotyped groups. See Todd D. Nelson,
      ed., *Handbook of Prejudice, Stereotyping, and Discrimination*
      (New York: Psychology Press, 2009), 4–5; David J. Schneider,
      The Psychology of Stereotyping, Distinguished Contributions in
      Psychology (New York: Guilford Press, 2004), 5–7, 11, 16–19,
      22–24. For an illustration of how stereotypes almost always
      get something critically wrong and disguise diversity within

stereotyped groups, see Kwame Anthony Appiah, *The Lies That Bind: Rethinking Identity: Creed, Country Colour, Class, Culture* (London: Profile Books, 2018), 30–32, 39–44, 52–58.

171 Gandhi, 'Hindu–Muslim Tension', 142–43.

172 Gandhi, 141–42.

173 Gandhi, 142; Devji, *Impossible Indian*, 59; Gould, *Religion and Conflict in Modern South Asia*, 117; Karuna Mantena, 'Another Realism: The Politics of Gandhian Nonviolence', *American Political Science Review* 106, no. 2 (2012): 460.

174 Mantena, 'Another Realism', 463; Dustin Ells Howes, *Toward a Credible Pacifism: Violence and the Possibilities of Politics* (New York: Suny Press, 2010), 125–26.

175 Devji, *Impossible Indian*, 128–30. For the argument that Gandhian non-violent satyagraha indeed stood as much a chance of practically slowing or stopping the Holocaust as violence, see Dustin Ells Howes, *Toward a Credible Pacifism: Violence and the Possibilities of Politics* (Albany: State University of New York Press, 2009), 8, 132–35.

176 Devji, *Impossible Indian*, 58–62.

177 Hardiman, *Gandhi in His Time and Ours: The Global Legacy of His Ideas*, 240.

178 For more on Gandhi's criticism of shuddhi, see Adcock, *Limits of Tolerance*, 144, 160. Religious studies scholar C.S. Adcock has recently rightly argued that, here, Gandhi's criticism of shuddhi as 'intolerant' overlooked another significant aspect of it i.e., how some Arya Samajists as well as 'Untouchable' castes were also using shuddhi as part of their own *caste*-related politics to strongly challenge humiliating and exclusionary caste practices of untouchability. In other words, shuddhi was utilized for struggles for equality and dignity by 'low' castes. Adcock argues that Gandhi's criticism of shuddhi (and his advocacy of tolerance) tacitly subsumed 'Untouchable' castes (whose religious affiliation was sometimes uncertain) into the 'Hindu community', and thus helped realize a Hindu majority (and a Muslim

minority) in politics. Gandhian tolerance (and therefore Gandhian secularism) rested on the implicit assumption of a Hindu majority. While this may have been true, as Adcock herself admits, shuddhi indeed was *also* a religious (and not just a caste-related) matter, and was defended by many Arya Samajists as so. It did aim at converting Indian Muslims (and was perceived by several Muslims as guided by this intention), engaged in 'hateful anti-Muslim rhetoric', and played a significant role in escalating Hindu–Muslim polarization and violence. See Adcock, 145–50, 152, 155, 157, 160–61, 164–66. As such, Gandhian tolerance/secularism was more than just about ignoring attempts by Untouchable castes to use shuddhi for their own purposes of caste emancipation. Its insistence on non-violence, self-restraint, self-suffering and self-sacrifice were still substantive, meaningful responses to very real conditions of polarization and violence that were tearing apart Indian society and politics in the 1920s.

179 Nathuram Godse, *Why I Assassinated Mahatma Gandhi* (New Delhi: Surya Bharti Parkashan, 1993), 83, 85–86, 90, 94–96, 105.

180 Mantena, 'Another Realism', 466.

181 Mantena, 456–58. Also see Howes, *Credible Pacifism*. Gandhi understood the limits of idealism, and emphasized that he was a 'practical idealist', wishing to give ideals a specific *practical* shape in political work and action.

182 Mantena, 'Another Realism', 457–60.

183 Mantena, 459, 461–64.

184 That Gandhi's approach was failing in the 1920s in north India can be read as suggesting its inefficacy. But the success of any political method and action—whether based on a politics of distrust/extremism/violence *or* trust/moderation/non-violence—ultimately depends on how many other join, support and consent to those who spearhead either type of politics. See Howes, *Credible Pacifism*, 127–28. Gandhi's recommended methods in the early 1920s were being dismissed by more

individuals than those who approved of them, which in turn diminished their capacity for powerful effectiveness.

185 Referred to as 'Pathans' in much of the subcontinent, the people of the region call themselves 'Pashtun' or 'Pakhtun'. I use Pashtun instead of Pathan to affirm Pashtun self-description and avoid the stereotypes (of inherent bravery, martialness or violence) that often accompany the term 'Pathan'.

186 Hardiman, *Gandhi in His Time and Ours: The Global Legacy of His Ideas*, 237–39. For more details, see Mukulika Banerjee, *The Pathan Unarmed: Opposition & Memory in the North West Frontier*, World Anthropology (Oxford: James Currey, 2000); Amar Sohal, *The Muslim Secular*, 229–51, 278–86.

187 Mantena, 'Another Realism', 463. Also see David Hardiman, 'Gandhi's Global Legacy', in *The Cambridge Companion to Gandhi*, ed. Judith Brown and Anthony Parel (Cambridge: Cambridge University Press, 2011); Thomas Weber, 'Gandhian Philosophy, Conflict Resolution Theory and Practical Approaches to Negotiation', *Journal of Peace Research* 38, no. 4 (2001): 493–513; Mark Juergensmeyer, *Gandhi's Way: A Handbook of Conflict Resolution* (New Delhi: Oxford University Press, 2003).

188 Lala Lajpat Rai, 'Hindu–Muslim Unity, The Tribune, November–December 1924', in *CWLLR*, vol. 11, 2008, 136.

189 Lajpat Rai, 136.

190 Travelling to England in April 1924, Lajpat Rai had met Labour Prime Minister Ramsay MacDonald, his old friends the Webbs and other contacts among labour and radical circles. Here, Rai had also joined the Independent Labour Party. He then travelled to Switzerland where he met Shyamji Krishnavarma; Germany, where he met Virendranath Chattopadhyay and Agnes Smedley who were working towards a communist world revolution; Paris, where he met the revolutionary Madam Cama, and then further travelled to Denmark, Austria and Hungary. Rai then visited Istanbul (now ruled by the Young Turks), Syria and Palestine, and ended his trip in Egypt, from

where he returned to Bombay on 20 September 1924. Through his trip, Lajpat Rai had remained in regular touch with Malaviya and particularly Motilal Nehru on matters regarding the Swaraj Party (which Rai did not formally join but assisted). Chand, *Lajpat Rai*, 439–45, 451; Lajpat Rai, 'Hindu–Muslim Unity', 163.

191 Lajpat Rai, *CWLLR*, vol. 11, pp. xxiii, 135.

Chapter 15

1 Lala Lajpat Rai, 'Hindu–Muslim Unity, The Tribune, November–December 1924', in *CWLLR*, vol. 11, 2008 [hereafter cited as 'Hindu–Muslim Unity'], 140–42.

2 Lajpat Rai, 142.

3 Lajpat Rai, 143.

4 Lajpat Rai, 143, 145.

5 Lajpat Rai, 143.

6 M.K. Gandhi, 'Hindu–Muslim Tension: Causes and Cure, Young India, 29 May 1924', in *CWMG*, vol. 24 (Ahmedabad: Navajivan Trust, 1965).

7 Farzana Shaikh, *Community and Consensus in Islam: Muslim Representation in Colonial India, 1860–1947* (Delhi: Imprint One, 2012), 182.

8 Lajpat Rai, 'Hindu–Muslim Unity', 144. That the Khilafat movement—despite the intentions of Gandhi and leaders like Azad and the Ali brothers—did also bring in other, more narrow-minded and divisive religious voices into politics on a large scale has been highlighted by some contemporary historians of modern India. See Sumit Sarkar, *Modern India: 1886–1947* (Delhi: Macmillian, 1983), 234; Sekhar Bandyopadhyay, *From Plassey to Partition: A History of Modern India* (New Delhi: Orient Longman, 2004), 304; Suranjan Das, 'Communal Violence in Twentieth Century Colonial Bengal: An Analytical Framework', *Social Scientist* 18, no. 6/7 (June–July 1990): 30; Ayesha Jalal, *Self and Sovereignty: Individual*

and Community in South Asian Islam since 1850 (London: Routledge, 2002), 374. Yet, it would be reductive to pin all the blame for the polarization occurring between 'Hindus' and 'Muslims' only on Gandhi's Khilafat movement, whose aim after all was Hindu–Muslim (and, therefore, Indian national) unity. Doing so obfuscates the complex range of factors and socio-political actors which encouraged this polarization. To recall, see Chapter 14, n. 54 and n. 94.

9 Lajpat Rai, 'Hindu–Muslim Unity', 146.

10 Lajpat Rai, 144–46.

11 Lajpat Rai, 143.

12 Lajpat Rai, 151.

13 Lajpat Rai, 146.

14 Lajpat Rai, 150.

15 As noted by the historian Neeti Nair, Lajpat Rai's suggestion to eliminate the 'non-essentials' of religion drew criticism from some Arya Samajists. One Mr Chamupati would remark that Rai was 'on insecure ground . . . it is only those whose life's work is study, practice and guidance in the religious sphere that can determine which rite or form is essential and which is not'. Cited in Neeti Nair, *Changing Homelands: Hindu Politics and the Partition of India* (Cambridge, MA: Harvard University Press, 2011), 75, 283, n. 76.

16 Lajpat Rai, 'Hindu–Muslim Unity', 150.

17 Lajpat Rai, 'Hindu–Muslim Unity', 148.

18 Lajpat Rai, 'Hindu–Muslim Unity', 149–150.

19 Elaine M. Fisher, *Hindu Pluralism: Religion and the Public Sphere in Early Modern South India* (Oakland, California: University of California Press, 2017), chap. 1; Wendy Doniger, *On Hinduism*, 2016, 132.

20 Anantanand Rambachan, 'The Co-Existence of Violence and Non-Violence in Hinduism', *The Ecumenical Review* 55, no. 2 (2003): 115–22; Also see Upinder Singh, *Political Violence in Ancient India* (Cambridge, Massachusetts: Harvard University Press, 2017).

21 John L. Esposito, *Unholy War: Terror in the Name of Islam* (Oxford: Oxford University Press, 2002), 29–33; John L Esposito, *What Everyone Needs to Know about Islam* (New York: Oxford University Press, 2011), 137–38.

22 Esposito, *Unholy War*, 34–35.

23 Esposito, 36.

24 Esposito, 41–42; *What Everyone Needs to Know about Islam*, 245.

25 Esposito, *Unholy War*, 43.

26 Esposito, 44–46.

27 Esposito, 46.

28 Esposito, 47–48.

29 Esposito, 32, 158; *What Everyone Needs to Know about Islam*, 74–75, 138, 140.

30 Esposito, *Unholy War*, 28.

31 Esposito, 28.

32 Esposito, 42; *What Everyone Needs to Know about Islam*, 43.

33 Malise Ruthven, *Islam: A Very Short Introduction* (New York: Oxford University Press, 1997), 8–9.

34 Ruthven, 6.

35 Esposito, *Unholy War*, 67.

36 Esposito, 35. In using the term 'discriminatory', I follow Raziuddin Aquil. See his *Lovers of God: Sufism and the Politics of Islam in Medieval India* (New Delhi: Oxford University Press, 2020), 61.

37 Ruthven, *Islam*, 119; Esposito, *What Everyone Needs to Know about Islam*, 79, 84; *Unholy War*, 121.

38 Hardip Singh Syan, *Sikh Militancy in the Seventeenth Century: Religious Violence in Mughal and Early Modern India* (London: I.B. Tauris, 2013); Balbinder Singh Bhogal, 'Text as Sword: Sikh Religious Violence Taken for Wonder', in *Religion and Violence in South Asia: Theory and Practice*, ed. John R. Hinnells and Richard King (Routledge, 2007), 101.

39 Esposito, *Unholy War*, 122.

40 Ruthven, *Islam*, 2.

41 Ruthven, 1.

42 Sunaina Maira, 'Islamophobia and the War on Terror: Youth, Citizenship and Dissent', in *Islamophobia: The Challenge of Pluralism in the 21st Century*, ed. John L. Esposito and Ibrahim Kalin (USA: Oxford University Press, 2011), 109–10; Kate Zebiri, 'Orientalist Themes in Contemporary British Islamophobia', in *Islamophobia: The Challenge of Pluralism in the 21st Century*, ed. John L. Esposito and Ibrahim Kalin (New York: Oxford University Press, 2011), 175–76.

43 Esposito, *Unholy War*, chap. 3.

44 Esposito, *What Everyone Needs to Know about Islam*, 141–42.

45 Esposito, *Unholy War*, 64.

46 Esposito, 63–65, Chap. 4; John L. Esposito and Ibrahim Kalin, 'Introduction', in *Islamophobia: The Challenge of Pluralism in the 21st Century*, ed. John L. Esposito and Ibrahim Kalin (USA: Oxford University Press, 2011), xxii, xxxiii; Peter Gottschalk and Gabriel Greenberg, 'From Muhammad to Obama: Caricatures, Cartoons, and Stereotypes of Muslims', ed. John L. Esposito and Ibrahim Kalin, *Islamophobia: The Challenge of Pluralism in the 21st Century*, 2011, 194; Zebiri, 'Orientalist Themes', 183.

47 Sufi anecdotes do exist regarding occasional attempts at forced conversion. There is also a record of one Sufi shaikh's anguish over his failure to win over Hindu religious leaders to Islam even after defeat in a rational debate and contest around miracle-working abilities, which is how awe-inspired individual and group conversions to Sufi Islam in medieval times often seem to have occurred. See Raziuddin Aquil, *Lovers of God: Sufism and the Politics of Islam in Medieval India* (New Delhi: Oxford University Press, 2020), 126–29, 131–32, 139. The point that the story of Sufi Islam's encounter with the Hindu faith, while producing a composite culture, also involved a measure of competition, clash and

conflict (which was then accommodated) is similarly made
by historian Shahid Amin. See *Conquest and Community: The
Afterlife of Warrior Saint Ghazi Miyan* (New Delhi: Orient
Blackswan, 2015), 5–8.

48 These details are drawn from Aquil, *Lovers of God*, chap. 1,
pp. 179–80; *The Muslim Question: Understanding Islam and
Indian History* (Penguin Random House India, 2017), 34–36,
38–39. Also see Richard Eaton, *India in the Persianate Age:
1000–1765*, 2020, 31–41.

49 Lajpat Rai, 'Hindu–Muslim Unity', 150.

50 Lajpat Rai, 'Hindu–Muslim Unity', 150.

51 Lajpat Rai, 'Hindu–Muslim Unity', 160.

52 Lajpat Rai, 'Hindu–Muslim Unity', 160.

53 Iqbal, 'tarana-e-hindi', www.rekhta.org/nazms/taraana-e-hindii-
saare-jahaan-se-achchhaa-hindostaan-hamaaraa-allama-iqbal-
nazms (accessed 29 July 2023).

54 Lajpat Rai, 'Hindu–Muslim Unity', 160.

55 Iqbal, 'hindustani bachchon ka qaumi git', www.rekhta.org/
nazms/hindustaanii-bachchon-kaa-qaumii-giit-chishtii-ne-
jis-zamiin-men-paigaam-e-haq-sunaayaa-allama-iqbal-nazms
(accessed on 29 July 2023).

56 Lajpat Rai, 'Hindu–Muslim Unity', 162.

57 Dayne E. Nix, 'Muhammad Iqbal: Restoring Muslim Dignity
through Poetry, Philosophy and Religious Political Action',
in H. Chad Hillier and Basit Bilal Koshul (ed.), *Muhammad
Iqbal: Essays on the Reconstruction of Modern Muslim Thought*
(Edinburgh: Edinburgh University Press, 2015), 216–25.

58 The rest of this paragraph is based on my reading of Iqbal Singh
Sevea, *The Political Philosophy of Muhammad Iqbal: Islam and
Nationalism in Late Colonial India* (Cambridge; New York:
Cambridge University Press, 2012), chaps 3–5; Faisal Devji,
'Secular Islam', *Political Theology* 19, no. 8 (2018): 704–18.

59 See the introduction in Sohal, *The Muslim Secular: Parity and
the Politics of India's Partition* (Oxford: Oxford University Press,
2023).

60 Lajpat Rai, 'Hindu–Muslim Unity', 162.
61 Ayesha Jalal, *Self and Sovereignty: Individual and Community in South Asian Islam since 1850* (London: Routledge, 2002), 215–16.
62 Jalal, 216.
63 Jalal, 216.
64 Jalal, 224.
65 The aforementioned details about the hijrat movement are drawn from: M. Naeem Qureshi, 'The 'Ulamā'of British India and the Hijrat of 1920', *Modern Asian Studies* 13, no. 1 (1979): 41–59; Jalal, *Self and Sovereignty*, 214–18, 223–24. Also see Shabnum Tejani, *Indian Secularism: A Social and Intellectual History, 1890–1950* (Bloomington: Indiana University Press, 2008), 164–65.
66 Rajmohan Gandhi, *Ghaffar Khan: Nonviolent Badshah of the Pakhtuns*, Penguin Lives (New Delhi; New York: Penguin Viking, 2004), 73.
67 Lajpat Rai, 'Hindu–Muslim Unity', 159. Charges of divided loyalties arise due to the assumption that individuals cannot have multiple, coexisting identifications, and that one must necessarily override or deplete the other. Such charges have been faced, among countless others, by the Catholics and Jews of the United States (JFK faced the charge that, being Catholic, he would be more loyal to the Vatican than to America); Catholics and, more recently, British Indians and Pakistanis of Britain; the Jews of France; the Tamils and Muslims of Sri Lanka; and the Hindus of Bangladesh. The reductive nature of the charge might perhaps be understood by those second- or third-generation American and British Hindus who dislike the assumption that they are less committed to America or Britain simply because they have some attachments to Hindu holy places in India or to India more broadly. For what is only a small glimpse into this complex issue, see Ilan Zvi Baron, 'The Problem of Dual Loyalty', *Canadian Journal of Political Science* 42, no. 4 (2009): 1025–44; Thomas Fletcher, 'Who Do

"They" Cheer for? Cricket, Diaspora, Hybridity and Divided Loyalties amongst British Asians', *International Review for the Sociology of Sport* 47, no. 5 (2012): 612–31, https://doi.org/10.1177/1012690211416556. Pre-conceived, prejudiced assumptions about Indian Muslims' lack of attachment to India have persisted till today, but recent research shows that 95 per cent of Indian Muslims are very proud to be Indian, and 85 per cent agree with the statement that 'Indian culture is superior to others'. Pew Research Centre, 'Religion in India: Tolerance and Segregation', 29 June 2021, 18, 127.

68 See Chapter 12, pp. 221, 224; and Chapter 13, pp. 243–44.

69 Similar assumptions also marked the thought of certain other Congress leaders. For example, see Sarojini Naidu's Presidential Address Indian National Congress, *Report of the Indian National Congress: Fortieth Session, Cawnpore, 1925* (Madras: General Secretary, All India Congress, 1926), 10, 20.

70 Jalal, 224.

71 Lajpat Rai, 'Hindu–Muslim Unity', 158–59, 165.

72 The idea of a Muslim world (centred around the Ottoman caliphate) had not been confined to Indian Muslims. Upheld by many Muslims in other parts of Asia and Africa, it was often leveraged to demand dignity and equality for Muslims living under European empires. At the same time, the myth of a united Muslim world was clearly visible in the differences between the secular modernist turn in Turkey, Afghanistan and Iran; the secular socialist turn among Soviet Muslims; and the Salafi bent of Saudi Arabia and Yemen. The Saudi capture of Mecca and Medina, their lack of interest in resurrecting a caliphate, and their Wahabi-inspired destruction of the shrines of Muhammad and his companions, which had traumatized several South Asian and African Muslims, similarly punctured a hole in the myth of a united Muslim world. See Cemil Aydin, *The Idea of the Muslim World:*

A Global Intellectual History (Cambridge, Massachusetts: Harvard University Press, 2017), 127, 134–40; Gail Minault, *The Khilafat Movement: Religious Symbolism and Political Mobilization in India* (Delhi: Columbia University Press, 1982), 206.

73 Aydin, *Idea of the Muslim World*, 130.

74 David Page, *Prelude to Partition: The Indian Muslims and the Imperial System of Control, 1920-1932* (New Delhi: Oxford University Press, 1982), 101; For a statement by Azad asking Muslims to concentrate on matters at home, see Minault, *Khilafat Movement*, 205.

75 Mushirul Hasan, 'A Nationalist Conscience: M.A. Ansari, the Congress and The Raj', in *The Mushirul Hasan Omnibus* (New Delhi: Oxford University Press, 2010), 103.

76 Minault, *Khilafat Movement*, 205; Mushirul Hasan, 'Secular and Communitarian Representations of Indian Nationalism: Ideology and Praxis of Azad and Mohamed Ali', in *Islam and Indian Nationalism Reflections on Abul Kalam Azad*, ed. Mushirul Hasan (New Delhi: Manohar, 1992), 89.

77 'Maulana Shaukat Ali's Statement, All-India Khilafat Conference, Bombay, 10 May 1924', in A.M. Zaidi (ed.), *Evolution of Muslim Political Thought in India*, vol. 2 (New Delhi: Michiko and Panjathan, 1975), 628–29.

78 Jalal, *Self and Sovereignty*, 276.

79 Lajpat Rai, 'Hindu–Muslim Unity', 168.

80 Lajpat Rai, 165.

81 Lajpat Rai, 165, 169.

82 Lajpat Rai, 165, 171.

83 Lajpat Rai, 153–54.

84 Lajpat Rai, 152.

85 Lajpat Rai, 155.

86 Chetan Bhatt, *Hindu Nationalism: Origins, Ideologies and Modern Myths* (Oxford: Berg, 2001), 73; Ghazala Wahab, 'The Fine Line', *Force India*, September 2021, https://forceindia.

net/firstperson/the-fine-line/; Neha Sinha, 'Partition Wasn't Jinnah's Brainchild, Say Experts', *Indian Express*, 10 September 2009, http://archive.indianexpress.com/news/partition-wasn-t-jinnah-s-brainchild-say-experts/515243/.

87 Lajpat Rai, 'Hindu–Muslim Unity', 174; Also see Nair, *Changing Homelands*, 77. Emphasis mine.

88 Jalal, *Self and Sovereignty*, 274.

89 Lajpat Rai, 'Hindu–Muslim Unity', 174.

90 Sevea, *Muhammad Iqbal*, chap. 5; Jalal, *Self and Sovereignty*, 324–29; Devji, 'Secular Islam', 708.

Chapter 16

1 Neeti Nair, *Changing Homelands: Hindu Politics and the Partition of India* (Cambridge, MA: Harvard University Press, 2011), 55–57. It was later claimed that the bhajan was a response to a poem published in a Punjabi Muslim newspaper *Lahaul* that asked Muslims to burn the Gita, break Krishna's flute and destroy Hindu goddesses. Others would point out that *Lahaul* had little circulation in Kohat, and therefore little to do with Kohat's Muslims. Neeti Nair, *Changing Homelands: Hindu Politics and the Partition of India* (Cambridge, MA: Harvard University Press, 2011), 282, n. 15.

2 Nair, 55.

3 Nair, 57.

4 Nair, 57.

5 Nair, 58.

6 Nair, 58.

7 Nair, 58.

8 Nair, 58.

9 Nair, 58.

10 Nair, 59.

11 Nair, 59.

12 Nair, 59.

13 For details up to here, see Nair, 55–59.

14 Nair, 61.
15 Nair, 61–62.
16 Nair, 62.
17 Nair, 62.
18 Nair, 284, n. 44.
19 Nair, 283, n. 37.
20 Nair, 63.
21 Nair, 59–64, 66. After the event, the British focused on absolving themselves of responsibility. The government of India pressured the local British authorities in Kohat to rewrite reports that had initially spoken of lapses such as the failure to report escalating tensions from 3 September to the higher-ups, the imprudent release of Jivan Das on 8 September, and the lack of security precautions after the violence on 9 September to prevent violence on 10 September. Instead, revised reports pinned the blame on Hindus for provoking the riots. Nair, 65. It might be mentioned here that the fact that the British government had evacuated Kohat's Hindus was not disputed. The government openly stated that it had evacuated Hindus 'at the earnest entreaty of Hindus themselves'. See Nair, 66. And Hindus like Rai would criticize the government's decision. See Lala Lajpat Rai, 'Hindu–Muslim Unity, The Tribune, November–December 1924', in CWLLR, vol. 11, 2008, 138–39; 'Duty towards Hindus of Kohat, The Tribune, 19 November 1924', in CWLLR, vol. 11, 2008, 185–86. The departure of Kohat's Hindus in 1924 evokes the Kashmiri Pandit (KP) exodus in early 1990. However, there were important differences. The little research on the KP exodus argues that targeted killings of senior Hindu officials/notables, branded agents of the Indian state, by some militant groups, and threats by two newspapers to KPs asking them to leave, deeply frightened them. Legitimate fear led them to leave the Valley en masse. This happened, understandably, despite most Pandits not having been personally harmed or threatened, despite the entreaties of their Muslim neighbours to stay and despite Kashmiri Muslim delegations seeking to

prevent the exodus. While evidence suggests that the Indian government did not discourage, even inadvertently encouraged, the departure of Pandits, there is little that points to a state-administered evacuation. See Alexander Evans, 'A Departure from History: Kashmiri Pandits, 1990–2001', *Contemporary South Asia* 11, no. 1 (2002): 19–23. The context of 1924 Kohat was different. There was no militant secessionist movement. In fact, large numbers of Kohat's Muslims would soon, under Ghaffar Khan's leadership, affirm their faith in a non-violent, pluralist Indian nationalism, ally with the Congress and oppose the Muslim League. This nationalism was based on a reading of Islam that prioritized restraint, reciprocity and forgiveness, and on taking non-violence and friendship as intrinsic Pashtun values. In 1931, Kohat would be the site of brutal British repression of the Indian nationalist Khudai Khitmatgars [See Mukulika Banerjee, *The Pathan Unarmed: Opposition & Memory in the North West Frontier*, World Anthropology (Oxford: James Currey, 2000), 70. For more on the nationalism of Ghaffar Khan and his Khudai Khitmatgars, see Safoora Arbab, 'Nonviolence, Pukhtunwali and Decolonization', in *Muslims against the Muslim League*, ed. Ali Usman Qasmi and Robb, Megan Eaton (Cambridge University Press, 2017), 220; Amar Sohal, *The Muslim Secular*, 1–33, Chap. 4.]. There had been no threats issued by any newspapers, as in 1990. And the British government, by its own admission, had evacuated Kohat's fearful Hindus. Still, some similarities exist between the events in 1924 and 1990: fears of a Hindu minority, in the midst of violence and the government's lack of guarantee of safety, causing them to flee, and the powerlessness, in the face of louder extremists, of members of the Muslim majority, who tried to protect their Hindu neighbours or prevent them from leaving.

22 M.K. Gandhi, 'Statement Announcing 21-Day Fast, Young India, 25 September 1924', in *CWMG*, vol. 25 (Ahmedabad: Navajivan Trust, 1965), 171–72.

23 M.K. Gandhi, 'Discussion with Shaukat Ali, Navajivan, 28 September 1924', in *CWMG*, vol. 25 (Ahmedabad: Navajivan Trust, 1965), 181–84.

24 M.K. Gandhi, 'All About the Fast, Young India, 25 September 1924', in *CWMG*, vol. 25 (Ahmedabad: Navajivan Trust, 1965), 199–201.

25 Bhikhu C. Parekh, *Gandhi: A Very Short Introduction*, Very Short Introductions (Oxford; New York: Oxford University Press, 2001), 15. Also see Karuna Mantena, 'Another Realism: The Politics of Gandhian Nonviolence', *American Political Science Review* 106, no. 2 (2012): 468.

26 Anwesha Roy, *Making Peace, Making Riots: Communalism and Communal Violence, Bengal 1940-1947* (Cambridge University Press, 2018), 237.

27 Parekh, *Gandhi*, 15.

28 Ramachandra Guha, *Gandhi: The Years That Changed the World, 1914-1948* (Vintage, 2018), 414.

29 Lajpat Rai, 'Hindu–Muslim Unity', 138. See chapter 15.

30 Lajpat Rai, 139.

31 David Hardiman, *Gandhi in His Time and Ours: The Global Legacy of His Ideas* (Ranikhet: Permanent Black, 2003), 259–60; Roy, *Making Peace, Making Riots*, 236.

32 Hardiman, *Gandhi in His Time and Ours: The Global Legacy of His Ideas*, 343–46. The following details about the effects of the Delhi fast are from Gyanendra Pandey, *Remembering Partition: Violence, Nationalism, and History in India* (Cambridge; New York: Cambridge University Press, 2001), 143–44.

33 Guha, *Gandhi: The Years*, 416; Gail Minault, *The Khilafat Movement: Religious Symbolism and Political Mobilization in India* (Delhi: Columbia University Press, 1982), 200.

34 Mahadev Desai, *Maulana Abul Kalam Azad: The President of the Indian National Congress* (London: G. Allen and Unwin limited, 1941), 96.

35 M.K. Gandhi, 'Hindu–Muslim Unity, Young India, 14 September 1924', in *CWMG*, vol. 25 (Ahmedabad: Navajivan Trust, 1965),

136–37; 'Question of Questions, Young India, 18 September 1924', in *CWMG*, vol. 25 (Ahmedabad: Navajivan Trust, 1965), 168–69.

36 M.K. Gandhi, 'Notes, Young India, 18 September 1924', in *CWMG* (Ahmedabad: Navajivan Trust, 1965), 163.

37 M.K. Gandhi, 'Letter to Private Secretary to Viceroy, 16 October 1924', in *CWMG*, vol. 25 (Ahmedabad: Navajivan Trust, 1965), 238; 'Telegram to Private Secretary to Viceroy, 27 October 1924', in *CWMG*, vol. 25 (Ahmedabad: Navajivan Trust, 1965).

38 M.K. Gandhi, 'Letter to Lajpat Rai, 27/28 October 1924', in *CWMG*, vol. 25 (Ahmedabad: Navajivan Trust, 1965).

39 M.K. Gandhi, 'Letter to Lajpat Rai, 28 October 1924', in *CWMG*, vol. 25 (Ahmedabad: Navajivan Trust, 1965), 267.

40 Guha, *Gandhi: The Years*, 308–09; Sumit Sarkar, *Modern India: 1886–1947* (Delhi: Macmillian, 1983), 227–28. The two sides fought for control of the Congress organization and often carried out propaganda against each other. B.R. Nanda, *The Nehrus: Motilal and Jawaharlal*, New ed, Oxford India Paperbacks (New Delhi: Oxford University Press, 2008), 206–07.

41 Sarkar, *Modern India*, 226; Guha, *Gandhi: The Years*, 312.

42 Ajay Skaria, 'Gandhi's Politics: Liberalism and the Question of the Ashram', *The South Atlantic Quarterly* 101, no. 4 (2003): 968.

43 V. Geetha and S.V. Rajadurai, *Towards a Non-Brahmin Millennium: From Iyothee Thass to Periyar* (Calcutta: Bhatkal & Sen, 1998), 283, 293.

44 M.K. Gandhi, 'Letter to Lajpat Rai, 12 November 1924', in *CWMG*, vol. 25 (Ahmedabad: Navajivan Trust, 1965); 'Statement on Kohat, New India, 17 November 1924', in *CWMG*, vol. 25 (Ahmedabad: Navajivan Trust, 1965).

45 Nanda, *The Nehrus*, 242.

46 M.K. Gandhi, 'Letter to Lajpat Rai, 12 November 1924', in *CWMG*, vol. 25 (Ahmedabad: Navajivan Trust, 1965).

47 Lala Lajpat Rai, 'Telegram to Mahatma Gandhi, 14 November 1924', in *CWLLR*, vol. 11, 2008, 185. J.P. Misra, *Madan Mohan Malaviya and the Indian Freedom Movement* (New Delhi: Oxford University Press, 2016), 170.

48 Gandhi, 'Statement on Kohat', 327–28.

49 For British repression in Bengal, see Durba Ghosh, *Gentlemanly Terrorists: Political Violence and the Colonial State in India, 1919–1947* (Cambridge: Cambridge University Press, 2017), 98–118.

50 B.R. Nanda, *The Nehrus: Motilal and Jawaharlal*, Oxford India Paperbacks (New Delhi: Oxford University Press, 2008), 242; Sugata Bose, *His Majesty's Opponent: Subhas Chandra Bose and India's Struggle Against Empire* (Harvard University Press, 2011), 55.

51 Gandhi, 'Statement on Kohat', 327–28.

52 Lajpat Rai, 'Duty towards Hindus of Kohat', 186–88.

53 Lajpat Rai, 185–86.

54 Lajpat Rai, 186.

55 Lajpat Rai, 186. I owe this point to Nair, *Changing Homelands*, 70.

56 Lajpat Rai, 'Duty towards Hindus of Kohat', 186–88.

57 Lajpat Rai, 188.

58 Lajpat Rai, 186, 188.

59 Rakhahari Chatterji, *Gandhi and the Ali Brothers: Biography of a Friendship* (New Delhi: SAGE, 2013), 169.

60 M.K. Gandhi, 'Speech at Rawalpindi, Navajivan, 14 December 1924', in *CWMG*, vol. 25 (Ahmedabad: Navajivan Trust, 1965), 414–16.

61 Gandhi, 414–16; Chatterji, *Gandhi and the Ali Brothers*, 169.

62 M.K. Gandhi, 'Interview to "The Tribune", The Tribune, 13 December 1924', in *CWMG*, vol. 25 (Ahmedabad: Navajivan Trust, 1965), 426; Guha, *Gandhi: The Years*, 420.

63 M.K. Gandhi, 'The Kohat Tragedy, Young India, 18 December 1924', in *CWMG*, vol. 25 (Ahmedabad: Navajivan Trust, 1965), 440.

64 Nair, *Changing Homelands*, 67.

65 M.K. Gandhi, 'Presidential Address at Belgaum Congress, Young India, 26 December 1924', in *CWMG*, vol. 25 (Ahmedabad: Navajivan Trust, 1965), 478.

66 See his letter as cited in M.K. Gandhi, 'My Punjab Diary, Young India, 11 December 1924', in *CWMG*, vol. 25 (Ahmedabad: Navajivan Trust, 1965), 416–17; Nanda, *The Nehrus*, 224–26. That year, Motilal Nehru had also worked to secure the cooperation of Jinnah and 'moderates' like Malaviya to outvote the government. Nanda, 228.

67 See 'Speech on Resolution on Kohat and Gulbarga Riots, Belgaum Congress, 27 December 1924', in *CWMG* (Ahmedabad: Navajivan Trust, 1965), 499.

68 Nanda, *The Nehrus*, 249–51.

69 Rajmohan Gandhi, *Patel: A Life*, 1991, 134.

70 Semanti Ghosh, *Different Nationalisms: Bengal, 1905–1947* (New Delhi: Oxford University Press, 2017), 143.

71 Nanda, *The Nehrus*, 208, 242.

72 Subhas Chandra Bose, *The Indian Struggle, 1920–1942* (Delhi; New York: Oxford University Press, 1997), 95, 106.

73 Bose, 103.

74 Gandhi, *Patel*, 132–34.

75 Zafar Ahmad Nizami, *Hakim Ajmal Khan* (Publications Division Ministry of Information & Broadcasting, 1988), 221–22.

76 Nizami, 222–24.

77 Nizami, 217–18.

78 Shan Muhammad, ed., 'Muslim Reaction on Kohat Riots, The Comrade, April 1925', in *The Indian Muslims: A Documentary Record (1900–1947)*, vol. 8 (Meerut: Meenakshi Prakashan, 1980), 6–7.

79 Nair, *Changing Homelands*, 71.

80 Desai, *Azad*, 126–27.

81 Mushirul Hasan, *M.A. Ansari* (New Delhi: Publications Division Ministry of Information & Broadcasting, 1995), 90; Nizami, *Hakim Ajmal Khan*, 218.

82 Desai, *Azad*, 91–93.

83 Pradip Kumar Datta, 'War over Music: The Riots of 1926 in Bengal', *Social Scientist*, no. No. 6/7 (1990): 47.

84 Desai, *Azad*, 96.

85 Gail Minault, 'The Elusive Maulana: Reflections on Writing Azad's Biography', in *Islam and Indian Nationalism Reflections on Abul Kalam Azad*, ed. Mushirul Hasan (New Delhi: Manohar, 1992), 25–26; Ali Ashraf, 'Islam and Indian Nationalism Reflections on Abul Kalam Azad', ed. Mushirul Hasan (New Delhi: Manohar, 1992), 114.

86 Barbara Metcalf, 'Nationalist Muslims in British India: The Case of Hakim Ajmal Khan', *Modern Asian Studies* 19, no. 1 (1985): 26; Nizami, *Hakim Ajmal Khan*, 224.

87 'Appeal for Contributions for Relief of Hindus of Kohat', The Tribune, 22 November 1924, Lala Lajpat Rai, *The Collected Works of Lala Lajpat Rai*, ed. B.R. Nanda (New Delhi: Manohar, 2003), vol. 11, p. 189.

88 Lala Lajpat Rai, 'The Hindu Mahasabha and Muslim League, Bombay Chronicle, 22 December 1924', in *CWLLR*, vol. 11, 2008, 203.

89 Vikram Sampath, *Savarkar: A Contested Legacy, 1924–66* (Gurugram: Viking, 2021), 37–38.

90 See Chapter 14, p. 275.

91 Lala Lajpat Rai, 'The Kohat Tragedy and the Responsibility of Hindu and Muslim Leaders, Speech at Belgaum Congress, 27 December 1924. Report of the Indian National Congress, Belgaum, December 1924', in *CWLLR*, vol. 11, 2008 [hereafter cited as 'The Kohat Tragedy'], 23–29; 'Degradation of Hindus, Bombay Chronicle, 27 December 1924', in *CWLLR*, vol. 11, 2008 [Hereafter cited as 'Degradation of Hindus'], 203–04.

92 Lajpat Rai, 'The Kohat Tragedy', 24.

93 Lajpat Rai, 26–27.

94 Lajpat Rai, 28.

95 Lajpat Rai, 29.

96 Lajpat Rai, 'Degradation of Hindus', 204.

97 See the resolutions passed by the Mahasabha at its Belgaum session as reproduced in Shan Mohammad, ed., 'Kohat and the Muslim League: An Explanation by Mohamed Ali, Comrade, January 1925', in *Indian Muslims: A Documentary Record (1900–1947)*, vol. 8 (Meerut: Meenakshi Prakashan, 1980), 81–82.

98 Gandhi, 'Hindu–Muslim Unity, 14 September 1924'.

99 Gandhi, 'Question of Questions', 166–69; 'Hindus and Muslims, Navajivan. 26 October 1924', in *CWMG*, vol. 25 (Ahmedabad: Navajivan Trust, 1965), 166–69.

100 M.K. Gandhi, 'Notes, Young India, 18 December 1924', in *CWMG* (Ahmedabad: Navajivan Trust, 1965).

101 Gandhi, 'The Kohat Tragedy', 439–41.

102 Gandhi, 'Speech at Rawalpindi', 414–16.

103 Gandhi, 'Interview to "The Tribune"', 425–27; 'The Kohat Tragedy', 439–41; 'Presidential Address at Belgaum Congress', 477–78.

104 Lala Lajpat Rai, 'Mahatma Gandhi and the Kohat Hindus, The Tribune, 1 January 1925', in *CWLLR*, vol. 11, 2008, 191.

105 Lala Lajpat Rai, 'From Ravi to Brahmaputra, The Bombay Chronicle, 21/23/26 May 1925', in *CWLLR*, vol. 11, 2008, 243.

106 Lajpat Rai, 'Mahatma Gandhi and the Kohat Hindus', 191.

107 Ibid.

108 Lala Lajpat Rai, 'The Need for Hindu Organisation, The Bombay Chronicle, 5 January 1925', in *CWLLR*, vol. 11, 2008, 205–06.

109 A.M. Zaidi, ed., 'Presidential Address of Syed Reza Ali, All-India Muslim League, Bombay, 30-1 December 1924', in *Evolution of Muslim Political Thought in India*, vol. 2 (New Delhi: Michiko & Panjathan, 1975), 633.

110 Zaidi, 303–05.

111 Neeti Nair, *Changing Homelands: Hindu Politics and the Partition of India* (Cambridge, MA: Harvard University Press, 2011), 71.

112   Shan Mohammad, ed., 'Kohat and the Muslim League: An Explanation by Mohamed Ali, Comrade, January 1925', in *Indian Muslims: A Documentary Record (1900-1947)*, vol. 8 (Meerut: Meenakshi Prakashan, 1980), 84.

113   Shan Mohammad, ed., 'Kohat and the Muslim League: An Explanation by Mohamed Ali, Comrade, January 1925', in *Indian Muslims: A Documentary Record (1900-1947)*, vol. 8 (Meerut: Meenakshi Prakashan, 1980), 86.

114   Mohammad, 86.

115   Mohammad, 86.

116   Mohammad, 87.

117   'All India Muslim League, Sixteenth Session, Bombay, 30-31 December 1924' in A.M. Zaidi (ed.), *Evolution of Muslim Political Thought in India*, vol. 2 (New Delhi: Michiko & Panjathan, 1975), 315.

118   Chatterji, *Gandhi and the Ali Brothers*, 189.

119   Lajpat Rai, 'Need for Hindu Organisation', 206.

120   Lala Lajpat Rai, 'The Hindu Sabha and Hindu Community, The Tribune, 16 January 1925', in *CWLLR*, vol. 11, 2008, 210.

121   Lajpat Rai, 210; Lajpat Rai, 'Need for Hindu Organisation', 205.

122   Lajpat Rai, 'The Hindu Mahasabha and Muslim League', 202-03; Lajpat Rai, 'The Hindu Sabha and Hindu Community', 210.

123   See Chapter 10, pp. 176, 195, 197.

124   See Chapter 10, pp. 182-83.

125   See Chapter 13, pp. 241-42.

126   Mushirul Hasan, 'A Nationalist Conscience: M.A. Ansari, the Congress and The Raj', in *The Mushirul Hasan Omnibus* (New Delhi: Oxford University Press, 2010), 104-05.

127   Farzana Shaikh, *Community and Consensus in Islam: Muslim Representation in Colonial India, 1860-1947* (Delhi: Imprint One, 2012), 181-82.

128   Repelled by Gandhian mass politics and the entry of the ulema into politics, Jinnah had resigned from the Congress in 1920, withdrawn from politics in 1921, and even abandoned the Muslim League which was presided by Khilafatists like

Mohani with whom Jinnah did not agree. As Gandhi had drawn up plans for civil disobedience, which were eventually called off after Chauri Chaura, Jinnah, along with Malaviya, had attempted to convince the British government to arrange a Round Table Conference to discuss future constitutional reforms for India. These efforts were struck down by the non-cooperators. By mid-1922, Jinnah was trying to organize a new moderate party. He had invited Jayakar and Motilal Nehru to join, but both declined, leaving Jinnah isolated from his former Congress colleagues. In 1923, Jinnah stood from Bombay as an independent Muslim candidate. In 1924, Jinnah got his swing bloc of 'independents' to merge with the Swaraj Party to defeat official appointees and British imperial interests in the Central Legislative Assembly. Historian Stanley Wolpert argues that the influence Gandhi (and his insistence on non-cooperation) continued to have on even a Swarajist like Motilal Nehru eventually had him abandon his alliance with Jinnah in favour of a strategy of using the council to non-cooperate by throwing out all legislation. Converging with Lajpat Rai who would soon similarly criticize this Swarajist strategy, Jinnah and his independents refused to engage in obstructionist tactics in the Assembly. See *Jinnah of Pakistan* (New York: Oxford University Press, 1984), 73–80, 84–86. Ayesha Jalal suggests that Jinnah had hoped that his resignation from the Congress in 1920 would be only a temporary parting of ways. See *The Sole Spokesman: Jinnah, the Muslim League and the Demand for Partition* (Cambridge: Cambridge University Press, 1985), 8. While this question needs further research, it has also been cursorily suggested that Jinnah sought to act as a broker between various Muslim politicians and Congressmen, and did not re-join the Congress because he wished not to compromise his chances of negotiating Muslim demands with the Congress as an equal by becoming party to its decisions. See

David Page, *Prelude to Partition: The Indian Muslims and the Imperial System of Control, 1920–1932* (New Delhi: Oxford University Press, 1982), 118–19; Also see Ayesha Jalal and Anil Seal, 'Alternative to Partition: Muslim Politics between the Wars', *Modern Asian Studies* 15, no. 03 (1981): 433.

129   Lajpat Rai, 'The Hindu Sabha and Hindu Community', 210.

130   Jalal and Seal, 'Alternative to Partition', 417–18, 429–30.

131   Jalal and Seal, 429–30.

132   Page, *Prelude to Partition*, 139–42.

133   Jalal and Seal, 'Alternative to Partition', 421–27.

134   Page, *Prelude to Partition*, 39; Jalal and Seal, 'Alternative to Partition', 429–30.

135   Jalal and Seal, 418.

136   Jalal and Seal, 'Alternative to Partition', 418–23.

137   Jalal and Seal, 'Alternative to Partition 431. Ayesha Jalal, *Self and Sovereignty: Individual and Community in South Asian Islam since 1850* (London: Routledge, 2002), 301–02.

138   Farzana Shaikh, *Community and Consensus in Islam: Muslim Representation in Colonial India, 1860–1947* (Delhi: Imprint One, 2012), 185–87; Jalal and Seal, 'Alternative to Partition', 434–54.

139   Shaikh, *Community and Consensus*, 183–84; Jalal and Seal, 'Alternative to Partition', 417; Minault, *Khilafat Movement*, 181–82, 186–88, 201–04.

140   Shaikh, *Community and Consensus*, 183.

141   Page, *Prelude to Partition*, 98–101.

142   Ayesha Jalal and Anil Seal, 'Alternative to Partition: Muslim Politics between the Wars', *Modern Asian Studies* 15, no. 03 (1981): 417.

143   'All-India Muslim League, Fifteenth Session, Lahore, 24-25 May 1924' in A.M. Zaidi, (ed.), *Evolution of Muslim Political Thought in India*, vol. 2 (New Delhi: Michiko and Panjathan, 1975), 272.

144 The Lucknow Pact granted Muslims in Punjab, with their population of 55 per cent, 50 per cent reservations, while in Bengal, with their population of 52.6 per cent, Muslims were given 40 per cent. Holding that they had been asked to concede too much and were vulnerable, Punjabi and Bengali Muslim leaders sought revision of the Lucknow Pact. See Hugh Owen, 'Negotiating the Lucknow Pact', *The Journal of Asian Studies* 31, no. 03 (1972): 561–87; Zaidi, 'All-India Muslim League, Sixteenth Session', 305–06.

145 David Page, *Prelude to Partition: The Indian Muslims and the Imperial System of Control, 1920–1932* (New Delhi: Oxford University Press, 1982), 120.

146 Owen, 'Lucknow Pact', 586.

147 A.M. Zaidi, ed., 'Presidential Address of Syed Reza Ali, All-India Muslim League, Bombay, 30-1 December 1924', in *Evolution of Muslim Political Thought in India*, vol. 2 (New Delhi: Michiko & Panjathan, 1975), 309, 314.

148 Rajeev Bhargava, *The Promise of India's Secular Democracy* (New Delhi: Oxford University Press, 2010), 13; Shabnum Tejani, 'Defining Secularism in the Particular: Caste and Citizenship in India, 1909–1950', *Politics and Religion* 6, no. 4 (2013): 717–20.

149 Rochana Bajpai, *Debating Difference: Group Rights and Liberal Democracy in India* (Oxford: Oxford University Press, 2011), 37; Susan Bayly, *Caste, Society and Politics in India from the Eighteenth Century to the Modern Age* (Cambridge: Cambridge University Press, 1999), 242.

150 Gail Omvedt, *Ambedkar: Towards an Enlightened India* (London: Penguin UK, 2008), 24.

151 V. Geetha and S.V. Rajadurai, *Towards a Non-Brahmin Millennium: From Iyothee Thass to Periyar* (Calcutta: Bhatkal & Sen, 1998), 142-43,156, 168–69, 173, 225.

152 V. Geetha and S.V. Rajadurai, *Towards a Non-Brahmin Millennium*, 173.

153 Page, *Prelude to Partition*, 114. Historians have so far not given a clear answer to why Jinnah wanted to now re-negotiate the Lucknow Pact which he had so painstakingly crafted along with Tilak in 1916 (see Chapter 10, p. 176). Was he helplessly compelled to relent to new provincial forces as hinted by Ayesha Jalal, or did he have a little more agency, as suggested by David Page? The answers to these questions require further investigation by historians of political history. It must also be remembered that agreement between Jinnah and other provincial Muslim leaders at Lahore remained somewhat vague and fragile, as would be proved by the difficulty Jinnah faced subsequently from intransigent Bengali Muslim leaders. Thus, while Jinnah sought a relatively more reasonable revision of the Lucknow Pact and a settlement with the Congress, Bengali Muslim politicians were less compromising and an obstacle to cooperation with the Congress. David Page, *Prelude to Partition*, 116–17.

154 David Page, *Prelude to Partition*, 106, 120–21. At the League's 1924 Lahore session, Jinnah set up a committee to formulate a new constitution in consultation with the Congress and other organizations. It was snubbed by the Congress, under leaders such as Mohamed Ali and Jawaharlal Nehru. Yet, for the sake of a peaceful, stable India, the Congress too remained anxious for an agreement with Jinnah and the League. When Jinnah re-fashioned the original constitution committee to accommodate a larger Congress Muslim component, it was co-opted—at Gandhi's behest—on to a Unity Committee of the All-Parties Conference called in November 1924 in Bombay to devise a united front against the government. *Prelude to Partition*, 118, 120–21.

155 Syed Sharifuddin Pirzada, ed., 'All-India Muslim League, Fifteenth Session, Lahore, 24–25 May 1924', in *Foundations of Pakistan: All-India Muslim League Documents, 1906–1947*, vol. 1 (Karachi: National Publishing House, 1970), 577.

156 Syed Sharifuddin Pirzada, ed., 'All-India Muslim League, Fifteenth Session, Lahore, 24–25 May 1924', 581.

157 David Page, *Prelude to Partition*, 116–17.

158 Syed Sharifuddin Pirzada, ed., 'All-India Muslim League, Fifteenth Session, Lahore, 24–25 May 1924', 581.

159 David Page, *Prelude to Partition*, 113.

160 Lajpat Rai, 'Need for Hindu Organisation', 205; Lajpat Rai, 'The Hindu Sabha and Hindu Community', 211.

161 Lajpat Rai, 'The Hindu Mahasabha and Muslim League', 202.

162 Page, *Prelude to Partition*, 88.

163 David Page, *Prelude to Partition*, 120. The Ali brothers were party to Gandhi's offer.

164 Lala Lajpat Rai, 'The Hindu Sabha and Hindu Community', in *CWLLR*, vol. 11, 2008, 211; 'Nagpur Constitution, Article XXIX' in N.V. Rajkumar, *Development of the Congress Constitution* (New Delhi: All India Congress Committee, 1949), 58–59. Such a veto was accepted by the Congress in the Lucknow Pact. Rochana Bajpai, *Debating Difference*, 41.

165 Rochana Bajpai, *Debating Difference*; Arend Lijphart, 'The Puzzle of Indian Democracy: A Consociational Interpretation', *American Political Science Review* 90, no. 2 (1996): 258–68.

166 Lajpat Rai, 'The Hindu Mahasabha and Muslim League', 203.

167 Gould, *Language of Politics*, 14–17; Jalal, 'Exploding Communalism: The Politics of Muslim Identity in South Asia', 78, 89, 100, 102.

168 Jayakar, *The Story of My Life*, 2: 484.

169 Lala Lajpat Rai, 'To Purushottamdas Thakurdas, 13 December 1924', in *CWLLR*, vol. 11, 2008, 201.

170 Lajpat Rai, 'The Hindu Sabha and Hindu Community', 209.

Chapter 17

1 David Page, *Prelude to Partition: The Indian Muslims and the Imperial System of Control, 1920–1932* (New Delhi: Oxford University Press, 1982), 121–22.

2 M.R. Jayakar, *The Story of My Life*, vol. 2 (Bombay: Asia Publishing House, 1959), 517.

3 Lala Lajpat Rai, 'To Purushottamdas Thakurdas, 13 December 1924', in *CWLLR*, vol. 11, 2008, 202; 'The Hindu Mahasabha and Muslim League, Bombay Chronicle, 22 December 1924', in *CWLLR*, vol. 11, 2008, 202; 'The Need for Hindu Organisation, The Bombay Chronicle, 5 January 1925', in *CWLLR*, vol. 11, 2008, 205.

4 Lala Lajpat Rai, 'Circular Letter to Provincial Hindu Leaders, The Bombay Chronicle, 6 February 1925', in *CWLLR*, vol. 11, 2008 [hereafter cited as 'Circular to Provincial Hindu Leaders'], 217–20.

5 Richard Gordon, 'The Hindu Mahasabha and the Indian National Congress, 1915–26', *Modern Asian Studies* 9, no. 2 (1975): 173.

6 Gordon, 173–74.

7 Page, *Prelude to Partition*, 174.

8 Lajpat Rai, 'Circular to Provincial Hindu Leaders', 217–20.

9 Lala Lajpat Rai, 'Presidential Speech at the Punjab Provincial Hindu Conference, Lahore, The Tribune, 5 June 1925', in *CWLLR*, vol. 11, 2008, 249; 'On Sarojini Naidu's Criticism of the Leaders of the Hindu Sabha Movement, The Tribune, 24 October 1925', in *CWLLR*, vol. 11, 2008, 261.

10 Lala Lajpat Rai, 'Religion and Politics, The People, 22 August 1926', in *CWLLR*, vol. 12, 2009, 354.

11 Lala Lajpat Rai, 'Hindu–Muslim Unity, *The Tribune*, November-December 1924', in *CWLLR*, vol. 11, 2008, 172.

12 Lala Lajpat Rai, 'My Political Creed, *The People*, 26 July 1925', in *CWLLR*, vol. 11, 2008, 383; 'Communal Representation—a Negation of Nationalism, *Hindustan Times*, 27 January 1925', in *CWLLR*, vol. 11, 2008, 217.

13 Lajpat Rai, 'My Political Creed', 383.

14 Lala Lajpat Rai, 'Communal Representation, *The People*, 19 December 1926', in *CWLLR*, vol. 12, 2009, 358.

15 Lajpat Rai, 'Communal Representation—a Negation', 217; 'Communalism, Nationalism and Internationalism, The People,

27 September 1925', in *CWLLR*, vol. 11, 2003, 403–04; 'My Political Creed', 383.

16 Lala Lajpat Rai, 'Presidential Address to the Eighth Session of the Hindu Mahasabha, Calcutta, Amrita Bazar Patrika, 12 April 1925', in *CWLLR*, vol. 11, 2008 [hereafter cited as 'Presidential Address, Eighth Hindu Mahasabha'], 228; 'Communalism, Nationalism and Internationalism', 403.

17 Lajpat Rai, 'Presidential Address, Eighth Hindu Mahasabha', 228; 'Two Wrongs?, *The Tribune*, 10 November 1925', in *CWLLR*, vol. 11, 2008, 267.

18 Lala Lajpat Rai, 'Concluding Speech at the Bombay Hindu Mahasabha Conference, *The Bombay Chronicle*, 8 December 1925', in *CWLLR*, vol. 11, 2008 [hereafter cited as 'Concluding Speech at the Bombay Hindu Mahasabha Conference'], 284.

19 Shan Muhammad, ed., 'Mohammad Ali on Hindus and Mussulmans, *The Comrade*, January 1926', in *Indian Muslims: A Documentary Record (1900-1947)*, vol. 8 (Meerut: Meenakshi Prakashan, 1980), 127.

20 William Gould, *Hindu Nationalism and the Language of Politics in Late Colonial India* (Cambridge: Cambridge University Press, 2004), 96.

21 In the South, a 3–4 per cent minority of Brahmins held a massively disproportionate number—55–72 per cent—of government posts. Here, fear that self-government would quickly turn hereditary Brahmin privilege into oppressive Brahmin rule drove the majority of underprivileged non-Brahmins to organize to demand communal representation to safeguard against future Brahmin domination. Charges of divisive 'communalism' were levelled at non-Brahmins by Brahmin Congressmen. Non-Brahmin representatives refuted charges of communalism, and/or argued that communalism (in the form of communal representation) and nationalism were perfectly reconcilable. See V. Geetha and S.V. Rajadurai,

Towards a Non-Brahmin Millennium: From Iyothee Thass to Periyar (Calcutta: Bhatkal & Sen, 1998), 142, 208, 292.

22 In humanities and social science research, to say a phenomenon is 'constructed' is to question its supposed given-ness and self-evident-ness, and assert that it is a historically and socially created and contingent phenomenon.

23 Gyanendra Pandey, *The Construction of Communalism in Colonial North India* (New Delhi: Oxford University Press, 2006), 234–42.

24 Pandey, 240, 255.

25 Pandey, 255–57.

26 Lajpat Rai, 'Hindu–Muslim Unity', 167.

27 Lala Lajpat Rai, 'What Is Political Work, The People, 8 November 1925', in *CWLLR*, vol. 11, 2008, 417.

28 Ernest Gellner, *Nations and Nationalism* (Ithaca, New York: Cornell University Press, 1983), 35–55.

29 Craig J. Calhoun, Mark Juergensmeyer, and Jonathan VanAntwerpen, 'Introduction', in *Rethinking Secularism*, ed. Craig J. Calhoun, Mark Juergensmeyer, and Jonathan VanAntwerpen (Oxford, NY: Oxford University Press, 2011), 15; Wolfgang Reinhard, 'Reformation, Counter-Reformation, and the Early Modern State a Reassessment', *The Catholic Historical Review* 75, no. 3 (1989): 384, 393, 398; Joel F. Harrington and Helmut Walser Smith, 'Confessionalization, Community, and State Building in Germany, 1555–1870', *The Journal of Modern History* 69, no. 1 (1997): 86; Daniel Nexon, 'Religion, European Identity, and Political Contention in Historical Perspective', in *Religion in an Expanding Europe*, ed. Timothy Byrnes and Peter Katzenstein (Cambridge University Press, 2006), 258–61, 277–78; Philip Gorski, 'Historicizing the Secularization Debate: Church, State, and Society in Late Medieval and Early Modern Europe, ca. 1300 to 1700', *American Sociological Review*, 2000, 157–58. The 'confessionalisation of Europe' saw the emergence of three mono-confessional

blocs: the Lutheran north (Denmark, Norway, Sweden), the Catholic south (France, Italy, Spain, Portugal) and the Orthodox east. In between, there was also a belt of 'bi-' and 'multi-confessional' lands. This included England and Ireland, south Germany, Switzerland, Bohemia, Poland and Hungary. However, Ireland was a colony of a Britain that was dominated by Anglican England, and, as such, saw efforts at Protestantization, with Catholics being subject to social and political discrimination for a long time. Even in 'multi-confessional' German lands, there were Lutheran, Reformed and Catholic states with tendencies towards disciplining, assimilation, and homogenization. Policies of religious homogenization were similarly undertaken in Hungary and Bohemia. See Anja Hennig, 'Zum Verhältnis von Religion Und Politik in Europa', *Aus Politik Und Zeitgeschichte*, no. 63 (10 June 2013): 44; Gorski, 'Historicizing the Secularization Debate: Church, State, and Society in Late Medieval and Early Modern Europe, ca. 1300 to 1700', 147–48, 157–58; Harrington and Smith, 'Confessionalization, Community, and State Building in Germany, 1555–1870', 82–86; Nexon, 'Religion, European Identity', 278. In the 'multi-confessional' German lands, the assumed need to manage sectarian diversity and conflict led to confessional (not secular) states. These confessional German states resulted in 'confessional cleansing', forced migration, expulsion, homogenization, unequal treatment of minorities, and the hardening of confession-specific Protestant and Catholic identities, which reproduced confessional conflicts and intolerance. Harrington and Smith, 'Confessionalization, Community, and State Building in Germany, 1555–1870', 77–78. 84–92.

30 See Rajeev Bhargava, 'Is European Secularism Secular Enough?', 167; Calhoun, Juergensmeyer, and VanAntwerpen, 'Introduction', 7, 15; Mark Juergensmeyer, 'Rethinking the Secular and Religious Aspects of Violence', in *Rethinking*

Secularism, ed. Craig J. Calhoun, Mark Juergensmeyer, and Jonathan VanAntwerpen (Oxford, NY: Oxford University Press, 2011), 187; Andrew Copson, *Secularism: A Very Short Introduction* (New York, NY: Oxford University Press, 2019), 61–70.

31 Juergensmeyer, 'Secular and Religious Aspects of Violence', 187.

32 Lajpat Rai, 'Religion and Politics', 352–53.

33 Scholars of secularism/secularization draw a distinction between 'secularism' and 'secularization'. Secularism is an ideology seeking the separation of religion and politics for particular normative purposes like individual freedom, non-domination, equal citizenship or peace. Secularization is not an ideology, but a societal process. This process involves either or all of the three components: 1) decline in religious beliefs and practices 2) the differentiation of secular spheres (state, economy, science) from religious institutions and norms, and 3) the privatization of religion. See Rajeev Bhargava, 'Introduction', in *Secularism and Its Critics*, ed. Rajeev Bhargava (Delhi: Oxford University Press, 1998); José Casanova, 'Rethinking Secularization: A Global Comparative Perspective', *The Hedgehog Review* 8, no. 1–2 (Spring–Summer 2006): 7–22; Christoph Kleine and Monika Wohlrab-Sahr, *Research Program of the Humanities Centre for Advanced Studies,* 'Multiple Secularities – Beyond the West, Beyond Modernities', 2016.

34 Both Skinnerian and German conceptual history approaches to the study of ideas allow for a concept to be possessed even in the absence of a word to express it. Melvin Richter, *The History of Political and Social Concepts: A Critical Introduction* (Oxford University Press on Demand, 1995), 9, 133.

35 Lajpat Rai, 'My Political Creed', 382.

36 Lajpat Rai, 382; 'Hindu–Muslim Unity', 145–46.

37 Lajpat Rai, 'Hindu–Muslim Unity', 145–46.

38 Lajpat Rai, 147.

39 Lajpat Rai, 'Religion and Politics', 352–53.
40 Lajpat Rai, 'What Is Political Work', 417–18.
41 Rai had presided over the first session of the All-India Trade Union Congress (AITUC) when it was founded in 1920. According to his biographer, after this, he also took a broad interest in the organization of trade unions in Punjab, continued to support labour and socialist movements through his newspaper *The People*, and dreamt of creating a parliamentary labour group. At the AITUC session held in 1925 under C.F. Andrews's presidentship, Rai was named the workers' delegate for the 1926 Geneva Conference of the International Labour Organization, founded by the League of Nations in 1919. During Lajpat Rai's trip to Paris before the Conference, he met Jean Longuet, Karl Marx's grandson and top leader of the French Socialist Party. At the conference, he demanded an inquiry into the conditions of native and coloured labour in Africa and America, and spoke on forced labour in British India. He made contacts with socialists and trade unionists from across Europe, met the left-wing and Nobel Prize-winning dramatist–novelist Romain Rolland and the young Jawaharlal Nehru. Rai stayed in England for two months where he represented the Indian working class at the World Migration Congress and came in contact with a transnational network of labour and socialist movements. See Feroz Chand, *Lajpat Rai: Life and Work* (New Delhi: Publications Division, Ministry of Information and Broadcasting, Government of India, 1978), 466–73, 498.
42 Lala Lajpat Rai, 'Religionism vs. Secularism, The People, 8 September 1927', in *CWLLR*, vol. 13, 2010; 'All-India Muslim League, 12 February 1928', in *CWLLR*, vol. 15, 2010, 222–23.
43 The mere separation of religion from the state or from politics does not amount to secularism, which requires such a project to be guided by a commitment to values such as the protection of individual liberty, the promotion of equality

and equal citizenship, the promotion of peace or tolerance, or respect for diversity. See Rajeev Bhargava, *The Promise of India's Secular Democracy* (Oxford: Oxford University Press, 2010), 67, 76–77. As we shall see, however, Rai's secularism was grounded in certain normative values and not simply an unthinking call for the separation of religion from politics.

44 See Chapter 14, pp. 276.

45 See Chapter 14, p. 277.

46 See Chapter 14, p. 277.

47 Lajpat Rai, 'Hindu–Muslim Unity', 173.

48 Lajpat Rai, 'On Sarojini Naidu's Criticism', 261.

49 Lala Lajpat Rai, 'Need to Protect Hindu Interests, Hindustan Times, 22 October 1926', in *CWLLR*, vol. 12, 2009, 146.

50 Mohammad Ali Jinnah, 'Jinnah's Presidential Address to the Muslim League, Lucknow, December 1916', in *Mohammad Ali Jinnah An Ambassador of Unity: His Speeches and Writings (1912–1917)*, ed. Sarojini Naidu (Madras: GA Natesan and Co., 1918), 46.

51 See her portrayal of Jinnah in her edited volume of Jinnah's speeches published in 1918: *Mohammad Ali Jinnah An Ambassador of Unity: His Speeches and Writings (1912–1917)*, ed. Sarojini Naidu (Madras: GA Natesan and Co., 1918).

52 'Jinnah's Presidential Address, All-India Muslim League, Fifteenth Session, Lahore, 24–25 May 1924', in A.M. Zaidi (ed.), *Evolution of Muslim Political Thought in India*, vol. 2 (New Delhi: Michiko and Panjathan, 1975), 270.

53 'Jinnah on Nehru Committee Recommendations', in Shan Mohammad (ed.), *Indian Muslims: A Documentary Record (1900–1947)*, vol. 9, 1980, 91.

54 Jinnah, 'Jinnah's Presidential Address to the Muslim League, Lucknow, December 1916', 46.

55 Francis Robinson, *The Muslim World in Modern South Asia: Power, Authority, Knowledge* (Albany: State University of New York Press, 2021), 292.

56 Lala Lajpat Rai, 'Presidential Address to the Bombay Hindu Mahasabha Conference, Supplement to The People, 5 December 1925', in *CWLLR*, vol. 11, 2008 [hereafter cited as 'Presidential Address to the Bombay Hindu Mahasabha Conference'], 272.

57 Lajpat Rai, 'Presidential Address, Eighth Hindu Mahasabha', 229.

58 Lajpat Rai, 'Presidential Address to the Bombay Hindu Mahasabha Conference', 272; Lajpat Rai, 'Hindu–Muslim Unity', 172–78.

59 Chapter 14, pp. 274–75.

60 Neeti Nair, *Changing Homelands: Hindu Politics and the Partition of India* (Cambridge, MA: Harvard University Press, 2011), 78.

61 Lajpat Rai, 'Hindu–Muslim Unity', 172–73.

62 Lajpat Rai, 'Presidential Address to the Bombay Hindu Mahasabha Conference', 271.

63 Lajpat Rai, 272.

64 That no majority would be reduced to a minority was reiterated by Jinnah during the discussions of the Reforms Enquiry Committee in 1924. See Page, *Prelude to Partition*, 117.

65 Lajpat Rai, 'Presidential Address to the Bombay Hindu Mahasabha Conference', 273–74.

66 Lajpat Rai, 273.

67 Lala Lajpat Rai, 'Sir Abdur Rahim's Speech and Mr. Jinnah's Comments, The People, 24 January 1926', in *CWLLR*, vol. 12, 2009 [hereafter cited as 'Abdur Rahim's Speech and Jinnah's Comments'], 323.

68 'Presidential Address of Sir Abdur Rahim, Seventeenth Session of the All India Muslim League, Aligarh, 30 December 1925' in Shan Mohammad (ed.), *Indian Muslims: A Documentary Record (1900–1947)*, vol. 8 (Meerut: Meenakshi Prakashan, 1980), 41.

69 Syed Sharifuddin Pirzada, ed., 'Presidential Address of Sir Abdur Rahim, All-India Muslim League, Seventeenth Session,

Aligarh, December 1925', in *Foundations of Pakistan: All-India Muslim League Documents, 1906–1947*, vol. 2 (Karachi: National Publishing House, 1970), 41, 43.

70 Pirzada, 41, 46.

71 Abdur Rahim is an under-studied politician, but for a little more information, see Pradip Kumar Datta, 'War over Music: The Riots of 1926 in Bengal', *Social Scientist*, no. No. 6/7 (1990): 47; Ayesha Jalal and Anil Seal, 'Alternative to Partition: Muslim Politics between the Wars', *Modern Asian Studies* 15, no. 03 (1981): 428–29. In 1925, the year he presided over the Muslim League, Rahim had played his part in the polarization of Bengali politics along community lines, and had begun to make communally divisive appeals through the press to launch his own party for the 1926 elections. He would very soon also play an incendiary role in the riots in Calcutta in 1926 alongside his son-in-law, H.S. Suhrawardy, who would himself become famous two decades later for his role in the Great Calcutta Killings in 1946. Page, *Prelude to Partition*, 44–45. (Influenced by Gandhi, in 1947, Suhrawardy would publicly regret and take responsibility for violence in Calcutta in 1946, an act that would actively reduce communal tensions in the city. Roy, *Making Peace, Making Riots*, 233.).

72 Page, *Prelude to Partition*, 116–17.

73 Lajpat Rai, 'Two Wrongs?', 267.

74 Lajpat Rai, 'Abdur Rahim's Speech and Jinnah's Comments', 324.

75 Lajpat Rai, 325–26.

76 'All India Muslim League, Fifteenth Session' in A.M. Zaidi (ed.), *Evolution of Muslim Political Thought in India*, vol. 2 (New Delhi: Michiko and Panjathan, 1975), 272–73.

77 All-India Muslim League, 'Resolutions Passed at the Seventeenth Session', in Syed Sharifuddin Pirzada (ed.), *Foundations of Pakistan: All-India Muslim League Documents, 1906–1947*, vol. 2 (Karachi: National Publishing House, 1970), 272–73.

78 Lajpat Rai, 'Abdur Rahim's Speech and Jinnah's Comments', 325.

79 Lajpat Rai, 324.

80 Lajpat Rai, 324.

81 Lajpat Rai, 'On Sarojini Naidu's Criticism', 261.

82 Pirzada, 'Presidential Address of Sir Abdur Rahim, All-India Muslim League, Seventeenth Session, Aligarh, December 1925', 42.

83 Lajpat Rai, 'Presidential Address, Eighth Hindu Mahasabha', 230.

84 Lajpat Rai, 'Two Wrongs?', 267.

85 Lajpat Rai, 'Presidential Address to the Bombay Hindu Mahasabha Conference', 272.

86 See Chapter 16, p. 330.

87 M.K. Gandhi, 'Hindu–Muslim Question, Young India, 19 February 1925', in *CWMG*, vol. 26 (Ahmedabad: Navajivan Trust, 1965), 162.

88 Gandhi, 162.

89 Gandhi, 160–63; 'Hindu–Muslim Tension: Causes and Cure, Young India, 29 May 1924', in *CWMG*, vol. 24 (Ahmedabad: Navajivan Trust, 1965), 153.

90 B.R. Nanda, *The Nehrus: Motilal and Jawaharlal*, Oxford India Paperbacks (New Delhi: Oxford University Press, 2008), chaps 23–26; J.C. Johari, ed., 'Battle for Liberty, Presidential Address by Sarojini Naidu at Kanpur Congress, 26–28 December 1925', in *Voices of Indian National Movement*, vol. 9.1 (New Delhi: Akashdeep Publishing House, 1993); J.C. Johari, ed., 'A Charter of Constructive Program Presidential Address by Srinivas Iyenger at Gauhati Congress, 26–28 December 1926', in *Voices of Indian National Movement*, vol. 9.1 (New Delhi: Akashdeep Publishing House, 1993); Subhas Chandra Bose, *The Indian Struggle, 1920–1942* (Delhi; New York: Oxford University Press, 1997), chaps 4–8; Hindol Sengupta, *The Man Who Saved India: Sardar Patel and His Idea of India* (Gurgaon: Penguin/Viking, 2018), chap. 5; Rajmohan Gandhi, *Patel: A Life*, 1991, 2–3.

91 Ayesha Jalal, *Self and Sovereignty: Individual and Community in South Asian Islam since 1850* (London: Routledge, 2002), 300–301; For the original, see Shan Mohammad, ed., 'Delhi Muslim Proposals, 20 March 1927', in *Indian Muslims: A Documentary Record (1900–1947)*, vol. 8 (Meerut: Meenakshi Prakashan, 1980).

92 Lajpat Rai, 'Abdur Rahim's Speech and Jinnah's Comments', 325.

93 Lajpat Rai, 325–26.

94 Ayesha Jalal, *Self and Sovereignty: Individual and Community in South Asian Islam since 1850* (London: Routledge, 2002), 435; Ayesha Jalal and Anil Seal, 'Alternative to Partition: Muslim Politics between the Wars', *Modern Asian Studies* 15, no. 03 (1981): 425–26, 439; Nonica Datta, *Forming an Identity: A Social History of the Jats* (New Delhi: Oxford University Press, 1999), 8, 82, 95, 109–10, 114–15, 120–21, 125, 148.

95 Hugh Owen, 'Negotiating the Lucknow Pact', *The Journal of Asian Studies* 31, no. 03 (1972): 565.

96 Neeti Nair, *Changing Homelands: Hindu Politics and the Partition of India* (Cambridge, MA: Harvard University Press, 2011), 4; Hugh Owen, 'Negotiating the Lucknow Pact', *The Journal of Asian Studies* 31, no. 03 (1972): 565; Ayesha Jalal and Anil Seal, 'Alternative to Partition: Muslim Politics between the Wars', *Modern Asian Studies* 15, no. 03 (1981): 430–31.

97 Lala Lajpat Rai, 'From Ravi to Brahmaputra, The Bombay Chronicle, 21/23/26 May 1925', in *CWLLR*, vol. 11, 2008, 241–45. As mentioned earlier in this book, this image of the medieval 'Muslim' invasions and subsequent 'Muslim' rule over Hindus is a ruler-centric, elite history that distorts our understanding. It obscures the fact that the majority of medieval India's Muslims were indigenous low castes and tribals, who were poor and marginal, had no access to political power, and were not beneficiaries of Muslim rule. Raziuddin Aquil, *Lovers of God: Sufism and the Politics of Islam in Medieval India* (New Delhi: Oxford University Press, 2020), 32; Hilal Ahmed,

'Hindutva Opponents Must Go beyond Muslims as Invaders vs Legal Citizens Categories', ThePrint, 30 August 2021, https://theprint.in/opinion/hindutva-opponents-must-go-beyond-muslims-as-invaders-vs-legal-citizens-categories/724400/.

98 Lajpat Rai, 'Concluding Speech at the Bombay Hindu Mahasabha Conference', 283–84.

99 Lajpat Rai, 'Concluding Speech at the Bombay Hindu Mahasabha Conference', 283.

100 Pirzada, 'Presidential Address of Sir Abdur Rahim, All-India Muslim League, Seventeenth Session, Aligarh, December 1925', 41–42; Shan Mohammad, ed., 'Tanzim Conference, Aligarh, 29 December 1925', in *Indian Muslims: A Documentary Record (1900–1947)*, vol. 8 (Meerut: Meenakshi Prakashan, 1980), 113.

101 Jalal, *Self and Sovereignty*, 267.

102 Jalal, 276.

103 A political culture which valorized power, domination and violence would flourish among extremist *sections* of Muslim and Hindu middle-class circles in the 1930s and 1940s. Inspired by fascism and dismissive about a democratic politics of negotiation, they saw the world in Social Darwinian terms, as an apocalyptic struggle and war for the 'survival of the fittest'. See Markus Daechsel, *The Politics of Self-Expression: The Urdu Middle-Class Milieu in Mid-Twentieth Century India and Pakistan* (London; New York: Routledge, 2006), 1–2, 10, 18. 42–51. Punjab became an important centre of this new form of radical politics, and in the late 1930s saw extremist Muslim pamphlets call for the establishment of Muslim supremacy in India (56–59.). Calls for Muslim or Hindu Raj reflected a politics whose main aim was to demonstrate a will to be free from the rule of the Other and a will to rule and exercise power over the Other (38, 58–59, 69, 76–79.). Research on this radical political culture by historian Markus Daechsel focuses on the 1930s and 1940s. However, as we saw in Chapter 13, fears about Muslim and Hindu Raj were beginning to be expressed by

some sections during the Khilafat/non-cooperation movement itself. This perhaps shows that some sections among both communities, however small, had begun to also express ideas about instituting Muslim and Hindu rule or domination. Indeed, Daechsel notes that this new radical politics had begun to take root in the 'climate of despair' that followed the collapse of the movement (35.). Flickers of such politics had likely begun to appear in *particular* organs of the Punjabi Muslim press in the mid-1920s. Lajpat Rai was probably reacting to these.

104 Lajpat Rai, 'Presidential Address to the Bombay Hindu Mahasabha Conference', 271–72.

105 Lajpat Rai, 'Presidential Address, Eighth Hindu Mahasabha', 230.

106 Lajpat Rai, 231. For original see *Report of the North-West Frontier Enquiry Committee and Minutes of Dissent* (Delhi, 1924), 74, 122–23.

107 Cited in Sengupta, *The Man Who Saved India*, 230.

108 Vikram Sampath, *Savarkar: A Contested Legacy, 1924–66* (Gurugram: Viking, 2021), 159.

109 *Report of the North-West Frontier Enquiry Committee and Minutes of Dissent*, 68–83, 147–54.

110 Amar Sohal, *The Muslim Secular*, chap. 4.

111 See Chapter 14, pp. 266–70.

112 See Chapter 15, pp. 295–301.

113 Gandhi, 'Hindu–Muslim Question', 162.

114 Jawaharlal Nehru, 'Evolution of British Policy in India, September 1927', in *Selected Works of Jawaharlal Nehru*, ed. Sarvepalli Gopal, vol. 2, 1 (Delhi: B.R. Publishing Corporation, 1974), 361.

115 Bose, *The Indian Struggle, 1920–1942*, chaps 4–8; Subhas Chandra Bose, *Subhas Chandra Bose Netaji: Collected Works*, ed. Sisir Kumar Bose, vol. 2 (Calcutta: Netaji Research Bureau, 1994), 129.

116 Sugata Bose, *His Majesty's Opponent: Subhas Chandra Bose and India's Struggle Against Empire* (Harvard University Press, 2011), 54.

117 Muslim leaders calling for the organization and physical training of Muslims as part of tanzim also rationalized this as a response to the Mahasabha's sangathan and in terms of 'self-defence'. See A.M. Zaidi, ed., 'Presidential Address of Syed Reza Ali, All-India Muslim League, Bombay, 30-1 December 1924', in *Evolution of Muslim Political Thought in India*, vol. 2 (New Delhi: Michiko & Panjathan, 1975), 302; Pirzada, 'Presidential Address of Sir Abdur Rahim, All-India Muslim League, Seventeenth Session, Aligarh, December 1925', 42; Mohammad, 'Tanzim Conference, 1925', 113.

Chapter 18

1 Lala Lajpat Rai, 'Presidential Address to the Eighth Session of the Hindu Mahasabha, Calcutta, Amrita Bazar Patrika, 12 April 1925', in *CWLLR*, vol. 11, 2008, 232; Lala Lajpat Rai, 'Two Wrongs?, The Tribune, 10 November 1925', in *CWLLR*, vol. 11, 2008, 267.

2 By 'sub-political' realm, I mean a domain of life existing or seen as existing *below* the political domain.

3 Lajpat Rai, 'Presidential Address, Eighth Hindu Mahasabha', 233; 'The Need for Hindu Organisation, The Bombay Chronicle, 5 January 1925', in *CWLLR*, vol. 11, 2008, 206.

4 Neeti Nair, *Changing Homelands: Hindu Politics and the Partition of India* (Cambridge, MA: Harvard University Press, 2011), 70–71.

5 Nair, *Changing Homelands*, 52.

6 See Chapter 16, pp. 305–07.

7 Nair, *Changing Homelands*, 70.

8 David Page, *Prelude to Partition: The Indian Muslims and the Imperial System of Control, 1920–1932* (New Delhi: Oxford University Press, 1982), 74, 85; Pradip Kumar Datta, 'War over

Music: The Riots of 1926 in Bengal', *Social Scientist*, no. No. 6/7 (1990): 38.

9 Margrit Pernau, 'Riots, Masculinity, and the Desire for Passions: North India 1917–1946', *South Asian History and Culture* 12, no. 2–3 (2021): 244–60; William Gould, *Religion and Conflict in Modern South Asia* (Cambridge University Press, 2011), 69.

10 Lala Lajpat Rai, 'Reflections on the Lahore Riots, Lahore, The People, 15 May 1927', in *CWLLR*, vol. 13, 2010, 264.

11 Ayesha Jalal and Anil Seal, 'Alternative to Partition: Muslim Politics between the Wars', *Modern Asian Studies* 15, no. 03 (1981): 415–54; Page, *Prelude to Partition*, 41–42. For Muslim politics in Bihar, see Mohammad Sajjad, *Muslim Politics in Bihar: Changing Contours* (New Delhi, India; Oxfordshire, England: Routledge, 2014).

12 Jalal and Seal, 'Alternative to Partition', 419–23.

13 Soheb Niazi, 'Sayyids and Social Stratification of Muslims in Colonial India: Genealogy and Narration of the Past in Amroha', *Journal of the Royal Asiatic Society*, 3, 2020, 15; Nandini Gooptu, *The Politics of the Urban Poor in Early Twentieth-Century India* (Cambridge; New York: Cambridge University Press, 2001), 265–66; Khalid A. Ansari, 'Pasmanda Politics and Muslim (Minority) Discourse in India', in *Gender, Caste and the Imagination of Equality*, ed. Anupama Rao, 2018, 311–12. For a quick overview of Momin politics in the 1930s and 1940s and its opposition to the Muslim League, see 'How IndianPolitics Uses Hindu vs Muslim To Cover Up Caste', 20 August 2021, https://www.youtube.com/watch?v=SZDCYGVm5E4&ab_channel=IndiaInk. As historian Nita Kumar has shown, the term 'momin' means honest and true to tradition, faithful and honourable, and refers to the ordinary good, pious and god-fearing people. See as cited in Gooptu, *Politics of the Urban Poor*, 266.

14 Gould, *Religion and Conflict in Modern South Asia*, 93.

15 V. Geetha and S.V. Rajadurai, *Towards a Non-Brahmin Millennium: From Iyothee Thass to Periyar* (Calcutta: Bhatkal & Sen, 1998), 321.

16 Lala Lajpat Rai, 'Exhortation to Hindus to Give Up Passive Mentality, The Bombay Chronicle, 6 April 1927', in *CWLLR*, vol. 13, 2010, 211.

17 For details, see Yoginder Sikand, 'Arya Shuddhi and Muslim Tabligh: Muslim Reactions to Arya Samaj Proselytization (1923–30)', in *Religious Conversion in India: Modes, Motivations, and Meanings*, ed. Rowena Robinson and Sathianathan Clarke (New Delhi: Oxford University Press, 2003), 106–07.

18 Sikand, 106–07.

19 C.S. Adcock, *The Limits of Tolerance: Indian Secularism and the Politics of Religious Freedom* (New York: Oxford University Press, 2013), 148.

20 Sikand, 'Arya Shuddhi and Muslim Tabligh', 103.

21 J.T.F. Jordens, *Swāmī Shraddhānanda: His Life and Causes* (Delhi: Oxford University Press, 1981), 164.

22 Nair, *Changing Homelands*, 109, 292 n. 54.

23 Jordens, *Swāmī Shraddhānanda*, 66; Ayesha Jalal, *Self and Sovereignty: Individual and Community in South Asian Islam since 1850* (London: Routledge, 2002), 295. As Savarkar's most recent biographer, Vikram Sampath, argues, the 1920s also saw the publication of books and pamphlets that were offensive about Prophet Mohammed. These included *Vichitra Jeevan* (Weird Life) by Pandit Kalicharan Sharma (Agra, 1923), *Rangila Rasul* (The Colourful Prophet) by Pandit Chamupati (Lahore, 1924), and *Sair-i-Dozakh* by Devi Saran Sharma (Amritsar, 1927). Sampath writes: 'that many of the writers were, publishers, or distributors were directly or remotely linked with the Arya Samaj made matters worse for the communal situation in the country. If *shuddhi* was the main area of grouse, these publications added fuel to the communal fire . . . the backlash of the *shuddhi* movement was what ultimately led to the assassination of Swami

Shraddhanand'. Vikram Sampath, *Savarkar: A Contested Legacy, 1924–66* (Gurugram: Viking, 2021), 92–93.

24 M.K. Gandhi, 'Speech at A.I.C.C Meeting, Gauhati, Hindi Navajivan, 6 January 1927', in *CWMG*, vol. 37, n.d., 434–37, https://www.gandhiashramsevagram.org/gandhi-literature/mahatma-gandhi-collected-works-volume-37.pdf.

25 M.K. Gandhi, 'Resolution and Speech at Congress Session, Gauhati, 26 December 1926', in *CWMG*, vol. 37, n.d., 443, https://www.gandhiashramsevagram.org/gandhi-literature/mahatma-gandhi-collected-works-volume-37.pdf.

26 M.K. Gandhi, 'Shraddhanandji — The Martyr, Young India, 30 December 1926', in *CWMG*, vol. 37, 457, https://www.gandhiashramsevagram.org/gandhi-literature/mahatma-gandhi-collected-works-volume-37.pdf.

27 M.K. Gandhi, 'Shraddhanandji — The Martyr, Young India, 30 December 1926', in *CWMG*, vol. 37, 455-57, https://www.gandhiashramsevagram.org/gandhi-literature/mahatma-gandhi-collected-works-volume-37.pdf.

28 Shan Mohammad, ed., 'Eighteenth Session of the All-India Muslim League, Delhi, 29 December 1926', in *Indian Muslims: A Documentary Record (1900-1947)*, vol. 8 (Meerut: Meenakshi Prakashan, 1980), 191.

29 Mohammad, 208-09.

30 Shan Mohammad, ed., 'Press Version of the League Session, Aligarh Mail, January 1927', in *Indian Muslims: A Documentary Record (1900–1947)*, vol. 8 (Meerut: Meenakshi Prakashan, 1980) [hereafter cited as 'Press Version'], 217.

31 Shan Mohammad, ed., 'Campaign of Vilification, Aligarh Mail, January 1927', in *Indian Muslims: A Documentary Record (1900–1947)*, vol. 8 (Meerut: Meenakshi Prakashan, 1980), 227.

32 Sampath, *Savarkar: A Contested Legacy*, 87–89, 91–92. To make his argument about Gandhi's softness towards Muslims in the face of Shraddhanand's assassination, Sampath also draws on Ambedkar's impressions fourteen years later in 1940. A closer

analysis of Gandhi's statements after the event challenges Ambedkar's reading as much as Savarkar's.

33 Lala Lajpat Rai, 'Determination to Protect Interests of Non-Hindus, The Tribune, 30 December 1926', in *CWLLR*, vol. 12, 2009, 368.

34 Lajpat Rai, 368.

35 M.K. Gandhi, 'Letter to Mazharul Haque, 1 January 1927', in CWMG, vol. 37, n.d., 482–83, https://www.gandhiashramsevagram.org/gandhi-literature/mahatma-gandhi-collected-works-volume-37.pdf.

36 Sajjad, *Muslim Politics in Bihar: Changing Contours*, 112.

37 Lala Lajpat Rai, 'Need for Hindus to Organise Themselves, The Bombay Chronicle, 19 April 1927', in *CWLLR*, vol. 13, 2010, 215.

38 Mohammad, 'Press Version', 1980, 227.

39 Shan Mohammad, ed., 'Special Session of the All-India Khilafat Conference, Delhi, 8-9 May 1926', in *Indian Muslims: A Documentary Record (1900–1947)*, vol. 8 (Meerut: Meenakshi Prakashan, 1980) [hereafter cited as 'Special Session, Khilafat Conference, Delhi, 1926'], 130.

40 Lajpat Rai, 'Determination to Protect Interests of Non-Hindus', 368.

41 Lajpat Rai, 368.

42 Feroz Chand, *Lajpat Rai: Life and Work* (New Delhi: Publications Division, Ministry of Information and Broadcasting, Government of India, 1978), 493–94. The young Chand had been closely associated with Rai during the last eight years of his life, working with him in the Servants of the People Society founded by Rai and inaugurated by Gandhi in Lahore in November 1921. Chand, viii–ix, xiii, xiv.

43 Charu Gupta, 'Articulating Hindu Masculinity and Femininity: "Shuddhi" and "Sangathan" Movements in United Provinces in the 1920s', *Economic and Political Weekly*, 1998, 730. The following three paragraphs draw heavily on Gupta's research.

44 Gupta, 730.

45 Gupta, 731.

46 Gupta, 730.

47 Gupta, 731.

48 Gupta, 731.

49 Gupta, 731.

50 Gupta, 731.

51 Gupta, 731.

52 Gupta, 731.

53 Gupta, 731.

54 Gupta, 730–31. The 1920s saw women beginning to mobilize in their own right. These years also saw efforts, evident in popular journal literature and political organizations, to assert patriarchal control. Men of the community attempted to, through a 'totalizing paternalism', control women in different aspects of life. This was true of sections of both the Hindu and the Muslim communities. Drawing on Gupta's research, scholars have argued that the assertion of Hindu communal identity through sangathan was linked to male anxieties about domestic control. Gould, *Religion and Conflict in Modern South Asia*, 114–15.

55 Gupta, 'Articulating Hindu Masculinity', 730–31. Also see, Pradip Kumar Datta, '"Dying Hindus": Production of Hindu Communal Common Sense in Early 20th Century Bengal', *Economic and Political Weekly* 28, No., no. 25 (1993): 1314–15; Nandini Gooptu, 'The Urban Poor and Militant Hinduism in Early Twentieth-Century Uttar Pradesh', *Modern Asian Studies* 31, no. 4 (1997): 912.

56 Gupta, 'Articulating Hindu Masculinity', 731.

57 Pradip Kumar Datta, *Carving Blocs: Communal Ideology in Early Twentieth-Century Bengal* (New Delhi: Oxford University Press, 1999), chap. 4. The following three paragraphs draw heavily on Datta's research.

58 Datta, 'War over Music: The Riots of 1926 in Bengal', 46; *Carving Blocs*, 185.

59 Datta, *Carving Blocs*, 171.

60 Datta, 150.

61 Datta, 151.

62 Datta, 152.
63 Datta, 237.
64 Datta, 194, 214.
65 Datta, 184–87.
66 Datta, 196.
67 Datta, 194–95.
68 Datta, 212.
69 I am thankful to P.K. Datta for clarifying this point.
70 Datta, *Carving Blocs*, 197, 210–11.
71 Datta, 157–63.
72 Datta, 164.
73 Datta, 171–74.
74 Datta, 178–82. For details of the Bengal Pact, see Chapter 14, p. 276, n. 142 (p. 636).
75 Jason Stanley, *How Fascism Works: The Politics of Us and Them*, First edition (New York: Random House, 2018), 128.
76 Stanley, 129.
77 Stanley, 129.
78 Stanley, 129–30.
79 Jonathan Hyslop, 'White Working-Class Women and the Invention of Apartheid:'Purified'Afrikaner Nationalist Agitation for Legislation against 'Mixed'Marriages, 1934–39', *The Journal of African History* 36, no. 1 (1995): 57–81.
80 Stanley, *How Fascism Works*, 127–28, 131, 135, 139.
81 Datta, *Carving Blocs*, chap. 4.
82 Datta, 154; Datta, '"Dying Hindus"', 1314; Gupta, 'Articulating Hindu Masculinity', 730.
83 Lajpat Rai, 'Need for Hindus to Organise Themselves', 214–15.
84 Syed Sharifuddin Pirzada, ed., 'Presidential Address of Sir Abdur Rahim, All-India Muslim League, Seventeenth Session, Aligarh, December 1925', in *Foundations of Pakistan: All-India Muslim League Documents, 1906–1947*, vol. 2 (Karachi: National Publishing House, 1970), 41–42; Shan Mohammad, ed., 'Tanzim Conference, Aligarh, 29 December 1925', in *Indian Muslims: A Documentary Record (1900–1947)*, vol. 8 (Meerut: Meenakshi Prakashan, 1980), 113. See Chapter 17, p. 354.

85 Jalal, *Self and Sovereignty*, 267. Violent rhetoric demanding that the 'beards and moustaches of Muslims should be pulled out and ... their houses and shops ... set on fire' continued into the late 1920s and beyond. Jalal, 314. Rhetoric about how 'peace in the country would only be attained when other religions had been absorbed in Hinduism' continued as well. 315.

86 Sikand, 'Arya Shuddhi and Muslim Tabligh', 102.

87 Sikand, 104.

88 Sikand, 103–04, 110.

89 Mohammad, 'Special Session, Khilafat Conference, Delhi, 1926', 128–29.

90 Mohammad, 130.

91 Mohammad, 131.

92 Mohammad, 129, 134.

93 Sumit Sarkar, *Modern India: 1886-1947* (Delhi: Macmillian, 1983), 239–42.

94 Sarkar, 244–47.

95 Sarkar, 247–51.

96 Sarkar, 251–52; Kama Maclean, *A Revolutionary History of Interwar India: Violence, Image, Voice and Text* (New York: Oxford University Press, 2015), 28.

97 Nair, *Changing Homelands*, 112–13. As Bhagat Singh would clarify later, the revolution he dreamt of was one where India would be free and organized along socialist lines, where labourers, peasants, weavers, masons, smiths and carpenters would no longer remain the exploited class. 116–17, 125.

98 Mark Juergensmeyer, *Religious Rebels in the Punjab: The Ad Dharm Challenge to Caste*, New Delhi (Berkeley: Navayana Publishing, 2009), 24–26; Sarkar, *Modern India*, 158–68, 242–44; Gail Omvedt, *Ambedkar: Towards an Enlightened India* (London: Penguin UK, 2008), 27–32; Geetha and Rajadurai, *Towards a Non-Brahmin Millennium*, chaps 2–7; Gooptu, *Politics of the Urban Poor*, 265; Ansari, 'Pasmanda Politics and Muslim (Minority) Discourse in India', 311–12.

99 Lajpat Rai, 'Presidential Address, Eighth Hindu Mahasabha', 226.

100 Lala Lajpat Rai, 'Ahimsa Paramodharmah, The People, 18 October 1925', in *CWLLR*, vol. 11, 2008, 406.

101 Lajpat Rai, 406.

102 Lajpat Rai, 407.

103 Patrick Olivelle, *The Āśrama System: The History and Hermeneutics of a Religious Institution* (New York ; Oxford: Oxford University Press, 1993), 53–55.

104 Olivelle, 131–32, 165.

105 Lajpat Rai, 'Ahimsa Paramodharmah', 407.

106 Lajpat Rai, 'Presidential Address, Eighth Hindu Mahasabha', 227.

107 M.K. Gandhi, 'Hindu–Muslim Unity, Young India, 18 September 1924', in *Communal Unity* (Ahmedabad: Navajivan Publishing House), 1949, 80.

108 M.K. Gandhi, 'Hindu-Muslim Tension: Causes and Cure, Young India, 29 May 1924', in *CWMG*, vol. 24 (Ahmedabad: Navajivan Trust, 1965); 'Notes, Young India, 18 December 1924', in *CWMG*, vol. 25, 1965, 436–37; 'Hindu–Muslim Unity, 18 September 1924', 80. Also see Chapter 14, pp. 280, 282–83.

109 Parmananda, *Mahamana Madan Mohan Malaviya: An Historical Biography*, vol. 1 (Varanasi: Malaviya Adhyayan Sansthan: Banaras Hindu University, 1985), vol. 2, 626, 651.

110 Gooptu, 'The Urban Poor and Militant Hinduism in Early Twentieth-Century Uttar Pradesh', 906–10; Prabhu Bapu, *Hindu Mahasabha in Colonial North India, 1915–1930: Constructing Nation and History*, Routledge Studies in South Asian History (London: Routledge, 2013), 83–84.

111 Gupta, 'Articulating Hindu Masculinity', 730.

112 Lala Lajpat Rai, 'From Ravi to Brahmaputra, The Bombay Chronicle, 21/23/26 May 1925', in *CWLLR*, vol. 11, 2008, 241–45.

113 See Chapter 7, pp. 117–20.

114 Lala Lajpat Rai, 'From Ravi to Brahmaputra, The Bombay Chronicle, 21/23/26 May 1925', in *CWLLR*, vol. 11, 2008, 241–45.

115 Lajpat Rai, 'Exhortation to Hindus to Give Up Passive Mentality', 211; Lala Lajpat Rai, 'Militancy No Crime, The Tribune, 15 April 1927', in *CWLLR*, vol. 13, 2010, 213–14; Lala Lajpat Rai, 'Presidential Address to the Provincial Hindu Conference, Sind, The Hindustan Times, 5 May 1927', in *CWLLR*, vol. 13, 2010, 219.

116 Christophe Jaffrelot, ed., 'Madan Mohan Malaviya: Presidential Speech as Reported (1923)', in *Hindu Nationalism: A Reader* (Princeton: Princeton University Press, 2007), 38–39.

117 'Presidential Address of Sir Abdur Rahim, Seventeenth Session of the All India Muslim League, Aligarh, 30 December 1925', in Shan Mohammad (ed.), *Indian Muslims: A Documentary Record (1900–1947)*, vol. 8, 1980, 115; 'Tanzim Conference, Aligarh, 29 December 1925', in Shan Mohammad (ed.), *Indian Muslims: A Documentary Record (1900–1947)*, vol. 8, 1980, 113.

118 John Zavos, *The Emergence of Hindu Nationalism in India* (Oxford: Oxford University Press, 2000), 189; Christophe Jaffrelot, *The Hindu Nationalist Movement and Indian Politics: 1925 to the 1990s* (New Delhi: Penguin Books, 1999), 36; Gooptu, 'The Urban Poor and Militant Hinduism in Early Twentieth-Century Uttar Pradesh', 905.

119 Zavos, *Emergence of Hindu Nationalism*, 189; Jaffrelot, *Hindu Nationalist Movement*, 36; Gooptu, 'The Urban Poor and Militant Hinduism in Early Twentieth-Century Uttar Pradesh', 905.

120 Lajpat Rai, 'Presidential Address, Eighth Hindu Mahasabha', 227.

121 Joseph Alter, 'Somatic Nationalism: Indian Wrestling and Militant Hinduism', *Modern Asian Studies* 28, no. 3 (1994): 572–76.

122 Bapu, *Hindu Mahasabha in Colonial North India, 1915–1930*, 83.

123 Bapu, 83.

124 See Chapter 4, pp. 70–3.

125 Sikata Banerjee, *Make Me a Man!: Masculinity, Hinduism, and Nationalism in India*, SUNY Series in Religious Studies (Albany, NY: State University of New York Press, 2005), 51–57; Chetan Bhatt, *Hindu Nationalism: Origins, Ideologies and Modern Myths* (Oxford: Berg, 2001), 89–91.

126 Banerjee, *Make Me a Man*, 51–57; Bhatt, *Origins*, 89–91.

127 Banerjee, *Make Me a Man*, 51–57; Vinayak Chaturvedi, 'Violence as Civility: VD Savarkar and the Mahatma's Assassination', *South Asian History and Culture* 11, no. 3 (2020): 239–53; Bhatt, *Origins*, 103–04; Gyanendra Pandey, 'Hindus and Others: The Militant Hindu Construction', *Economic and Political Weekly* 26, no. 52 (1991): 3001; Shruti Kapila, *Violent Fraternity: Indian Political Thought in the Global Age* (Princeton: Princeton University Press, 2021), 91, 97–98, 104, 109, 114–16. For a glimpse into Savarkar's emphasis on the need for training in arms, rifles and guns, and how he saw Hindu militarization as relevant for a power struggle with Muslims in even a future independent India which the British had left, see Vikram Sampath, *Savarkar: Echoes from a Forgotten Past, 1883–1924* (Gurgaon: Viking, 2019), 186, 190, 204, 236, 239, 243, 245, 252.

128 Kapila, *Violent Fraternity*, 104, 115–16.

129 See Chapter 14, pp. 282–83 and Chapter 16, p. 318.

130 Gandhi, 'Hindu–Muslim Tension', 142–44; 'Hindu–Muslim Unity, 18 September 1924', 76–77; 'Question of Questions, Young India, 18 September 1924', in *CWMG*, vol. 25 (Ahmedabad: Navajivan Trust, 1965), 166–69.

131 Gandhi, 'Hindu–Muslim Tension', 142; Devji, *Impossible Indian*, 59; Gould, *Religion and Conflict in Modern South Asia*, 117; Karuna Mantena, 'Another Realism: The Politics of Gandhian Nonviolence', *American Political Science Review* 106, no. 2 (2012): 460.

132 A person engaged in Gandhi's method of *satyagraha* or truth-based, non-violent resistance.

133 Arafaat Valiani, *Militant Publics in India: Physical Culture and Violence in the Making of a Modern Polity* (Palgrave Macmillan, 2011), 12–13.

134 By 'bio-political' vision, I mean a political vision that relies on disciplining and training human bodies.

135 Lajpat Rai, 'Militancy No Crime', 213.

136 Chapter 14, p. 265.

137 Certainly, the conversions of Hindus by Mappilas in 1921 provided a massive fillip to the campaign to convert Malkanas en masse. It was reported that between 1923 and 1927, 1,63,000 Malkanas (of a 3,00,000 strong community) entered the Hindu fold. At the same time, to say that shuddhi among Malkanas was a response to the Mappila conversions would be slightly simplistic. Already in 1910, 1052 Malkanas were claimed to have been converted with the help of the Arya Samaj. Yoginder Sikand and Manjari Katju, 'Mass Conversions to Hinduism among Indian Muslims', *Economic and Political Weekly* 29, no. 34 (20 August 1994): 2216; Sikand, 'Arya Shuddhi and Muslim Tabligh', 103. Whatever else it was, the shuddhi of Malkanas in the 1920s was also a logical outcome of the Arya Samajist ideological framework which had always sought to preach 'Vedic' Hinduism to India's Muslim population. The earliest recorded shuddhi of a born Muslim was undertaken by Swami Dayanand Saraswati in 1877. This was followed by a 'few more such individual conversions', after which, the first decade of the twentieth century witnessed Arya Samajist attempts at mass conversions of entire Muslim *biradris* or groups. Arya Samajists had, then, largely concentrated their efforts on 'neo-Muslim' groups in Rajasthan and the western United Provinces. Sikand, 102–03. They converted groups like the Sheikhs of Larkana (Sind), the Subrai Lubanas of Ludhiana (Punjab) and the Maiwaris of Ajmer (Rajputana), many of whom followed a mix of Hindu and Islamic practices. Often such group conversions involved urging these groups to renounce Islamic customs rather

than preaching Hindu religious knowledge to them. Sikand and Katju, 'Mass Conversions', 2215. In the 1920s, apart from Malkanas, the Arya Samaj also carried out shuddhi conversions among the Muslim Jats of Rohtak, Haryana (Punjab). This attempt, however, proved unsuccessful since Hindu Jats refused to accept them as social equals. The group was eventually reconverted back to Islam by tabligh organizations. Sikand and Katju, 2216. The Samaj was more successful in the de-Islamicization and fuller Hinduization of groups on the margins of caste Hindu society, such as the Bhangis (sweepers) of Jodhpur, who although non-Muslim had practised many Islamic customs and practices. Sikand and Katju, 2217. Interestingly, in post-Independence India, mass conversion drives among Muslim Mer Rajputs of Rajasthan have been undertaken by the Vishwa Hindu Parishad (VHP). Although considered a gross exaggeration, the VHP claims to have converted 47,000 mers, which in turn spurred efforts by Islamic organizations like the Jamiat to reconvert them to Islam. Conversions of Muslims were also undertaken in Gujarat and UP. Sikand and Katju, 2218.

138 The successful shuddhi of Malkanas notwithstanding, Hindu Rajputs apparently do not inter-marry Malkanas to this day. Sikand and Katju, 'Mass Conversions', 2216. Interestingly, it was in response to the shuddhi campaign that, in mid-1923, the Jami'at-i-Ulama-i-Hind, the organization of mostly reformist Deobandi ulema, set up 'The Department for the Propagation and Protection of Islam'. Sikand, 'Arya Shuddhi and Muslim Tabligh', 114. It despatched ulema to areas inhabited by 'neo-Muslims' like the Malkanas, where they established mosques and schools. Here, they aimed to counter what they saw as Arya attempts to take advantage of the poverty of neo-Muslims by offering them monetary inducements. Sikand, 114–15. The Tablighi Jama'at, which over time would evolve into the largest Islamic movement in the world, active in 200 countries, also emerged in the wake of the shuddhi movement

as a means to counter it. Sikand, 115. It largely eschewed conversion of non-Muslims and concentrated on making Muslims better Muslims. See Ziya Us Salam, *Inside the Tablighi Jamaat* (HarperCollins, 2020), 66, 151, 154–55. The Deendar Anjuman (Religious Association) was also founded in 1924 as a response to the Arya shuddhi campaign. Sikand, 'Arya Shuddhi and Muslim Tabligh', 108. If the aim was to reduce the influence of Islam, whether shuddhi campaign produced counter-productive outcomes is a question that needs serious consideration.

139 Sikand, 'Arya Shuddhi and Muslim Tabligh', 98–99, 104.

140 Sikand, 107, 115–16.

141 For details, see Sikand, 104, 107, 109–14. Some tabligh activists accepted Hindu holy books as divine and legitimate, but reinterpreted them to suggest that they predicted the arrival of Prophet Mohammad as 'World Teacher', whom Hindus should accept and whose community they should join. Sikand, 113–14. Here, Islam was presented as not a repudiation but a fulfilment of Hindu beliefs and scriptures. Sikand, 111–12. Most of the ulema engaged in tabligh disagreed with such 'un-Islamic' methods, and insisted that the way to counter shuddhi and lead tabligh was to preach the basics of Islam and the shariat among the population. Sikand, 114.

142 Sikand, 'Arya Shuddhi and Muslim Tabligh', 99, 111, 113, 115.

143 The following description draws heavily from Adcock, *Limits of Tolerance*, 147, 150, 152–54. It also relies on John Zavos, on whose research Adcock builds. Zavos, *Emergence of Hindu Nationalism*, 173–75.

144 For the original words, see Zavos, *Emergence of Hindu Nationalism*, 176.

145 Zavos, 175.

146 Zavos, 175–76.

147 Adcock, *Limits of Tolerance*, 154. To recall the meaning of vertical and horizontal approaches to the caste hierarchy and Hindu unity, see Chapter 9, pp. 162–63.

148 Lajpat Rai, 'Presidential Address, Eighth Hindu Mahasabha', 232–34.

149 Lajpat Rai, 'Presidential Address, Eighth Hindu Mahasabha', 234.

150 Emphasis mine.

151 Lala Lajpat Rai, 'Presidential Address to the Bombay Hindu Mahasabha Conference, Supplement to The People, 5 December 1925', in *CWLLR*, vol. 11, 2008, 277–79.

152 Lajpat Rai, 275–77.

153 Lajpat Rai, 'Presidential Address to the Bombay Hindu Mahasabha Conference', 274.

154 Sarkar, *Modern India*, 158.

155 Sarkar, 159; Geetha and Rajadurai, *Towards a Non-Brahmin Millennium*, 31.

156 Sarkar, 159, 167; Geetha and Rajadurai, *Towards a Non-Brahmin Millennium*, 137–74.

157 Sarkar, *Modern India*, 244; Geetha and Rajadurai, *Towards a Non-Brahmin Millennium*, chaps 6–7.

158 Sarkar, *Modern India*, 160.

159 Sarkar, 160–61.

160 Sarkar, *Modern India*, 244.

161 Sarkar, 162, 242.

162 Lajpat Rai, 'Presidential Address to the Bombay Hindu Mahasabha Conference', 274–75.

163 Mahars were one of the largest Untouchable castes, and widespread in Maharashtra. Gail Omvedt, a scholar who has researched the history of Mahars in Maharashtra, writes: 'Mahars were 'village servants who performed hereditary duties for the headman, higher political overlords, and dominant groups of the village. They held small allotments of land in exchange for these services, and were also agricultural labourers . . . In Bombay and Nagpur, Mahars provided a good proportion of labourers in the textile mills'. Interestingly, not only did some Mahars become wealthy farmers and acquire large landholdings but (alongside Mangs) had a tradition of

military service (serving as soldiers, squadron leaders, or guard posts) dating back to the sixteenth and seventeenth centuries. In fact, both Ambedkar's grandfather and father had held jobs related to military service. However, the military recruitment of 'Untouchables' was discontinued in 1893, two years after Ambedkar's birth, as Untouchables were excluded from definitions of 'martial races'. See Omvedt, *Ambedkar*, 2–3.

164 Zavos, *Emergence of Hindu Nationalism*, 176.

165 Zavos, 177; Adcock, *Limits of Tolerance*, 154–55.

166 Sampath, *Savarkar: A Contested Legacy*, 43–59; Chaturvedi, *Hindutva and Violence: VD Savarkar and the Politics of History*, 338–40.

167 Lajpat Rai, 'Two Wrongs?', 267.

168 See Chapter 17, p. 349.

169 Lala Lajpat Rai, 'Presidential Speech at the Punjab Provincial Hindu Conference, Lahore, The Tribune, 5 June 1925', in *CWLLR*, vol. 11, 2008, 246–47.

170 Lajpat Rai, 'Presidential Speech, Punjab Provincial Hindu Conference', in *CWLLR*, vol. 11, 2008, 246–48; 'Presidential Address, Provincial Hindu Conference of Agra', in *CWLLR*, vol. 15, 2010, 219.

171 Lajpat Rai, 248; 'Need for Hindus to Organise Themselves', 214.

172 Jyotirmaya Sharma, *Hindutva: Exploring the Idea of Hindu Nationalism* (New Delhi: Viking, 2003), 152–55.

173 Sharma, 156; Pandey, 'Hindus and Others', 3005.

174 Shruti Kapila argues that Savarkar saw violence, civil war and the shedding of blood, as a necessary condition for forging a Hindutva brotherhood. Given that Buddhism and Islam had held political sway over the Indian subcontinent for a long period of time, Savarkar found it difficult to argue that Hindus had an exclusive claim over India. Additionally, Hindus and Muslims shared common blood, and a history of inter-mixing. These facts were obstacles for anyone wishing to argue that, by virtue of their exclusive bonds of common blood, Hindus

formed an exclusive Hindu nation. And so, violence in the form of a civil war was envisioned by Savarkar as a necessary prerequisite to establish a Hindutva national brotherhood and enable its complete attachment to the Indian homeland. Kapila, *Violent Fraternity*, 104, 111–17.

175 Kapila, 117.

176 Rao, *Caste Question*, 2.

177 Rao, 48, 74; Omvedt, *Ambedkar*, 22.

178 Rao, *Caste Question*, 12–14, 40, 44–45, 47–49, 296.

179 Rao, 32–33, 46; Omvedt, *Ambedkar*, 22.

180 Geetha and Rajadurai, *Towards a Non-Brahmin Millennium*, 175.

181 Anand Teltumbde, *Dalits: Past, Present and Future* (Routledge India, 2020), 57–58; Gail Omvedt, *Understanding Caste: From Buddha to Ambedkar and Beyond* (New Delhi: Orient Blackswan, 2011), 59.

182 Geetha and Rajadurai, *Towards a Non-Brahmin Millennium*, 46, 72, 91–92, 96–98, 104, 108.

183 Geetha and Rajadurai, 63–65.

184 Ramnarayan S. Rawat, 'Colonial Archive versus Colonial Sociology: Writing Dalit History', in *Dalit Studies*, ed. Ramnarayan S. Rawat and Kusuma Satyanarayana (Duke University Press, 2016), 63. The word 'Chamar' is often used in India as a pejorative word for Dalits in general. When used with the intent to insult or humiliate, it is considered a casteist slur in violation of the Scheduled Castes and Scheduled Tribes (Prevention of Atrocities) Act, 1889. I do not use the word in a pejorative sense, but follow scholars such as Ramnarayan Rawat who use it descriptively to refer to a particular caste group among Dalits. As Rawat shows, despite their popular image as being engaged in leatherwork, Chamars are actually engaged in agriculture. See Ramnarayan S. Rawat, *Reconsidering Untouchability: Chamars and Dalit History in North India*, Contemporary Indian Studies (Bloomington: Indiana University Press, 2011), 5.

185 Gooptu, *Politics of the Urban Poor*, 148–49, 152–53; Ramnarayan Rawat, 'Genealogies of the Dalit Political: The Transformation of

Achhut from 'Untouched' to 'Untouchable' in Early Twentieth-Century North India', *The Indian Economic & Social History Review* 52, no. 3 (2015): 337.

186 The term 'Dalit', widely used today across India to refer to groups who have suffered the stigma of being considered 'untouchable', gained widespread prominence from the 1970s. But it had already begun to be used in some regions in the 1920s. See Rawat, 'Genealogies', 343; Teltumbde, *Dalits*, 15; Rao, *Caste Question*, xx–xxi.

187 Juergensmeyer, *Religious Rebels*, 24; Geetha and Rajadurai, *Towards a Non-Brahmin Millennium*, 175.

188 Adcock, *Limits of Tolerance*, 52; Raj Sekhar Basu, 'The Making of Adi Dravida Politics in Early Twentieth Century Tamil Nadu', *Social Scientist* 39, no. 7/8 (2011): 21.

189 Geetha and Rajadurai, *Towards a Non-Brahmin Millennium*, 50–51, 70, 106.

190 Geetha and Rajadurai, 176–77; Basu, 'Making of Adi Dravida Politics', 21, 38.

191 Geetha and Rajadurai, *Towards a Non-Brahmin Millennium*, 177, 233, 242.

192 Omvedt, *Understanding Caste*, 40–41; *Dalits and the Democratic Revolution: Dr. Ambedkar and the Dalit Movement in Colonial India* (New Delhi; Newbury Park: Sage Publications, 1994), 211, 218–20.

193 Adcock, *Limits of Tolerance*, 156–57; Rawat, 'Colonial Archive versus Colonial Sociology: Writing Dalit History', 68–69.

194 Gooptu, 'The Urban Poor and Militant Hinduism in Early Twentieth-Century Uttar Pradesh', 156–57; Rawat, *Reconsidering Untouchability*, 137; Adcock, *Limits of Tolerance*, 156, 159.

195 Rawat, 'Genealogies', 348; Gooptu, *Politics of the Urban Poor*, 152.

196 A Chamar leader, Swami Achhutanand had been educated through the Arya Samaj, had worked in it and left it. He adopted this title to highlight his *acchut* (Untouchable) identity.

197 Gooptu, *Politics of the Urban Poor*, 152, 158, 163–66.

Endnotes

Gooptu, 152–53.
199 Rawat, 'Genealogies', 349; Gooptu, 'The Urban Poor and Militant Hinduism in Early Twentieth-Century Uttar Pradesh', 170, 173.
200 Juergensmeyer, *Religious Rebels*, 27, 35, 37–40.
201 Juergensmeyer, 45, 50, 55. In 1909, Mangoo Ram had been contracted to work in the orchards of California. He returned to Punjab sixteen years later, in 1925, after witnessing the absence of caste discrimination in American society and among the Ghadar revolutionaries with whom he was deeply involved. 35–37, 42–44.
202 Juergensmeyer, *Religious Rebels*, 45–49, 51–52.
203 Mark Juergensmeyer, *Religion as Social Vision: The Movement against Untouchability in 20th Century Punjab* (Berkeley: University of California Press, 1982)t, 53–54.
204 Omvedt, *Ambedkar*, 26–27; Eleanor Zelliot, *From Untouchable to Dalit: Essays on the Ambedkar Movement* (New Delhi: Manohar, 1992), 66, 98.
205 Rao, *Caste Question*, 80; Omvedt, *Ambedkar*, 28.
206 Rao, *Caste Question*, 33, 77; Omvedt, *Ambedkar*, 29.
207 Omvedt, *Ambedkar*, 29–30; Rao, *Caste Question*, 77–79, 84–85; Adcock, *Limits of Tolerance*, 156.
208 Omvedt, *Ambedkar*, 27–28, 32; Rao, *Caste Question*, 50, 79–80, 83.
209 Omvedt, *Ambedkar*, 31; Rao, *Caste Question*, 79, 83.
210 Omvedt, *Ambedkar*, 31.
211 Omvedt, 36; *Understanding Caste*, 49; Zelliot, *From Untouchable to Dalit*, 101–02.
212 Juergensmeyer, *Religious Rebels*, 25–26, 136.
213 Adcock, *Limits of Tolerance*, 53, 155, 159. A confluence of several factors produced this newly assertive Dalit politics in the 1920s. These varied from region to region, but often included a combination of the following: the cumulative efforts of earlier generations of 'low caste' activists; migration to towns and cities (or sometimes, even overseas) and employment in factories, which brought

a new awareness of rights; discriminatory urban local policies that involved displacement and dispossession; increased access to education and upward social mobility which produced activist–leaders; the influence of ideas of upper-caste-led reformist organizations and eventual disillusionment with them (this was true for the Arya Samaj in UP and Punjab, and the Prarthana Samaj-backed Depressed Classes Mission in Maharashtra); and the rise of Gandhian mass nationalism and other mass struggles of workers and peasants. Juergensmeyer, *Religious Rebels*, 26–27, 36–39, 42, 52, 57; Gooptu, *Politics of the Urban Poor*, 153–57; Omvedt, *Understanding Caste*, 42–43; *Dalits and the Democratic Revolution*, 195–97, 201–04, 210, 211–12, 214, 247–48, 260–73; *Ambedkar*, 22. A strong political 'Non-Brahminism' also encouraged Dalit activism in southern and western India. Basu, 'Making of Adi Dravida Politics', 11–12, 20; Omvedt, *Dalits and the Democratic Revolution*, 196–97, 202, 205, 210, 260. In Punjab, a distinctive factor was the communal competition between upper caste organizations of the Arya Samaj, Sikh Khalsa Diwan, Ahmaddiyas and the Christian missionaries, which involved vying for lower caste allegiance, and in turn provoked lower caste thinking about their identity. Juergensmeyer, *Religious Rebels*, 22–23, 27–28, 31–32. Yet another important stimulus for Dalit mobilization were the deliberations around the Montagu–Chelmsford reforms and the reforms' eventual and full recognition in 1919 of the principle of communal representation i.e., that Indians would be granted representation communally in accordance to the numbers of Hindus, Muslims, Sikhs and others. This focused attention on the relative numbers of different religious communities, and made the so-called 'Untouchables' more aware of the political value of their numbers in a context where how they were divided up among these different religious communities had tremendous political implications. This further encouraged the formation of several new radical Dalit political organizations, which realized that their numbers, if unified and mobilized autonomously, could be politically potent. In the latter half of the 1920s, in anticipation of the next stage of reforms approached, these radical Dalit movements were asserting a non-Hindu identity and demanding separate political representation from the colonial state. Gooptu, *Politics of the Urban Poor*, 153–57; Omvedt, *Ambedkar*, 22; *Dalits and the Democratic Revolution*, 268; Juergensmeyer, *Religious Rebels*, 22–23, 29-30; Adcock, *Limits of Tolerance*, 52, 155.

214　Rao, *Caste Question*, 33, 39–40, 46, 49, 51–52, 60, 261, 270; Omvedt, *Ambedkar*, 23–25; *Dalits and the Democratic Revolution*, 13, 181–82, 202, 204–6, 209; Zelliot, *From Untouchable to Dalit*, 37, 39–41, 43, 271.

215　Omvedt, *Ambedkar*, 24; *Dalits and the Democratic Revolution*, 13, 210, 334, 387.

216　Omvedt, *Ambedkar*, 23–24.

217　Geetha and Rajadurai, *Towards a Non-Brahmin Millennium*, 129, 139–49, 155–57; Basu, 'Making of Adi Dravida Politics', 16, 18; Rochana Bajpai, *Debating Difference: Group Rights and Liberal Democracy in India* (Oxford: Oxford University Press, 2011), 35.

218　Geetha and Rajadurai, *Towards a Non-Brahmin Millennium*, 163–67.

219　Geetha and Rajadurai, 168–74, 207–08.

220　Omvedt, *Understanding Caste*, 59–60; *Dalits and the Democratic Revolution*, 214.

221　Omvedt, *Understanding Caste*, 59–60; Geetha and Rajadurai, *Towards a Non-Brahmin Millennium*, 220–25, 230, 284, 288–90, 295–97, 299–300, 302–50.

222　Lala Lajpat Rai, 'Presidential Address at the Provincial Hindu Conference of Agra, The Tribune, 30 October 1928', in *CWLLR*, vol. 15, 2010, 240.

223　Rajah had been the best-known spokesperson for 'Untouchables' until the rise of Ambedkar. Juergensmeyer, *Religion as Social Vision*, 24, 136–39, 159.

224 Lajpat Rai, 'Presidential Address, Provincial Hindu Conference of Agra', 239–41.

225 Juergensmeyer, *Religious Rebels*, 30–31.

226 Farzana Shaikh, *Community and Consensus in Islam: Muslim Representation in Colonial India, 1860–1947* (Delhi: Imprint One, 2012), 153; Shabnum Tejani, *Indian Secularism: A Social and Intellectual History, 1890-1950* (Bloomington: Indiana University Press, 2008), 202; Rao, *Caste Question*, 131, 134–35.

227 Lajpat Rai, 'Presidential Address to the Bombay Hindu Mahasabha Conference', 275.

228 Lajpat Rai, 274.

229 Broadly, 'majoritarianism' is the tendency to believe that a majority (often based on religion, culture, language, race, and so on) must have primacy in a society and the right to make decisions that affect that society. It involves believing that a majority can rule a country however it pleases, no matter its adverse effects on groups that happen to be in a minority.

230 To recall, see Chapter 17, pp. 345–58.

231 See Chapter 17, p. 342.

232 For more on the link between democracy and the politics of numbers, see Shaikh, *Community and Consensus*, 114, 158. Also see Sudipta Kaviraj, "On Thick and Thin Religion: Some Critical Reflections on Secularization Theory," in *Religion and the Political Imagination*, ed. Ira Katznelson and Gareth Stedman Jones (New York: Cambridge University Press, 2010), 352; Arjun Appadurai, "Number in the Colonial Imagination," in *Orientalism and the Post-Colonial Predicament*, ed. Carol Breckenridge and Peter van der Veer (Philadelphia: University of Pennsylvania Press, 1993), 332.

233 See Chapter 17, p. 349. Also see: Lajpat Rai, 'Two Wrongs?', 267; 'On Sarojini Naidu's Criticism of the Leaders of the Hindu Sabha Movement, The Tribune, 24 October 1925', in *CWLLR*, vol. 11, 2008, 261.

234 Lajpat Rai, 'Presidential Address, Provincial Hindu Conference of Agra', 241.

235 In its desire to contain community-based rights, Rai's secular Indian nationalism overlapped with the secularism eventually enshrined in India's constitution in 1950. See Tejani, *Indian Secularism*; Bajpai, *Debating Difference*, chap. 2.

236 Lala Lajpat Rai, 'Hindu–Muslim Unity, The Tribune, November-December 1924', in *CWLLR*, vol. 11, 2008, 181.

237 Lala Lajpat Rai, 'Need to Protect Hindu Interests, Hindustan Times, 22 October 1926', in *CWLLR*, vol. 12, 2009, 146.

238 See Chapter 14, pp. 276, and Chapter 17, pp. 338, 341–42.

239 NWFP was annexed by the British in 1849 and was originally part of the Punjab province. In 1901, it was carved out as a separate province. Because it flanked British India's north-west frontier—hence, its name—NWFP was vital to the strategic interests of the British Empire. This province was therefore directly, militarily and oppressively governed by the British. Democratic reforms would eventually be extended to NWFP, and it would be made a province like other British Indian provinces, only in 1935. See the introduction in Sohal, *The Muslim Secular*. In 1926, during the debate over the introduction of democratic reforms to NWFP, such that it would get its own legislative council, and become a province like any other, Lajpat Rai had gone against several Hindus to argue in favour of extending democracy to this Muslim-majority province. Nair, *Changing Homelands*, 54, 78–79. Conquered by the British in 1859, Baluchistan, like NWFP, was considered too backward, tribal and turbulent to be granted full provincial status. It was therefore ruled by 'centrally-appointed military autocrats' and without provincial legislatures accountable to their people. Stanley Wolpert, *Jinnah of Pakistan* (New York: Oxford University Press, 1984), 94. Sindh was annexed by the British and made part of Bombay Presidency in 1843. Since 1917, demands had emerged for the creation of Sindh as a separate province. This proposal had also been recommended by a government reforms committee in 1917. Tejani, *Indian Secularism*, 188–89. It is unclear how far Rai was, in the

mid-1920s, consciously imagining Baluchistan as part of his vision of a federal India and aware of efforts to create Sindh as a separate province. But Rai eventually supported Jinnah's 1927 Delhi proposals, which demanded the creation of Muslim-majority NFWP, Sindh and Baluchistan as full democratic provinces. It is quite possible that he was already working with such a vision of substantial Muslim majority autonomy at the regional level even before 1927.

Chapter 19

1 Lala Lajpat Rai, 'Two Wrongs?, *The Tribune*, 10 November 1925', in *CWLLR*, vol. 11, 2008, 267.
2 Lala Lajpat Rai, 'The Hindu Sabha and Hindu Community, *The Tribune*, 16 January 1925', in *CWLLR*, vol. 11, 2008, 211.
3 Richard Gordon, 'The Hindu Mahasabha and the Indian National Congress, 1915–26', *Modern Asian Studies* 9, no. 2 (1975): 179–80, 200, 202; Prabhu Bapu, *Hindu Mahasabha in Colonial North India, 1915–1930: Constructing Nation and History*, Routledge Studies in South Asian History (London: Routledge, 2013), 38.
4 Lala Lajpat Rai, 'Congress and Communal Organisations, *The Bombay Chronicle*, 12 May 1925', in *CWLLR*, vol. 11, 2008, 45.
5 David Page, *Prelude to Partition: The Indian Muslims and the Imperial System of Control, 1920-1932* (New Delhi: Oxford University Press, 1982), 120; M.K. Gandhi, 'Hindu–Muslim Question, Young India, 19 February 1925', in *CWMG*, vol. 26 (Ahmedabad: Navajivan Trust, 1965), 162.
6 M.R. Jayakar, *The Story of My Life*, vol. 2 (Bombay: Asia Publishing House, 1959), 527.
7 Lala Lajpat Rai, 'Hindu Sabha and Council Elections, *The Tribune*, 2 March 1926', in *CWLLR*, vol. 12, 2003, 111–13; 'Hindu Sabha and Elections, The Hindustan Times, 16 March 1926', in *CWLLR*, vol. 12, 2003, 113–14; 'The Hindu Mahasabha, The People, 21 March 1926', in *CWLLR*, vol. 12, 2003, 328–30.
8 Lajpat Rai, 'Hindu Sabha and Council Elections', 112.

9 Bhai Parmanand, *The Story of My Life* (New Delhi: S. Chand and Company Ltd., 1982), 167.

10 As Neeti Nair has noted, Lajpat Rai declared that politics was like 'chess, a game of moves' and held that those who did not know how to change their moves constantly should not be in politics. *Changing Homelands: Hindu Politics and the Partition of India* (Cambridge, MA: Harvard University Press, 2011), 81.

11 Gordon, 'Hindu Mahasabha', 192, 195.

12 Gordon, 146, 180, 184.

13 B.R. Nanda, *The Nehrus: Motilal and Jawaharlal*, Oxford India Paperbacks (New Delhi: Oxford University Press, 2008), 456–57.

14 Gordon, 'Hindu Mahasabha', 146, 180, 184.

15 Lala Lajpat Rai, 'Need for Careful Selection of Candidates, The Tribune, 30 September 1926', in *CWLLR*, vol. 12, 2009, 124–26; 'To Motilal Nehru, The People, 29 August 1926', in *CWLLR*, vol. 12, 2009, 5–6.

16 Ayesha Jalal, *Self and Sovereignty: Individual and Community in South Asian Islam since 1850* (London: Routledge, 2002), 300.

17 Lala Lajpat Rai, 'The Real Issue, The Tribune, 28 September 1926', in *CWLLR*, vol. 12, 2009, 131; Nair, *Changing Homelands*, 78; Gordon, 'Hindu Mahasabha', 191–92.

18 Lala Lajpat Rai, 'To Motilal Nehru, The People, 29 August 1926', in *CWLLR*, vol. 12, 2009, 6; Neeti Nair, *Changing Homelands: Hindu Politics and the Partition of India* (Cambridge, MA: Harvard University Press, 2011), 81; Richard Gordon, 'The Hindu Mahasabha and the Indian National Congress, 1915–26', *Modern Asian Studies* 9, no. 2 (1975): 191–92.

19 Gordon, 'Hindu Mahasabha', 192, 200, 202. The creation of the ICP as a faction inside the Congress has been seen as illustrating the Hindu Mahasabha's link with the Congress. See William Gould, *Hindu Nationalism and the Language of Politics in Late Colonial India* (Cambridge: Cambridge University Press, 2004), 93. While this certainly had political consequences, often taking the Congress towards Hindu politics, such a straightforward portrayal disguises the tension and conflict that existed between

the ICP and the Swaraj-dominated Congress. This conflict too had political implications, revealing continued and meaningful internal opposition to rightward pulls.

20 Cited in Nair, *Changing Homelands*, 81.

21 Nair, 81.

22 Lala Lajpat Rai, 'The Hindu Mahasabha and Muslim League, Bombay Chronicle, 22 December 1924', in *CWLLR*, vol. 11, 2008, 202; 'Hindu Sabha a Unifying Force, 8 February 1925', in *CWLLR*, vol. 11, 2008, 208.

23 Lajpat Rai, 'The Hindu Sabha and Hindu Community', 212–14.

24 Sarojini Naidu, 'Sarojini Naidu's Rejoinder, The Tribune, 25 October 1925', in *CWLLR*, vol. 11, 2008, 310–12.

25 Lala Lajpat Rai, 'On Sarojini Naidu's Criticism of the Leaders of the Hindu Sabha Movement, The Tribune, 24 October 1925', in *CWLLR*, vol. 11, 2008, 261.

26 Gyanendra Pandey, *The Construction of Communalism in Colonial North India* (New Delhi: Oxford University Press, 2006), 257.

27 Gould, *Language of Politics*, 14, 16–17, 32–33, 98, 181–83, 200, 265, 271; Chetan Bhatt, *Hindu Nationalism: Origins, Ideologies and Modern Myths* (Oxford: Berg, 2001), 61–63; Shabnum Tejani, *Indian Secularism: A Social and Intellectual History, 1890–1950* (Bloomington: Indiana University Press, 2008), 182–85; Jalal, *Self and Sovereignty*, 310. In the 1920s, the Hindu Mahasabha influenced the Congress through individuals such as Malaviya and Lajpat Rai, members of both the Mahasabha (and its electoral front, the ICP) and the Congress. However, Motilal Nehru's and broader Swarajist opposition to the Mahasabha, the Swarajist monopoly over the Congress, the failure of Malaviya and Lajpat Rai to break it, the resultant formation of the ICP, and the ICP's contestation of the Swarajist Congress vision suggest that things were more complicated. See Gordon, 'Hindu Mahasabha', 180, 192. Similarly, recent scholarship rightly notes Gandhi's closeness to Mahasabhites like Malaviya and Lajpat Rai. Tejani, *Indian Secularism*, 182–85.

But it ignores Gandhi's continued closeness with Swarajists like Motilal Nehru, the left-leaning Jawaharlal Nehru, apart from 'Gandhians' like Patel and C. Raja, whose politics had its own focus and integrity. Also left out are the consequences of Gandhi's retreat from overt politics in the mid-1920s. During 1925–27, Gandhi had retired to Sabarmati Ashram to realize his vision of Indian nation-building through his 'constructive programme'. This reduced the effects his closeness with Rai and Malaviya could have on politics in the mid-1920s. More importantly, the monochromatic view of the Hindu Mahasabha influencing the Congress overlooks the implications of the conflict *within* the Congress between Mahasabhaites (like Lajpat Rai, Malaviya, Jayakar, N.C. Kelkar and B.S. Moonje) and those Swarajists and Gandhians who explicitly opposed them or even implicitly contested their visions of nationalism. This internal conflict reflected ideological tension, difference and contestation. To get a preliminary sense of this internal tension, see Gordon, 'Hindu Mahasabha', 180, 192; Nanda, *The Nehrus*, 265–69; Feroz Chand, *Lajpat Rai: Life and Work* (New Delhi: Publications Division, Ministry of Information and Broadcasting, Government of India, 1978), 450, 455–57, 462. As I see it, revisionist historical research—whether seeking to contribute to political or intellectual history—needs to build on, rather than circumvent, these facts and nuances. Indeed, as I mentioned in the introduction, even William Gould, a historian whose research has questioned a necessary oppositional binary between Congress's secular Indian nationalism and Hindu communalism/nationalism (*Language of Politics*, 14, 16–17, 33.), has highlighted the Congress's links with Hindu Sabhas at the local level in UP, and argued that individual Congressmen at this local level often articulated forms of Hindu politics or loose ideas of a 'Hindu nation', acknowledges that the Congress was a broad-based movement from which a heterogeneity of political languages emanated. Gould's research focuses on a *particular* form of Hindu nationalist language originating from within the Congress (which he clarifies is distinct from 'the harder, exclusivist Hindu nationalism of the Sangh Parivar'). But he acknowledges the simultaneous existence within the Congress of secular Indian nationalist ideologies, particularly at the level of provincial and all-India politics. Gould, 1–2, 4, 7, 8–9, 20, 160, 179, 266–67, 274. The primary focus and weight of Gould's research, highlighting overlaps between the Congress and Mahasabha, have overshadowed his acknowledgement of the continuing secular nationalism of the Congress. For more details of the sometimes-explicitly, often-implicitly exclusionary Hindu nationalist idiom that occasionally emanated from inside the Congress, see Gould, 37, 40–42, 69–75, 78, 81–83, 132–33, 135–36, 155–56, 175–76, 188, 190–91, 266–69, 274.

28 Bapu, *Hindu Mahasabha in Colonial North India, 1915–1930*, 38. Nath was president of the Mahasabha in 1926, Moonje in 1927, Kelkar in 1928, and Parmanand in 1933. See Nair, *Changing Homelands*, 79; Bapu, *Hindu Mahasabha in Colonial North India, 1915–1930*, 33, 39–40; Vikram Sampath, *Savarkar: A Contested Legacy, 1924–66* (Gurugram: Viking, 2021), 42; Chand, *Lajpat Rai*, 465. These men took over the leadership of the Mahsabha after Malaviya and Lajpat Rai, and led it before Savarkar took over in 1937. Moonje, a close associate of K.B. Hedgewar, founded the RSS in 1925 alongside V.D. Savarkar's brother, Babarao, with his brother's Hindutva ideology as its creed. Kelkar too had close ties with V.D. Savarkar. Sampath, *Savarkar: A Contested Legacy*, 8, 39.

29 Bapu, *Hindu Mahasabha in Colonial North India, 1915–1930*, 38.

30 Bapu, 38–39; Bhatt, *Origins*, 100. Prabhu Bapu, a historian of the Hindu Mahasabha, has acknowledged that Rai and Malaviya wished that the Hindu Mahasabha conduct itself as subordinate to the Congress, and respect its sanctity as the only true Indian nationalist political organization. However, he argues that these moderate Mahasabha leaders did play a role in the anti-INC direction that the Hindu Mahasabha, and its electoral front, the

ICP, took in the 1926 elections. This, Bapu argues, contributed to the emergence of the Mahasabha as an anti-Congress political party under the hard-liners. See *Hindu Mahasabha in Colonial North India, 1915–1930*, 39.

31 Bapu, *Hindu Mahasabha in Colonial North India, 1915–1930*, 40.

32 Lala Lajpat Rai, 'Law of Love, The People, 19 July 1925', in *CWLLR*, vol. 11, 2008, 378.

33 Lala Lajpat Rai, 'My Political Creed, The People, 26 July 1925', in *CWLLR*, vol. 11, 2008, 382.

34 For one example, see 'Sarojini Naidu's Presidential Address', in *Report of the Indian National Congress: Fortieth Session, Cawnpore, 1925* (Madras: General Secretary, All India Congress, 1926), 9–10.

35 See Chapter 18, pp. 376–99.

36 Lala Lajpat Rai, 'Presidential Address to the Eighth Session of the Hindu Mahasabha, Calcutta, Amrita Bazar Patrika, 12 April 1925', in *CWLLR*, vol. 11, 2008, 229.

37 See Chapter 18, p. 399.

38 To recall, see Chapter 17, p. 341–42, and Chapter 18, p. 400.

39 Lala Lajpat Rai, 'False Gods, The People, 7 July 1927', in *CWLLR*, vol. 13, 2010, 271.

40 Lala Lajpat Rai, 'All-India Muslim League, The People, 12 January 1928', in *CWLLR*, vol. 15, 2010 [hereafter cited as 'All-India Muslim League'], 222–23.

41 Jalal, *Self and Sovereignty*, 300–01.

42 According to Ayesha Jalal, this group included certain members of the central legislative assembly and state council, Congress Muslims, Islamic universalists and those interested in all-India constitutional arrangements. Muslims representatives from Muslim-majority provinces were under-represented. Jinnah's position as a politician with an all-India lens and with no regional base, and his primary interest in the grant of power to Indians at the centre, meant that Jinnah did not fully understand the politics of Muslims at the regional

or provincial levels. This is why his proposals would be soon rejected by Punjabi Muslim leaders. See Jalal, 300–02.

43 Now part of Pakistan, Sind (Sindh) had been occupied by the British and made part of Bombay Presidency in 1843. Bapu, *Hindu Mahasabha in Colonial North India, 1915–1930*, 218, n. 66. It would be created as a separate province under the Government of India Act, 1935. Sampath, *Savarkar: A Contested Legacy*, 172.

44 Now part of Pakistan, Baluchistan was conquered by the British in 1859. Like NWFP, Baluchistan was considered too backward, tribal and turbulent to be granted full provincial status. Both regions were therefore currently ruled by 'centrally-appointed military autocrats' and without provincial legislatures accountable to their people. Stanley Wolpert, *Jinnah of Pakistan* (New York: Oxford University Press, 1984), 94.

45 David Page, *Prelude to Partition: The Indian Muslims and the Imperial System of Control, 1920–1932* (New Delhi: Oxford University Press, 1982), 145; Nair, *Changing Homelands*, 82; Jalal, *Self and Sovereignty*, 300–01; Ayesha Jalal and Anil Seal, 'Alternative to Partition: Muslim Politics between the Wars', *Modern Asian Studies* 15, no. 03 (1981): 430; Bapu, *Hindu Mahasabha in Colonial North India, 1915–1930*, 141; Sumit Sarkar, *Modern India: 1886–1947* (Delhi: Macmillian, 1983), 262; Wolpert, *Jinnah*, 94–95; Tejani, *Indian Secularism*, 186. Jinnah's biographer, Stanley Wolpert, notes that he had always been ambivalent about separate electorates, viewing them as a 'necessary evil' and protection required by Muslims only as long as they 'remained too weak and too educationally backward to aspire to anything approaching equality with Hindus'. Jinnah's Delhi proposals reflected his belief that there were other means by which Muslims could be protected, which made mechanisms like separate electorates dispensable. *Jinnah*, 94.

46 Jalal, *Self and Sovereignty*, 301.

47 Bapu, *Hindu Mahasabha in Colonial North India, 1915–1930*, 141; Jalal, *Self and Sovereignty*, 299.

48 Lajpat Rai, 'All-India Muslim League', 221.

49 Nair, *Changing Homelands*, 78.

50 Chand, *Lajpat Rai*, 497–98.

51 Nair, *Changing Homelands*, 80. Nair writes that Lajpat Rai recognized that as 'a highly accomplished barrister, Jinnah could have minted money if he chose to work in the courts; instead, he sat in the legislative chambers, through dull debate after dull debate, working the reforms'. This reflected 'his sacrifice and his contribution to India's slowly awakening representative democracy'.

52 Lajpat Rai, 'All-India Muslim League', 221–22.

53 Page, *Prelude to Partition*, 158.

54 Lajpat Rai, 'All-India Muslim League', 221.

55 Neeti Nair, *Changing Homelands: Hindu Politics and the Partition of India* (Cambridge, MA: Harvard University Press, 2011), 82–83, 86–87.

56 After 1915, Rai used the term 'nation', 'nationalist' and 'nationalism' only to signify an *Indian* nation, *Indian* nationalists, and *Indian* nationalism. By 'Hindu nationalist', Lajpat Rai meant not individuals subscribing to the ideology of Hindu nationalism but an (Indian) 'nationalist' who was Hindu. Similarly, by 'Muslim nationalists' Rai meant not individuals subscribing to an ideology that India's Muslims constituted a separate Muslim nation, but only Muslims whom he believed were Indian 'nationalists'. Lajpat Rai's use of the terms 'Hindu nationalist' and 'Muslim nationalist' reflects his position as an unselfconscious politician–thinker rather than a self-conscious academic thinker/theorist or a systematic ideologue.

57 Lala Lajpat Rai, 'The Political Situation and the Hindus of Punjab, 9 February 1928', in *CWLLR*, vol. 15, 2010, 206; Lajpat Rai, 'All-India Muslim League', 221–22.

58 Lajpat Rai, 'The Political Situation and the Hindus of Punjab', 205–08.

59 Lala Lajpat Rai, 'Raja Narendra Nath and the Simon Commission, 7 August 1928', in *CWLLR*, vol. 15, 2010, 148–49.

60 Jalal, *Self and Sovereignty*, 301; Bapu, *Hindu Mahasabha in Colonial North India, 1915–1930*, 141; Uma Kaura, *Muslims and Indian Nationalism: The Emergence of the Demand for India's Partition, 1928–40* (New Delhi: Monahar Book Service, 1977), 30–31; Tejani, *Indian Secularism*, 186. The All-India Congress Committee accepted the Proposals in May 1927, as did the Madras Congress session in December 1927.

61 Bapu, *Hindu Mahasabha in Colonial North India, 1915–1930*, 142; Jalal, *Self and Sovereignty*, 300; Tejani, *Indian Secularism*, 186; Wolpert, *Jinnah*, 95. The Hindu Mahasabha opposed the Proposals throughout 1927 and in early 1928. Some scholars argue that by late February 1928 the Congress had begun to renege on its acceptance of Jinnah's proposals in the face of Mahasabha opposition, and point to Gandhi's disapproval of this backtracking. See Wolpert, 95; Kaura, *Muslims and Indian Nationalism: The Emergence of the Demand for India's Partition, 1928–40*, 33–35. It may be argued that the Congress should have held its ground in the face of Mahasabha pressure. Yet, the question of what Jinnah could and would be able to do in the face of steadfast opposition to his Delhi proposals by an ascendant and powerful Punjabi Muslim leadership remains.

62 Page, *Prelude to Partition*, 150, 164–66; Jalal, *Self and Sovereignty*, 301–02; Jalal and Seal, 'Alternative to Partition', 431–32. Contrary to Jinnah's 1927 proposals, Punjabi Muslim leaders insisted on separate electorates and a majority for Muslims of one seat over other communities in reformed legislatures. This was considered necessary due to the presence of a small Sikh minority and sizeable (and economically and educationally more advanced) Hindu minority in Punjab.

63 Wolpert, *Jinnah*, 95–96; Bapu, *Hindu Mahasabha in Colonial North India, 1915–1930*, 143.

64 Bapu, *Hindu Mahasabha in Colonial North India, 1915–1930*, 143.

65 These were: Sir Ali Imam and Shauib Qureshi (the Muslim group); M.R. Jayakar and M.S. Aney (Mahasabha); Sardar

Mangal Singh (Sikh League); Tej Bahadur Sapru (Liberals); G.R. Pradhan (Non-Brahmins); N.M. Joshi (trade unions). Bapu, 143, 218 n. 91; Wolpert, *Jinnah*, 96–97; Arvind Elangovan, *Norms and Politics: Sir Benegal Narsing Rau in the Making of the Indian Constitution, 1935–50* (New Delhi: Oxford University Press, 2019), 197–98.

66 Jalal and Seal, 'Alternative to Partition', 432; Bapu, *Hindu Mahasabha in Colonial North India, 1915–1930*, 143.

67 Elangovan, *Norms and Politics*, 197; Wolpert, *Jinnah*, 96. According to Stanley Wolpert, Jinnah refused invitations from Motilal Nehru, Ansari and Azad to join the committee's meetings before the separate meetings of the League and Congress in December, and before the All-Parties Convention met later that month. 97–99. The Nehru Committee produced its report not only in the absence of major Muslim leaders but in the face of the Mahasabha's continued opposition to the League's demands (relating to Punjab and Bengal, Sindh, and one-third reservation at the centre). Bapu, *Hindu Mahasabha in Colonial North India, 1915–1930*, 143; Wolpert, *Jinnah*, 96.

68 According to Wolpert, it was Jinnah's now-rebellious assistant M.C. Chagla, who was present at the committee's sessions, who convinced the elder Nehru not to concede separate electorates. Wolpert, *Jinnah*, 97.

69 For the Report's reasoning behind its dismissal of reservations for Muslim majorities in Punjab and Bengal, see Elangovan, *Norms and Politics*, 199–201; Nair, *Changing Homelands*, 288, n. 134. For a critique of this reasoning, see Elangovan, *Norms and Politics*, 199–201.

70 The details of the Nehru Report are collectively drawn from Nair, *Changing Homelands*, 88–89; Sarkar, *Modern India*, 263; Jalal, *Self and Sovereignty*, 303; Tejani, *Indian Secularism*, 187; Bapu, *Hindu Mahasabha in Colonial North India, 1915–1930*, 143–44; Rochana Bajpai, *Debating Difference: Group Rights and Liberal Democracy in India* (Oxford: Oxford University Press, 2011), 40–41; Elangovan, *Norms and Politics*, 99–201.

71 Nair, *Changing Homelands*, 89.

72 Jalal, *Self and Sovereignty*, 303; Bajpai, *Debating Difference*, 41; Elangovan, *Norms and Politics*, 197–98.

73 Jalal and Seal, 'Alternative to Partition', 432; Rakhahari Chatterji, *Gandhi and the Ali Brothers: Biography of a Friendship* (New Delhi: SAGE, 2013), 193.

74 Jalal, *Self and Sovereignty*, 303–04, 310–11, 317.

75 Jalal, 303, 307, 310; Jalal and Seal, 'Alternative to Partition', 433–34; Bapu, *Hindu Mahasabha in Colonial North India, 1915–1930*, 145; Elangovan, *Norms and Politics*, 197–98; Chatterji, *Gandhi and the Ali Brothers*, 194.

76 Chatterji, *Gandhi and the Ali Brothers*, 193, 195, 198, 200.

77 Lala Lajpat Rai, 'Speech at the Political Conference, The Tribune, 5 October 1928', in *CWLLR*, vol. 15, 2010, 172.

78 Lala Lajpat Rai, 'Punjab Hindus and the Nehru Report, The People, 25 October 1928', in *CWLLR*, vol. 15, 2010, 176; Neeti Nair, *Changing Homelands: Hindu Politics and the Partition of India* (Cambridge, MA: Harvard University Press, 2011), 91.

79 Lajpat Rai, 'Punjab Hindus and the Nehru Report', 198.

80 Lajpat Rai, 'Speech at the Political Conference', 171.

81 Lala Lajpat Rai, 'Nehru Report—Solution to the Communal Problem, The Tribune, 7 October 1928', in *CWLLR*, vol. 15, 2010, 176.

82 Lala Lajpat Rai, 'Presidential Address at the Provincial Hindu Conference of Agra, The Tribune, 30 October 1928', in *CWLLR*, vol. 15, 2010, 236.

83 Parmanand, *Story of My Life*, 168.

84 Nair, *Changing Homelands*, 90–91.

85 Chand, *Lajpat Rai*, chap. 64. For a depiction of the event in popular cinema, see S. Ram Sharma, *Shaheed*, 1965, https://www.youtube.com/watch?v=9k6-3XlAU7s&ab_channel=FILMISONGfilmoraSUBSCRIBNOW; Rajkumar Santoshi, *The Legend of Bhagat Singh*, 2002; Guddu Dhanoa, *23rd March 1931: Shaheed*, 2002.

86 Lala Lajpat Rai, 'To G.D. Birla, 16 November 1928', in *CWLLR*, vol. 15, 2010, 201.

87 Bapu, *Hindu Mahasabha in Colonial North India, 1915–1930*, 144; Jalal and Seal, 'Alternative to Partition', 433–34; Tejani, *Indian Secularism*, 187.

88 Bapu, *Hindu Mahasabha in Colonial North India, 1915–1930*, 145. Punjabi Muslim leaders insisted on separate electorates, reservations for Punjabi and Bengali Muslim majorities, and a weak federation of autonomous provinces (rather than the strong centre proposed by the Report).

89 Bapu, 145; Tejani, *Indian Secularism*, 194.

90 Barbara Daly Metcalf and Thomas R. Metcalf, *A Concise History of Modern India* (Cambridge [England]; New York: Cambridge University Press, 2012), 191. Muslim alienation from the Congress would have far-reaching political consequences. In contrast to the non-cooperation movement of 1920–22, many Muslims stayed away from the civil disobedience movement of the early 1930s. Sekhar Bandyopadhyay, *From Plassey to Partition: A History of Modern India* (New Delhi: Orient Longman, 2004), 338; Tejani, *Indian Secularism*; Metcalf and Metcalf, *A Concise History of Modern India*, 192.

91 Bapu, *Hindu Mahasabha in Colonial North India, 1915–1930*, 146; Jalal, *Self and Sovereignty*, 321–22; Tejani, *Indian Secularism*, 187; Sarkar, *Modern India*, 263.

92 Wolpert, *Jinnah*, 102; Bapu, *Hindu Mahasabha in Colonial North India, 1915–1930*, 144.

93 Cited in Page, *Prelude to Partition*, 200.

94 Amar Sohal, 'Ideas of Parity: Muslims, Sikhs and the 1946 Cabinet Mission Plan', *South Asia: Journal of South Asian Studies* 40, no. 4 (2017): 707–08.

95 Pandey, *Construction of Communalism*, 235–36, 239–40; Sohal, 'Ideas of Parity', 707–08; Nair, *Changing Homelands*, 159.

Chapter 20

1 Bhatt, *Origins*, 4, 39, 41–43, 84, 110; Pandey, *Construction of Communalism*, 234–35; 'Hindus and Others: The Militant Hindu

Construction', *Economic and Political Weekly* 26, no. 52 (1991): 2998–99; John Zavos, *The Emergence of Hindu Nationalism in India* (Oxford: Oxford University Press, 2000), 167, 177.

2 Christophe Jaffrelot, *The Hindu Nationalist Movement and Indian Politics: 1925 to the 1990s* (New Delhi: Penguin Books, 1999), 33; Vikram Sampath, *Savarkar: Echoes from a Forgotten Past, 1883–1924* (Gurgaon: Viking, 2019), 419. Hedgewar was close to the Savarkar brothers, with this association helping the RSS establish branches in western and coastal Maharashtra. Sampath, *Savarkar: A Contested Legacy*, 40.

3 Jaffrelot, *Hindu Nationalist Movement*, 19; C.S. Adcock, *The Limits of Tolerance: Indian Secularism and the Politics of Religious Freedom* (New York: Oxford University Press, 2013), 151; Bapu, *Hindu Mahasabha in Colonial North India, 1915–1930*, 61, 73.

4 Bhatt, *Origins*, 61.

5 See Chapter 15, pp. 295–301.

6 Muzaffar Alam, *Languages of Political Islam in India 1200–1800* (Orient Blackswan, 2004); Raziuddin Aquil, *Lovers of God: Sufism and the Politics of Islam in Medieval India* (New Delhi: Oxford University Press, 2020); *The Muslim Question: Understanding Islam and Indian History* (Penguin Random House India, 2017), 25–26, 28; Richard Eaton, *India in the Persianate Age: 1000–1765*, 2020.

7 Sampath, *Savarkar: A Contested Legacy*, 407.

8 See Chapter 14, pp. 266–69, and Chapter 17, pp. 345, 354–56.

9 Chapter 18, pp. 378–79.

10 Chapter 18, pp. 387–88.

11 Chand, *Lajpat Rai*, xv–xvi.

12 Lala Lajpat Rai, 'Hindu History, The People, 14 March 1926', in *CWLLR*, vol. 12, 2009, 413.

13 Lajpat Rai, 'Hindu History'.

14 All these men had close ties with Vinayak Savarkar. Having lived with Savarkar in London's India House in 1907, Parmanand was an old friend. Kelkar had started a fund for Savarkar in 1924. Moonje and Hedgewar founded the RSS alongside Vinayak

Savarkar's brother, Babarao, with Vinayak's Hindutva ideology as its creed. Nair, *Changing Homelands*, 289 see n. 147 ; Sampath, *Savarkar: A Contested Legacy*, 8, 13, 38–40.

15 V.D. Savarkar, '19th Session of the Hindu Mahasabha, Karnavati (Ahmedabad), 1937', in *Hindu Rashtra Darshan* (Poona: Maharashtra Prantik Hindusabha, 2020), 8, 11, 13–14, https://archive.org/details/hindu-rashtra-darshan-en-v002/mode/2up; Chetan Bhatt, *Hindu Nationalism: Origins, Ideologies and Modern Myths* (Oxford: Berg, 2001), 100, 103–04; Vikram Sampath, *Savarkar: A Contested Legacy, 1924–66* (Gurugram: Viking, 2021), 195–97.

16 Jyotirmaya Sharma, *Hindutva: Exploring the Idea of Hindu Nationalism* (New Delhi: Viking, 2003), 156; Chetan Bhatt, *Hindu Nationalism: Origins, Ideologies and Modern Myths* (Oxford: Berg, 2001), 100, 102, 105; Shruti Kapila, *Violent Fraternity: Indian Political Thought in the Global Age* (Princeton: Princeton University Press, 2021), 104, 115–16.

17 Jyotirmaya Sharma, *Hindutva: Exploring the Idea of Hindu Nationalism* (New Delhi: Viking, 2003), 156; Bhatt, *Origins*, 100, 102, 105.

18 Lajpat Rai, 'Hindu History', 413.

19 V.D. Savarkar, '21st Session of the Hindu Mahasabha, 1939', in *Hindu Rashtra Darshan* (Poona: Maharashtra Prantik Hindusabha, 2020), 44, https://archive.org/details/hindu-rashtra-darshan-en-v002/mode/2up.

20 Jaffrelot, *Hindu Nationalist Movement*, 27; Janaki Bakhle, 'Country First? Vinayak Damodar Savarkar (1883–1966) and the Writing of Essentials of Hindutva', *Public Culture* 22, no. 1 (2010): 159, 165–66, 179–80; Kapila, *Violent Fraternity*, 111, 114–15. The concept of 'monogamous' love, that Savarkar believed was given to India by Hindus alone, is borrowed from historian Janaki Bakhle, who has researched and interpreted Savarkar's *Hindutva* tract in the article cited here.

21 Savarkar, '19th Session of the Hindu Mahasabha, Karnavati (Ahmedabad), 1937', 3–4; '20th Session of the Hindu Mahasabha,

Nagpur, 1938', in *Hindu Rashtra Darshan* (Poona: Maharashtra Prantik Hindusabha, 2020), 51–52, https://archive.org/details/hindu-rashtra-darshan-en-v002/mode/2up; *Savarkar: A Contested Legacy*, 159, 164; '22nd Session of the Hindu Mahasabha, Madura, 1940', in *Hindu Rashtra Darshan* (Poona: Maharashtra Prantik Hindusabha, 2020), 74, https://archive.org/details/hindu-rashtra-darshan-en-v002/mode/2up; '23rd Session of the Hindu Mahasabha, Bhagalpur, 1941', in *Hindu Rashtra Darshan* (Poona: Maharashtra Prantik Hindusabha, 2020), 97–98, https://archive.org/details/hindu-rashtra-darshan-en-v002/mode/2up.

22 Sampath, *Savarkar: A Contested Legacy*, 164.

23 '20th Session of the Hindu Mahasabha, Nagpur, 1938', 29; Sampath, *Savarkar: A Contested Legacy*, 219. In 1937, Savarkar would argue that India is inhabited by two religiously and culturally conflictual and antagonistic Hindu and Muslim nations. Savarkar, '19th Session of the Hindu Mahasabha, Karnavati (Ahmedabad), 1937', 11, 13–14; also cited in Sampath, *Savarkar: A Contested Legacy*, 198. It therefore seems that Savarkar oscillated between holding that India was inhabited by two clashing Hindu and Muslim nations, and insisting that Hindus were *the* nation in India and Muslims only a minority community. Either way, he seemed to believe that the Hindu nation had special and superior claims over the land of India, and was more devoted to it than Muslims.

24 Chetan Bhatt, *Hindu Nationalism: Origins, Ideologies and Modern Myths* (Oxford: Berg, 2001), 102; V.D. Savarkar, '20th Session of the Hindu Mahasabha, Nagpur, 1938', in *Hindu Rashtra Darshan* (Poona: Maharashtra Prantik Hindusabha, 2020), 32, https://archive.org/details/hindu-rashtra-darshan-en-v002/mode/2up; '21st Session of the Hindu Mahasabha, 1939', in *Hindu Rashtra Darshan* (Poona: Maharashtra Prantik Hindusabha, 2020), 39, https://archive.org/details/hindu-rashtra-darshan-en-v002/mode/2up; '23rd Session of the Hindu Mahasabha, Bhagalpur, 1941', in *Hindu Rashtra Darshan* (Poona: Maharashtra Prantik

Hindusabha, 2020), 99, https://archive.org/details/hindu-rashtra-darshan-en-v002/mode/2up.

25 Reflecting his own social background, Savarkar defined 'Hindu culture' in largely upper-caste terms to the neglect of shudra, untouchable and tribal cultures. See Bhatt, *Origins*, 96–97.

26 Sampath, *Savarkar: A Contested Legacy*, 193–95.

27 Sampath, 193–94.

28 Sampath, 195, 197, 218–19.

29 Sampath, 217.

30 Sampath, 218.

31 Sampath, 194–95, 219.

32 Sampath, 195–96.

33 Sampath, *Savarkar: A Contested Legacy*, 261–62. In line with Ambedkar's reading, it has been argued that the presence of the Muslim other was essential for Savarkar's political vision because, for him, it was in their domination and humiliation that Hindu glory was realized. See Vikram Visana, 'Glory and Humiliation in the Making of V.D. Savarkar's Hindu Nationalism', *The Historical Journal*, 2022, 3, 7, 9, 12, 17–21. Savarkar also made other statements apparently urging 'enraged intolerance', wiping out of 'existence all masjids without exception', and worse. Visana, 18–20; Luna Sabastian, 'Women, Violence, Sovereignty:"Rakshasa" Marriage by Capture in Modern Indian Political Thought', *Modern Intellectual History* 19, no. 3 (2022): 761, 776–77, 780; Purushottam Agarwal, 'Surat, Savarkar and Draupadi: Legitimising Rape as a Political Weapon', in *Women and the Hindu Right: A Collection of Essays*, ed. Tanika Sarkar and Urvashi Butalia (New Delhi: Kali for Women, 1995), 43, 48–52, 54.

34 Also see Pandey, 'Hindus and Others', 3000; Jaffrelot, *Hindu Nationalist Movement*, 29.

35 These were the kind of overlaps recognized early on in the nineteenth century by the Bengali Hindu essayist–novelist Bhudev Mukhopadhyay. As a Hindu, Mukhopadhyay had argued that people living together in and sharing the same

natural and historical environment, over time, acquire an organic sameness. Everyday practices create deep cultural similarities between people (for instance, in what they wear or eat or how they build their houses) such that they see themselves as more similar to each other than to another set of people. Such cultural similarities were shared by India's Hindus and Muslims, who therefore constituted an Indian people and nation, despite their differences. Mukhopadhyay argued that while outwardly it may seem that India's Muslims shared religious belief and conduct with Islamic societies outside India, because of their shared living with Hindus over centuries, they were in fact culturally and even religiously more similar to India's Hindus. For more on Mukhopadhyay, see Sudipta Kaviraj, 'The Reversal of Orientalism: Bhudev Mukhopadhyay and the Project of Indigenist Social Theory', in *Representing Hinduism: The Construction of Religious Traditions and National Identity*, ed. Vasudha Dalmia and Heinrich von Stietencron (London: SAGE, 1995), 257–58; 'Contradictions of Conservatism', *Studies in Indian Politics* 6, no. 1 (2018): 6–9. India's 'composite culture'—evident in many of its regions, shared by its Hindus and Muslims, and the outcome of centuries-old interaction of Hindu and Islamic influences—has been repeatedly noted by researchers. It is reflected in a significant part of India's architecture, music, painting, languages, knowledge systems, literature, syncretic religiosity (as reflected, for instance, in the Kabirpanth, other *nirguna bhakti* groups, and numerous Sufi orders), and vernacular cultures (as in Benaras). See Philippa Williams, *Everyday Peace? Politics, Citizenship and Muslim Lives in India*, RGS-IBG Book Series (Chichester, UK; Malden, MA: Wiley Blackwell, 2015), 38–39, 146; Peter Gottschalk, *Beyond Hindu and Muslim: Multiple Identity in Narratives from Village India* (New Delhi: Oxford Univ. Press, 2001), 22–23, 37; Eaton, *India in the Persianate Age*, 10–11, 13, 18, 61, 114, 117–18, 152, 193–94, 220, 386–91, 393. Also see historian Muzaffar Alam's argument about Indian Islam being the result of a syncretic mix with local influences, as summarized in Neeladri Bhattacharya, 'Predicaments of Secular Histories', *Public Culture* 20, no. 1 (2008): 59–60; For the original see Alam, *Languages of Political Islam in India 1200–1800*.

36 *The Nehru Report: An Anti Separatist Manifesto* (New Delhi: Michiko & Panjathan, 1928), 185, https://archive.org/details/ in.ernet.dli.2015.212381/mode/2up.

37 Here, religion was conceived not in terms of belief but simply as a form of identity.

38 Mark Juergensmeyer, 'Rethinking the Secular and Religious Aspects of Violence', in *Rethinking Secularism*, ed. Craig J. Calhoun, Mark Juergensmeyer, and Jonathan VanAntwerpen (Oxford, NY: Oxford University Press, 2011); Ashis Nandy, 'The Politics of Secularism and the Recovery of Tolerance', in *Secularism and Its Critics*, ed. Rajeev Bhargava (Delhi: Oxford University Press, 1998); Triloki N. Madan, 'Secularism in Its Place', *The Journal of Asian Studies* 46, no. 4 (1987): 747–59.

39 Juergensmeyer, 'Secular and Religious Aspects of Violence', 192, 196.

40 Some varieties of secularism have been recognized as hostile and even oppressive towards religion. Prominent examples include China, Soviet Russia, France, and Turkey. For more, see Peter van der Veer, 'Smash Temples, Burn Books: Comparing Secularist Projects in India and China', in *Rethinking Secularism*, ed. Craig J. Calhoun, Mark Juergensmeyer, and Jonathan VanAntwerpen (Oxford, NY: Oxford University Press, 2011); Geoffrey Hosking, 'The Russian Orthodox Church and Secularisation', in *Religion and the Political Imagination*, ed. Ira Katznelson and Gareth Stedman Jones (Cambridge; New York: Cambridge University Press, 2010); Rajeev Bhargava, 'Political Secularism', in *The Oxford Handbook of Political Theory*, ed. John S. Dryzek, Bonnie Honig, and Anne Phillips (Oxford: Oxford University Press, 2008), 642; Alfred Stepan, 'The Multiple Secularisms of Modern Democratic and Non-Democratic Regimes', in *Rethinking Secularism*, ed. Craig J. Calhoun, Mark Juergensmeyer, and

Jonathan VanAntwerpen (Oxford, NY: Oxford University Press, 2011). Indian secularism is recognized by secularism scholars as more accommodative of religion.

41 New scholarship seeking to challenge and *revise* the long- and widely-held view of professional historians about a historical event, phenomenon or process, by introducing new evidence or by reinterpreting old evidence. Such historical revisionism often complicates older, more simplistic understandings, culminating in new and often more nuanced understanding.

42 Ayesha Jalal, 'Exploding Communalism: The Politics of Muslim Identity in South Asia', in *Nationalism, Democracy and Development: State and Politics in India*, ed. Sugata Bose and Ayesha Jalal (Delhi: Oxford University Press, 1999).

43 Tejani, *Indian Secularism*, 236, 255–56; Adcock, *Limits of Tolerance*.

44 Partha Chatterjee, 'Secularism and Tolerance', in *Secularism and Its Critics*, ed. Rajeev Bhargava (Delhi: Oxford University Press, 1998), 347–60.

45 Perry Anderson, *The Indian Ideology* (Verso Books, 2013); for a similar view, see Jalal, 'Exploding Communalism: The Politics of Muslim Identity in South Asia'. Shubnam Tejani's argument about secular Indian nationalism and Indian secularism has also been read in this light. See Nandini Chatterjee, *The Making of Indian Secularism: Empire, Law and Christianity, 1830–1960*, Cambridge Imperial and Post-Colonial Studies Series (Basingstoke, Hampshire; New York: Palgrave Macmillan, 2011), 4–5.

46 For more on the difference between preference-based and identity-based majorities and minorities, see Rajeev Bhargava, *The Promise of India's Secular Democracy* (Oxford: Oxford University Press, 2010), 16–19.

47 Bhargava, 'Political Secularism', 645, 647–48; Bhargava, *Promise*, 69, 187; 'Is European Secularism Secular Enough?', 171, 174–76; 'Secular Politico-Legal Regimes in Religiously Homogenous and Diverse Societies', in *Routledge Handbook of Law and Religion*,

ed. Silvio Ferrari (London: Routledge, 2015), 238–40, 242; Also see 'Defenders of Secularism Need to Make a Course Correction', *The Hindu*, 23 September 2019, https://www.thehindu.com/news/cities/Vijayawada/defenders-of-secularism-need-to-make-a-course-correction/article29484623.ece.

48 Rajeev Bhargava, 'Should We Abandon the Majority-Minority Framework?', in *Minority Identities and the Nation–State*, ed. D.L. Sheth and Gurpreet Mahajan (Oxford University Press, 1999), 169–205; *Promise*, 16–33.

49 Bhargava, *Promise*, 65.

50 See Chapter 17, p. 338.

51 Pakistan is not a theocracy, but that does not make it a secular state. This is because although it is not run by a priestly order or Islamic authority, the Pakistani state still 'establishes' or officially privileges Islam. For a clear explanation of the analytical distinction between theocracies and states with 'established religions', see Bhargava, *Promise*, 70–75, 83.

52 Bhargava, 74–75.

53 For contemporary theorists of secularism, mechanical separation does not, in itself, amount to secularism. The latter involves separation for the sake of some *values*. Once again, see Bhargava, 67, 76–77.

54 Lala Lajpat Rai, 'Problem of National Education in India, 1918', in *CWLLR*, vol. 7, 2005, 32. Also see Chapter 10, p. 195.

55 *The Nehru Report: An Anti Separatist Manifesto*, 183.

56 For the distinction between passive and active citizenship rights, see Bhargava, *Promise*, 78–79.

57 See Chapter 17, pp. 339–40.

58 By 'communitarian', I broadly mean a way of thinking or being that assumes that belonging to a community is important to a person's identity, development and well-being.

59 By 'multi-value', I mean something driven or guided by multiple values or principles.

60 Chand, *Lajpat Rai*, chap. 64.

61 A lesser known fact, Jinnah had strongly defended Bhagat Singh in the Central Legislative Assembly and the courts. Sampath,

Savarkar: A Contested Legacy, 128; Aparna Vaidik, *Waiting for Swaraj: Inner Lives of Indian Revolutionaries* (Cambridge University Press, 2021), 38.

62 At his trial, Singh would clarify that for him revolution was not the 'cult of the bomb or the pistol' but a total change of society culminating in the overthrow of foreign and Indian capitalism and the establishment of the dictatorship of the proletariat. Sarkar, *Modern India*, 268; Kama Maclean, *A Revolutionary History of Interwar India: Violence, Image, Voice and Text* (New York: Oxford University Press, 2015), 6.

63 Vaidik, *Waiting for Swaraj: Inner Lives of Indian Revolutionaries*, 76.

64 Vaidik, 76–77.

65 Chris Moffat, 'The Itinerant Library of Lala Lajpat Rai', *History Workshop Journal*, no. 89 (Spring 2020): 121, 130, 138 (n. 41).

66 Moffat, 130, 133; See Introduction of Chaman Lal, ed., *The Bhagat Singh Reader* (Noida, Uttar Pradesh, India: HarperCollins Publishers India, 2019); Shiv Verma, Oral History Transcript at Nehru Memorial Musuem and Library. Interviewed by Hari Dev Sharma and S.L. Manchanda, Acc. No 50., 16 February 1972. I am thankful to Kama Maclean, a historian of Indian revolutionaries in the 'inter-war period' (the late 1920s and 1930s), for pointing me to this fact.

67 Jalal, *Self and Sovereignty*, 307, 317; Elangovan, *Norms and Politics*, 198–99; Bapu, *Hindu Mahasabha in Colonial North India, 1915–1930*, 146.

68 The Congress Working Committee offered a resolution in 1931 which conceded virtually all of Jinnah's 'Fourteen Points' except one-third seats at the centre. This were objected to by Bhai Parmanand of the Hindu Mahasabha alongside other Punjabi Hindus. In 1935, Congress president Rajendra Prasad came very close to negotiating a settlement with Jinnah, the League's president. While Prasad considered Jinnah's demands 'essentially fair', nothing came of the agreement as the seventy-four-year-old Madan Mohan Malaviya wanted Jinnah to concede more. Nair, *Changing Homelands*, 139–40, 149–51; Bandyopadhyay,

From Plassey to Partition: A History of Modern India, 340. Even as late as 1946, both the All-India Congress and Muslim League would initially accept the Cabinet Mission Plan. However, this concord too did not last. Nair, *Changing Homelands*, 169; Bhatt, *Origins*, 101; Sohal, 'Ideas of Parity'.

69 Farzana Shaikh, *Making Sense of Pakistan* (New York: Columbia University Press, 2009), 34, 38–39.

70 Faisal Devji, *Muslim Zion: Pakistan as a Political Idea* (Cambridge, Massachusetts: Harvard University Press, 2013), 103–5; See the introduction of Amar Sohal, *The Muslim Secular: Parity and the Politics of India's Partition* (Oxford: Oxford University Press, 2023).

71 Ayesha Jalal, *The Sole Spokesman: Jinnah, the Muslim League and the Demand for Partition* (Cambridge: Cambridge University Press, 1985), 52; Shaikh, *Making Sense of Pakistan*, 39–40, 42; Sohal, 'Ideas of Parity', 709; Devji, *Muslim Zion*, 102–06.

72 Devji, *Muslim Zion*, 187. Jinnah had envisioned neither the mass migration of Indian Muslims to his imagined Muslim 'homeland', nor that of non-Muslims out of it. Instead, his demand had taken for granted the existence of vast numbers of Muslim and non-Muslim minorities in the successor states of India and Pakistan. Shaikh, *Making Sense of Pakistan*, 37. Indeed, historians have pointed to the ambiguities in Jinnah's Pakistan demand, suggesting that it was never completely clear whether Jinnah was insisting on a separate Muslim nation–state partitioned from an Indian nation–state or a substantially autonomous Muslim political entity and 'homeland' *within* a single radically federalized state. Shaikh, *Making Sense of Pakistan*, 39; Devji, *Muslim Zion*, 17, 26–28, 87. Either way, without sustained clarification or qualification, Jinnah often enough engaged in perilous rhetoric about his goal being the 'division of India', about the impossibility of 'one united India', the need for the Muslim nation to have 'their homelands, their territory and their state', and for a separate homeland of Pakistan in the face of what he insisted would be assured Hindu tyranny

in its absence. *Making Sense of Pakistan*, 37, 48, 60; See Jinnah's words as cited in Ishtiaq Ahmed, *Jinnah: His Successes, Failures and Role in History* (Gurgaon, Haryana, India: Penguin Random House, 2020), p. 187, 197, 207.

73 See the introduction in Sohal, *The Muslim Secular*. Despite their basis in Hindu and Muslim majorities respectively, the Indian and Pakistani states remained distinct. India chose to follow secularism and aspired to not collapse into Hindu majoritarianism. Pakistan established Islam as its official state religion and had fewer checks against Muslim majoritarianism.

74 Bajpai, *Debating Difference*, 46–47.

75 For more details, see Rajeev Bhargava, ed., *Politics and Ethics of the Indian Constitution* (Oxford: Oxford University Press, 2009); Sujit Choudhry, Madhav Khosla, and Pratap Bhanu Mehta, eds., *The Oxford Handbook of the Indian Constitution*, First edition, Oxford Handbooks (Oxford New York, NY: Oxford University Press, 2016). For basic introductions for unacquainted adults as much as for children, see Subhadra Sen Gupta and Tapas Guha, *The Constitution of India for Children* (India Puffin, 2020); Leila Seth and Bindia Thapar, *We, The Children Of India: The Preamble to Our Constitution* (India Puffin, 2019).

76 Bhargava, *Promise*, 158; Tejani, *Indian Secularism*, 258–59; Bajpai, *Debating Difference*, 52–53.

77 For further details on how the Indian constitution represented a radical scaling back of community-based rights, and particularly the safeguard of guaranteed community-based political representation, which had been gained by minorities in colonial times, see Bajpai, *Debating Difference*, Chapter 2.

78 Bajpai, 56–58; Bhargava, *Promise*, 159.

79 Tejani, *Indian Secularism*, chap. 6. The Indian constitution and Indian secularism have been recently critiqued by several scholars for rejecting reservations for Muslims, even as these were provided for Dalits. They argue that while Dalits were granted reservations, the language of secularism, with its emphasis on the separation of religion and politics, was

complicit in denying these to Indian Muslims, even as they were and remain as economically and educationally 'backward' and underprivileged. As already noted, sophisticated theorists of secularism argue that secularism is not just mechanical separation of religion and politics, but is guided by values like peace, tolerance, equal citizenship, liberty, justice, fraternity, and so on. Bhargava, *Promise*, 67, 76–77. Moreover, they argue that while secularism requires the state to disconnect from religion at the two levels of the state's goals and institutions, a certain measure of religion–state connection at a third level of law and public policy (say, in the form of reservations) is compatible with the concept of secularism. This means a policy of reservation for religious minorities is compatible with secularism if guided by values like equality and justice. Bhargava, 74–75, 212–13. One effect of the Indian constitution's denial of Muslim reservations has been the severe under-representation of India's Muslims in its Parliament, where the people's representatives make laws to govern the people. In 1980, Muslims constituted 11 per cent of India's population and 9 per cent of its Lok Sabha. This percentage declined to 4.42 per cent in 2019, despite Muslims constituting 14.2 per cent of the population, according to the 2011 census. Shakil Sana, 'Yet Again, No Muslim Face in BJP's Bandwagon Headed to Parliament', *The New Indian Express*, 24 May 2019, https://www.newindianexpress.com/nation/2019/may/24/yet-again-no-muslim-face-in-bjps-bandwagon-headed-to-parliament-1981129.html; Katharina Buchholz, 'Number of Muslim MPs Stagnating Despite Faith Growing', 4 March 2020, https://www.statista.com/chart/21025/muslim-representation-lok-sabha-parliament-india/; Adnan Farooqui and E. Sridharan, 'The Rajya Sabha as a Corrective Mechanism for Muslim Underrepresentation?', in *Minorities and Populism : Critical Perspectives from South Asia and Europe [Electronic Resource]*, ed. Volker Kaul and Ananya Vajpeyi, Philosophy and Politics, Critical Explorations ; v. 10 (Cham: Springer, 2020), 114. That said, equally complicit in this development has been the role of

Partition and the creation of Pakistan. This strengthened India's Hindu majority, while thoroughly weakening the position of those Muslims who remained in India, who were overnight reduced to a radically smaller and weaker minority much more vulnerable to Hindu majority domination. Moreover, more than any deep flaw in India's secular constitution, the political under-representation of India's Muslims has been caused by the irregular enforcement of its constitution's Secularism-related articles (and the values they encourage), and the uneven commitment to them by India's political class. Nor can we overlook the primary role of the political actors who attack or undermine India's secular constitution through ideologies that seek to link one religion to India's state and national identity and consider one religious community as hierarchically superior to others.

80 Bajpai, *Debating Difference*, 49–53.

81 Bhargava, *Promise*, 81, 84.

82 Bhargava, 84.

83 See Chapter 15, pp. 287–90.

84 Bhargava, *Promise*, 84–86.

85 Here, I am somewhat warily accepting Lajpat Rai as part of the Hindu Right. Lajpat Rai's complex evolving thought defies categorical classification as Left or Right. His turn to militant Hindu politics in the mid-1920s may lead us to view him as part of the Hindu Right. But we may equally ask: why does his attraction to socialist/labour politics and his secularism not make him part of the Hindu Left?

86 See the following sources for the percentage of Muslims in the— **Parliament:** https://www.cfr.org/backgrounder/india-muslims-marginalized-population-bjp-modi, https://www.tandfonline.com/doi/full/10.1080/14736489.2020.1744996, Sana, 'Yet Again, No Muslim Face in BJP's Bandwagon Headed to Parliament'; Farooqui and Sridharan, 'The Rajya Sabha as a Corrective Mechanism for Muslim Underrepresentation?', 114. **Army:** https://www.tni.org/es/node/7883, https://thediplomat.

com/2014/05/indias-muslim-soldiers/, **media:** https://www.
tandfonline.com/doi/full/10.1080/13602004.2011.556, **police:**
https://www.commoncause.in/uploadimage/page/Status_
of_Policing_in_India_Report_2019_by_Common_Cause_
and_CSDS.pdf, https://www.tni.org/my/node/8559, **judiciary:**
https://www.thequint.com/voices/opinion/muslim-population-
at-15-but-minority-representation-in-judiciary-poor-muslim-
judge-supreme-court-altamas-kabir#read-more, https://indian
express.com/article/opinion/columns/muslims-in-prison-
india-judiciary-supreme-court-5347728, https://twocircles.net/
2016jan13/1452681363.html, https://www.dailypioneer.com/
2021/sunday-edition/need-to-promote-diversity-in-judiciary.
html, https://www.barandbench.com/columns/disproportionate-
representation-supreme-court-caste-and-religion-of-judges,
bureaucracy: https://www.tni.org/my/node/8559, https://www.
epw.in/journal/2006/08/commentary/representation-minorities-
civil-services.html. Also see: https://www.minorityaffairs.gov.in/
sites/default/files/sachar_comm.pdf

87 For one example, see Shashi Holla, 'Anti-Hindu Psuedo-
Secularism of India [Sic]', *Hindu Council of Australia* (blog),
18 July 2019, https://hinducouncil.com.au/new/anti-hindu-
psuedo-secularism-of-india/.

88 Tejani, *Indian Secularism*, 9.

89 Lajpat Rai supported the Nehru Report which granted freedom
of worship, propagation, association and education as a
constitutional right to minorities. It also committed itself to
protecting the language, script and culture of minorities, as well
as their 'personal laws'. See Bajpai, *Debating Difference*, 51, 102.
Today considered by the Hindu Right as offensive to their ideal
of an integrationist, homogenous (and Hindu-dominated and
diversity-averse) Indian nation, Lajpat Rai seemed to comfortably
take for granted the right of minorities to live by their own
religiously-coded, community-based personal laws and their
culture, a continuation of an earlier attitude first revealed in
his initial intervention on the separate electorates controversy

in 1909. See Chapter 8, pp. 136–37, 139. Here, it is worth also pausing to briefly clarify that at least on one occasion in the late 1930s, Savarkar spoke about 'guaranteeing special protection for the language, culture and religion of Mohammedans as a minority'. Sampath, *Savarkar: A Contested Legacy*, 197. But this was made conditional upon Muslims not wanting to humiliate and dominate others, a condition Savarkar never saw Muslims as meeting. Moreover, such a statement again needs to be read alongside his championing of his Hindutva ideology, which saw Hindu culture as *the* culture of India and required religious minorities to assimilate into it to become part of the Hindu nation. It must also be read next to his belief in '*Hindusthan Hinduon Ka*', and the existence of either separate antagonistic Hindu and Muslim nations or one supreme Hindu nation in India with Muslims constituting merely a community.

90 In making this argument, I disagree with Partha Chatterjee who views the phenomenon of self-proclaimed proponents of 'secularism' seeking assimilation and domination as a flaw of secularism itself. As noted on p. 432 of this chapter, preventing inter-religious domination is a core value of secularism. Any individual or group claiming to be a champion of 'secularism' while actually seeking assimilation and domination is thus in fact anti-secular.

91 For one example of this assimilationist mentality of domination today, see 'By 2024, Muslims Who Assimilate into Hindu Culture Can Stay in India: BJP MLA', *Hindustan Times*, 14 January 2018, https://www.hindustantimes.com/india-news/by-2024-muslims-who-assimilate-into-hindu-culture-can-stay-in-india-bjp-mla/story-UOukyntsgtrzgfqc59gJdP.html.

92 'India: Citizenship Bill Discriminates Against Muslims', *Human Rights Watch*, 11 December 2019, https://www.hrw.org/news/2019/12/11/india-citizenship-bill-discriminates-against-muslims; Gautam Bhatia, 'A Bill That Undercuts Key Constitutional Values', *The Hindu*, 7 October 2019, https://www.thehindu.com/opinion/lead/a-bill-that-undercuts-key-

constitutional-values/article29611770.ece; Christophe Jaffrelot, 'Citizenship Law in India, a Populist Polarization?', 6 February 2020, https://carnegieendowment.org/2020/02/06/citizenship-law-in-india-populist-polarization-pub-81023; Mehal Jain, 'Citizenship Amendment Act(CAA) Is Unconstitutional Since It Distinguishes Between Persons On The Basis Of Religion:Justice Gopala Gowda', *LiveLaw.In* (blog), 21 March 2021, https://www.livelaw.in/top-stories/supreme-court-justice-v-gopala-gowda-national-register-of-citizensnrc-citizenship-amendment-actcaa-171500; Barkha Dutt, 'Gandhi Would Be Fasting against India's Discriminatory New Citizenship Law', *Washington Post*, 8 October 2019, https://www.washingtonpost.com/opinions/2019/10/08/gandhi-would-be-fasting-against-indias-discriminatory-new-citizenship-law/; Jeffrey Gettleman and Suhasini Raj, 'India Steps Toward Making Naturalization Harder for Muslims', *New York Times*, 9 December 2019, https://www.nytimes.com/2019/12/09/world/asia/india-muslims-citizenship-narendra-modi.html; Niraja Gopal Jayal, 'Faith-Based Citizenship', *The India Forum*, 31 October 2019, https://www.theindiaforum.in/article/faith-criterion-citizenship; Abhinav Chandrachud, 'Secularism and the Citizenship Amendment Act', *Indian Law Review* 4, no. 2 (2020): 159, https://doi.org/10.1080/24730580.2020.1757927.

93 Santosh Singh, 'Bihar BJP MLA Says Take Away Muslims' Voting Rights, Gets Party Notice', *Indian Express*, 25 February 2022; Rajeev Mani, 'Won't Let Minorities Vote: Hindu Rashtra Statute Draft', *Times of India*, 13 August 2022. Such fantasies align with the Hindu nationalist vision of M.S. Golwalkar (1906–73), the second *sarsanghchalak* (chief) of RSS, one of its most prominent ideologues, and a significant influence on some among the Hindu right. Referring to India's Muslims and Christians in his 1939 book *We or Our Nationhood Defined*, he wrote: 'the foreign races of Hindusthan must either adopt the Hindu culture and language, must learn to respect and hold in reverence Hindu religion, must entertain no ideas but

those of glorification of the Hindu race and culture [. . .] or may stay in the country, wholly subordinated to the Hindu nation, claiming nothing, deserving no privileges, far less any preferential treatment—not even citizen's rights'. See as cited in Jaffrelot, *Hindu Nationalist Movement*, 56. This effectively meant a choice between hierarchical reverence for Hinduism and complete assimilation into Hindu culture, on the one hand, and living in India under clear Hindu domination and without citizenship rights, on the other. Such visions are far from Lajpat Rai's envisioned India, where individual Indians, regardless of religion, would constitute equal citizens of the secular Indian nation–state, religious and cultural diversity sincerely respected, and dreams of Hindu cultural and political domination ruled out as insanity, ruinous to both Hinduism and India.

Conclusion

1 To be sure, it also arises when all the people in India are deemed as constituting an 'Indian nation' but their distinctive cultural character is defined in Hindu terms. See William Gould, *Hindu Nationalism and the Language of Politics in Late Colonial India* (Cambridge: Cambridge University Press, 2004).

2 Faisal Devji, *The Impossible Indian: Gandhi and the Temptation of Violence* (London: Harvard University Press, 2012), 51–53, 64; Ajay Skaria, 'Gandhi's Politics: Liberalism and the Question of the Ashram', *The South Atlantic Quarterly* 101, no. 4 (2003): 957, 968, 978–79.

3 Nehru explicitly refused to term the continuing cultural essence of the Indian nation as 'Hindu', holding that ancient and present Indian culture, larger than 'Hinduism' or 'Hindu culture', was a sum of India's multiple historical layers, with each layer enriching India's national culture, and adding to India's complex 'personality'. Jawaharlal Nehru, *Discovery of India* (Calcutta: Signet Press, 1946), 72–75.

4 While hard-line secularisms insist on a hard religion–state separation, other forms of secularism (while requiring substantial religion–state separation) allow a degree of religion-state connection at the level of law or public policy as long as this is guided by core values of secularism (e.g., justice, religious freedom, equal citizenship, peace, tolerance, fraternity, and so on). Rajeev Bhargava, *The Promise of India's Secular Democracy* (Oxford: Oxford University Press, 2010), 74–80, 212–13. For multiple forms of secularism, see Rajeev Bhargava, 'Is European Secularism Secular Enough?', 157–181; Alfred Stepan, 'The Multiple Secularisms of Modern Democratic and Non-Democratic Regimes'.

5 For details, see Chapter 20, n. 86 (p. 727).

6 The conflation of the possibly true historical effect of an author's work with the author's intention, the conflation of what the author's writing achieved with what the author intended, is referred to by intellectual historian Quentin Skinner as the 'mythology of prolepsis'. Quentin Skinner, *Visions of Politics*, vol. 1 (Cambridge: Cambridge University Press, 2002), 72–74.

7 Skinner, 1: 67–72.

8 Margaret MacMillan, *The Uses and Abuses of History* (Profile Books, 2016), 81–83.

9 For an introduction, see Alexander J. Motyl, ed., *Encyclopedia of Nationalism*, vol. 2 (San Diego, Calif.; London: Academic Press, 2001), 23, 57, 105, 241–44, 394–95, 471–72, 597–98, 604–05.

10 For a glimpse, see Motyl, 2:10, 20, 27–28, 84, 99, 115, 146, 150–52, 183–84, 187–90, 202, 341, 435, 471–72, 538, 558–60, 573–74, 596–98.

11 Motyl, 2:20, 57, 94–95, 105, 202, 229, 248, 352–53, 577–78, 471–72; For the relationship between nationalism and war, also see Margaret MacMillan, *War: How Conflict Shaped Us*, 2020, 106–08, 121. For a window into the vast body of research of nationalism, see John Breuilly, ed., *The Oxford Handbook of the History of Nationalism* (Oxford: Oxford University Press, 2013).

12 For recent examples, see 'How Cynical Leaders Are Whipping up Nationalism to Win and Abuse Power', *The Economist*, 31 August 2023, https://www.economist.com/briefing/2023/08/31/how-cynical-leaders-are-whipping-up-nationalism-to-win-and-abuse-power?giftId=844f613b-ccab-4b67-b410-d2c1be7a46bb.

Index

secular Indian nationalism,
   xxvi, 342, 346, 348–49, 399,
   437, 452, 477
Indian National Social
   Conference, 102
Intellectual history, xxxv–xxxviii
Iqbal, Mohammad
   and nationalism, 296–97
   and Pan-Islamism, 296–97
Islam, 291–93
   and Indian subcontinent, 91,
   186, 293–94
Iyengar, Srinivas, 350

Jallianwala Bagh massacre, 222
Jayakar, M.R., 279, 331, 402, 415
Jinnah, Mohammad Ali, 135,
   167, 173, 175–76, 220, 265,
   268, 288, 304, 316, 321, 323,
   325–27, 329, 343–50, 352,
   360, 362, 403, 408–16,
   438–39, 452, 455, 479, 550
   n. 73, 552 n. 1, 558 n. 43,
   577 n. 33, 601 n. 56, 606
   n. 93, 610 n. 115, 624
   n. 56, 626 n. 68, 662 n. 128,
   665 n. 153 and 154, 708
   n. 42, 709 n. 45, 710 n. 51,
   711 n. 61, 712, n. 67, 723
   n. 68, 724 n. 72
Jones, William, 62
Justice Party, 242, 384, 393

Karmayoga, 116–17, 549 n. 53
Kelkar, N.C., 316, 407, 419, 706
   n. 27, 707 n. 28

Khan, Abdul Ghaffar, 187, 285,
   299, 356, 627 n. 71, 654 n. 21
Khan, Aga, 130
Khan, Hakim Ajmal, 220–21,
   224, 241, 262, 264, 268,
   273–74, 280, 309, 315, 325,
   327, 600 n. 54
Khan, Sardar
   Muhammad Gul, 355
Khan, Sir Syed Ahmed, xxxix,
   4, 7–8, 19
   and Aligarh college and
   Muslim modernism, 22–23,
   29, 52, 516 n. 31, 464
   on Congress and elective
   representation, 22–45, 133
   disinterest in Pan-Islamism,
   300, 599 n. 41
   and Lajpat Rai, 22–45, 59–62,
   64, 78–79, 182, 192, 234,
   300, 335, 447
   ideas of 'nation',
   30–33, 39, 130
   and pre-modern/aristocratic
   nominated representation,
   26–27, 30, 42
Khilafat/non-cooperation
   movement xvii, xxv–xxvi,
   xxx, xxxiv, xxxvi, 129, 214,
   220–22, 224, 226–27, 231,
   238, 243–45, 249, 254, 259,
   261–64, 266–67, 269, 272,
   276, 279, 288, 298, 319,
   323–26, 330, 338, 406, 423,
   476, 638 n. 154, 679 n. 103.
Kidd, Benjamin, 98–101, 103–4

Scan QR code to access the
Penguin Random House India website